Cheltenham & Gloucester

Cricket Year

Cheltenham & Gloucester

Cricket Year

Twenty-Fifth Edition
September 2005 to September 2006

Edited by **Jonathan Agnew**

with additional contributions by
Qamar Ahmed
Charlie Austin
Mark Baldwin
Tony Cozier
Gulu Ezekiel
Vic Marks
Jim Maxwell
Telford Vice
Bryan Waddle

A & C Black • London

Edited by Jonathan Agnew
Assistant editing by Mark Baldwin
with additional contributions by
Qamar Ahmed
Charlie Austin
Tony Cozier
Gulu Ezekiel
Vic Marks
Jim Maxwell
Telford Vice
Bryan Waddle
With special thanks to Pat Gibson and Andrew Hignell

The publishers would also like to thank *The Times* for their kind permission to
reproduce the photograph of Mark Baldwin on page 70.

First published in 2006 by
A & C Black Ltd
38 Soho Square
London W1D 3HB

www.acblack.com

A copy of the CIP entry for this book is available from the British Library.

ISBN-13: 978-0-7136-7972-4
ISBN-10: 0-7136-7972-7

10 9 8 7 6 5 4 3 2 1

This book is produced using paper that is made from wood grown in managed,
sustainable forests. It is natural, renewable and recyclable. The logging and
manufacturing processes conform to the environmental regulations of the
country of origin.

Project editor: Julian Flanders at Butler and Tanner
Design: Kathie Wilson at Butler and Tanner
Statistics and County information: Press Association
Pictures researched and supplied by David Munden at Sportsline Photographic:
www.sportsline.org.uk and Graham Morris: www.cricketpix.com – except those
on the following pages which are copyright © Empics: 9, 12 both, 13 top, 16 top,
19 bottom, 32 top, 36 both, 37 all, 49, 54, 55, 60, 62–4, 73, 80, 83, 86, 91, 92, 95,
96, 111, 113, 114, 124, 126, 127, 139, 142, 156, 162, 163, 165, 167, 168, 170, 171,
174, 185, 189, 191, 192, 200, 201, 224, 231, 237 both, 238 both, 246, 247, 248,
252–55, 261–64, 268, 269, 270–72, 276, 277 both

Printed and bound in Great Britain by Butler and Tanner, Frome and London

CONTENTS

A MESSAGE FROM
CHELTENHAM & GLOUCESTER

The England team faces a wonderful challenge this winter, as Andrew Flintoff and company first attempt to retain the Ashes which were won so memorably in 2005, and then try to win the World Cup in the West Indies.

As one of English cricket's main sponsors for the past six years, we at Cheltenham & Gloucester are hugely proud of the successes that England – and English cricket – have achieved in recent times. Under Duncan Fletcher's canny stewardship as head coach, and with the likes of Nasser Hussain, Michael Vaughan, Andrew Strauss and Flintoff proving themselves to be highly inspirational captains both on and off the field, England are currently enjoying a

true golden era. Long may it continue.

The emergence of Monty Panesar this year has been one of the joys of English sport, underlining yet again the advances which cricket in this country has made in terms of player development, grass roots initiatives and the game's general profile. And for our fourth Man of the Year award – following on from Vaughan last year, Flintoff in 2004 and Alec Stewart in 2003 – we had no hesitation in choosing Monty, a cricketer whose marvellous enthusiasm and affection for his sport is so evident in everything he does.

When we took over the sponsorship of *Cricket Year*, four years ago, we initiated a new award designed to recognise the outstanding contribution to cricket of a player, or personality, who had been prominent to the public during the previous year.

Monty, superbly profiled in these pages by Jonathan Agnew, will be as popular a winner as any of his three distinguished predecessors. Can there have been a player who has so quickly been taken to the public's hearts as the first Sikh to represent England?

In the meantime, the likes of Panesar, Strauss, Kevin Pietersen, Ian Bell, Alastair Cook and Chris Read will all be relishing their first Ashes series in Australia. It will be a massive test of England's skill, courage and resilience, but the Ashes heroes of 2005 provide the backbone of the tour squad and Australia know that these days – even on their home soil – they will not have it all their own way.

We are very pleased that Cheltenham & Gloucester's support for English cricket has coincided with such an exciting and uplifting time for the game, but also sad, of course, that our six-year association is now coming to an end.

It was a privilege to see Sussex and Lancashire produce such a nerve tingling and closely fought affair in the last C&G Trophy final at Lord's in late August. As ever, the cup final occasion was eagerly awaited by players and supporters alike, but to have one of the most memorable of all finals as our last game made it a poignant and emotional day for all of us associated with Cheltenham & Gloucester.

Andrew Flintoff, England's captain in India last winter and in Australia in 2006–07.

Above: James Kirtley, just visible under a pile of bodies, has just taken the wicket which clinched the C&G Trophy for Sussex at Lord's.

Much was made in the media, meanwhile, about the changed format adopted for this past summer's C&G Trophy. There was widespread criticism of the England and Wales Cricket Board's decision to split the qualifying process into just two groups – a North and South conference – and to scrap both a quarter-final and semi-final round. As it was, Sussex and Lancashire qualified directly for the final as a result of winning their respective conferences, leaving counties without the opportunity to host popular and lucrative knockout matches in between the group stage and the final itself.

Obviously, in the future, the competition will no longer bear our name, but we are pleased for cricket fans that the ECB has taken the decision to re-introduce at least one of the knockout stages (the semi-finals) for next season.

Despite our decision to end the sponsorship of the C&G Trophy, we as a company remain committed to supporting English cricket at county and grass roots level. We have just signed a further two-year deal to sponsor the C&G Cheltenham Cricket Festival – which in 2006 saw Gloucestershire hosting matches against Glamorgan, Yorkshire, Leicestershire and Somerset – and we also support Gloucestershire Young Cricketers, Cheltenham Cricket Club, the Gloucester Club Cricket Federation and the Cheltenham & District Cricket League.

We are also proud of our association with *Cricket Year*, especially as the book has now reached its 25th anniversary edition. Congratulations to Jonathan Agnew, Mark Baldwin, the global editorial team, and all at A&C Black for guiding this popular and much-respected annual to such a significant landmark. As ever, this current edition is published within weeks of the end of the English season and serves as the perfect reminder of all the worldwide cricketing action of the previous 12 months.

Congratulations, also, to Sussex for their magnificent double of Liverpool Victoria County Championship and C&G Trophy, to Leicestershire for a second Twenty20 Cup triumph, and to Essex for winning the inaugural NatWest Pro40 League. An in-depth review of the English domestic summer makes up the bulk of these pages, while there is also comprehensive coverage of England's progress throughout the year plus reports on every other Test nation.

Special features have been a part of *Cricket Year* since we became involved, and Tony Cozier writes a fascinating preview of the 2007 World Cup while Vic Marks effortlessly straddles the past 25 years to make a telling Ashes link.

Finally, we would like to express our thanks to A&C Black for producing this traditional autumn delight and to wish the England team the very best of luck for the Ashes, the World Cup and beyond.

Ian Whittaker
Head of Marketing
Cheltenham & Gloucester

AGGERS' VIEW

The summer of 2006 was not meant to have been like this. It was the time to sit back, basking in the glory of the previous year's Ashes success, and enjoy the visits of Sri Lanka and Pakistan: two entertaining cricket teams. At the same time, of course, we could savour the prospect of the return trip to Australia this winter in what must be the most gloriously anticipated cricket tour there has ever been.

But sport would be nothing without controversy, and the unprecedented and deeply depressing scenes that accompanied the premature end to the final Test of the summer at The Oval must never again be witnessed on a cricket ground.

The background to the saga of the first Test match ever deemed to have been forfeited is well documented. Inzamam-ul-Haq was subsequently cleared of the ball-tampering charge that, in the light of a lack of specific evidence against an individual, was brought against him as captain, but he was found guilty of bringing the game into disrepute for failing to take the field, and was banned for four one-day internationals.

The sub-plot to the drama was the role of umpire Darrell Hair – no stranger to controversy, and in whom Pakistan had lost confidence before the series started. It was almost entirely overlooked throughout that Billy Doctrove, the West Indian umpire, was equally involved in the decision to change the ball and award England five penalty runs. After the hearing, Doctrove was publicly defiant, saying that he stood by his judgement. Those words were lost in the maelstrom that engulfed Hair, who was coming to terms with the fact that he had been stood down from the Champions Trophy.

Pakistan's mistrust of Hair was widely known on the circuit long before the International Cricket Council entrusted him with the last two Tests in this series, and yet he was the umpire most regularly employed to officiate Pakistan's Tests. The Oval was his ninth match out of their last 17 games. Why? It would not be right for any team to dictate which umpire is acceptable to them or not – and there is an irony to the fact that Pakistan, having campaigned so hard for independent umpires, is now the first team

to object to a neutral – but there is a balance to be struck, and Pakistan might be forgiven for feeling at the very least that the ICC was too dogmatic and dictatorial in trying to prove a point.

Hair has always firmly denied the allegations of bias made against him, and argues that he is an umpire who does not shy away from making the tough decisions. It is interesting that the two incidents that attract the most attention from his detractors do little to support their claims. It is true that Hair no-balled Muttiah Muralitharan for throwing. This occurred ten years ago when the law merely stated that there should be no straightening or even partial straightening of the bowling arm, and Hair is hardly the only person in the cricketing world to suspect that Muralitharan's action is not legal. As we know, Hair is simply not the type of man to turn a blind eye for the sake of expediency or in the interest of diplomacy. He could and should consider more carefully the impact his decisions might have, especially those that court controversy, but he would argue that to do that would be to chicken out.

The second example used by Hair's detractors is the infamous run out of Inzamam by England in Faisalabad earlier this year. In fact, the mistake in ignoring the fact that the batsman was taking evasive action rather than taking a run was made by Simon Taufel. He then asked Hair at square leg for a line decision. Given his remit, Hair referred it to the third umpire – a former Pakistan Test player – who, acting on the same terms as Hair, gave Inzamam out. Taufel made the error, but it is always Hair who gets the blame.

It seems that it is not so much Hair's decision-making ability that Pakistan objects to, but his manner. Hair is big, burly and brusque, and he could certainly be viewed as overbearing in Asia where any suggestion of throwing one's weight around quickly stirs up unpleasant memories of its colonial past. No individual is bigger than the game itself, and Inzamam was rightly punished for refusing to take the field: to have let him off would be to establish a situation in which the umpire's authority is permanently compromised. However, both umpires need closely and honestly to examine the preamble to their changing of the ball that day. Surely a firm and obvious warning first would have been more sensible?

One lesson of all of this must be that Hair, Inzamam and Bob Woolmer, the Pakistan coach, badly needed a sit-down together before the Test at Headingley to bury any differences, and the ICC should have made that happen. Currently, it seems

Flashpoint: umpires Darrell Hair (second left) and Billy Doctrove (left) inform Inzamam–ul–Haq and his Pakistan team-mates that they are unhappy with the condition of the match ball at The Oval.

team, helpless, with cries of 'cheats' ringing in their ears. I asked Andrew Strauss how he might have reacted had he been in Inzamam's shoes that afternoon, and he could not come up with an explanation.

I am not of the view that ball-tampering should be allowed simply because it makes everyone's life easier. One proposition is to allow ball-tampering, but to give the fielding team only one ball in each innings. If they choose to scratch it to bits, that is up to them. But that would do nothing for the game in that the ball would become very soft and impossible to hit to the boundary. Besides, the decision whether or not to take the second new ball is one of the game's more intriguing talking points.

One of the umpires needs to see the ball at the end of every over and if any suspicions of sharp practice are aroused, he could raise it with the fielding captain who should then be seen to gather his team together, and warn them. I am also of the view that the captain needs to be held responsible for any ball-tampering incident and always to be punished alongside the offending bowler or fielder, if one is identified. Those two procedures would place heavily the responsibility on the captain to police his team, rather than the current practice of trying to conceal any surreptitious scratching and scraping from the umpires. It would not eliminate ball-tampering overnight, but I would not mind betting it would have a marked impact.

that no sooner has an umpire arrived for a Test match than he is on his way to stand in part of another series elsewhere in the world. Such is the hurly-burly of international cricket these days that the niceties are becoming things of the past, and there is no opportunity to nip festering disquiet in the bud. But this is just one area in which the role of the match referee should be expanded. Currently, his position is grey and undefined in that he is supposed to be in overall charge of the event, and yet, as we saw at The Oval, he defers to the umpires on playing matters. Mike Procter should have been empowered with the means to continue the match, even if it meant overruling Hair and Doctrove and getting the two reserve umpires to stand in their place. Laws need to be implemented, and Pakistan's refusal to play would still have stood on the charge sheet to be dealt with later but, for the time being, the game had to go on.

And so to the real issue: that of ball-tampering. As it stands at present, the Law is unworkable and must be changed. It is not right to have a situation in which two umpires can suddenly act as prosecutor, judge and jury and declare that a team is cheating without giving the captain any opportunity to defend himself, or have the decision overturned. Instead, he stands out there with his

Jonathan Agnew, Leicestershire, October 2006

CHELTENHAM & GLOUCESTER MAN OF THE YEAR AWARD

JONATHAN AGNEW profiles Monty Panesar, the 2006 C&G Man of the Year in succession to the 2003–2005 award winners Alec Stewart, Andrew Flintoff and Michael Vaughan.

Many people have been rightly praised for their part in the startling rise of Mudhsuden Singh Panesar in 2006, but the man who had the biggest hand in ensuring that Monty's international career was not snuffed out virtually the moment it started is rarely mentioned.

There is Monty's father, Paramjit, who first instilled the love of cricket in the youngster. When he travelled to his native Punjab to watch 24-year-old Monty play the Second Test against India in Mohali, Paramjit sat wide-eyed in the company of his own childhood hero, Bishen Bedi. He simply could not take it all in.

Then there is Hitu Naik, the hard-working coach at Luton Town & Indians Cricket Club. Naik is one of those men that have a knack of rarely appearing satisfied – no matter what his charge might have achieved – and he has also devoted a great deal of time and energy to improving Panesar's dreadful fielding. The results of that hard labour speak for themselves.

Nick Cook, the second XI coach at Northamptonshire and himself a former left-arm spinner, played his part too. But none of these individuals have had quite such an influence on Monty's career as the Indian wicketkeeper, Mahendra Dhoni.

In searing heat on an early Bombay afternoon in March, Dhoni – who was supposed to be staving off defeat – had a moment of madness for which he is unhappily renowned, and slogged a catch high into the clear blue sky. You could detect the moment from 100 yards away that England's fielders stopped preparing for their animated celebrations – it was when they realised that Monty was the man circling uneasily underneath it.

In fact, he never got near the catch. To gales of laughter

Above: The first of Monty's now-familiar celebratory routines, after he had dismissed Sachin Tendulkar to take his maiden Test wicket in Nagpur in March 2006.

Left: Monty Panesar's classical action has had the purists purring. An English Bedi?

from 30,000 Indian supporters and crushing embarrassment all round, Monty could only watch as after what seemed an age the ball finally plopped to the ground ten yards to his right. It was as grotesque a fielding blunder as there ever can have been. It also confirmed that while he appeared to be a promising bowler – he did claim Sachin Tendulkar as his first victim after all – Panesar was unselectable for Test cricket because of his dreadful fielding. Duncan Fletcher, the coach, simply would not sanction his inclusion.

And yet, only three balls later, Monty's world was turned on its head. Barely had the laughter subsided in the Wankhede Stadium than Dhoni inexplicably charged Shaun Udal again and produced an identically mis-hit high catch to exactly the same place. This time everybody held their breath as Panesar hovered beneath the catch: one can only imagine the terror he was feeling. But triumphantly and against all the odds he clutched on to the ball, demonstrating a nerve of steel that certainly had not been evident before. Suddenly, this was a man to be taken seriously and although he immediately dashed from the field to the dressing room, we are assured this was purely to restore his patka – which had been knocked out of position by his boisterous team-mates – rather than the result of an errant bodily function.

Panesar's fielding continued to entertain and frustrate in equal measure at the start of the summer. At Lord's against Sri Lanka, he was jeered every time the ball went close to him, and at Edgbaston he dropped a sitter at mid-off. And yet curiously, every time he came on to bowl, Panesar looked like a man entirely confident and comfortable with life in Test cricket. Indeed, a cricket ball appears to be his comfort blanket, for this ease is the absolute antithesis of his appearance and demeanour on the field when he does not have one in his hand.

The Third Test against Sri Lanka at Trent Bridge was an unhappy game for England. Not only was the Test lost, but Andrew Flintoff limped away and did not appear again for the rest of the summer. It was, however, a huge milestone in Panesar's fledgling career for not only did he take five wickets in the second innings but also conceded only 78 runs from 37 overs while doing so. Moreover, he gave an indication of some prowess with the bat, even hitting Muralitharan for six over deep midwicket during a 28-ball whirlwind innings of 26.

This was the confirmation that Panesar needed truly to believe that he is good enough to succeed at Test level. His bowling became even more intense and aggressive – yes, spinners can be combative characters – and with England only able to field four bowlers in Flintoff's absence, Panesar's ability to exert control as well as take key wickets was crucially important to England's success.

The Second Test against Pakistan at Old Trafford will be remembered for Steve Harmison's remarkable 6 for 19 in the first innings, but of equal value was Panesar's five-wicket haul in the second, in which he dismissed Nos. 2 to 7. At Headingley, he recorded what must rank as one of the most entertaining dismissals in Test cricket when Inzamam-ul-Haq fell on to his stumps but, far better, he produced the ball of the summer which pitched on middle stump and brushed the off bail to clean bowl Younis Khan. This was a classic piece

of left-arm spin bowling and the delivery which finally persuaded even the most ardent Ashley Giles supporter that, in seven short months, Panesar had seized the King of Spain's crown.

More than that, Panesar has overcome a personal battle to prove that there is room in the game for the traditionalist: that you do not have to be an all-rounder to bowl spin for England. To be fair, Daniel Vettori apart, the world lacks bowlers of his type so to claim that Panesar is now the best left-arm spinner on the planet does not say a great deal. However, the fact that we are still talking about him at all owes a great deal to the harebrained Dhoni, and whatever little prayer it was that Panesar offered when that second catch was launched in his direction.

The catch that made a man of Monty? Panesar is mobbed after clinging on to a skyer from Mahendra Dhoni in Mumbai, three balls after completely missing a similar chance.

IN PICTURES

In celebration of this 25th edition of *Cricket Year*, Jonathan Agnew and Mark Baldwin look back at the highs and lows of domestic and international cricket during the last 25 years.

1982
Fresh from his Ashes heroics in 1981,
Ian Botham hits his highest Test score against
India the following summer: 208 at The Oval.
Syed Kirmani is the wicketkeeper.

1983
Kapil Dev, India's captain,
holds the World Cup aloft on
the Lord's balcony after his side's
shock defeat of West Indies.

1984
Even one-handed, the West Indies of 1984 were more than a match for England as they completed a 5–0 'blackwash'. Malcolm Marshall later bowled out England in the Headingley Test despite having his injured left hand encased in plaster.

1985
David Gower (above) salutes The Oval crowd as England regain the Ashes.

Ian Botham (right), or 'Rambotham' as he was dubbed here in his 'Hollywood' years, enjoyed his last hurrah as a strike bowler in the 1985 Ashes series, taking 31 wickets.

1986
England's woes against the great West Indies teams of the 1980s continued in early 1986, their second successive 5–0 series thrashing following the other 'blackwash' of 1984. Mike Gatting (top left), meanwhile, came off second best against Malcolm Marshall in the Jamaica Test.

The picture says it all: Viv Richards (above) is ecstatic after smashing a 56-ball century, Test cricket's fastest ton, against England in his home island of Antigua.

Elton John (left), pictured with Ian Botham and Mike Gatting, was a big supporter of the England team in Australia during the 1986–87 Ashes series.

1987

The year got off to a good start for England (above), following their retaining of the Ashes in Australia ...

... but it did not end too well. After being beaten in the 1987 World Cup final by Australia, the England team were caught up in a controversial series in Pakistan. Here, Chris Broad (left) refuses to walk after being given out in the Lahore Test. His fellow England opener, Graham Gooch, eventually had to persuade him to leave the field.

The bad blood over umpiring decisions in the series finally boiled over when England captain Mike Gatting (left) had a stand-up row with Pakistan umpire Shakoor Rana at Faisalabad. As a result, the Test was held up for a day before Gatting was forced by the TCCB (under pressure from the Foreign Office) to apologise to Rana.

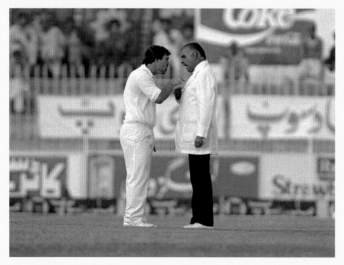

1988
Malcolm Marshall goes down on his knees in thanks
after dismissing Mike Gatting soon after he had been
sacked as England captain following the 'barmaid affair'
at Rothley Court Hotel during the First Test of the series
against West Indies. It was a summer in which England,
beaten 4–0, were to have four captains – Gatting, John
Emburey, Chris Cowdrey and Graham Gooch – with a fifth,
Derek Pringle, standing in as a temporary skipper when
Gooch was off the field nursing an injury during the final
Test at The Oval.

1989
Allan Border not only denied England the
World Cup in late 1987. He also rebuilt
Australia's Test side to the point where, in
1989, they won back the Ashes under his
gritty leadership in England ... a triumph
which started 16 long years of English hurt.

1990
The Lord's scoreboard
tells the tale as
Graham Gooch walks off
to a standing ovation at
the end of his epic 333
against India.

1991
Viv Richards, who took on and tamed the world's best bowlers in his maroon West Indies cap, ended his great Test career against England at The Oval in August 1991. He scored 8,540 runs in 121 Tests, at an average of 50.23, and also won 27 and lost only eight of his 50 Tests as captain.

1992
Pipped at the post by Pakistan's brilliance, England players (from left to right) Graham Gooch, Alec Stewart, Robin Smith and coach Mickey Stewart trudge a sad farewell lap of the Melbourne Cricket Ground after losing the World Cup final in a tournament they dominated.

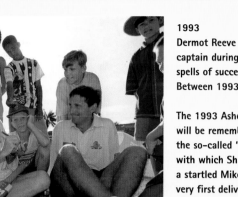

1993

Dermot Reeve (centre) was the Warwickshire captain during one of the most remarkable spells of success enjoyed by any county. Between 1993 and 1995 they won six titles.

The 1993 Ashes series, won again by Australia, will be remembered in particular for the so-called 'ball of the century' with which Shane Warne clean bowled a startled Mike Gatting with his very first delivery against England.

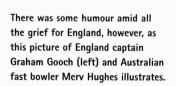

There was some humour amid all the grief for England, however, as this picture of England captain Graham Gooch (left) and Australian fast bowler Merv Hughes illustrates.

1994
Alec Stewart was a world-class performer with both bat and wicketkeeping gloves for England in a Test career which stretched from 1990 to 2003. Perhaps his greatest individual achievement came when he hit two hundreds in a Test match – the first Englishman ever to do so – as England beat the West Indies in Barbados for the first time.

An incredible year for Brian Lara (right and below) began when he scored a then world Test record 375 against England in Antigua.

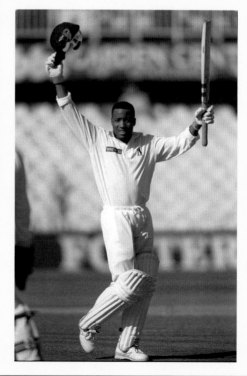

Lara's year continued when, playing for Warwickshire against Durham at Edgbaston in June, he hit 501 not out to eclipse Hanif Mohammad's 499; he also became the new holder of the highest first-class score.

1995
Dominic Cork made a dramatic entry
into Test cricket against the West Indies
in the summer of 1995. After taking
7 for 43 on his debut at Lord's
he picked up a hat-trick
in the Old Trafford Test (right).

Graham Gooch's great Test career
came to a close after
the 1994–95 Ashes series
in Australia.

1996
Arjuna Ranatunga raises the
1996 World Cup into the Lahore night sky
after Sri Lanka, ranked 66–1 outsiders
before the tournament, had beaten
Australia in the final.

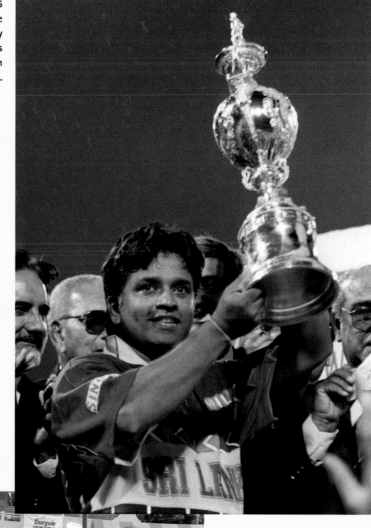

England's rancorous tour of
Zimbabwe in late 1996 included an
awkward moment for England captain
Mike Atherton in Harare. Should he
shake Zimbabwean president Robert
Mugabe's hand or not? In the end, he
offered a perfunctory handshake before
walking off as Mugabe greeted Zimbabwe's
captain Alistair Campbell. Sadly for
Zimbabwe and its cricket, the political
turmoil of Mugabe's years in power
continues still.

1997
Australia celebrate as England
last man Devon Malcolm walks off,
and the Ashes are secured by
Mark Taylor's men for the fifth
successive series.

Basil D'Oliveira, the
Cape Coloured former England
batsman and an important VIP,
surveys the scene at Newlands
in Cape Town as South African
cricket continues to heal the
wounds of its divisive past.

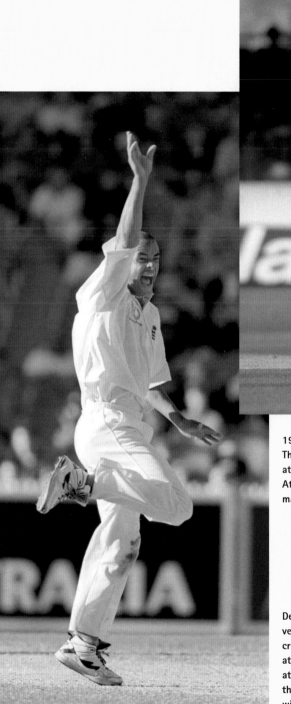

1998
The duel between Mike Atherton (above) and Allan Donald at Trent Bridge in July 1998 has gone down in cricket lore. Atherton's bravery, as well as Donald's ferociousness, made it compelling viewing.

Dean Headley could have become one of England's very best fast bowlers but for the back injury which cruelly cut short his career after just 15 Tests, and at the age of 29. Happily for him, though, he was at least able to take with him into premature retirement the memory of winning the 1998 Ashes Test at Melbourne with a heroic 6 for 66.

1999
The year started with a bang as England's
Darren Gough took an Ashes hat-trick
at Sydney in the final Test of the series.

The World Cup captains (below) pose with the trophy
before the start of the tournament in England.

South Africa's Allan Donald (right) walks off distraught,
as Australia's players celebrate, and one of the most
exciting World Cup matches ever played is over.
The semi-final at Edgbaston ended with scores level
after Donald and Lance Klusener had suffered
a mid-pitch mix-up and Donald, South Africa's
last wicket, was run out.

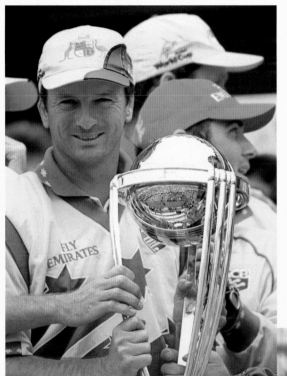

Steve Waugh (left) achieved yet another of his ambitions by leading Australia to victory in the World Cup final against Pakistan at Lord's.

England's lowest point of modern times? After flopping in the World Cup, England suffered defeat in the four-match Test series against New Zealand which followed it, and slumped to the bottom of the Test-match rankings. In contrast to the New Zealand celebrations at the end of The Oval Test (below), Nasser Hussain, the new England captain, was booed during the after-match presentations and vowed to lead England back to better times.

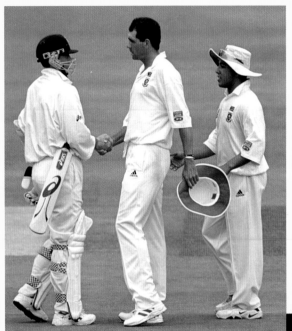

2000
Hansie Cronje (centre), South Africa's captain, shakes hands with Darren Gough after England had won the Centurion Test following Cronje's extraordinary last-morning declaration.
South Africa had already won the series, but Cronje's action led to more allegations of match-fixing. By April, Cronje was in the dock and in disgrace after admitting that he received gifts and money from bookmakers.

The year ended with England's upturn in fortunes continuing. After an exciting home series win against West Indies, Nasser Hussain's team went to Pakistan and won the deciding Test of a three-match series in a remarkable finish in near darkness in Karachi.

2001
Steve Waugh (far left), iron man captain of Australia, led his team to Ashes victory once more.

Darren Gough's bowling action (left) is a mixture of controlled power and balletic grace, as he leaps into the crease at Kandy during England's memorable 2-1 series win in Sri Lanka.

2002
Matthew Hoggard can only watch in wonderment as New Zealand's Nathan Astle cracks yet another six (left) during his amazing 153-ball double-hundred in Christchurch in early 2002. Unsurprisingly, it is the fastest 200 in Test history.

Rahul Dravid (right), along with Sachin Tendulkar, has provided cricket lovers with the best in Indian batsmanship for more than a decade now. In the summer of 2002 Dravid was prolific against England and fully lived up to his nickname of 'The Wall'.

2003
South Africa's patriotic and committed young captain, Graeme Smith, kicked off the summer series in England with innings of 277 at Edgbaston and 259 at Lord's.

2004

Cooley & The Gang: England's formidable pace quintet of Andrew Flintoff, Steve Harmison, Simon Jones, Matthew Hoggard and James Anderson pose with bowling coach Troy Cooley (centre) in the Caribbean, where England began a year of huge success by beating West Indies 3-0.

Brian Lara (above), however, prevented England from completing a 4-0 'whitewash' by scoring the little matter of 400 not out in the final Test in Antigua. On the same ground that he had made 375 ten years earlier, Lara reclaimed the world individual Test record from Matthew Hayden – whose 380 had come against the pop-gun attack of Zimbabwe seven months earlier.

Nasser Hussain (left), in his final Test appearance before announcing his retirement from all cricket, completes his hundred as England close in on victory in the opening Test of the summer against New Zealand at Lord's.

2005

After beating West Indies 4–0 at home in late 2004, and then defeating South Africa during the winter of 2004–05, England under Michael Vaughan were ready for the challenge of regaining the Ashes. A pulsating series duly followed, felt by many to be the greatest ever played, and many of the images from the five matches at Lord's, Edgbaston, Old Trafford, Trent Bridge and The Oval have already achieved iconic status. Here are just a few.

And, to cap a memorable 2005 summer for England, Clare Connor's women's team won back their version of the Ashes from Australia's women too.

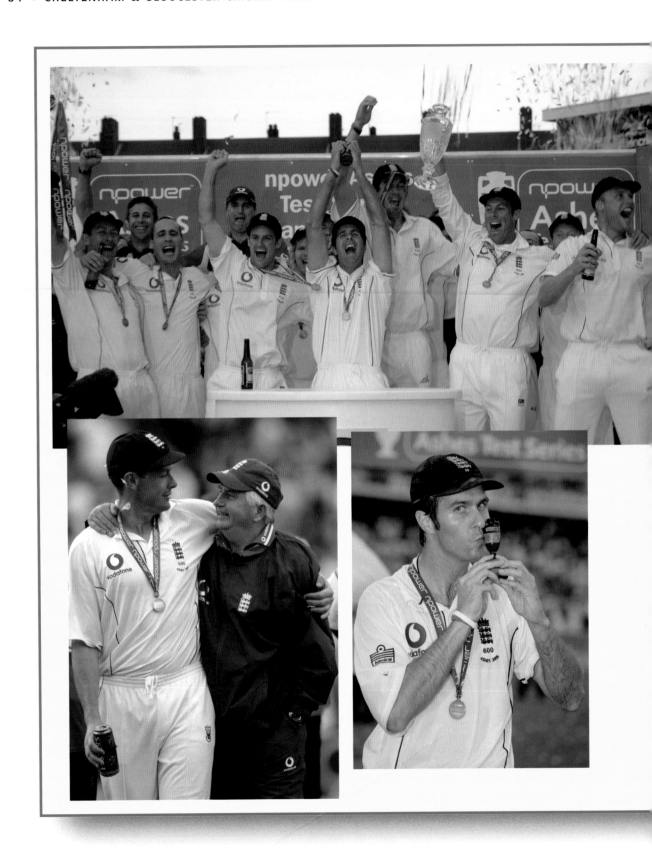

Scenes of jubilation followed England's
heart-stopping 2–1 series victory.

2006

The death on 1 July of Fred Trueman, one of England's finest cricketers, hit his family and many friends very hard. His, arguably, was the most classical bowling action there has ever been: perfectly side-on at the moment of delivery – illustrated below as he bowls for Yorkshire against Sussex at Middlesbrough in June 1960 – which helped to produce his dangerous outswinger. Fred was also the first bowler to take 300 Test wickets – at a rate of one in every 50 deliveries – but he will be remembered equally fondly as an entertaining contributor and great raconteur on *Test Match Special*.

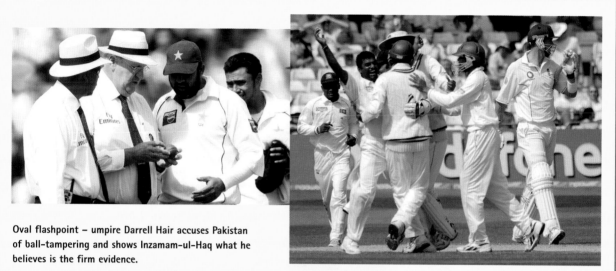

Oval flashpoint – umpire Darrell Hair accuses Pakistan of ball-tampering and shows Inzamam-ul-Haq what he believes is the firm evidence.

Kevin Pietersen exits stage right after enjoying a thrilling duel with Muttiah Muralitharan during England's early-season series against Sri Lanka which ended 1-1. Pietersen even played the shot of the summer against Murali – an astonishing switch-handed sweep for six way over the head of a startled cover point – but the Kandy Man won this battle.

Pakistan batsman Younis Khan looks back at his off stump in disbelief, but Monty Panesar is already away and running in jubilation after producing the ball of the summer – it pitched on middle-and-leg and clipped the top of the off bail – in the Headingley Test.

Mushtaq Ahmed, perhaps symbolically, single-handedly lifts the Liverpool Victoria County Championship trophy aloft after Sussex clinched the title by thrashing Nottinghamshire at Trent Bridge. Yet, while critics say Sussex are basically a one-man team on the back of the remarkable wicket-taking exploits of their Pakistani leg spinning wizard, skipper Chris Adams (applauding) knows that the county's successes of 2003 and now 2006 have been built upon many more vital factors, such as team spirit and thorough preparation.

ENGLAND

SRI LANKA IN ENGLAND
PAKISTAN IN ENGLAND
NATWEST TWENTY20 INTERNATIONALS
NATWEST ONE-DAY SERIES

SRI LANKA IN ENGLAND
By Jonathan Agnew

npower FIRST TEST
11–15 May 2006 at Lord's

The England team that reconvened at Lord's for the opening Test of the summer was very different to the one that beat up Bangladesh the previous year and which, almost to a man, went on to win the Ashes. An injury cloud continued to hang darkly over the squad, with Michael Vaughan, Ashley Giles and Simon Jones still appearing to be long-term absentees, while James Anderson was sidelined with a stress fracture in his back and Steve Harmison was still unavailable for England because of the shin problem that forced him back early from India.

Although Andrew Flintoff had done a sterling job with the captaincy on that trip, Vaughan's continued absence was now asking serious questions of the wisdom of Flintoff becoming what appeared increasingly to be England's full-time leader. Flintoff himself always spoke with great enthusiasm about the role, and certainly gave the impression of being entirely happy with the additional responsibility. At the same time, he made it quite clear that he believed Vaughan was needed back at the helm as quickly as possible.

Sri Lanka's build-up to the first match had hardly been auspicious, and the new chairman of selectors – the former fast bowler, Asantha de Mel – ruffled a few feathers when he unilaterally persuaded Sanath Jayasuriya out of retirement and flew him to England to join the tour. Jayasuriya arrived too late for the First Test, but the move was seen as being one in the eye for the coach, the affable Australian Tom Moody. In fact, Moody was to have the last laugh when his young batsmen made amends for a hideous collective first innings, and survived for 199 overs – and more than 14

hours – in their second innings to earn one of the hardest fought draws in cricket history.

Early May is hardly the best time for a team from the subcontinent to tour England. In fact, being 11 May, this was the earliest start to a Test summer ever, and the game appeared to be following its expected course as England rattled up 551 for 6, and promptly bowled Sri Lanka out for just 192.

Apart from the nightwatchman, Matthew Hoggard, everyone who batted for England made a decent contribution. Strauss and Trescothick's opening stand was worth 86 when Strauss was well taken at slip for 48 off Muttiah Muralitharan in the over before lunch. Trescothick and Cook took the score to 213 after tea when Trescothick, who really should have been given out lbw on 28, was well taken by Mahela Jayawardene – again off Muralitharan – for 106. It seemed to be a cast-iron certainty that Cook would score his second Test century in only his third match, but after a stand of 99 with Pietersen, he surprised everyone by flashing at a wide delivery from Farveez Maharoof, and was caught behind for 89 from 184 balls.

The sight of Hoggard plodding to the crease did little to quicken the pulse but he departed mercifully swiftly on the second morning, enabling the crowd to enjoy a stand of 173 for the fifth wicket that was ruthlessly dominated by Pietersen. He was very fortunate to survive a confident lbw appeal on 4, and was caught off a no-ball on 52, but he produced his usual array of outrageous shots as he raced to 158 from 205 balls, including 19 fours and two sixes. Collingwood was more than happy to play second fiddle – he scored a patient 57 – and when Flintoff had bludgeoned 33 from 29 balls, the captain declared 20 minutes before tea on 551 for 6.

By the close of the second day, Sri Lanka were already looking at certain defeat on 91 for 6, the small matter of 460 behind, and with 261 needed to avoid the follow-on. Apart from Jayawardene, the batsmen all looked hopelessly inadequate against the swinging ball, and a lively burst from Sajid Mahmood nipped out Sangakkara, Samaraweera and Kapugedera before the close.

By lunch on the third day Sri Lanka were dismissed with a massive deficit of 359 – Hoggard finished with 4 for 27 – and Flintoff had no option but to enforce the follow-on. The game, we felt, would end by lunch on the fourth day at the very latest.

But Sri Lanka had lost only three wickets when that interval came and went, with Jayawardene on 70. The captain reached his second century at Lord's just before tea, and was very unlucky to be given out caught behind down the legside after

FIRST TEST – ENGLAND v. SRI LANKA
11–15 May 2006 at Lord's

ENGLAND

	First Innings	
ME Trescothick	c Jayawardene b Muralitharan	106
AJ Strauss	c Jayawardene b Muralitharan	48
AN Cook	c Sangakkara b Maharoof	89
KP Pietersen	lbw b Vaas	158
MJ Hoggard	b Vaas	7
PD Collingwood	b Muralitharan	57
A Flintoff (capt)	not out	33
*GO Jones	not out	11
LE Plunkett		
SI Mahmood		
MS Panesar		
Extras	b 16, lb 7, w 4, nb 15	42
	(6 wkts dec 143 overs)	**551**

First Innings	O	M	R	W
Vaas	36	2	124	2
Maharoof	28	4	125	1
Kulasekara	25	3	89	0
Muralitharan	48	10	158	3
Dilshan	6	0	32	0

Fall of Wickets
1-86, 2-213, 3-312, 4-329, 5-502, 6-502

SRI LANKA

	First Innings		Second Innings (following on)	
J Mubarak	lbw b Hoggard	0	b Hoggard	6
WU Tharanga	lbw b Hoggard	10	c Jones b Panesar	52
*KC Sangakkara	c Trescothick b Mahmood	21	c Jones b Panesar	65
DPMD J'wardene (capt)	c Jones b Flintoff	61	c Jones b Flintoff	119
TT Samaraweera	lbw b Mahmood	0	(6) c Jones b Mahmood	6
TM Dilshan	run out	0	(7) c Trescothick b Plunkett	69
CK Kapugedera	lbw b Mahmood	0	(8) c Jones b Flintoff	10
MF Maharoof	c & b Hoggard	22	(5) c Pietersen b Mahmood	59
WPUJC Vaas	c Trescothick b Hoggard	31	not out	50
KMDN Kulasekara	c Strauss b Flintoff	29	c Pietersen b Hoggard	64
M Muralitharan	not out	0	not out	1
Extras	lb 8, nb 10	18	b 9, lb 19, w 3, nb 5	36
	(all out 55.3 overs)	**192**	(9 wkts 199 overs)	**537**

	First Innings				Second Innings			
	O	M	R	W	O	M	R	W
Hoggard	14	4	27	4	46	11	110	2
Flintoff	17.3	2	55	2	51	11	131	2
Plunkett	11	0	52	0	31	10	85	1
Mahmood	13	2	50	3	35	5	118	2
Collingwood	-	-	-	-	9	2	16	0
Panesar	-	-	-	-	27	10	49	2

Fall of Wickets
1-0, 2-21, 3-81, 4-81, 5-85, 6-85, 7-129, 8-131, 9-192
1-10, 2-119, 3-178, 4-291, 5-303, 6-371, 7-405, 8-421, 9-526

Umpires: Aleem Dar (Pakistan) & RE Koertzen (South Africa)
Toss: England
Debuts: SI Mahmood & CK Kapugedera
Man of the Match: DPMD Jayawardene

Match drawn

Another 158 ... and Kevin Pietersen, who famously made the same score at The Oval eight months earlier to help England to clinch the Ashes, celebrates reaching three figures against Sri Lanka at Lord's.

more than six hours at the crease when the ball appeared to brush his sweater.

England needed only four wickets on the final day, but by lunch Sri Lanka led by 70 runs with two wickets left. Vaas – normally a free-scoring tail-ender – knuckled down with Kulasekara, and defied England for 52 overs. It was clear that the lead would be beyond England when Kulasekara eventually pulled Hoggard to deep square leg for 64 from 133 balls, and bad light ended proceedings with Vaas on 50, having defied England for four hours and 13 minutes.

Depending upon the severity of one's assessment, England dropped nine chances, the most important being Jayawardene on 58, Kapugedera on 5 and Kulasekara on 14. When Vaas was put down – by Collingwood of all people – England would have needed to score 169 from 24 overs to win. It was a chastening experience for England's exhausted bowlers, with Hoggard, Flintoff and Mahmood all conceding more than a hundred runs each as Sri Lanka recorded the highest ever second-innings Test score made at Lord's.

npower SECOND TEST
25–28 May 2006 at Edgbaston

After the disappointment of Lord's, where England were unable to bowl Sri Lanka out a second time to win the match, Flintoff's team made no mistake at Birmingham and took the lead in the series midway through the fourth afternoon. It was not as one-sided as that suggests, however, with Muralitharan taking ten wickets in the game and forcing England unnecessarily to bat a second time.

Liam Plunkett, who was somewhat overshadowed by Mahmood at Lord's, was quickly among the wickets as, again, the Sri Lankans showed a naivety against the swinging ball. Flintoff's captaincy was more imaginative than at Lord's – he took himself off after only three overs at the start of the game in order to get Plunkett into the action – and although Vaas was again a determined adversary, batting two hours for his unbeaten 30, Sri Lanka were bundled out in only 51.2 overs for 141 – their second-lowest total against England – with Plunkett taking 3 for 43. It should be noted that Monty Panesar's fielding bordered on the woeful as he dropped a sitter at mid-off, but this did not noticeably appear to affect his bowling.

England were batting after tea on the first day, and were within three runs of level terms at the close, with seven wickets in hand. As at Lord's, Hoggard's

Liam Plunkett made an immediate impact with the ball in the Second Test against Sri Lanka.

SECOND TEST – ENGLAND v. SRI LANKA
25–28 May 2006 at Edgbaston

SRI LANKA

	First Innings		Second Innings	
MG Vandort	c Collingwood b Plunkett	9	c Jones b Plunkett	105
WU Tharanga	b Hoggard	0	c Jones b Hoggard	0
*KC Sangakkara	c Jones b Plunkett	25	c Collingwood b Panesar	18
DPMD J'wardene (capt)	c Jones b Plunkett	0	lbw b Hoggard	5
TT Samaraweera	c Collingwood b Hoggard	3	st Jones b Panesar	8
TM Dilshan	c Trescothick b Flintoff	27	lbw b Hoggard	59
MF Maharoof	c Jones b Mahmood	5	c & b Flintoff	13
WPUJC Vaas	not out	30	c Collingwood b Plunkett	1
KMDN Kulasekara	c Trescothick b Mahmood	3	c Collingwood b Plunkett	0
SL Malinga	lbw b Panesar	26	c Strauss b Flintoff	2
M Muralitharan	c Plunkett b Flintoff	1	not out	0
Extras	lb 6, nb 6	12	lb 8, w 1, nb 11	20
	(all out 51.2 overs)	141	(all out 93.2 overs)	231

	First Innings				Second Innings			
	O	M	R	W	O	M	R	W
Hoggard	15	4	32	2	22	8	64	3
Flintoff	13.2	4	28	2	19	3	50	2
Plunkett	12	1	43	3	13.2	6	17	3
Mahmood	9	1	25	2	9	2	19	0
Panesar	2	0	7	1	28	6	73	2
Collingwood	-	-	-	-	2	2	0	0

Fall of Wickets
1-3, 2-16, 3-16, 4-25, 5-46, 6-65, 7-79, 8-82, 9-132
1-2, 2-38, 3-43, 4-56, 5-181, 6-219, 7-223, 8-223, 9-231

ENGLAND

	First Innings		Second Innings	
ME Trescothick	c Sangakkara b Muralitharan	27	lbw b Muralitharan	0
AJ Strauss	run out	30	c Jayawardene b Muralitharan	16
AN Cook	lbw b Muralitharan	23	not out	34
KP Pietersen	lbw b Muralitharan	142	lbw b Muralitharan	13
MJ Hoggard	b Vaas	3		
PD Collingwood	c Tharanga b Muralitharan	19	(5) c Sangakkara b Muralitharan	3
A Flintoff (capt)	b Malinga	9	(6) not out	4
*GO Jones	c Samaraweera b Muralitharan	4		
LE Plunkett	c Vandort b Muralitharan	0		
SI Mahmood	not out	0		
MS Panesar	lbw b Malinga	0		
Extras	b 6, lb 13, nb 14, p 5	38	b 2, nb 9	11
	(all out 78.3 overs)	295	(4 wkts 27.2 overs)	81

	First Innings				Second Innings			
	O	M	R	W	O	M	R	W
Vaas	16	6	30	1	7	2	12	0
Malinga	13.3	3	68	2	7	1	29	0
Maharoof	11	3	42	0	-	-	-	-
Muralitharan	25	2	86	6	12.2	3	29	4
Kulasekara	13	2	45	0	-	-	-	-
Dilshan	-	-	-	-	1	0	9	0

Fall of Wickets
1-56, 2-69, 3-125, 4-169, 5-238, 6-290, 7-290, 8-293, 9-294
1-9, 2-35, 3-63, 4-73

Umpires: Aleem Dar (Pakistan) & DB Hair (Australia)
Toss: Sri Lanka
Man of the Match: KP Pietersen

England won by 6 wickets

contribution as nightwatchman was agreeably brief, and Pietersen's amazing hitting was again the highlight of England's first innings. He even contrived to reverse sweep Muralitharan for six – surely a first in Test cricket – as he made 142 from only 157 balls. In all he hit 20 fours and three sixes, but he also had a stroke of luck because on two occasions he might well have been given out lbw off Muralitharan. That was how he perished in the end as Murali's doosra trapped him in front, but there was no doubt about who had dominated the contest.

The rest of England's batting was a huge disappointment with the next-highest score being 30. On a pitch that appeared to be deteriorating quickly, batting demanded discipline, not least to leave oneself exposed to batting a second time against Murali. The last five wickets fell for only five runs in 29 balls as the champion off spinner claimed 6 for 86.

Sri Lanka were quickly reduced to 56 for 4, and struggled to 86 for 4 at the close of the second day, but they lost only one more wicket on a rain-hit third day, with the towering opener, Michael Vandort, on 89 not out. By then Sri Lanka were 40 runs ahead, and having already seen the danger that Muralitharan represented, it was clear that England had to polish off the lower order very quickly. Vandort duly reached his well-deserved century from 294 balls, and was well set to carry his bat when the last man, Muralitharan, joined him with Sri Lanka's lead standing at 77. But on 105, Vandort edged Plunkett to Jones, to give the Durham swing bowler the excellent figures of 3 for 17, and to set England an easy target of 78 to win.

Murali was quickly into the attack – and among the wickets. Trescothick was trapped lbw for a duck to his fourth delivery, and Strauss edged him to slip for 16. Fifteen runs were needed when Pietersen was lbw to the doosra for the second time in the game – this time for just 13. And with five to win, Collingwood was caught behind for 3. But Cook again displayed a maturity beyond his 21 years to finish unbeaten on 34 as England won by six wickets.

npower THIRD TEST
2–5 June 2006 at Trent Bridge

When Sri Lanka, who needed to win the final Test in order to level the series, were reduced to 139 for 8 before tea on the first day, not many pundits would seriously have given them a prayer of achieving their aim. But, due to the two constants in the series – England's fickle batting and Muralitharan's bowling,

Sri Lanka completed their remarkable victory soon after tea on the fourth afternoon.

This England team was so far removed from the Ashes-winning unit as to be unrecognisable, and yet seven of the players involved in this game had featured in the series against Australia the previous summer. The problem remained the absence of key players – Vaughan, Giles, Harmison and Simon Jones who, shortly after this match, was to be ruled out of the forthcoming Ashes tour because of further knee surgery.

Sri Lanka managed to struggle to 231 thanks, yet again, to another excellent innings by Vaas who scored an unbeaten 38 as the last two wickets added 92. Even Murali managed to swipe 33 as the gloss was taken off England's effort, which was led on his debut by the redoubtable Jon Lewis who, with 3 for 68, enjoyed the morning's favourable conditions. He took a wicket with only his fourth ball when Vandort – a centurion at Edgbaston – played-on for a single. Jayawardene's precious wicket was taken by Flintoff who, for the first time in the series, regularly bowled in excess of 90 mph. It was much more like the conquering hero of the previous summer and yet he was to break down and be ruled out of the one-day NatWest Series which followed this Test.

England had already lost two wickets by the close of the first day – the openers, Strauss and Trescothick for

Muttiah Muralitharan greets the demise of yet another victim during his decisive 8 for 70 at Trent Bridge.

7 and 24 respectively. Trescothick's run out – taking a completely unnecessary second to fine leg, was one of the most gormless examples of running between the wickets to have been seen for a long time.

Even so, if this game was to follow the pattern of the previous two, England would build a lead and put Sri Lanka under pressure in their second innings. In fact, England lost eight wickets for 156 in 73 overs, with Pietersen scoring 41 from 58 balls and then, as the innings started to unfold, Collingwood faced 184 balls and batted for three and three-quarter hours for his 48. It was tortuous stuff, as only 52 runs were scored in the 35 overs between lunch and tea, and only a feisty 20 from Lewis lifted England to within two runs of Sri Lanka. A potentially awkward session of 14 overs remained on the second day giving England a chance to fight back. But they managed to claim only one wicket and Sri Lanka, with an overnight lead of 47, were well placed to press on.

The following morning the top order all contributed as the runs were added steadily, yet Panesar and Plunkett chipped away to the extent that at tea the game was superbly set up with Sri Lanka 221 in the lead, but with only five wickets left. By the close, that had been extended to 288 thanks to Kapugedera's 50 and another solid and supporting 24 from the reinvented Vaas. With the ball now spinning sharply at times, it was already looking to be a long shot for England, and when Panesar had taken the last two wickets to claim his first five-wicket haul in Test cricket, England needed 325 to win, which would have represented England's second-highest successful run chase.

Despite an encouraging start, they got nowhere near, of course, as Murali got to work. Strauss and Trescothick cruelly raised English hopes as, untroubled, they put on 84. But after them only two batsmen – Plunkett and, bizarrely, Panesar – reached double figures. Their unlikely last-wicket stand of 37 spared England from a complete rout as Muralitharan took the first seven wickets to fall. Hoggard's run out eliminated the chance of Murali becoming only the third Test bowler in history to take all ten in an innings, but he finished with the amazing figures of 8 for 70 from 30 overs and, clearly, none of England's batsmen could read him either in the air or off the pitch.

Excellent catching by Dilshan close to the wicket gave Murali excellent support as England caved in and lost eight wickets for 49, leaving Sri Lanka to celebrate what was only their second Test victory in England.

THIRD TEST – ENGLAND v. SRI LANKA
2–5 June 2006 at Trent Bridge

SRI LANKA

	First Innings		Second Innings	
MG Vandort	b Lewis	1	b Hoggard	5
WU Tharanga	c Jones b Hoggard	34	c Cook b Panesar	46
*KC Sangakkara	c Jones b Flintoff	36	c Trescothick b Flintoff	66
DPMD J'wardene (capt)	c Jones b Flintoff	0	c Jones b Plunkett	45
TM Dilshan	c Flintoff b Lewis	8	(6) c Jones b Hoggard	32
ST Jayasuriya	c Pietersen b Flintoff	4	(5) lbw b Panesar	4
CK Kapugedera	c Strauss b Plunkett	14	c Cook b Plunkett	50
MF Maharoof	c Flintoff b Hoggard	13	b Panesar	6
WPUJC Vaas	not out	38	not out	34
SL Malinga	c Pietersen b Lewis	21	b Panesar	22
M Muralitharan	c Flintoff b Plunkett	33	c Strauss b Panesar	2
Extras	b 4, lb 3, w 2, nb 20	29	b 1, lb 3, w 1, nb 5	10
	(all out 66.2 overs)	231	(all out 113.1 overs)	322

	First Innings				Second Innings			
	O	M	R	W	O	M	R	W
Hoggard	17	3	65	2	22	4	71	2
Lewis	21	3	68	3	20	6	54	0
Plunkett	8.2	1	36	2	19	2	65	2
Flintoff	15	2	52	3	13	1	38	1
Panesar	5	3	3	0	37.1	13	78	5
Pietersen	-	-	-	-	2	0	12	0

Fall of Wickets
1-2, 2-84, 3-85, 4-86, 5-97, 6-105, 7-129, 8-139, 9-169
1-6, 2-100, 3-143, 4-148, 5-191, 6-223, 7-238, 8-287, 9-320

ENGLAND

	First Innings		Second Innings	
ME Trescothick	run out	24	b Muralitharan	31
AJ Strauss	b Vaas	7	c Jayawardene b Muralitharan	55
AN Cook	b Malinga	24	lbw b Muralitharan	5
KP Pietersen	c Jayawardene b Muralitharan	41	c Dilshan b Muralitharan	6
PD Collingwood	lbw b Vaas	48	c Dilshan b Muralitharan	9
A Flintoff (capt)	c Jayawardene b Jayasuriya	1	c Dilshan b Muralitharan	0
*GO Jones	st Sangakkara b Muralitharan	19	b Muralitharan	6
LE Plunkett	b Jayasuriya	9	not out	22
MJ Hoggard	c Jayawardene b Muralitharan	10	run out	4
J Lewis	c Dilshan b Malinga	20	lbw b Muralitharan	7
MS Panesar	not out	0	lbw b Jayasuriya	26
Extras	b 2, lb 13, w 3, nb 8	26	b 13, lb 1, w 1, nb 4	19
	(all out 91.1 overs)	229	(all out 68.5 overs)	190

	First Innings				Second Innings			
	O	M	R	W	O	M	R	W
Vaas	26	5	71	2	9	1	28	0
Malinga	23.1	5	62	2	7	0	24	0
Muralitharan	31	10	62	3	30	10	70	8
Jayasuriya	11	4	19	2	22.5	3	54	1

Fall of Wickets
1-25, 2-39, 3-73, 4-117, 5-118, 6-151, 7-184, 8-196, 9-229
1-84, 2-104, 3-111, 4-120, 5-120, 6-125, 7-132, 8-136, 9-153

Umpires: DB Hair (Australia) & RE Koertzen (South Africa)
Toss: Sri Lanka
Debut: J lewis
Man of the Match: M Muralitharan
Men of the Series: M Muralitharan & KP Pietersen

Sri Lanka won by 134 runs

SERIES AVERAGES
England v. Sri Lanka

ENGLAND

Batting	M	Inns	NO	Runs	HS	Av	100	50	c/st
KP Pietersen	3	5	0	360	158	72.00	2	-	4/-
AN Cook	3	5	1	175	89	43.75	-	1	2/-
ME Trescothick	3	5	0	188	106	37.60	1	-	6/-
AJ Strauss	3	5	0	156	55	31.20	-	1	4/-
PD Collingwood	3	5	0	136	57	27.20	-	1	5/-
A Flintoff	3	5	2	47	33*	15.66	-	-	4/-
LE Plunkett	3	3	1	31	22*	15.50	-	-	1/-
J Lewis	1	2	0	27	20	13.50	-	-	-/-
GO Jones	3	4	1	40	19	13.33	-	-	16/1
MS Panesar	3	3	1	26	26	13.00	-	-	-/-
MJ Hoggard	3	4	0	24	10	6.00	-	-	1/-
SI Mahmood	2	1	1	0	0*	-	-	-	-/-

Bowling	Overs	Mds	Runs	Wkts	Av	Best	5/inn	10m
MS Panesar	99.1	32	210	10	21.00	5-78	1	-
MJ Hoggard	136	34	369	15	24.60	4-27	-	-
LE Plunkett	94.4	20	298	11	27.09	3-17	-	-
A Flintoff	128.5	23	354	12	29.50	3-52	-	-
SI Mahmood	66	10	212	7	30.28	3-50	-	-
J Lewis	41	9	122	3	40.66	3-68	-	-

Also bowled: KP Pietersen 2-0-12-0, PD Collingwood 11-4-16-0.

SRI LANKA

Batting	M	Inns	NO	Runs	HS	Av	100	50	c/st
WPUJC Vaas	3	6	4	184	50*	92.00	-	1	-/-
KC Sangakkara	3	6	0	231	66	38.50	-	2	3/-
DPMD Jayawardene	3	6	0	230	119	38.33	1	1	7/-
TM Dilshan	3	6	0	195	69	32.50	-	2	4/-
MG Vandort	2	4	0	120	105	30.00	1	-	1/-
KMDN Kulasekara	2	4	0	96	64	24.00	-	1	-/-
WU Tharanga	3	6	0	142	52	23.66	-	1	1/-
MF Maharoof	3	6	0	118	59	19.66	-	1	-/-
CK Kapugedera	2	4	0	74	50	18.50	-	1	-/-
SL Malinga	2	4	0	71	26	17.75	-	-	-/-
M Muralitharan	3	6	3	37	33	12.33	-	-	-/-
TT Samaraweera	2	4	0	17	8	4.25	-	-	1/-
ST Jayasuriya	1	2	0	8	4	4.00	-	-	-/-
J Mubarak	1	2	0	6	6	3.00	-	-	-/-

Bowling	Overs	Mds	Runs	Wkts	Av	Best	5/inn	10m
M Muralitharan	146.2	35	405	24	16.87	8-70	2	2
ST Jayasuriya	33.5	7	73	3	24.33	2-19	-	-
SL Malinga	50.4	6	183	4	45.75	2-62	-	-
WPUJC Vaas	94	16	265	5	53.00	2-71	-	-
MF Maharoof	39	7	167	1	167.00	1-125	-	-

Also bowled: TM Dilshan 7-0-41-0, KMDN Kulasekara 38-5-134-0.

NATWEST SERIES v. Sri Lanka
By Jonathan Agnew

With Andrew Flintoff sidelined for the rest of the summer following an operation on his left foot, it was left to Andrew Strauss to shoulder the burden of leading England's one-day team in the NatWest Series against Sri Lanka. And what an onerous task this proved to be as the bowlers – inexperienced, maybe – produced possibly the worst attempt at displaying the required skills at this level of limited-overs cricket there has ever been. Words cannot adequately describe quite how badly they bowled.

The Twenty20 international match at the Rose Bowl, preceding the NatWest Series, was a decent game in which Sri Lanka won by just two runs. Jayasuriya caned 41 from 30 balls as Sri Lanka set England 164 to win and, despite Trescothick's 57-ball 72, Tim Bresnan found himself with the unlikely task of hitting the last ball for six.

On a glorious morning at Lord's, in the opening NatWest Series match, England conceded a record number of extras – 42, including a staggering 23 wides – as Sri Lanka notched up 257 for 9. Tharanga cut and carved an entertaining 120, and although Trescothick again replied positively with 67, England were always behind the rate. Dalrymple made an encouraging 67, but England fell 20 runs short.

At The Oval, Sri Lanka made 319 for 8, their highest score against England, and a total that included another 21 wides. Jayasuriya returned to his blistering best form with a magnificent century, and his assault on Sajid Mahmood – who conceded 80 from seven overs – bordered on cruelty. Pietersen scored 73, and Collingwood 56, and although Dalrymple impressed again, it was in another losing cause, this time by 46 runs.

And things got worse still. At the Riverside, England set a decent target of 262 to win, thanks to 77 from Bell – but it was knocked off in only the 43rd over. Jayawardene was Sri Lanka's centurion this time, his 126 not out coming from just 127 balls. At Old Trafford, it was Kabir Ali's turn to go round the park. His last over disappeared for 20 as Jayawardene made another hundred – this time from only 83 balls. A further 21 wides were delivered by England's errant bowlers who by now were so shell-shocked that they were on the verge of ducking each time they released the ball. Trescothick and Strauss both passed 40 but, unlike their opponents, no one went on to make a big score and England fell short by 33 runs to go 4–0 down in the series.

And so to Headingley, the coup de grâce, where England's bowlers were mercilessly crucified. Trescothick scored a very good hundred (121 from 118 balls) to set up a commanding target of 322. Incredibly, this was knocked off with almost 12 overs to spare as a rampant Jayasuriya scored 152 in an opening stand of 286 with Tharanga (109). It is the biggest opening partnership in the history of one-day international cricket, and came at an astonishing rate. The hundred was posted in only the eighth over, and after ten overs Sri Lanka were 133 for no wicket. Harmison broke the record for the most expensive analysis in internationals – ten overs for 97 – and to complete a bleak day, he was then able to watch England's footballers being knocked out of the World Cup by Portugal.

NatWest Twenty20 International

15 June 2006
at the Rose Bowl
Sri Lanka 163 all out (20 overs)
(PD Collingwood 4 for 22)
England 161 for 5 (20 overs)
(ME Trescothick 72)
Sri Lanka won by 2 runs

NatWest One-Day Series

Match One
17 June 2006 at Lord's
Sri Lanka 257 for 9 (50 overs)
(WU Tharanga 120)
England 237 for 9 (50 overs)
(ME Trescothick 67,
JWM Dalrymple 67)
Sri Lanka won by 20 runs

Match Two
20 June 2006 at The Oval
Sri Lanka 319 for 8 (50 overs)
(ST Jayasuriya 122,
DPMD Jayawardene 66,
KC Sangakkara 51)
England 273 all out (46.4 overs)
(KP Pietersen 73,
PD Collingwood 56)
Sri Lanka won by 46 runs

Match Three
24 June 2006
at Chester-le-Street
England 261 for 7 (50 overs)
(IR Bell 77)
Sri Lanka 265 for 2 (42.2 overs)
(DPMD Jayawardene 126*,
KC Sangakkara 58*)
Sri Lanka won by 8 wickets

Match Four
28 June 2006 at Old Trafford
Sri Lanka 318 for 7 (50 overs) (DPMD Jayawardene 100, WU Tharanga 60, MF Maharoof 58*)
England 285 all out (48.4 overs)
Sri Lanka won by 33 runs

Match Five
1 July 2006 at Headingley
England 321 for 7 (50 overs) (ME Trescothick 121, SL Malinga 4 for 44)
Sri Lanka 324 for 2 (37.3 overs) (ST Jayasuriya 152, WU Tharanga 109)
Sri Lanka won by 8 wickets

Sri Lanka won the series 5–0

Marcus Trescothick is pictured during his 118-ball 121 against Sri Lanka at Headingley, a fine innings ultimately overshadowed by the record-breaking stand of 286 between Sanath Jayasuriya and Upul Tharanga.

OF ENGLAND

By Jonathan Agnew

There is a symmetrical feel to the last 25 years of English cricket in that the period began with an Ashes summer which gripped the nation and ends at a time when interest in sport's greatest contest has never been higher.

Interestingly, a larger-than-life all-rounder called Ian Botham dominated the 1981 Ashes with performances that, in all likelihood, will never quite be matched again. Could anyone ever do another Headingley 1981? Surely not, but if history ever does repeat itself, chances are that a certain Andrew Flintoff – a chip off the old block if ever there was one – will be the man responsible.

It would not be accurate to dwell on the last 25 years of Ashes cricket and feel any smugness, however. The victories in question are two of only four completed by England in that time, compared to nine by Australia. With the West Indies, who repeatedly crushed England (and everyone else) in the 1980s, Australia enjoyed an unprecedented superiority over the old enemy.

Eras are all about the characters that dominate them. Botham, David Gower, Allan Lamb, Mike Gatting and Graham Gooch entertained us all in the 1980s in their very different ways. Lamb's record against the West Indies is astonishing, while Gooch's 154 not out against them at Headingley in 1991 was one of the greatest innings I have seen. Mike Atherton produced another – a typically cussed 185 not out against South Africa at the Wanderers in 1995 – which stands out from the crowd, as did Alec Stewart's two hundreds in Barbados the previous winter to set up England's first victory there for 60 years.

The twilight image of Gatting arguing passionately with umpire Shakoor Rana in Faisalabad in 1987 reminds us of the various controversies of the time, including the dirt-in-the-pocket saga, as well as the spectre of match-fixing. Umpire Javed Akhtar was widely accused of corruption following his one-off match against South Africa at Headingley in 1998 – a performance so ghastly and inept as to beggar belief – but the charges against him were never proven. Two years later England gained an unlikely victory in Pretoria, only to discover later that South African captain Hansie Cronje had sold out to the bookies.

Overall, results in the1990s gave rise to the realisation that English cricket needed a complete overhaul if it were to become competitive again. Lord MacLaurin, the chairman of the newly formed England and Wales Cricket Board, introduced central contracts to control the amount of county cricket that the top players feature in, and a

Mike Atherton and Jack Russell are captured in perfect harmony at Johannesburg in 1995, deep into their epic Test-saving partnership against South Africa.

magnificently equipped Academy was set up. Whether or not these measures are entirely responsible for the recent upturn is open to debate, but it is no coincidence that ten years after a period of ridicule and criticism, national pride has been restored in cricket once again.

The appointment as captain of the popular, thoughtful and determined Michael Vaughan after a necessary period of butt-kicking by Nasser Hussain played its part – as did the emergence of Steve Harmison who led England's resurgence with a blistering year in which he shot to number one in the international rankings. His effectiveness has dwindled, but Matthew Hoggard, Simon Jones and Flintoff also came to the fore, fuelled by his example.

Nothing has changed more in the last 25 years than the incredible level of support that England's cricketers now enjoy overseas. Whether they be housed in the 'posh seats' or are members of the Barmy Army singing and sweltering on the terraces, cricket fans young and old have discovered that there is little to beat some winter sunshine while cheering on their national team. Former strongholds including Barbados, Johannesburg and Sydney have been transformed into a sea of red, white and blue reflecting the view that while participation at school level remains a concern, English cricket has never been so popular as it is now.

PAKISTAN IN ENGLAND
By Jonathan Agnew

npower FIRST TEST
13–17 July 2006 at Lord's

Test cricket is played at such a fast pace these days that old-fashioned, solid draws are few and far between. With neither side wanting to give anything away in the first of four matches, the outcome at Lord's was entirely predictable once Pakistan had responded strongly to England's first innings total of 528 for 9 declared.

Pakistan put down five chances on the opening day – shades of England against Sri Lanka on the same ground earlier in the summer. Alastair Cook benefited to an almost embarrassing degree, being dropped on 0, 45 and 81, so it would have been criminal had he not battled through to his third hundred in only his sixth Test match. He reached the milestone just before the close of the first-day's play, and shortly after Collingwood had beaten him to it. At stumps England were 309 for 3, and the foundation for a very large first innings had been laid.

Five overs into the second day, Cook was bowled by Mohammad Sami for 105, but Bell and Collingwood – who had also received reprieves on 79 and 131 – added 120 before, 14 runs short of a maiden double-hundred, Collingwood was surprised by a ball from Danish Kaneria which spun sharply, and he was stumped by Kamran Akmal after a stay of seven hours and 20 minutes. Flintoff's absence had provided Bell with a lifeline, and batting at No. 6 he suddenly appeared liberated. Driving classically, and working smoothly off his pads, Bell became the third centurion of the innings, enabling Strauss to declare with 19 overs of the second day remaining.

It was a difficult period for Pakistan to negotiate, and with Harmison working up a welcome head of steam, they lost Salman Butt for 10, Imran Farhat for 33 and finally Faisal Iqbal to a screamer of a catch by Collingwood at third slip. They hobbled to 66 for 3 at the end of the day, but could easily have lost another wicket or two.

With only four frontline bowlers to choose from, Strauss had his work cut out on the third day, which was dominated by the prolific Mohammad Yousuf. The heavily bearded right-hander, who recently denounced his position as the only Christian in the team and converted to Islam, has a remarkable tendency to convert centuries into big hundreds. Never flustered, he duly reached his fourth double-century with a rare edge off Hoggard, having faced 325 balls. With Inzamam-ul-Haq, he added 173, before the captain was bowled in rather strange fashion behind his legs by Plunkett, and then Akmal scored 58 in a stand of 99, which ended when Yousuf edged Harmison to Jones for 202. Hoggard wrapped up the innings for 445, dismissing Afridi for 17 and Gul for a duck to finish with 3 for 117, while Harmison took 4 for 94.

England pressed on cautiously throughout the fourth day, with Strauss becoming only the third Englishman to score a hundred in his first Test as captain. Wary of being bowled out cheaply themselves, England's policy was to ensure that Pakistan were not given even a remote sniff of victory. Strauss scored 128 from 214 balls after Pietersen had been stumped by Akmal for 41 and Bell was run out for 28 as Strauss chased the second run to bring up his hundred. By the close, England led by 341, which surely would have been enough to guarantee their safety, but they chose to bat on into the fifth morning, adding a further 38 in 35 minutes. It was a disappointingly negative approach, but

What a take: Paul Collingwood produces a trademark leaping effort at Lord's to catch Faisal Iqbal off the bowling of Steve Harmison.

Strauss – under the impression at the time that this would be his only Test in charge – clearly did not want a record of played one, lost one. Finally the declaration came, setting Pakistan an impossible 380 to win in 80 overs.

When Hoggard had Butt lbw to the first ball of Pakistan's innings, followed by Farhat, caught at slip for 18, England's hopes soared. The important wicket was Yousuf who made 48 in typically assured style before playing no stroke to Panesar and falling lbw. The left-arm spinner struck again with the score on 141 when Faisal Iqbal was taken at gully for 48, but Inzamam remained immovable at the other end. After he and Razzaq had occupied the crease for 29 overs, Strauss called a halt to proceedings with eight overs remaining.

Mohammad Yousuf: the faith may have changed, but the class and skill of his batsmanship have remained the same. He scored a total of 250 runs in the Lord's Test.

FIRST TEST – ENGLAND v. PAKISTAN
13–17 July 2006 at Lord's

ENGLAND

	First Innings			Second Innings	
ME Trescothick	c Kamran Akmal b Umar Gul	16		b Umar Gul	18
AJ Strauss (capt)	lbw b Abdul Razzaq	30		c Imran Farhat b Danish Kaneria	128
AN Cook	b Mohammad Sami	105		c Mohammad Yousuf b Umar Gul	4
KP Pietersen	lbw b Abdul Razzaq	21		st Kamran Akmal b Shahid Afridi	41
PD Collingwood	st Kamran Akmal b Danish Kaneria	186		c Salman Butt b Danish Kaneria	3
IR Bell	not out	100		run out	28
*GO Jones	lbw b Danish Kaneria	18		c Kamran Akmal b Danish Kaneria	16
LE Plunkett	c Imran Farhat b Danish Kaneria	0		c Kamran Akmal b Abdul Razzaq	28
MJ Hoggard	lbw b Shahid Afridi	13		not out	12
SJ Harmison	run out	2			
MS Panesar	not out	0			
Extras	b 8, w 15, nb 14	37		b 5, lb 6, w 1, nb 6	18
	(9 wkts dec 158.3 overs)	528		(8 wkts dec 84.5 overs)	296

	First Innings				Second Innings			
	O	M	R	W	O	M	R	W
Mohammad Sami	28	4	116	1	6	1	23	0
Umar Gul	33	6	133	1	19	4	70	2
Abdul Razzaq	25	2	86	2	9.5	0	45	1
Danish Kaneria	52	6	119	3	30	4	77	3
Shahid Afridi	19.3	0	63	1	19	1	65	1
Imran Farhat	1	0	3	0	1	0	5	0

Fall of Wickets
1-60, 2-60, 3-88, 4-321, 5-441, 6-469, 7-473, 8-515, 9-525
1-38, 2-64, 3-141, 4-146, 5-203, 6-250, 7-253, 8-296

PAKISTAN

	First Innings			Second Innings	
Salman Butt	c Strauss b Harmison	10		lbw b Hoggard	0
Imran Farhat	b Plunkett	33		c Collingwood b Hoggard	18
Faisal Iqbal	c Collingwood b Harmison	0		c Cook b Panesar	48
Mohammad Yousuf	c Jones b Harmison	202		lbw b Panesar	48
Mohammad Sami	c Jones b Hoggard	0			
Inzamam-ul-Haq (capt)	b Plunkett	69		(5) not out	56
Abdul Razzaq	c Jones b Harmison	22		(6) not out	25
*Kamran Akmal	c Jones b Pietersen	58			
Shahid Afridi	c Bell b Hoggard	17			
Umar Gul	c Jones b Hoggard	0			
Danish Kaneria	not out	1			
Extras	b 7, lb 14, w 7, nb 5	33		b 1, lb 8, w 6, nb 4	19
	(all out 119.3 overs)	445		(4 wkts 73 overs)	214

	First Innings				Second Innings			
	O	M	R	W	O	M	R	W
Hoggard	33	3	117	3	12	3	31	2
Harmison	29.3	6	94	4	15	3	43	0
Panesar	27	3	93	0	27	7	60	2
Plunkett	21	3	78	2	12	2	41	0
Collingwood	7	1	31	0	2	0	11	0
Pietersen	2	0	11	1	5	1	19	0

Fall of Wickets
1-28, 2-28, 3-65, 4-68, 5-241, 6-300, 7-399, 8-435, 9-436
1-0, 2-33, 3-116, 4-141

Umpires: SA Bucknor (West Indies) & SJA Taufel (Australia)
Toss: England
Man of the Match: Mohammad Yousuf

Match drawn

npower SECOND TEST
27–29 July at Old Trafford

A stunning bowling performance by Steve Harmison – who relished a bone-hard pitch and some uneven bounce – condemned Pakistan to an overwhelming defeat within three days by an innings and 120 runs. One had to question the lack of resolve by one or two of Pakistan's top order, who clearly did not have the stomach for a fight, while Alastair Cook became the first Englishman since Ian Botham to record three centuries in his first seven Tests.

Inzamam won the toss and chose to bat first, but his team was soon in disarray at 93 for 6. It would be wrong to suggest that Harmison was back to his best – there were far too many wayward deliveries for that – but this was a reminder of the danger he is still capable of producing when the mood takes him. Inzamam, who failed to score, was the sixth out with the score on only 93. The previous delivery from Harmison, which bounced prodigiously, clearly unsettled him and although the next ball lifted a little more than he might have expected, his limp prod to gully did little to calm the fears of the batsmen that remained. As it was, they were cleared up in no time with Harmison finishing with the remarkable figures of 6 for 19 from 13 overs – his seventh five-wicket bag in Tests. Panesar claimed three wickets, including that of Yousuf for 38, which ended a partnership of 81 with Younis Khan, who top scored with 44. The rest of the team managed 33 between them, as eight wickets fell for only 29 runs in 85 balls.

To complete a bizarre day, England, having lost Trescothick to a catch behind off Sami for a laboured 5 and Strauss for 42, then closed on 168 for 2 having scored 119 runs in the final session – the same number of runs that Pakistan scored in their first innings.

Pakistan lacked England's firepower – and especially a tall pace bowler to make the most of the variable bounce, and England batted them out of the game on the second day, despite Pietersen falling to only the second ball of the morning and a brilliant catch in the gully by Farhat. Collingwood continued his good progress and added 119 with Cook before he fell to the second new ball for 48. England were 288 for 4, already leading by 169 runs and, having faced 259 balls, Cook was finally bowled by the persevering Gul for 127. When Jones – whose place was now under real threat because of his poor batting form – scratched about for 8, it was just possible for Pakistan to keep England's lead within limits. But Bell, who was on only 19 when he was joined by the No. 8, Mahmood, produced a quite superb innings of 106 not out from 135 balls. Bell batted brilliantly, driving handsomely through the covers, and he was well supported by Harmison who stayed with him for an hour while 73 runs were added. Strauss decided to give Pakistan's openers an uncomfortable four overs to bat on the second evening by declaring on 461 for 9, a lead of 342.

Alastair Cook's great natural talent brought him a third Test hundred in just his seventh match – his 127 enabling him to equal Ian Botham's feat of almost 30 years previously.

Harmison's first loosener of a delivery flew directly to a startled second slip, and the fast bowler immediately clutched his left side, suggesting that he had suffered a serious injury. He managed to complete the over, and received treatment, but England anxiously awaited news of any adverse overnight reaction.

In fact there was none, and Harmison was fit to bowl straight away, removing Akmal in the fourth over when he edged to Jones for 4. But overall, Pakistan made a better fist of their second innings, as Harmison struggled to find a controlled line, and it was left to Panesar to come into his own with an aggressive and mightily effective spell of spin

bowling. He claimed five middle-order wickets on the trot, again removing the cream of the batting, and including the curious dismissal of Yousuf who was stumped for 15 off the first delivery after lunch. Inzamam was caught off his boot at silly point for 13, and when Pakistan had lurched towards defeat on 174 for 6, Strauss brought Harmison back to deal with the somewhat reluctant lower order. Afridi slogged, but the plan worked as the last five wickets fell for only 48 runs after tea. Harmison – who completed his first ten-wicket haul for England – took 5 for 57, but the real star was Panesar whose 5 for 72 was, in truth, the most consistent bowling performance of the match.

England's players begin their celebrations as Steve Harmison takes the final Pakistan wicket, and his own 11th of the match, to clinch the drubbing of Pakistan at Old Trafford.

SECOND TEST – ENGLAND v. PAKISTAN
27–29 July 2006 at Old Trafford

PAKISTAN

	First Innings		Second Innings	
*Kamran Akmal	c Trescothick b Harmison	4	c Jones b Harmison	4
Imran Farhat	c Pietersen b Harmison	0	c Bell b Panesar	34
Younis Khan	c Collingwood b Harmison	44	lbw b Panesar	62
Mohammad Yousuf	c Jones b Panesar	38	st Jones b Panesar	15
Inzamam-ul-Haq (capt)	c Pietersen b Panesar	0	c Cook b Panesar	13
Faisal Iqbal	c Jones b Panesar	3	c Trescothick b Panesar	29
Abdul Razzaq	b Harmison	9	c Jones b Harmison	13
Shahid Afridi	c Pietersen b Panesar	15	c Strauss b Harmison	17
Mohammad Sami	c Strauss b Harmison	1	c Jones b Harmison	0
Umar Gul	not out	1	c Jones b Harmison	13
Danish Kaneria	run out	0	not out	4
Extras	lb 2, w 2	4	b 4, lb 4, w 6, nb 4	18
	(all out 38.4 overs)	119	(all out 67.1 overs)	222

	First Innings				Second Innings			
	O	M	R	W	O	M	R	W
Hoggard	9	1	30	0	14	2	52	0
Harmison	13	7	19	6	18.1	3	57	5
Mahmood	6	1	33	0	6	1	22	0
Collingwood	3	0	14	0	-	-	-	-
Panesar	7.4	3	21	3	27	4	72	5
Pietersen	-	-	-	-	2	0	11	0

Fall of Wickets
1-4, 2-9, 3-90, 4-90, 5-93, 6-93, 7-112, 8-113, 9-118
1-21, 2-60, 3-101, 4-117, 5-161, 6-174, 7-194, 8-194, 9-208

ENGLAND

	First Innings	
ME Trescothick	c Kamran Akmal b Mohammad Sami	5
AJ Strauss (capt)	c Kamran Akmal b Abdul Razzaq	42
AN Cook	lbw b Umar Gul	127
KP Pietersen	c Imran Farhat b Umar Gul	38
PD Collingwood	c Mohammad Sami b Umar Gul	48
IR Bell	not out	106
*GO Jones	lbw b Mohammad Sami	8
SI Mahmood	c & b Abdul Razzaq	12
MJ Hoggard	lbw b Shahid Afridi	6
SJ Harmison	c Kamran Akmal b Danish Kaneria	26
MS Panesar	not out	3
Extras	b 9, lb 10, w 7, nb 14	40
	(9 wkts dec 133 overs)	461

	First Innings			
	O	M	R	W
Mohammad Sami	28	5	92	2
Umar Gul	28	2	96	3
Abdul Razzaq	19	4	72	2
Danish Kaneria	37	8	106	1
Shahid Afridi	21	0	76	1

Fall of Wickets
1-30, 2-95, 3-169, 4-288, 5-304, 6-321, 7-357, 8-384, 9-457

Umpires: SA Bucknor (West Indies) & SJA Taufel (Australia)
Toss: Pakistan
Man of the Match: SJ Harmison

England won by an innings and 120 runs

npower THIRD TEST
4–8 August at Headingley

The selectors finally bowed to the inevitable and, after a run of 31 consecutive Tests, dropped Geraint Jones for Chris Read. Ironically, Jones had been keeping wicket more tidily than at any other stage in his Test career – and he was passed fit for this match despite breaking a finger at Old Trafford. Although Duncan Fletcher resisted – he is, after all, the man who infuriated Rod Marsh when he replaced Read with Jones in the first place – Jones's figures spoke for themselves. Brought in to bolster England's lower-order batting, Jones's average had slipped to 25 and he had scored just one fifty in his last nine Tests. What an irony, then, that Read's batting for Nottinghamshire should secure his position in the England team once again, and he showed in the course of his return match that the decision was not misguided. Meanwhile Pakistan rang the changes once again, unveiling another opening combination while dropping Razzaq and Afridi.

At first glance, the foundation for England's series-clinching victory was the imposing first innings score of 515, but that score – at Headingley, don't forget – was overtaken by Pakistan who, from that position, really should have made a better fist of the match.

England battled to 110 for 3 with Trescothick (28), Strauss (36) and Cook (23) all contriving to get out when they had made starts, and Pietersen really should have been given out by Darrell Hair when he had scored just 2. The ball flicked the inside edge before brushing his leg, but this was not picked up by the umpire. Pakistan's fury increased when Billy Doctrove immediately turned down another perfectly good appeal for caught behind against Cook – Inzamam was positively animated at slip – but then the Pakistanis already had an issue about Hair standing in this series. This was due to perceived bias against them – something Hair would refute absolutely – but this mutual mistrust would spill over and cause the unprecedented scenes which brought the following Test at The Oval to a premature end.

Although Cook did not last much longer, Pietersen – who had stood his ground angelically – rubbed salt into Inzamam's wounds by scoring a typically bullish century. This was his fourth in Tests, and came from only 123 balls and dominated a partnership of 82 with Collingwood for the fourth wicket. Collingwood fell for 31, but Bell – in rampant form – joined Pietersen shortly before tea and the pair seemed destined to bat out the day until Pietersen was suddenly hit by cramp in his forearm. After receiving

Sealed with a kiss: Ian Bell celebrates becoming only the tenth Englishman to score a century in three successive Tests.

treatment on the field, he was then immediately dropped on 104 and wisely felt that he should retire hurt. This was followed by a curious passage of play in which Inzamam – desperate for the second new ball – introduced his part-time spinners, Taufeeq and Butt. All the pressure on Read was lifted at a stroke as six overs of assorted rubbish conceded 26 runs, and Read gently returned to Test cricket equalling his top score – 38 – as he and Bell added 86 together. Hoggard's attempt at nightwatchman was snuffed out by what became the last ball of the day.

Pietersen was fit enough to resume first thing on the second morning. He moved aggressively on to 135 before holing out on the long off boundary, leaving Mahmood to escort Bell to his third successive hundred – the tenth Englishman to achieve this record. After he was bowled by Kaneria for 119 from 206 balls, Harmison and Mahmood slogged an entertaining 56 together before England were dismissed for 515 shortly after lunch on the second day.

THIRD TEST – ENGLAND v. PAKISTAN
4–8 August 2006 at Headingley

ENGLAND

	First Innings		Second Innings	
ME Trescothick	c & b Mohammad Sami	28	c Salman Butt b Umar Gul	58
AJ Strauss (capt)	c Younis Khan b Shahid Nazir	36	c Kamran Akmal b M Sami	116
AN Cook	c & b Umar Gul	23	c Faisal Iqbal b Danish Kaneria	21
KP Pietersen	c Shahid Nazir b Mohammad Sami	135	b Danish Kaneria	16
PD Collingwood	c Taufeeq Umar b Umar Gul	31	b Shahid Nazir	25
IR Bell	b Danish Kaneria	119	c Kamran Akmal b M Sami	4
*CMW Read	lbw b Umar Gul	38	b Mohammad Sami	55
MJ Hoggard	b Umar Gul	0	(9) c Younis Khan b Shahid Nazir	8
SI Mahmood	b Umar Gul	34	(8) c Kamran Akmal b Shahid Nazir	2
SJ Harmison	c M Sami b Danish Kaneria	36	c sub b Umar Gul	4
MS Panesar	not out	5	not out	5
Extras	b 13, lb 6, nb 11	30	b 8, lb 3, w 1, nb 19	31
	(all out 123 overs)	515	(all out 88.3 overs)	345

	First Innings				Second Innings			
	O	M	R	W	O	M	R	W
Mohammad Sami	26	1	135	2	21.3	4	100	3
Umar Gul	29	4	123	5	20	1	76	2
Shahid Nazir	28	7	101	1	14	4	32	3
Danish Kaneria	34	4	111	2	33	2	126	2
Taufeeq Umar	2	0	8	0	–	–	–	–
Salman Butt	4	0	18	0	–	–	–	–

Fall of Wickets
1-67, 2-67, 3-110, 4-192, 5-345, 6-347, 7-421, 8-445, 9-501
1-158, 2-190, 3-214, 4-237, 5-248, 6-299, 7-301, 8-323, 9-332

PAKISTAN

	First Innings		Second Innings	
Salman Butt	run out	20	c Trescothick b Hoggard	16
Taufeeq Umar	c Read b Hoggard	7	c Cook b Panesar	11
Younis Khan	run out	173	b Panesar	41
Mohammad Yousuf	c Read b Harmison	192	run out	8
Inzamam-ul-Haq (capt)	hit wkt b Panesar	26	(7) st Read b Panesar	37
Faisal Iqbal	lbw b Collingwood	0	(5) c Read b Mahmood	11
*Kamran Akmal	c Trescothick b Mahmood	20	(6) c Read b Mahmood	0
Mohammad Sami	c Harmison b Panesar	19	run out	0
Shahid Nazir	not out	13	c Trescothick b Mahmood	17
Umar Gul	c Panesar b Mahmood	7	c Collingwood b Mahmood	0
Danish Kaneria	c Trescothick b Panesar	29	not out	0
Extras	b 1, lb 20, w 5, nb 6	32	lb 6, w 5, nb 3	14
	(all out 141.4 overs)	538	(all out 47.5 overs)	155

	First Innings				Second Innings			
	O	M	R	W	O	M	R	W
Hoggard	29	4	93	1	7	3	26	1
Harmison	30	1	142	1	15	3	62	0
Mahmood	24	1	108	2	8	2	22	4
Panesar	47.4	13	127	3	17.5	4	39	3
Pietersen	1	0	14	0	–	–	–	–
Collingwood	10	1	33	1	–	–	–	–

Fall of Wickets
1-34, 2-36, 3-399, 4-447, 5-447, 6-451, 7-481, 8-489, 9-496
1-23, 2-52, 3-68, 4-80, 5-80, 6-112, 7-113, 8-148, 9-149

Umpires: BR Doctrove (West Indies) & DB Hair (Australia)
Toss: England
Man of the Match: Younis Khan

England won by 167 runs

Pakistan's reply recovered from a shaky start (36 for 2) to the small matter of 399 for 2. This now stands as the seventh-highest third-wicket partnership in Test cricket and, for a long time, never seemed as if it would end as Yousuf and Younis batted brilliantly in their individual styles for five hours and 43 minutes to put on 363 – this after Collingwood had put down Yousuf on 5 at third slip. Harmison finally snared him as he gloved a lifter down the leg side for 192 from 261 balls, and then the fun started.

Bearing in mind that Inzamam was in a filthy mood anyway, his run out of Younis for 192 was a fine achievement. Younis, who is always all smiles, managed to retain his humour at least until he had left the ground, but he was shortly to be joined in the pavilion by Inzamam, whose dismissal must rank as one of the most hilarious and embarrassing in Test cricket. Aiming to sweep Panesar, Inzamam lost his balance and slowly, inexorably and with an absolute lack of dignity, collapsed on to his stumps which, at the very last moment, he attempted hopelessly to hurdle. It was a glorious spectacle and one which, to be fair, Inzamam admitted seeing the funny side to later in the game. Inzamam departed at 451 for 6 – Pakistan having lost three wickets for four runs in two overs – but the tail added a further 87 to give Pakistan a narrow lead of 23.

Despite Trescothick being dropped on 6 and 7, he and Strauss constructed their eighth century opening stand together and took England comfortably ahead before Trescothick was taken low at second slip for 58. Cook fell for 21 ten overs later, at which point Pakistan chipped away by taking England's last nine wickets for 187. In scoring his second century of the series, Strauss confirmed that he was thriving on the responsibility of leadership, but the other crucial contribution came lower down the order at No. 7 where Read made an excellent 55. Unlike the first innings, this was a pressure situation because England's lead

had stood merely at 225. With what remained of England's batting, Read added 97 priceless runs in 28 overs before being the last man out.

Thanks to Read, Pakistan's victory target now stood at 323 in 91 overs – a very different proposition – and after they had lost Butt in the tenth over to a good catch at first slip by Trescothick, their attempt at victory quickly unravelled. Yousuf was run out by a direct hit by Collingwood in the gully for 8, and Mahmood nipped out Faisal Iqbal and Kamran Akmal within three balls to leave Pakistan floundering on 80 for 5. The prize wicket was that of Younis Khan, who was clean bowled by the delivery of the summer from Panesar. Pitching on middle stump, the ball turned and bounced to miss the outside edge of the bat and knock off the off bail. It was an unplayable delivery, and Pakistan's slide to defeat was hastened when a disgruntled Inzamam was stumped off Panesar to give the spinner 3 for 39, while Mahmood's 4 for 22 was comfortably his most assured effort in Test cricket.

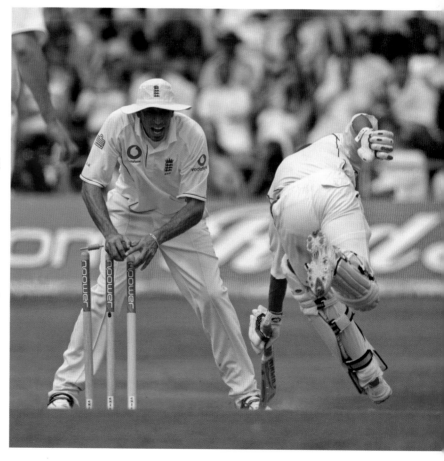

Howzat! England's Sajid Mahmood runs out Mohammad Sami as Pakistan slip to defeat at Headingley.

npower FOURTH TEST
17–20 August at The Oval

A Test match that was dominated throughout by Pakistan ended both suddenly and dramatically on the fourth afternoon when the umpires, Darrell Hair and Billy Doctrove, ruled that the game had been forfeited by Pakistan – the first time a Test had ended in such a manner in the history of the game. The decision crowned one of the most controversial days in Test cricket, during which the umpires charged Pakistan with ball-tampering, and awarded five penalty runs to England. Such is the framework of the Law that the effect of this was to pronounce Pakistan guilty of cheating without any opportunity for them to defend themselves.

Play continued until the tea interval, at which point a decision was taken in the Pakistan dressing room that a protest would be mounted. Rather than issue a firm statement of denial, and taking up the matter with the referee at the end of the day – which is the correct procedure – Inzamam and his team stayed in their dressing room when the umpires took the field at the end of the tea break. Four minutes later, the umpires walked off, and there was a short break of ten minutes during which Pakistan were warned of the consequences of failing to take the field a second time. The umpires and the England batsmen – Collingwood and Bell – then returned to the pitch. Again there was no movement from the Pakistan dressing room, so the umpires removed the bails and awarded the match to England. A further 20 minutes passed before Inzamam led his team on to a deserted field, but the decision had already been taken.

Now the arguments began, and behind the scenes there were frantic efforts as officials both at The Oval and in Dubai – the home of the ICC – tried in vain to convince the umpires to change their minds. An announcement that play had been abandoned for the day was finally made at a quarter past six to an increasingly angry and frustrated crowd which, shamefully, had been kept in the dark throughout. Still the arguments raged in the pavilion until 10.10 pm, when an exasperated ICC official confirmed that the umpires would not budge, and that the game had been awarded to England.

Umpire Darrell Hair confers with England batsmen Paul Collingwood and Ian Bell while, in the background, his fellow umpire Billy Doctrove removes the bails to signify that The Oval Test has been officially forfeited by Pakistan for refusing to play on.

Twenty minutes after Hair and Doctrove made their fateful ruling, Pakistan captain Inzamam-ul-Haq led his team out on to the field. When the umpires did not appear again, he then led his players back to their dressing room once more.

Depending on your view, this was an example of grotesque intransigence and a lack of common sense by the umpires, or a case of adhering to the fundamental principle of the game that the umpire's word is final, and that refusing to play in protest at an umpiring decision can bring only one outcome.

Needless to say, the issue dominated the cricket world for the five weeks it took for the disciplinary hearing to take place, in which Inzamam – representing his team – was cleared of ball tampering, but found guilty of bringing the game into disrepute. This is discussed in greater depth in Aggers' View at the beginning of this book.

When the match was abandoned, England were battling for their lives at 298 for 4 – still 33 runs behind – and, with a full day left, Pakistan might very well have completed their first victory of the series.

Inzamam won the toss on the first damp and overcast morning, and put England in to bat. With his attack reinforced by the return of Mohammad Asif, Inzamam's decision paid off with England limping to 134 for 6 at tea. Pietersen was out first ball to Asif, and only Strauss and Cook managed to reach double figures until Read played another valuable lower-order knock of 33 to add 46 with Mahmood. But the wicketkeeper chopped the ball into his stumps and England were quickly polished off for 173, with Asif taking 4 for 56 and Gul 4 for 46.

Pakistan seized their chance to pile the pressure on England by replying with the small matter of 504. Mohammad Hafeez and Imran Farhat both fell in the nineties, while Mohammad Yousuf, having been dropped on 5 and 9, continued his excellent tour with his third score of a hundred or more to give him a series average of 90.14. Faisal Iqbal chipped in with an unbeaten 58 after Yousuf fell to Hoggard for 128 from 236 balls. Pakistan lost their last seven wickets for 125 runs, but their lead of 331 was

FOURTH TEST – ENGLAND v. PAKISTAN
17–20 August 2006 at The Oval

ENGLAND

	First Innings		Second Innings	
ME Trescothick	c Mohammad Hafeez b Umar Gul	6	c Kamran Akmal b M Asif	4
AJ Strauss (capt)	c Kamran Akmal b M Asif	38	lbw b Danish Kaneria	54
AN Cook	lbw b Shahid Nazir	40	lbw b Umar Gul	83
KP Pietersen	c Kamran Akmal b M Asif	0	c Kamran Akmal b Shahid Nazir	96
PD Collingwood	lbw b Mohammad Asif	5	not out	26
IR Bell	c Faisal Iqbal b Danish Kaneria	9	not out	9
*CMW Read	b Umar Gul	33		
SI Mahmood	b Umar Gul	15		
MJ Hoggard	c Kamran Akmal b M Asif	3		
SJ Harmison	not out	8		
MS Panesar	b Umar Gul	0		
Extras	b 4, lb 5, nb 7	16	b 8, lb 3, nb 10, p 5	26
	(all out 53.2 overs)	173	(4 wkts 72 overs)	298

	First Innings				Second Innings			
	O	M	R	W	O	M	R	W
Mohammad Asif	19	6	56	4	17	1	79	1
Umar Gul	15.2	3	46	4	14	1	70	1
Shahid Nazir	11	1	44	1	8	1	26	1
Danish Kaneria	8	1	18	1	29	6	94	1
Mohammad Hafeez	-	-	-	-	4	1	13	0

Fall of Wickets
1-36, 2-54, 3-54, 4-64, 5-91, 6-112, 7-158, 8-163, 9-173
1-8, 2-115, 3-218, 4-277

PAKISTAN

	First Innings	
Mohammad Hafeez	c Strauss b Hoggard	95
Imran Farhat	c Trescothick b Hoggard	91
Younis Khan	c Read b Mahmood	9
Mohammad Yousuf	c Read b Hoggard	128
Inzamam-ul-Haq (capt)	c Strauss b Harmison	31
Faisal Iqbal	not out	58
*Kamran Akmal	c Collingwood b Harmison	15
Shahid Nazir	c Hoggard b Mahmood	17
Umar Gul	lbw b Panesar	13
Danish Kaneria	c Trescothick b Harmison	15
Mohammad Asif	c Cook b Harmison	0
Extras	b 4, lb 9, w 11, nb 8	32
	(all out 129.5 overs)	504

	First Innings			
	O	M	R	W
Hoggard	34	2	124	3
Harmison	30.5	6	125	4
Mahmood	27	3	101	2
Panesar	30	6	103	1
Collingwood	6	0	29	0
Pietersen	2	0	9	0

Fall of Wickets
1-70, 2-148, 3-325, 4-379, 5-381, 6-398, 7-444, 8-475, 9-504

Umpires: BR Doctrove (West Indies) & DB Hair (Australia)
Toss: Pakistan
Man of the Series: Mohammad Yousuf

England won by default

SERIES AVERAGES
England v. Pakistan

ENGLAND

Batting	M	Inns	NO	Runs	HS	Av	100	50	c/st
IR Bell	4	7	3	375	119	93.75	3	-	2/-
AJ Strauss	4	7	0	444	128	63.42	2	1	5/-
AN Cook	4	7	0	403	127	57.57	2	1	4/-
PD Collingwood	4	7	1	324	186	54.00	1	-	5/-
KP Pietersen	4	7	0	347	135	49.57	1	1	3/-
CMW Read	2	3	0	126	55	42.00	-	1	6/1
ME Trescothick	4	7	0	135	58	19.28	-	1	8/-
SJ Harmison	4	5	1	76	36	19.00	-	-	1/-
SI Mahmood	3	4	0	63	34	15.75	-	-	-/-
GO Jones	2	3	0	42	18	14.00	-	-	11/1
LE Plunkett	1	2	0	28	28	14.00	-	-	-/-
MS Panesar	4	5	4	13	5*	13.00	-	-	1/-
MJ Hoggard	4	6	1	42	13	8.40	-	-	1/-

Bowling	Overs	Mds	Runs	Wkts	Av	Best	5/inn	10m
SJ Harmison	151.3	29	542	20	27.10	6-19	2	1
MS Panesar	184.1	40	515	17	30.29	5-72	1	-
SI Mahmood	71	11	286	8	35.75	4-22	-	-
MJ Hoggard	138	18	473	10	47.30	3-117	-	-
LE Plunkett	33	5	119	2	59.50	2-78	-	-
KP Pietersen	12	1	64	1	64.00	1-11	-	-
PD Collingwood	28	2	118	1	118.00	1-33	-	-

PAKISTAN

Batting	M	Inns	NO	Runs	HS	Av	100	50	c/st
Mohammad Hafeez	1	1	0	95	95	95.00	-	1	1/-
Mohammad Yousuf	4	7	0	631	202	90.14	3	-	1/-
Younis Khan	3	5	0	329	173	65.80	1	1	2/-
Inzamam-ul-Haq	4	7	1	232	69	38.66	-	2	-/-
Imran Farhat	3	5	0	176	91	35.20	-	1	3/-
Faisal Iqbal	4	7	1	149	58*	24.83	-	1	2/-
Shahid Nazir	2	3	1	47	17	23.50	-	-	1/-
Abdul Razzaq	2	4	1	69	25*	23.00	-	-	1/-
Kamran Akmal	4	6	0	101	58	16.83	-	1	14/2
Shahid Afridi	2	3	0	49	17	16.33	-	-	-/-
Danish Kaneria	4	6	3	49	29	16.33	-	-	-/-
Salman Butt	2	4	0	46	20	11.50	-	-	2/-
Taufeeq Umar	1	2	0	18	11	9.00	-	-	1/-
Umar Gul	4	6	1	34	13	6.80	-	-	1/-
Mohammad Sami	3	5	0	20	19	4.00	-	-	3/-
Mohammad Asif	1	1	0	0	0	0.00	-	-	-/-

Bowling	Overs	Mds	Runs	Wkts	Av	Best	5/inn	10m
Mohammad Asif	36	7	135	5	27.00	4-56	-	-
Shahid Nazir	61	13	203	6	33.83	3-32	-	-
Umar Gul	158.2	21	614	18	34.11	5-123	1	-
Abdul Razzaq	53.5	6	203	5	40.60	2-72	-	-
Danish Kaneria	223	31	651	13	50.07	3-77	-	-
Mohammad Sami	109.3	15	466	8	58.25	3-100	-	-
Shahid Afridi	59.3	15	204	3	68.00	1-63	-	-

Also bowled: Imran Farhat 2-0-8-0, Taufeeq Umar 2-0-8-0, Mohammad Hafeez 4-1-13-0, Salman Butt 4-0-18-0.

substantial, and by the close of the third day, England had already lost Trescothick, who was caught behind off Asif for 4.

The dramatic fourth day began with England battling to stave off defeat. Strauss fell in the morning session, lbw to Kaneria for 54, but chances went begging. Cook should have been given out caught at silly point on 33, was bowled by a no-ball on 40 and Faisal dropped a sitter at square leg when he had 47. Pietersen was dropped by Akmal off Kaneria on 15, but when Cook was yorked for 83 with England 119 behind, Pakistan were still in command.

Four overs later, the umpires consulted and held a brief discussion with a bemused Inzamam. Umpire Hair signalled a five-run penalty to the scorers, and the batsmen – Collingwood and Pietersen – chose the replacement ball, confirming to onlookers that this was indeed the implementation of Law 42.3.

Pietersen set about a dispirited attack, reaching 96 before edging a catch behind the wicket, but all the while resentment and frustration was building up in the Pakistan dressing room. As the players left the field for tea, however, nobody was to know that we had seen the last of the action in a Test match that has now gained notoriety for all the wrong reasons.

NATWEST SERIES v. Pakistan
By Jonathan Agnew

After fears that the one-day series might not proceed following the debacle at The Oval – the West Indies were prepared to stand in if Pakistan had flown home – it was with great relief that common sense prevailed.

Having lost every one-day game to Sri Lanka earlier in the summer, it was crucial that England started to find a winning formula in the limited-overs arena, but a straightforward victory for Pakistan in the Twenty20 International opener in Bristol confirmed that this would be another tough series for Andrew Strauss's team.

Pakistan would probably have won the first 50-over match at Cardiff, too, had rain not washed it out. England made only 202, with Bell scoring 88, and Pakistan were romping along at 46 for 1 from 7 overs, chasing a revised target of 159 from 32, when the heavens opened. Duckworth-Lewis intervened at Lord's, too, but this time Pakistan comfortably knocked off their target of 167 in 40 overs. Shoaib Akhtar tore in to claim four wickets, and had it not been for a stand of 53 between Clarke and Read, the game would have been over very early indeed. As it was, Younis Khan (55), Mohammad Yousuf (49 not out) and Inzamam (42 not out from 26 balls) confirmed Pakistan's superiority.

Back in action: Shoaib Akhtar returned from a lengthy injury lay-off to spearhead Pakistan's attack in the NatWest Series.

Ian Bell, England's best batsman in the NatWest Series games against Pakistan, sweeps Shahid Afridi for four during the unbeaten 86 which guided his side to victory at Trent Bridge.

To the Rose Bowl, and a closer contest. Pakistan seemed to be easing to a second comfortable win when they suddenly lost their way in the closing stages, and limped home with an over to spare. Strauss, Collingwood and Dalrymple all hit half-centuries, but they were put well in the shade by a brilliant hundred by the effervescent Younis Khan. With Broad, Mahmood and Lewis taking late wickets, it was left to Inzamam to negotiate his way to victory with an unbeaten 44.

Strauss finally broke his duck in the fourth match at Trent Bridge – his 11th one-day game as captain. It was also England's first win in 12 one-day internationals and came despite some fantastic hitting by Razzaq. Rescuing Pakistan from 117 for 6, he scored 75 from 72 balls. No fewer than 47 runs were smashed from the last 12 balls of the innings,

with Razzaq scoring 45 from 16 deliveries. His sixes got bigger and bolder, and the last ball of the innings landed in the top tier of the pavilion. Strauss and Bell put England on course with a solid second-wicket stand of 110, and when the captain was bowled by Hafeez for 78, Pietersen and Bell added 89. In the end, Bell was on 86 not out as England won with 22 balls remaining.

Pakistan had started strongly in the tournament, but now it seemed as if they were starting to run out of steam. England had to win the final game at Edgbaston to level the series, and a desperately close tussle it turned out to be. Pakistan struggled to post only 154 for 9, but the conditions remained awkward for batting and England slipped to 49 for 3. Pietersen and Collingwood made 34 and 22 respectively, but Razzaq and Afridi both took two wickets to leave England floundering on 118 for 7 – still needing 37 to win with only three wickets left. Yardy and Mahmood, however, kept their cool, and carefully saw England to victory with 19 overs remaining.

NatWest Twenty20 International

28 August 2006 at Bristol
England 144 for 7 (20 overs) (ME Trescothick 53, Abdul Razzaq 3 for 30)
Pakistan 148 for 5 (17.5 overs)
Pakistan won by 5 wickets

NatWest One-Day Series

Match One
30 August 2006 at Cardiff
England 202 all out (49.2 overs)
(IR Bell 88)
Pakistan 46 for 1 (7 overs)
Match abandoned – rain

Match Two
2 September 2006 at Lord's
England 166 all out (39.1 overs)
(Shoaib Akhtar 4 for 28)
Pakistan 169 for 3 (36.4 overs)
(Younis Khan 55)
*Pakistan won by 7 wickets
– DL Method: target 167
from 40 overs*

Match Three
5 September 2006
at the Rose Bowl
England 271 for 9 (50 overs)
(JWM Dalrymple 62,
PD Collingwood 61, AJ Strauss 50,
Naved-ul-Hasan 4 for 57)
Pakistan 274 for 8 (48.5 overs)
(Younis Khan 101,
Mohammad Yousuf 60)
Pakistan won by 2 wickets

Match Four
8 September 2006 at Trent Bridge
Pakistan 235 for 8 (50 overs) (Abdul Razzaq 75*)
England 237 for 2 (46.2 overs) (IR Bell 86*,
AJ Strauss 78)
England won by 8 wickets

Match Five
10 September 2006 at Edgbaston
Pakistan 154 for 9 (50 overs)
England 155 for 7 (31 overs)
England won by 3 wickets

Series drawn

Younis Khan, a century-maker at the Rose
Bowl, unleashes another flamboyant stroke.

OTHER TOUR MATCHES

SRI LANKA IN ENGLAND

24–26 April 2006
at Fenner's
Sri Lanka 289 all out (74.2 overs) (WU Tharanga 100,
RMR Braithwaite 3 for 61, MA Richards 3 for 62)
& 256 for 6 dec (67 overs) (TT Samaraweera 114,
HAPW Jayawardene 52*, DJ Balcombe 3 for 67)
British Universities 125 all out (49.4 overs)
(WPUJC Vaas 4 for 34, DNT Zoysa 4 for 38)
& 130 for 8 (56 overs)
Match drawn

The British Universities hung on for a draw as
Sri Lanka made a useful start to their tour at
Fenner's. Ninth-wicket pair Paul Harrison and
David Balcombe stayed for 12 overs and put on 38
to thwart the tourists at the end of three worthwhile
days. Upul Tharanga was the star of the opening
day, hitting an attractive century, and Thilan
Samaraweera also made it to three figures in the
second innings. There were four wickets apiece
for Chaminda Vaas and Nuwan Zoysa as the
Universities crumbled to 125 all out on the
second morning.

30 April–2 May 2006
at Derby
Derbyshire 219 all out (84 overs)
(M Muralitharan 3 for 47, SL Malinga 3 for 59)
& 208 for 4 dec (44 overs) (TR Birt 83, CR Taylor 53)
Sri Lanka 166 for 7 dec (47.5 overs)
& 262 for 4 (58.1 overs) (MG Vandort 90*)
Sri Lanka won by 6 wickets

Two imaginative declarations beat some weather
interruptions and kept alive a match that Sri Lanka
won on the final afternoon with 11 balls to spare.
Michael Vandort played the anchor role to
perfection with an unbeaten 90, adding 86 with
Kumar Sangakkara for the second wicket, while
19-year-old Chamara Kapugedera revealed his high
promise with a 45-ball 44 not out at the end.
Derbyshire, who had been bowled out for just 219
on the first day despite reaching 88 without loss,
thanks to three wickets each for Lasith Malinga and
Muttiah Muralitharan, had earlier declared their
second innings on 208 for 4. Travis Birt and Chris
Taylor had added 126 for the second wicket, and
there was also some good batting earlier on the
second day from the Sri Lankan sixth-wicket pair

Thilan Samaraweera gave the Sri Lankans a good start to
their tour with a hundred against the British Universities.

Kapugedera and Farveez Maharoof, who had rallied
their side from 69 for 5 to an eventual declaration at
166 for 7.

4–6 May 2006
at Worcester
Sri Lanka 179 all out (58.5 overs) (J Lewis 6 for 49,
LE Plunkett 3 for 47) & 118 all out (50.3 overs)
(SCJ Broad 3 for 17, J Lewis 3 for 41)
England A 259 all out (87.3 overs) (RWT Key 63,
KMDN Kulasekara 4 for 83, MF Maharoof 3 for 41)
& 41 for 0 (8 overs)
England A won by 10 wickets

Jon Lewis led an England A seam bowling
destruction of the Sri Lankans on a juiced-up pitch
at New Road. Gloucestershire captain Lewis did his

senior international claims no harm with nine wickets in the match, which England A won easily by ten wickets after bowling out their opponents for 179 and 118. Lewis's initial new-ball burst on the first morning was 4 for 22 in eight overs, and he returned later to finish with 6 for 49. Only Tillekeratne Dilshan and Chamara Kapugedera, who added 76 for the sixth wicket, resisted for long as Lewis and Liam Plunkett made hay. Robert Key, the England A captain, then contributed a solid 63 and, with Ed Joyce and Ravi Bopara both getting into the 40s, England A were 225 for 4 at one stage in reply before subsiding to 259 all out. The lead of 80 assumed match-winning proportions, however, as soon as the Sri Lankan second innings also hit the buffers. Again Dilshan batted well, but no one else could keep out Lewis, Stuart Broad and the rest of the England A attack.

18–21 May 2006
at Hove
Sri Lanka 521 for 5 dec (161.4 overs)
(WU Tharanga 140, CK Kapugedera 134*,
TT Samaraweera 100*)
& 5 for 1 (2 overs)
Sussex 262 all out (85.5 overs) (OP Rayner 101,
SL Malinga 5 for 79, KMDN Kulasekara 3 for 35)
Match drawn

Sri Lanka had much the best of their match against a second-string Sussex side until rain washed away the fourth and final day to prevent the chance of a positive finish. Upul Tharanga lit up the first day with a majestic 140, and Sri Lanka were then further boosted by an unbroken sixth-wicket partnership of 238 between Thilan Samaraweera and the precociously talented Chamara Kapugedera. Both scored hundreds, with Kapugedera's his maiden ton in just his eighth first-class match. Lasith Malinga's unique sling-action and genuine pace then took centre stage as Sussex initially struggled in reply, although the county was thrilled when Ollie Rayner strode in at No. 8 to hit his maiden first-class century. Rayner struck a six and 12 fours in a 134-ball 101.

9 June 2006
at Chelmsford
Sri Lanka 172 all out (43.3 overs) (JS Ahmed 4 for 32,
RS Bopara 3 for 23)
Essex 174 for 4 (38 overs) (ML Pettini 69,
RN ten Doeschate 63*)
Essex won by 6 wickets

In search of limited-overs practice ahead of the NatWest Series matches against England, the Sri Lankans were embarrassed to be beaten by six wickets by Essex – for whom young fast bowler Jahid Ahmed took 4 for 32 from his ten overs and Ravi Bopara snapped up three wickets in 14 balls to further undermine the tourists' innings. In the end, Sri Lanka did not even bat out their 50 overs, and Essex cruised to victory as Mark Pettini made a 59-ball 50 and Ryan ten Doeschate hit out to reach 63.

11 June 2006
at Taunton
Somerset 332 for 6 (50 overs) (MJ Wood 116,
AV Suppiah 72, CL White 64, SL Malinga 3 for 55)
Sri Lanka 281 all out (46.3 overs) (TM Dilshan 97,
HAPW Jayawardene 55, KC Sangakkara 52,
CM Willoughby 6 for 43)
Somerset won by 51 runs

Sri Lanka's self-confidence was not helped by a 51-run loss to Somerset in a high-scoring affair before a 5,500 crowd at Taunton. The county, who in 2005 had beaten the Australians in a one-day fixture, raced to 332 for 6 against an attack badly missing the rested pair of Chaminda Vaas and Muttiah Muralitharan. Matthew Wood's 101-ball century provided a lot of the early fireworks, while Arul Suppiah joined him in a second-wicket stand worth 164 before Cameron White arrived to thrash 64 off 48 balls. Kumar Sangakkara sparkled briefly, Tillekeratne Dilshan hit an impressive 87-ball 97 and reserve wicketkeeper Prasanna Jayawardene contributed 55 from 59 balls, but Sri Lanka kept losing wickets – mainly to Charl Willoughby, who finished with 6 for 43 – and always looked like falling short.

PAKISTAN IN ENGLAND

1–3 July 2006
at Leicester
Leicestershire 315 for 9 dec (81 overs) (D Mongia 129*,
JL Sadler 92, Mohammad Sami 3 for 53)
& 191 all out (43 overs) (TJ New 67, JL Sadler 51,
Danish Kaneria 4 for 32)
Pakistan 304 for 5 dec (85 overs) (Imran Farhat 81,
Salman Butt 68, Kamran Akmal 62*,
NGE Walker 3 for 47)
& 207 for 2 (40.2 overs) (Shoaib Malik 110*,
Younis Khan 55*)
Pakistan won by 8 wickets

Pakistan won by an impressive eight-wicket margin at Grace Road to kick off their tour in some style. Yet, as lunchtime approached on the final day, with Leicestershire having recovered from their overnight 45 for 2 to reach 160 for 4 thanks to a 105-run stand for the fifth wicket between Tom New and John Sadler, a draw had seemed the only possibility. Danish Kaneria, however, took 4 for 32 to spearhead a dramatic turnaround and, soon, Leicestershire were all out for 191 and Pakistan were chasing 203 to win from 56 overs. They did it at a canter, with Shoaib Malik hitting three sixes and 12 fours in his brilliant 110 not out from 124 balls, and Younis Khan weighed in with an unbeaten 55 as victory was clinched with almost 16 overs to spare. Earlier in the game, as the Pakistanis found their feet on day one, Dinesh Mongia had struck an unbeaten 129 and featured in a 174-run fourth-wicket stand with Sadler during Leicestershire's first innings. But Pakistan's batsmen had replied with a solid first innings of their own, Salman Butt and Imran Farhat putting on 145 for the opening wicket and Kamran Akmal thumping Claude Henderson for three sixes in his 62 not out.

6–9 July 2006
at Canterbury
England A 595 for 9 dec (173 overs)
(CMW Read 150*, RWT Key 136, IR Bell 74,
SCJ Broad 54*,
AGR Loudon 51, Danish Kaneria 4 for 158)
& 153 for 1 dec (44.1 overs) (AN Cook 80*, IR Bell 50*)
Pakistan 242 all out (73.1 overs) (Faisal Iqbal 82,
Salman Butt 63, JWM Dalrymple 4 for 61,
AGR Loudon 3 for 28)
& 154 for 2 (50 overs) (Salman Butt 50)
Match drawn

Robert Key, leading England A on his home ground, put down a marker for Ashes winter tour selection with a determined first-day century at Canterbury. Key, on 128 at the close after he and Ian Bell had offset the early loss of Alastair Cook with a second-wicket stand of 160, fell early on day two for 136 but the stage was then set for Chris Read to showcase his improved batting ability. Batting on into a third day, in an England A tactic which left the tourists furious, Read reached an

Robert Key, who had earlier in the summer led England A to victory against the Sri Lankans, hits out as his 136 helps to put Pakistan on the back foot at Canterbury.

Chris Read signals his intent to get back in England's Test team by hitting a century against Pakistan in A team colours at Canterbury. Here he acknowledges the applause as he reaches three figures.

unbeaten 150 before the declaration eventually came. Stuart Broad had also taken the opportunity to show he could hold a bat, and it was no surprise that Pakistan looked a trifle demotivated as, despite fluent half-centuries from both Salman Butt and Faisal Iqbal, they fell away to 242 all out. Rejecting the chance to enforce the follow-on, England's management clearly seemed more intent on denying the Pakistanis batting practice ahead of the opening Test at Lord's than on actually winning the game. As Pakistan's occasional spinners Butt and Farhat sent down over after over, Cook and Bell batted throughout the final morning. Then, after a declaration did come, the England A team served up an even more unseemly collection of dross as the game petered out amid unedifying scenes.

20–22 July 2006
at Northampton
Northamptonshire 269 for 3 dec (62.3 overs)
(SD Peters 142, U Afzaal 71*)
& 140 all out (38.3 overs) (Shahid Nazir 3 for 33)
Pakistan 250 for 9 dec (64.5 overs) (Younis Khan 58, DH Wigley 5 for 77)
& 160 for 3 (40.2 overs) (Salman Butt 84, Imran Farhat 64)
Pakistan won by 7 wickets

A superb bowling performance on the second afternoon, following a lunchtime visit to a local mosque for Friday prayers, sped Pakistan to a seven-wicket win against Northamptonshire. Shahid Nazir and Iftikhar Anjum found pace and movement on a previously sluggish surface to sent Northants tumbling to 43 for 6. The tourists had themselves struggled to 250 for 9 declared, with David Wigley picking up 5 for 77, in reply to a Northants first innings of 269 for 3 declared, when the sudden collapse occurred. Northants, who also lost Sourav Ganguly to a gashed chin after he had been struck by a ball from Nazir, were eventually all out for 140 and Pakistan were propelled to victory on the back of an opening stand of 118 between Salman Butt and Imran Farhat. What a changearound it had been, following a first day in which Stephen Peters had stroked 26 fours in a 195-ball 142 and Usman Afzaal had also prospered before the county reduced the tourists to 97 for 3 by the close.

12 August 2006
at Shenley
West Indies A 214 for 4 (40 overs)
(LMP Simmons 108*, DR Smith 55*, Samiullah Khan 3 for 30)
Pakistan 123 for 3 (22 overs)
(Imran Farhat 62*)
No result

The first of two scheduled one-day matches against their fellow tourists, West Indies A, fell foul of the weather – but not before the match was tilting Pakistan's way thanks to Imran Farhat's unbeaten 62. Earlier, Shoaib Akhtar had bowled 11 overs on his comeback from a lengthy injury lay-off, taking a wicket with his fifth ball. Lendl Simmons and Dwayne Smith had, however, taken West Indies A to 214 for 4 with a counter-attacking fifth-wicket partnership. The scheduled second match, on 13 August, was washed out completely.

THE ASHES: PAST AND PRESENT

VIC MARKS, the former Somerset and England all-rounder and now cricket correspondent of the *Observer*, played most of his cricket alongside Ian Botham and has since written on the game for many years as a colleague of Mike Brearley. Here, in a special Ashes feature, he remembers the impact that Botham and Brearley had on English cricket in the great summer of 1981 ... and also draws some modern parallels as he considers the latest Ashes confrontation.

At the time we decided that we would never see anything like it again. In the summer of 1981 the preparations for the Royal Wedding of Prince Charles and Lady Diana Spencer were in full swing. Shakin' Stevens topped the charts with 'Green Door' and the Ashes series was well under way. Actually, the Ashes barely pierced the consciousness of the nation until the two teams met at Headingley for the Third Test match. Until then it had been a desultory affair between two mediocre sides. The Wedding most certainly took priority. Maybe Shakin' Stevens did as well.

In the Test series Australia had won by four wickets at Nottingham; it had rained at Lord's, where the England captain, one I. T. Botham, bagged a pair, icy silence greeting his forlorn passage through the Long Room to the dressing room after his second duck. There followed an unseemly race between the Chairman of Selectors, Alec Bedser, and Botham to see who could get their sacking/resignation in first.

Three days into the Headingley Test and the England players – Botham included – were checking out of their Leeds hotel, another doleful defeat on the horizon. Mike Brearley's recall as England captain had not worked any magic. And then it happened. It was the Monday and Tuesday of 20 and 21 July. Where were you when English cricket was resuscitated? Well, I was at Taunton playing in a forgettable Championship match against Derbyshire, witnessing two contrasting hundreds: one by David Steele, and one by

Ian Botham hooks a ball from Rodney Hogg for four during the Fourth Test against Australia at Edgbaston in 1981 – the series which became known as 'Botham's Ashes'.

Viv Richards, which did not take quite so long. Richards had been particularly severe on Steele's left-arm spinners ('Doesn't he know you're not supposed to knock down conkers until September?').

At Taunton, we had seen the desolation of Botham after his fall from grace as England captain. But he would soldier on anyway. Brearley rang him to check that he was still hungry to be included in the Test team. He was. Playing for Somerset against Sussex the week before Headingley he took six wickets and hit a belligerent 72. (In those pre-central contract days I notice that Botham played nine Championship matches for Somerset in a six-Test summer, which would be regarded as slave labour today.)

Now the images of Headingley 1981 flood back: Botham guffawing with Graham Dilley as another heave slices over the slips for four; a rather better straight drive that ended up in the Rugby Stand. Brearley appearing on the balcony when Botham reached his hundred, applauding and, starting to smell something special on the horizon, urging him to keep going. Then there was Bob Willis in his zombie state pounding down the hill, Bob Taylor leaping high to take the catches, Mike Gatting diving forward at mid-on and Willis, still in a trance, being dragged in front of a startled Peter West of the BBC after he had taken the final wicket. Willis was deadpan, drained and distinctly un-ecstatic (whoever took care of those boys' media training?). 'Probably an ill-judged interview', he acknowledged some time afterwards, but on the rest day the press had terminated his Test career – along with one or two others – and so an unsuspecting Peter West paid the price.

The Ashes were rekindled and Botham prevailed like a bull at Edgbaston with the ball and a musketeer at Old Trafford with the bat. The combination of Botham and Brearley gelled magnificently. 'He needs a father figure, I need a younger brother', observed Brearley, who soon acquired wizard status. A correspondent to the *Guardian* wrote after the Edgbaston Test, 'On Friday I watched J. M. Brearley directing his fieldsmen very carefully. He then looked up at the sun and made a gesture, which seemed to indicate that it should move a little squarer. Who is this man?'

I once asked Ian which Test in his career he looked back on with most affection. He did not mention any of those in 1981. And you can understand why. His astonishing feats in that series tossed him into a nasty Catch 22 scenario. By performing so miraculously he added force to the argument that he was unable to play to his potential when captain; that he was at his most lethal when he had leeway to be irresponsible. If he had been captain at Headingley he would have felt duty bound to bat properly rather than slog merrily and England would have

The brains behind the brawn: Mike Brearley, England's captain in the 1981 Ashes series.

lost. Botham has always been reluctant to accept this theory; he wanted to be captain. Indeed the heroics of 1981 haunted him for the rest of his career. After that, every time he entered the arena he was expected to produce the extraordinary. It is remarkable how often he achieved it. Yet he must have known that he could never surpass 1981.

And, for our part, we all thought that 1981 could never be surpassed as well – until 2005. In between there had been some diverting Ashes series, but too often they had been one-sided, an anti-climax. The Australians started to regard fixtures against India as the sternest and most important on their cricket calendar – until 2005. It was always possible to find a seat for an Ashes Test match in Australia – until 2005.

In so many ways 2005, with Botham now in the commentary box and Brearley a sporadic and excited visitor to the press box, outstripped 1981. In 2005 Australia and England were the two best teams in the world; in 1981 they were way behind the West Indies. In 2005 there was never a day when the cricket was not mesmerising. In 1981 there were three extraordinary games, at Headingley, Edgbaston and Old Trafford, and three drab ones – at Nottingham, Lord's and The Oval. And it was a

Return of the Ashes: England captain Michael Vaughan holds the urn aloft at The Oval in September 2005 as Australia are beaten at last amid widespread English ecstasy.

closer contest in 2005, the outcome in doubt until teatime on the final day of the final Test. For the Australians, Shane Warne and Brett Lee could enhance reputations that were already sky-high. For England, the Ashes-winning crew – and there were only 12 of them – started to slip off the tongue like 'Banks, Cohen, Wilson ... etc' of 40 years previously. Michael Vaughan and his team were summoned to Trafalgar Square, and to 10 Downing Street. For once Beckham and Rooney were relegated to the inside pages. 'Fred' was king.

The Aussies, meanwhile, took it all pretty well. No whingeing. 'At least we won't have to watch endless replays of 1981 when it rains on our next trip here', said one, determined to look on the bright side.

For the commercial wing of the ACB it was not so difficult to look on the bright side; this defeat was like gold dust to them. Suddenly everyone in Australia wanted to witness their team restoring the natural order; everyone in England wanted to winter in Australia – from Brisbane in November to Sydney in January – just in case the Poms pulled it off again. Tickets were as rare as a penitent politician.

And so we have prepared for the sequel. Surely it couldn't be as melodramatic, as unbearably thrilling as 2005, could it? It was obviously going to be different from previous Ashes trips, however. For a start England had not been branded by the locals as the 'worst side ever to be sent to Australia', which is the usual template. Moreover, in August of 2006 the Australian players had been sent to the depths of the Queensland jungle to bond in a 'boot camp'. Usually a carton of tinnies was sufficient for a bit of Aussie-bonding before an Ashes series.

One further oddity: you would have expected the Australian side to have been overhauled after their defeat in 2005 and England's XI to be the same. The opposite is true. After a mini-purge, the Aussies – with the oldest side in their history – have more or less reverted to their 2005 Ashes team. Only Mike Hussey had penetrated into their first-choice Test XI. The flops of the 2005 tour, Jason Gillespie and Damien Martyn, seem to be back in favour. England would have liked the same side, too, but fragile bodies have not permitted that. The most striking absentees are Simon Jones, whose reverse swing had all the Australians scratching their heads, and

The new Captain Fantastic: Andrew Flintoff, pictured here in the 2005 series, is the man charged with keeping the Ashes in England hands this winter.

Michael Vaughan, a nerveless, supremely confident leader throughout the 2005 campaign, in which he outshone his opposite number Ricky Ponting.

The England selectors agonised long and hard over who should replace Vaughan. In the end they did not pay much heed to the echoes of 1981, when the graduate Middlesex opener took over from the barnstorming all-rounder with such astonishing effect. Andrew Strauss, once of Durham University, once captain of Middlesex and a sound, erudite man, was by-passed, and they went for Andrew 'Freddie' Flintoff, the charismatic national hero.

The parallels with Botham should not be overstated, of course. This pair had contrasting routes to the top, for instance, for while Flintoff tiptoed gently up the scale Botham exploded on to the international scene. In India last winter the signs were that Flintoff the batsman was enhanced by the captaincy, whereas 25 years ago Botham's batting appeared to be neutered by it. England's captaincy might actually give Flintoff greater confidence; Botham did not need it. Moreover, Flintoff was taking over in a well-ordered, sophisticated regime, a far cry from the haphazard days of the early 1980s. Everywhere he turned, Flintoff was in receipt of better advice.

This winter's 2006–07 expedition to Australia is bound to be a defining tour for Flintoff. If successful he would achieve one goal that eluded Botham in his illustrious career: captaining England effectively against Australia. For Flintoff and his team this was and is the ultimate challenge. There has never been a more enticing Ashes contest, which is why expectations are so high.

ASHES SERIES 2006–07
First Test 23–27 November 2006, Brisbane
Second Test 1–5 December 2006, Adelaide
Third Test 14–18 December 2006, Perth
Fourth Test 26–30 December 2006, Melbourne
Fifth Test 2–6 January 2007, Sydney

Vic Marks played six Tests and 34 one-day internationals for England in the 1980s. He scored 12,419 first-class runs at 30.29 and took 859 wickets at 33.28. Since retiring at the end of the 1989 season, after 15 summers with Somerset, he has forged a much-respected media career with the Observer *and as a wise, witty and whimsical member of BBC Radio's* Test Match Special *team.*

CRICKET WORLD CUP 2007

TONY COZIER, one of the Caribbean's leading sports journalists and for millions the voice of West Indies cricket, looks ahead to the 2007 World Cup.

They have become inevitable questions prior to any major, international sporting event. Will everything be in ready in time? Will all the money spent be worth it? Six months before the start of cricket's ninth World Cup next March and April, the first in the West Indies, there were similar reservations. The general opinion was best summed up by Mike Atherton, the former England captain whose connections with the region extend beyond his cricketing tours. 'The West Indies World Cup has the potential to be a terrific celebration of cricket,' he wrote in his newspaper column. 'It also has all the makings of a shambles.'

As the time approached and preparations intensified, those closest to the tournament were becoming inclined to the more positive of Atherton's alternatives. On a reconnaissance visit to Jamaica in August, new ICC president Percy Sonn and chief executive Malcolm Speed proclaimed themselves satisfied with the way things were going – even if with lingering reservations. 'We are very pleased with the progress that is being made but there is still much to be done,' Speed told the media. 'The message we bring is that we are happy with progress but that we can't relax. There must now be great attention to detail.' Guided by second-hand reports, Sonn, the former president of the South African Board, raised some concerns soon after he took office in July. He was more assured once he saw and heard for himself. 'I think the West Indies is, relatively speaking, ahead of where South Africa was at this stage (in 2003), vis-à-vis the final stages,' he said. 'South Africa didn't build any new stadiums; they just improved on the old ones. Several new ones are being built here. I think they are fine and further than where South Africa was.'

Such confidence mirrored that of Chris Dehring, the investment banker who has been at the centre of the preparations since he successfully argued the case for staging the Cup in the Caribbean on behalf of the West Indies Cricket Board (WICB) before the ICC seven years earlier. He has been the managing director and chief executive officer of the company managing the Cup on behalf of the ICC and the WICB for the past three years.

'Cricket World Cup 2007 is very much on track,' he said during the Sonn-Speed visit. 'We are now moving into a much more intense operational phase.' Sales of the 800,000 tickets for the 51 matches at the eight venues, mainly booked through the Internet on a lottery basis, indicated strong international interest. By the end of the first phase, on 1 September, only the more expensive corporate packages remained for the final on 28 April at Barbados' Kensington Oval. Dehring and his group have the advantage that the tournament is being staged in a region where cricket holds a special place in the hearts of the people, for social and political, as much as sporting, reasons. Owen Arthur, prime minister of Barbados, the island that has produced more great players per square mile than anywhere else on earth, emphasised just how much it means to the small, scattered territories that were bequeathed the game by British colonialism. 'It's an expression of confidence of who we are and what we can do as a people that the Caribbean governments, no matter how financially strapped our circumstances may be, should not only act on the belief, but pursue the belief, that this region should host something as important as a cricket World Cup.'

Yet no previous tournament has had to cope with such unique complexities. Although the West Indies have played as a unified cricket team for more than a century, there is no such political entity. After more than one failed attempt at integration, most notably a federation from 1958 to 1962, all the constituents went their separate ways into full independence, all with their own governments, flags, anthems, currencies, seats at the UN and, except for cricket, their own individual sporting teams. The populations of tiny St Kitts (35,000), where Australia will begin their defence of the championship, and Antigua (70,000), which hosts a second round Super Eight group at the new Sir Vivian Richards Stadium, could be comfortably accommodated in the Melbourne Cricket Ground or Kolkata's Eden Gardens. Barbados (population 270,000) stages the final that has previously been held in some of the great cities of the world – London, Kolkata, Melbourne, Lahore and Johannesburg – with their several millions and their experience of handling such extravaganzas.

The ICC made the job that much harder by increasing the number of teams from 14 to 16, rendering it the biggest World Cup ever. The first round is divided into groups of four with the top two from each moving on to the Super Eight phase and ultimately the semi-final and final. The catchphrase Dehring used in 1998 to win the ICC's unanimous approval for locating the game's premier event in the Caribbean was, 'A great place for the cricket World

Cup'. Given its rich cricket history and its status as one of the planet's favourite holiday destinations, it was an assertion that could not be challenged. The trick was to make it work.

Although Barbados and Antigua have had virtual trial runs, hosting as many as the 10,000 supporters following England on recent tours, this time the invasion will be larger and more cosmopolitan. The cricket-starved, expatriate Commonwealth populations on the Caribbean's doorstep in the US and Canada are likely to outnumber all others. While their presence will boost local economies, they will place a strain on accommodation, both in and away from the stadiums, stretch the infrastructure of the small host countries and test the capacity of overburdened internal airlines. New stadiums were commissioned in St Kitts, Antigua, Guyana and Jamaica (at Trelawney on the north coast, strictly for the opening ceremony). All but a couple of stands at Kensington Oval in Bridgetown were demolished and the ground reconfigured and rebuilt so that 26,000 can be seated for the final, double the previous capacity. Kingston's Sabina Park would have a new grandstand covering the northern end. The stadium in Grenada, opened in 1999 but almost completely destroyed by a hurricane in 2004, had to be raised again from the rubble. The Queen's Park Oval in Port of Spain and the Beausejour Stadium in St Lucia needed no more than upgrades, including a new pavilion for the former. St Kitts' Warner Park proved its readiness by putting on the first international matches in the island's history, a Test and a one-day international against India last July. The others were in varying states of completion as the deadline for ICC inspections in January 2006 approached.

Away from the stadiums, local organising committees (the LOCs) encouraged locals to convert their homes into bed-and-breakfast operations during the tournament to supplement hotels and guesthouses. Additionally, tour operators have leased cruise liners to act as floating hotels, simultaneously overcoming the shortage of rooms in some destinations and offering the ability to move easily from island to island. By August 2006, Bridgetown port authorities reported it had bookings for 12 such vessels, with an estimated 20,000 passengers, for the day of the final. The importance of the World Cup persuaded the governments, through CARICOM (the Caribbean Community), to agree to a special passport that players, officials, media and supporters would present only at their original point of entry. It would eliminate the annoying and time-consuming process of clearing immigration and customs in every island, a change that regular travellers in the area hope will become

permanent. The most frequent Cup-related phrase used by international travel agents seeking to satisfy their cricket clients was 'logistical nightmare'. Given that the tournament covers eight venues, separated by water, from Guyana on the South American mainland, to Jamaica, in the northern Caribbean, the inadequacy of many airports and the unenviable reputation of regional airlines for delays, the apprehension was not misplaced.

Dehring has predicted an 'economic windfall' for the region of around US$500 million, based on ticket sales, sponsorship, broadcasting rights, concessions, merchandising and tourism. This has to be set against a final, collective bill of US$300 million, mostly underwritten by the relevant governments. Cynics add on another US$100 million or so for the inevitable cost overruns. The WICB is banking on a sizeable profit. It has acknowledged that, for a variety of reasons, it is all but bankrupt, a position that has contributed to the decline of the team to the lower rungs of the ICC's ratings ladder.

But whatever happens off the field, with accommodation, transport and the hundred and one other factors that make such a major tournament tick, Dehring cites the importance of a strong West Indies showing in it. 'To have a successful tournament we have to have an enthusiastic local population – and so we have to have a successful West Indies team'. It is the last piece in the intricate jigsaw that would make it live up to Dehring's claim that it will be 'the best World Cup ever'.

2007 WORLD CUP TEAM GROUPINGS

GROUP A
St Kitts & Nevis
Australia (1)
South Africa (5)
Scotland (12)
The Netherlands (16)

GROUP B
Trinidad & Tobago
Sri Lanka (2)
India (8)
Bangladesh (11)
Bermuda (15)

GROUP C
St Lucia
New Zealand (3)
England (7)
Kenya (10)
Canada (14)
(Seedings in brackets)

GROUP D
Jamaica
Pakistan (4)
West Indies (6)
Zimbabwe (9)
Ireland (13)

ENGLAND DOMESTIC SEASON INTRODUCTION
By Mark Baldwin

When the Professional Cricketers' Association chose Mark Ramprakash as its Player of the Year for 2006, the reaction of members and guests at a packed Royal Albert Hall told of a popular decision and a popular, and massively respected, recipient. Yet was it the right choice?

Even though the ballot papers had to be in by mid-August, a month before the glitzy end-of-season awards bash and before Sussex had confirmed their domination of the domestic scene with the two biggest trophies and almost a third thrown in for good measure, it is hard to see why a certain little Pakistani leg spinner did not get the nod.

Mushtaq Ahmed not only took 102 wickets at 19.91 runs each in the Liverpool Victoria County Championship (in 15 matches, too, and with neck and groin injuries troubling him significantly in at least three of those games), but he underlined a quality of bowling apparent in the first division that was simply not matched by that of the second tier.

Look at the national first-class averages, based on those who batted in at least six completed innings and bowled in at least ten, and this imbalance is striking. No fewer than 20 of the top 25 in the bowling averages are from Division One counties, whereas 15 of the top 25 in the batting averages (excluding players who performed wholly or largely at international level during the summer) are from Division Two.

Ramprakash's remarkable haul of 2,278 first-class runs from 24 innings at an average of 103.54 is, of course, an accurate reflection of his technique, talent and huge powers of concentration – plus the desire to strive for the greatest achievements well into his 37th year. But, to my mind, Darren Lehmann's 1,706 runs at 77.54 for Yorkshire or John Crawley's 1,737 runs for Hampshire at 66.80 – made for the most part on far trickier pitches and against far superior bowling attacks – are just as worthy of mention.

The reasons, meanwhile, that Sussex won both the Championship and C&G Trophy titles, besides coming second in the NatWest Pro40 League only because of an inexplicable batting collapse against Nottinghamshire in the final round of matches, are many and varied.

Chief among them, though, are the fact that four of their bowlers were among the top 10 in the country. Mushtaq, the highest wicket-taker by a distance, finished second in the averages to Rana Naved-ul-Hasan, whose 35 wickets at the start of the season cost a mere 16.71 runs apiece. Jason Lewry, bowling his pacy left-arm swingers better than at any stage of his career at the age of 35, occupied sixth position with 57 scalps at 23.17, and Yasir Arafat, Naved's replacement, ended up in tenth place himself with 41 wickets at 24.85.

When Chris Adams, the no-nonsense Sussex captain, looked around the field and wondered who to throw the ball to, he was seldom wondering for long. Great captains, of great teams, usually have above-average bowling attacks to call upon – and, for the past four seasons, Adams has had in Mushtaq in particular the best bowler of the lot.

In 2003, when he re-launched his flagging career by taking 103 wickets and spearheading Sussex's drive to their historic first Championship, Mushtaq set in train an astounding run of personal success which – with 84 in 2004 and 80 in 2005 – has seen him finish as the country's leading wicket-taker for four successive summers. Bounding in with seemingly limitless energy and enthusiasm (apart from when his wear-and-tear injuries prompted Sussex sensibly to give him a couple of weeks off in July), Mushtaq has enriched English domestic cricket by his presence and his wonderful repertoire of skills.

To have him and Shane Warne operating at county level at the same time is a considerable bonus for the first-class game in England and Wales, and for young English batsmen in the first division it is nothing short of a God-given opportunity to advance their own knowledge and careers.

What a shame, of course, and this includes Ramprakash, that the batsmen of the second division have not in recent times had this same opportunity to test themselves against Mushtaq and Warne. And the fact that Lehmann made his runs last season despite having to face both great leg spinners, plus the rest of the Sussex, Hampshire and Lancashire attacks – members of whom dominate the top 40 places in the bowling averages – counts even more in his favour.

With apologies to the likes of Zaheer Khan, Kabir Ali, Charl Willoughby and a past-his-best

Darren Gough, the only bowlers in last summer's second division likely to achieve world-class status in the foreseeable future are Monty Panesar and Stuart Broad. Happily, both will do so for England, and their rise over the past two seasons at two unfashionable counties like Northamptonshire and Leicestershire is further evidence that the 18-county system is – in its entirety – the great and particular strength of English cricket.

Northants and Leicestershire, moreover, are to be commended for the way they have nurtured Panesar and Broad's exciting talents during the past few years. Neither have been overplayed or overbowled, although as a spinner Panesar has thrived on bowling for long spells at county level, at Loughborough University and at the National Academy.

But back to the first division, and to a story to set alongside the emergence of Panesar and Broad in its importance to the future both of county cricket and – by definition – England. Yorkshire's survival in the top tier resulted as much from the performances of two leg spinners of their own cultivation, aged 18 and 20, as from the masterful batting of Lehmann and the efforts of other senior professionals such as Craig White, the captain, and Anthony McGrath. How magical it was for all supporters of England to see, and at Headingley of all places, the precocious pair of Adil Rashid and Mark Lawson spinning Nottinghamshire to defeat in the crucial relegation battle of mid-September. Rashid's 25 wickets at 25.16 and Lawson's 26 at 34.50 are, hopefully, just a forerunner of many more in tandem for the White Rose and, who knows, alongside Panesar in England colours.

With iconic overseas players to watch and to learn from, with a successful team like Sussex to show what can be done even at a smaller county with no Test match staging ambitions, with a flourishing England team bursting with recognisable and charismatic stars, and with the youthful likes of Rashid, Lawson, Broad, Liam Plunkett and Steven Davies – to name but a handful – coming up fast behind them, there is much at present for English cricket to be thankful for.

Mark Baldwin, a former cricket correspondent of the Press Association, has covered county cricket for The Times *since 1998.*

WEATHER WATCH

By Andrew Hignell

A study of where the rain fell in the Championship summer of 2006, and on whom, reveals a clear north-south divide, with Lancashire, Nottinghamshire, Yorkshire and Leicestershire losing most time, and Essex, Surrey and Sussex losing least.

Looking simply at the time lost at home, Lancashire (53.00 hours) are the 'raining champions', followed by Yorkshire (41.50), Nottinghamshire (39.25) and Derbyshire (35.25). In contrast, the driest home locations in 2006 were Glamorgan (3 hours), Warwickshire (8.25), Gloucestershire and Sussex (8.5).

Estimates of Lost Playing Time in County Championship Cricket – 2006

KEY: Total (hours)
At home
Away

Derbyshire	Kent	Somerset
57.00	44.75	52.50
35.25	10.00	34.75
21.75	34.75	17.75

Durham	Lancashire	Surrey
41.25	68.75	19.75
18.25	53.00	12.75
23.00	15.75	7.00

Essex	Leicestershire	Sussex
25.50	60.00	11.00
11.75	31.00	8.50
13.75	29.00	2.50

Glamorgan	Middlesex	Warwickshire
32.00	37.50	36.50
3.00	15.75	8.25
29.00	21.75	33.25

Gloucestershire	Northamptonshire	Worcestershire
32.50	46.25	50.00
8.50	31.25	21.25
24.00	15.00	28.75

Hampshire	Nottinghamshire	Yorkshire
47.50	68.50	60.75
23.50	39.25	41.50
24.00	29.25	19.25

MCC v. Nottinghamshire

14–17 April 2006 at Lord's

A remarkable exhibition of hitting by Mark Ealham, plus eye-catching batting from Jason Gallian and Chris Read and fine left-arm swing bowling from Ryan Sidebottom, put the young thrusters of English cricket in their place in the cricket season's traditional curtain-raiser. County champions Nottinghamshire began the new summer with a pleasing 142-run victory over an MCC side packed with recent England A tourists to the West Indies, but all the talk afterwards was of the 45-ball hundred struck by the 36-year-old all-rounder Ealham.

The onslaught, late on the third day, contained seven sixes and 11 fours and – before the Championship had got under way – the destination of the Walter Lawrence Trophy for the season's fastest first-class century looked beyond doubt. Ealham finished on 112 not out, totally dominating an unbroken sixth-wicket stand of 139 in 20 overs with Read in which the wicketkeeper scored just 25. Those runs, however, were enough to take Read into three figures himself, and his 110 not out from 156 balls, with two sixes and 14 fours – added to yet another display of fine glovework in this match – further fanned the flames of those crying out for his return to the Test side.

Ealham's assault followed a partnership of 160 between Read and Gallian, who had shown immense application and skill to steady the Notts second innings after a shaky start on the second evening. By then, indeed, 23 wickets had fallen despite lengthy bad weather interruptions on both the first two days, but Gallian got his head down and went from 40 not out to 171 on day three before leaving the stage free for Ealham's pyrotechnics. Monty Panesar, who had only a fortnight earlier returned as one of the heroes of England's courageous fightback to 1-1 in their Test series in India, was in one over despatched for 4, 6, 4, 4, and 4 in successive balls by Ealham.

To make matters worse for MCC, they lost Ravi Bopara before the close of that third day – but then fought hard to delay the Notts victory as Alastair Cook passed 50 and Alex Loudon was joined in a stand worth 111 for the seventh wicket by Tim Bresnan. The cool, elegant Loudon did his own international prospects no harm with a fine 123 while the 21-year-old Bresnan underlined his genuine all-round talents by hitting three sixes and 11 fours in a robust 94.

There were three more wickets for Sidebottom, however, to add to the 4 for 42 he had taken when MCC had slid to 168 all out first time around in reply to a Notts first day total of 191, in which Darren Bicknell's 36 was the top score.

MCC v. NOTTINGHAMSHIRE – at Lord's

NOTTS	First Innings		Second Innings	
DJ Bicknell	c Davies b Clarke	36	b Bresnan	0
JER Gallian (capt)	c Davies b Footitt	20	c Cook b Panesar	171
RJ Warren	c Davies b Bresnan	0	c Davies b Bresnan	4
DJ Hussey	c Davies b Bopara	21	b Bopara	19
WR Smith	c Bopara b Bresnan	29	c Clarke b Footitt	39
*CMW Read	c Panesar b Bresnan	12	not out	110
MA Ealham	c Loudon b Clarke	25	not out	112
PJ Franks	not out	30		
GP Swann	c Clarke b Stephenson	8		
GJ Smith	lbw b Stephenson	0		
RJ Sidebottom	lbw b Stephenson	1		
Extras	lb 3, nb 6	9	b 2, lb 7, w 3, nb 4	16
	(all out 60.4 overs)	191	(5 wkts dec 93.4 overs)	471

Bowling
Bresnan 16-2-60-3. Footitt-10-2-34-1. Bopara 6-0-34-1. Clarke 16-6-34-2. Panesar 8-3-20-0. Stephenson 4.4-3-6-3.
Bresnan 20-5-81-2. Footitt 17-2-79-1. Bopara 7-2-33-1. Clarke 14.4-1-92-0. Panesar 23-3-113-1. Stephenson 6-0-28-0. Joyce 3-0-12-0. Loudon 3-0-24-0.
Fall of Wickets: 1-44, 2-45, 3-77, 4-89, 5-122, 6-129, 7-168, 8-181, 9-181 1-0, 2-10, 3-54, 4-172, 5-332

MCC	First Innings		Second Innings	
RS Bopara	c Hussey b Ealham	18	c Ealham b Smith GJ	2
AN Cook	c Ealham b Sidebottom	1	lbw b Sidebottom	51
MS Panesar	c Gallian b Sidebottom	1	(10) c Swann b Smith GJ	3
AGR Loudon	c Hussey b Sidebottom	18	(3) c Read b Franks	123
EC Joyce	c Swann b Sidebottom	4	(4) c Read b Sidebottom	0
R Clarke	c Read b Ealham	25	(5) b Swann	32
LC Parker	c Read b Ealham	32	(6) lbw b Ealham	21
*SM Davies	b Smith GJ	42	(7) b Sidebottom	6
TT Bresnan	c Read b Franks	21	(8) c Sidebottom b Hussey	94
JP Stephenson (capt)	c Swann b Franks	1	(9) b Franks	0
MHA Footitt	not out	0	not out	5
Extras	lb 5	5	lb 7, w 4, nb 4	15
	(all out 55.2 overs)	168	(all out 82 overs)	352

Bowling
Sidebottom 16-6-42-4. Smith GJ 13-3-57-1. Ealham 14-7-26-3. Franks 11.2-2-34-2. Swann 1-0-4-0.
Sidebottom 18-2-77-3. Smith GJ 17-2-54-2. Ealham 10-4-34-1. Franks 15-0-87-2. Swann 21-7-88-1. Hussey 1-0-5-1.
Fall of Wickets: 1-5, 2-7, 3-37, 4-43, 5-43, 6-100, 7-107, 8-163, 9-167 1-7, 2-71, 3-71, 4-132, 5-179, 6-195, 7-306, 8-306, 9-343

Nottinghamshire won by 142 runs

Mark Ealham took a heavy toll of Monty Panesar's left-arm spinners during his 45-ball hundred against MCC.

LIVERPOOL VICTORIA COUNTY CHAMPIONSHIP
By Mark Baldwin

Round One: 18–22 April 2006

Division One

The only first division county to force victory in this opening round of games was Durham, newly promoted and a team who had finished bottom of Division Two in 2004. The side they defeated, Kent, were on home soil and had begun the campaign as the only county never to have played their Championship cricket outside Division One. Yet if it was a harrowing experience for Kent, the innings-and-56-run win achieved by Durham was a triumph for Martyn Moxon, their long-serving and assiduous coach, and a real early-season morale-booster for a predominantly young and locally raised team and for cricket in the North East generally.

Star of the show was Gordon Muchall, a 23-year-old from Tyneside who had shown much promise for several seasons – following his days playing for England Under 19s – without really establishing himself at county level. His career-best 219 – he finished the opening day on 193 not out in a Durham score of 401 for 5 – was, however, the work of a man suddenly at ease with the first-class cricket environment while also hinting that he could go even higher up the ladder.

Gary Pratt, England's Ashes super-sub of the previous summer, kept Muchall company for a while as he contributed a useful 52, but it was wicketkeeper Phil Mustard who helped to propel the game beyond Kent's reach. Mustard, just a month older than Muchall and yet another Geordie lad of immense talent, caned the tiring home attack for 130 as a Durham record sixth-wicket stand of 249 was rattled up in 58 overs. Both scores were career-bests, and Kent were left facing an uphill struggle to save the match.

For a while, led by David Fulton and Martin van Jaarsveld, they made a good fist of it. Darren Stevens was a third Kent batsman to pass 50, but from 230 for 2 the pressure of the situation began to tell, and a slide to 340 condemned them to a follow-on. By the close of the third day, moreover, Kent's hopes had virtually vanished. Both openers had fallen early to Graham Onions, the lively seamer and yet another 23-year-old raised in the North East, and at stumps Kent were 98 for 6. Min Patel fought hard to reach 61, but in the end there were three wickets for the

Gordon Muchall was the star of Durham's significant win at Canterbury with a career-best 219.

veteran Ottis Gibson, a shrewd winter signing from Leicestershire, and on the final morning Durham were soon celebrating a magnificent start to their second stint in the top division.

Sussex's oldest-surviving record wicket stand was shattered at Hove as Murray Goodwin and Michael Yardy thwarted Warwickshire's attempt to force victory in what up to then had been an attritional contest. Goodwin finished on 214 not out and Yardy was unbeaten on 159, and the pair batted right through the final day to put on an unbroken 385. They had come together late on the third afternoon, with Sussex tottering unsteadily on 32 for 2 as they faced a first-innings deficit of 147. Yardy batted for 498 minutes in total and repelled 384 deliveries. Goodwin was characteristically more aggressive, hitting two sixes and 23 fours in his 472-minute and 359-ball stay, but both players demonstrated superb concentration to erase from the county's record books the 1901 third-wicket stand of 298 between Ranjitsinhji and Ernest Killick. In their first innings, only bright batting down the order by the fast-improving Luke Wright and the effervescent Mushtaq Ahmed hauled Sussex above 300, and then

Round One: 18–22 April 2006 Division One

KENT v. DURHAM – at Canterbury

DURHAM	First Innings	
JJB Lewis	b Cook	20
JP Maher	lbw b Joseph	25
GJ Muchall	c Key b Dexter	219
GJ Pratt	b Patel	52
DM B'kenstein (capt)	b Patel	22
GR Breese	c Patel b Dexter	11
*P Mustard	c Stevens b Joseph	130
OD Gibson	st O'Brien b Patel	33
CD Thorp	c van Jaarsveld b Joseph	12
G Onions	not out	17
N Killeen	b Patel	5
Extras	b 5, lb 15, w 3, nb 6	29
	(all out 138 overs)	575

Bowling
Khan 32-2-115-0. Cook 19-2-85-1. Joseph 29-7-124-3. Patel 28-5-100-4. Stevens 10-0-55-0. Dexter 20-5-76-2.
Fall of Wickets: 1-46, 2-52, 3-170, 4-206, 5-233, 6-482, 7-512, 8-530, 9-565

KENT	First Innings		Second Innings (following on)	
DP Fulton	c Mustard b Benkenstein	62	c Lewis b Onions	13
RWT Key (capt)	c Mustard b Killeen	23	b Onions	1
M van Jaarsveld	c Breese b Gibson	83	c Benkenstein b Gibson	37
MJ Walker	st Maher b Breese	27	c Benkenstein b Breese	14
DI Stevens	c Pratt b Benkenstein	62	c Gibson b Thorp	7
NJ Dexter	b Onions	6	c Muchall b Thorp	5
*NJ O'Brien	c Pratt b Onions	3	c Pratt b Breese	13
MM Patel	c sub b Onions	19	b Gibson	61
SJ Cook	c Onions b Thorp	27	lbw b Killeen	2
A Khan	not out	0	not out	15
RH Joseph	lbw b Gibson	4	lbw b Gibson	0
Extras	b 4, lb 8, nb 12	24	lb 9, nb 2	11
	(all out 118 overs)	340	(all out 54.4 overs)	179

Bowling
Gibson 26-7-81-2. Onions 20-3-91-3. Thorp 23-9-50-1. Killeen 30-11-63-1. Breese 8-3-14-1. Benkenstein 11-3-29-2.
Gibson 13.4-2-58-3. Onions 11-0-47-2. Killeen 8-2-19-1. Breese 13-2-28-2. Thorp 6-2-11-2. Benkenstein 3-1-7-0.
Fall of Wickets: 1-60, 2-135, 3-230, 4-230, 5-239, 6-243, 7-277, 8-333, 9-335
1-2, 2-23, 3-59, 4-68, 5-80, 6-93, 7-101, 8-116, 9-179

Durham won by an innings and 56 runs – Kent (5 pts), Durham (22 pts)

Warwickshire's batsmen followed up the five-wicket return of their new captain, Heath Streak, by constructing an excellent reply. Nick Knight, Alex Loudon and Jim Troughton all made half-centuries but Jonathan Trott – the South African who becomes England-qualified by the end of the summer – took the majority of the plaudits with a superb 109.

A washed-out final day at Old Trafford meant that a hard-fought and low-scoring affair between Lancashire and Hampshire ended in a draw. Bad weather interruptions on each of the previous three days had meant that a draw was the likeliest outcome, but at 54 without loss in their second innings, Hampshire had by then responded well to conceding a first-innings deficit of 30. Tom Smith, the 20-year-old Lancashire all-rounder fresh out of the England Under 19s, impressed with both ball and bat, while Glen Chapple completed the double of 5,000 first-class runs and 500 wickets during his fine 70 and Sean Ervine proved his recovery from a serious operation to repair torn knee ligaments the previous October. Nic Pothas became the first Hampshire wicketkeeper to hold seven catches in an innings.

Champions Nottinghamshire, meanwhile, had to endure the huge frustration of seeing their opening fixture, against Yorkshire at Trent Bridge, almost completely decimated by rain. Days one and three were washed out, and only 14 overs were possible in between. On that second day Mitchell Claydon, a burly England-qualified Australian, had taken a wicket with his 12th ball in Championship cricket –

SUSSEX v. WARWICKSHIRE – at Hove

SUSSEX	First Innings		Second Innings	
RR Montgomerie	c Knight b Streak	2	(2) run out	9
CD Hopkinson	c Klokker b Streak	39	(1) c Loudon b Carter	7
MH Yardy	lbw b Streak	48	not out	159
MW Goodwin	c Klokker b Brown	37	not out	214
CJ Adams (capt)	c Loudon b Brown	23		
RSC Martin-Jenkins	c Klokker b Brown	4		
*AJ Hodd	lbw b Troughton	18		
LJ Wright	c Brown b Streak	54		
DJ Spencer	lbw b Brown	16		
Mushtaq Ahmed	not out	42		
JD Lewry	b Anyon	13		
Extras	lb 3, w 1, nb 2	6	b 7, lb 11, w 2, nb 8	28
	(all out 90.5 overs)	302	(2 wkts 136 overs)	417

Bowling
Streak 22-4-72-5. Anyon 16.5-1-66-1. Carter 15-4-39-0. Brown 19-3-68-3. Loudon 14-5-39-0. Troughton 4-1-15-1.
Streak 22-8-52-0. Brown 15-6-21-0. Carter 20-8-71-1. Loudon 31-3-95-0. Anyon 25-7-74-0. Troughton 12-3-41-0. Powell 11-0-45-0.
Fall of Wickets: 1-2, 2-89, 3-108, 4-138, 5-145, 6-162, 7-207, 8-239, 9-268
1-12, 2-32

WARWICKSHIRE	First Innings	
NV Knight	c Adams b Martin-Jenkins	73
IJ Westwood	lbw b Spencer	4
*FA Klokker	c Hodd b Wright	40
IJL Trott	c Hodd b Martin-Jenkins	109
AGR Loudon	c Hodd b Wright	51
JO Troughton	c M'gomerie b Mushtaq Ahmed	58
MJ Powell	lbw b Martin-Jenkins	42
DR Brown	c Spencer b Martin-Jenkins	7
HH Streak (capt)	c Adams b Lewry	20
NM Carter	lbw b Mushtaq Ahmed	4
JE Anyon	not out	6
Extras	b 4, lb 18, w 3, nb 10	35
	(all out 144.2 overs)	449

Bowling
Lewry 28.2-14-58-1. Spencer 13-1-70-1. Mushtaq Ahmed 43-5-128-2. Martin-Jenkins 33-10-78-4. Wright 25-4-88-2. Yardy 2-0-5-0.
Fall of Wickets: 1-19, 2-99, 3-161, 4-295, 5-302, 6-412, 7-412, 8-421, 9-425

Match drawn – Sussex (9 pts), Warwickshire (12 pts)

LANCASHIRE v. HAMPSHIRE – at Old Trafford

HAMPSHIRE	First Innings		Second Innings	
MJ Brown	lbw b Chapple	23	not out	21
JHK Adams	c Sutton b Chapple	2	not out	26
JP Crawley	b Smith	20		
DJ Thornely	c Sutcliffe b Newby	31		
MA Carberry	lbw b Smith	30		
*N Pothas	run out	6		
SM Ervine	not out	44		
AD Mascarenhas	c Sutton b Smith	0		
SD Udal (capt)	c Loye b Cork	8		
RJ Logan	c Smith b Chapple	4		
JTA Bruce	c Cork b Newby	5		
Extras	b 8, lb 3, nb 10	21	lb 3, nb 4	7
	(all out 68 overs)	194	(0 wkts 22 overs)	54

Bowling
Chapple 19-5-46-3. Cork 19-4-47-1. Smith 13-4-29-3. Keedy 8-1-21-0. Newby 9-1-40-2.
Chapple 6-2-13-0. Cork 7-1-14-0. Smith 5-3-4-0. Newby 2-0-14-0. Keedy 2-0-6-0.
Fall of Wickets: 1-7, 2-44, 3-68, 4-101, 5-125, 6-126, 7-127, 8-140, 9-153

LANCASHIRE	First Innings	
MJ Chilton (capt)	c Pothas b Bruce	11
IJ Sutcliffe	c Pothas b Bruce	39
MB Loye	c Pothas b Bruce	0
SG Law	c Pothas b Ervine	30
PJ Horton	c Pothas b Ervine	8
*LD Sutton	lbw b Thornely	1
G Chapple	c Carberry b Logan	70
DG Cork	c Pothas b Mascarenhas	7
TC Smith	c Pothas b Bruce	26
OJ Newby	lbw b Logan	4
G Keedy	not out	0
Extras	lb 5, w 4, nb 18	27
	(all out 79.3 overs)	224

Bowling
Logan 16-3-71-2. Bruce 22.3-4-52-4. Mascarenhas 21-8-40-1. Ervine 11-2-38-2. Thornely 5-2-11-1. Udal 4-1-7-0.
Fall of Wickets: 1-23, 2-24, 3-61, 4-87, 5-88, 6-142, 7-159, 8-199, 9-213

Match drawn – Lancashire (8 pts), Hampshire (7 pts)

NOTTINGHAMSHIRE v. YORKSHIRE – at Trent Bridge

NOTTS	First Innings	
DJ Bicknell	lbw b Blain	95
JER Gallian (capt)	c Brophy b Claydon	5
RJ Warren	b McGrath	93
DJ Hussey	c Bresnan b McGrath	31
WR Smith	c Brophy b Bresnan	60
*CMW Read	not out	102
MA Ealham	b Bresnan	2
PJ Franks	lbw b Bresnan	1
GJ Smith	c Brophy b McGrath	0
RJ Sidebottom	not out	0
AJ Harris		
Extras	lb 5, w 1, nb 22	28
	(8 wkts dec 105.1 overs)	417

Bowling
Claydon 21-1-92-1. Bresnan 25.1-7-85-3. Blain 10-0-95-1. Dawson 13-0-53-0. McGrath 20-2-64-3. Lehmann 7-1-23-0.
Fall of Wickets: 1-11, 2-181, 3-225, 4-253, 5-356, 6-366, 7-400, 8-411

YORKSHIRE	
MJ Wood	
JJ Sayers	
A McGrath	
MJ Lumb	
DS Lehmann	
C White (capt)	
*GL Brophy	
RKJ Dawson	
TT Bresnan	
JAR Blain	
ME Claydon	

Match drawn – Nottinghamshire (9 pts), Yorkshire (6 pts)

but on the final day it was the Notts batsmen who prospered most in the hunt for bonus points. Darren Bicknell and Russell Warren both fell in the 90s, but added 170 for the second wicket before leaving the stage for the promising Will Smith, who scored 60, and the rapidly maturing Chris Read, who finished 102 not out, to underline their batting skills.

Division Two

Not even a wonderful career-best 172 from Cameron White, the 22-year-old Victoria captain marking his debut for Somerset with an eye-catching performance, could deny Jon Lewis and Gloucestershire in the West Country derby at Bristol. Lewis took a Championship best 7 for 38 as Somerset were initially tumbled out for 143 in reply to a Gloucestershire first innings of 437 built around centuries from Craig Spearman and Alex Gidman. White scored 36 in that innings but, with Somerset following on, he found himself at the crease again for much of the rest of the third day to walk off at stumps on 154 not out. Unfortunately for his new county, White could find no one capable of staying with him and, at 268 for 8 at the close, Somerset had nowhere to go. After a bit more defiance from White the next morning, Gloucestershire's innings-and-seven-run victory was soon confirmed, with Lewis and Ian Harvey each picking up three wickets.

Jon Lewis: ten wickets for the Gloucestershire captain in the West Country derby win against Somerset.

Round One: 18–22 April 2006 Division One

GLOUCESTERSHIRE v. SOMERSET – at Bristol

GLOS	First Innings	
CM Spearman	c White b Willoughby	109
WPC Weston	b Trego	54
MGN Windows	c Trescothick b Caddick	20
CG Taylor	c White b Willoughby	10
APR Gidman	run out	103
IJ Harvey	c Francis b Johnson	45
*SJ Adshead	lbw b White	7
MA Hardinges	lbw b Willoughby	16
MCJ Ball	b Willoughby	15
J Lewis (capt)	not out	21
SP Kirby	lbw b Willoughby	3
Extras	b 8, lb 13, w 3, nb 10	34
	(all out 120.4 overs)	437

Bowling
Caddick 34-7-104-1. Willoughby 33.4-7-125-5. Johnson 28-2-105-1. Trego 19-4-65-1. White 6-1-17-1.
Fall of Wickets: 1-135, 2-196, 3-206, 4-211, 5-295, 6-325, 7-361, 8-403, 9-416

SOMERSET	First Innings		Second Innings (following on)	
ME Trescothick	lbw b Lewis	12	lbw b Lewis	4
MJ Wood (capt)	c Adshead b Lewis	9	b Gidman	27
JD Francis	lbw b Lewis	2	run out	4
JC Hildreth	b Lewis	9	c Spearman b Lewis	8
CL White	lbw b Harvey	36	c Lewis b Harvey	172
WJ Durston	c Weston b Harvey	2	lbw b Harvey	21
*CM Gazzard	lbw b Hardinges	21	c Adshead b Lewis	9
PD Trego	c Adshead b Lewis	4	c Ball b Hardinges	15
RL Johnson	not out	9	c Adshead b Hardinges	11
AR Caddick	b Lewis	2	not out	7
CM Willoughby	b Lewis	21	c Taylor b Harvey	0
Extras	b 1, lb 2, w 5, nb 8	16	lb 5, nb 4	9
	(all out 40.3 overs)	143	(all out 85 overs)	287

Bowling
Lewis 14.3-1-4-38-7. Kirby 14-2-49-0. Harvey 7-2-21-2. Hardinges 5-0-32-1.
Lewis 15-5-37-3. Kirby 16-4-51-0. Harvey 16-2-39-3. Hardinges 17-4-69-2.
Gidman 5-1-21-1. Ball 13-1-54-0. Taylor 3-2-11-0.
Fall of Wickets: 1-17, 2-25, 3-35, 4-61, 5-68, 6-85, 7-108, 8-108, 9-111
1-6, 2-10, 3-28, 4-69, 5-123, 6-153, 7-196, 8-222, 9-286

Gloucestershire won by an innings and 7 runs –
Gloucestershire (22 pts), Somerset (3 pts)

ESSEX v. NORTHAMPTONSHIRE – at Chelmsford

NORTHANTS	First Innings		Second Innings	
SD Peters	c Flower b Adams	8	(2) c Pettini b Gough	7
CJL Rogers	lbw b Gough	9	(1) b Bopara	9
BM Shafayat	c Bopara b Adams	118	c Cook b ten Doeschate	43
U Afzaal	c Cook b Gough	5	c Foster b ten Doeschate	28
DJG Sales (capt)	lbw b ten Doeschate	75	not out	157
*MH Wessels	lbw b ten Doeschate	9	c Foster b ten Doeschate	11
L Klusener	not out	126	lbw b ten Doeschate	62
BJ Phillips	c Foster b Gough	9	c Pettini b Middlebrook	1
SP Crook	c Cook b Adams	0		
MJ Nicholson	lbw b Gough	5	(9) not out	29
MS Panesar	c Foster b Gough	2		
Extras	b 1, lb 15, w 1, nb 14	31	b 5, lb 7, w 1, nb 4	17
	(all out 110.5 overs)	397	(7 wkts dec 86 overs)	364

Bowling
Gough 25.5-7-82-5. Adams 24-4-66-3. Bopara 15-1-54-0. Napier 13-2-67-0.
ten Doeschate 13-2-53-2. Middlebrook 20-2-59-0.
Gough 14-4-43-1. Adams 15-5-42-0. Bopara 10-2-46-1. Napier 12-4-39-0.
ten Doeschate 19-2-99-4. Middlebrook 16-0-83-1.
Fall of Wickets: 1-9, 2-21, 3-31, 4-183, 5-195, 6-341, 7-376, 8-377, 9-389
1-13, 2-18, 3-68, 4-133, 5-147, 6-291, 7-295

ESSEX	First Innings		Second Innings	
ML Pettini	c Wessels b Nicholson	12	c Sales b Phillips	7
AN Cook	c Wessels b Klusener	88	not out	103
RS Bopara	b Crook	9	c Wessels b Klusener	7
A Flower	c Afzaal b Panesar	51	c Sales b Crook	7
RC Irani (capt)	c Sales b Klusener	2	not out	20
*JS Foster	c Phillips b Klusener	7		
RN ten Doeschate	c Wessels b Phillips	4		
JD Middlebrook	c Wessels b Klusener	59		
GR Napier	c Nicholson b Phillips	52		
AR Adams	b Phillips	16		
D Gough	not out	52		
Extras	b 7, lb 10, w 1, nb 18	36	b 4, nb 10	14
	(all out 110.5 overs)	381	(3 wkts 49 overs)	158

Bowling
Nicholson 26-7-92-1. Phillips 23-7-69-3. Crook 14-1-57-1. Klusener 21.5-4-70-4.
Panesar 26-5-76-1.
Nicholson 6-1-18-0. Phillips 5-1-12-1. Panesar 19-6-47-0. Klusener 7-3-17-1.
Crook 11-0-59-1. Sales 1-0-1-0.
Fall of Wickets: 1-46, 2-81, 3-163, 4-173, 5-173, 6-176, 7-180, 8-277, 9-299
1-23, 2-64, 3-96

Match drawn – Essex (11 pts), Northamptonshire (11 pts)

SURREY v. DERBYSHIRE – at The Oval

DERBYSHIRE	First Innings	
SD Stubbings	c Batty b Ormond	7
MJ Di Venuto	c Brown b Azhar Mahmood	60
CR Taylor	lbw b Azhar Mahmood	45
TR Birt	c Batty b Ormond	99
Hassan Adnan	c Batty b Azhar Mahmood	88
AG Botha	c Newman b Doshi	100
G Welch (capt)	c Butcher b Azhar Mahmood	0
*DJ Pipe	b Azhar Mahmood	16
MA Sheikh	not out	51
PS Jones	lbw b Salisbury	0
ID Hunter	lbw b Salisbury	6
Extras	b 4, lb 11, w 1, nb 4	20
	(all out 142.1 overs)	492

Bowling
Ormond 32-8-93-2. Akram 3.2-0-17-0. Azhar Mahmood 28.4-10-69-5.
Clarke 17-0-94-0. Doshi 38-4-135-1. Salisbury 23.1-2-69-2.
Fall of Wickets: 1-13, 2-101, 3-162, 4-245, 5-353, 6-353, 7-395, 8-481, 9-482

SURREY	First Innings		Second Innings (following on)	
SA Newman	c Stubbings b Jones	66	b Botha	90
*JN Batty	lbw b Welch	22	b Hunter	96
MR Ramprakash	c Pipe b Sheikh	71	b Jones	12
MA Butcher (capt)	c Di Venuto b Jones	2	c Welch b Botha	19
R Clarke	c Botha b Sheikh	59	(6) b Birt	130
Azhar Mahmood	b Sheikh	37	(7) lbw b Welch	46
AD Brown	c Di Venuto b Sheikh	26	(5) c Birt b Botha	15
IDK Salisbury	c Di Venuto b Welch	14	c Di Venuto b Welch	2
J Ormond	c Stubbings b Welch	0	not out	41
ND Doshi	not out	1	not out	1
Mohammad Akram	b Sheikh	1		
Extras	b 1, lb 1, w 2, nb 6	10	b 4, lb 16, w 2, nb 2	24
	(all out 88.5 overs)	308	(8 wkts 155 overs)	476

Bowling
Jones 17-5-48-2. Hunter 18-5-63-0. Sheikh 22.5-8-65-5. Welch 19-5-72-3.
Botha 12-4-58-0.
Jones 25-5-78-1. Hunter 22-3-89-1. Sheikh 22-9-48-0. Welch 26-8-58-2.
Botha 54-11-159-3. Birt 6-1-24-1.
Fall of Wickets: 1-42, 2-108, 3-114, 4-201, 5-265, 6-266, 7-297, 8-307, 9-307
1-152, 2-181, 3-218, 4-243, 5-246, 6-371, 7-377, 8-442

Match drawn – Surrey (9 pts),
Derbyshire (12 pts)

An eighth first-class hundred by Alastair Cook, which England's new batting star added to a first-innings 88, provided most of the interest as Essex's high-scoring meeting with Northamptonshire ended in a tame draw at Chelmsford. David Sales, the Northants captain, technically set Essex 381 to win in 53 overs after himself romping to an unbeaten second-innings 157 from 174 balls, with three sixes and 22 fours. But Cook, striking Monty Panesar for ten of his 15 boundaries, merely settled for batting practice. Essex, in fact, were perhaps the more grateful for the draw: in their first innings they had slid to 180 for 7 despite Cook's runs in reply to a Northants total of 397 in which Sales made 75, Bilal Shafayat an assured 118 and Lance Klusener a typically powerful 126 not out. Klusener did some damage with the ball, too, but Essex were rallied by James Middlebrook and Graham Napier, who put on 97 for the eighth wicket, before Darren Gough strode out at No. 11 to add a half-century of his own, from 48 balls, as another 82 was added for the final wicket.

Derbyshire, having asked to switch their match against Surrey to The Oval because of a waterlogged pitch and outfield at their own Derby headquarters, gave their opponents a harsh lesson about life in the second division. Batting first, in what was the 2,000th first-class match staged at The Oval, Derbyshire batted with great consistency and no little style to amass a total of 492. Travis Birt, the new overseas-player signing from Tasmania, became the first Derbyshire cricketer to be out for 99 on his debut for the county, while Ant Botha went one run better to claim the third century of his career. Azhar Mahmood bowled heroically to take 5 for 69, especially after Mohammad Akram had broken down with a groin strain in his fourth over, but Mo Sheikh also took a five-wicket haul as Surrey found themselves following on despite fine batting from Scott Newman, Mark Ramprakash and Rikki Clarke. Newman then made 90 from 145 balls and, with his opening partner Jon Batty finishing on 95 not out, Surrey ended the third day with some hope of saving the game at 217 for 2. Batty went for 96 the next morning, but then Clarke produced a superb innings of 130, containing 20 fours and a six, to deny Derbyshire. The final afternoon session was

particularly tense and hard-fought: at lunch Surrey were only 131 runs ahead, but by tea they had stretched that lead to 213 with three wickets still intact and the draw was more or less secured.

Round Two: 26–29 April 2006

Division One

Spectators of a certain age were all misty-eyed at Lord's as, for the first time for 49 summers, a Compton hit a hundred there. The batsman was, moreover, the grandson of the great Denis Compton – and he went to three figures with an appropriately dashing straight six, off Min Patel. Nick Compton's maiden first-class hundred possibly lacked just one thing: his memorable six was deposited into the Warner Stand and not the Compton Stand. Denis, who hit 47 first-class centuries in all at his beloved Lord's, would also have been disappointed that his grandson's fine 124 did not, in the end, prevent Middlesex from losing a match that – until Kent pulled away on the final afternoon – had been closely fought. Compton's 88-run eighth-wicket stand with a spirited Chris Wright had presented Kent with what seemed to be a stiff last-innings target, but Martin van Jaarsveld stroked a 26th first-class hundred and featured in three-figure stands with both David Fulton and Matthew Walker. Darren Stevens then joined

Yet another hundred for Compton at Lord's ... although, this time, it was by Denis's grandson Nick.

Walker to see Kent home, with Walker adding an unbeaten 84 to his superb first-innings 123. Ed Joyce was the other batting star of the match, dominating Middlesex's first innings with a fluent 130, but Robbie Joseph bowled his outswingers consistently and well to claim four-wicket hauls in both innings while Amjad Khan also impressed for Kent.

A virtuoso 150 from Darren Lehmann, occupying just 174 balls and with four sixes and 17 fours, took Yorkshire to within 67 runs of the mammoth 500 victory target set by Warwickshire at Edgbaston. With Anthony McGrath hitting 84 and Michael Lumb 71, Yorkshire found themselves needing only another 145 from 28 overs shortly after tea, but in the end it was a fairly relieved Warwickshire who took the points which propelled them into an early lead in the Championship. Fine batting from Nick Knight and Jonathan Trott was mainly responsible for putting them into what they had thought was an impregnable position: the pair added 249 for the third wicket, with Trott finishing up on 177 not out at the second-innings declaration.

Hampshire, still waiting for their captain Shane Warne to join them, found a Sussex side spearheaded by Pakistani duo Naved-ul-Hasan and Mushtaq Ahmed too hot to handle at the Rose Bowl. Naved, available for seven Championship fixtures before Pakistan's tour, took 5 for 63 to undermine Hampshire's first innings, while the irrepressible Mushtaq wrecked what – at 144 for 3

– had looked like a decent chase by the home side to finish with 7 for 64. On what was never a straightforward pitch, the batting efforts of both Chris Adams and Robin Martin-Jenkins were also vital components of Sussex's 94-run win.

Round Two: 26–29 April 2006 Division One

MIDDLESEX v. KENT – at Lord's

MIDDLESEX	First Innings		Second Innings	
ET Smith	c van Jaarsveld b Joseph	36	c van Jaarsveld b Khan	2
BL Hutton (capt)	c Joseph b Kemp	47	c Key b Joseph	8
OA Shah	c van Jaarsveld b Khan	12	lbw b Khan	16
EC Joyce	c Kemp b Joseph	130	c van Jaarsveld b Joseph	9
JWM Dalrymple	c O'Brien b Cook	17	lbw b Joseph	64
NRD Compton	c O'Brien b Kemp	13	b Khan	124
*BJM Scott	b Kemp	12	c & b Kemp	14
J Louw	c O'Brien b Stevens	1	c O'Brien b Joseph	2
CJC Wright	c van Jaarsveld b Joseph	10	c sub b Walker	42
CEW Silverwood	c Stevens b Joseph	2	not out	1
Mohammad Ali	not out	19	c & b Khan	19
Extras	lb 13, w 5, nb 16	34	b 1, lb 13, w 4, nb 8	26
	(all out 101.1 overs)	333	(all out 93.1 overs)	327

Bowling
Khan 23-4-82-1. Cook 18-4-48-1. Joseph 22.1-2-62-4. Kemp 20-3-72-3. Patel 12-1-42-0. Stevens 6-0-14-1.
Joseph 23-3-67-4. Khan 17.1-3-58-4. Cook 15-1-48-0. Kemp 12-1-51-1. Stevens 9-1-19-0. Patel 12-1-52-0. Walker 5-1-18-1.
Fall of Wickets: 1-67, 2-91, 3-154, 4-191, 5-232, 6-255, 7-268, 8-289, 9-295
1-11, 2-23, 3-45, 4-45, 5-140, 6-182, 7-210, 8-298, 9-307

KENT	First Innings		Second Innings	
DP Fulton	c Dalrymple b Wright	30	c Scott b Louw	77
RWT Key (capt)	lbw b Silverwood	4	lbw b Silverwood	19
M van Jaarsveld	c Smith b Silverwood	63	lbw b Louw	104
MJ Walker	c Joyce b Mohammad Ali	123	not out	84
DI Stevens	c Scott b Louw	15	not out	35
JM Kemp	c Hutton b Dalrymple	13		
*NJO'Brien	b Mohammad Ali	10		
MM Patel	c Hutton b Dalrymple	2		
SJ Cook	c Shah b Silverwood	6		
A Khan	b Dalrymple	11		
RH Joseph	not out	0		
Extras	b 4, lb 6, w 1, nb 20	31	lb 17, w 2, nb 18	37
	(all out 85.5 overs)	308	(3 wkts 92.4 overs)	356

Bowling
Silverwood 17-3-55-3. Louw 20-5-69-1. Wright 15-3-64-1.
Mohammad Ali 13.5-2-71-2. Hutton 3-2-6-0. Dalrymple 17-6-33-3.
Louw 19-1-83-2. Silverwood 16-2-42-1. Wright 10-0-48-0.
Mohammad Ali 15-1-49-0. Dalrymple 26-4-77-0. Hutton 2-1-14-0. Shah 4.4-0-26-0.
Fall of Wickets: 1-9, 2-69, 3-145, 4-162, 5-184, 6-211, 7-224, 8-251, 9-296
1-63, 2-166, 3-267

Kent won by 7 wickets – Middlesex (6 pts), Kent (20 pts)

WARWICKSHIRE v. YORKSHIRE – at Edgbaston

WARWICKSHIRE	First Innings		Second Innings	
NV Knight	c Brophy b McGrath	30	(3) c Bresnan b Gillespie	126
IJ Westwood	c Brophy b Blain	25	c McGrath b Gillespie	4
UL Trott	lbw b McGrath	43	(4) not out	177
AGR Loudon	b White	73	(5) b McGrath	29
JO Troughton	run out	73	(6) c Brophy b McGrath	2
MJ Powell	c McGrath b White	7	(7) not out	12
*TR Ambrose	lbw b Blain	13		
HH Streak (capt)	lbw b McGrath	9		
TD Groenewald	b McGrath	10		
NM Carter	c Blain b Gillespie	10	(1) c Dawson b Bresnan	36
JE Anyon	not out	0		
Extras	b 2, lb 18, w 7	27	b 2, lb 8	10
	(all out 99.1 overs)	316	(5 wkts dec 95 overs)	399

Bowling
Gillespie 22.1-4-50-1. Bresnan 21-5-81-0. Blain 20-3-72-2. McGrath 22-7-62-4. White 6-3-11-2. Dawson 8-1-20-0.
Gillespie 19.5-2-73-1. Bresnan 15-2-73-1. Blain 8-0-41-0. McGrath 19-1-65-2. Dawson 17-2-78-0. Lehmann 13-1-48-0. White 4-1-12-0.
Fall of Wickets: 1-60, 2-64, 3-153, 4-215, 5-221, 6-251, 7-272, 8-296, 9-315
1-41, 2-61, 3-310, 4-370, 5-378

YORKSHIRE	First Innings		Second Innings	
MJ Wood	c Knight b Streak	15	c Westwood b Anyon	18
JJ Sayers	c Knight b Streak	11	lbw b Streak	10
A McGrath	lbw b Carter	48	lbw b Anyon	84
MJ Lumb	c Knight b Groenewald	11	st Ambrose b Troughton	71
DS Lehmann	c Trott b Groenewald	6	c Ambrose b Carter	150
C White (capt)	run out	23	b Carter	2
*GL Brophy	b Loudon	40	c Trott b Anyon	19
TT Bresnan	c Ambrose b Anyon	10	(10) c Trott b Loudon	9
RKJ Dawson	b Carter	10	(8) c & b Loudon	1
JN Gillespie	not out	6	(9) not out	10
JAR Blain	lbw b Streak	12	lbw b Streak	10
Extras	b 4, lb 6, w 3, nb 4	17	b 2, lb 7, w 1, nb 10	20
	(all out 73 overs)	216	(all out 135.3 overs)	433

Bowling
Streak 16-1-47-3. Anyon 17-3-60-1. Carter 20-6-48-2. Groenewald 14-4-36-2. Loudon 6-3-15-1.
Streak 28.3-5-77-2. Carter 27-4-120-2. Anyon 22-6-66-3. Groenewald 16-5-34-0. Loudon 27-7-65-2. Powell 1-0-4-0. Troughton 14-3-58-1.
Fall of Wickets: 1-18, 2-53, 3-88, 4-96, 5-104, 6-149, 7-171, 8-195, 9-197
1-15, 2-61, 3-165, 4-241, 5-305, 6-353, 7-380, 8-392, 9-396

Warwickshire won by 66 runs – Warwickshire (20 pts), Yorkshire (4 pts)

HAMPSHIRE v. SUSSEX – at the Rose Bowl

SUSSEX	First Innings		Second Innings	
RR Montgomerie	c Pothas b Bruce	9	(2) c Adams b Ervine	35
CD Hopkinson	c Ervine b Thornely	45	(1) c Ervine b Tremlett	5
MH Yardy	c Pothas b Ervine	12	b Thornely	38
MW Goodwin	c Thornely b Ervine	0	lbw b Bruce	8
CJ Adams (capt)	c Pothas b Udal	64	c Pothas b Thornely	31
RSC Martin-Jenkins	c Adams b Thornely	3	(7) c Carberry b Bruce	91
LJ Wright	c Mascarenhas b Thornely	5	(8) c sub b Ervine	30
Naved-ul-Hasan	c Thornely b Udal	38	(3) c Adams b Udal	8
*AJ Hodd	c Pothas b Ervine	8	(6) c Pothas b Bruce	5
Mushtaq Ahmed	c Crawley b Bruce	1	c Thornely b Udal	2
JD Lewry	not out	12	not out	1
Extras	lb 5, w 2, nb 6	13	lb 12, nb 4	16
	(all out 84.3 overs)	211	(all out 74 overs)	262

Bowling
Bruce 19-9-35-2. Tremlett 16-7-30-0. Ervine 16-4-57-3. Mascarenhas 13-4-34-0. Thornely 13-5-38-3. Udal 7-3-2-12-2.
Bruce 17-6-59-3. Tremlett 12-3-4-24-1. Ervine 13.3-3-60-2. Udal 9-2-27-2. Thornely 11-2-52-2. Mascarenhas 11-0-28-0.
Fall of Wickets: 1-15, 2-36, 3-40, 4-114, 5-130, 6-152, 7-152, 8-178, 9-179
1-5, 2-55, 3-92, 4-112, 5-119, 6-149, 7-209, 8-229, 9-246

HAMPSHIRE	First Innings		Second Innings	
MJ Brown	c Hodd b Naved-ul-Hasan	0	(2) c Adams b Lewry	37
JHK Adams	lbw b Naved-ul-Hasan	13	(1) c Mgomerie b Naved-ul-Hasan	2
JP Crawley	c Adams b Naved-ul-Hasan	18	c Yardy b Wright	14
DJ Thornely	c Hodd b Lewry	18	lbw b Mushtaq Ahmed	1
MA Carberry	c Yardy b Lewry	43	b Mushtaq Ahmed	39
*N Pothas	c Hodd b Mushtaq Ahmed	9	lbw b Mushtaq Ahmed	7
SM Ervine	c Wright b Naved-ul-Hasan	3	lbw b Mushtaq Ahmed	7
AD Mascarenhas	c Hodd b Martin-Jenkins	11	lbw b Mushtaq Ahmed	7
SD Udal (capt)	c Adams b Martin-Jenkins	3	b Mushtaq Ahmed	13
CT Tremlett	c Yardy b Naved-ul-Hasan	4	lbw b Mushtaq Ahmed	23
JTA Bruce	not out	5	not out	1
Extras	lb 5, w 1	6	b 2, lb 7, nb 6	15
	(all out 64.2 overs)	168	(all out 59.2 overs)	211

Bowling
Naved-ul-Hasan 23.2-9-63-5. Lewry 14-1-56-2. Mushtaq Ahmed 5-2-6-1. Martin-Jenkins 14-10-19-2. Wright 8-2-19-0.
Naved-ul-Hasan 19-3-52-1. Lewry 13-1-31-1. Mushtaq Ahmed 15.2-1-64-7. Martin-Jenkins 7-2-23-0. Wright 5-0-32-1.
Fall of Wickets: 1-0, 2-34, 3-37, 4-76, 5-103, 6-129, 7-149, 8-155, 9-159
1-33, 2-61, 3-77, 4-144, 5-148, 6-152, 7-164, 8-175, 9-190

Sussex won by 94 runs – Hampshire (3 pts), Sussex (18 pts)

DURHAM v. LANCASHIRE – at the Riverside

LANCASHIRE	First Innings		Second Innings	
MJ Chilton	c Breese b Killeen	44	lbw b Onions	57
IJ Sutcliffe	c Breese b Onions	6	(1) c Muchall b Onions	17
MB Loye	c Maher b Breese	114	lbw b Onions	3
SG Law	c Mustard b Thorp	45	not out	111
PJ Horton	lbw b Gibson	21	run out	19
*LD Sutton	b Gibson	58	c Breese b Killeen	23
G Chapple	c Muchall b Thorp	82	b Mustard b Thorp	27
DG Cork	b Gibson	16		
TC Smith	b Onions	2	(8) not out	1
SI Mahmood	lbw b Gibson	7		
G Keedy	not out	5		
Extras	lb 0, w 1, nb 10	21	b 1, lb 1, lb 7, nb 2	10
	(all out 113.5 overs)	421	(6 wkts dec 77 overs)	268

Bowling
Gibson 28.5-1-106-4. Onions 24-2-117-2. Thorp 23-8-58-2. Killeen 19-5-47-1. Benkenstein 10-2-40-0. Breese 9-1-43-1.
Gibson 17-4-34-1. Onions 16-4-46-2. Thorp 12-1-48-1. Killeen 13-0-39-1. Breese 18-3-87-0. Benkenstein 1-0-6-0.
Fall of Wickets: 1-10, 2-107, 3-194, 4-243, 5-243, 6-353, 7-388, 8-391, 9-406
1-23, 2-32, 3-133, 4-180, 5-218, 6-265

DURHAM	First Innings		Second Innings	
JJB Lewis	c Law b Smith	33	lbw b Mahmood	2
JP Maher	c Sutton b Smith	22	c Law b Keedy	63
GJ Muchall	c Horton b Chapple	102	c Sutton b Keedy	1
GJ Pratt	c Sutcliffe b Keedy	25	b Chapple	20
DM B'kenstein (capt)	lbw b Smith	37	lbw b Mahmood	88
GR Breese	c Sutton b Chilton	26	c Sutton b Chapple	33
*P Mustard	c Sutton b Chapple	10	c Sutton b Chapple	4
OD Gibson	lbw b Cork	6	c Chapple b Mahmood	11
CD Thorp	c Sutton b Chapple	10	lbw b Mahmood	10
G Onions	lbw b Chapple	9	b Chapple	10
N Killeen	not out	5	not out	0
Extras	b 5, lb 8	13	b 5, lb 13, n 4, nb 2	21
	(all out 95.4 overs)	289	(all out 93.4 overs)	272

Bowling
Chapple 27.4-5-74-4. Mahmood 22-5-62-0. Smith 21-4-72-4. Keedy 22.3-3-67-1. Chilton 2-1-1-0.
Chapple 22-6-54-4. Mahmood 18.4-7-46-4. Keedy 28-5-82-2. Smith 9-3-29-0. Cork 13-3-36-0. Chilton 3-0-7-0.
Fall of Wickets: 1-47, 2-72, 3-110, 4-183, 5-232, 6-251, 7-259, 8-277, 9-277
1-7, 2-14, 3-63, 4-129, 5-195, 6-205, 7-238, 8-239, 9-264

Lancashire won by 128 runs – Durham (5 pts), Lancashire (22 pts)

OF DERBYSHIRE

S mall of population and small of membership, Derbyshire have nevertheless made it a habit throughout their long and proud history to punch well above their weight. It is a characteristic which in the summer of 2006 they have happily begun to demonstrate again under the shrewd leadership of David Houghton and Graeme Welch, the captain.

In the recent past, the best of Derbyshire cricketers have tended to be tempted elsewhere. Chris Adams, successful and long-serving captain of Sussex, played for his native county from 1988 until 1997; Dominic Cork,

who gave sterling service from 1990 to 2003, and was captain for his last six seasons, has sought pastures new at Lancashire; Chesterfield-born Ian Blackwell left after three years to join Somerset in 2000; Andrew Harris went to Nottinghamshire in 1999 after six seasons; Luke Sutton, Derbyshire's captain after Cork in 2004 and 2005, also decided to go to Old Trafford after six years.

But with new young talent now beginning to emerge under Houghton amid the cast-offs and inspired signings from other counties, a return to the modern golden age of 1983–1995 – when Kim Barnett was as influential a county captain as the game has seen – cannot be ruled out.

In that time Derbyshire, having just won the NatWest Trophy in 1981, were often among the leading teams in the County Championship as well as winning the Sunday League in 1990 and the Benson and Hedges Cup in 1993. The 1990 side included West Indies fast bowler Ian Bishop and big-hitting South African all-rounder Adrian Kuiper as overseas players, consistent run-scorers in John Morris, Peter Bowler, the young Adams and skipper Barnett, and also the likes of Devon Malcolm, Ole Mortensen, Simon Base and Allan Warner to bowl the seam and swing that is traditionally required at Derby.

The success of 1993 was achieved without a significant overseas player contribution, with Bishop prevented by injury from playing any more than just a single one-day match. But the core of English-qualified talent remained from 1990, and by now Cork had become such an all-round force that it was his rumbustious 92 not out in the Lord's final against overwhelming favourites Lancashire that, in the end, proved decisive in the six-run Benson and Hedges Cup triumph.

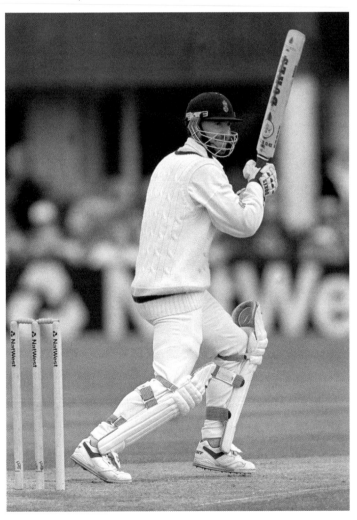

Kim Barnett, the inspirational Derbyshire captain for 13 seasons in the 1980s and 1990s.

Durham battled hard, but Lancashire's all-round strength always kept them in control of their match at the Riverside and in the end they won by 128 runs with an hour to spare. Mal Loye's rapier, in a fine 114, and Glen Chapple's bludgeon – with 68 of his first-innings 82 coming in boundaries – gave Lancashire the early advantage, and then 20-year-old Tom Smith's high promise ensured a decent lead despite the in-form Gordon Muchall's 102. Stuart Law's unbeaten 111 kept Durham on the back foot before Chapple and Sajid Mahmood shared eight wickets to secure victory.

Division Two

The rich promise of 20-year-old Ravi Bopara shone out from Essex's innings-and-30-run thrashing of Glamorgan at Cardiff, plus the experience of Andy Flower and the better variety of the visiting attack. Initially, however, it was all about Bopara and Flower as 339 runs were added for Essex's third wicket in 86 overs. Bopara scored 159, a career-best, and Flower 169, but Essex were not finished there. After Ronnie Irani's 73 came an unbeaten 102 from the hard-hitting Ryan ten Doeschate and a declaration on 639 for 8 challenged a demoralised Glamorgan side to bat out the remaining two and a half days. The 22-year-old opener Ryan Watkins did

his best with a career-best 87, while Mark Wallace played two spirited hands and featured in a defiant eighth-wicket stand of 90 with his captain, Robert Croft, in the Welsh county's second innings. Despite this it was all over midway through the final day.

Surrey found Leicestershire a tough nut to crack at Grace Road, but crack it they did on the back of four days' hard graft. Mark Ramprakash, with the 80th first-class hundred of his career, set things rolling for Surrey while – in both innings – new captain Mark Butcher showed that he was well on the road back from the wrist injury which had cost him his England place in late 2004. Butcher's 77 and unbeaten 85 helped to engineer a second-innings declaration which gave Surrey enough time to work their way through a stubborn Leicestershire rearguard action, led by Darren Maddy and Hylton Ackerman, and triumph in the end by 99 runs. The highly rated Stuart Broad took a maiden five-wicket haul in Surrey's first innings of 370.

Brian Rose, Somerset's director of cricket, spoke of the club's 'nursemaid' strategy for Andrew Caddick in the 2006 season following the former England fast bowler's match-winning display against Worcestershire at New Road, and it was easy to understand why. At 37, Caddick was just as dangerous as the Indian left-arm seamer Zaheer Khan, whose second-innings 6 for 40 made him the

Round Two: 26–29 April 2006 Division Two

GLAMORGAN v. ESSEX – at Cardiff

ESSEX	First Innings		
ML Pettini	b Wharf		22
AN Cook	c Wallace b Davies		35
RS Bopara	c Powell b Wharf		159
A Flower	lbw b Jones		169
RC Irani (capt)	c Hemp b Davies		73
*JS Foster	c Wallace b Watkins		4
RN ten Doeschate	not out		102
JD Middlebrook	c Watkins b Croft		19
TJ Phillips	lbw b Grant		6
AR Adams	not out		15
D Gough			
Extras	b 9, lb 7, w 1, nb 18		35
	(8 wkts dec 158.3 overs)		639

Bowling
Jones 28-4-96-1. Wharf 26-5-82-2. Davies 39-3-147-2. Watkins 19-2-77-1. Croft 33.3-1-139-1. Grant 13-0-82-1.
Fall of Wickets: 1-56, 2-60, 3-399, 4-420, 5-435, 6-548, 7-583, 8-599

GLAMORGAN	First Innings		Second Innings (following on)	
DD Cherry	c Foster b Gough	12	c Cook b Phillips	7
RE Watkins	c Pettini b Phillips	87	b Adams	5
DL Hemp	c Bopara b ten Doeschate	31	c Flower b Middlebrook	36
MJ Powell	b Gough	38	lbw b Gough	36
N Peng	b Middlebrook	39	(6) lbw b Gough	2
RN Grant	c Phillips b Middlebrook	25	(7) c Adams b Phillips	28
*MA Wallace	not out	47	(8) c Phillips b ten Doeschate	48
RDB Croft (capt)	lbw b Adams	7	(9) b Phillips	71
AG Wharf	c Pettini b ten Doeschate	31	(5) lbw b Bopara	4
AP Davies	c & b Phillips	1	c Foster b ten Doeschate	7
SP Jones	c Flower b Phillips	0	not out	4
Extras	b 1, lb 9, w 1, nb 8	19	b 16, lb 4, nb 4	24
	(all out 109.5 overs)	337	(all out 94 overs)	272

Bowling
Gough 22-5-58-2. Adams 25-7-59-1. Phillips 22.5-2-69-3. Middlebrook 12-5-30-2. ten Doeschate 21-3-79-2. Bopara 7-1-32-0.
Gough 12-4-31-2. Adams 17-5-3-171-1. Phillips 25-3-103-3. Middlebrook 16-8-16-1. ten Doeschate 17-3-51-2. Bopara 7-2-20-1.
Fall of Wickets: 1-16, 2-85, 3-171, 4-197, 5-249, 6-252, 7-285, 8-336, 9-337
1-10, 2-23, 3-86, 4-96, 5-96, 6-99, 7-145, 8-235, 9-263

Essex won by an innings and 30 runs – Glamorgan (4 pts), Essex (22 pts)

LEICESTERSHIRE v. SURREY – at Leicester

SURREY	First Innings		Second Innings	
SA Newman	c Maddy b Masters	9	c Nixon b Mohammad Asif	75
*JN Batty	b Broad	54	lbw b Maddy	41
MR Ramprakash	lbw b Maddy	113	b Masters	22
MA Butcher (capt)	b Broad	77	not out	85
AD Brown	c Nixon b Broad	25	b Masters	0
R Clarke	c Robinson b Broad	45	c Nixon b Masters	4
Azhar Mahmood	c Ackerman b Mohammad Asif	1	b Mohammad Asif	0
IDK Salisbury	lbw b Mohammad Asif	4	lbw b Broad	8
TJ Murtagh	run out	4	not out	37
J Ormond	c Nixon b Broad	6		
ND Doshi	not out	6		
Extras	b 5, lb 14, w 2, nb 8	29	b 10, lb 3, nb 2	15
	(all out 112.5 overs)	370	(7 wkts dec 83.5 overs)	287

Bowling
Mohammad Asif 28-4-76-2. Masters 22-11-33-1. Maunders 12-2-29-0.
Broad 22.5-2-94-5. Henderson 10-1-43-0. Maddy 15-1-53-1. Mongia 3-0-23-0.
Mohammad Asif 17-4-40-2. Broad 7-0-48-1. Masters 14-4-47-3.
Henderson 21-1-64-0. Maddy 12-0-37-1. Snape 12.5-1-38-0.
Fall of Wickets: 1-15, 2-90, 3-252, 4-292, 5-335, 6-340, 7-346, 8-354, 9-358
1-113, 2-130, 3-156, 4-156, 5-160, 6-161, 7-187

LEICESTERSHIRE	First Innings		Second Innings	
DDJ Robinson	b Ormond	9	lbw b Azhar Mahmood	13
DL Maddy	b Azhar Mahmood	43	c Azhar Mahmood b Ormond	97
HD Ackerman	c & b Murtagh	15	b Azhar Mahmood	55
D Mongia	c Ramprakash b Murtagh	4	b Clarke	15
JK Maunders	c Butcher b Doshi	87	lbw b Ormond	7
JN Snape (capt)	c Batty b Murtagh	4	b Clarke	4
*PA Nixon	c Butcher b Doshi	20	not out	31
CW Henderson	lbw b Doshi	14	b Ormond	0
SCJ Broad	c Butcher b Salisbury	24	c Azhar Mahmood b Clarke	11
DD Masters	not out	6	c Azhar Mahmood b Salisbury	1
Mohammad Asif	c Batty b Doshi	1	st Batty b Salisbury	21
Extras	b 4, lb 11, nb 2	17	b 7, lb 21, nb 6	34
	(all out 88.1 overs)	244	(all out 97.5 overs)	314

Bowling
Ormond 16-3-52-1. Azhar Mahmood 14-5-36-1. Murtagh 16-6-48-3.
Clarke 10-2-32-1. Salisbury 22-7-40-1. Doshi 10.1-4-21-3.
Ormond 18-6-39-3. Azhar Mahmood 24-5-66-2. Doshi 4-0-18-0.
Murtagh 9-1-37-0. Clarke 20-7-44-3. Salisbury 22.5-1-82-2.
Fall of Wickets: 1-22, 2-62, 3-67, 4-78, 5-88, 6-126, 7-173, 8-229, 9-243
1-21, 2-107, 3-132, 4-158, 5-224, 6-246, 7-246, 8-273, 9-280

Surrey won by 99 runs – Leicestershire (4 pts), Surrey (21 pts)

WORCESTERSHIRE v. SOMERSET – at Worcester

SOMERSET	First Innings		Second Innings	
ME Trescothick	c Smith b Khan	0	lbw b Kabir Ali	5
MJ Wood (capt)	c Davies b Malik	36	lbw b Khan	44
JD Francis	c Batty b Mason	27	lbw b Khan	0
JC Hildreth	c Mason b Kabir Ali	28	c Batty b Mason	10
CL White	b Malik	65	b Malik	0
WJ Durston	c Hick b Kabir Ali	74	c Davies b Malik	35
*CM Gazzard	lbw b Khan	22	c Davies b Khan	4
PD Trego	b Malik	51	c Hick b Khan	0
RL Johnson	c Hick b Khan	51	c Solanki b Malik	13
AR Caddick	not out	39	not out	0
CM Willoughby	c Solanki b Khan	0	c Davies b Khan	4
Extras	lb 2, nb 1	13	lb 3, w 1	5
	(all out 101.1 overs)	406	(all out 46.3 overs)	120

Bowling
Khan 25.1-8-100-4. Kabir Ali 26-5-99-2. Mason 24-4-65-1. Malik 18-5-104-3.
Batty 8-0-26-0.
Khan 16.3-4-40-6. Kabir Ali 6-1-19-1. Mason 7-3-16-1. Malik 12-3-29-2.
Batty 5-0-13-0.
Fall of Wickets: 1-8, 2-63, 3-67, 4-124, 5-168, 6-235, 7-299, 8-321, 9-404
1-5, 2-10, 3-34, 4-39, 5-75, 6-83, 7-83, 8-111, 9-115

WORCS	First Innings		Second Innings	
DKH Mitchell	c Caddick b Trego	52	c Durston b Caddick	5
SC Moore	c Hildreth b Johnson	24	lbw b Caddick	24
VS Solanki (capt)	c Trescothick b Caddick	34	c Trescothick b Caddick	0
BF Smith	c White b Caddick	0	c Trescothick b Caddick	0
GA Hick	c Gazzard b Caddick	8	lbw b Trego	6
*SM Davies	c Gazzard b Caddick	1	c Gazzard b Willoughby	37
GJ Batty	c Gazzard b Johnson	9	lbw b Johnson	10
Kabir Ali	c Gazzard b Willoughby	0	c Trescothick b Willoughby	0
MS Mason	c White b Trego	14	c Wood b Willoughby	10
Z Khan	not out	0	not out	30
MN Malik	not out	0	c Gazzard b Caddick	4
Extras	b 1, lb 4, w 2, nb 4	11	w 3, nb 4	7
	(all out 63.2 overs)	161	(all out 47.1 overs)	138

Bowling
Caddick 18.2-5-40-5. Willoughby 19-6-40-1. Johnson 15-4-41-2. Trego 10-1-26-2.
White 1-0-9-0.
Caddick 12.1-4-25-4. Willoughby 14-3-43-3. Johnson 14-2-53-2. Trego 7-2-17-1.
Fall of Wickets: 1-38, 2-79, 3-89, 4-105, 5-107, 6-122, 7-123, 8-154, 9-161
1-32, 2-37, 3-37, 4-39, 5-48, 6-92, 7-92, 8-95, 9-111

Somerset won by 227 runs – Worcestershire (3 pts), Somerset (22 pts)

Somerset's Andrew Caddick follows up his first-innings five-wicket haul by removing Worcestershire opener Daryl Mitchell.

Round Three: 3–6 May 2006

Division One

Shane Warne's best bowling figures for Hampshire, 7 for 99, completed Middlesex's downfall at the Rose Bowl – despite a high-class, fighting 141 from England opener Andrew Strauss. However, it was Strauss's first-innings duck, lbw to James Bruce, which had set Middlesex on their way to a pathetic opening-day collapse to 98 all out – a performance which, on a decent pitch, condemned them to their fate. Billy Taylor was Hampshire's first-day hero, taking a hat-trick and finishing with 6 for 32 overall in his first Championship appearance since the previous July. There were six ducks in the Middlesex first innings as they crashed from the relative security of 50 for 1, and Taylor's maiden first-class hat-trick victims were Nick Compton, caught at short leg, Paul Weekes, who lost his middle stump, and Ben Scott, bowled off an inside-edge. Hampshire then set about building a match-winning lead, with Nic Pothas leading the way with 100, and Warne needed no second invitation to work his way relentlessly through the Middlesex second innings.

The Nottinghamshire top order batting also showed worrying frailty as the champions slipped to a 60-run defeat to Warwickshire at Trent Bridge. The visitors' first innings was boosted to 248 by the unlikely seventh-wicket alliance of Dougie Brown and Moeen Ali, who at 18 was exactly half his veteran partner's age. The pair both scored half-centuries, with Moeen hitting ten boundaries in his fifty and going on to reach 68 in his Championship debut innings. Notts were soon 36 for 6 in reply, with only robust knocks by David Alleyne and Paul Franks hauling them up to 157. Ian Bell and Jonathan Trott quickly underlined Warwickshire's advantage, however, with excellent innings of 79 and 84 respectively and, during the third afternoon, Notts had crumbled to 77 for 5 in their second innings as they sought a win target of 377. Mark Ealham's 56 rallied them, and for the second time in the match it was 30-year-old reserve wicketkeeper Alleyne who showed up the best. In only his 12th first-class appearance, he fought on splendidly to an unbeaten 109 from 257 balls, but sadly for Notts the tail could not wag hard enough in support.

Wounded fatally by an early injury to Min Patel, their senior spinner, Kent slid to a six-wicket defeat at Lancashire after folding to a disappointing second-innings 124 on an Old Trafford pitch by

first bowler to take a ten-wicket match haul for Worcestershire since George Wilson against Yorkshire in 1899. After warming up with a cavalier unbeaten 39 as a ferociously wagging Somerset tail swept them to 406 on the opening day, Caddick took 5 for 40 as Worcestershire plunged to 161 all out in reply. Then came another 4 for 25 as the match came to a swift conclusion on a pitch growing increasingly tricky for batting. Cameron White and Wes Durston impressed with the bat for Somerset, while both Pete Trego and Richard Johnson struck 36 and 38-ball fifties respectively, but it was Caddick who was the real difference. 'As a matter of policy this summer, we're going to try to keep Andy fresh,' said Rose.

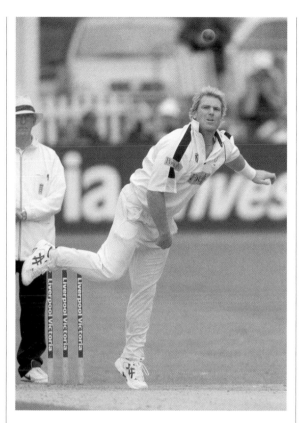

Shane Warne spins his way to another match-winning bag of 7 for 99 as Hampshire beat Middlesex.

then assisting the left-arm spin of Gary Keedy and the reverse swing of Sajid Mahmood, who both picked up four wickets. That left Lancashire with a small win target, which they reached in some comfort despite the off-spin of James Tredwell

Round Three: 3–6 May 2006 Division One

HAMPSHIRE v. MIDDLESEX – at the Rose Bowl

MIDDLESEX	First Innings		Second Innings	
AJ Strauss	lbw b Bruce	0	lbw b Warne	141
BL Hutton (capt)	b Bruce	24	b Udal	20
ET Smith	lbw b Taylor	32	b Warne	22
JWM Dalrymple	c Pothas b Taylor	0	c Pothas b Ervine	27
NRD Compton	c Crawley b Taylor	0	lbw b Taylor	31
PN Weekes	b Taylor	0	c Adams b Warne	8
*BJM Scott	b Taylor	0	lbw b Warne	23
J Louw	c Bruce b Ervine	12	b Warne	35
CEW Silverwood	c Thornely b Taylor	0	c Mascarenhas b Warne	4
MM Betts	c Carberry b Ervine	7	c Ervine b Warne	4
Mohammad Ali	not out	12	not out	13
Extras	lb 1, nb 10	11	b 2, lb 2, w 2, nb 10	16
	(all out 32.3 overs)	98	(all out 109.1 overs)	344

Bowling
Bruce 7.3-1-33-2. Taylor 12-2-32-6. Mascarenhas 8-2-12-0. Ervine 5-0-20-2.
Bruce 14-2-47-0. Ervine 11-3-26-1. Taylor 12-0-61-1. Thornely 5-0-16-0.
Mascarenhas 10-1-26-0. Udal 20-3-65-1. Warne 37.1-5-99-7.
Fall of Wickets:
1-0, 2-50, 3-50, 4-52, 5-52, 6-52, 7-75, 8-75, 9-84
1-79, 2-130, 3-188, 4-252, 5-256, 6-277, 7-304, 8-321, 9-327

HAMPSHIRE	First Innings		Second Innings	
JHK Adams	c Strauss b Louw	11	not out	14
MA Carberry	c Scott b Betts	29	not out	0
JP Crawley	c Scott b Louw	55		
SM Ervine	c & b Betts	34		
DJ Thornely	b Louw	65		
*N Pothas	c Smith b Silverwood	100		
AD Mascarenhas	b Louw	38		
SK Warne (capt)	c Strauss b Louw	22		
SD Udal	c Hutton b Silverwood	28		
JTA Bruce	not out	16		
BV Taylor	b Mohammad Ali	0		
Extras	b 1, lb 6, w 7, nb 14	28	nb 4	4
	(all out 109.4 overs)	426	(0 wkts 2.4 overs)	18

Bowling
Silverwood 20-2-86-2. Louw 29-5-117-5. Betts 17-3-59-2.
Mohammad Ali 18.4-1-70-1. Dalrymple 16-1-52-0. Hutton 9-0-35-0.
Hutton 1.4-0-17-0. Dalrymple 1-0-1-0.
Fall of Wickets: 1-31, 2-45, 3-122, 4-158, 5-286, 6-343, 7-382, 8-382, 9-412

Hampshire won by 10 wickets – Hampshire (22 pts),
Middlesex (3 pts)

NOTTINGHAMSHIRE v. WARWICKSHIRE – at Trent Bridge

WARWICKSHIRE	First Innings		Second Innings	
NV Knight	c Alleyne b Sidebottom	0	c Hussey b Harris	20
IJ Westwood	c Smith b Harris	14	c Alleyne b Harris	5
IR Bell	c Gallian b Harris	8	c Sidebottom b Ealham	79
IJL Trott	c Gallian b Ealham	30	lbw b Franks	84
JO Troughton	c Alleyne b Harris	11	c Warren b Sidebottom	10
MJ Powell	lbw b Franks	36	c Hussey b Ealham	29
DR Brown	c Alleyne b Ealham	53	c Hussey b Ealham	5
MM Ali	c Alleyne b Sidebottom	68	c Alleyne b Ealham	3
*T Frost	c Alleyne b Harris	3	(10) st Alleyne b Swann	12
HH Streak (capt)	c Ealham b Harris	0	(9) not out	27
JE Anyon	not out	2	st Alleyne b Swann	1
Extras	b 4, lb 8, w 7, nb 4	23	b 5, lb 2, w 1, nb 2	10
	(all out 104.5 overs)	248	(all out 79 overs)	285

Bowling
Sidebottom 22.5-5-73-2. Harris 27.9-9-53-5. Ealham 18-6-45-2. Franks 14-6-28-1.
Swann 23-9-37-0.
Sidebottom 21-2-77-1. Harris 13-0-51-3. Franks 12-1-60-1. Ealham 16-6-43-3.
Swann 17-3-47-2.
Fall of Wickets: 1-0, 2-15, 3-44, 4-58, 5-83, 6-133, 7-203, 8-224, 9-224
1-14, 2-33, 3-181, 4-193, 5-201, 6-213, 7-226, 8-257, 9-279

NOTTS	First Innings		Second Innings	
DJ Bicknell	c Ali b Anyon	0	b Anyon	17
JER Gallian (capt)	c Frost b Anyon	25	lbw b Streak	8
RJ Warren	lbw b Streak	9	b Streak	0
DJ Hussey	b Brown	2	c Bell b Anyon	21
WR Smith	lbw b Brown	0	b Streak	16
MA Ealham	c Frost b Bell	4	c Trott b Anyon	56
*D Alleyne	c Streak b Anyon	57	not out	109
PJ Franks	c Powell b Brown	38	c Bell b Troughton	1
GP Swann	not out	15	c Troughton b Bell	30
RJ Sidebottom	b Brown	1	b Anyon	26
AJ Harris	b Anyon	0	run out	3
Extras	b 3, lb 3, w 5, nb 2	13	b 11, lb 8, w 2, nb 8	29
	(all out 53.3 overs)	157	(all out 111 overs)	316

Bowling
Streak 16-6-40-2. Brown 17-4-49-4. Bell 6-2-18-1. Anyon 12.3-3-33-3. Ali 2-1-11-0.
Streak 26-4-78-3. Brown 20-7-49-0. Anyon 27-8-48-4. Ali 16-3-52-0. Bell 5-2-10-1.
Troughton 17-6-60-1.
Fall of Wickets: 1-8, 2-8, 3-11, 4-21, 5-36, 6-36, 7-103, 8-143, 9-156
1-13, 2-13, 3-38, 4-47, 5-77, 6-200, 7-201, 8-254, 9-310

Warwickshire won by 60 runs –
Nottinghamshire (3 pts), Warwickshire (18 pts)

LANCASHIRE v. KENT – at Old Trafford

KENT	First Innings		Second Innings	
DP Fulton	st Sutton b Keedy	40	c Horton b Mahmood	7
NJ Dexter	c Chapple b Keedy	34	c Law b Mahmood	5
M van Jaarsveld	lbw b Mahmood	87	b Keedy	15
MJ Walker	c Law b Keedy	41	c Smith b Chapple	2
DI Stevens	lbw b Keedy	10	c Sutcliffe b Chapple	0
*GO Jones	c Horton b Hogg	29	b Keedy	60
JM Kemp	not out	54	lbw b Keedy	7
JC Tredwell	c Chilton b Hogg	2	lbw b Keedy	7
MM Patel (capt)	c Hogg b Mahmood	8	(11) not out	0
SJ Cook	lbw b Mahmood	6	(9) b Mahmood	10
RH Joseph	run out	4	(10) b Mahmood	0
Extras	b 1, lb 10, w 1	12	b 8, lb 3	11
	(all out 114.3 overs)	327	(all out 46.2 overs)	124

Bowling
Mahmood 24.3-4-71-3. Chapple 23-6-59-0. Smith 20-5-59-0. Hogg 19-5-56-2.
Keedy 28-5-71-4.
Chapple 10-5-13-2. Mahmood 11-2-24-4. Smith 7-1-20-0. Keedy 13.2-3-44-4.
Hogg 5-0-12-0.
Fall of Wickets: 1-69, 2-97, 3-187, 4-199, 5-237, 6-252, 7-258, 8-290, 9-305
1-10, 2-17, 3-22, 4-26, 5-59, 6-79, 7-91, 8-120, 9-124

LANCASHIRE	First Innings		Second Innings	
MJ Chilton (capt)	lbw b Dexter	131	(2) b Tredwell	33
IJ Sutcliffe	c Jones b Cook	5	(1) c Dexter b Tredwell	27
MB Loye	c Kemp b Joseph	44	c sub b Tredwell	4
SG Law	c van Jaarsveld b Kemp	39	c Fulton b Stevens	4
PJ Horton	c van Jaarsveld b Joseph	79	not out	5
*LD Sutton	c Dexter b Kemp	11	not out	1
G Chapple	c van Jaarsveld b Dexter	0		
KW Hogg	not out	19		
TC Smith	c Jones b Cook	0		
SI Mahmood	c sub b Tredwell	4		
G Keedy	c Walker b Tredwell	4		
Extras	b 2, lb 12, w 3, nb 10	27	lb 1, nb 4	5
	(all out 121.3 overs)	363	(4 wkts 22.2 overs)	89

Bowling
Joseph 25-5-84-2. Cook 23-6-60-2. Tredwell 27.3-3-102-2. Kemp 24-3-63-2.
Walker 1-1-0-0. Dexter 21-4-40-2.
Joseph 7-2-18-0. Cook 6-0-31-0. Tredwell 7-1-34-3. Stevens 2.2-1-5-1.
Fall of Wickets: 1-8, 2-94, 3-154, 4-307, 5-326, 6-326, 7-338, 8-343, 9-353
1-59, 2-77, 3-83, 4-83

Lancashire won by 6 wickets – Lancashire (21 pts), Kent (6 pts)

YORKSHIRE v. SUSSEX – at Headingley

YORKSHIRE	First Innings		Second Innings	
MJ Wood	c Prior b Lewry	5	lbw b Naved-ul-Hasan	0
JJ Sayers	c Hopkinson b Naved-ul-Hasan	8	c M'gomerie b Naved-ul-Hasan	8
A McGrath	c Hopkinson b Mushtaq Ahmed	80	(4) c Prior b Naved-ul-Hasan	20
MJ Lumb	lbw b Lewry	1	(5) b Lewry	69
DS Lehmann	c & b Wright	64	(6) c Wright b Naved-ul-Hasan	87
C White (capt)	c & b Naved-ul-Hasan	37	(7) b Lewry	7
TT Bresnan	b Mushtaq Ahmed	11	(8) c Prior b Naved-ul-Hasan	6
*SM Guy	c Prior b Naved-ul-Hasan	25	(9) b Naved-ul-Hasan	9
RKJ Dawson	c Prior b Naved-ul-Hasan	0	(10) not out	4
JN Gillespie	lbw b Mushtaq Ahmed	1	(3) lbw b Lewry	1
MJ Hoggard	not out	0	c Yardy b Naved-ul-Hasan	0
Extras	b 10, lb 9, nb 6, p 10	35	b 4, lb 1, w 3, nb 2	10
	(all out 82.3 overs)	272	(all out 67 overs)	221

Bowling
Naved-ul-Hasan 18-5-86-4. Lewry 13-3-34-2. Mushtaq Ahmed 28.3-7-68-3.
Martin-Jenkins 15-3-32-0. Wright 8-2-23-1.
Naved-ul-Hasan 22-5-62-7. Lewry 22-10-49-3. Martin-Jenkins 7-1-12-0.
Wright 5-1-14-0. Mushtaq Ahmed 11-1-79-0.
Fall of Wickets: 1-9, 2-17, 3-24, 4-150, 5-182, 6-214, 7-233, 8-242, 9-263
1-0, 2-1, 3-15, 4-40, 5-176, 6-197, 7-204, 8-212, 9-221

SUSSEX	First Innings		Second Innings	
RR Montgomerie	lbw b Hoggard	14	(2) lbw b Hoggard	1
CD Hopkinson	c Guy b Bresnan	65	(1) c Guy b Gillespie	41
LJ Wright	c Lumb b Hoggard	2		
MH Yardy	c Bresnan b Gillespie	23	(3) c Guy b Hoggard	11
MW Goodwin	lbw b Bresnan	0	(4) c Dawson b Bresnan	23
CJ Adams (capt)	c Wood b McGrath	12	(5) st Guy b Lehmann	44
*MJ Prior	b White	124	(6) not out	55
RSC Martin-Jenkins	c Wood b Lehmann	29	(7) not out	17
Naved-ul-Hasan	c Lumb b Hoggard	1		
Mushtaq Ahmed	c Lumb b Gillespie	13		
JD Lewry	not out	2		
Extras	b 4, lb 9, w 1, nb 2	16	lb 3	3
	(all out 114.3 overs)	301	(5 wkts 56 overs)	195

Bowling
Gillespie 28-8-64-2. Hoggard 30-11-63-3. Dawson 18-1-69-0. Bresnan 21-4-53-2.
McGrath 5-1-11-1. White 4.3-0-8-1. Lehmann 8-1-20-1.
Gillespie 14-4-27-1. Hoggard 15-0-58-2. Bresnan 11-1-60-1. McGrath 0-0-17-0.
White 7-0-18-0. Lehmann 6-0-12-1.
Fall of Wickets: 1-25, 2-39, 3-79, 4-80, 5-115, 6-166, 7-223, 8-230, 9-252
1-12, 2-26, 3-64, 4-94, 5-133

Sussex won by 5 wickets –Yorkshire (5 pts),
Sussex (20 pts)

25 years OF DURHAM

Durham's ninth Minor Counties title was secured in 1984 – their fourth success in nine summers, in fact – and in 1985 they beat a first-class county for the second time in the Gillette Cup/NatWest Trophy competition by dispatching Derbyshire by seven wickets at Derby. But on 19 April 1992, Durham put 97 years of official competition in minor counties cricket behind them by playing their first match as a major county. It was a Sunday League match against Lancashire, played at the Durham University ground, and it resulted in a narrow, dramatic nine-run win for the home side.

Durham, the first new first-class county since Glamorgan's elevation in 1921, had arrived. Little more than 13 years later, when England played Pakistan at Lahore, there were three Durham players in the England XI: all three, moreover, were born and bred within the county's own territory of Northumberland, Tyne & Wear, Cleveland and Durham itself. The recent international successes of Steve Harmison, Paul Collingwood and Liam Plunkett, however, merely underlines a historical fact: the North East has always produced fine cricketers – from A. E. Stoddart to fellow England captains Tom Graveney and Bob Willis, from Colin Milburn to Peter Willey.

Now Durham have a fine, custom-built Test match ground at the Riverside, under the shadow of Lumley Castle at Chester-le-Street, to go with a team full of yet more young local promise.

They may not yet have won a title – and, in truth, the best part of their last 15 seasons has been spent struggling in the lower regions of the Championship – but the very emergence of Harmison, Collingwood and Plunkett has already established their right to be placed at the top table of English cricket.

Life as a first-class county began with more than a touch of stardust. Ian Botham played for a season and a half before retiring at the end of the county's match against the 1993 Australians, Dean Jones was a popular and highly effective first overseas recruit and David Graveney was the first captain of the new era. Now, though, they have homegrown stars of their own.

The Riverside, at Chester-le-Street, is already establishing itself as one of England's Test match grounds as well as being home to Durham, the newest of the country's 18 first-class counties.

claiming three wickets. Keedy had also taken 4 for 71 in Kent's first innings, but Martin van Jaarsveld's 87 and an unbeaten half-century from Justin Kemp pushed the visitors up to 327 and what might have been a match-winning total had Patel been fit to bowl. As it was, Mark Chilton compiled a determined 131 and added a vital 153 for the fourth wicket with Peter Horton. Then, despite Geraint Jones's spirited second-innings 60, Kent's challenge faded still further.

The batting of Matt Prior, and the pace and bounce of Rana Naved-ul-Hasan, were the major ingredients in a fine Sussex victory against Yorkshire at Headingley. In the end, the margin was five wickets, but that arrived only after a second highly impressive display with the bat by Prior, who added a nerveless unbeaten 55 from 90 balls to his first-innings 124. Sussex were also indebted to the steady support for Prior by Robin Martin-Jenkins on a tense final morning and to the belligerent 44 from Chris Adams, their captain, as they rallied to 139 for 5 by the close of the third day. Darren Lehmann also batted brilliantly for Yorkshire in both their innings, each time resuscitating a situation that had seemed

desperate. Anthony McGrath was Lehmann's first-innings accomplice, and Michael Lumb his partner second time around, but Naved's second-innings 7 for 62 – and Prior's calm assurance – ultimately made the difference.

Division Two

Derbyshire continued their promising start to the new season with an exciting 28-run victory over Glamorgan at Cardiff, which owed much to the club's very own Welshman, Steffan Jones. Bowling with fire and no little skill, Jones wrecked Glamorgan's second innings to finish with career-best figures of 6 for 25. Robert Croft was left stranded on 41 not out and Nicky Peng made 56, but the Welsh county had little answer to Derbyshire's dragon. Jones produced an initial spell of 7-6-4-2 as Glamorgan tottered to 16 for 2 in the 13 overs available to them on the third evening and then, next morning, Jones raced in again to further incapacitate Glamorgan with another burst of 7-5-10-3. Ian Hunter, who added three more wickets to his first-innings 4 for 47, supported Jones excellently. The first day of the match had seen a

Mark Ramprakash was in total command as he thrashed Gloucestershire's bowlers for a career-best 292 at The Oval.

remarkable collapse by Derbyshire from 247 for 1 after Chris Taylor had joined Steve Stubbings in a second-wicket partnership worth 198. Taylor, run out by new partner Hassan Adnan, publicly rebuked his team-mate before leaving the field. Glamorgan,

Round Three: 3–6 May 2006 Division Two

```
                GLAMORGAN v. DERBYSHIRE – at Cardiff

DERBYSHIRE    First Innings              Second Innings
MJ Di Venuto  lbw b Waters          26   (2) c Wallace b Watkins    33
SD Stubbings  b Croft               97   (1) lbw b Croft            52
CR Taylor     run out              121   st Wallace b Cosker        10
TR Birt       lbw b Croft            0   lbw b Croft                1
Hassan Adnan  b Waters               9   lbw b Croft               33
AG Botha      c Watkins b Cosker     0   c Cosker b Davies          2
G Welch (capt) b Davies             10   (8) c Powell b Cosker     15
*DJ Pipe      lbw b Cosker           0   (2) c Cosgrove b Cosker   20
MA Sheikh     not out               36   (7) lbw b Cosker           8
PS Jones      c Hemp b Croft        16   c Hemp b Cosker            4
ID Hunter     c Hemp b Cosker       11   not out                    4
Extras        lb 5, w 4              9   b 1, lb 1, w 3, nb 4      9
              (all out 131.5 overs) 335  (all out 80.4 overs)     192
Bowling
Davies 21-7-55-1. Watkins 8-3-36-0. Waters 22-7-49-2. Cosgrove 9-2-35-0.
Croft 37-8-86-3. Cosker 34.5-7-69-3.
Davies 9-2-33-1. Waters 4-0-18-0. Cosker 30.4-7-78-4. Croft 34-10-51-4.
Watkins 3-2-10-1.
Fall of Wickets: 1-49, 2-247, 3-247, 4-251, 5-251, 6-267, 7-268, 8-279, 9-308
1-62, 2-79, 3-80, 4-124, 5-138, 6-138, 7-158, 8-171, 9-178

GLAMORGAN    First Innings              Second Innings
MJ Cosgrove  c Welch b Botha       114  (2) c Botha b Jones        18
DD Cherry    c Pipe b Jones          5  (1) c Hunter b Jones        5
DL Hemp      b Jones                 0  c Welch b Jones             0
MJ Powell    c Sheikh b Botha      100  (5) c sub b Jones          10
N Peng       c Di Venuto b Botha     6  (6) lbw b Hunter           56
RE Watkins   lbw b Welch            7   (7) c sub b Hunter          5
*MA Wallace  c Welch b Hunter       52  (8) lbw b Sheikh            6
HT Waters    b Hunter                0  (11) c sub b Hunter         2
RDB Croft (capt) c Botha b Hunter    2  not out                   41
DA Cosker    lbw b Hunter            0  (4) b Jones                 0
AP Davies    not out                 2  (10) c Di Venuto b Jones   16
Extras       b 3, w 6, nb 18        27  b 8, lb 8, w 4, nb 4      24
             (all out 85.1 overs)  315  (all out 75.4 overs)     184
Bowling
Jones 19-4-86-2. Hunter 15.1-5-47-4. Sheikh 10-4-34-0. Welch 14-1-62-1.
Botha 27-8-83-3.
Jones 20-14-25-6. Hunter 22.4-10-52-3. Botha 17-4-48-0. Sheikh 8-3-17-1.
Welch 8-3-26-0.
Fall of Wickets: 1-45, 2-53, 3-158, 4-222, 5-233, 6-292, 7-300, 8-306, 9-306
1-12, 2-16, 3-22, 4-37, 5-42, 6-58, 7-69, 8-160, 9-181

Derbyshire won by 28 runs – Glamorgan (6 pts), Derbyshire (20 pts)
```

however, could not get past Derbyshire's eventual first-innings total despite centuries from both Mark Cosgrove and Michael Powell, and a second-innings half-century from Stubbings gave Derbyshire enough runs – just. Cosgrove, the 21-year-old South Australian, became only the fifth Glamorgan player to score a hundred on his Championship debut – and it took him only 93 balls.

An epic, nine-and-a-quarter hour 292 from Mark Ramprakash, unsurprisingly a career-best, allowed Surrey to ease to a crushing innings-and-297-run win against Gloucestershire at The Oval. It was Ramprakash's 11th double-hundred, and with James Benning also hitting 112 on his 23rd birthday, the second day of the match brought 476 Surrey runs. Ramprakash ended the day's carnage on 276 not out, having begun it on 54, and at that stage he had struck six sixes and 32 fours. Surrey's eventual 639 for 8 declared was their highest total against Gloucestershire for whom, in the circumstances, Martyn Ball produced worthy figures of 6 for 134. Mohammad Akram then skittled what remained of Gloucestershire's resistance, with 6 for 34, leaving Phil Weston – with a stubborn first-day 102 – as the only Gloucestershire batsman to even approach the standards set by Ramprakash, Benning and Scott Newman, who went past 500 first-class runs for the season during his 81.

Not even a magnificent 154 from Marcus Trescothick, who came good spectacularly after

```
            SURREY v. GLOUCESTERSHIRE – at The Oval

GLOS         First Innings              Second Innings
WPC Weston   c Ramprakash b Doshi  102  (2) c Butcher b Doshi     28
CM Spearman  c Batty b Azhar Mahmood  3 (1) lbw b Akram           13
MGN Windows  c Batty b Akram         0  c Batty b Benning          1
CG Taylor    lbw b Benning           8  c Batty b Doshi           11
APR Gidman (capt) lbw b Benning     10  not out                  39
IJ Harvey    c Butcher b Azhar Mahmood 0 (11) absent hurt
*SJ Adshead  c Brown b Benning      22  (6) c Batty b Akram       22
MCJ Ball     c Newman b Salisbury   16  (7) b Akram               0
CG Greenidge lbw b Salisbury         5  (9) c Salisbury b Akram    8
JMM Averis   c Azhar Mahmood b Salisbury 21 (10) lbw b Akram      8
SP Kirby     not out                 0
Extras       lb 7, w 2, nb 14       23  b 4, lb 10, nb 10        24
             (all out 72.2 overs)  207  (all out 42.5 overs)    135
Bowling
Akram 18-7-43-2. Azhar Mahmood 17-4-44-2. Ormond 8-2-18-0. Benning 11-0-58-2.
Salisbury 14-5-29-3. Doshi 4.2-0-8-1.
Akram 12.5-5-34-6. Azhar Mahmood 9-3-20-0. Doshi 9-3-18-2. Benning 7-1-32-1.
Salisbury 5-0-17-0.
Fall of Wickets: 1-6, 2-14, 3-31, 4-60, 5-61, 6-109, 7-145, 8-145, 9-195
1-20, 2-37, 3-42, 4-45, 5-113, 6-121, 7-121, 8-135, 9-135

SURREY       First Innings
SA Newman    lbw b Ball             81
*JN Batty    c Adshead b Kirby       4
MR Ramprakash c Weston b Ball      292
MA Butcher (capt) c Windows b Ball  47
AD Brown     b Ball                  4
JGE Benning  c Gidman              112
Azhar Mahmood c b b Ball            39
IDK Salisbury c Greenidge b Ball     4
J Ormond     not out                15
ND Doshi
Mohammad Akram
Extras       b 4, lb 9, w 2, nb 26  41
             (8 wkts dec 144.1 overs) 639
Bowling
Kirby 30-2-132-1. Greenidge 28-0-146-0. Averis 24-4-111-0. Gidman 16-0-85-1.
Ball 42.1-7-134-6. Taylor 4-0-18-0.
Fall of Wickets: 1-13, 2-182, 3-295, 4-303, 5-490, 6-600, 7-606, 8-639

Surrey won by an innings and 297 runs –
Surrey (22 pts), Gloucestershire (2 pts)
```

```
        NORTHAMPTONSHIRE v. SOMERSET – at Northampton

SOMERSET      First Innings              Second Innings
ME Trescothick c Phillips b Brown  154   c & b Phillips           12
MJ Wood (capt) lbw b Phillips        0   b Panesar                24
JD Francis    lbw b Klusener        10   lbw b Brown              12
JC Hildreth   c Wessels b Klusener  10   b Nicholson               0
CL White      b Brown               26   b Brown                  19
WJ Durston    b Brown                2   c Shafayat b Panesar     41
*CM Gazzard   c Wessels b Brown      9   b Nicholson               5
PD Trego      c Shafayat b Panesar   2   b Panesar                18
AR Caddick    c Wessels b Phillips  13   lbw b Panesar             1
DJ Cullen     not out               24   not out                   4
CM Willoughby b Brown                4   c Klusener b Panesar      2
Extras        b 2, lb 3             5    b 5, lb 1, nb 2          7
              (all out 77.3 overs) 258  (all out 61.3 overs)    145
Bowling
Nicholson 11-2-47-0. Phillips 13-3-28-2. Klusener 8-1-44-2. Brown 25.3-4-82-5.
Panesar 20-6-52-1.
Nicholson 12-2-50-2. Phillips 4-1-11-1. Brown 19-6-47-2. Panesar 26.3-12-32-5.
Fall of Wickets: 1-2, 2-27, 3-53, 4-98, 5-106, 6-132, 7-141, 8-186, 9-249
1-19, 2-44, 3-47, 4-70, 5-77, 6-113, 7-137, 8-138, 9-141

NORTHANTS    First Innings
CJL Rogers   lbw b Cullen           36
RA White     c Cullen b Willoughby   0
BM Shafayat  c Hildreth b Cullen   101
U Afzaal     c Francis b Cullen     26
DJG Sales (capt) c Trescothick b White 88
*MH Wessels  lbw b White             1
L Klusener   not out               147
BJ Phillips  c Trego b Caddick      11
MJ Nicholson lbw b Cullen           26
MS Panesar   c sub b Durston         1
JF Brown     b Cullen                3
Extras       lb 4, w 1, nb 4        9
             (all out 126 overs)  449
Bowling
Caddick 26-4-113-1. Willoughby 16-4-44-1. Cullen 43-10-137-5. Trego 16-2-70-0.
White 10-0-71-2. Durston 8-2-10-1.
Fall of Wickets: 1-6, 2-41, 3-87, 4-210, 5-215, 6-314, 7-333, 8-406, 9-407

Northamptonshire won by an innings and 46 runs –
Northamptonshire (22 pts), Somerset (5 pts)
```

```
          ESSEX v. LEICESTERSHIRE – at Chelmsford

LEICESTERSHIRE First Innings              Second Innings
DDJ Robinson  c Foster b ten Doeschate 53 b Palladino             13
DL Maddy      c Foster b Adams      2   lbw b Napier              16
HD Ackerman   c Foster b Phillips  111   not out                 14
D Mongia      lbw b Palladino      165
JK Maunders   c Flower A b Phillips  5   (4) not out               4
JN Snape (capt) lbw b Palladino     29
*PA Nixon     c Flower GW b Palladino 18
CW Henderson  c Foster b Palladino   0
DD Masters    c & b Palladino       15
Mohammad Asif b Palladino            3
RAG Cummins   not out                1
Extras        b 1, lb 10, w 2, nb 8 21  lb 1                     1
              (all out 116.4 overs) 417  (2 wkts dec 10.4 overs) 48
Bowling
Palladino 24.4-6-68-6. Adams 29-5-79-1. Napier 11-0-40-0. Middlebrook 21-2-66-0.
ten Doeschate 14-0-81-1. Phillips 15-3-57-2. Flower GW 2-1-15-0.
Palladino 5-1-16-1. Adams 4-0-19-0. Napier 1-0-6-1. Phillips 0.4-0-6-0.
Fall of Wickets: 1-16, 2-97, 3-267, 4-267, 5-343, 6-393, 7-393, 8-406, 9-412
1-16, 2-38

ESSEX         First Innings              Second Innings (following on)
GW Flower     c Mohammad Asif       1   b Nixon b Henderson      59
ML Pettini    c Mohammad Asif      19   c Robinson b Henderson   30
A Flower      c Maddy b Masters     5   (4) c & b Cummins        26
RC Irani (capt) c Nixon b Masters   2   (5) c Maddy b Masters    24
*JS Foster    c Robinson b Cummins 30   (6) c Nixon b Henderson  25
RN ten Doeschate b Mohammad Asif   33   (7) c M Asif b Henderson 25
JD Middlebrook c Nixon b Henderson 21   (8) b Cummins            0
TJ Phillips   c Maunders b Mongia  49   (9) c Ackerman b Cummins 0
GR Napier     c Henderson b Mohammad Asif 62 (10) not out        17
AR Adams      c Nixon b Mohammad Asif 18 (11) c M Asif b Henderson 7
AP Palladino  not out               0   (3) c Maddy b Mohammad Asif 7
Extras        lb 2                  2   b 1, lb 1                2
              (all out 62.1 overs) 242  (all out 87 overs)     222
Bowling
Mohammad Asif 15.1-0-56-5. Masters 14-4-44-2. Cummins 6-0-44-1.
Maddy 5-1-14-0. Henderson 15-5-40-1. Mongia 6-1-26-1.
Mohammad Asif 22-5-74-1. Masters 20-13-23-1. Cummins 20-4-54-3.
Henderson 24-6-69-5. Mongia 1-1-0-0.
Fall of Wickets: 1-12, 2-23, 3-27, 4-29, 5-90, 6-92, 7-142, 8-220, 9-224
1-67, 2-75, 3-122, 4-136, 5-153, 6-183, 7-184, 8-198, 9-198

Leicestershire won by 8 wickets – Essex (4 pts),
Leicestershire (22 pts)
```

scoring just 21 runs from his previous four Championship innings of the season, could prevent Somerset from being humbled by an innings and 46 runs by Northamptonshire at Wantage Road. Spinners Jason Brown and Monty Panesar were Somerset's undoing – Brown taking 5 for 82 on the opening day as none of the visiting batsmen could follow Trescothick's lead, and then Panesar mesmerising the West Countrymen with 5 for 32 from 26.3 beautifully controlled overs on day three. In between, there was a rumbustious unbeaten 147 from 184 balls by Lance Klusener, a century for Bilal Shafayat and a powerful 88 from David Sales as Northamptonshire assumed total control.

Centuries for both Hylton Ackerman and Dinesh Mongia, who added 170 for the third wicket, set up Leicestershire for a convincing eight-wicket win against Essex at Chelmsford. Missing Darren Gough, who was nursing a hamstring strain, the Essex attack could not contain Ackerman and Mongia despite a brave six-wicket haul by Tony Palladino. Then, undone by the pace of Mohammad Asif, Essex only made it as far as 242 due to some lusty lower order blows from Graham Napier and Tim Phillips and, following on, had lost Mark Pettini by the close of the second day. Claude Henderson's left-arm spin confirmed their demise on day three, with only Grant Flower resisting for long.

Round Four: 9–13 May 2006

Division One

The skill and drive of Shane Warne, as captain and leg spinner, lay behind Hampshire's 193-run win against Warwickshire at Edgbaston. Warne's 5 for 52 gave his side the initial advantage, following good first-day batting by Michael Carberry and John Crawley, and then Jimmy Adams' 105-ball 85, and three successive sixes by Dominic Thornely off Dougie Brown, set up Warne's second-innings declaration. Jim Troughton had used his left-handedness and his pads to frustrate Warne in Warwickshire's first innings while making a fine 103, but Warne got his man in the end on the final day, for 25, as Hampshire's bowlers worked their way determinedly through the home side's lengthy batting order.

A tricky pitch at Hove, where low bounce made for largely attritional cricket, saw Sussex dismissed for just 143 on day one but then rally so well that, in the end, they defeated champions Nottinghamshire

by 41 runs. Chris Read earned himself three points on his player licence for an uncharacteristic outburst at Mushtaq Ahmed, after being one of the Pakistani leg spinner's six victims on the second day, but Notts looked in control after Mark Ealham's battling half-century gave them an 86-run lead at the halfway point. Carl Hopkinson, however, then grafted four and a quarter hours for a career-best 74 and, despite four-wicket hauls for both Ealham and Graeme Swann, it was Hopkinson's dedication and aggressive contributions from Matt Prior and Chris Adams which tilted the game back towards Sussex. Although they reached 49-1, chasing 162 to win, Notts then had no answer to the pace and reverse swing of Rana Naved-ul-Hasan, the swing of Jason Lewry and the spin of Mushtaq.

Eight wickets in the match for Graham Onions put Middlesex into a stew at the Riverside.

OF ESSEX

Between 1979, when they won the first two titles in the county's long history, and 1992, when the Championship was taken for the sixth time, Essex brought home 11 trophies to their Chelmsford stronghold. Since then, there have been further wins too in the NatWest Trophy (1997), Benson and Hedges Cup (1998) and National League (2005).

The reason that Essex became, out of nothing, one of the powerhouse counties of modern times boils down to the outstanding contributions of three men in particular. Others can claim significant credit, of course, but it was the leadership qualities of Keith Fletcher, Graham Gooch and – off the field – the late Peter Edwards as secretary, which created a team, and an environment, capable of achieving sustained success.

Fletcher, already a fine international batsman, was elevated to the county captaincy in 1974, the summer he turned 30. By the time he stood down in favour of Gooch, after the 1985 season, Essex had already won eight trophies. Gooch led Essex to their fourth Championship title in his first season as captain in 1986, but stood down

for a while in the 1988 season to concentrate again fully on his batting and allow Fletcher to resume on-field control. But with the 44-year-old Fletcher by now struggling on the playing front, Gooch found himself captaining the side anyway for more than half the time.

Further Championships were won under Gooch's command in 1991 and 1992 and, although the most prolific run-scorer in the history of the game (he scored more than 65,000 runs in all cricket) resigned from the captaincy following the 1994 season and retired midway through 1997, no one was more pleased than Gooch when Essex, under Paul Prichard, gained further cup honours later that summer and again in 1998.

Lately, under Ronnie Irani's popular leadership, Essex have once more rejoiced in that winning feeling and, throughout the past 25 years, they have also contributed hugely to the overall health of English cricket. There have not just been the England captains: Fletcher, Gooch and Nasser Hussain. They have also produced a succession of international cricketers of the calibre of John Lever, Neil Foster, Derek Pringle, Nick Knight, Mark Ilott, James Foster, and latterly, Alastair Cook.

An Essex first team squad photograph from 1983 captures for posterity the talented group who won so much silverware. Back row (left to right): Alan Lilley, Graham Gooch, Derek Pringle, Neil Foster, Keith Pont, Brian Hardie, David East; front row (left to right): Ken McEwan, David Acfield, John Lever, Keith Fletcher, Ray East, Stuart Turner.

Match figures of 8 for 138 for seamer Graham Onions were instrumental in earning Durham a fine 135-run win over Middlesex at the Riverside. Owais Shah and Jamie Dalrymple batted well for the visitors, and Chris Silverwood and Alan Richardson had their moments with the ball, but Durham were always in control from the moment that Jimmy Maher's 106 and Phil Mustard's 78 took them to 348 all out on day one and Onions and Callum Thorp ensured a three-figure lead. The determination of Jon Lewis, meanwhile, meant that this advantage was not wasted – and although Lewis was dismissed one run short of a deserved hundred, he was more than happy with the eventual outcome.

Kent, stripped of most of their first-choice bowling attack by injury and the delayed arrival from South Africa of Andrew Hall, were content to engage Yorkshire in a high-scoring draw at Canterbury. The visitors, in fact, were 34 for 4 after less than an hour's play but recovered magnificently through a fifth-wicket stand of 229 between Darren Lehmann and Craig White. Lehmann was often imperious during his 193, but Kent hit back with a 153-run opening partnership between David Fulton and Rob Key and, after further half-centuries from Martin van Jaarsveld and Matthew Walker, were propelled to a lead of 151 by Justin Kemp. The big-hitting South African went to his century with three sixes off Richard Dawson in an over which cost the off-spinner 24, and struck five sixes and seven fours

overall in an unbeaten 124 from 152 balls. In theory, Kent had a chance of forcing victory on the final day, but in truth they did not have the firepower to unsettle century-maker Anthony McGrath or Matthew Wood, who made 92.

Round Four: 9–13 May 2006 Division One

WARWICKSHIRE v. HAMPSHIRE – at Edgbaston

HAMPSHIRE	First Innings		Second Innings	
JHK Adams	lbw b Carter	40	c Frost b Brown	85
MA Carberry	c Trott b Loudon	102	lbw b Streak	11
JP Crawley	lbw b Loudon	96	(6) c Anyon b Brown	0
SM Ervine	c Trott b Loudon	7	c & b Brown	23
DJ Thornely	c Frost b Brown	42	not out	30
CT Tremlett	c Frost b Brown	5		
*N Pothas	not out	67	b Streak	9
AD Mascarenhas	c Frost b Brown	5	(3) c Carter b Trott	41
SK Warne (capt)	c Knight b Loudon	17		
SD Udal	c Loudon b Brown	4		
JTA Bruce	b Loudon	0		
Extras	b 7, lb 7, nb 6	20	lb 12, w 1, nb 6	19
	(all out 144 overs)	405	(6 wkts dec 35.2 overs)	218

Bowling
Streak 21-3-66-0. Carter 28-8-58-1. Brown 35-6-87-4. Anyon 16-1-42-0. Loudon 36-1-109-5. Powell 6-0-16-0. Troughton 2-0-3-0. Brown 9-1-61-3. Streak 9.2-3-22-2. Carter 6-0-29-0. Troughton 3-0-24-0. Loudon 5-0-33-0. Trott 2-0-22-1. Powell 1-0-15-0.
Fall of Wickets: 1-113, 2-180, 3-196, 4-276, 5-282, 6-353, 7-368, 8-391, 9-400 1-25, 2-118, 3-166, 4-184, 5-186, 6-218

WARWICKSHIRE	First Innings		Second Innings	
NV Knight	c Ervine b Bruce	20	(4) c Adams b Ervine	34
IJ Westwood	c Mascarenhas	21	c Ervine b Warne	23
IJL Trott	lbw b Bruce	0	b Tremlett	6
JO Troughton	b Warne	103	(6) b Warne	25
AGR Loudon	b Mascarenhas	15	c Pothas b Udal	11
MJ Powell	c Carberry b Warne	10	(7) lbw b Udal	6
DR Brown	c Pothas b Warne	15	(8) lbw b Bruce	26
*T Frost	c Ervine b Udal	19	(9) lbw b Bruce	29
HH Streak (capt)	lbw b Warne	4	(10) not out	12
NM Carter	not out	2	(1) c Udal b Tremlett	23
JE Anyon	not out	0	b Tremlett	4
Extras	lb 8	8	lb 12, nb 2	14
	(all out 91.2 overs)	217	(all out 99.5 overs)	213

Bowling
Tremlett 10-2-34-0. Bruce 11-1-42-2. Ervine 15-5-28-0. Mascarenhas 16-5-38-2. Warne 27.2-9-52-5. Udal 12-6-15-1.
Tremlett 16.5-2-50-3. Bruce 15-5-37-2. Udal 17-8-23-2. Warne 33-12-58-2. Ervine 11-5-25-1. Mascarenhas 7-2-8-0.
Fall of Wickets: 1-31, 2-33, 3-52, 4-84, 5-128, 6-166, 7-204, 8-212, 9-214 1-28, 2-38, 3-80, 4-92, 5-131, 6-135, 7-140, 8-187, 9-202

Hampshire won by 193 runs –
Warwickshire (3 pts), Hampshire (21 pts)

SUSSEX v. NOTTINGHAMSHIRE – at Hove

SUSSEX	First Innings		Second Innings	
RR Montgomerie	b Sidebottom	8	(2) c Gallian b Swann	29
CD Hopkinson	b Harris	0	(1) c & b Swann	74
MH Yardy	b Franks	25	c Read b Ealham	7
MW Goodwin	c Read b Franks	29	c & b Harris	5
CJ Adams (capt)	c Gallian b Sidebottom	6	c Harris b Swann	37
*MJ Prior	b Swann	33	b Hussey	42
RSC Martin-Jenkins	b Hussey	17	b Swann	22
LJ Wright	lbw b Swann	13	lbw b Swann	3
Naved-ul-Hasan	lbw b Ealham	11	b Ealham	2
Mushtaq Ahmed	c Gallian b Ealham	1	not out	0
JD Lewry	not out	0	c Read b Ealham	0
Extras	lb 3, nb 4	7	b 5, lb 6, nb 6	17
	(all out 66.3 overs)	143	(all out 94.4 overs)	247

Bowling
Sidebottom 16-6-36-2. Harris 12-3-33-1. Ealham 13.3-7-17-2. Swann 15-4-25-2. Franks 9-5-24-2. Hussey 1-0-5-1.
Sidebottom 13-7-17-0. Harris 14-3-47-1. Swann 43-8-114-4. Franks 12-1-50-0. Ealham 12.4-0-29-4. Hussey 4-0-10-1.
Fall of Wickets: 1-8, 2-10, 3-64, 4-75, 5-75, 6-114, 7-138, 8-140, 9-142 1-68, 2-77, 3-91, 4-154, 5-185, 6-233, 7-233, 8-242, 9-247

NOTTS	First Innings		Second Innings	
DJ Bicknell	c Yardy b Naved-ul-Hasan	28	lbw b Lewry	28
JER Gallian (capt)	lbw b Mushtaq Ahmed	19	lbw b Mushtaq Ahmed	15
RJ Warren	b Lewry	9	c Hopkinson b Lewry	7
DJ Hussey	lbw b Naved-ul-Hasan	15	lbw b Lewry	4
GP Swann	lbw b Mushtaq Ahmed	37	(9) b Naved-ul-Hasan	14
WR Smith	c M'gomerie b Mushtaq Ahmed	16	(5) c Lewry b Naved-ul-Hasan	13
*CMW Read	b Mushtaq Ahmed	0	(6) b Naved-ul-Hasan	15
MA Ealham	c Lewry b Mushtaq Ahmed	52	(7) lbw b Mushtaq Ahmed	4
PJ Franks	b Naved-ul-Hasan	1	(8) b Naved-ul-Hasan	3
RJ Sidebottom	not out	21	not out	6
AJ Harris	c Prior b Mushtaq Ahmed	2	b Naved-ul-Hasan	3
Extras	b 10, lb 5, nb 8	23	b 6, lb 2, w 2	10
	(all out 80.5 overs)	229	(all out 45.3 overs)	120

Bowling
Naved-ul-Hasan 24-4-89-3. Lewry 17-5-38-1. Mushtaq Ahmed 28.5-6-72-6. Martin-Jenkins 4-2-5-0. Wright 7-3-10-0.
Naved-ul-Hasan 13-4-29-4. Lewry 10-2-23-3. Mushtaq Ahmed 18.3-4-58-3. Martin-Jenkins 4-2-2-0.
Fall of Wickets: 1-34, 2-54, 3-70, 4-114, 5-131, 6-131, 7-148, 8-159, 9-227 1-32, 2-49, 3-52, 4-55, 5-83, 6-86, 7-89, 8-96, 9-111

Sussex won by 41 runs – Sussex (17 pts),
Nottinghamshire (4 pts)

DURHAM v. MIDDLESEX – at the Riverside

DURHAM	First Innings		Second Innings	
JJB Lewis	lbw b Dalrymple	21	c Hutton b Richardson	99
JP Maher	c Scott b Louw	106	lbw b Silverwood	8
GJ Muchall	c Scott b Silverwood	17	c Hutton b Richardson	5
GJ Pratt	lbw b Betts	8	c Hutton b Silverwood	20
DM B'kenstein (capt)	c Hutton b Betts	19	c Hutton b Dalrymple	48
GR Breese	b Dalrymple	8	c Scott b Richardson	2
*P Mustard	b Silverwood	78	c Scott b Richardson	9
OD Gibson	c Scott b Silverwood	38	b Silverwood	17
CD Thorp	lbw b Silverwood	4	b Silverwood	9
G Onions	not out	0	c Shah b Silverwood	4
ML Lewis	lbw b Louw	6	not out	5
Extras	lb 4, w 1, nb 16	21	b 12, lb 15, w 2, nb 6	35
	(all out 106 overs)	348	(all out 93.2 overs)	261

Bowling
Silverwood 27-4-88-4. Louw 30-6-99-2. Betts 9-1-29-2. Richardson 18-4-71-0. Dalrymple 22-4-57-2.
Louw 21-7-46-0. Silverwood 19.2-3-47-5. Richardson 22-6-50-4. Dalrymple 23-2-70-1. Hutton 8-1-21-0.
Fall of Wickets: 1-78, 2-119, 3-131, 4-159, 5-192, 6-208, 7-296, 8-302, 9-327 1-16, 2-27, 3-84, 4-170, 5-193, 6-217, 7-239, 8-243, 9-248

MIDDLESEX	First Innings		Second Innings	
ET Smith	lbw b Onions	5	b Onions	3
BL Hutton (capt)	lbw b Thorp	9	b Onions	4
OA Shah	c Mustard b Lewis ML	68	lbw b Lewis ML	5
EC Joyce	c Mustard b Onions	14	c Breese b Lewis ML	7
JWM Dalrymple	lbw b Onions	36	c Mustard b Benkenstein	71
NRD Compton	b Breese	48	c Mustard b Gibson	33
*BJM Scott	c Mustard b Thorp	4	b Thorp	49
J Louw	c Mustard b Thorp	0	lbw b Onions	25
CEW Silverwood	not out	10	c Benkenstein b Onions	8
MM Betts	b Onions	0	b Gibson	0
A Richardson	b Lewis ML	9	not out	0
Extras	b 1, lb 11, w 1, nb 26	39	b 12, lb 3, nb 4	13
	(all out 63.1 overs)	242	(all out 59.3 overs)	232

Bowling
Lewis ML 13.1-4-49-2. Onions 16-2-82-4. Thorp 15-9-19-3. Gibson 13-1-66-0. Breese 6-2-14-1.
Lewis ML 15-2-63-2. Onions 11.3-1-56-4. Thorp 8-1-28-1. Gibson 14-5-49-2. Benkenstein 9-4-22-1. Breese 2-0-5-0.
Fall of Wickets: 1-11, 2-54, 3-101, 4-137, 5-149, 6-161, 7-215, 8-219, 9-219 1-7, 2-8, 3-24, 4-41, 5-126, 6-166, 7-197, 8-225, 9-232

Durham won by 135 runs – Durham (20 pts), Middlesex (4 pts)

KENT v. YORKSHIRE – at Canterbury

YORKSHIRE	First Innings		Second Innings	
MJ Wood	lbw b Kemp	11	b Stevens	92
JJ Sayers	c Kemp b Cook	1	c Key b Kemp	5
A McGrath	c Kemp b Cook	5	not out	123
MJ Lumb	c O'Brien b Dexter	3	not out	24
DS Lehmann	c Key b Cook	193		
C White (capt)	b Stevens	79		
TT Bresnan	b Stevens	33		
*SM Guy	c O'Brien b Cook	6		
RKJ Dawson	b Stevens	12		
JN Gillespie	not out	1		
GJ Kruis	b Stevens	1		
Extras	b 13, lb 10, w 4, nb 4	31	b 9, lb 3, w 5, nb 2	19
	(all out 127.3 overs)	382	(2 wkts 96 overs)	263

Bowling
Joseph 26-5-86-0. Cook 27-8-67-4. Kemp 20-3-56-1. Dexter 17-2-55-1. Stevens 17.3-3-36-4. Ferley 14-3-42-0. Walker 6-1-17-0.
Joseph 7-0-23-0. Cook 9-1-21-0. Kemp 2-0-7-1. Ferley 42-10-94-0. Stevens 14-3-33-1. van Jaarsveld 19-2-60-0. Walker 3-0-13-0.
Fall of Wickets: 1-6, 2-18, 3-26, 4-34, 5-263, 6-334, 7-342, 8-369, 9-378 1-21, 2-198

KENT	First Innings		
DP Fulton	c Guy b Dawson	75	
RWT Key (capt)	c Guy b Bresnan	81	
M van Jaarsveld	c Sayers b Dawson	82	
SJ Cook	lbw b Lehmann	0	
MJ Walker	c Wood b Dawson	60	
DI Stevens	lbw b McGrath	3	
JM Kemp	not out	124	
NJ Dexter	b Kruis	39	
*NJO'Brien	run out	6	
RS Ferley	c Guy b Dawson	14	
RH Joseph	c Guy b White	29	
Extras	b 2, lb 5, w 1, nb 12	20	
	(all out 177.5 overs)	533	

Bowling
Gillespie 31-9-86-0. Kruis 27-5-91-1. Bresnan 26-5-67-1. McGrath 17-4-38-1. Dawson 43-3-151-4. Lehmann 21-2-60-1. White 10.5-0-26-1. Sayers 2-0-7-0.
Fall of Wickets: 1-153, 2-183, 3-186, 4-304, 5-307, 6-317, 7-398, 8-420, 9-449

Match drawn – Kent (11 pts),
Yorkshire (10 pts)

OF GLAMORGAN

The highlight of the last quarter-century for Welsh cricket undoubtedly came at 6.18 pm on Saturday 20 September 1997, when Steve James hit the four to fine leg which brought Glamorgan the crushing ten-wicket victory over Somerset at Taunton that was required to clinch only the third Championship in their history.

Glamorgan had begun that last match of the season just one point ahead of Kent and therefore needing a full 24 points to guarantee the title. Fine seam bowling from Waqar Younis, their star overseas fast bowler, the ever-dependable Steve Watkin and promising 22-year-old Darren Thomas – who took 5 for 38 in Somerset's second innings – meant that the home side were always on the back foot as they were dismissed for 252 and 285.

And, in between, came some magnificent strokeplay from Hugh Morris and Matthew Maynard, the captain, in a third-wicket stand of 235, which ensured Glamorgan kept control of their own destiny. Morris, in his last game for the county, scored 165 and Maynard 142 from just 117 balls. Robert Croft, meanwhile, came in at No. 6 to thump 86 and add a further 111 with Morris and 71 with wicketkeeper Adrian Shaw, who finished on 53 not out in an eventual total of 527.

Around 4,000 spectators – with the vast majority of them Welsh – were present to witness the winning stroke from opener James, and a Championship title to follow those of 1948 and 1969 was the perfect reward for a true team effort over the previous six months by a happy, tight-knit unit.

The bulk of that Glamorgan side had also tasted success in 1993 when, with Viv Richards on board as a hugely popular overseas player, they had won the Sunday League. And players such as Maynard, Croft, Thomas and Cosker were still to the fore when, in 2002 and 2004, further National League titles were secured.

The emergence of fast bowler Simon Jones in recent years, culminating in his superb performances as part of

Hugh Morris is already celebrating as Steve James hits the winning four to confirm Glamorgan's 1997 Championship triumph.

England's Ashes-winning attack in 2005, has also provided Welsh cricket with much to celebrate – alongside, of course, the successes as England head coach of Duncan Fletcher, who was coach to Glamorgan's Championship team of 1997, and of Morris as the ECB's technical director and, latterly, as the Board's acting chief executive and now deputy chief executive.

Indeed, the Welsh influence on what is always called 'English cricket' has become so strong – with former county chairman David Morgan a long-serving ECB chairman and Maynard installed as England batting coach – that the decision earlier this year to award a 2009 Ashes Test match to Cardiff provoked cries of a 'Taffia' existing in the Lord's corridors of power!

Division Two

Derbyshire confirmed their emergence as the season's surprise package with an exciting 35-run win against Worcestershire at New Road that made them joint leaders of the division alongside Surrey. It was a second successive victory for Derbyshire and achieved despite the best efforts of Zaheer Khan and Kabir Ali, who were outstanding with the ball for Worcestershire, and the home side's captain, Vikram Solanki, who hit 24 boundaries in his first Championship hundred for two years. Michael Di Venuto, however, scored half-centuries in both innings for the visitors, while skipper Graeme Welch led from the front by making 94 on the opening day and taking 4 for 33 as Worcestershire chased 210 in vain on the third afternoon. There were seven wickets in the match, too, for the wholehearted Steffan Jones.

Essex, set 347 in 96 overs at Taunton, eased home by three wickets as Somerset's Australian spinners, Dan Cullen and Cameron White, failed to impress after Andrew Caddick had removed both Andy Flower and Ronnie Irani cheaply. Mark Pettini, the 22-year-old opener, led the successful Essex chase with a maiden first-class hundred in his 15th match, while Ryan ten Doeschate added late order aggression with a 46-ball 50 and James Foster supplied class and a steadying hand on the tiller with an unbeaten 82. Earlier, in a match dominated by the bat, there were also centuries for Somerset's Keith Parsons (with a Championship-best 153) and Peter Trego, and Essex's Irani and Andy Flower.

Round Four: 9–13 May 2006 Division Two

WORCESTERSHIRE v. DERBYSHIRE – at Worcester

DERBYSHIRE	First Innings		Second Innings	
SD Stubbings	lbw b Khan	8	(2) lbw b Kabir Ali	9
MJ Di Venuto	c Hick b Khan	56	(1) c Hick b Kabir Ali	58
CR Taylor	lbw b Khan	11	c Hick b Khan	9
TR Birt	b Price	39	c Davies b Khan	7
Hassan Adnan	c Davies b Malik	42	c Hick b Kabir Ali	0
AG Botha	lbw b Kabir Ali	0	lbw b Khan	3
MA Sheikh	lbw b Kabir Ali	0	c Hick b Kabir Ali	13
G Welch (capt)	c Davies b Khan	94	not out	4
*DJ Pipe	c Mitchell b Khan	57	b Kabir Ali	12
PS Jones	lbw b Khan	0	c Mitchell b Kabir Ali	8
ID Hunter	not out	5	b Kabir Ali	8
Extras	b 1, lb 11, w 2, nb 12	26	b 3, lb 4, w 3, nb 8	18
	(all out 100.1 overs)	**338**	(all out 53.4 overs)	**149**

Bowling
Khan 22.1-6-60-6. Kabir Ali 21-6-69-2. Malik 17-3-76-1. Sillence 13-1-49-0. Price 25-6-58-1. Moore 2-0-14-0.
Khan 16.2-7-58-3. Kabir Ali 17.4-3-43-7. Malik 6.4-2-25-0. Price 13-5-16-0.
Fall of Wickets: 1-8, 2-30, 3-100, 4-131, 5-132, 6-132, 7-235, 8-311, 9-319
1-38, 2-60, 3-75, 4-80, 5-89, 6-112, 7-113, 8-127, 9-137

WORCS	First Innings		Second Innings	
DKH Mitchell	c Di Venuto b Hunter	2	c Pipe b Welch	11
SC Moore	c Stubbings b Jones	0	c Pipe b Jones	24
VS Solanki (capt)	c Botha b Hunter	110	c Stubbings b Welch	0
BF Smith	lbw b Hunter	5	b Welch	18
GA Hick	c Pipe b Sheikh	6	c Pipe b Jones	4
*SM Davies	c Taylor b Welch	49	c Pipe b Jones	5
RJ Sillence	c Hassan Adnan b Hunter	20	c Pipe b Welch	9
Kabir Ali	c Pipe b Jones	15	b Sheikh	13
RW Price	not out	34	c Pipe b Hunter	56
Z Khan	c Pipe b Jones	12	b Jones	10
MN Malik	st Pipe b Botha	0	not out	6
Extras	b 6, lb 4, w 5, nb 10	25	b 5, lb 9, nb 4	18
	(all out 81.4 overs)	**278**	(all out 40.2 overs)	**174**

Bowling
Hunter 20-5-92-4. Jones 17-3-58-3. Sheikh 18-9-44-1. Welch 17-5-50-1. Botha 9.4-1-24-1.
Jones 15-1-62-4. Hunter 4.2-0-33-1. Welch 11-2-33-4. Sheikh 10-3-32-1.
Fall of Wickets: 1-2, 2-6, 3-36, 4-65, 5-173, 6-209, 7-218, 8-261, 9-275
1-45, 2-45, 3-46, 4-51, 5-61, 6-82, 7-91, 8-101, 9-114

Derbyshire won by 35 runs – Worcestershire (5 pts), Derbyshire (20 pts)

SOMERSET v. ESSEX – at Taunton

SOMERSET	First Innings		Second Innings	
MJ Wood (capt)	b Adams	49	lbw b Adams	1
AV Suppiah	c Foster b Phillips	27	lbw b Palladino	10
CL White	c Pettini b ten Doeschate	41	c Foster b Phillips	58
JC Hildreth	c Flower GW b Middlebrook	57	c Palladino b Phillips	69
KA Parsons	c Foster b Bopara	153	c Phillips b Bopara	59
WJ Durston	c Pettini b Middlebrook	21	not out	69
*CM Gazzard	lbw b Phillips	102	not out	5
PD Trego	c Adams b Palladino	102		
RL Johnson	lbw b Phillips	1		
AR Caddick	lbw b Palladino	11		
DJ Cullen	not out	1		
Extras	b 2, lb 3, w 4	9	lb 3, w 1	4
	(all out 137.3 overs)	**471**	(5 wkts dec 67.2 overs)	**275**

Bowling
Palladino 22-7-53-3. Adams 24-4-93-1. Middlebrook 20-2-69-2. Phillips 29-6-86-2. Bopara 22.3-3-79-1. ten Doeschate 20-0-86-1.
Palladino 13-2-54-1. Adams 7-3-11-1. ten Doeschate 4-0-20-0. Phillips 21-1-100-2. Middlebrook 17-0-68-0. Bopara 5.2-1-19-1.
Fall of Wickets: 1-69, 2-95, 3-140, 4-202, 5-204, 6-244, 7-446, 8-451, 9-453
1-7, 2-11, 3-131, 4-156, 5-263

ESSEX	First Innings		Second Innings	
GW Flower	lbw b Caddick	8	lbw b Trego	8
ML Pettini	c Parsons b Caddick	22	run out	124
RS Bopara	lbw b Caddick	29	c Gazzard b Cullen	27
A Flower	c Trego b Durston	161	c Gazzard b Caddick	1
RC Irani (capt)	not out	141	lbw b Caddick	15
*JS Foster	not out	26	not out	82
RN ten Doeschate			lbw b White	50
JD Middlebrook			b Johnson	20
TJ Phillips			not out	4
AR Adams				
AP Palladino				
Extras	b 1, lb 3, w 1, nb 8	13	b 2, lb 8, nb 6	16
	(4 wkts dec 106.5 overs)	**400**	(7 wkts 90.4 overs)	**347**

Bowling
Caddick 20-3-79-3. Johnson 15-1-57-0. Cullen 26-4-84-0. Trego 14-2-31-0. White 12-2-44-0. Suppiah 6-0-41-0. Durston 11-0-45-1. Parsons 2.5-0-15-0.
Caddick 24-7-64-2. Johnson 19.4-2-69-1. Trego 12-4-48-1. Cullen 14-0-54-1. White 9-0-49-1. Suppiah 5-0-26-0. Durston 1-0-6-0. Parsons 6-0-21-0.
Fall of Wickets: 1-20, 2-46, 3-80, 4-358
1-24, 2-108, 3-109, 4-125, 5-224, 6-311, 7-340

Essex won by 3 wickets – Somerset (6 pts), Essex (21 pts)

GLOUCESTERSHIRE v. NORTHAMPTONSHIRE – at Bristol

NORTHANTS	First Innings		Second Innings	
CJL Rogers	c Adshead b Greenidge	16	(2) lbw b Lewis	4
SD Peters	c Taylor b Greenidge	33	(1) b Harvey	10
BM Shafayat	c Taylor b Kirby	15	lbw b Lewis	0
U Afzaal	c Adshead b Harvey	40	b Harvey	2
DJG Sales (capt)	lbw b Harvey	22	c Spearman b Lewis	4
L Klusener	b Hardinges	5	c Ball b Lewis	0
*MH Wessels	c Adshead b Harvey	8	c Adshead b Kirby	49
BJ Phillips	not out	47	b Hardinges	6
MJ Nicholson	c Harvey b Hardinges	3	c Adshead b Harvey	18
DH Wigley	c Ball b Greenidge	12	not out	6
JF Brown	b Kirby	0	b Lewis	0
Extras	b 2, lb 5, w 1, nb 10	18	b 2, lb 1, w 4, nb 8	15
	(all out 72.3 overs)	**219**	(all out 40.5 overs)	**114**

Bowling
Kirby 20.3-7-67-2. Greenidge 15-4-50-3. Hardinges 18-7-52-2. Harvey 15-2-40-3. Ball 4-2-3-0.
Lewis 16.5-2-36-5. Kirby 10-3-27-1. Harvey 8-1-25-3. Hardinges 6-2-23-1.
Fall of Wickets: 1-57, 2-62, 3-83, 4-126, 5-139, 6-147, 7-151, 8-158, 9-215
1-11, 2-13, 3-21, 4-30, 5-30, 6-70, 7-40, 8-100, 9-113

GLOS	First Innings		Second Innings	
WPC Weston	c Wessels b Brown	54	(2) b Brown	21
CM Spearman	c Wessels b Nicholson	11	(1) c Wessels b Nicholson	5
MGN Windows	b Nicholson	6	not out	38
CG Taylor	lbw b Klusener	7	lbw b Phillips	5
APR Gidman (capt)	c Phillips b Brown	8	c Peters b Wigley	12
CG Greenidge†	c Wessels b Nicholson	5		
IJ Harvey	not out	102	(6) not out	12
*SJ Adshead	c Rogers b Brown	4		
MA Hardinges	c Rogers b Brown	8		
MCJ Ball	c Wigley b Klusener	5		
SP Kirby	c Nicholson b Klusener	5		
J Lewis				
Extras	lb 5, w 2, nb 10	17	w 1, nb 8	9
	(all out 84.4 overs)	**232**	(4 wkts 34.5 overs)	**102**

Bowling
Nicholson 22-12-43-3. Phillips 9-2-41-0. Wigley 9-2-37-0. Klusener 18.4-1-67-3. Brown 26-8-39-4.
Nicholson 8-1-22-1. Klusener 9-2-20-0. Phillips 7-2-20-1. Brown 8-2-22-1. Wigley 2.5-0-18-1.
Fall of Wickets: 1-11, 2-25, 3-50, 4-65, 5-73, 6-171, 7-185, 8-197, 9-214
1-8, 2-63, 3-68, 4-88
† Replaced by J Lewis

Gloucestershire won by 6 wickets – Gloucestershire (18 pts), Northamptonshire (4 pts)

LEICESTERSHIRE v. GLAMORGAN – at Leicester

LEICESTERSHIRE	First Innings	
JK Maunders	c Wallace b Wharf	71
DL Maddy	c Wallace b Davies	26
A Habib	lbw b Watkins	4
D Mongia	c Wallace b Davies	161
JL Sadler	lbw b Watkins	77
JN Snape (capt)	lbw b Cosgrove	19
*PA Nixon	not out	70
CW Henderson	b Croft	26
SCJ Broad	lbw b Croft	14
DD Masters	run out	19
Mohammad Asif	c Croft b Cosker	8
Extras	b 8, lb 17, w 5	30
	(all out 167.2 overs)	**525**

Bowling
Wharf 31-8-100-1. Davies 29-9-70-2. Watkins 25-5-78-2. Cosgrove 15-2-53-1. Croft 23-9-66-2. Cosker 28.2-1-93-1.
Fall of Wickets: 1-38, 2-57, 3-148, 4-331, 5-381, 6-381, 7-446, 8-474, 9-510

GLAMORGAN	First Innings		Second Innings (following on)	
DD Cherry	lbw b Masters	66	(2) lbw b Henderson	91
MJ Cosgrove	c Nixon b Masters	5	(4) not out	54
DL Hemp	c Maunders b Mohammad Asif	38	c Nixon b Maddy	86
DA Cosker	b Broad	9		
MJ Powell	c Nixon b Mohammad Asif	73	(7) not out	4
N Peng	c Maunders b Henderson	7	(5) lbw b Mongia	0
RE Watkins	c Habib b Henderson	18	(6) lbw b Maddy	1
*MA Wallace	c Maddy b Henderson	2		
RDB Croft (capt)	c Maddy b Henderson	27	(1) lbw b Mohammad Asif	0
AG Wharf	lbw b Broad	19		
AP Davies	not out	11		
Extras	b 10, lb 11, nb 2	23	b 9, lb 2, w 1, nb 2, p 5	19
	(all out 124.2 overs)	**297**	(5 wkts 108 overs)	**267**

Bowling
Mohammad Asif 26-8-61-2. Masters 20-5-45-2. Broad 21-8-49-2. Henderson 38.2-9-77-4. Maddy 13-5-39-0. Mongia 6-3-5-0.
Mohammad Asif 12-4-29-1. Masters 15-6-25-0. Henderson 37-12-75-1. Snape 15-4-24-0. Broad 3-0-19-0. Maddy 18-2-71-2. Mongia 4-4-8-1.
Fall of Wickets: 1-14, 2-88, 3-110, 4-169, 5-202, 6-230, 7-236, 8-244, 9-285
1-0, 2-173, 3-223, 4-249, 5-250

Match drawn – Leicestershire (12 pts), Glamorgan (8 pts)

Above: Mark Pettini, the Essex opener who scored a maiden first-class hundred in the fine win against Somerset.

Below: Tom Smith's command of swing and seam impressed Roses Match observers at Headingley.

Jon Lewis, unwanted by England in the Lord's Test against Sri Lanka, drove down the M4 from London to Bristol and took four wickets in 25 balls to set up a straightforward six-wicket victory for his Gloucestershire side against Northamptonshire. Allowed by the regulations to join a match already in progress, once the Test XI had been decided, Lewis ended up with 5 for 36 as Northants were tumbled out for 114 in their second innings on the second afternoon. Up until then, it had looked like being a close contest in difficult conditions – with Gloucestershire only earning a small first-innings lead thanks to an astonishing unbeaten 102 from 136 balls by Ian Harvey. Coming in at 73 for 5, Harvey opened up with four fours in an over off Matt Nicholson, who at that stage had figures of 12-9-6-3. Harvey helped to add 98 for the sixth wicket with Phil Weston before single-handedly ensuring the lead, and then snapping up three second-innings Northants wickets himself.

Dan Cherry batted for 148 overs in all, adding 91 to his first-innings 66 as Glamorgan held on for a draw at Leicester. Dinesh Mongia's 161 spearheaded Leicestershire's progress to 525, and, despite first-innings resistance from Cherry and Michael Powell, the Welsh county soon found themselves following on. In the end, though, a 173-run partnership between Cherry and David Hemp, who made 86, denied the home team.

Round Five: 16–20 May 2006 Division One

YORKSHIRE v. LANCASHIRE – at Headingley

LANCASHIRE	First Innings	
MJ Chilton (capt)	c McGrath b Kruis	4
IJ Sutcliffe	hit wkt b Gillespie	12
MB Loye	c Kruis b Bresnan	138
BJ Hodge	b Blain	27
SG Law	lbw b Blain	101
*LD Sutton	lbw b Kruis	46
G Chapple	c Bresnan b Gillespie	35
KW Hogg	c Brophy b Bresnan	12
DG Cork	c Blain b Bresnan	11
TC Smith	not out	1
G Keedy	not out	4
Extras	b 1, lb 3, nb 22	26
	(9 wkts dec 111 overs)	417

Bowling
Gillespie 33-7-97-2. Kruis 29-4-135-2. Bresnan 22-2-65-3. Blain 12-0-79-2. McGrath 10-0-28-0. Lehmann 5-0-9-0.
Fall of Wickets: 1-15, 2-17, 3-86, 4-292, 5-300, 6-381, 7-385, 8-411, 9-412

YORKSHIRE	First Innings		Second Innings (following on)	
MJ Wood	b Smith	13	c Sutton b Hogg	14
JJ Sayers	b Hogg	23	not out	75
A McGrath	lbw b Keedy	64	not out	81
MJ Lumb	c Sutton b Smith	20		
DS Lehmann	st Sutton b Keedy	33		
C White (capt)	lbw b Cork	1		
*GL Brophy	b Keedy	1		
TT Bresnan	b Smith	13		
JN Gillespie	c Smith b Chapple	45		
JAR Blain	lbw b Smith	2		
GJ Kruis	not out	28		
Extras	b 4, lb 4, nb 14	22	b 6, lb 1	7
	(all out 100 overs)	265	(1 wkt 59 overs)	177

Bowling
Cork 19-2-58-1. Chapple 24-9-58-1. Smith 25-12-57-4. Hogg 14-5-44-1. Keedy 18-3-40-3.
Chapple 9-3-23-0. Smith 9-1-24-0. Hogg 9-1-30-1. Cork 9-2-18-0. Keedy 14-0-42-0. Hodge 6-0-20-0. Chilton 2-0-12-0. Sutcliffe 1-0-1-0.
Fall of Wickets: 1-34, 2-46, 3-99, 4-156, 5-157, 6-164, 7-181, 8-185, 9-189
1-30

Match drawn – Yorkshire (9 pts), Lancashire (12 pts)

NOTTINGHAMSHIRE v. DURHAM – at Trent Bridge

DURHAM	First Innings	
JJB Lewis	lbw b Franks	61
JP Maher	c Gallian b Franks	33
GJ Muchall	run out	88
GJ Pratt	c Read b Harris	26
DM B'kenstein (capt)	lbw b Ealham	73
GR Breese	lbw b Ealham	16
*P Mustard	c Read b Harris	19
OD Gibson	not out	49
SJ Harmison	c & b Ealham	18
G Onions	not out	4
ML Lewis		
Extras	b 2, lb 2, w 1, nb 12	17
	(8 wkts dec 127.2 overs)	404

Bowling
Sidebottom 22-5-65-0. Harris 33.2-7-133-2. Ealham 24-10-53-3. Franks 20-0-83-2. Swann 28-6-66-0.
Fall of Wickets: 1-62, 2-165, 3-196, 4-260, 5-307, 6-318, 7-333, 8-384

NOTTS	First Innings	
DJ Bicknell	b Onions	40
JER Gallian	c Mustard b Lewis ML	114
WR Smith	c Pratt b Breese	41
SP Fleming (capt)	c Pratt b Breese	7
DJ Hussey	b Breese	15
*CMW Read	c Muchall b Breese	23
MA Ealham	c Mustard b Onions	7
PJ Franks	c Mustard b Lewis ML	12
GP Swann	lbw b Onions	2
RJ Sidebottom	not out	18
AJ Harris	c Lewis JJB b Gibson	19
Extras	b 5, lb 4, nb 6	15
	(all out 90.1 overs)	313

Bowling
Onions 19-2-65-3. Harmison 15-4-52-0. Lewis ML 15-1-60-2. Gibson 9.1-2-38-1. Breese 32-9-89-4.
Fall of Wickets: 1-52, 2-163, 3-175, 4-204, 5-248, 6-248, 7-256, 8-260, 9-285

Match drawn – Nottinghamshire (9 pts), Durham (12 pts)

Round Five: 16–20 May 2006

Division One

Lancashire had much the better of a Roses Match against Yorkshire at Headingley, which, due to constant weather interruptions, ended in a tame draw. Fine hundreds by Mal Loye and Stuart Law took full toll of some moderate home bowling, and 20-year-old Tom Smith then impressed hugely for Lancashire with a superbly-controlled exhibition of seam and swing in just his fifth first-class appearance. Yorkshire only made it as far as 265 thanks to a 76-run last-wicket stand between Jason Gillespie and Deon Kruis but, following on, they were never in trouble as Anthony McGrath made his second half-century of the game and Joe Sayers also dug in.

There was even less play possible at Trent Bridge, where Nottinghamshire again suffered with the weather and their overall form. Jason Gallian made the 34th first-class hundred of his career but Notts were already coming off second best against a Durham side who had made sure of maximum batting points through solid contributions from Jon Lewis, Gordon Muchall, Dale Benkenstein and Ottis Gibson.

Below: Phil Jaques was the catalyst of a remarkable Worcestershire win at The Oval.

Division Two

Rain also ruined Derbyshire's match with Leicestershire at Derby, where no play was possible at all on the fourth day after hundreds from Steve Stubbings and Travis Birt – with his first ton for the county in his fourth game – had put the visitors under pressure, but at The Oval there was one of the most astonishing Championship victories in history for Worcestershire. Set to score 285 in a mere 32 overs by Surrey, following yet another rain break, Worcestershire galloped to their target with one ball to spare – Zaheer Khan clinching the thrilling two-wicket win by hitting the penultimate delivery, from Nayan Doshi, for six.

It had been openers Phil Jaques and Stephen Moore who had set up the remarkable chase, however, by putting on 171 and treating the Surrey attack with disdain. Jaques, in particular, scored freely all round the wicket on his Worcestershire debut with two sixes and 14 fours, and his 107 needed only 69 balls. Ben Smith took control of the later stages with an unbeaten 46 that revealed all his experience. Earlier in the game, Jaques and Moore had featured in another century stand as Worcestershire battled to stay in contention following a Surrey thrust to 501 for 7 declared. Mark Ramprakash passed 27,000 first-class runs

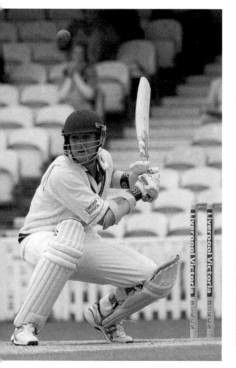

Round Five: 16–20 May 2006 Division Two

DERBYSHIRE v. LEICESTERSHIRE – at Derby

DERBYSHIRE	First Innings	
MJ Di Venuto	c Nixon b Masters	93
SD Stubbings	lbw b Mohammad Asif	119
CR Taylor	c Ackerman b Masters	23
TR Birt	run out	119
Hassan Adnan	lbw b Masters	2
MA Sheikh	c Maddy b Masters	1
G Welch (capt)	not out	4
*DJ Pipe	not out	15
AKD Gray		
PS Jones		
ID Hunter		
Extras	b 6, lb 17, nb 2	25
	(6 wkts dec 120.2 overs)	401

Bowling
Mohammad Asif 32-4-109-1. Masters 40-10-89-4. Broad 16.2-1-89-0. Maddy 15-3-51-0. Henderson 17-4-40-0.
Fall of Wickets: 1-145, 2-189, 3-337, 4-354, 5-378, 6-378

LEICESTERSHIRE	First Innings	
JK Maunders	c Hunter b Jones	0
DL Maddy	c Stubbings b Hunter	1
HD Ackerman	b Welch	13
D Mongia	c Birt b Hunter	10
JL Sadler	not out	52
JN Snape (capt)	not out	30
*PA Nixon		
CW Henderson		
SCJ Broad		
DD Masters		
Mohammad Asif		
Extras	b 9, lb 10, nb 12	31
	(4 wkts 55 overs)	137

Bowling
Jones 11-4-30-1. Hunter 16-7-26-2. Sheikh 14-1-49-0. Welch 12-5-11-1. Gray 2-0-2-0.
Fall of Wickets: 1-2, 2-2, 3-21, 4-49

Match drawn – Derbyshire (10 pts), Leicestershire (6 pts)

SURREY v. WORCESTERSHIRE – at The Oval

SURREY	First Innings		Second Innings	
SA Newman	c Hick b Khan	74		
*JN Batty	c Price b Batty	69		
MR Ramprakash	b Kabir Ali	118		
MA Butcher (capt)	c Hick b Price	74	(3) c Solanki b Smith	20
AD Brown	c Hick b Batty	17	(2) c sub b Moore	11
R Clarke	b Kabir Ali	38	(4) not out	57
JGE Benning	st Davies b Batty	52	(1) c Moore b Khan	0
Azhar Mahmood	not out	16	(5) not out	40
IDK Salisbury	not out	3		
Mohammad Akram				
ND Doshi				
Extras	b 2, lb 19, w 5, nb 14	40	nb 8	8
	(7 wkts dec 124.3 overs)	501	(3 wkts dec 8.2 overs)	136

Bowling
Khan 27-7-110-1. Kabir Ali 29-7-101-2. Mason 13-5-34-0. Batty 27-3-120-3. Price 25.3-4-104-1. Moore 3-1-11-0.
Khan 1-0-8-1. Kabir Ali 1-0-13-0. Moore 3-0-61-1. Smith 3-0-39-1. Jaques 0.2-0-15-0.
Fall of Wickets: 1-144, 2-201, 3-357, 4-381, 5-385, 6-459, 7-488
1-0, 2-27, 3-41

WORCS	First Innings		Second Innings	
PA Jaques	c Doshi b Salisbury	61	c Clarke b Salisbury	107
SC Moore	c Azhar Mahmood b Salisbury	61	run out	57
VS Solanki (capt)	b Doshi	16	c Benning b Salisbury	11
BF Smith	c Akram b Doshi	34	(5) not out	46
GA Hick	c Azhar Mahmood b Doshi	26	(4) c Ramprakash b Doshi	20
*SM Davies	not out	61	st Batty b Doshi	1
GJ Batty	c Azhar Mahmood b Doshi	4	c b Doshi	0
Kabir Ali	c Azhar Mahmood b Doshi	14	c Batty b Azhar Mahmood	8
RW Price	c Azhar Mahmood b Doshi	0	c sub b Doshi	5
Z Khan	c Benning b Doshi	18	not out	6
MS Mason	not out	0		
Extras	b 8, lb 8, w 2, nb 26	44	lb 5, w 3, nb 18	26
	(9 wkts dec 108.1 overs)	353	(8 wkts 31.5 overs)	287

Bowling
Akram 15-1-73-0. Azhar Mahmood 17-3-56-0. Doshi 36-7-91-6. Salisbury 36.1-5-104-3. Benning 2-0-9-0. Clarke 2-1-4-0.
Akram 6-0-53-0. Azhar Mahmood 10-0-79-1. Doshi 7.5-0-68-4. Clarke 1-0-22-0. Salisbury 7-0-60-2.
Fall of Wickets: 1-109, 2-140, 3-210, 4-249, 5-259, 6-273, 7-316, 8-317, 9-349
1-171, 2-200, 3-200, 4-241, 5-252, 6-252, 7-275, 8-280

Worcestershire won by 2 wickets – Surrey (8 pts), Worcestershire (20 pts)

OF GLOUCESTERSHIRE

The golden age of Gloucestershire cricket is popularly held to be the days of W. G. Grace and Gilbert Jessop, although in the century or so since there has also been the heady strokeplay of Walter Hammond and Tom Graveney, and the brilliance of South African all-rounder Mike Procter, which was instrumental in securing the county's first-ever trophies in the 1970s. Yet the famous Gillette Cup success of 1973, followed four years later by another Lord's triumph in the Benson and Hedges Cup, have now been overshadowed by the remarkable run of one-day victories achieved by the Gloucestershire teams of 1999–2004.

In what truly was a golden age for a county far more used to being the perennial underdog, Gloucestershire won seven titles in those six summers. At the heart of it was Mark Alleyne, the captain in limited-overs cricket from 1997 to 2004, the former England wicketkeeper and urger-on-in-chief Jack Russell, and the coach John Bracewell.

Alleyne and Bracewell, a hard-nosed, often abrasive but eminently likeable New Zealander, saw in Gloucestershire's seemingly rag-tag collection of honest county cricketers a group which, together, was capable of a level of one-day performance which far outstripped the sum of its constituent parts. Russell, at the tail-end of his great career, was still good enough to stand up for most of the time to all of Gloucestershire's battery of accurate seamers, which included the talented Australian all-rounder Ian Harvey, the unsung Jon Lewis – fated not to win England recognition of his skills until 2005 – and Alleyne himself.

The dashing strokeplay of the likes of Matt Windows, Phil Weston, Craig Spearman, Chris Taylor, Alex Gidman, Tim Hancock, Harvey and Alleyne, plus the dependency of support acts like James Averis and Martyn Ball, made the team a potent force in the pressure-cooker atmosphere of a big one-day game. The fielding, too, often took the breath away while – relentlessly from behind the stumps – came the yapping

and the demands for focus and concentration from the emotional heartbeat that was Russell.

The NatWest/C&G Trophy was won four times in 1999, 2000, 2003 and 2004, the Benson and Hedges Cup was claimed in 1999 and 2000 and – completing a unique domestic treble in 2000 – came the National League too. They also reached the Benson and Hedges final in 2001, only to be beaten by Surrey, but this golden Gloucestershire side seldom came off second best in the one-day arena.

That winning feeling is sweet indeed for Jack Russell (left) and Mark Alleyne at Lord's in 2000, when the Benson and Hedges Cup formed the first leg of an unprecedented domestic one-day treble for Gloucestershire.

while compiling the 82nd hundred of his career, and four other players hit half-centuries. Only a fine 61 not out from Steven Davies enabled Worcestershire to get past the follow-on mark, and then some unattractive declaration bowling – Moore went for 61 off his three overs and Smith for 39 off his three – allowed Rikki Clarke (57 not out from 23 balls, with five sixes and four fours) and Azhar Mahmood (40 not out off 15 balls, with six fours and a six) to set up the memorable last act.

Round Six: 23–27 May 2006

Division One

Sussex stole a march on the rest of the division when they crushed Durham inside two days at the Riverside, and then saw the remaining three matches in this round of games finish as weather-affected draws. The demolition of Durham, in which Rana Naved-ul-Hasan and his Pakistani compatriot Mushtaq Ahmed took 19 of the 20 home wickets to tumble, in fact lasted a mere four and a half sessions. First, on a reasonable surface, Durham were shot out for 110 and, by the end of a truncated first day, Sussex were already ahead with Murray Goodwin hitting an aggressive unbeaten 38. Goodwin fell early the next morning as Durham, led by Steve Harmison, attempted to

fight back, but Robin Martin-Jenkins put together a valuable 49 and earned Sussex a lead of 119. At 47 for 1, Durham looked to be capable of a second-innings recovery but then Mushtaq came on for the 16th over and – by the end of it – the

Round Six: 23–27 May 2006 Division One

DURHAM v. SUSSEX – at the Riverside

DURHAM	First Innings		Second Innings	
JJB Lewis	lbw b Naved-ul-Hasan	5	st Prior b Mushtaq Ahmed	28
JP Maher	c Prior b Wright	23	c Adams b Mushtaq Ahmed	22
GJ Muchall	c Prior b Naved-ul-Hasan	0	lbw b Mushtaq Ahmed	0
GJ Pratt	c Adams b Mushtaq Ahmed	9	c Wright b Mushtaq Ahmed	0
DM B'kenstein	lbw b Mushtaq Ahmed	18	c Adams b Naved-ul-Hasan	7
GR Breese	lbw b Mushtaq Ahmed	0	c Yardy b Naved-ul-Hasan	4
*P Mustard	c Prior b Mushtaq Ahmed	15	lbw b Naved-ul-Hasan	0
OD Gibson	c Prior b Naved-ul-Hasan	8	b Naved-ul-Hasan	2
SJ Harmison	b Mushtaq Ahmed	8	not out	3
G Onions	b Naved-ul-Hasan	4	st Prior b Mushtaq Ahmed	9
ML Lewis	not out	0	lbw b Naved-ul-Hasan	2
Extras	b 5, lb 13, nb 2	20	b 1, lb 2	3
	(all out 52.5 overs)	110	(all out 29.1 overs)	80

Bowling
Naved-ul-Hasan 12.5-5-28-4. Lewry 11-4-27-0. Wright 7-3-6-1.
Martin-Jenkins 9-5-6-0. Mushtaq Ahmed 13-4-25-5.
Naved-ul-Hasan 9.1-0-42-5. Lewry 3-0-9-0. Martin-Jenkins 7-1-9-0. Wright 3-1-5-0.
Mushtaq Ahmed 7-4-12-5.
Fall of Wickets: 1-12, 2-18, 3-40, 4-53, 5-59, 6-75, 7-92, 8-92, 9-106
1-47, 2-47, 3-47, 4-58, 5-62, 6-62, 7-66, 8-66, 9-77

SUSSEX	First Innings	
RR Montgomerie	c Mustard b Lewis ML	28
CD Hopkinson	lbw b Gibson	20
MH Yardy	lbw b Onions	17
MW Goodwin	c Mustard b Harmison	42
CJ Adams (capt)	lbw b Harmison	19
*MJ Prior	c Mustard b Harmison	2
RSC Martin-Jenkins	c Mustard b Lewis ML	49
LJ Wright	c Mustard b Onions	1
Naved-ul-Hasan	c Gibson b Lewis ML	7
Mushtaq Ahmed	c Muchall b Harmison	8
JD Lewry	not out	0
Extras	b 4, lb 10, w 2, nb 20	36
	(all out 63.2 overs)	229

Bowling
Onions 17.2-1-67-2. Harmison 17-5-43-4. Gibson 15-4-51-1. Lewis ML 13-4-43-3.
Breese 1-0-11-0.
Fall of Wickets: 1-57, 2-57, 3-123, 4-135, 5-137, 6-158, 7-181, 8-207, 9-227

*Sussex won by an innings and 39 runs – Durham (3 pts),
Sussex (18 pts)*

HAMPSHIRE v. KENT – at the Rose Bowl

HAMPSHIRE	First Innings		Second Innings	
JHK Adams	b Hall	0	b Hall	4
MA Carberry	b Hall	17	c Stevens b Hall	7
MJ Brown	c Kemp b Cook	0	b Stevens	2
JP Crawley	c O'Brien b Joseph	43	not out	83
DJ Thornely	c O'Brien b Stevens	13	c Fulton b Patel	34
SM Ervine	lbw b Stevens	12	(8) not out	16
*N Pothas	c Stevens b Joseph	96		
AD Mascarenhas	c O'Brien b Cook	34	(6) b Hall	20
SK Warne (capt)	c Kemp b Joseph	9	(7) st O'Brien b Patel	3
JTA Bruce	b Patel	17		
BV Taylor	not out	0		
Extras	b 3, lb 18, w 7, nb 2	30	lb 6, w 1	7
	(all out 95.5 overs)	271	(6 wkts dec 34 overs)	176

Bowling
Hall 30-10-62-2. Cook 22-6-62-2. Kemp 5-1-13-0. Joseph 19.5-4-68-3.
Stevens 17-5-35-2. Patel 2-0-10-1.
Hall 9-3-27-3. Stevens 8-2-31-1. Joseph 2-0-18-0. Cook 6-0-40-0. Patel 9-0-54-2.
Fall of Wickets: 1-0, 2-3, 3-38, 4-72, 5-92, 6-108, 7-156, 8-171, 9-246
1-6, 2-15, 3-15, 4-108, 5-152, 6-155

KENT	First Innings		Second Innings	
DP Fulton	c Warne b Bruce	0	b Ervine	18
RWT Key (capt)	b Taylor	28	b Warne	17
M van Jaarsveld	c Thornely b Mascarenhas	15	lbw b Mascarenhas	24
MJ Walker	c Mascarenhas b Ervine	26	c Pothas b Ervine	1
DI Stevens	c Adams b Ervine	10	not out	17
JM Kemp	b Warne	16	not out	9
AJ Hall	not out	61		
*NJ O'Brien	c Bruce b Warne	38		
MM Patel	lbw b Warne	4		
SJ Cook	lbw b Mascarenhas	4		
RH Joseph	b Warne	2		
Extras	b 3, lb 3, nb 12	19	lb 2, nb 6	8
	(all out 81.4 overs)	223	(4 wkts 34 overs)	94

Bowling
Bruce 16-1-49-1. Mascarenhas 16-4-35-2. Taylor 11-2-41-1. Thornely 8-4-10-0.
Ervine 15-3-43-2. Warne 15.4-2-38-4.
Bruce 5-1-9-0. Taylor 6-0-23-0. Ervine 8-1-35-2. Warne 11-4-16-1.
Mascarenhas 4-0-9-1.
Fall of Wickets: 1-0, 2-27, 3-69, 4-92, 5-95, 6-125, 7-189, 8-207, 9-212
1-38, 2-50, 3-51, 4-84

Match drawn – Hampshire (9 pts), Kent (8 pts)

LANCASHIRE v. NOTTINGHAMSHIRE – at Old Trafford

NOTTS	First Innings		Second Innings	
DJ Bicknell	b Newby	30	lbw b Smith	28
JER Gallian	c Cork b Chapple	4	lbw b Newby	7
WR Smith	c Sutton b Cork	10	c Sutton b Smith	2
SP Fleming (capt)	c Chilton b Newby	42	lbw b Newby	0
DJ Hussey	c Smith b Keedy	19	not out	38
*CMW Read	b Newby	53	not out	22
MA Ealham	c Cork b Smith	33		
PJ Franks	c Cork b Chapple	1		
GP Swann	c Hodge b Newby	26		
GJ Smith	b Cork	17		
AJ Harris	not out	6		
Extras	lb 8, nb 4	12	lb 3, nb 2	5
	(all out 82.3 overs)	253	(4 wkts 37 overs)	102

Bowling
Chapple 18-3-64-2. Cork 25.3-7-49-2. Newby 12-2-58-4. Smith 21-7-46-1.
Keedy 6-1-28-1.
Chapple 7-3-10-0. Cork 7-1-25-0. Newby 9-3-32-2. Smith 8-4-11-2. Keedy 4-0-19-0.
Hodge 2-0-2-0.
Fall of Wickets: 1-5, 2-24, 3-50, 4-81, 5-154, 6-173, 7-179, 8-211, 9-242
1-33, 2-38, 3-41, 4-41

LANCASHIRE	First Innings	
MJ Chilton	c Read b Ealham	11
IJ Sutcliffe	c Read b Ealham	50
MB Loye	c Read b Harris	53
BJ Hodge	c Fleming b Ealham	115
SG Law	c Read b Ealham	0
*LD Sutton	lbw b Smith GJ	13
G Chapple	c Smith WR b Harris	31
DG Cork	c Read b Ealham	1
TC Smith	lbw b Harris	6
OJ Newby	not out	12
G Keedy	c Read b Harris	2
Extras	b 2, lb 3, w 1, nb 8	14
	(all out 116.1 overs)	308

Bowling
Harris 34.5-7-76-4. Smith GJ 16.2-8-28-1. Ealham 29-6-75-5. Franks 24-3-85-0.
Swann 12-1-39-0.
Fall of Wickets: 1-31, 2-115, 3-125, 4-126, 5-183, 6-259, 7-264, 8-283, 9-301

*Match drawn – Lancashire (10 pts),
Nottinghamshire (9 pts)*

MIDDLESEX v. WARWICKSHIRE – at Lord's

MIDDLESEX	First Innings	
ET Smith	lbw b Brown	166
BL Hutton (capt)	c Knight b Brown	24
OA Shah	lbw b Streak	73
EC Joyce	c Knight b Streak	9
JWM Dalrymple	lbw b Carter	69
SB Styris	c Trott b Streak	13
NRD Compton	lbw b Bell	40
*BJM Scott	c Knight b Bell	39
J Louw	c Frost b Carter	28
CB Keegan	not out	34
CEW Silverwood		
Extras	lb 16, nb 9	25
	(9 wkts dec 139.3 overs)	520

Bowling
Streak 33-11-113-3. Carter 25.3-4-104-2. Brown 26-6-85-2. Vettori 31-4-92-0.
Bell 12-1-59-2. Loudon 12-1-51-0.
Fall of Wickets: 1-72, 2-205, 3-227, 4-351, 5-368, 6-380, 7-453, 8-456, 9-520

WARWICKSHIRE	First Innings	
NV Knight	c Scott b Keegan	14
MA Wagh	b Keegan	16
IR Bell	lbw b Keegan	14
IJL Trott	c Hutton b Dalrymple	139
AGR Loudon	b Silverwood	68
JO Troughton	c Smith b Louw	9
DR Brown	c Keegan b Silverwood	69
DL Vettori	c Smith b Silverwood	27
HH Streak (capt)	lbw b Louw	6
*T Frost	not out	5
NM Carter	not out	5
Extras	b 3, lb 11, w 1, nb 6	21
	(9 wkts 114 overs)	401

Bowling
Silverwood 27-5-92-3. Keegan 25-5-76-3. Louw 25-3-102-2. Styris 13-3-65-0.
Dalrymple 24-5-52-1.
Fall of Wickets: 1-21, 2-44, 3-51, 4-232, 5-261, 6-281, 7-343, 8-379, 9-395

*Match drawn – Middlesex (12 pts),
Warwickshire (11 pts)*

Danger: whirring wizard approaching. Mushtaq Ahmed's match figures of 10 for 37 amply demonstrated how quickly Durham were blown away by Sussex's Pakistani leg spinner.

home team were 47 for 4. The leg spinner's 5 for 12 from seven overs gave him remarkable match figures of 10 for 37, and it was clear that the Durham batsmen had no idea how to cope against him. Naved, meanwhile, added 5 for 42 to his four-

wicket first-innings haul as Sussex bowled out their opponents for 80 to complete a victory by an innings and 39 runs.

Kent's decision to turn down Shane Warne's offer of a run chase at the Rose Bowl after three days of miserable weather and constant interruptions, left the Hampshire captain complaining, 'We were the only team out there trying to win the game'. But there was no chance of any result either at Trent Bridge, where Lancashire's young seamer Oliver Newby took career-best figures against Nottinghamshire, or at Lord's as Middlesex and Warwickshire were also forced to settle for a draw. Ed Smith made a first-day century and 25-year-old South African Jonathan Trott also caught the eye with 139 from 194 balls, with 15 fours, in a summer during which he completes his England qualification period.

Division Two

There were no positive results in the second division at all, with the game between Northamptonshire and Derbyshire at Wantage Road suffering the most as days three and four were washed out entirely by rain.

The best match was undoubtedly at Worcester, where Glamorgan came agonisingly close to a first win of the season. When opener Stephen Moore, the one man who stood firm amid the ruins of Worcestershire's second innings, blocked out the final over of the game from Alex Wharf it left the Welsh county wishing they had been a bit bolder with their last-day declaration. As it was, Robert Croft waited until his side were 268 runs ahead before giving himself 38 overs to bowl Worcestershire out. Perhaps watching Mark Cosgrove thump a six and 11 fours on his way to 71 not out immediately before the declaration had persuaded him that conditions were more favourable for batting than they really were, but when Worcestershire lost nine wickets attempting to play out time, it became evident that this was very much a missed opportunity for Glamorgan. Cosgrove also hit a six and 11 fours in his first-innings 61, and David Harrison's five wickets and Ryan Watkins' all-round abilities kept Glamorgan on top despite a fluent 73 from Phil Jaques.

Varun Chopra, the 19-year-old opener, became the youngest Essex player to hit a Championship century as a Chelmsford meeting with Gloucestershire held the possibility of a positive

Varun Chopra: Essex's youngest Championship century-maker.

result until midway through the final day. Chopra, the former England Under 19 captain, was on 80 not out at the close of the second day and went to three figures the following morning to put his name in the county's record books ahead of that

Round Six: 23–27 May 2006 Division Two

NORTHAMPTONSHIRE v. DERBYSHIRE – at Northampton

NORTHANTS — First Innings

CJL Rogers	c Pipe b Welch	30
SD Peters	c Stubbings b Welch	33
BM Shafayat	c Di Venuto b Hunter	18
U Afzaal	c Taylor b Jones	68
DJG Sales (capt)	b Hunter	0
*MH Wessels	c Pipe b Jones	6
L Klusener	c Hunter b Jones	49
BJ Phillips	lbw b Hunter	7
MJ Nicholson	not out	106
GG White	b Hunter	37
JF Brown	b Jones	9
Extras	b 1, lb 6, nb 16	23
	(all out 130.4 overs)	386

Bowling
Jones 30.4-6-109-4. Hunter 30-5-93-4. Welch 22-9-57-2. Sheikh 22-6-67-0. Gray 26-8-53-0.
Fall of Wickets: 1-65, 2-78, 3-110, 4-110, 5-136, 6-214, 7-222, 8-232, 9-359

DERBYSHIRE — First Innings

SD Stubbings	not out	10
MJ Di Venuto	c Klusener b Phillips	23
CR Taylor	c Rogers b Phillips	4
TR Birt	not out	16
Hassan Adnan		
G Welch (capt)		
*DJ Pipe		
MA Sheikh		
AKD Gray		
PS Jones		
ID Hunter		
Extras	b 5	5
	(2 wkts 32 overs)	58

Bowling
Nicholson 4-1-23-0. Klusener 7-5-8-0. Phillips 7-4-5-2. Brown 9-5-9-0. White 5-1-8-0.
Fall of Wickets: 1-33, 2-38

Match drawn – Northamptonshire (8 pts), Derbyshire (7 pts)

WORCESTERSHIRE v. GLAMORGAN – at Worcester

GLAMORGAN

	First Innings		Second Innings	
MJ Cosgrove	c Davies b Khan	61	not out	71
DD Cherry	b Kabir Ali	33	c Davies b Kabir Ali	40
DL Hemp	c Hick b Khan	29	c Davies b Khan	10
MJ Powell	c Davies b Khan	4	c Davies b Kabir Ali	20
N Peng	c Smith b Kabir Ali	8	c Ett b Khan	49
RE Watkins	c Davies b Kabir Ali	8	c Davies b Khan	41
*MA Wallace	c Ett b Sillence	37	not out	31
RDB Croft (capt)	c Batty b Khan	10		
AG Wharf	b Malik	2		
DS Harrison	lbw b Malik	4		
AP Davies	not out	14		
Extras	b 10, lb 4, w 2, nb 13	19	lb 2, w 1, nb 16	19
	(all out 72.5 overs)	239	(5 wkts dec 65.2 overs)	281

Bowling
Khan 26-10-65-4. Kabir Ali 24-6-74-3. Malik 9-0-46-2. Sillence 10.5-3-36-1. Batty 3-2-4-0.
Khan 20-6-88-3. Kabir Ali 17-4-56-2. Batty 10.2-1-39-0. Malik 9-2-46-0. Sillence 7-1-28-0. Moore 2-0-22-0.
Fall of Wickets: 1-102, 2-104, 3-109, 4-134, 5-160, 6-160, 7-180, 8-182, 9-190
1-47, 2-90, 3-97, 4-170, 5-199

WORCS

	First Innings		Second Innings	
PA Jaques	b Harrison	73	c Ett b Davies	6
SC Moore	lbw b Harrison	16	not out	53
VS Solanki (capt)	c Wallace b Harrison	31	c Wallace b Harrison	4
BF Smith	b Watkins	21	c sub b Harrison	5
GA Hick	c Cosgrove b Wharf	23	c Wallace b Davies	7
*SM Davies	c Peng b Watkins	11	c Cherry b Watkins	12
GJ Batty	c Wharf b Watkins	10	c Peng b Wharf	1
RJ Sillence	c Peng b Harrison	27	c Powell b Watkins	0
Kabir Ali	not out	25	c Cherry b Croft	19
Z Khan	c Croft b Watkins	4	lbw b Croft	5
MN Malik	c Watkins b Harrison	2	not out	0
Extras	b 1, lb 4, nb 4	9	lb 5	5
	(all out 62.4 overs)	252	(9 wkts 38 overs)	117

Bowling
Harrison 20.4-3-76-5. Davies 16-1-69-0. Wharf 13-0-62-1. Watkins 13-1-40-4.
Harrison 10-2-33-2. Davies 10-2-28-2. Wharf 11-4-27-1. Watkins 4-1-19-2. Croft 3-1-5-2.
Fall of Wickets: 1-29, 2-115, 3-132, 4-164, 5-182, 6-182, 7-207, 8-225, 9-236
1-9, 2-15, 3-21, 4-30, 5-60, 6-63, 7-70, 8-107, 9-117

Match drawn – Worcestershire (9 pts), Glamorgan (8 pts)

ESSEX v. GLOUCESTERSHIRE – at Chelmsford

GLOS

	First Innings		Second Innings	
WPC Weston	c Bopara b ten Doeschate	62	(2) c Phillips b Adams	23
CM Spearman	c Foster b Adams	19	(1) c Flower b Adams	30
MGN Windows	c Chopra b Bopara	12	c Phillips b Adams	0
CG Taylor	b Phillips	66	c Foster b Phillips	27
APR Gidman (capt)	c Foster b ten Doeschate	4	b ten Doeschate	10
IJ Harvey	b Adams	114	c Chopra b Adams	27
*SJ Adshead	c Foster b ten Doeschate	36	c Palladino b ten Doeschate	58
MA Hardinges	lbw b Tudor	16	not out	107
MCJ Ball	not out	33	c ten Doeschate b Tudor	29
CG Greenidge	c Foster b Phillips	8	c Foster b Tudor	4
SP Kirby	lbw b Adams	3	c Foster b Tudor	0
Extras	b 6, lb 7, nb 10	23	lb 4, nb 4	8
	(all out 112.1 overs)	396	(all out 78.5 overs)	323

Bowling
Tudor 19-2-74-1. Palladino 27-4-80-0. Adams 26.1-5-71-3. Bopara 13-3-56-1.
ten Doeschate 19-6-75-3. Phillips 8-2-27-2.
Tudor 9.5-1-61-3. Palladino 16-4-66-0. Adams 19-2-72-4. Phillips 12-6-28-1.
ten Doeschate 16-2-57-2. Bopara 6-0-35-0.
Fall of Wickets: 1-35, 2-58, 3-130, 4-174, 5-196, 6-279, 7-319, 8-368, 9-385
1-48, 2-54, 3-57, 4-87, 5-95, 6-149, 7-208, 8-305, 9-323

ESSEX

	First Innings		Second Innings	
V Chopra	c Greenidge b Hardinges	106	not out	50
ML Pettini	b Kirby	33	c Adshead b Greenidge	8
RS Bopara	lbw b Hardinges	1	lbw b Hardinges	19
A Flower	c Spearman b Greenidge	0	not out	19
RC Irani (capt)	b Gidman	87		
*JS Foster	c Adshead b Gidman	0		
RN ten Doeschate	lbw b Ball	30		
TJ Phillips	c Adshead b Kirby	37		
AJ Tudor	c Spearman b Gidman	21		
AR Adams	not out	44		
AP Palladino	lbw b Kirby	0		
Extras	b 2, lb 3, w 1, nb 18	29	nb 6	6
	(all out 109.2 overs)	388	(2 wkts 24 overs)	102

Bowling
Kirby 23.2-5-91-3. Greenidge 23-4-91-1. Hardinges 21-4-77-2. Harvey 12-3-31-0.
Gidman 19-8-38-3. Ball 11-0-50-1.
Kirby 8-1-39-0. Greenidge 5-0-24-1. Hardinges 4-2-5-1. Gidman 4-0-30-0. Taylor 3-1-4-0.
Fall of Wickets: 1-69, 2-76, 3-85, 4-128, 5-221, 6-267, 7-283, 8-327, 9-375
1-20, 2-63

Match drawn – Essex (11 pts), Gloucestershire (11 pts)

SOMERSET v. LEICESTERSHIRE – at Taunton

LEICESTERSHIRE

	First Innings		Second Innings	
JK Maunders	lbw b Johnson	27	c Johnson b Willoughby	7
DL Maddy	lbw b Willoughby	3	lbw b Caddick	5
HD Ackerman	b Johnson	25	c Gazzard b Willoughby	64
D Mongia (capt)	c Gazzard b Willoughby	41	lbw b Johnson	49
JL Sadler	lbw b Trego	18	c Gazzard b Caddick	29
*PA Nixon	c Ett b Caddick	72	not out	71
S Clark	c Gazzard b Caddick	12	not out	23
CW Henderson	c White b Willoughby	29		
SCJ Broad	lbw b Willoughby	2		
DD Masters	c Gazzard b Caddick	0		
Mohammad Asif	not out	4		
Extras	b 2, lb 12, w 3, nb 4	21	lb 1, w 1, nb 4	6
	(all out 84.5 overs)	254	(5 wkts 77.3 overs)	254

Bowling
Caddick 20.5-4-58-3. Willoughby 27-10-86-4. Johnson 8-0-25-2. Trego 16-3-38-1. Blackwell 6-1-17-0. Parsons 3-0-10-0. White 4-1-6-0.
Caddick 28-5-85-2. Willoughby 23-4-70-2. Johnson 10.3-2-38-1. Trego 7-0-29-0. White 2-0-8-0. Suppiah 4-0-11-0. Hildreth 3-0-12-0.
Fall of Wickets: 1-6, 2-50, 3-63, 4-109, 5-134, 6-155, 7-231, 8-238, 9-239
1-7, 2-14, 3-113, 4-138, 5-178

SOMERSET — First Innings

MJ Wood	c Maunders b Mohammad Asif	11
AV Suppiah	c Ett b Henderson	99
CL White	c Nixon b Broad	0
JC Hildreth	b Maddy b Broad	4
KA Parsons	c Maddy b Broad	0
ID Blackwell (capt)	c Nixon b Maddy	49
PD Trego	c Ett b Mohammad Asif	31
*CM Gazzard	c Nixon b Clark	35
RL Johnson	c Maddy b Masters	40
AR Caddick	b Broad	25
CM Willoughby	not out	6
Extras	b 6, lb 8	14
	(all out 95 overs)	314

Bowling
Mohammad Asif 25-5-94-2. Broad 20-4-62-4. Masters 21-5-48-1.
Henderson 19-4-58-1. Maddy 4-0-9-1. Clark 6-1-29-1.
Fall of Wickets: 1-20, 2-23, 3-31, 4-31, 5-129, 6-186, 7-226, 8-254, 9-308

Match drawn – Somerset (10 pts), Leicestershire (9 pts)

OF HAMPSHIRE

Inspired by one of the greatest fast bowlers ever to grace the cricket grounds of the world, Hampshire were always a force to be reckoned with in the Malcolm Marshall years between 1979 and 1993. Indeed, under the stabilising and often inspirational captaincy of Mark Nicholas, who led the club from 1985 to 1995, Hampshire won four one-day trophies.

A Sunday League triumph in 1986 followed those of 1975 and 1978, but it was at Lord's that Hampshire won the prizes that defined the side that grew up under Nicholas. The team also had in Robin Smith one of the best and most destructive batsmen in the game and, for four seasons in the early 1990s, one of the most naturally gifted in David Gower. In 1988 Hampshire won the Benson and Hedges Cup when Derbyshire were swept aside by the swing bowling of South African Steve Jefferies. Then, in 1991, came the NatWest Trophy as Surrey were beaten, and finally, a year later, another Benson and Hedges Cup was won as Kent were seen off by 41 runs.

Smith was named Man of the Match in both the 1991 and 1992 finals and the sight of Nicholas brandishing a trophy aloft on the Lord's pavilion balcony – although, in 1992, Marshall was summoned by his skipper to share the honour – became a familiar and joyous one for Hampshire followers.

Marshall's tragic and premature death in November 1999, from cancer, hit as hard in Hampshire as in his native Barbados, but renewal came a year later when the club left the cramped confines of its century-long Northlands Road home for the splendour and sylvan setting of the Rose Bowl. Custom-built as a venue capable of attracting international cricket as well as providing for future generations of Hampshire players, it was a ground that also served to illustrate in tangible form the vaulting ambition of Rod Bransgrove, the club chairman.

It was he who had sought the signature of the great Shane Warne, to provide a compelling focus on the field for the start of the new century, and it was largely as a result of Warne's enthusiasm for Hampshire cricket that England's new batting star, Kevin Pietersen, joined the growing number of Southern Hemisphere-raised players for the start of the 2005 season. Since then Hampshire have threatened to begin another era of sustained success, starting with the C&G Trophy in 2005, ironically in Warne's absence with Australia.

Mark Nicholas (far left) holds the Benson and Hedges Cup aloft in 1992 as he and his Hampshire team gather on the Lord's dressing room balcony following their victory over Kent.

of Arthur Turner, the previous youngest century-maker in 1897. Ronnie Irani made 87 and helped the youngster to add 133 for the fourth wicket, and Andre Adams then biffed 44 not out from 46 balls to take Essex almost up to parity on first innings. Gloucestershire, for whom Ian Harvey had struck 114 and Phil Weston and Chris Taylor attractive half-centuries on the opening day, then slumped to 95 for 5 on the third evening to raise the prospect of an Essex win. But, after a delayed start, Steve Adshead hit 58 and Mark Hardinges rushed to a maiden Championship hundred from only 97 balls before celebrating with glee. In the time left, Chopra underlined his immense promise with a further unbeaten 50, while the match also featured the first-class return of former England paceman Alex Tudor, who bowled for the first time in the Championship since 30 April 2005.

At Taunton, where Arul Suppiah was out just one run short of a maiden hundred and Stuart Broad again impressed with the ball, Somerset's draw with Leicestershire also included a bad moment for the home team as Ian Blackwell, their captain, was forced from the field with a shoulder injury that was to rule him out of the remainder of the season. Paul Nixon batted well in both Leicestershire innings but the game was over as a contest well before its end.

Round Seven: 31 May–3 June 2006

Division One

Hampshire stepped up their Championship challenge by scoring more runs to beat Yorkshire in the fourth innings than anyone else had ever done. Set 404 in seven hours by Yorkshire's declaration on the third evening, Shane Warne's side shocked the Headingley faithful by romping home by five wickets. Not that it was easy. Michael Carberry, with ten fours in his 62, and Dominic Thornely, with 71 from 110 balls, played important parts, but it was the magnificent anchor role of opener Jimmy Adams which was the key – plus the aggressive input at the end by Greg Lamb, whose 18-ball 32 not out made mincemeat of a final equation of 33 runs from the last five overs. Adams's effort, however, was the true match-winning one, especially as his previous Championship best was a mere 85. Here, his unbeaten 168 from 313 balls, with 13 fours, plus his powers of concentration and stamina throughout a tense afternoon, took his batting to another level. The ultimate disbelief at Headingley was not just as a result of Adams's epic, however. For the first three days Yorkshire had been in charge, reaching 350 in their first innings thanks largely to a ninth-wicket stand of 144

Round Seven: 31 May–3 June 2006 Division One

YORKSHIRE v. HAMPSHIRE – at Headingley

YORKSHIRE	First Innings		Second Innings	
MJ Wood	lbw b Taylor	9	c Pothas b Bruce	0
MP Vaughan	c Pothas b Taylor	1	b Mascarenhas	56
A McGrath	c Pothas b Bruce	0	c Logan b Warne	127
MJ Lumb	c Warne b Thornely	67	c Thornely b Mascarenhas	5
DS Lehmann	run out	37	c Lamb b Warne	18
C White (capt)	c Lamb b Warne	57	b Thornely	35
*GL Brophy	c Adams b Warne	6	c Pothas b Warne	13
TT Bresnan	lbw b Warne	91	not out	14
RKJ Dawson	c Pothas b Warne	7	c Taylor b Thornely	5
JN Gillespie	c Pothas b Warne	44	not out	2
GJ Kruis	not out	0		
Extras	b 6, lb 9, w 6, nb 10	31	b 6, lb 7, w 7, nb 6	26
	(all out 115.1 overs)	350	(8 wkts dec 82 overs)	301

Bowling
Bruce 20-3-55-1. Taylor 22-4-64-2. Mascarenhas 17-4-51-0. Logan 15-1-58-1. Warne 28.1-8-68-4. Thornely 7-1-14-1. Lamb 3-0-13-0. Adams 2-0-8-0. Carberry 1-0-4-0.
Bruce 12-1-60-1. Taylor 14-2-42-0. Logan 5-0-22-0. Warne 25-1-83-3. Mascarenhas 14-1-47-2. Thornely 12-1-34-2.
Fall of Wickets: 1-8, 2-9, 3-13, 4-55, 5-175, 6-187, 7-192, 8-205, 9-349 1-0, 2-128, 3-136, 4-173, 5-253, 6-272, 7-277, 8-283

HAMPSHIRE	First Innings		Second Innings	
JHK Adams	c Brophy b Kruis	30	not out	168
MA Carberry	c Brophy b Gillespie	52	lbw b McGrath	62
JP Crawley	b Kruis	54	c Wood b McGrath	19
DJ Thornely	c Brophy b Bresnan	76	c Kruis b Lehmann	71
GA Lamb	lbw b McGrath	0	(7) not out	32
*N Pothas	c Wood b Bresnan	10	st Brophy b Lehmann	23
AD Mascarenhas	b Gillespie	3	(5) b Kruis	2
SK Warne (capt)	c Wood b Bresnan	0		
RJ Logan	b Bresnan	0		
JTA Bruce	c Brophy b Kruis	0		
BV Taylor	not out	0		
Extras	b 1, nb 22	23	b 3, lb 6, w 2, nb 16	27
	(all out 92 overs)	248	(5 wkts 111.2 overs)	404

Bowling
Gillespie 19-6-39-2. Kruis 20-3-71-3. Bresnan 19-3-36-4. Dawson 18-3-41-0. Lehmann 6-0-13-0. McGrath 10-0-47-1.
Gillespie 24-6-66-0. Kruis 21-3-75-1. Bresnan 18.2-2-74-0. Lehmann 16-0-70-2. Dawson 14-3-37-0. McGrath 18-0-73-2.
Fall of Wickets: 1-60, 2-109, 3-188, 4-189, 5-219, 6-226, 7-227, 8-227, 9-246 1-133, 2-164, 3-301, 4-309, 5-357

Hampshire won by 5 wickets – Yorkshire (7 pts), Hampshire (18 pts)

SUSSEX v. MIDDLESEX – at Horsham

SUSSEX	First Innings		Second Innings	
RR Montgomerie	c Scott b Dalrymple	26	lbw b Keegan	98
CD Hopkinson	c Compton b Louw	62	c Scott b Keegan	4
MW Goodwin	c Keegan b Dalrymple	55	c Compton b Dalrymple	57
CJ Adams (capt)	b Hutton	31	b Louw	59
*MJ Prior	b Hutton	3	(6) c Hutton b Louw	77
RSC Martin-Jenkins	c & b Mohammad Ali	37	(5) c Scott b Mohammad Ali	27
OP Rayner	lbw b Dalrymple	0	lbw b Louw	4
LJ Wright	c Scott b Silverwood	59	c Silverwood b Mohammad Ali	13
Naved-ul-Hasan	lbw b Silverwood	64	c Joyce b Dalrymple	3
Mushtaq Ahmed	not out	27	b Dalrymple	6
JD Lewry	c Joyce b Silverwood	0	not out	5
Extras	lb 8, nb 4	12	b 1, lb 12, nb 4	17
	(all out 104.5 overs)	376	(all out 88 overs)	370

Bowling
Silverwood 20.5-5-61-3. Keegan 17-4-80-0. Louw 21-4-65-1.
Mohammad Ali 18-4-61-1. Dalrymple 20-2-81-3. Hutton 8-2-20-2.
Keegan 17-8-50-2. Silverwood 19-4-74-0. Mohammad Ali 9-0-56-2. Louw 21-2-87-3. Hutton 3-0-19-0. Dalrymple 18-2-69-3. Shah 1-0-2-0.
Fall of Wickets: 1-57, 2-107, 3-156, 4-160, 5-209, 6-209, 7-231, 8-347, 9-348 1-8, 2-122, 3-190, 4-297, 5-321, 6-333, 7-355, 8-361, 9-361

MIDDLESEX	First Innings		Second Innings	
ET Smith	c Rayner b Naved-ul-Hasan	0	c Prior b Lewry	0
BL Hutton (capt)	c M'gomerie b Mushtaq Ahmed	18	c Rayner b Mushtaq Ahmed	16
OA Shah	c Lewry b Mushtaq Ahmed	126	c Lewry b Wright	4
EC Joyce	lbw b Wright	42	b Mushtaq Ahmed	92
JWM Dalrymple	run out	28	b Lewry	37
NRD Compton	lbw b Mushtaq Ahmed	4	b Wright	1
*BJM Scott	b Mushtaq Ahmed	0	c M'gomerie b Mushtaq Ahmed	1
J Louw	c Prior b Wright	5	b Mushtaq Ahmed	8
CB Keegan	b Wright	4	b Mushtaq Ahmed	8
CEW Silverwood	not out	24	st Prior b Mushtaq Ahmed	50
Mohammad Ali	b Lewry	1	not out	23
Extras	lb 3, w 1, nb 10	14	lb 6, lb 2, nb 6	14
	(all out 71.4 overs)	266	(all out 68 overs)	256

Bowling
Naved-ul-Hasan 12-0-69-1. Lewry 12.4-2-36-1. Martin-Jenkins 5-1-17-0. Mushtaq Ahmed 29-6-92-4. Wright 13-2-39-3. Rayner 2-0-10-0.
Lewry 20-6-49-2. Wright 15-1-60-2. Mushtaq Ahmed 24-3-110-6. Martin-Jenkins 5-2-15-0. Rayner 4-0-14-0.
Fall of Wickets: 1-4, 2-79, 3-188, 4-208, 5-208, 6-215, 7-222, 8-230, 9-264 1-16, 2-21, 3-46, 4-121, 5-126, 6-134, 7-146, 8-156, 9-199

Sussex won by 224 runs – Sussex (21 pts), Middlesex (5 pts)

KENT v. WARWICKSHIRE – at Tunbridge Wells

WARWICKSHIRE	First Innings		Second Innings	
NV Knight	c Hall b Khan	0	(3) lbw b Tredwell	24
MA Wagh	b Tredwell	48	run out	8
IR Bell	b Hall	20	(4) c O'Brien b Hall	8
IJL Trott	b Hall	31	(5) b Tredwell	40
AGR Loudon (capt)	c van Jaarsveld b Khan	11	(6) lbw b Tredwell	0
JO Troughton	lbw b Patel	29	(7) c Stevens b Patel	22
DR Brown	b Kemp	10	(8) st O'Brien b Patel	38
*T Frost	not out	66	(9) not out	34
NM Carter	c Key b Patel	27	(1) c O'Brien b Hall	6
JE Anyon	c Walker b Patel	2	c van Jaarsveld b Tredwell	1
LM Daggett	b Hall	7	b Patel	3
Extras	b 4, lb 6, w 1, nb 6	17	b 4, lb 3, w 1	8
	(all out 100.2 overs)	237	(all out 77.3 overs)	192

Bowling
Khan 20-5-43-2. Hall 18.2-7-43-3. Stevens 4-0-17-0. Patel 26-6-48-3. Kemp 9-1-25-1. Tredwell 29-8-51-1.
Khan 7-2-29-0. Hall 10-1-19-2. Patel 28.3-5-68-3. Kemp 4-1-8-0. Tredwell 28-6-61-4.
Fall of Wickets: 1-4, 2-40, 3-40, 4-72, 5-84, 6-109, 7-151, 8-181, 9-185 1-7, 2-26, 3-35, 4-80, 5-84, 6-95, 7-129, 8-172, 9-177

KENT	First Innings		Second Innings	
DP Fulton	c Trott b Brown	10	b Loudon	31
RWT Key (capt)	b Daggett	12	not out	98
M van Jaarsveld	c Troughton b Daggett	9	not out	57
MJ Walker	c Frost b Daggett	57		
DI Stevens	c Knight b Daggett	24		
JM Kemp	c Knight b Brown	28		
AJ Hall	b Carter	27		
*NJO'Brien	not out	26		
MM Patel	c Frost b Carter	0		
JC Tredwell	b Brown	10		
A Khan	lbw b Brown	0		
Extras	lb 14, w 5, nb 12	31	lb 5, nb 6	11
	(all out 91.5 overs)	234	(1 wkt 65.5 overs)	197

Bowling
Brown 27.5-11-45-4. Daggett 24-6-81-4. Loudon 10-4-13-0. Anyon 15-4-35-0. Carter 15-3-46-2.
Brown 9-2-21-0. Daggett 3-0-14-0. Loudon 22-3-63-1. Troughton 12-2-38-0. Anyon 9.5-2-26-0. Carter 10-2-30-0.
Fall of Wickets: 1-22, 2-22, 3-42, 4-101, 5-155, 6-171, 7-200, 8-204, 9-234 1-84

Kent won by 9 wickets – Kent (18 pts), Warwickshire (4 pts)

25 years OF KENT

Kent may have been the team of the 1970s, but in the quarter-century since then they have had to endure long years of frustration and near misses. They have, of course, managed Sunday League and National League titles – in 1995 and 2001 – yet overall it has been a bridesmaid's story.

Ten trophies between 1970 and 1978 seemed to have set up Kent for many more years of success, especially with genuine young talents like Chris Tavare, Graham Dilley, Richard Ellison, Chris Cowdrey and Paul Downton already emerging in the second half of that decade, but nothing seemed to go right. In 1983 and 1984 Kent were beaten by Somerset and Middlesex respectively in the Lord's finals of the NatWest Trophy, and worse was to come in the Benson and Hedges Cup.

Four times – in 1986, 1992, 1995 and 1997 – Kent battled through to the midsummer Lord's cup final. And four times they were beaten as, successively, the spoils went instead to Middlesex, Hampshire, Lancashire and Surrey. In 1995, Aravinda de Silva also hit one of the greatest and most thrilling cup final centuries in cricket history, but not even that could reverse the trend afflicting Kent.

It was not as if the Kent team of recent memory did not have the undeniable star turns of the Underwood/Knott/Denness/ Luckhurst/Asif Iqbal/Woolmer/Shepherd era either. In the likes of Mark Ealham, Matthew Fleming, Carl Hooper, Dean Headley, Martin McCague, Steve Marsh – notwithstanding De Silva – the county had some of the best and most consistent one-day cricketers in the land.

At least, though, many of that particular group of players had their one-day league wins of 1995 and 2001 to salve the wounds of those Lord's disappointments – although, since that

last trophy was won five years ago, there are many who feel that a first Championship title since 1978 should have been possible for the team led by David Fulton from 2002 to 2005.

As the only county who have never played outside the first division of the two-tier Championship, Kent still hold a certain cachet in the domestic game. And in players such as Robert Key, Geraint Jones, Amjad Khan, Martin van Jaarsveld and Matthew Walker they possess established cricketers still with much to offer and worthy of the county's proud history and traditionally passionate support. Fulton, Martin Saggers and Min Patel have been other fine and talented servants in the past decade, but Kent urgently need to start producing quality young players of their own again – and they need more silverware than the past 25 years have brought.

Even Aravinda de Silva's brilliance at Lord's in 1995 could not prevent the tide of history continuing to turn against Kent.

Jimmy Adams played the anchor role to perfection with 168 not out as Hampshire shocked Yorkshire at Headingley.

could be seen to have turned on the moment that Shah, on 122 and with his side on 192 for 3, was forced to leave the field suffering from severe cramps in his hands. It was a similar affliction to that which had caused him to retire hurt during his Test debut innings of 88 against India at Mumbai in March, but Shah said later that he had since been trying to eliminate the problem by keeping himself hydrated during a lengthy innings. Soon, after some massage and a few swigs of Lucozade, Shah was able to resume – but, by then, Middlesex had slumped to 215 for 6. To make matters worse for the visitors, Shah, who had struck four sixes and 15 fours, added just four more runs before he also fell and – at 266 all out – Middlesex suddenly found themselves nursing a first-innings deficit of 110. Mushtaq Ahmed, passing 300 first-class wickets for Sussex in little more than three and a half seasons, added a further four-wicket haul to his season's tally while, in the absence of groin injury victim Naved-ul-Hasan, Luke Wright also impressed with his energetic medium pace. Wright had made good runs the previous day, too, when he and Naved added 116 for the eighth wicket to boost a Sussex innings that had looked to be falling away at 231 for 7. Richard Montgomerie, Murray Goodwin, with his second half-century of the match, Chris Adams, and Matt Prior, who thumped three sixes and seven fours in a 57-ball 77, then all but took the game out of Middlesex's reach. On the evidence of the first innings, everything depended on Shah, whose batting had looked on a different plane from everyone else in the game. And so, when he departed to a quite stunning, leaping catch by Jason Lewry at deepish mid-off from a shell of a drive, only Ed Joyce stood between Mushtaq and another Sussex win. With Mushtaq completing his ten-wicket match haul on the fourth morning, even Joyce's excellent 92 did not delay the inevitable for long.

between Jason Gillespie and the fast-improving young English all-rounder Tim Bresnan. Then, with Bresnan also to the fore with the ball, Hampshire were forced to concede a 102-run first innings deficit despite half-centuries from Thornely, Carberry and John Crawley. When Anthony McGrath produced an excellent second-innings century, and Michael Vaughan made a measured 56 in his first first-class match since the Third Test against Pakistan in Lahore the previous December (on the opening day he had been out for a single, three balls after being bowled by a Billy Taylor no-ball), Yorkshire looked in complete command. In hindsight, Craig White might have wished he had not declared when he did – but, then again, no one could have foreseen the sting in the tail that lay ahead.

Sussex, however, went 23 points clear of Hampshire and 30 points clear of second-placed Lancashire with their fifth successive win. Middlesex, rooted to the bottom of the first division, were their latest victims, beaten by 224 runs at Horsham despite a scintillating first innings century from Owais Shah. The match, indeed,

An attritional contest at the Nevill Ground in Tunbridge Wells, where groundsman Dave Tankard had performed miracles to get conditions fit for four-day play after having his preparations severely hampered by a week of almost continuous rain, ended with a well-earned win for the home side. Kent owed much to their spinners, James Tredwell and Min Patel, who always held the upper hand against a Warwickshire side badly missing New Zealand slow left-armer Daniel Vettori, sadly returning home after just one Championship match because of a stress fracture of the back. Off spinner Tredwell was particularly impressive in a match which his captain, Rob Key, felt could prove to be a turning point in the 24-year-old's career. Key himself looked like reaching his first Championship hundred of the season as Kent romped towards victory in the sunshine which at last appeared on the final day, but Martin van Jaarsveld left his partner stranded on 98 by driving a ball towards mid-off – and then watching in horror as it beat the fielder and rolled away for four.

Division Two

At a St Helen's ground that had been flooded a week before, the seam and swing bowling of Andy Caddick and Charl Willoughby proved too potent a combination for Glamorgan's batsmen. Caddick took eight wickets in the match, and Willoughby six, as Somerset completed an ultimately comfortable six-wicket win. The pitch was not reported by John Jameson, the ECB pitch inspector, despite 15 wickets falling on day one and then 19 more on the second (and final) day. Swing rather than exaggerated movement off the pitch was the chief danger, but a lack of batting technique also contributed to the early finish. Alex Wharf's 49 from No. 9 ensured Glamorgan a first innings total big enough to give them a halfway lead, but Cameron White's 86 included a six and 11 fours and kept Somerset in the game. Caddick, with 5 for 55, then precipitated a Glamorgan second innings slide to 103 all out and Somerset – despite slipping initially to a worrying 22 for 4 – were guided home safely by Wes Durston and Keith Parsons.

Ian Salisbury took his first-class career wicket-tally beyond 800 as he spearheaded Surrey's hard-fought six-wicket win over Essex at Whitgift School. Ronnie Irani scored a brilliant 122 not out on the opening day and, with Andre Adams thumping 75 from 98 balls in a stand of 124 for the ninth wicket with his captain, Essex totalled 365 despite Salisbury's 5 for

46. But an opening partnership of 194 between Scott Newman and Jon Batty set up Surrey for an eventual 433 in reply, and not even the supreme skill against the turning ball of Andy Flower, who made 111, could then deny the home side. Salisbury finally defeated the former Zimbabwe captain, having him caught off the glove at short leg, and a steadying

Joining the 800 club: Ian Salisbury took decisive wickets in Surrey's win over Essex to go past 800 first-class victims.

fourth-wicket stand between Mark Ramprakash and James Benning, whose unbeaten 63 was scored off just 43 balls with three sixes and ten fours, made sure that Surrey reached their modest victory target.

Lance Klusener hit his third hundred in only seven innings, and followed it up with 6 for 69 and an unbeaten 51 later in the match, but Northamptonshire could still not get the better of Leicestershire in an eventual draw at Oakham School. Ben Phillips's 72 helped Klusener to rally Northants from 144 for 6 to an eventual 331 all out on day one, which ended with Leicestershire rocking at 18 for 2 after two new-ball strikes from Matt Nicholson. But John Maunders and Hylton Ackerman then added 173 for the third wicket and, try as Northants and Klusener might after that, the visitors could not be broken.

Gloucestershire's draw with Worcestershire at Bristol was dominated by the bat on a slow surface, and will be chiefly remembered for the hundred which New Zealand batsman Hamish Marshall made for the home side on his Championship debut and for the hugely-promising career-best 192 put together by Worcestershire's then 19-year-old wicketkeeper Steven Davies. He joined his captain Vikram Solanki in a fifth-wicket stand finally worth 345, with Solanki also posting a career-best 222 – from 295 balls, with two sixes and 28 fours – and Davies taking only 44 balls over his second fifty in an innings in which overall he faced 254 deliveries

and struck 30 boundaries. A characteristic, aggressive 192 from Craig Spearman helped Marshall to fashion a worthy Gloucestershire reply and, set 364 in 58 overs to win on the last afternoon, the home side quite understandably shut up shop.

Round Seven: 31 May–3 June 2006 Division Two

GLAMORGAN v. SOMERSET – at Swansea

GLAMORGAN	First Innings		Second Innings	
DD Cherry	b Parsons	20	c Durston b Caddick	6
RE Watkins	b Willoughby	7	c Hildreth b Willoughby	0
DL Hemp	c Gazzard b Parsons	12	lbw b Caddick	21
MJ Powell	b Caddick	31	lbw b Caddick	4
MJ Cosgrove	b Trego	19	lbw b Caddick	5
*MA Wallace	lbw b Willoughby	5	run out	9
JEC Franklin	lbw b Parsons	37	lbw b Parsons	4
RDB Croft (capt)	c Suppiah b Willoughby	17	lbw b Willoughby	10
AG Wharf	c Parsons b Caddick	49	c Durston b Caddick	4
DS Harrison	not out	4	not out	4
DA Cosker	c Gazzard b Caddick	3	b Willoughby	11
Extras	b 8, lb 2, nb 4	14	lb 15, nb 10	25
	(all out 65.3 overs)	223	(all out 32.5 overs)	103

Bowling
Caddick 22.3-5-79-3. Willoughby 17-6-39-3. Cullen 10-2-33-0. Parsons 13-5-43-3. Trego 3-0-19-1.
Willoughby 10.5-2-24-3. Caddick 16-3-55-5. Parsons 6-4-9-1.
Fall of Wickets: 1-18, 2-34, 3-49, 4-74, 5-101, 6-105, 7-141, 8-174, 9-219
1-3, 2-17, 3-27, 4-39, 5-48, 6-55, 7-60, 8-73, 9-85

SOMERSET	First Innings		Second Innings	
MJ Wood	c Wallace b Franklin	6	lbw b Franklin	9
AV Suppiah	c Croft b Cosker	26	b Harrison	5
WJ Durston	c Wallace b Harrison	4	not out	52
JC Hildreth	c Wallace b Watkins	24	b Franklin	0
CL White (capt)	lbw b Cosker	86	c Wallace b Franklin	0
KA Parsons	b Cosker	1	not out	46
PD Trego	c Wallace b Franklin	15		
*CM Gazzard	lbw b Franklin	12		
AR Caddick	c Wallace b Franklin	0		
DJ Cullen	c Franklin b Croft	7		
CM Willoughby	not out	5		
Extras	b 1, lb 4, w 1, nb 18	24	lb 1, w 1, nb 4	6
	(all out 64.2 overs)	210	(4 wkts 21.4 overs)	118

Bowling
Harrison 13-3-32-1. Franklin 14-3-53-4. Wharf 10-2-33-0. Watkins 6-1-19-1.
Cosker 14-4-38-3. Croft 7.2-0-30-1.
Harrison 8-2-24-1. Franklin 5-1-27-3. Watkins 2-0-16-0. Cosker 3.4-0-31-0.
Wharf 2-0-15-0. Croft 1-0-4-0.
Fall of Wickets: 1-11, 2-25, 3-50, 4-91, 5-93, 6-127, 7-153, 8-155, 9-202
1-18, 2-22, 3-22, 4-22

Somerset won by 6 wickets – Glamorgan (4 pts), Somerset (18 pts)

SURREY v. ESSEX – at Whitgift School

ESSEX	First Innings		Second Innings	
V Chopra	c Azhar Mahmood b Doshi	42	c Butcher b Azhar Mahmood	20
ML Pettini	c Azhar Mahmood b Clarke	44	c Batty b Azhar Mahmood	4
RS Bopara	b Azhar Mahmood	14	c Bicknell b Akram	5
A Flower	lbw b Clarke	13	c Newman b Salisbury	111
RC Irani (capt)	not out	122	lbw b Akram	20
*JS Foster	c Batty b Salisbury	34	c Benning b Salisbury	4
RN ten Doeschate	lbw b Salisbury	0	c Clarke b Doshi	4
JD Middlebrook	c Batty b Salisbury	2	run out	16
TJ Phillips	lbw b Salisbury	0	c Ramprakash b Doshi	16
AR Adams	c Newman b Clarke	75	b Doshi	38
AP Palladino	not out	0	not out	0
Extras	b 4, lb 6, w 5, nb 4	19	lb 2, nb 12	14
	(all out 105.3 overs)	365	(all out 89.3 overs)	244

Bowling
Akram 22-2-83-0. Azhar Mahmood 17-3-52-1. Bicknell 14-3-56-0. Clarke 22-8-68-3.
Doshi 13-2-50-1. Salisbury 17.3-1-46-5.
Azhar Mahmood 12-0-43-2. Akram 12-3-32-2. Clarke 7-1-26-0. Bicknell 7-3-10-0.
Benning 5-3-5-0. Salisbury 25-5-52-2. Doshi 21.3-1-74-3.
Fall of Wickets: 1-81, 2-92, 3-117, 4-129, 5-213, 6-213, 7-227, 8-227, 9-351
1-28, 2-33, 3-35, 4-87, 5-125, 6-132, 7-148, 8-182, 9-232

SURREY	First Innings		Second Innings	
SA Newman	b Foster b Adams	97	c Foster b ten Doeschate	1
*JN Batty	c Bopara b Phillips	87	b Middlebrook	32
MR Ramprakash	c ten Doeschate b Palladino	14	c Foster b ten Doeschate	48
MA Butcher (capt)	st Foster b Middlebrook	71	c Pettini b Middlebrook	4
JGE Benning	c Foster b ten Doeschate	35	not out	63
R Clarke	c Foster b ten Doeschate	13	not out	12
Azhar Mahmood	lbw b ten Doeschate	42		
MP Bicknell	lbw b Adams	24		
IDK Salisbury	c Palladino b ten Doeschate	27		
ND Doshi	not out	1		
Mohammad Akram	lbw b ten Doeschate	0		
Extras	b 2, lb 7, w 1, nb 10	20	b 5, lb 2, w 1, nb 10	18
	(all out 113 overs)	433	(4 wkts 43.2 overs)	178

Bowling
Palladino 9-2-40-1. Adams 25-8-59-2. ten Doeschate 31-2-143-5. Bopara 3-0-19-0.
Phillips 22-3-91-1. Middlebrook 23-5-72-1.
ten Doeschate 11-1-67-2. Adams 9.2-2-25-0. Palladino 6-3-9-0. Phillips 11-3-41-0.
Middlebrook 6-0-29-2.
Fall of Wickets: 1-194, 2-196, 3-226, 4-294, 5-312, 6-367, 7-391, 8-413, 9-431
1-16, 2-60, 3-87, 4-155

Surrey won by 6 wickets – Surrey (22 pts), Essex (7 pts)

LEICESTERSHIRE v. NORTHAMPTONSHIRE – at Oakham School

NORTHANTS	First Innings		Second Innings	
SD Peters	c Maunders b Mohammad Asif	0	lbw b Mohammad Asif	63
CJL Rogers	c Nixon b Mohammad Asif	9	c Nixon b Mohammad Asif	7
BM Shafayat	c Nixon b Broad	32	st Nixon b Henderson	66
U Afzaal	c Sadler b Mohammad Asif	1	b Mohammad Asif	53
DJG Sales (capt)	c Nixon b Broad	46	c Sadler b Henderson	31
L Klusener	c New b Henderson	122	not out	51
*MH Wessels	c Maunders b Clark	22	c Mohammad Asif b Henderson	0
BJ Phillips	b Henderson	72	c Nixon b Mohammad Asif	7
MJ Nicholson	c Sadler b Masters	18	c Sadler b Henderson	40
GG White	c Nixon b Masters	7	c Maunders b Mohammad Asif	0
JF Brown	not out	0	not out	2
Extras	lb 9	9	b 4, lb 15, w 1	20
	(all out 89.4 overs)	331	(9 wkts dec 99 overs)	334

Bowling
Mohammad Asif 26-6-67-3. Broad 16-4-49-2. Masters 23-4-91-2. Clark 6-0-40-1.
Henderson 22.4-3-75-2.
Mohammad Asif 31-3-132-5. Broad 11-1-48-0. Masters 14-1-80-0.
Henderson 32-8-75-4. Mongia 11-3-27-0.
Fall of Wickets: 1-0, 2-9, 3-19, 4-86, 5-91, 6-144, 7-284, 8-315, 9-319
1-35, 2-104, 3-175, 4-230, 5-234, 6-234, 7-270, 8-331, 9-331

LEICESTERSHIRE	First Innings		Second Innings	
TJ New	c Peters b Nicholson	6	c Wessels b Klusener	47
JK Maunders	c Rogers b Klusener	78	b Nicholson	80
S Clark	c Sales b Nicholson	92	(3) not out	55
HD Ackerman	c Sales b Klusener	92		
JL Sadler	lbw b Klusener	0		
D Mongia (capt)	c Phillips b Klusener	26	(4) not out	54
*PA Nixon	not out	40		
CW Henderson	run out	2		
SCJ Broad	c Wessels b Klusener	6		
DD Masters	b Klusener	12		
Mohammad Asif	st Wessels b Brown	15		
Extras	b 4, lb 7, w 2, nb 4	17	lb 3, w 1, nb 4	8
	(all out 102 overs)	294	(2 wkts 75 overs)	244

Bowling
Nicholson 24-7-59-2. Phillips 19-7-30-0. Brown 25-5-88-1. Klusener 25-5-69-6.
Shafayat 1-0-8-0. White 8-0-29-0.
Nicholson 12-2-31-1. Phillips 8-1-28-0. Brown 27-5-72-0. Klusener 12-3-46-1.
White 13-0-42-0. Afzaal 1-0-8-0. Shafayat 2-0-14-0.
Fall of Wickets: 1-8, 2-8, 3-181, 4-181, 5-186, 6-221, 7-227, 8-249, 9-279
1-107, 2-152

Match drawn – Leicestershire (9 pts), Northamptonshire (10 pts)

GLOUCESTERSHIRE v. WORCESTERSHIRE – at Bristol

WORCS	First Innings		Second Innings	
PA Jaques	c Adshead b Hardinges	58	c Taylor b Greenidge	7
SC Moore	lbw b Hardinges	14	c Spearman b Kirby	15
VS Solanki (capt)	c Adshead b Hardinges	222	c Weston b Greenidge	29
BF Smith	lbw b Hardinges	5	c Adshead b Ball	59
GA Hick	c Ball b Harvey	20	c Adshead b Greenidge	64
*SM Davies	c Eb b Ball	192	c Adshead b Hardinges	22
GJ Batty	not out	12	not out	14
RJ Sillence	c Marshall b Gidman	32	c Greenidge b Ball	12
Kabir Ali	c Weston b Ball	0	lbw b Kirby	0
RW Price			c Adshead b Kirby	0
Z Khan			not out	12
Extras	b 1, lb 5, w 6, nb 20	32	lb 11, nb 2	13
	(8 wkts dec 132.5 overs)	587	(9 wkts dec 63 overs)	247

Bowling
Kirby 23-4-105-0. Greenidge 13-2-91-0. Hardinges 27-3-127-4. Harvey 18.2-5-61-1.
Gidman 18.4-2-72-1. Ball 29.5-5-107-2. Taylor 3-0-18-0.
Kirby 16-4-54-3. Greenidge 15-2-56-3. Hardinges 11-1-40-1. Ball 21-1-86-2.
Fall of Wickets: 1-57, 2-86, 3-94, 4-173, 5-518, 6-550, 7-585, 8-587
1-15, 2-33, 3-76, 4-151, 5-198, 6-213, 7-232, 8-232, 9-232

GLOS	First Innings		Second Innings	
WPC Weston	c Davies b Kabir Ali	13	(2) c Jaques b Price	61
CM Spearman	c Hick b Batty	192	(1) b Kabir Ali	14
HJH Marshall	c Davies b Khan	102	c Jaques b Batty	9
CG Taylor	c Davies b Kabir Ali	24	c Jaques b Batty	58
APR Gidman (capt)	c Davies b Kabir Ali	6	not out	5
*SJ Adshead	c Davies b Batty	13	not out	0
MA Hardinges	lbw b Sillence	35		
IJ Harvey	not out	50		
MCJ Ball	c Hick b Sillence	12		
CG Greenidge	c Sillence b Kabir Ali	2		
SP Kirby	c Smith b Kabir Ali	1		
Extras	b 5, lb 10, nb 6	21	b 6, lb 1, w 1, nb 2	10
	(all out 115.3 overs)	471	(4 wkts 58 overs)	163

Bowling
Khan 26-3-122-1. Kabir Ali 23.3-3-78-5. Batty 31-3-101-2. Sillence 15-0-65-2.
Price 17-2-74-0. Solanki 10-3-33-0.
Khan 16-3-55-0. Kabir Ali 9-2-34-1. Batty 16-4-33-2. Sillence 2-1-3-0.
Price 16-2-51-1.
Fall of Wickets: 1-23, 2-276, 3-315, 4-323, 5-359, 6-378, 7-437, 8-467, 9-470
1-19, 2-31, 3-131, 4-151

Match drawn – Gloucestershire (11 pts), Worcestershire (12 pts)

OF LANCASHIRE

L ike Kent, it is often said that Lancashire enjoyed a golden age in the 1970s. In fact, the real golden age of modern times came from 1989 until 1999 when no fewer than nine one-day titles were plundered. The five Championships won between 1926 and 1934 might represent spoils of a more precious and weighty nature – especially given the county's terrible struggles to subsequently add anything other than the shared county title of 1950 – but the achievements of the players in the last century's final decade should also be applauded.

Wasim Akram, the magnificent Pakistan all-rounder who represented Lancashire from 1988 to 1998 and finished up as club captain, was at the heart of this sustained period of success, but Lancashire had plenty of other stars too. Neil Fairbrother was perhaps the best one-day batsman of his generation, while runs in general were never much of a problem for a side also usually containing the likes of Mike Atherton, Jason Gallian, John Crawley and Graham Lloyd as well as all-rounders such as wicketkeeper Warren Hegg, Ian Austin, Glen Chapple, Mike Watkinson, Wasim and latterly Andrew Flintoff. The Lancashire bowling attack, for instance, which destroyed Derbyshire

in the 1998 NatWest Trophy final – they were dismissed for just 108 after reaching 70 without loss – was Wasim, Peter Martin, Chapple, Austin and Flintoff, with off spinner Gary Yates unused.

A Sunday League win in 1989 was the catalyst for this great run of trophy hunting. Then came a memorable Lord's double of Benson and Hedges Cup and NatWest Trophy in 1990 – an achievement, moreover, which was matched in 1996. The other titles were another Benson and Hedges Cup victory in 1995, that crushing NatWest Trophy win in 1998 – the year that the Sunday League was taken too – and finally a National League Division One trophy in 1999.

Flintoff's rise to superstardom in the early part of the new century savagely cut back the number of appearances for his county, sadly, but Lancashire are still producing their own genuine talent: witness the arrivals since 2002 of the likes of James Anderson, Sajid Mahmood and Tom Smith. Older hands like Dominic Cork, Stuart Law, Mal Loye and Luke Sutton have also been attracted to Lancashire from other counties, and the Red Rose looks like reaching full bloom again soon.

Lancashire's players celebrate at Lord's after winning the 1998 NatWest Trophy final against Derbyshire.

Round Eight: 6–11 June 2006

Division One

Lancashire's challenge for the title gained significant momentum when leaders Sussex were cut down to size at Aigburth. The Liverpool pitch had bounce and good carry and Sussex, still missing their injured Pakistan paceman Naved-ul-Hasan, could not compete with a pumped-up home team. Glen Chapple led the way on day one as Sussex were bundled out for 218, despite a solid half-century from Richard Montgomerie, and by the close Mal Loye's remarkable 61-ball 80 had ensured the early initiative remained with Lancashire. From an overnight 133 for 4, Lancashire reached 317 with the lower middle-order efforts of Chapple and Dominic Cork further frustrating Sussex, for whom both Jason Lewry and Mushtaq Ahmed picked up five wickets. Sussex needed a big second-innings total to get themselves back into the match, but only skipper Chris Adams looked capable of providing it as Sajid Mahmood and Chapple sliced through their batting. Iain Sutcliffe then rushed Lancashire to the small total they needed for an emphatic nine-wicket win.

Hampshire crushed champions Nottinghamshire by 299 runs at the Rose Bowl after opting not to enforce the follow-on. Centuries from John Crawley and Nic Pothas, who added a ground record 217

for the fifth wicket, gave Hampshire early control and then Notts' brittle batting was exposed by Dimitri Mascarenhas and the rest of the Hampshire attack. Crawley then compiled his second hundred of the match and, despite reaching 164 for 2 at one

Round Eight: 6–11 June 2006 Division One

LANCASHIRE v. SUSSEX – at Liverpool

SUSSEX	First Innings		Second Innings	
RR Montgomerie	c Cork b Chapple	56	(2) c & b Mahmood	27
CD Hopkinson	lbw b Chapple	2	(1) lbw b Chapple	4
MW Goodwin	c Smith b Chapple	1	(4) lbw b Mahmood	2
CJ Adams (capt)	c Law b Smith	30	(5) c Sutcliffe b Mahmood	68
*MJ Prior	b Chapple	37	(6) c Hodge b Keedy	9
CD Nash	c Sutton b Mahmood	29	(3) c Sutton b Mahmood	7
RSC Martin-Jenkins	c Smith b Cork	3	c Loye b Keedy	6
LJ Wright	c Sutton b Keedy	28	c Smith b Chapple	4
Mushtaq Ahmed	c Hodge b Cork	22	c Sutton b Chapple	14
RJ Kirtley	lbw b Keedy	2	c Smith b Mahmood	12
JD Lewry	not out	1	not out	1
Extras	b 3, lb 2, nb 4	7	lb 1, w 1, nb 10	12
	(all out 68.5 overs)	218	(all out 42.3 overs)	166

Bowling
Chapple 17-5-35-4. Cork 13.5-4-44-2. Smith 12-5-39-1. Mahmood 13-1-59-1.
Keedy 13-3-38-2.
Chapple 12-3-47-3. Cork 4-0-26-0. Smith 6-3-8-0. Mahmood 10.3-0-52-5.
Keedy 10-0-32-2.
Fall of Wickets: 1-11, 2-15, 3-55, 4-122, 5-137, 6-142, 7-188, 8-206, 9-213
1-4, 2-40, 3-44, 4-49, 5-72, 6-92, 7-96, 8-112, 9-137

LANCASHIRE	First Innings		Second Innings	
MJ Chilton (capt)	b Lewry	4	(2) c Prior b Kirtley	10
IJ Sutcliffe	lbw b Mushtaq Ahmed	10	(1) not out	45
MB Loye	b Mushtaq Ahmed	80	not out	10
BJ Hodge	b Lewry	47		
SG Law	c & b Mushtaq Ahmed	21		
TC Smith	c Adams b Mushtaq Ahmed	1		
*LD Sutton	c Prior b Lewry	23		
G Chapple	c Montgomerie b Lewry	47		
DG Cork	st Prior b Mushtaq Ahmed	53		
SI Mahmood	c Adams b Lewry	11		
G Keedy	not out	11		
Extras	b 3, lb 10, nb 2, p 5	20	lb 1, w 1, nb 2	4
	(all out 79.4 overs)	317	(1 wkt 19 overs)	69

Bowling
Lewry 23.5-5-75-5. Kirtley 20-4-74-0. Wright 4-0-38-0. Mushtaq Ahmed 32.4-4-112-5.
Lewry 4-1-13-0. Kirtley 8-1-25-1. Martin-Jenkins 4-1-11-0. Hopkinson 2-0-19-0.
Nash 1-1-0-0.
Fall of Wickets: 1-6, 2-56, 3-107, 4-133, 5-135, 6-180, 7-239, 8-260, 9-260
1-35

*Lancashire won by 9 wickets –
Lancashire (20 pts), Sussex (4 pts)*

HAMPSHIRE v. NOTTINGHAMSHIRE – at the Rose Bowl

HAMPSHIRE	First Innings		Second Innings	
JHK Adams	lbw b Harris	21	c Fleming b Swann	80
MA Carberry	c Read b Harris	15	c Smith b Shreck	23
JP Crawley	c Hussey b Shreck	106	c Gallian b Swann	116
DJ Thornely	c Read b Shreck	19	not out	10
SM Ervine	c Fleming b Ealham	13		
*N Pothas	b Harris	117		
AD Mascarenhas	c Fleming b Harris	25		
SK Warne (capt)	c Gallian b Shreck	19		
SD Udal	not out	17		
JTA Bruce	c Read b Shreck	4		
BV Taylor	lbw b Shreck	0		
Extras	b 3, lb 2, w 2, nb 38	45	b 1, lb 1, nb 20	22
	(all out 117.3 overs)	401	(3 wkts dec 64.1 overs)	251

Bowling
Harris 30-3-114-4. Shreck 32.3-2-94-5. Franks 20-4-72-0. Ealham 20-6-70-1.
Swann 15-2-46-0.
Harris 4.1-0-20-0. Shreck 13-2-60-1. Franks 9.5-1-56-0. Ealham 14-3-45-0.
Swann 18.1-1-51-2. Hussey 5-1-17-0.
Fall of Wickets: 1-38, 2-41, 3-64, 4-92, 5-309, 6-358, 7-380, 8-380, 9-401
1-52, 2-220, 3-251

NOTTS	First Innings		Second Innings	
DJ Bicknell	c Pothas b Taylor	15	c Ervine b Warne	22
JER Gallian	c Ervine b Mascarenhas	16	c & b Warne	67
WR Smith	b Mascarenhas	14	lbw b Bruce	40
SP Fleming (capt)	lbw b Mascarenhas	10	lbw b Thornely	29
DJ Hussey	lbw b Bruce	26	c Pothas b Bruce	13
*CMW Read	c Ervine b Mascarenhas	14	c Udal b Bruce	1
MA Ealham	c Pothas b Bruce	2	c Pothas b Bruce	0
PJ Franks	c Ervine b Taylor	15	not out	15
GP Swann	c & b Thornely	15	c Pothas b Bruce	2
AJ Harris	b Thornely	11	b Udal	2
CE Shreck	not out	0	lbw b Warne	1
Extras	b 5, nb 6	11	b 1, lb 5, w 2, nb 8	16
	(all out 42.4 overs)	147	(all out 74.1 overs)	206

Bowling
Bruce 10-2-52-2. Taylor 8-1-25-2. Mascarenhas 12-4-25-4. Ervine 9-0-31-0.
Warne 1-0-2-0. Thornely 2.4-0-7-2.
Bruce 16-3-43-5. Taylor 6-3-16-0. Mascarenhas 9-3-15-0. Warne 18.1-3-53-3.
Ervine 9-2-41-0. Udal 8-1-21-1. Thornely 8-2-11-1.
Fall of Wickets: 1-23, 2-44, 3-60, 4-65, 5-93, 6-96, 7-111, 8-123, 9-142
1-70, 2-101, 3-164, 4-165, 5-170, 6-170, 7-187, 8-187, 9-201

*Hampshire won by 299 runs –
Hampshire (22 pts), Nottinghamshire (3 pts)*

MIDDLESEX v. YORKSHIRE – at Southgate

YORKSHIRE	First Innings		Second Innings	
AW Gale	lbw b Silverwood	4	b Silverwood	2
MP Vaughan	c Smith b Dalrymple	99	b Shah b Louw	4
A McGrath (capt)	c Shah b Silverwood	0	c Scott b Silverwood	2
MJ Lumb	lbw b Silverwood	144	c Hutton b Peploe	12
DS Lehmann	c Compton b Peploe	35	c Styris b Dalrymple	26
TT Bresnan	c & b Silverwood	31	st Scott b Peploe	10
*GL Brophy	c Styris b Louw	8	c Hutton b Dalrymple	3
RKJ Dawson	lbw b Silverwood	8	c Styris b Peploe	12
JN Gillespie	c Joyce b Louw	1	not out	34
MAK Lawson	not out	0	c Hutton b Dalrymple	3
GJ Kruis	c Styris b Silverwood	1	c Scott b Peploe	7
Extras	b 5, lb 4, w 1, nb 18	28	lb 9, nb 6	15
	(all out 116.2 overs)	355	(all out 45.5 overs)	130

Bowling
Silverwood 22.2-6-51-6. Louw 22-10-30-2. Styris 19-3-70-0. Peploe 24-6-89-1.
Hutton 11-0-13-0. Dalrymple 22-4-55-1. Shah 5-1-29-0. Compton 1-0-9-0.
Silverwood 7-1-13-2. Louw 8-3-21-1. Dalrymple 16-1-56-3. Peploe 14.5-4-31-4.
Fall of Wickets: 1-8, 2-103, 3-116, 4-269, 5-333, 6-338, 7-348, 8-354, 9-354
1-12, 2-14, 3-15, 4-45, 5-59, 6-65, 7-67, 8-96, 9-117

MIDDLESEX	First Innings		Second Innings	
ET Smith	lbw b Gillespie	0	c Lumb b Dawson	44
BL Hutton (capt)	st Brophy b Lawson	59	not out	19
OA Shah	c Brophy b Dawson	30	c Lawson b Dawson	0
EC Joyce	c Brophy b Kruis	155	not out	7
JWM Dalrymple	b Lehmann	4		
SB Styris	c Gillespie b McGrath	33		
NRD Compton	run out	34		
*BJM Scott	b Kruis	0		
J Louw	not out	34		
CT Peploe	lbw b Lawson	43		
CEW Silverwood	c Lumb b Lawson	5		
Extras	b 5, lb 11, nb 5	21	nb 4	4
	(all out 122.2 overs)	415	(2 wkts 16.3 overs)	74

Bowling
Gillespie 22-7-58-1. Kruis 19-2-59-2. Bresnan 11-2-33-0. Dawson 33-2-102-1.
Lawson 19.2-1-98-2. Lehmann 14-1-40-2. McGrath 4-1-9-1.
Gillespie 4-0-15-0. Kruis 3-0-15-0. Dawson 50-30-2. Lehmann 4.3-1-14-0.
Fall of Wickets: 1-0, 2-53, 3-184, 4-194, 5-261, 6-333, 7-335, 8-335, 9-413
1-67, 2-67

*Middlesex won by 8 wickets –
Middlesex (22 pts), Yorkshire (7 pts)*

WARWICKSHIRE v. DURHAM – at Edgbaston

WARWICKSHIRE	First Innings		Second Innings	
NV Knight	c Thorp b Onions	37	lbw b Onions	41
MA Wagh	c Mustard b Thorp	12	b Onions	5
IR Bell	b Gibson	53	c Maher b Gibson	32
IJL Trott	c Pratt b Lewis ML	7	(5) c & b Breese	14
AGR Loudon	lbw b Gibson	11	(6) lbw b Breese	14
JO Troughton	b Gibson	0	(7) lbw b Breese	6
DR Brown	run out	30	(8) lbw b Breese	20
*T Frost	lbw b Onions	12	(9) c Lewis JJB b Gibson	96
HH Streak (capt)	lbw b Onions	12	(10) b Gibson	37
JE Anyon	b Onions	2	(4) c Mustard b Lewis ML	5
LM Daggett	c Pratt b Gibson	0	not out	2
Extras	lb 10, nb 12	22	b 11, lb 14, w 2, nb 8	35
	(all out 77 overs)	208	(all out 106.2 overs)	310

Bowling
Lewis ML 18-4-49-1. Onions 17-7-45-3. Thorp 13-5-25-1. Gibson 18-4-45-4.
Benkenstein 8-1-31-0. Breese 3-1-3-0.
Lewis ML 23-8-56-1. Onions 18-3-72-2. Gibson 22.2-7-39-3. Thorp 12-2-33-0.
Breese 27-4-75-4. Benkenstein 4-1-10-0.
Fall of Wickets: 1-36, 2-103, 3-116, 4-133, 5-138, 6-141, 7-179, 8-191, 9-207
1-27, 2-80, 3-104, 4-108, 5-138, 6-141, 7-154, 8-177, 9-290

DURHAM	First Innings		Second Innings	
JJB Lewis	lbw b Streak	12	lbw b Brown	24
JP Maher	lbw b Streak	10	(5) c Trott b Anyon	12
GJ Muchall	lbw b Brown	9	b Daggett	1
GJ Pratt	c Frost b Daggett	9	(2) c Trott b Streak	21
DM B'kenstein (capt)	not out	144	(6) not out	23
GR Breese	lbw b Daggett	1	(4) c Frost b Anyon	33
*P Mustard	c Streak b Brown	45	c Knight b Daggett	13
OD Gibson	c Frost b Troughton	81	c Frost b Daggett	6
CD Thorp	b Bell	0	b Daggett	2
G Onions	b Anyon	40	c Frost b Daggett	2
ML Lewis	lbw b Anyon	0	c Troughton b Daggett	0
Extras	lb 10	10	lb 4	4
	(all out 101.5 overs)	359	(all out 49.4 overs)	141

Bowling
Streak 18-2-80-2. Brown 21-3-64-2. Daggett 16-5-52-2. Anyon 21.5-4-59-2.
Loudon 14-0-54-0. Bell 7-0-24-1. Troughton 4-0-16-1.
Brown 7-1-16-1. Streak 11-2-44-1. Daggett 14.4-5-30-6. Anyon 5-1-36-2.
Loudon 2-0-11-0.
Fall of Wickets: 1-14, 2-27, 3-29, 4-58, 5-62, 6-132, 7-269, 8-281, 9-359
1-28, 2-33, 3-70, 4-93, 5-96, 6-113, 7-121, 8-137, 9-141

*Warwickshire won by 18 runs –
Warwickshire (18 pts), Durham (7 pts)*

Lee Daggett swept Warwickshire to a dramatic 18-run win over Durham with 6 for 30.

Yorkshire, suddenly, fell away against the Middlesex spinners and – midway through the third day – the match was over.

Durham left Edgbaston wondering how they had managed to lose by 18 runs a game that, for the first three days, they had seemed in total control of. A magnificent 144 not out by Dale Benkenstein, plus the bowling and batting efforts of Ottis Gibson and Graham Onions, dominated the first two days, and when Warwickshire continued to lose wickets after beginning day three still 69 runs adrift at 82 for 2, it seemed as if a Durham victory was inevitable. But Tony Frost, coming in at No. 9, hit a gutsy 96 and added 113 for the ninth wicket with Heath Streak and Durham had been set 160. At the close they were 62 for 2 and on target, but the following morning saw Lee Daggett, a 23-year-old seamer in only his second Championship appearance, grab the moment with a dramatic burst that brought him final figures of 6 for 30.

Division Two

Glamorgan recorded their first win of the season thanks largely to the efforts of Mark Cosgrove, their squat 21-year-old South Australian opener, and skipper Robert Croft. Cosgrove's superlative 233, in which he reached 200 off just 203 balls, contained two sixes and 28 fours and enabled Glamorgan to romp past Derbyshire's first innings 327, in which Croft's off-spin had brought him his 900th first-class wicket as well as figures of 5 for 56. Cosgrove was joined in a third-wicket stand of 235 by Michael Powell, who made 90, and a total of 470 gave the Welsh county an advantage that Croft and his spin partner Dean Cosker were quick to drive home. Michael Di Venuto battled valiantly for 95, as did Graeme Welch for his 63, but Croft and Cosker shared eight wickets to leave Glamorgan seeking only a modest last innings total for victory. At 78 for 4 they were looking a tad shaky, but Powell and Mark Wallace soon steadied the nerves.

The 129th first-class hundred of Graeme Hick's career, taking him past Graham Gooch and alongside Sir Len Hutton in the elite list of century-makers, made Worcestershire's ten-wicket win over Somerset at Taunton even more memorable. Hick, back on the ground where in 1988 he had hit his epic 405 not out against a suffering Somerset attack of an earlier era, this time went on to make 182 from 213 balls while adding 330 in 74 overs for the fourth wicket with Ben Smith, who scored a superb 203. Cameron White,

stage in their own second innings, Notts were soon being dismantled again as James Bruce took 5 for 43 and Shane Warne weighed in with three wickets of his own.

A miserable start to the season brightened up a little for Middlesex when they defeated Yorkshire by eight wickets at Southgate. For two days the contest was very even, with Michael Vaughan missing out on his first Championship hundred for three years by just one run and Michael Lumb hitting 24 fours in a career-best 144 as Yorkshire built a decent first innings total. But Chris Silverwood's wholehearted 6 for 51, against his former county, kept Middlesex in the game and a brilliant 155 by Ed Joyce then enabled the home team to gain a useful 60-run lead.

Power play: Glamorgan's exciting South Australian, Mark Cosgrove, thumps another boundary during his rumbustious 233 at Derby.

with 131 not out from 157 balls, and Wes Durston did their best to fashion some sort of Somerset response to Worcestershire's mammoth 618, but Roger Sillence ran in spiritedly to return career-best figures of 7 for 96 and, by the end of day three, Somerset were down and out at 246 for 8 after following on. Entertaining hitting by Andy Caddick and last man Charl Willoughby, whose 47 from 43 balls included three sixes and six fours, forced Worcestershire to bat again but still only delayed the inevitable on the final morning.

Surrey overwhelmed Leicestershire at The Oval, and the final margin of victory (an innings and 158 runs) summed up the difference between the two sides. Ian Salisbury was effective with his leg spin in both Leicestershire innings but it was the all-round performance of Rikki Clarke, which most caught the eye ahead of Salisbury, Alistair Brown's powerful 215 and further fine innings from Mark Butcher and Mark Ramprakash. Clarke took 4 for 45 on the opening day, plus four catches – two of them quite brilliant – and then struck a career-best 165 as he and Brown drove home Surrey's advantage in a fifth-wicket stand of 226.

Round Eight: 6–11 June 2006 Division Two

DERBYSHIRE v. GLAMORGAN – at Derby

DERBYSHIRE	First Innings		Second Innings	
MJ Di Venuto	c Wharf b Franklin	18	(2) lbw b Wharf	95
SD Stubbings	c Wallace b Cosker	98	(1) b Cosker	8
CR Taylor	c Wallace b Cosgrove	18	lbw b Croft	14
TR Birt	lbw b Croft	16	c Peng b Cosker	12
Hassan Adnan	c Wharf b Cosker	52	c Powell b Cosker	4
MA Sheikh	c Wallace b Croft	38	c & b Croft	15
G Welch (capt)	c Peng b Croft	15	c Cosgrove b Croft	63
*DJ Pipe	c Wallace b Harrison	28	c Cherry b Croft	3
AKD Gray	not out	6	run out	25
PS Jones	b Croft	3	c Croft b Cosker	9
ID Hunter	b Croft	0	not out	4
Extras	b 3, lb 14, nb 18	35	b 14, lb 8, w 2, nb 6	30
	(all out 119.5 overs)	**327**	(all out 103 overs)	**282**

Bowling
Harrison 23-6-49-1. Franklin 20-2-80-1. Wharf 9-0-56-0. Cosgrove 4-1-8-1. Croft 34.5-14-56-5. Cosker 29-9-61-2.
Cosker 41-7-119-4. Croft 39-10-73-4. Harrison 3-1-2-0. Franklin 8-1-27-0. Wharf 12-3-39-1.
Fall of Wickets: 1-47, 2-96, 3-131, 4-202, 5-268, 6-274, 7-317, 8-318, 9-327
1-26, 2-55, 3-76, 4-88, 5-135, 6-179, 7-205, 8-250, 9-278

GLAMORGAN	First Innings		Second Innings	
DD Cherry	c Pipe b Jones	3	(2) c Welch b Gray	20
MJ Cosgrove	st Pipe b Sheikh	233	(1) c Pipe b Gray	21
DL Hemp	c Pipe b Welch	19	c Hunter b Jones	8
MJ Powell	lbw b Hunter	90	not out	38
N Peng	c Di Venuto b Hunter	33	run out	6
*MA Wallace	lbw b Sheikh	0	not out	34
JEC Franklin	st Pipe b Gray	36		
AG Wharf	lbw b Welch	9		
RDB Croft (capt)	c Di Venuto b Gray	8		
DS Harrison	not out	8		
DA Cosker	st Pipe b Gray	0		
Extras	b 5, lb 11, w 5, nb 10	31	b 1, lb 10, nb 2	13
	(all out 116.2 overs)	**470**	(4 wkts dec 37.2 overs)	**140**

Bowling
Jones 29-3-106-1. Hunter 23-2-97-2. Welch 21-4-81-2. Sheikh 15-4-64-2.
Gray 28.2-6-106-3.
Jones 10-2-33-1. Sheikh 2-1-5-0. Gray 16.2-3-62-2. Hunter 7-2-24-0.
Hassan Adnan 2-0-5-0.
Fall of Wickets: 1-34, 2-76, 3-311, 4-380, 5-384, 6-432, 7-450, 8-462, 9-462
1-31, 2-48, 3-62, 4-78

Glamorgan won by 6 wickets – Derbyshire (6 pts), Glamorgan (22 pts)

SOMERSET v. WORCESTERSHIRE – at Taunton

WORCS	First Innings		Second Innings	
PA Jaques	b Willoughby	88	not out	15
SC Moore	c Gazzard b Willoughby	53	not out	27
VS Solanki (capt)	c Durston b Willoughby	5		
BF Smith	c Gazzard b Willoughby	203		
GA Hick	c Gazzard b Willoughby	182		
*SM Davies	c Willoughby b Cullen	11		
GJ Batty	c Hildreth b Parsons	15		
RJ Sillence	c Wood b Willoughby	20		
Kabir Ali	b Parsons	1		
RW Price	c Suppiah b Parsons	1		
Z Khan	not out	1		
Extras	b 4, lb 8, w 4, nb 22	38		0
	(all out 149.5 overs)	**618**	(0 wkts 4.3 overs)	**42**

Bowling
Caddick 26-1-145-0. Willoughby 32-5-104-6. Cullen 26-1-73-1. Trego 18-1-106-0.
Parsons 10.5-0-33-3. White 20-0-74-0. Suppiah 13-2-50-0. Durston 4-0-21-0.
Trego 2.3-0-22-0. Willoughby 2-0-20-0.
Fall of Wickets: 1-123, 2-129, 3-170, 4-500, 5-529, 6-570, 7-608, 8-612, 9-616

SOMERSET	First Innings		Second Innings (following on)	
MJ Wood	b Khan	8	c Khan	27
AV Suppiah	c Davies b Sillence	16	lbw b Price	4
WJ Durston	lbw b Kabir Ali	89	c Smith b Batty	40
JC Hildreth	c Batty b Sillence	34	c Moore b Batty	17
CL White (capt)	not out	131	b Batty	1
KA Parsons	c Davies b Sillence	5	lbw b Kabir Ali	37
PD Trego	c Davies b Sillence	8	c Hick b Batty	67
*CM Gazzard	b Kabir Ali	1	b Kabir Ali	0
AR Caddick	c Davies b Sillence	7	c Hick b Batty	43
DJ Cullen	c Davies b Sillence	19	not out	16
CM Willoughby	c Jaques b Sillence	2	c & b Khan	47
Extras	b 9, lb 6, w 3, nb 8	26	b 8, w 2, nb 4	14
	(all out 93.1 overs)	**346**	(all out 89 overs)	**313**

Bowling
Khan 21-1-93-1. Kabir Ali 26-5-87-2. Sillence 22.1-3-96-7. Batty 12-4-22-0.
Price 12-1-33-0.
Khan 11-2-48-1. Kabir Ali 13-4-50-2. Sillence 5-1-21-0. Price 24-8-67-1.
Batty 36-8-119-6.
Fall of Wickets: 1-16, 2-67, 3-136, 4-216, 5-227, 6-237, 7-241, 8-266, 9-336
1-36, 2-56, 3-87, 4-89, 5-121, 6-175, 7-175, 8-229, 9-250

Worcestershire won by 10 wickets – Somerset (4 pts), Worcestershire (22 pts)

SURREY v. LEICESTERSHIRE – at The Oval

LEICESTERSHIRE	First Innings		Second Innings	
DDJ Robinson (capt)	b Clarke	31	c Batty b Salisbury	106
JK Maunders	c Clarke b Akram	27	c Batty b Bicknell	7
TJ New	c Clarke b Doshi	8	b Akram	9
HD Ackerman	lbw b Salisbury	58	c Batty b Doshi	23
D Mongia	c & b Clarke	20	c Doshi b Salisbury	22
JL Sadler	c Clarke b Bicknell	13	c Newman b Salisbury	12
*PA Nixon	lbw b Salisbury	1	b Akram	12
DD Masters	st Batty b Salisbury	0	lbw b Akram	12
CW Henderson	not out	46	c Salisbury b Doshi	34
SCJ Broad	c Batty b Clarke	20	c & b Salisbury	12
Mohammad Asif	c Batty b Clarke	6	not out	0
Extras	b 4, lb 14, w 1, nb 2	21	b 5, lb 3, nb 2	10
	(all out 80 overs)	**251**	(all out 88.1 overs)	**259**

Bowling
Akram 14-0-64-1. Azhar Mahmood 11-1-37-0. Bicknell 13-4-30-1. Clarke 16-4-45-4.
Doshi 8-3-22-1. Salisbury 18-6-35-3.
Bicknell 7-2-20-1. Akram 20-6-61-3. Azhar Mahmood 2-0-9-0. Doshi 17.1-2-60-2.
Salisbury 33-12-64-4. Brown 1-0-9-0. Clarke 8-2-28-0.
Fall of Wickets: 1-63, 2-63, 3-93, 4-147, 5-161, 6-163, 7-171, 8-171, 9-231
1-13, 2-34, 3-83, 4-118, 5-132, 6-160, 7-192, 8-231, 9-259

SURREY	First Innings			
SA Newman	lbw b Mohammad Asif	8		
*JN Batty	c Maunders b Broad	39		
MR Ramprakash	lbw b Mongia	73		
MA Butcher (capt)	c Robinson b Mongia	105		
AD Brown	lbw b Henderson	215		
R Clarke	c Sadler b Henderson	165		
Azhar Mahmood	c Robinson b Henderson	0		
MP Bicknell	not out	27		
IDK Salisbury				
ND Doshi				
Mohammad Akram				
Extras	b 11, lb 10, w 7, nb 8	36		
	(7 wkts dec 174.2 overs)	**668**		

Bowling
Mohammad Asif 10-2-50-1. Broad 36-11-112-1. Henderson 54.2-5-235-3.
Masters 33-3-117-0. Mongia 33-7-105-2. Maunders 8-1-28-0.
Fall of Wickets: 1-22, 2-106, 3-146, 4-363, 5-589, 6-593, 7-668

Surrey won by an innings and 158 runs – Surrey (22 pts), Leicestershire (3 pts)

OF *LEICESTERSHIRE*

Two Championships in three years – 1996 and 1998 – are the highlights of Leicestershire's last 25-year history. Under James Whitaker's captaincy, a tight-knit team achieved great consistency of performance in the mid-1990s. There were no 'stars' in the teams, just a collective determination and belief that was fostered by Whitaker's energy and passion and the shrewd off-field leadership also shown by Jack Birkenshaw, the coach.

Whitaker, in fact, played no active part at all in the 1998 triumph – though still club captain – because of a chronic knee injury which required two operations. He did, however, stay with the side all season and he and Birkenshaw formed a strong alliance in their dual off-field roles. Chris Lewis and, latterly, Phil Simmons, provided the on-field captaincy for that Championship campaign – the title being clinched in the most satisfactory way possible when nearest challengers Surrey were beaten by an innings in the last match of the season at The Oval.

Ben Smith scored a double-hundred in the match, and both Aftab Habib and Paul Nixon hit centuries, but runs during the season also came from the likes of Vince Wells, Darren Maddy and Iain Sutcliffe at the top of the order and Lewis, Simmons and David Millns lower down. Alan Mullally, Millns, Lewis and James Ormond were the frontline seamers, while Wells and Simmons also picked up their fair share of wickets with their medium-pacers and slow left-armer Matthew Brimson claimed 31 victims with spin.

Sadly for Leicestershire's supporters, that team soon broke up with Whitaker forced to bow to his injury problems and the likes of Mullally, Smith, Sutcliffe, Habib, Ormond and Nixon all departing over the

next few years for the bigger pay cheques available at other counties. Nixon, however, after three years at Kent, returned to Grace Road in 2003 and latterly – along with the faithful Maddy – has provided the focal point of the club's new-found successes in the Twenty20 Cup. In 2006, following an initial win in 2004, Leicestershire became the first county to win domestic cricket's newest and best-supported trophy for the second time.

For a small county Leicestershire can more than hold its head up for what it has achieved over the past 25 years, especially as immediately before that – in the 1970s – the team had won five titles in six years, including the 1975 Championship.

In 1985 a side featuring the likes of David Gower, Peter Willey, Jonathan Agnew, Les Taylor and a young Whitaker, meanwhile, won that year's Benson and Hedges Cup – and Leicestershire's capacity for unearthing world-class young talent did not stop with the likes of Gower, Phillip DeFreitas and Lewis. This season's Twenty20 Cup was won with a significant contribution from opening bowler Stuart Broad who, at 20, seems to have a long and successful international career ahead of him.

Leicestershire's injured captain James Whitaker makes an emotional appearance on the field at The Oval to join in the Championship-winning celebrations of 1998.

Round Nine: 13–17 June 2006

Division One

Lancashire pushed themselves six points clear of Sussex at the top of the table after brushing aside Warwickshire by seven wickets at Edgbaston. A superb opening-day, new-ball spell of 12-4-17-4 by Dominic Cork, who finished with 6 for 53, immediately put Warwickshire on the back foot, and fine innings from Iain Sutcliffe and especially Stuart Law underlined Lancashire's dominance. Nick Knight then led a home rally, but Gary Keedy and Brad Hodge then teamed up to spark a dramatic Warwickshire slide which saw them lose their last eight wickets for 53 runs. Keedy ended with 6 for 81 and Lancashire were left with a simple run chase for victory.

A pitch inspection by Chris Wood, the ECB's Pitches Consultant, and his panel followed a match at Stockton which Durham looked to be winning until Kent's Justin Kemp intervened with as sustained a piece of hitting as the grand old Championship has ever witnessed. Wood's panel decided no action should be taken on the surface, perhaps as a result of Kent's Kemp-inspired rally and then Durham's brave effort to score 364 in the last innings. The ball was on top until, at 24 for 3 in their second innings and still behind overall, Kent captain Rob Key sent in James Tredwell at No. 5 to have a swing. This he did to great effect while making 47. At 101 for 5, Kemp joined Darren Stevens in a partnership that realised 174 runs in just 18 overs. Stevens made 70 but it was South African all-rounder Kemp, with 118, who took the match away from the home side. He reached his century from a mere 56 balls, with 88 of those runs in boundaries, and when Andrew Hall and Niall O'Brien also hit out successfully Kent's total had been boosted to a scarcely believable 411. Jimmy Maher and Dale Benkenstein were initially undeterred, however, adding 141 for the fourth wicket from the unpromising beginning of 51 for 3, but Benkenstein's run out by a direct hit was a bitter blow for Durham and when Maher fell one short of a hundred it was all but over.

One of the best individual bowling displays of the summer, by Nottinghamshire's 6ft 7in Cornish paceman Charlie Shreck, blew Middlesex away in highly dramatic fashion at Trent Bridge. Shreck took 8 for 31, unsurprisingly a career-best, and was on for all ten wickets until Graeme Swann dismissed Chris Silverwood. Middlesex, with only Nick Compton reaching double figures, crumpled to an embarrassing 49 all out and Notts had won by an innings and 33 runs. Shreck, who had done most of the damage with swing, claimed match figures of 12 for 129. Compton's first innings unbeaten 69, plus a fine 66 from Owais Shah, had initially seen Middlesex start the game quite comfortably, but Shreck and Mark Ealham then bowled Notts back

Round Nine: 13–17 June 2006 Division One

WARWICKSHIRE v. LANCASHIRE – at Edgbaston

WARWICKSHIRE	First Innings			Second Innings	
NV Knight	b Cork	0		b Hodge	80
IJ Westwood	b Cork	26		c Sutton b Smith	27
MA Wagh	c Hodge b Cork	4		b Sutcliffe b Keedy	13
IJL Trott	b Smith	7		lbw b Keedy	33
JO Troughton	c Sutton b Cork	2		lbw b Keedy	7
DR Brown	c Sutton b Cork	0		lbw b Keedy	0
*T Frost	c Cork b Newby	63		(8) not out	22
MM Ali	c Sutton b Cork	5		(7) lbw b Keedy	6
HH Streak (capt)	c Law b Keedy	29		c Chilton b Hodge	1
JE Anyon	not out	18		lbw b Hodge	0
LM Daggett	b Keedy	0		c Chilton b Keedy	12
Extras	lb 13, nb 6	19		b 4, lb 14, nb 6	24
	(all out 75.4 overs)	173		(all out 83.5 overs)	225

Bowling
Cork 25-7-53-6. Hogg 19-9-27-0. Smith 15-9-31-1. Newby 10-2-31-1. Keedy 6.4-0-18-2.
Cork 14-3-43-0. Hogg 11-1-31-0. Smith 7-0-20-1. Keedy 30.5-5-81-6.
Newby 5-1-11-0. Hodge 16-5-21-3.
Fall of Wickets: 1-0, 2-12, 3-35, 4-43, 5-43, 6-82, 7-92, 8-132, 9-173
1-65, 2-96, 3-172, 4-176, 5-176, 6-184, 7-189, 8-192, 9-196

LANCASHIRE	First Innings			Second Innings	
MJ Chilton (capt)	lbw b Brown	3		(2) lbw b Streak	8
IJ Sutcliffe	c Knight b Troughton	69		(1) b Streak	8
MB Loye	c Frost b Brown	5		b Troughton	15
BJ Hodge	lbw b Streak	2		not out	20
SG Law	b Ali	121		not out	31
*LD Sutton	b Troughton	2			
KW Hogg	c sub b Streak	44			
DG Cork	c Trott b Ali	1			
TC Smith	not out	35			
OJ Newby	lbw b Anyon	19			
G Keedy	b Streak	1			
Extras	b 4, lb 7, nb 4	15		nb 2	2
	(all out 108.5 overs)	317		(3 wkts 18.4 overs)	84

Bowling
Streak 26.5-7-37-3. Brown 24-3-82-2. Daggett 10-2-37-0. Anyon 21-2-74-1.
Ali 15-4-50-2. Troughton 12-2-26-2.
Streak 8-1-30-2. Daggett 4-2-9-0. Troughton 5-0-22-1. Ali 1.4-0-23-0.
Fall of Wickets: 1-7, 2-15, 3-22, 4-187, 5-199, 6-207, 7-217, 8-265, 9-300
1-10, 2-31, 3-37

Lancashire won by 7 wickets –
Warwickshire (3 pts), Lancashire (20 pts)

DURHAM v. KENT – at Stockton-on-Tees

KENT	First Innings			Second Innings	
DP Fulton	c Mustard b Benkenstein	27		c Gibson b Onions	29
RWT Key (capt)	b Lewis ML	0		c Mustard b Franks	4
M van Jaarsveld	lbw b Gibson	59		c Mustard b Gibson	2
MJ Walker	c Maher b Gibson	2		c sub b Gibson	2
DI Stevens	c Gibson b Benkenstein	1		(6) c Benkenstein b Gibson	70
JM Kemp	lbw b Gibson	0		(7) c sub b Gibson	118
AJ Hall	b Onions	36		(8) c Maher b Iqbal	45
*NJ O'Brien	c & b Benkenstein	0		(9) c Mustard b Gibson	62
JC Tredwell	c Mustard b Onions	16		(5) c Iqbal b Breese	47
MM Patel	c Mustard b Onions	11		c Maher b Iqbal	0
A Khan	not out	0		not out	0
Extras	lb 6, w 1, nb 20	27		b 6, lb 18, nb 4	28
	(all out 61.2 overs)	179		(all out 70.4 overs)	411

Bowling
Lewis ML 6-2-24-1. Onions 10.2-3-43-3. Gibson 16-7-25-3. Benkenstein 20-10-52-3.
Breese 7-1-18-0. Iqbal 2-0-11-0.
Onions 18-3-86-1. Gibson 20.4-2-110-6. Breese 16-1-73-1. Benkenstein 4-0-39-0.
Iqbal 10-2-57-2. Muchall 2-0-22-0.
Fall of Wickets: 1-11, 2-82, 3-109, 4-112, 5-112, 6-112, 7-114, 8-161, 9-172
1-4, 2-10, 3-24, 4-87, 5-101, 6-275, 7-290, 8-411, 9-411

DURHAM	First Innings			Second Innings	
JJB Lewis	b Khan	4		lbw b Khan	8
JP Maher	c Stevens b Kemp	27		c van Jaarsveld b Khan	99
GJ Muchall	c Hall b Kemp	61		c van Jaarsveld b Patel	1
GM Scott	c O'Brien b Stevens	21		c van Jaarsveld b Khan	2
DM B'kenstein (capt)	lbw b Stevens	12		run out	70
GR Breese	c O'Brien b Khan	15		b Tredwell	31
*P Mustard	not out	41		st O'Brien b Tredwell	3
OD Gibson	c Kemp b Khan	4		c van Jaarsveld b Patel	0
G Onions	c Kemp b Stevens	8		b Patel	4
MM Iqbal	lbw b Hall	0		not out	0
ML Lewis	c & b Stevens	14		not out	1
Extras	b 2, lb 8, w 2, nb 8	20		b 7, lb 12, w 3, nb 2, p 5	29
	(all out 81.4 overs)	227		(all out 75.2 overs)	268

Bowling
Khan 23-3-70-3. Hall 18-5-39-1. Stevens 27.4-4-71-4. Kemp 12-3-33-2. Patel 1-0-4-0.
Khan 17-3-52-3. Hall 7-2-38-0. Patel 26-2-83-4. Tredwell 19.2-7-58-2.
Kemp 3-0-5-0. Stevens 3-0-8-0.
Fall of Wickets: 1-4, 2-56, 3-110, 4-135, 5-148, 6-178, 7-190, 8-207, 9-210
1-39, 2-46, 3-51, 4-192, 5-203, 6-206, 7-217, 8-221, 9-266

Kent won by 95 runs – Durham (4 pts), Kent (17 pts)

NOTTINGHAMSHIRE v. MIDDLESEX – at Trent Bridge

MIDDLESEX	First Innings			Second Innings	
ET Smith	c Read b Ealham	31		lbw b Shreck	4
BL Hutton (capt)	c Swann b Franks	22		(11) absent hurt	
OA Shah	b Franks	66		lbw b Shreck	1
NRD Compton	not out	69		c Read b Shreck	11
SB Styris	c Gallian b Shreck	20		c Ealham b Shreck	7
EJG Morgan	c Read b Shreck	7		lbw b Shreck	5
*BJM Scott	c Fleming b Shreck	6		(2) c Read b Shreck	6
J Louw	c Read b Shreck	5		(7) c Read b Shreck	0
CT Peploe	c Gallian b Ealham	9		(8) b Shreck	0
CJC Wright	c Read b Ealham	0		(9) not out	7
CEW Silverwood	b Ealham	13		(10) c Hussey b Swann	8
Extras	lb 7, w 1, nb 20	28			0
	(all out 75.5 overs)	276		(all out 27.4 overs)	49

Bowling
Shreck 27-5-98-4. Footitt 11-0-62-0. Ealham 17.5-7-48-4. Franks 20-4-61-2.
Shreck 14-5-31-8. Ealham 8-4-8-0. Franks 4-1-3-0. Swann 1.4-0-7-1.
Fall of Wickets: 1-51, 2-75, 3-178, 4-219, 5-233, 6-241, 7-249, 8-260, 9-260
1-4, 2-6, 3-17, 4-27, 5-33, 6-33, 7-33, 8-34, 9-49

NOTTS	First Innings		
DJ Bicknell	b Louw	40	
JER Gallian	c Scott b Louw	0	
WR Smith	c Shah b Silverwood	4	
SP Fleming (capt)	lbw b Louw	75	
DJ Hussey	c Morgan b Silverwood	107	
*CMW Read	c Styris b Silverwood	0	
MA Ealham	c Scott b Wright	41	
PJ Franks	c Scott b Shreck	8	
GP Swann	b Silverwood	62	
CE Shreck	c Scott b Silverwood	0	
MHA Footitt	not out	0	
Extras	b 6, lb 4, nb 11	21	
	(all out 96.4 overs)	358	

Bowling
Silverwood 22.4-5-79-5. Louw 24-7-74-3. Wright 17-2-100-2. Styris 14-5-51-0.
Peploe 19-6-44-0.
Fall of Wickets: 1-4, 2-35, 3-71, 4-158, 5-165, 6-226, 7-234, 8-351, 9-357

Nottinghamshire won by an innings and 33 runs –
Nottinghamshire (21 pts), Middlesex (5 pts)

Charlie Shreck took a second innings 8 for 31, and 12 wickets in the match, as Nottinghamshire thrashed Middlesex.

into contention and a solid batting display, headed by David Hussey's 107, earned them a halfway lead of 82. Thanks to Shreck's efforts, it was easily enough.

Division Two

Zaheer Khan almost became the first bowler to take all ten wickets in a Championship innings this season as Worcestershire eventually managed to see off a tenacious Essex side at Chelmsford. Zaheer, not required for India's tour of the West Indies, first produced a remarkable spell of bowling to reduce Essex single-handedly to 186 for 9 by the close of the second day. Worcestershire had declared midway through the day at a massive 650 for 7, a total based upon a career-best 244 by Phil Jaques and only the second hundred of his career by Gareth Batty. At first Essex seemed to be comfortable in reply as Varun Chopra and Mark Pettini built an opening

stand of 117. Then came Zaheer. Swinging the ball viciously both ways at a good pace, he induced six edges to either the keeper or the slip cordon as he picked up 9 for 28 in the space of 69 balls. The next morning dawned with all eyes on Zaheer, but Essex last man Darren Gough was dropped in his second over by Steven Davies, the wicketkeeper, and try as he might after that the Indian fast bowler could not complete the full set. Matt Mason eventually dismissed Gough for a hard-hit 50, off just 32 balls, and with Ravi Bopara standing firm from No. 3 on 67 not out, Essex had made it up to 283. Zaheer's final figures were 9 for 138, due to all the late punishment he had taken: he had, in fact, conceded 73 runs from his last 33 balls. Bopara was soon impressing again, in Essex's second innings as they followed on, as he and Ronnie Irani attempted to rebuild an innings that had subsided to 53 for 3. They put on 204 in the end, before Bopara fell for 127, and Irani was still there on 92 at the close of the third day when Essex – at 302 for 4 – were just 65 runs away from making Worcestershire bat again. Irani would have dearly wanted to have gone on to a big hundred – he had spent time off the field on day one with an understandably bad headache after inviting Worcestershire to bat first – but he could add only five runs to his overnight score. James Foster, however, made 61 and Alex Tudor struck a six and 15 fours in a superb 97-ball 93 before spearing a long hop to cover point. In the end, with some time lost to the weather on the last day too, Worcestershire were getting a little worried before finally finishing off the Essex second innings on 486. Furrowed brows soon disappeared, however, as Jaques and Vikram Solanki raced to the victory target.

Usman Afzaal led a remarkable Northamptonshire fightback against Glamorgan after the county had looked destined for defeat at the end of the second day. By then Northants, who had been dismissed for just 178 in their first innings, had struggled to 81 for 3 second time around after seeing David Hemp, Mark Wallace and Alex Wharf take Glamorgan to 354. Afzaal, however, stood firm throughout the whole of day three – finishing up at 148 not out – and he received particularly strong support from both Ben Phillips and Matt Nicholson. Afzaal only added three more runs on the final morning, but Northants' 400 had given them some hope and soon they were celebrating a headlong dash to a 168-run victory as Glamorgan's batting collapsed in a heap. Nicholson, the 31-year-old Australian seamer, took 6 for 23 and Monty Panesar's left-arm spin brought him three wickets as Glamorgan spiralled to a sad 56 all out.

Surrey's four-wicket win at Bath was also achieved against the odds, as they successfully chased down 353 on the final day. Once more, Alistair Brown was at the heart of the Surrey effort – after they had somewhat limped to 129 for 4. Brown ended on 126 not out, and was joined in a fifth-wicket stand of 189 by Rikki Clarke, who hit 77. Somerset's bowling, apart from the left-arm seam and swing of Charl Willoughby, was woeful, and the result was a major embarrassment for the home side after they had been in control of proceedings for the first three days. Peter Trego's flamboyant unbeaten 110 off 131 balls, with three sixes and 13 fours, had initially helped Somerset to rally from 38 for 4 to reach a first-innings 342, and then a century by Cameron White had kept the home side on top following Surrey's first-innings slide to 266 all out despite a stand of 106 between Brown and Mark Ramprakash, who remained 87 not out as the innings crumbled around him.

There was a tense finish at Bristol where Derbyshire, set 355 off 73 overs, finished on 286 for 8 after Travis Birt had threatened to run amok for the second time in the game. Birt had already made a career-best 181 in the first innings as Derbyshire replied to Gloucestershire's initial 456 by going past 400 themselves. Then, after Chris Taylor's 121 had set up a home-side declaration; Birt was joined by Derbyshire's Chris Taylor in a fine chase. But when Birt fell for 89 off 114 balls, featuring 14 fours, Derbyshire decided to play for the draw. In the end,

after sliding to 226 for 8, they needed a brave rearguard action by Andy Gray and Steffan Jones to earn them their four extra points. Steve Kirby was warned by the umpires for bowling two beamers, the second of which hit Gray in the chest.

Round Nine: 13–17 June 2006 Division Two

ESSEX v. WORCESTERSHIRE – at Chelmsford

WORCS	First Innings		Second Innings	
PA Jaques	c Foster b Gough	244	not out	60
SC Moore	c Foster b Phillips	62	c Chopra b Tudor	16
VS Solanki (capt)	c & b Phillips	32	not out	40
BF Smith	c Foster b Adams	50		
GA Hick	b Gough	37		
*SM Davies	c Phillips b Tudor	18		
GJ Batty	not out	112		
RJ Sillence	c & b Phillips	36		
Kabir Ali	not out	38		
MS Mason				
Z Khan				
SA Wedge				
Extras	lb 5, w 2, nb 14	21	lb 4, w 1	5
	(7 wkts dec 145.5 overs)	650	(1 wkt dec 18.4 overs)	121

Bowling
Gough 25.5-4-73-2. Tudor 26-5-115-1. Adams 29.5-5-113-1. ten Doeschate 17-1-114-0. Bopara 10-0-62-0. Phillips 38-5-168-3.
Gough 4-0-22-0. Tudor 4-0-28-1. Adams 5.4-1-34-0. Phillips 4-0-33-0. Flower 1-1-0-0.
Fall of Wickets: 1-122, 2-212, 3-358, 4-438, 5-441, 6-469, 7-549
1-26

ESSEX	First Innings		Second Innings (following on)	
V Chopra	lbw b Khan	53	c Jaques b Mason	4
ML Pettini	c Davies b Khan	48	c Hick b Batty	25
RS Bopara	not out	67	lbw b Sillence	127
A Flower	c Smith b Khan	5	st Davies b Batty	5
RC Irani (capt)	c Davies b Khan	0	c & b Khan	97
*JS Foster	c Smith b Khan	32	c Hick b Mason	61
RN ten Doeschate	c Smith b Khan	5	lbw b Khan	0
TJ Phillips	lbw b Khan	0	lbw b	31
AJ Tudor	c Hick b Khan	5	c Solanki b Sillence	93
AR Adams	lbw b Khan	16	c Hick b Mason	1
D Gough	c Smith b Mason	50	not out	12
Extras	b 9, lb 4, nb 26	39	b 4, lb 9, w 1, nb 16	30
	(all out 70.1 overs)	283	(all out 139.2 overs)	486

Bowling
Khan 27-7-138-9. Kabir Ali 13-2-48-0. Mason 11.1-2-34-1. Sillence 4-1-9-0.
Batty 14-5-38-0. Solanki 1-0-3-0.
Mason 21-7-84-3. Sillence 25.2-4-98-2. Batty 46-14-98-2. Wedge 12-0-53-1.
Khan 27-1-122-2. Solanki 8-2-18-0.
Fall of Wickets: 1-117, 2-132, 3-132, 4-134, 5-134, 6-142, 7-142, 8-150, 9-186
1-16, 2-33, 3-53, 4-257, 5-316, 6-322, 7-357, 8-455, 9-456

Worcestershire won by 9 wickets –
Essex (4 pts), Worcestershire (22 pts)

NORTHAMPTONSHIRE v. GLAMORGAN – at Northampton

NORTHANTS	First Innings		Second Innings	
CJL Rogers	lbw b Wharf	54	(2) lbw b Croft	36
SD Peters	b Franklin	3	(1) c Wallace b Harrison	6
BM Shafayat	c Hemp b Franklin	0	c Franklin b Wharf	59
U Afzaal	b Wharf	20	(5) c Powell b Croft	151
DJG Sales (capt)	b Wharf	20	(6) c Peng b Croft	42
L Klusener	c Powell b Harrison	15	(7) lbw b Croft	0
*MH Wessels	not out	28	(8) c Cherry b Cosgrove	9
BJ Phillips	c Wharf b Franklin	14	(9) c Croft b Cosker	25
MJ Nicholson	b b Franklin	6	(10) c Cosgrove b Cosker	35
MS Panesar	lbw b Croft	10	(4) c Peng b Cosker	0
JF Brown	b Wharf	0	not out	0
Extras	lb 2, w 2, nb 4	8	b 6, lb 8, w 3, nb 20	37
	(all out 56 overs)	178	(all out 142.5 overs)	400

Bowling
Harrison 23-7-61-1. Franklin 13-3-49-4. Wharf 15-0-56-3. Cosgrove 3-1-8-1. Croft 2-0-2-1.
Harrison 19-0-77-1. Franklin 14-5-27-0. Wharf 17-2-82-1. Croft 47.5-11-99-4. Cosker 39-7-86-3. Cosgrove 6-0-15-1.
Fall of Wickets: 1-4, 2-10, 3-42, 4-88, 5-106, 6-122, 7-144, 8-154, 9-177
1-6, 2-79, 3-80, 4-132, 5-206, 6-206, 7-242, 8-298, 9-381

GLAMORGAN	First Innings		Second Innings	
MJ Cosgrove	lbw b Nicholson	1	(2) b Nicholson	5
DD Cherry	c Wessels b Panesar	27	(1) c Wessels b Nicholson	2
DL Hemp	c Sales b Panesar	99	c Wessels b Nicholson	5
MJ Powell	c Rogers b Nicholson	40	c Klusener b Panesar	6
N Peng	c Wessels b Phillips	8	c Sales b Nicholson	6
*MA Wallace	lbw b Nicholson	64	c Rogers b Brown	7
JEC Franklin	lbw b Brown	3	c Shafayat b Panesar	0
AG Wharf	b Panesar	60	b Nicholson	4
RDB Croft (capt)	c Wessels b Brown	18	lbw b Nicholson	10
DS Harrison	c Shafayat b Klusener	3	c Shafayat b Panesar	1
DA Cosker	not out	20	not out	0
Extras	b 4, lb 5, nb 2	11	w 3	3
	(all out 125.4 overs)	354	(all out 26.2 overs)	56

Bowling
Nicholson 20-6-67-3. Phillips 20-6-51-1. Klusener 18-1-74-1. Brown 31.4-12-63-2. Panesar 36-7-90-3.
Nicholson 9.2-1-23-6. Phillips 5-1-15-0. Panesar 8-1-11-3. Brown 4-0-7-1.
Fall of Wickets: 1-2, 2-59, 3-135, 4-163, 5-210, 6-221, 7-275, 8-321, 9-324
1-8, 2-9, 3-21, 4-27, 5-27, 6-40, 7-40, 8-53, 9-56

Northamptonshire won by 168 runs –
Northamptonshire (17 pts), Glamorgan (7 pts)

SOMERSET v. SURREY – at Bath

SOMERSET	First Innings		Second Innings	
MJ Wood	c Batty b Bicknell	14	(2) lbw b Saker	69
AV Suppiah	lbw b Bicknell	9	(1) c Butcher b Saker	26
WJ Durston	c Butcher b Akram	7	c Batty b Saker	23
JC Hildreth	c Butcher b Akram	42	c Salisbury b Saker	0
CL White (capt)	c Salisbury b Akram	4	c Batty b Akram	108
KA Parsons	c Batty b Bicknell	54	lbw b Salisbury	4
PD Trego	c Brown b Akram	110	c Bicknell b Salisbury	4
*CM Gazzard	c Butcher b Clarke	32	c Ramprakash b Salisbury	20
RL Johnson	c Ramprakash b Bicknell	22	b Akram	0
AR Caddick	c Batty b Bicknell	16	c Clarke b Salisbury	10
CM Willoughby	not out	1	not out	1
Extras	b 4, lb 7, nb 20	31	lb 3, w 1, nb 2	6
	(all out 81.1 overs)	342	(all out 74.4 overs)	276

Bowling
Bicknell 27-7-93-5. Akram 25.1-5-81-4. Benning 5-0-43-0. Saker 8-1-37-0. Clarke 11-1-43-1. Salisbury 5-0-34-0.
Bicknell 13-3-31-0. Akram 19-5-76-2. Clarke 9-1-41-0. Saker 16-1-79-4. Benning 3-0-10-0. Salisbury 14.4-3-36-4.
Fall of Wickets: 1-17, 2-30, 3-34, 4-38, 5-135, 6-155, 7-222, 8-287, 9-331
1-40, 2-82, 3-82, 4-190, 5-232, 6-244, 7-250, 8-250, 9-271

SURREY	First Innings		Second Innings	
SA Newman	c Hildreth b Willoughby	25	c Durston b Willoughby	14
*JN Batty	c Hildreth b Willoughby	13	lbw b Johnson	27
MR Ramprakash	not out	87	c Gazzard b Willoughby	51
MA Butcher (capt)	c sub b Johnson	5	c Wood b Willoughby	19
AD Brown	lbw b Caddick	63	not out	126
R Clarke	c Gazzard b Caddick	39	c Hildreth b Durston	77
JGE Benning	c Parsons b Caddick	0	c Wood b Durston	4
MP Bicknell	b Willoughby	15	not out	5
IDK Salisbury	lbw b Willoughby	0		
NC Saker	c sub b Trego	0		
Mohammad Akram	lbw b Trego	0		
Extras	b 6, lb 5, nb 8	19	b 8, lb 12, w 5, nb 8	33
	(all out 59.5 overs)	266	(6 wkts 71.3 overs)	356

Bowling
Caddick 23-3-93-3. Willoughby 16-4-52-4. Johnson 11-1-62-1. Trego 5.5-0-24-2. Parsons 3-0-23-0. Suppiah 1-0-1-0.
Caddick 22-2-102-0. Willoughby 17-6-40-3. Johnson 10.2-1-49-1. Trego 4-0-23-0. White 7-0-40-0. Suppiah 5.4-1-36-0. Hildreth 2-0-15-0. Durston 3.3-0-31-2.
Fall of Wickets: 1-41, 2-56, 3-65, 4-171, 5-221, 6-221, 7-265, 8-265, 9-266
1-23, 2-60, 3-117, 4-129, 5-318, 6-341

Surrey won by 4 wickets – Somerset (6 pts), Surrey (19 pts)

GLOUCESTERSHIRE v. DERBYSHIRE – at Bristol

GLOS	First Innings		Second Innings	
CM Spearman	lbw b Sheikh	30	c Taylor b Birt	47
WPC Weston	retired hurt	3		
HJH Marshall	c Taylor b Gray	84	(2) b Welch	2
CG Taylor	c Pipe b Jones	39	(3) c sub b Sheikh	121
Kadeer Ali	c Di Venuto b Jones	68	(4) c Birt b Gray	55
APR Gidman	c Pipe b Gray	59	(5) not out	31
*SJ Adshead	lbw b Jones	13	(6) not out	32
MA Hardinges	c Pipe b Sheikh	0		
MCJ Ball	c Stubbings b Jones	58		
J Lewis (capt)	c Birt b Gray	57		
SP Kirby	not out	19		
Extras	lb 14, nb 12	26	b 5, lb 4, w 1, nb 2	12
	(all out 140.4 overs)	456	(4 wkts dec 61 overs)	300

Bowling
Jones 31.4-8-105-4. Hunter 14-4-58-0. Welch 31-4-83-0. Sheikh 25-4-71-2. Gray 38-7-121-3. Hassan Adnan 1-0-4-0.
Jones 6-0-36-0. Welch 10-0-54-1. Sheikh 8-0-45-1. Birt 11-0-49-1. Gray 21-2-83-1. Hassan Adnan 5-0-24-0.
Fall of Wickets: 1-47, 2-141, 3-174, 4-284, 5-312, 6-313, 7-313, 8-416, 9-456
1-4, 2-80, 3-232, 4-233

DERBYSHIRE	First Innings		Second Innings	
SD Stubbings	c Adshead b Kirby	7	(2) c Ball b Kirby	17
MJ Di Venuto	c Ball b Hardinges	37	(1) lbw b Lewis	0
CR Taylor	lbw b Kirby	9	c Lewis b Ball	51
TR Birt	c Adshead b Gidman	181	c sub b Lewis	89
Hassan Adnan	b Lewis	73	run out	29
MA Sheikh	not out	19	(8) b Kirby	0
G Welch (capt)	c Adshead b Lewis	19	c Adshead b Lewis	9
*DJ Pipe	b Kirby	11	(6) c Taylor b Ball	16
AKD Gray	c Spearman b Kirby	10	not out	23
PS Jones	not out	12	not out	23
ID Hunter				
Extras	b 4, lb 10, nb 10	24	b 5, lb 2, w 2, nb 20	29
	(8 wkts dec 110.1 overs)	402	(8 wkts 72.5 overs)	286

Bowling
Lewis 25-5-92-1. Kirby 19.1-4-87-4. Ball 25.2-10-67-1. Hardinges 15.4-5-70-1. Gidman 17-6-45-1. Kadeer Ali 7-1-22-0. Taylor 1-0-5-0.
Lewis 24.5-4-73-3. Kirby 20.4-2-97-2. Hardinges 10-2-37-0. Ball 17.2-3-72-2.
Fall of Wickets: 1-7, 2-21, 3-101, 4-316, 5-328, 6-352, 7-367, 8-377
1-6, 2-46, 3-130, 4-189, 5-214, 6-219, 7-224, 8-226

Match drawn – Gloucestershire (11 pts), Derbyshire (11 pts)

Round Ten: 20–24 June 2006

Division One

Durham put a large dent in Hampshire's Championship winning credentials by thumping Shane Warne's team in their own backyard. Their 227-run victory at the

Rose Bowl also went a long way to proving Durham's ability to compete in the first division, as well as being a massive personal triumph for Callum Thorp, their 31-year-old West Australian of British parentage. Thorp's first contribution was to come in at No. 9 on day one and carve his way to a career-best 75 that hauled Durham up to 234. Then, when Hampshire began the second day seemingly in control of the game at 123 for 3, the seamer produced career-best figures with the ball of 6 for 55 to limit the home lead to just 22 runs. Half-centuries from Jimmy Maher and Dale Benkenstein, plus some lusty strokeplay from a lower middle-order again featuring Thorp, took Durham to 353 in their second innings. Hampshire got nowhere near their fourth innings target as Thorp wrapped up the match of his life by taking a further 5 for 42 as the home side were bundled out for a paltry 104.

Both Lancashire and Sussex, by contrast, stepped up their title challenges by beating Middlesex and Yorkshire respectively. Dominic Cork was at the forefront of Lancashire's ten-wicket win at Lord's, his first-innings 4 for 61 instrumental in Middlesex being forced to follow on in reply to a Lancashire total of 505 built upon Mark Chilton's 93, Brad Hodge's high-class 161 and seventies from Luke Sutton and Kyle Hogg. Batting again, Middlesex were 47 for 1 by the close of the second day, but centuries from Ed Smith and Scott Styris held Lancashire up on day three. Cork, though, eventually finished with figures of 4 for 85 and Lancashire needed only required 83 to claim maximum points.

Round Ten: 20–24 June 2006 Division One

HAMPSHIRE v. DURHAM – at the Rose Bowl

DURHAM	First Innings		Second Innings	
JJB Lewis	c Warne b Thornely	10	c Pothas b Thornely	22
JP Maher	c Pothas b Mascarenhas	7	lbw b Mascarenhas	57
GJ Muchall	c Pothas b Mascarenhas	4	lbw b Warne	17
GM Scott	c Adams b Mascarenhas	7	lbw b Mascarenhas	40
DM B'kenstein (capt)	c Adams b Ervine	22	lbw b Thornely	61
GR Breese	c Pothas b Bruce	44	b Tremlett	5
*P Mustard	c Pothas b Tremlett	19	c Warne b Tremlett	43
OD Gibson	c Thornely b Tremlett	2	not out	37
CD Thorp	c Warne b Tremlett	75	c Carberry b Mascarenhas	28
M Davies	c Pothas b Ervine	10	b Mascarenhas	0
G Onions	not out	4	b Tremlett	4
Extras	b 5, lb 2, nb 12	19	b 6, lb 10, w 1, nb 22	39
	(all out 68.2 overs)	234	(all out 113.1 overs)	353

Bowling
Bruce 8–1–33–1. Mascarenhas 15–7–25–3. Tremlett 13.2–1–51–3. Ervine 16–3–45–2. Thornely 5–3–17–1. Warne 11–1–56–0.
Mascarenhas 32–5–93–4. Tremlett 28.1–5–101–3. Ervine 8–2–23–0. Thornely 24–10–61–2. Adams 4–0–13–0. Warne 17–1–46–1.
Fall of Wickets: 1–10, 2–14, 3–22, 4–56, 5–60, 6–92, 7–108, 8–149, 9–163
1–50, 2–86, 3–128, 4–192, 5–197, 6–278, 7–284, 8–339, 9–344

HAMPSHIRE	First Innings		Second Innings	
JHK Adams	lbw b Davies	29	c Thorp b Benkenstein	32
MA Carberry	c Mustard b Thorp	20	c Muchall b Onions	12
JP Crawley	b Thorp	93	c Maher b Thorp	31
DJ Thornely	c Mustard b Gibson	21	b Benkenstein	4
CC Benham	c Mustard b Thorp	13	c Lewis b Thorp	0
SM Ervine	c Mustard b Thorp	0	st Mustard b Benkenstein	0
AD Mascarenhas	c Mustard b Gibson	4	(8) c Scott b Thorp	0
*N Pothas	c Mustard b Onions	17	(7) c Breese b Thorp	7
SK Warne (capt)	c sub b Thorp	25	b Thorp	12
CT Tremlett	c Lewis b Thorp	12	b Onions	0
JTA Bruce	not out	0	not out	0
Extras	b 5, lb 7, nb 13	25	b 1, lb 2, w 3	6
	(all out 76.3 overs)	256	(all out 34.4 overs)	104

Bowling
Gibson 20–5–79–2. Onions 16–6–37–1. Davies 8–5–9–1. Thorp 18.3–7–55–6.
Benkenstein 11–3–37–0. Breese 3–0–27–0.
Gibson 11–5–27–0. Onions 6.4–1–16–2. Thorp 12–3–42–5. Benkenstein 5–2–16–3.
Fall of Wickets: 1–59, 2–59, 3–91, 4–126, 5–134, 6–151, 7–209, 8–244, 9–245
1–35, 2–71, 3–83, 4–83, 5–83, 6–83, 7–83, 8–97, 9–104

Durham won by 227 runs – Hampshire (5 pts), Durham (18 pts)

MIDDLESEX v. LANCASHIRE – at Lord's

LANCASHIRE	First Innings		Second Innings	
MJ Chilton (capt)	c Shah b Silverwood	93	(2) not out	39
IJ Sutcliffe	c Shah b Styris	40	(1) not out	34
MB Loye	c Styris b Louw	4		
BJ Hodge	b Mohammad Ali	161		
SG Law	c Mohammad Ali b Styris	17		
*LD Sutton	c Smith b Styris	72		
KW Hogg	c Mohammad Ali b Styris	70		
DG Cork	lbw b Styris	1		
TC Smith	lbw b Weekes	2		
OJ Newby	b Styris	15		
G Keedy	not out	8		
Extras	lb 7, w 1, nb 4	22	b 5, lb 3, w 1, nb 4	13
	(all out 142.3 overs)	505	(0 wkts 21.3 overs)	86

Bowling
Silverwood 30–5–105–1. Louw 33–8–121–1. Mohammad Ali 28–5–117–1.
Styris 27.3–6–71–6. Peploe 12–2–45–0. Weekes 12–1–29–1.
Louw 5–0–27–0. Silverwood 5–1–13–0. Peploe 6–2–18–0. Weekes 5.3–0–20–0.
Fall of Wickets: 1–71, 2–80, 3–198, 4–279, 5–350, 6–467, 7–469, 8–472, 9–484

MIDDLESEX	First Innings		Second Innings (following on)	
ET Smith	lbw b Cork	0	lbw b Cork	114
NRD Compton	b Cork	8	c Sutton b Smith	9
OA Shah	b Smith	19	(4) c Sutcliffe b Hodge	36
EJG Morgan	c Smith b Cork	4	(5) b Keedy	2
SB Styris (capt)	lbw b Hogg	19	(6) c sub b Cork	133
PN Weekes	c Sutton b Keedy	22	(7) c Chilton b Keedy	10
*DC Nash	not out	52	(8) b Keedy	39
J Louw	c Sutcliffe b Cork	20	(9) c Smith b Cork	2
CT Peploe	c Sutton b Hogg	0	(3) c Cork b Hodge	46
CEW Silverwood	c Loye b Newby	11	not out	17
Mohammad Ali	c Sutton b Newby	0	c sub b Cork	0
Extras	lb 2, nb 4	6	b 8, lb 7, w 1, nb 2	18
	(all out 51.3 overs)	161	(all out 108.4 overs)	426

Bowling
Cork 15–2–61–4. Smith 13–4–27–1. Hogg 10–2–35–2. Newby 5.3–1–16–2. Keedy 8–2–20–1.
Cork 26.4–3–85–4. Smith 20–3–54–1. Newby 16–2–68–0. Hogg 10–1–58–0.
Keedy 23–2–72–3. Hodge 11–1–54–2. Chilton 2–0–15–0.
Fall of Wickets: 1–0, 2–29, 3–33, 4–35, 5–72, 6–80, 7–126, 8–135, 9–161
1–26, 2–153, 3–213, 4–215, 5–227, 6–237, 7–371, 8–393, 9–426

Lancashire won by 10 wickets – Middlesex (1 pt), Lancashire (22 pts)

SUSSEX v. YORKSHIRE – at Arundel Castle

YORKSHIRE	First Innings		Second Innings	
C White (capt)	lbw b Mushtaq Ahmed	104	b Mushtaq Ahmed	49
MP Vaughan	b Lewry	14	(7) lbw b Yasir Arafat	4
A McGrath	lbw b Lewry	0	c Montgomerie b Lewry	58
MJ Lumb	lbw b Kirtley	2	c Adams b Martin-Jenkins	15
DS Lehmann	c Prior b Yasir Arafat	12	not out	130
AW Gale	c Prior b Kirtley	10	(2) b Lewry	4
*GL Brophy	c Prior b Lewry	4	(6) c Adams b Mushtaq Ahmed	0
RKJ Dawson	b Mushtaq Ahmed	56	b Yasir Arafat	4
JN Gillespie	c Adams b Mushtaq Ahmed	12	c Prior b Lewry	10
MJ Hoggard	b Lewry	4	b Kirtley	1
GJ Kruis	not out	0	lbw b Mushtaq Ahmed	0
Extras	lb 2, nb 8, nb 10	20	b 4, lb 7, w 1, nb 4	16
	(all out 78.1 overs)	238	(all out 78.4 overs)	287

Bowling
Lewry 19–6–54–4. Kirtley 20–7–53–2. Yasir Arafat 9–2–40–1. Martin-Jenkins 11–5–19–0.
Mushtaq Ahmed 18.1–3–58–3. Yardy 1–0–4–0.
Lewry 21–1–67–3. Kirtley 13–3–41–1. Yasir Arafat 11–3–36–2.
Mushtaq Ahmed 27.4–5–109–3. Martin-Jenkins 6–1–23–1.
Fall of Wickets: 1–37, 2–37, 3–48, 4–67, 5–92, 6–101, 7–200, 8–229, 9–238
1–13, 2–101, 3–135, 4–139, 5–143, 6–148, 7–162, 8–204, 9–266

SUSSEX	First Innings	
RR Montgomerie	c Lumb b Gillespie	9
CD Hopkinson	b Gillespie	25
MH Yardy	lbw b Kruis	12
MW Goodwin	c Brophy b Kruis	235
CJ Adams (capt)	c McGrath b Gillespie	107
*MJ Prior	c McGrath b Kruis	4
RSC Martin-Jenkins	b McGrath	32
Yasir Arafat	run out	86
RJ Kirtley	b Gillespie	14
Mushtaq Ahmed	c Hoggard b Dawson	11
JD Lewry	not out	0
Extras	b 3, lb 4, w 1, nb 7	15
	(all out 151 overs)	550

Bowling
Hoggard 22–5–75–0. Gillespie 35–9–89–4. Kruis 35–6–108–3. McGrath 21–1–107–1.
Dawson 20–5–82–1. Lehmann 17–0–76–0. Lumb 1–0–6–0.
Fall of Wickets: 1–13, 2–33, 3–87, 4–341, 5–352, 6–401, 7–455, 8–500, 9–517

Sussex won by an innings and 25 runs – Sussex (22 pts), Yorkshire (3 pts)

KENT v. NOTTINGHAMSHIRE – at Canterbury

KENT	First Innings	
DP Fulton	c Read b Sidebottom	65
RWT Key (capt)	c Read b Ealham	31
M van Jaarsveld	lbw b Shreck	108
MJ Walker	b Swann	141
SJ Cook	lbw b Sidebottom	8
DI Stevens	c Smith b Shreck	7
NJ Dexter	not out	131
AJ Hall	not out	68
*NJ O'Brien		
MM Patel		
A Khan		
Extras	b 8, lb 19, nb 14	41
	(6 wkts dec 176 overs)	600

Bowling
Sidebottom 32–10–76–2. Shreck 37–10–124–2. Smith 28–7–89–0. Ealham 29–3–97–1.
Swann 46–7–152–1. Hussey 4–0–35–0.
Fall of Wickets: 1–72, 2–118, 3–305, 4–329, 5–344, 6–467

NOTTS	First Innings		Second Innings (following on)	
DJ Bicknell	c Patel b Khan	85	c Hall b Patel	25
JER Gallian	c van Jaarsveld b Cook	7	b Dexter	42
D Alleyne	b Hall	41	b Cook	10
SP Fleming (capt)	st O'Brien b Patel	51	not out	63
DJ Hussey	lbw b Khan	32	not out	20
*CMW Read	lbw b Hall	67		
MA Ealham	c van Jaarsveld b Khan	4		
GP Swann	b Hall	85		
RJ Sidebottom	c van Jaarsveld b Khan	31		
GJ Smith	c van Jaarsveld b Khan	0		
CE Shreck	not out	0		
Extras	b 4, lb 19, w 3, nb 10	36	b 5, nb 2	7
	(all out 150.1 overs)	439	(3 wkts 70 overs)	167

Bowling
Khan 36–11–100–5. Hall 31.1–5–100–3. Cook 22–7–66–1. Patel 45–6–103–1.
Walker 4–1–6–0. Stevens 8–4–16–0. Dexter 3–0–16–0. van Jaarsveld 1–0–9–0.
Hall 5–1–6–0. Khan 6–2–12–0. Patel 20–6–44–1. Cook 8–1–18–1. Dexter 13–5–26–1.
Walker 9–1–36–0. Stevens 4–0–7–0. van Jaarsveld 3–0–7–0. Fulton 1–0–3–0. Key 1–0–3–0.
Fall of Wickets: 1–20, 2–109, 3–194, 4–194, 5–249, 6–293, 7–332, 8–414, 9–414
1–46, 2–57, 3–132

Match drawn – Kent (10 pts), Nottinghamshire (9 pts)

Callum Thorp had the match of his life, taking 11 wickets and hitting 103 runs from the lower order, as Durham won a famous victory at Hampshire.

Sussex remained six points behind Lancashire in second place despite themselves picking up 22 points from their innings and 25-run, three-day dismantling of Yorkshire at Arundel. Jason Lewry and Mushtaq Ahmed were the bowlers who mainly troubled the visitors, although Craig White in the first innings and Darren Lehmann on the third day both made fine hundreds. In between, however, Murray Goodwin hit a wonderful, fluent 235 and put on 254 for Sussex's fourth wicket with his captain Chris Adams, who made 107. When Yasir Arafat, the 24-year-old Pakistani fast bowling all-rounder, then struck 86 off 135 balls on his Championship debut, Sussex's first-innings total was pushed up to 550 and their lead beyond 300. England

captain Michael Vaughan was off the field for the two sessions after lunch on the second day, clearly troubled again by his chronic knee injury.

A placid pitch at Canterbury, and two largely toothless attacks, made for a bore draw between Kent and Nottinghamshire. Kent, though, still had their chances after running up a mammoth 600 for 6 declared on the back of excellent hundreds from Martin van Jaarsveld, Matthew Walker and the promising Neil Dexter. Dropped catches reprieved Darren Bicknell three times during his fighting 85, and Stephen Fleming was missed on both 0 and 31. Finally, Graeme Swann had made only 22 of his eventual 85 when he was also put down by Dexter at square leg. Notts still had to follow on, after totalling 439, but Amjad Khan's figures could have been even more impressive if catches had stuck. The final day became an academic exercise.

Division Two

Graeme Hick became the first Worcestershire player, and only the eighth batsman in history, to make 100 hundreds for a county when he hit the Northamptonshire attack for 139 at New Road. It was also the 130th first-class century of his remarkable career, putting him one ahead of Sir Len Hutton and into eighth place in the all-time list (see panel on page 113), and during the course of this innings he moved into the top 20 all-time run-scorers. The last man to reach the landmark of 100 hundreds for a county, Geoff Boycott, did so in August 1985 – a month before Hick made his own first Championship century. The run-scoring exploits in county cricket of Phil Jaques, moreover, are almost Hickesque: his 202 in this eventual innings and 222-run battering of Northants took the Australian's Championship tally to 4,807 in three and a half seasons at an average of 65.85. His 2006 summer tally was now 921 runs at 102.33. Thanks mainly to Jaques and Hick, Worcestershire ran up 543 for 9 declared – their lowest first innings total for four games – and then humiliated their opponents by dismissing them for a pathetic 67 in reply. Zaheer Khan took 5 for 27 and Stuart Wedge also picked up three cheap wickets, and at 4 for 2 in their second innings – after being invited to follow on – Northants looked as if all fight had been drained from them. But at least Bilal Shafayat and Usman Afzaal saw it to 76 for 2 by the close. However, the next day, Matt Mason and Gareth Batty worked their way through a line-up in which only Riki Wessels offered much further resistance.

A burst of 6 for 38 on the third afternoon by Andy Bichel, the former Australian Test bowler making his Championship debut for Essex, blew away Derbyshire's resistance in what – until then – had been a closely-fought affair. Darren Gough also picked up two wickets and Essex, who had battled hard through 121 overs in their first innings to get past Derbyshire's own first innings of 312, were left with a straightforward win target. Travis Birt's 130, from 198 balls, was the highlight of the opening day – with the Tasmanian going past 1,000 runs for all cricket in the process.

Gloucestershire withstood the loss of Hamish Marshall, to a broken finger suffered in the field on the opening day, and a sizeable first innings deficit, to emerge with a seven-wicket victory of great merit at Leicester. Jon Lewis was once again to the fore with the ball, taking eight wickets in the match, but it was the composed batting of Kadeer Ali and Alex Gidman on the third evening and fourth morning which set up a win that was completed with a flourish by Ian Harvey's 99-ball 72 not out. Kadeer scored a fine 83 and Gidman batted four and a quarter hours for his unbeaten 115 as Gloucestershire repelled a Leicestershire attack in which Stuart Broad had taken a career-best 5 for 83 in the first innings.

Surrey felt the wrath of a Welsh crowd at Swansea when, unaccountably, they decided to bat on in their second innings deep into the final day and pass up the chance of setting up a meaningful Glamorgan run chase. Glamorgan's supporters, desperate to see their own team kick-start a season so far short on achievement, had to settle instead for the sight of Mark Cosgrove thumping 80 off just 48 balls, with a six and 16 fours. Perhaps that was his way of registering his dissatisfaction with an eventual

Round Ten: 20–24 June 2006 Division Two

WORCESTERSHIRE v. NORTHAMPTONSHIRE – at Worcester

WORCS	First Innings	
PA Jaques	c sub b Panesar	202
SC Moore	run out	29
VS Solanki (capt)	c Peters b Nicholson	23
BF Smith	run out	21
GA Hick	b Panesar	139
*SM Davies	b Phillips	14
GJ Batty	b Nicholson	68
RJ Sillence	b Nicholson	18
Z Khan	b Panesar	3
MS Mason	not out	0
SA Wedge		
Extras	b 4, lb 13, w 5, nb 4	26
	(9 wkts dec 146.3 overs)	543

Bowling
Nicholson 38.3-8-127-3. Phillips 32-4-121-1. Klusener 2-0-11-0. Ganguly 9-3-23-0. Panesar 58-10-211-3. Shafayat 7-0-33-0.
Fall of Wickets: 1-43, 2-93, 3-139, 4-386, 5-410, 6-487, 7-514, 8-539, 9-543

NORTHANTS	First Innings		Second Innings (following on)	
SD Peters	b Mason	9	c Smith b Khan	4
RA White	lbw b Khan	0	c Davies b Mason	0
BM Shafayat	c Davies b Khan	0	c Hick b Mason	49
U Afzaal	c Batty b Khan	8	c Hick b Mason	27
DJG Sales (capt)	c Smith b Khan	2	c Mason b Batty	38
SC Ganguly	b Khan	2	c Jaques b Mason	0
L Klusener	lbw b Wedge	21	run out	28
*MH Wessels	c Hick b Mason	12	not out	59
BJ Phillips	lbw b Wedge	1	c & b Batty	10
MJ Nicholson	c Hick b Wedge	0	c Moore b Batty	19
MS Panesar	not out	0	b Mason	12
Extras	b 4, w 2	6	b 5, lb 2, w 1	8
	(all out 25.2 overs)	67	(all out 76.2 overs)	254

Bowling
Khan 8-1-27-5. Mason 9.2-4-19-2. Wedge 5-2-11-3. Sillence 2-0-6-0. Batty 1-1-0-0.
Khan 21-9-59-1. Mason 20.2-5-59-5. Wedge 10-1-44-0. Sillence 8-2-33-0. Batty 16-4-52-3. Solanki 1-1-0-0.
Fall of Wickets: 1-1, 2-1, 3-12, 4-22, 5-28, 6-40, 7-54, 8-67, 9-67
1-4, 2-4, 3-84, 4-100, 5-106, 6-151, 7-153, 8-185, 9-221

Worcestershire won by an innings and 222 runs –
Worcestershire (22 pts), Northamptonshire (1 pt)

DERBYSHIRE v. ESSEX – at Derby

DERBYSHIRE	First Innings		Second Innings	
MJ Di Venuto	c Middlebrook b Bopara	48	(2) c Flower b Bichel	1
SD Stubbings	c Foster b Tudor	23	(1) c Foster b Bichel	48
Hassan Adnan	lbw b Tudor	21	c Tudor b Gough	3
TR Birt	c Bopara b Bichel	130	b Bichel	3
AG Botha	c Flower b Middlebrook	2	lbw b Bichel	2
G Welch (capt)	b Tudor	2	lbw b Bichel	2
MA Sheikh	run out	37	c Middlebrook b Phillips	46
*DJ Pipe	c Foster b Tudor	0	lbw b Bichel	0
GG Wagg	c Irani b Bopara	5	b Middlebrook	3
AKD Gray	lbw b Bichel	12	c Foster b Gough	29
PS Jones	not out	4	not out	5
Extras	b 4, lb 8, w 6, nb 10	28	b 8, lb 10, nb 4	22
	(all out 99 overs)	312	(all out 55.3 overs)	162

Bowling
Gough 14-2-57-0. Tudor 22-6-76-4. Bopara 9.5-3-36-2. Bichel 17.1-5-54-2.
Phillips 8-0-22-0. Middlebrook 28-9-55-1.
Gough 15-6-33-2. Bichel 17.5-5-38-6. Middlebrook 12-5-23-1. Tudor 6-0-27-0.
Phillips 5.3-1-23-1.
Fall of Wickets: 1-65, 2-100, 3-129, 4-134, 5-141, 6-235, 7-235, 8-266, 9-307
1-4, 2-7, 3-12, 4-14, 5-20, 6-92, 7-92, 8-97, 9-152

ESSEX	First Innings		Second Innings	
V Chopra	c Di Venuto b Sheikh	65	lbw b Gray	39
ML Pettini	c Pipe b Wagg	30	c Di Venuto b Botha	40
RS Bopara	c Di Venuto b Welch	50	not out	6
A Flower	lbw b Gray	84	not out	6
RC Irani (capt)	c Pipe b Gray	8		
*JS Foster	b Wagg	19		
JD Middlebrook	c Birt b Wagg	31		
AJ Bichel	c Pipe b Jones	35		
TJ Phillips	c Pipe b Welch	11		
AJ Tudor	c Botha b Jones	26	w 1	1
D Gough	not out	1		
Extras	b 3, lb 12, w 1, nb 10	26		
	(all out 121 overs)	386	(2 wkts 19 overs)	92

Bowling
Jones 22-2-120-3. Wagg 26-4-74-3. Welch 26-8-58-2. Sheikh 25-6-50-1.
Botha 10-2-32-0. Gray 12-4-37-1.
Jones 6-0-24-0. Wagg 3-1-17-0. Gray 6-0-27-1. Botha 4-0-24-1.
Fall of Wickets: 1-92, 2-123, 3-223, 4-252, 5-272, 6-298, 7-313, 8-335, 9-375
1-78, 2-82

Essex won by 8 wickets –
Derbyshire (6 pts), Essex (21 pts)

LEICESTERSHIRE v. GLOUCESTERSHIRE – at Leicester

LEICESTERSHIRE	First Innings		Second Innings	
DDJ Robinson (capt)	c sub b Kirby	4	lbw b Lewis	7
JK Maunders	lbw b Lewis	6	lbw b Lewis	6
TJ New	c Adshead b Lewis	52	(4) b Gidman	25
HD Ackerman	c Spearman b Lewis	58	(5) c Spearman b Ball	59
D Mongia	b Gidman	7	(6) b Lewis	62
JL Sadler	c Adshead b Kirby	82	(7) not out	24
*PA Nixon	c Spearman b Hardinges	21	(8) c Adshead b Lewis	0
DD Masters	c Spearman b Shome	19	(3) c Adshead b Ball	7
CW Henderson	c Taylor b Lewis	40	(3) b Hardinges	5
SCJ Broad	c Adshead b Harvey	12	c Ball b Kirby	0
AR Griffith	not out	10	c Spearman b Ball	13
Extras	b 4, lb 13, w 2, nb 10	29	b 1, lb 4, nb 18	23
	(all out 109.4 overs)	371	(all out 76.3 overs)	233

Bowling
Lewis 27.4-6-93-4. Kirby 18-4-78-2. Harvey 12-6-25-1. Hardinges 23-5-82-1.
Gidman 16-3-40-2. Ball 13-3-36-0.
Lewis 23-12-36-4. Kirby 20-3-73-1. Hardinges 10-2-44-1. Harvey 7-2-16-0.
Gidman 6-0-23-1. Ball 10.3-3-36-3.
Fall of Wickets: 1-11, 2-17, 3-139, 4-146, 5-146, 6-205, 7-267, 8-290, 9-313
1-16, 2-17, 3-48, 4-88, 5-194, 6-194, 7-194, 8-215, 9-216

GLOS	First Innings		Second Innings	
CM Spearman	lbw b Masters	35	c Mongia b Masters	36
Kadeer Ali	b Griffith	42	c Nixon b Masters	83
CG Taylor	c Nixon b Broad	29	c Nixon b Masters	1
APR Gidman	b Mongia	32	not out	115
IJ Harvey	c Mongia b Maunders	17	not out	72
*SJ Adshead	b Broad	49		
MA Hardinges	c Sadler b Broad	24		
MCJ Ball	c Sadler b Broad	1		
J Lewis (capt)	b Broad	31		
SP Kirby	not out	2		
HJH Marshall	not out	0		
Extras	b 1, lb 11, nb 8	20	lb 8, w 6, nb 2	16
	(9 wkts dec 78.4 overs)	282	(3 wkts 81.5 overs)	323

Bowling
Griffith 21-3-49-1. Broad 19.4-2-83-5. Masters 19-3-78-1. Maunders 7-0-27-1.
Mongia 9-1-23-1. Henderson 3-0-10-0.
Griffith 19-2-81-0. Broad 15-1-78-0. Masters 17-3-57-3. Mongia 8-1-23-0.
Henderson 20.5-3-66-0. Maunders 2-0-10-0.
Fall of Wickets: 1-53, 2-108, 3-118, 4-144, 5-190, 6-233, 7-235, 8-269, 9-282
1-55, 2-60, 3-196

Gloucestershire won by 7 wickets –
Leicestershire (7 pts), Gloucestershire (19 pts)

GLAMORGAN v. SURREY – at Swansea

SURREY	First Innings		Second Innings	
SA Newman	lbw b Wharf	22	lbw b Croft	27
*JN Batty	c Hemp b Harrison	0	c Cosker b Wharf	73
MR Ramprakash	c Wallace b Harrison	20	b Wharf	156
MA Butcher (capt)	lbw b Croft	136	c Peng b Cosker	1
AD Brown	c Wharf b Harrison	4	b Wharf	73
R Clarke	c Peng b Harrison	14	b Wharf	5
JGE Benning	c Wallace b Wharf	11	lbw b Croft	29
MP Bicknell	c Wharf b Watkins	59	c Powell b Croft	26
IDK Salisbury	b Wharf	42	not out	26
Mohammad Akram	not out	9		
DS Harrison			(10) not out	16
Extras	b 4, lb 2, w 2, nb 2	10	lb 10, w 11	21
	(all out 83.3 overs)	348	(8 wkts dec 141.2 overs)	448

Bowling
Harrison 22-2-97-4. Wharf 26.3-1-126-3. Watkins 10-0-53-1. Cosgrove 3-0-13-0.
Cosker 9-2-20-0. Croft 13-4-33-2.
Harrison 23-5-73-0. Wharf 25-4-77-4. Croft 39-5-140-3. Cosgrove 8-1-25-0.
Cosker 35-2-96-1. Watkins 11-2-37-0.
Fall of Wickets: 1-1, 2-34, 3-67, 4-71, 5-85, 6-98, 7-250, 8-286, 9-316
1-54, 2-179, 3-182, 4-312, 5-312, 6-364, 7-400, 8-404

GLAMORGAN	First Innings		Second Innings	
MJ Cosgrove	c Ramprakash b Clarke	63	st Batty b Doshi	80
RE Watkins	c Batty b Clarke	3	st Batty b Doshi	48
DL Hemp	c Ramprakash b Doshi	21	not out	21
MJ Powell	c Brown b Doshi	27	not out	4
N Peng	lbw b Akram	59		
RN Grant	b Doshi	2		
*MA Wallace	lbw b Salisbury	0		
AG Wharf	c Clarke b Akram	60		
RDB Croft (capt)	c Salisbury b Akram	72		
DS Harrison	b Clarke	36		
DA Cosker	not out	28		
Extras	b 14, lb 3, nb 6	23	b 8, lb 1, nb 6	15
	(all out 111.3 overs)	410	(2 wkts 33 overs)	168

Bowling
Bicknell 16-3-49-0. Akram 21.3-4-64-3. Doshi 29-3-106-3. Clarke 14-0-93-3.
Salisbury 31-4-81-1.
Bicknell 4-1-14-0. Akram 5-0-25-0. Doshi 10-0-49-2. Clarke 8-0-44-0.
Salisbury 5-1-22-0. Clarke 3-0-5-0.
Fall of Wickets: 1-82, 2-91, 3-127, 4-144, 5-146, 6-147, 7-266, 8-267, 9-355
1-108, 2-162

Match drawn – Glamorgan (12 pts), Surrey (10 pts)

declaration that set Glamorgan 387 in a mere 40 overs. Cosgrove had also made 63 from 64 balls first time around, as Glamorgan went past Surrey's own first innings total of 348 with Nicky Peng, Alex Wharf and Robert Croft also contributing half-centuries. Surrey, in fact, had been in deep trouble on the opening day at 98 for 6 – with David Harrison grabbing three prime wickets in 15 balls – before skipper Mark Butcher compiled a masterly 136 from 175 balls, featuring a six and 20 fours, and was joined in a seventh-wicket stand of 152 by Martin Bicknell. Mark Ramprakash then hit the 83rd first-class hundred of his career, and became the first batsman past 1,000 first-class runs for the season, as he and Alistair Brown made the game safe for Surrey by putting on 130 for the fourth wicket in the county's second innings. Ramprakash, however, provoked Welsh ire by pottering along from his overnight 110 to an eventual 156, as Surrey showed no desire to make a game of it on that final day.

FIRST-CLASS HUNDREDS

100 first-class hundreds for a county:

Jack Hobbs   144
(Surrey)

Phil Mead   138
(Hampshire)

Frank Woolley   122
(Kent)

Patsy Hendren   119
(Middlesex)

Wally Hammond   113
(Gloucestershire)

Herbert Sutcliffe   112
(Yorkshire)

Geoff Boycott   103
(Yorkshire)

Graeme Hick   100
(Worcestershire)

The top eight places in the all-time list of first-class hundreds now reads:

Hobbs	197
Hendren	170
Hammond	167
Mead	153
Boycott	151
Sutcliffe	149
Woolley	145
Hick	130

Statistics correct at this stage of the Championship (22 June 2006)

Modern master: Graeme Hick joined an elite list with his 100th first-class hundred for Worcestershire.

OF MIDDLESEX

In the 1980s Middlesex were very much the team of Mike Gatting and John Emburey, and it was a golden era even for a club with a history of being one of the leading lights of English cricket. But it was Mike Brearley, in fact, who had laid the foundations of prolonged success by leading the county to their Championship wins of 1976, 1977, 1980 and 1982 – and to Gillette Cup victories in both 1977 and 1980.

Gatting, however, took over the captaincy in 1983 and immediately led Middlesex to their first Benson and Hedges Cup win that summer. Then, in chronological order, came the NatWest Trophy (1984), the Championship (1985), the Benson and Hedges Cup once more (1986), NatWest Trophy again (1988), Championship (1990), Sunday League (1992) and Championship yet again in 1993.

With Emburey as his on-field lieutenant, and with fellow England players of the calibre of Phil Edmonds, Clive Radley, Paul Downton, Norman Cowans, Angus Fraser and Mark Ramprakash around him, Gatting inspired an era of remarkably sustained success. He led the team until 1997, in fact, when Ramprakash succeeded him, and as player and captain Gatting was associated with no fewer than 14 title wins.

The last dozen years have not brought much further success, although Middlesex as a club are still producing leading English cricketers. Andrew Strauss, who made his county debut in 1998 and led the side during the 2002 and 2004 seasons, was elevated to the England captaincy (albeit on a temporary basis) in the summer of 2006 and, since scoring a hundred on debut at Lord's in 2004, has been one of the most successful opening batsmen in world cricket.

Though Owais Shah, Jamie Dalrymple and Ed Joyce have all won England recognition in 2006, Middlesex are in urgent need of producing a new side capable of winning trophies. Perhaps the return of a Compton to Lord's as South African-born Nick, grandson of the legendary Denis, has broken into the side this year, will herald a return to the glory days.

Mike Gatting and Justin Langer congratulate each other at Southgate in 1998 after posting a record Middlesex first wicket partnership. When Langer was out to the suffering Essex bowlers for 166 they had put on 372 – beating by five runs the previous record held by Wilf Slack and Graham Barlow.

Round Eleven: 13–17 July 2006

Division One

Sussex captain Chris Adams decided to bat on for six overs on the final morning of the match against Kent at Hove, probably as a result of being without Pakistan leg spinner Mushtaq Ahmed who had a neck injury, but this extreme caution cost him dear in the end as Kent struggled to see out time with just three wickets remaining. A sick David Fulton battled 15 overs for two runs but Kent had still slid to 245 for 7 when Tyron Henderson joined the staunch Matthew Walker to leave Sussex ultimately denied. It was difficult to see why Adams delayed his declaration while 25 more runs were accrued, and he should have declared the previous evening rather than waiting so long and leaving Kent an unlikely 457 in 88 overs. With Mushtaq, however, Sussex would undoubtedly have won although the 20-year-old Ollie Rayner picked up his first three Championship wickets in Kent's second innings. A dedicated 134 from Michael Yardy, and an explosive 82 from 108 balls by Murray Goodwin, had put Sussex in initial control, although Walker and Darren Stevens, who made a fine 118, fashioned a decent Kent reply. Further hundreds from both Goodwin and Matt Prior, who hit two sixes and 13 fours, then ensured an impregnable position which still failed to produce a victory.

Yorkshire produced the only first division victory in this round of games, by beating Durham by 145 runs at the Riverside, and it was an important result. Jason Gillespie led the way on the final day, picking up a season's best 6 for 37, but the 201 runs which

Round Eleven: 13–17 July 2006 Division One

SUSSEX v. KENT – at Hove

SUSSEX	First Innings		Second Innings	
RR Montgomerie	lbw b Khan	0	(2) st O'Brien b Patel	69
CD Hopkinson	b Henderson	20	(1) c & b Patel	57
MH Yardy	c O'Brien b Patel	134	lbw b Khan	4
MW Goodwin	st O'Brien b Patel	82	c Tredwell b Patel	122
CJ Adams (capt)	lbw b Khan	3		
*MJ Prior	c Tredwell b Bravo	15	(5) c Tredwell b Patel	108
LJ Wright	c Key b Patel	0	(6) lbw b Stevens	3
Yasir Arafat	c Stevens b Patel	31	(7) not out	5
OP Rayner	st O'Brien b Tredwell	23	(8) not out	5
RJ Kirtley	lbw b Patel	36		
JD Lewry	not out	17		
Extras	b 5, lb 17, w 2, nb 14	38	b 5, lb 3, nb 12	20
	(all out 121.4 overs)	399	(6 wkts dec 89 overs)	393

Bowling
Khan 28-3-75-3. Henderson 20-4-57-1. Bravo 16-1-74-1. Stevens 9-3-14-0. Tredwell 17-1-56-1. Patel 37.4-7-101-4.
Khan 16-2-60-1. Henderson 8-2-30-0. Patel 36-4-122-4. Bravo 6-0-51-0. Tredwell 17-1-90-0. Walker 4-0-26-0. Stevens 2-1-6-1.
Fall of Wickets: 1-0, 2-39, 3-180, 4-199, 5-223, 6-224, 7-268, 8-308, 9-377
1-129, 2-138, 3-152, 4-370, 5-383, 6-383

KENT	First Innings		Second Innings	
DP Fulton	lbw b Lewry	0	(8) c Goodwin b Rayner	2
RWT Key (capt)	run out	16	c & b Rayner	36
M van Jaarsveld	b Kirtley	10	c & b Wright	23
MJ Walker	c Prior b Yasir Arafat	87	not out	70
DI Stevens	c Prior b Yasir Arafat	118	b Rayner	43
DJ Bravo	c Kirtley b Yasir Arafat	31	c Prior b Yasir Arafat	31
JC Tredwell	lbw b Yasir Arafat	6	lbw b Yasir Arafat	0
*NJ O'Brien	c Wright b Yasir Arafat	16	(1) lbw b Kirtley	13
T Henderson	c Prior b Lewry	4	not out	31
MM Patel	c Prior b Kirtley	0		
A Khan	not out	10		
Extras	b 11, lb 17, w 1, nb 8	37	b 14, lb 3, nb 14	31
	(all out 102.4 overs)	336	(7 wkts 90 overs)	280

Bowling
Lewry 27-8-54-2. Kirtley 18.4-3-72-2. Wright 12-6-33-0. Yasir Arafat 29-3-84-5. Rayner 10-1-47-0. Yardy 5-0-16-0. Adams 1-0-2-0.
Lewry 13-4-29-0. Kirtley 15-3-37-1. Yasir Arafat 17-3-58-2. Rayner 31-15-89-3. Wright 6-0-21-1. Yardy 8-2-29-0.
Fall of Wickets: 1-0, 2-17, 3-34, 4-222, 5-266, 6-280, 7-297, 8-312, 9-312
1-29, 2-72, 3-82, 4-155, 5-226, 6-226, 7-245

Match drawn – Sussex (11 pts), Kent (10 pts)

DURHAM v. YORKSHIRE – at the Riverside

YORKSHIRE	First Innings		Second Innings	
C White (capt)	lbw b Gibson	5	c Mustard b Lewis ML	66
JJ Sayers	c Mustard b Gibson	4	lbw b Lewis ML	56
A McGrath	not out	140	lbw b Thorp	61
MJ Lumb	lbw b Thorp	14	c Breese b Thorp	18
DS Lehmann	b Gibson	58	(8) c Breese b Gibson	49
TT Bresnan	b Lewis ML	3	lbw b Lewis ML	5
*GL Brophy	b Lewis ML	1	(5) c Scott b Gibson	27
RKJ Dawson	c Mustard b Thorp	8	(7) b Thorp	4
JN Gillespie	b Benkenstein	18	not out	7
ME Claydon	c Muchall b Breese	38	lbw b Gibson	0
GJ Kruis	run out	0	c Mustard b Gibson	0
Extras	b 10, lb 15, w 1, nb 24	50	b 4, lb 8, w 5, nb 2	19
	(all out 86 overs)	339	(all out 93 overs)	312

Bowling
Lewis ML 23-7-84-2. Onions 14-3-46-0. Gibson 17-1-85-3. Thorp 15-5-35-2. Benkenstein 4-0-24-1. Breese 13-1-40-1.
Lewis ML 22-4-81-3. Onions 14-4-48-0. Thorp 18-3-53-3. Gibson 18-4-62-4. Breese 21-4-56-0.
Fall of Wickets: 1-15, 2-28, 3-51, 4-148, 5-159, 6-169, 7-186, 8-255, 9-335
1-115, 2-148, 3-205, 4-212, 5-217, 6-236, 7-290, 8-304, 9-304

DURHAM	First Innings		Second Innings	
JJB Lewis	lbw b Gillespie	6	b Gillespie	0
JP Maher	c Brophy b Kruis	16	c Brophy b Kruis	19
GJ Muchall	c Brophy b Gillespie	36	c Brophy b Gillespie	1
GM Scott	sub b Claydon	4	lbw b Bresnan	25
DM B'enstein (capt)	c Lumb b Bresnan	93	c Brophy b Kruis	96
GR Breese	lbw b Bresnan	21	b Gillespie	63
*P Mustard	c McGrath b Bresnan	17	lbw b Kruis	0
OD Gibson	b Bresnan	53	lbw b Gillespie	13
CD Thorp	b Bresnan	0	c McGrath b Gillespie	0
G Onions	b Kruis	0	not out	6
ML Lewis	not out	1	c Brophy b Gillespie	5
Extras	b 1, lb 7, nb 4	12	b 9, lb 3, nb 8	20
	(all out 62 overs)	258	(all out 64.2 overs)	248

Bowling
Claydon 11-2-42-1. Gillespie 17-1-74-2. Kruis 14-2-59-2. Bresnan 16-2-58-5. McGrath 4-1-17-0.
Gillespie 14.2-2-37-6. Kruis 18-1-95-3. Claydon 11-3-37-0. Bresnan 11-3-23-1. Dawson 7-0-38-0. McGrath 4-0-6-0.
Fall of Wickets: 1-13, 2-49, 3-66, 4-68, 5-106, 6-132, 7-253, 8-253, 9-254
1-12, 2-18, 3-22, 4-79, 5-205, 6-205, 7-235, 8-235, 9-242

Yorkshire won by 145 runs – Durham (5 pts), Yorkshire (20 pts)

WARWICKSHIRE v. MIDDLESEX – at Edgbaston

MIDDLESEX	First Innings		Second Innings	
ET Smith	lbw b Brown	30	c Ambrose b Carter	19
NRD Compton	c Ambrose b Carter	52	not out	100
OA Shah	c Anyon b Carter	10	c Trott b Loudon	20
EC Joyce	b Loudon	211	st Ambrose b Harris	6
JWM Dalrymple	c Brown b Harris	43	(4) c Knight b Loudon	33
SB Styris (capt)	b Harris	0	not out	80
*DC Nash	lbw b Harris	68		
J Louw	lbw b Streak	0		
CT Peploe	b Loudon	2		
CB Keegan	c Trott b Loudon	7		
CEW Silverwood	not out	2		
Extras	b 5, lb 7, w 7, nb 2	21	b 4, lb 11, w 7	22
	(all out 143.3 overs)	446	(4 wkts dec 78.3 overs)	280

Bowling
Streak 24-3-69-1. Brown 21-5-47-1. Carter 24-2-91-2. Anyon 20-5-65-0. Harris 36-5-109-3. Loudon 18.3-1-53-3.
Brown 5.4-0-37-0. Carter 18.1-3-54-1. Loudon 12.5-1-34-2. Harris 23-2-77-1. Streak 10-1-30-0. Troughton 8.3-0-33-0. Anyon 0.2-0-0-0.
Fall of Wickets: 1-41, 2-56, 3-127, 4-219, 5-247, 6-414, 7-419, 8-435, 9-443
1-21, 2-48, 3-123, 4-137

WARWICKSHIRE	First Innings		Second Innings	
NV Knight	c Nash b Keegan	10	(3) c Styris b Dalrymple	36
MA Wagh	c Smith b Keegan	111	lbw b Peploe	44
IJL Trott	c Dalrymple b Silverwood	16	(4) not out	46
AGR Loudon	c Joyce b Keegan	19		
JO Troughton	b Styris	93	(1) c Compton b Dalrymple	3
*TR Ambrose	b Silverwood	133		
DR Brown	b Styris	66	(6) not out	10
HH Streak (capt)	not out	44		
NM Carter	lbw b Louw	15	(1) c Shah b Keegan	8
PL Harris	lbw b Louw	0		
JE Anyon	c Nash b Louw	3		
Extras	b 4, lb 16, nb 10	30	b 5, lb 2	7
	(all out 123.5 overs)	391	(4 wkts 52 overs)	154

Bowling
Silverwood 23-3-97-2. Keegan 24-4-78-3. Louw 23.5-3-62-3. Dalrymple 21-3-64-0.
Styris 14-2-40-2. Peploe 13-6-18-0.
Silverwood 5-0-28-0. Keegan 7-1-20-1. Louw 8-1-24-0. Dalrymple 19-4-57-2. Peploe 13-6-18-1.
Fall of Wickets: 1-23, 2-46, 3-74, 4-82, 5-258, 6-288, 7-356, 8-375, 9-375
1-13, 2-65, 3-121, 4-128

Match drawn – Warwickshire (9 pts), Middlesex (12 pts)

NOTTINGHAMSHIRE v. HAMPSHIRE – at Trent Bridge

HAMPSHIRE	First Innings		Second Innings	
JHK Adams	not out	262	c Fleming b Sidebottom	4
MA Carberry	c Read b Sidebottom	49	c Read b Sidebottom	8
JP Crawley	c Alleyne b Ealham	148	c Gallian b Shreck	23
CC Benham	c Alleyne b Shreck	35	c Gallian b Shreck	15
DJ Thornely	not out	50	not out	43
*N Pothas			c Read b Shreck	46
SM Ervine			b Smith	11
AD Mascarenhas			c Swann b Shreck	11
SK Warne (capt)				
CT Tremlett				
SD Udal				
Extras	b 5, lb 19, nb 4	28	lb 10, nb 2	12
	(3 wkts dec 156 overs)	572	(8 wkts dec 40 overs)	173

Bowling
Sidebottom 32-6-88-1. Shreck 34-10-110-1. Smith 27-3-103-0. Ealham 28-7-74-1. Swann 20-0-85-0. Hussey 5-0-37-0.
Sidebottom 8-0-43-2. Shreck 10-0-35-4. Ealham 5-2-10-1. Swann 10-0-42-0. Smith 7-0-33-1.
Fall of Wickets: 1-111, 2-387, 3-496
1-4, 2-27, 3-50, 4-53, 5-56, 6-139, 7-150, 8-173

NOTTS	First Innings		Second Innings	
DJ Bicknell	b Tremlett	77	b Mascarenhas	9
JER Gallian	b Warne	23	lbw b Mascarenhas	18
D Alleyne	not out	0	c Benham b Warne	99
SP Fleming (capt)	c Thornely b Warne	81	b Pothas b Ervine	0
DJ Hussey	c Warne b Tremlett	4	not out	150
RJ Sidebottom	c Benham b Warne	3		
*CMW Read	c Pothas b Tremlett	5	(6) c Benham b Tremlett	6
MA Ealham	not out	101	(7) not out	15
GP Swann	c Pothas b Tremlett	54		
GJ Smith	lbw b Udal	2		
CE Shreck	c Carberry b Mascarenhas	0	b 4, w 11, nb 6	
Extras	lb 2, w 2, nb 12	16	lb 4, w 11, nb 6	21
	(all out 101 overs)	362	(5 wkts 103 overs)	318

Bowling
Tremlett 25-9-43-4. Ervine 12-0-66-0. Udal 17-2-97-1. Mascarenhas 8-2-19-1. Warne 26-6-128-3. Thornely 3-0-7-0.
Tremlett 21-3-50-1. Mascarenhas 19-6-35-2. Warne 24-4-92-1. Udal 12-2-60-0. Ervine 15-4-40-1. Thornely 8-2-29-0.
Fall of Wickets: 1-57, 2-57, 3-151, 4-157, 5-164, 6-183, 7-203, 8-306, 9-326
1-25, 2-32, 3-33, 4-272, 5-279

Match drawn – Nottinghamshire (8 pts), Hampshire (11 pts)

Anthony McGrath scored in the match for once out was perhaps the most significant contribution over the three days. A five-wicket return for Tim Bresnan ensured a good first innings lead, meanwhile, and not even two excellent innings of 93 and 96 by Dale Benkenstein could save Durham in the end.

Middlesex's failure to beat Warwickshire at Edgbaston, coupled with Yorkshire's win, meant that they dropped to the bottom of the table. The game was a personal triumph, though, for Middlesex batsman Ed Joyce who made 211 in a shade under eight hours, a month after his season was cruelly interrupted by a bad ankle injury on his England debut in the Twenty20 international against Sri Lanka at the Rose Bowl. Joyce's class, plus combative half-centuries from Nick Compton and David Nash, took Middlesex well beyond 400, but Warwickshire themselves replied with 391 as Mark Wagh and Tim Ambrose scored hundreds – in Ambrose's case his first for four summers in only his second Championship appearance for the county he joined from Sussex after the 2005 season. An unbeaten 100 by Compton in Middlesex's second innings, and a belligerent 80 not out in an unbroken stand of 143 from Scott Styris, then set up a declaration, but time soon ran out for the visitors.

Shane Warne was left seething in frustration as his Hampshire side was denied victory over Nottinghamshire at Trent Bridge by a defiant rearguard action from David Alleyne and David Hussey. Notts had begun the final day on 24 without loss, after being set a win target of 384 by the ever-imaginative Warne, but even began to think about an unlikely victory after the stand between Alleyne – dropped on six by wicketkeeper Nic Pothas – and Hussey flourished. At tea, Notts required another 153 in 34 overs, but Alleyne finally fell for 99 and Hussey decided to see it out for the draw on 150 not out. Earlier in the match there was magnificent career-best 262 not out from Hampshire opener Jimmy Adams, who batted for just under ten hours and hit two sixes and 34 fours from 446 balls, besides another fine hundred for John Crawley and Mark Ealham's twelfth first-class century.

Division Two

A startling last-day collapse by Gloucestershire brought Essex an exciting and promotion-boosting seven-wicket win at Bristol. The final day had begun with the home side on 70 without loss, still 84 runs behind but looking more than capable of forcing a draw on a pitch where 942 runs had been scored in the two first innings. At 154 for 2, and with the arrears having been knocked off, Gloucestershire seemed to have done the hardest part of their rearguard action. Cricket, however, is never that simple and in mid-afternoon wickets began to tumble as Andy Bichel, Grant Flower and Ravi Bopara all worked hard to bring Essex back into the game. Indeed, 15 minutes after tea Gloucestershire had been bowled out for just 251 and Mark Pettini emerged to lead a successful run chase. Pettini also scored a first innings 59 but it was Andy Flower's magnificent 190, from 358 balls, which ultimately proved to be the difference between the sides.

Mark Ramprakash hit the 84th first-class hundred of his career, and Alistair Brown and Jon Batty also scored centuries, as Surrey overwhelmed Northamptonshire by 229 runs at Wantage Road. Usman Afzaal's fine, unbeaten 136 had made sure of an even contest over the first two days, but then a second-wicket stand of 281 between Ramprakash and Batty saw Surrey accelerating away and not even fighting fifties from Lance Klusener and Ben Phillips could save Northants after an upper order second-innings slide which included another failure for Sourav Ganguly.

Jason Gillespie took a season's best 6 for 37 as Yorkshire beat Durham at the Riverside.

Long–distance runner: Hylton Ackerman hit an epic unbeaten 309 against Glamorgan at Cardiff.

Graham Wagg, beginning to put behind him the shame of a 15-month exile from the game following admission of cocaine use, took a career-best 6 for 38 on the last day at Taunton as Somerset collapsed in a heap. Derbyshire's 344-run win was well earned,

Round Eleven: 13–17 July 2006 Division Two

GLOUCESTERSHIRE v. ESSEX – at Bristol

GLOS	First Innings		Second Innings	
CM Spearman	c Pettini b Gough	70	c Foster b Bichel	51
Kadeer Ali	lbw b Tudor	28	lbw b Bopara	43
MGN Windows	lbw b Tudor	2	b Bopara	48
CG Taylor	c Flower GW b Tudor	9	b Flower GW	30
APR Gidman (capt)	b Middlebrook	87	c Foster b Bichel	4
IJ Harvey	c Foster b Gough	0	b Bopara	40
*SJ Adshead	c Flower A b Flower GW	68	not out	16
MA Hardinges	b Gough	27	c Bopara b Middlebrook	3
ID Fisher	c Bopara b Bichel	45	c Bopara b Flower GW	4
J Lewis	st Foster b Middlebrook	38	c Chopra b Bichel	0
SP Kirby	not out	3	lbw b Flower GW	1
WD Rudge				
Extras	w 5, nb 12	17	b 2, lb 1, nb 8	11
	(all out 120.3 overs)	394	(all out 85.1 overs)	251

Bowling
Gough 26-4-87-3. Bichel 23.3-0-101-1. Tudor 25-5-64-3. Middlebrook 38-9-94-2.
Bopara 2-0-12-0. Flower GW 11-1-36-1.
Gough 12-1-50-0. Bichel 18-5-50-3. Tudor 11-2-41-0. Middlebrook 22-7-63-1.
Flower GW 15.1-6-28-3. Bopara 7-2-16-3.
Fall of Wickets: 1-69, 2-79, 3-93, 4-139, 5-139, 6-268, 7-282, 8-321, 9-386
1-78, 2-145, 3-154, 4-158, 5-220, 6-226, 7-241, 8-249, 9-250

ESSEX	First Innings		Second Innings	
V Chopra	c Adshead b Lewis	7	b Lewis	6
ML Pettini	c Windows b Fisher	59	b Kirby	39
RS Bopara	c Adshead b Kirby	5	c Adshead b Lewis	14
A Flower	c Adshead b Gidman	190	not out	24
RC Irani (capt)	c Kadeer Ali b Fisher	12	not out	6
GW Flower	lbw b Lewis	58		
*JS Foster	lbw b Lewis	13		
JD Middlebrook	not out	73		
AJ Bichel	b Kirby	27		
AJ Tudor	c Adshead b Kirby	6		
D Gough	c Gidman b Kirby	37		
Extras	b 7, lb 10, w 8, nb 36	61	b 3, w 4, nb 2	9
	(all out 169 overs)	548	(3 wkts 22.5 overs)	98

Bowling
Lewis 32-3-93-3. Kirby 34-11-94-4. Hardinges 21-4-64-0. Harvey 16-5-51-0.
Fisher 48-5-178-2. Gidman 15-6-27-1. Taylor 2-0-20-0. Kadeer Ali 1-0-4-0.
Lewis 7-0-27-2. Kirby 7.5-1-36-1. Fisher 8-0-32-0.
Fall of Wickets: 1-16, 2-36, 3-147, 4-191, 5-332, 6-360, 7-441, 8-478, 9-490
1-14, 2-38, 3-91

Essex won by 7 wickets – Gloucestershire (6 pts), Essex (22 pts)

NORTHAMPTONSHIRE v. SURREY – at Northampton

SURREY	First Innings		Second Innings	
SA Newman	c Wessels b Phillips	23	b Nicholson	8
*JN Batty	c Wessels b Nicholson	8	b Ganguly	133
MR Ramprakash	c Wessels b Nicholson	51	c Nicholson b Brown	155
MA Butcher (capt)	b Nicholson	30	c Klusener b Brown	4
AD Brown	lbw b Nicholson	113	(7) not out	44
R Clarke	b Ganguly	47	c Shafayat b Brown	10
Azhar Mahmood	c Nicholson b Phillips	21	(5) c Sales b Phillips	52
IDK Salisbury	run out	1		
Mohammad Akram	lbw b Phillips	1		
NC Saker	c Wessels b Pietersen	13		
ND Doshi	not out	5		
Extras	b 7, nb 8	15	b 1, lb 7, w 4, nb 6	18
	(all out 88 overs)	328	(6 wkts dec 108.5 overs)	424

Bowling
Nicholson 24-5-84-4. Phillips 20-1-59-3. Pietersen 16-1-62-1. Ganguly 11-2-36-1.
Brown 8-1-47-0. Klusener 9-0-33-0.
Nicholson 14-1-31-1. Phillips 16.5-3-55-1. Brown 38-3-177-3. Pietersen 23-3-75-0.
Klusener 4-0-23-0. Ganguly 10-2-29-1. White 3-0-26-0.
Fall of Wickets: 1-29, 2-41, 3-119, 4-132, 5-215, 6-273, 7-274, 8-279, 9-310
1-14, 2-295, 3-304, 4-318, 5-330, 6-424

NORTHANTS	First Innings		Second Innings	
RA White	lbw b Azhar Mahmood	15	lbw b Azhar Mahmood	7
BM Shafayat	lbw b Akram	6	lbw b Azhar Mahmood	6
U Afzaal	not out	136	b Akram	0
SC Ganguly	c Batty b Azhar Mahmood	6	c sub b Akram	2
C Pietersen	c Batty b Akram	12	(10) not out	39
DJG Sales (capt)	lbw b Saker	23	(5) lbw b Salisbury	4
L Klusener	lbw b Salisbury	32	(6) c A Mahmood b Salisbury	58
*MH Wessels	c Butcher b Clarke	34	(7) b Batty b Clarke	22
BJ Phillips	c Batty b Salisbury	8	(8) c Batty b Clarke	52
MJ Nicholson	lbw b Salisbury	0	(9) lbw b Akram	0
JF Brown	b Akram	6	b Salisbury	10
Extras	lb 19, w 1, nb 8	28	b 9, lb 4, nb 10	23
	(all out 89.1 overs)	300	(all out 52.4 overs)	223

Bowling
Akram 15.1-3-53-3. Azhar Mahmood 19-2-61-2. Clarke 8-2-22-1. Doshi 14-4-40-0.
Salisbury 22.5-6-67-3. Saker 11-1-38-1.
Akram 14-4-49-3. Azhar Mahmood 7-2-36-2. Salisbury 16.4-4-62-3. Clarke 8-2-30-1.
Doshi 7-0-33-1.
Fall of Wickets: 1-1, 2-27, 3-43, 4-76, 5-124, 6-175, 7-249, 8-280, 9-280
1-11, 2-12, 3-20, 4-20, 5-52, 6-97, 7-125, 8-140, 9-181

Surrey won by 229 runs – Northamptonshire (6 pts), Surrey (20 pts)

SOMERSET v. DERBYSHIRE – at Taunton

DERBYSHIRE	First Innings		Second Innings	
SD Stubbings	c Gazzard b Willoughby	19	(2) b Trego	124
MJ Di Venuto	c Parsons b Willoughby	4	(1) lbw b Caddick	6
CR Taylor	c Francis JD b Caddick	60	(4) c Langer b White	74
MJ North	c Gazzard b Francis SRG	132	(5) c Gazzard b Trego	75
Hassan Adnan	c Gazzard b Francis SRG	20	(6) c Wood b Willoughby	42
G Welch (capt)	c Parsons b Francis SRG	20	(7) c Francis JD b Suppiah	53
*DJ Pipe	c Francis JD b Willoughby	24	(8) not out	32
GG Wagg	c Parsons b Caddick	17	(9) not out	20
AKD Gray	c Gazzard b Caddick	0	(3) run out	0
PS Jones	not out	34		
ID Hunter	lbw b White	48		
Extras	lb 11, w 1, nb 6	18	b 8, lb 10, w 3, nb 8	29
	(all out 113.5 overs)	396	(7 wkts dec 116 overs)	415

Bowling
Caddick 30-7-99-3. Willoughby 29-8-106-3. Francis SRG 21-8-61-3.
White 21.5-2-63-1. Trego 8-2-40-0. Parsons 3-0-15-0. Suppiah 1-0-1-0.
Caddick 21-3-78-1. Willoughby 27-7-80-1. Francis SRG 11-1-32-0.
Trego 17-5-44-2. White 19-0-92-1. Suppiah 20-3-62-1. Francis JD 1-0-9-0.
Fall of Wickets: 1-25, 2-30, 3-175, 4-244, 5-265, 6-274, 7-304, 8-304, 9-318
1-6, 2-6, 3-159, 4-286, 5-311, 6-326, 7-376

SOMERSET	First Innings		Second Innings	
JL Langer	lbw b Welch	18	c Di Venuto b Welch	30
MJ Wood	c North b Jones	2	(3) c Pipe b Wagg	14
AV Suppiah	lbw b Welch	50	c Pipe b Wagg	4
JD Francis	c Pipe b Hunter	30	(4) c Hassan Adnan b Wagg	4
CL White (capt)	c Pipe b Welch	2	c Pipe b Wagg	16
KA Parsons	retired hurt	9	(11) absent hurt	
PD Trego	c Welch b Hunter	135	(6) c Pipe b Welch	4
*CM Gazzard	c Stubbings b Welch	19	(7) c Di Venuto b Wagg	4
SRG Francis	c Pipe b Jones	36	(8) c Pipe b Wagg	4
AR Caddick	b Jones	0	(9) not out	13
CM Willoughby	not out	17	(10) c Taylor b Welch	4
Extras	lb 10, w 1, nb 12	23	b 1, lb 4, nb 10	15
	(all out 83.5 overs)	340	(all out 36.4 overs)	127

Bowling
Welch 20-3-72-3. Jones 19-2-88-4. Hunter 19.5-4-92-2. Wagg 16-1-56-0.
Gray 7-2-16-0. North 2-0-6-0.
Welch 6.4-1-24-3. Jones 12-2-48-0. Hunter 6-2-12-0. Wagg 12-3-38-6.
Fall of Wickets: 1-12, 2-20, 3-90, 4-91, 5-125, 6-149, 7-292, 8-292, 9-340
1-46, 2-56, 3-56, 4-72, 5-77, 6-85, 7-95, 8-123, 9-127

Derbyshire won by 344 runs – Somerset (6 pts), Derbyshire (21 pts)

GLAMORGAN v. LEICESTERSHIRE – at Cardiff

LEICESTERSHIRE	First Innings		Second Innings	
DDJ Robinson	b Cosker	29	run out	90
JK Maunders	c Harrison b Croft	32	lbw b Croft	34
HD Ackerman	not out	309	not out	62
D Mongia	c Wallace b Cosker	0	not out	20
JL Sadler	c Grant b Watkins	36	not out	15
JN Snape (capt)	lbw b Watkins	9		
*PA Nixon	c McCullum b Croft	60		
CW Henderson	c Hemp b Watkins	42		
DD Masters	c Wallace b Harrison	18		
SCJ Broad	c & b Cosker	15		
AR Griffith	c Grant b Croft	1		
Extras	b 2, lb 10, w 6	18	b 2, lb 4, w 1	7
	(all out 168 overs)	560	(3 wkts dec 54 overs)	228

Bowling
Harrison 30-7-83-1. Wharf 20-1-74-0. Watkins 19-2-67-3. Cosker 44-2-138-3.
Croft 55-6-186-3.
Cosker 18-2-74-0. Croft 22-5-105-1. Harrison 6-2-21-0. Watkins 8-2-22-0.
Fall of Wickets: 1-55, 2-91, 3-96, 4-178, 5-178, 6-338, 7-450, 8-501, 9-553
1-70, 2-183, 3-193

GLAMORGAN	First Innings		Second Innings	
RE Watkins	c Snape b Broad	20	c Ackerman b Griffith	6
BB McCullum	c Ackerman b Masters	160	lbw b Griffith	16
DL Hemp	c Nixon b Masters	29	b Griffith	7
MJ Powell	b Mongia	127	c Snape b Broad	4
RN Grant	run out	3	c Henderson b Snape	34
*MA Wallace	c Nixon b Griffith	1	c Henderson b Mongia	20
N Peng	c Ackerman b Henderson	43	c Sadler b Broad	23
AG Wharf	c Nixon b Griffith	14	not out	33
RDB Croft (capt)	c Broad b Mongia	17	not out	0
DS Harrison	b Henderson	2		
DA Cosker	not out	1		
Extras	b 6, lb 9, w 1, nb 6	22	b 1, lb 6, w 2, nb 2	11
	(all out 133.1 overs)	449	(7 wkts 47.4 overs)	154

Bowling
Broad 27-1-113-1. Griffith 26-5-82-1. Henderson 32-3-115-3. Masters 21-2-57-2.
Mongia 26.1-6-62-2. Snape 1-0-5-0.
Broad 9-11-21-2. Griffith 11-3-34-3. Masters 3-0-14-0. Henderson 13.4-4-45-0.
Mongia 8.5-14-1. Snape 2-0-47-0.
Fall of Wickets: 1-72, 2-114, 3-320, 4-332, 5-338, 6-381, 7-412, 8-425, 9-447
1-22, 2-27, 3-32, 4-36, 5-81, 6-116, 7-144

Match drawn – Glamorgan (11 pts), Leicestershire (11 pts)

OF NORTHAMPTONSHIRE

Northamptonshire had just won the 1980 Benson and Hedges Cup when this era began, with a team that they must have thought would go on and add to that success. As it turned out, they had to wait another 12 years – until 1992 – for what to date is their only subsequent trophy win. That was in the NatWest Trophy and was gained by a crushing, eight-wicket margin against Leicestershire. Allan Lamb, the captain, had also been the Man of the Match in the narrow 1980 Lord's final triumph against Essex, and this victory was a fitting one for a player who had given much to Northants cricket since he arrived from South Africa in 1978.

Lamb had an experienced and well-balanced team at his command, too, as Leicestershire were restricted to 208 for 7 from their 60 overs – after being put into bat. The attack was led by Curtly Ambrose, the great West Indies fast bowler, and also contained three international seamers in Paul Taylor, David Capel and Kevin Curran and international-class spin in the shape of slow left-armer Nick Cook. The loyal Tony Penberthy was a third seam-bowling all-rounder, coming in at No. 7 behind Capel and Curran, with wicketkeeper David Ripley also capable of significant runs at No. 8.

In the final, only the top four of Alan Fordham, Nigel Felton, Rob Bailey and Lamb were needed, with Fordham winning the match award for his 91 and putting on a decisive 144 for the second wicket with Bailey, who finished 72 not out.

Lamb scored 32,502 runs at an average of 48.94 and hit 89 hundreds in a first-class career that lasted from 1972 until 1995. He also captained the county from 1989 and it was not for want of his trying that Northants could not quite add more silverware to their 1980 and 1992 cup wins.

Two more Benson and Hedges Cup finals were reached, in 1987 and 1996, when they lost to Yorkshire and Lancashire respectively. The 1987 loss was particularly hard to take, as the scores had finished tied and Yorkshire were awarded the trophy as they had lost fewer wickets. Besides which, they also lost in that year's NatWest Trophy final, against Nottinghamshire, two months later. Northants were also runners-up in the 1979, 1981, 1990 and 1995 Gillette Cup or NatWest Trophy finals – completing a quarter-century in which they tasted disappointment far more than elation.

Heartbeat of Northants for 24 seasons, Allan Lamb averaged almost 50 in his first-class career for the county and England.

In more recent times they have often struggled to compete with the bigger counties, also losing players such as Mal Loye, Graeme Swann, Richard Montgomerie, Russell Warren and Gerard Brophy to other clubs. Before he parted company with Northants by mutual consent midway through this past summer, the former South African and Australia batsman Kepler Wessels was accused of stripping the county of its identity. But what Northants have done in these same past few years is unearth perhaps England's finest spinner since Derek Underwood in the lovable guise of Luton-born Monty Panesar, the first Sikh ever to play for England.

because they had batted strongly in both innings with Marcus North scoring more than 200 runs in the match, Chris Taylor also showing up well and Steve Stubbings hitting a fine third day century. They also bowled tenaciously on day two to keep Somerset to 340 – a first-innings deficit of 56. That was all the more creditable because Peter Trego had come in at No. 7 to thump 135 from only 166 balls, with 25 fours, but the home side had no answer at all to Wagg second time around as he and Graeme Welch cleaned up.

Over-caution cost Leicestershire dear at Sophia Gardens, where Jeremy Snape delayed his second-innings declaration until Glamorgan required a near-impossible 340 from 48 overs. The penalty for Snape and his side was a nervy Glamorgan slide to 154 for 7 before time ran out. No one would have deserved a Leicestershire win more than Hylton Ackerman, who finished day one on 177 not out and went on to make an unbeaten career-best 309 in a Leicestershire first innings of 560. He batted for 570 minutes, faced 446 balls and struck a six and 39 fours. Brendon McCullum, the New Zealand Test wicketkeeper playing for Glamorgan as a specialist batsman, replied with a career-best 160 of his own, while Michael Powell also made an excellent hundred after joining the fluent McCullum in a third-wicket stand of 206. Darren

Robinson's 90, plus more runs from the prodigious Ackerman, then set Glamorgan their target of sorts – but, even on a surface that had brought so many runs, the extent of Snape's safety-first approach was mystifying.

Round Twelve: 18–23 July 2006

Division One

High summer at Scarborough witnessed one of the more significant Championship debuts of recent years: that of the hugely talented 18-year-old from Bradford, Adil Rashid. A diminutive leg spinning all-rounder of equal promise and precociousness in both batting and bowling, the 5ft 7in Rashid not only became the first Asian-born Yorkshireman to play Championship cricket for the county; he ended the match leading the team from the field to ringing applause from the traditionally sizeable seaside crowd after bowling Yorkshire to an innings victory over Warwickshire by taking 6 for 67 from 28 consecutive overs. Nor was Rashid overawed either by the occasion or his dramatic success. 'I was loving it out there,' he said. 'At tea our captain, Craig White, asked how I was feeling and I said I was fresh. I wanted that fifth wicket.' Rashid's eye-catching control of flight and spin, as

Round Twelve: 18–23 July 2006 Division One

YORKSHIRE v. WARWICKSHIRE – at Scarborough

WARWICKSHIRE	First Innings		Second Innings	
IJ Westwood	c McGrath b Bresnan	31	lbw b Rashid	80
MA Wagh	c McGrath b Bresnan	18	b Gillespie	5
IJL Trott	c White b Bresnan	7	c & b Rashid	43
NV Knight	c Brophy b Gillespie	3	c Brophy b Rashid	58
LC Parker	b Gillespie	9	c Gale b Rashid	0
*TR Ambrose	c Brophy b Gillespie	4	b Bresnan	1
DR Brown	c Gale b Patterson	22	c White b Rashid	4
HH Streak (capt)	not out	68	not out	16
TD Groenewald	c Sayers b Gillespie	0	lbw b Rashid	14
NM Carter	run out	0	c Rashid b Bresnan	2
PL Harris	lbw b Rashid	32	lbw b Bresnan	0
Extras	b 1, lb 4, w 2	7	b 6, lb 6, w 2, nb 2	16
	(all out 65.2 overs)	201	(all out 81 overs)	239

Bowling
Gillespie 17-5-52-4. Kruis 19-4-57-0. Bresnan 14-3-37-3. Patterson 9-1-25-1. McGrath 5-1-17-0. Rashid 1-0-8-1.
Gillespie 14-3-29-1. Kruis 17-3-56-0. Bresnan 16-4-40-3. Patterson 5-0-26-0. Rashid 28-6-67-6. McGrath 1-0-9-0.
Fall of Wickets: 1-49, 2-60, 3-61, 4-68, 5-74, 6-85, 7-117, 8-122, 9-122 1-17, 2-116, 3-154, 4-158, 5-179, 6-186, 7-214, 8-232, 9-239

YORKSHIRE	First Innings	
C White (capt)	c Wagh b Brown	28
JJ Sayers	c Westwood b Carter	72
A McGrath	c Ambrose b Carter	15
JN Gillespie	c Ambrose b Carter	25
MJ Lumb	b Harris	57
AW Gale	b Harris	149
A Rashid	c Parker b Harris	10
*GL Brophy	b Harris	97
TT Bresnan	lbw b Harris	3
SA Patterson	c Ambrose b Carter	8
GJ Kruis	not out	10
Extras	b 23, lb 15, w 4, nb 20	62
	(all out 134 overs)	536

Bowling
Streak 19-2-93-0. Carter 31-7-101-4. Groenewald 16-1-78-0. Brown 20-2-80-1. Harris 44-12-134-5. Westwood 4-0-12-0.
Fall of Wickets: 1-73, 2-115, 3-131, 4-160, 5-277, 6-293, 7-455, 8-459, 9-517

Yorkshire won by an innings and 96 runs –
Yorkshire (22 pts), Warwickshire (3 pts)

KENT v. LANCASHIRE – at Canterbury

LANCASHIRE	First Innings		Second Innings	
MJ Chilton (capt)	c O'Brien b Saggers	31	(2) c O'Brien b Henderson	1
IJ Sutcliffe	b Khan	10	(1) b Khan	6
MB Loye	c O'Brien b Henderson	6	c O'Brien b Khan	98
SG Law	b Khan	53	c Stevens b Henderson	85
NJ Astle	c van Jaarsveld b Henderson	7	c van Jaarsveld b Khan	84
A Flintoff	c O'Brien b Henderson	4	c Henderson b Stevens	37
G Chapple	c Fulton b Henderson	0	b Saggers	50
*GD Cross	lbw b Khan	72	c van Jaarsveld b Khan	2
DG Cork	c Walker b Saggers	10	c van Jaarsveld b Saggers	23
SI Mahmood	c Henderson b Saggers	3	c Walker b Stevens	2
G Keedy	not out	2	not out	2
Extras	b 9, lb 4, w 3, nb 4	20	b 1, lb 10, w 5, nb 10	26
	(all out 57.5 overs)	218	(all out 114.4 overs)	436

Bowling
Khan 17-2-73-3. Henderson 14-5-29-4. Bravo 9-0-50-0. Saggers 12.5-4-38-3. Stevens 2-0-8-0. Patel 3-1-7-0.
Khan 26-4-129-4. Henderson 27-5-87-2. Bravo 6-2-16-0. Saggers 15-3-52-2. Stevens 15.4-0-72-2. Patel 24-0-68-0. van Jaarsveld 1-0-1-0.
Fall of Wickets: 1-21, 2-29, 3-58, 4-92, 5-102, 6-102, 7-184, 8-205, 9-216 1-2, 2-12, 3-202, 4-204, 5-282, 6-375, 7-385, 8-385, 9-412

KENT	First Innings		Second Innings	
DP Fulton	c Flintoff b Chapple	29	c Cork b Keedy	64
RWT Key (capt)	b Flintoff	16	c Cross b Chapple	2
M van Jaarsveld	lbw b Flintoff	6	c sub b Cork	59
MJ Walker	run out	197	c Sutcliffe b Keedy	1
DI Stevens	c Cross b Cork	25	c Law b Keedy	16
DJJ Bravo	c Law b Astle	76	c Cross b Chapple	6
*NJ O'Brien	c Chapple b Mahmood	10	c Cross b Mahmood	7
T Henderson	c Chapple b Mahmood	13	st Cross b Keedy	11
MM Patel	c Chapple b Mahmood	0	(10) not out	16
A Khan	c Flintoff b Keedy	38	(9) not out	19
MJ Saggers	not out	2		
Extras	b 8, lb 12, nb 8	28	b 1, lb 7, w 2, nb 4	14
	(all out 130.3 overs)	440	(8 wkts 76.5 overs)	215

Bowling
Cork 23-6-76-1. Chapple 21-5-75-1. Flintoff 19-4-45-2. Mahmood 20-2-79-3. Keedy 39.3-4-128-1. Astle 8-1-17-1.
Cork 19-6-45-1. Flintoff 4-0-11-0. Chapple 11-1-56-2. Mahmood 12-3-34-1. Keedy 26.5-9-61-4.
Fall of Wickets: 1-28, 2-42, 3-56, 4-109, 5-246, 6-283, 7-299, 8-301, 9-422 1-3, 2-122, 3-123, 4-138, 5-153, 6-159, 7-173, 8-179

Kent won by 2 wickets – Kent (22 pts), Lancashire (4 pts)

MIDDLESEX v. SUSSEX – at Southgate

SUSSEX	First Innings		Second Innings	
RR Montgomerie	lbw b Silverwood	0	(2) c Nash b Compton	61
CD Hopkinson	lbw b Silverwood	8	(1) c Dalrymple b Smith	68
MH Yardy	c Nash b Louw	97	not out	66
MW Goodwin	not out	69	st Morgan b Nash	156
CJ Adams (capt)	lbw b Louw	115	not out	16
*MJ Prior	b Dalrymple	43		
LJ Wright	b Silverwood	43		
Yasir Arafat	st Nash b Peploe	67		
OP Rayner	c Nash b Louw	0		
Mushtaq Ahmed	lbw b Dalrymple	12		
JD Lewry	not out	27		
Extras	b 6, lb 5, w 1, nb 14	26	b 2, lb 2, w 2, nb 6	12
	(all out 127.3 overs)	507	(3 wkts dec 56.5 overs)	379

Bowling
Silverwood 25-4-84-4. Louw 33-6-141-3. Styris 20-2-66-0. Dalrymple 23-2-102-1. Peploe 23.3-5-89-1. Shah 3-0-14-0.
Silverwood 6-2-7-0. Louw 5-0-27-0. Peploe 13-2-34-0. Styris 5-0-14-0. Dalrymple 8-1-26-0. Compton 6-0-94-1. Smith 5-0-60-1. Nash 4.5-0-53-1. Joyce 4-0-9-0.
Fall of Wickets: 1-0, 2-15, 3-174, 4-195, 5-284, 6-376, 7-400, 8-402, 9-419 1-132, 2-134, 3-329

MIDDLESEX	First Innings		Second Innings	
ET Smith	c Rayner b Lewry	75	run out	31
NRD Compton	lbw b Yasir Arafat	1	lbw b Lewry	86
OA Shah	c Goodwin b Yasir Arafat	85	c Adams b Mushtaq Ahmed	26
EC Joyce	st Prior b Yardy	68	c Adams b Mushtaq Ahmed	4
JWM Dalrymple	b Yasir Arafat	60	b Yasir Arafat	0
SB Styris (capt)	c Montgomerie b Wright	70	c Lewry b Rayner	16
EJG Morgan	st Prior b Rayner	27	c M'gomerie b Mushtaq Ahmed	5
*DC Nash	b Wright	12	c Hopkinson b Rayner	16
CT Peploe	lbw b Yasir Arafat	7	lbw b Yasir Arafat	0
J Louw	not out	10	not out	0
CEW Silverwood	lbw b Yasir Arafat	0	not out	0
Extras	b 10, lb 5, w 6, nb 30	51	b 2, lb 1, nb 7	10
	(all out 120.4 overs)	466	(9 wkts 73 overs)	208

Bowling
Lewry 18-5-55-1. Yasir Arafat 21.4-3-94-5. Mushtaq Ahmed 42-1-168-0. Wright 16-1-58-2. Rayner 9-1-33-1. Yardy 14-0-43-1. Lewry 13-1-39-1. Yasir Arafat 18-6-71-2. Wright 7-1-13-0. Mushtaq Ahmed 27-12-74-3. Rayner 8-4-8-2.
Fall of Wickets: 1-26, 2-112, 3-234, 4-259, 5-372, 6-411, 7-437, 8-443, 9-466 1-64, 2-105, 3-109, 4-138, 5-185, 6-185, 7-205, 8-208, 9-208

Match drawn – Middlesex (12 pts), Sussex (12 pts)

Matthew Walker's superb 197 at Canterbury was central to Kent's morale-boosting victory against Lancashire, and was yet another fine performance from one of county cricket's most underrated yet consistent players.

much as his self-confidence, was a thrill for the Yorkshire supporters as Warwickshire tumbled from 154 for 2 to 239 all out. Tim Bresnan, another fine young all-round Yorkshire cricketer back on the county stage after experiencing his first taste of representative cricket in England's NatWest Series defeat against Sri Lanka, took three wickets for the second time in the match, while another pair of youngsters – batsmen Andrew Gale and Joe Sayers – also enjoyed fine matches. Sayers contributed a solid and classy 72 at the top of the order after Bresnan and Jason Gillespie had combined to dismiss Warwickshire for just 201 in their first innings, and 22-year-old Dewsbury left-hander Gale converted a maiden first-class hundred into a 208-ball 149 as he and Gerard Brophy plundered 162 for the seventh wicket. Warwickshire, who had needed a last-wicket stand of 79 between Heath Streak and Paul Harris even to reach one batting

bonus point on the opening day, were soon looking a shambles in the field as Yorkshire totalled 536 in reply and set the stage for Rashid to announce himself to a wider cricket world with a considerable flourish.

Momentous happenings of far more immediate concern to English cricket were occurring at Canterbury, however, where Andrew Flintoff was attempting to prove his fitness for the second Test against Pakistan by coming through Lancashire's match against Kent. Sadly, the ankle injury which he had been resting since pulling out of the NatWest Series against Sri Lanka, flared up again and Flintoff was forced to face up to the surgery which would put him out of action for the remainder of the summer. Initially, though, it seemed as if Flintoff was once again approaching full pace and hostility with the ball. On the first evening, after he and Lancashire had disappointed with the bat,

Flintoff tore into the Kent top order and after bowling Robert Key with his first delivery – the ball nipping back off the seam as the opener shouldered arms – he went on to add the wicket of David Fulton and finish up with overnight figures of 10-3-16-2. On day two, however, he managed only another nine overs of lesser power as Kent, led by Matthew Walker's brilliant 197 and boosted further by 76 from Dwayne Bravo and 38 from No. 10 by Amjad Khan, took control of the match with 440. By the close, indeed, both Lancashire openers had fallen to Khan and Tyron Henderson – who had shared seven wickets in the visitors' first day 218 all out – and at 56 for 2 they looked destined for defeat inside three days. There then followed a thrilling counter-attack by Mal Loye and Stuart Law, who was desperate to atone for dropping Walker at slip when the left-hander had scored just one, while further aggressive batting from Nathan Astle, Flintoff and Glen Chapple eventually set Kent an awkward last day target. By then, though, Flintoff was so obviously struggling with his ankle that he bowled merely two tentative overs before leaving the field – never to return. At 122 for 1, with Fulton and Martin van Jaarsveld going to fine fifties, Kent were cruising, but in the end it required a gutsy unbroken stand of 36 in 19 tense overs for the ninth wicket by Khan and Min Patel to see them to the win which put them into third place in the Championship race. Gary Keedy's last-day spin heroics completed a truly excellent four-day contest but, of course, it was all rather overshadowed by the fresh injury worries surrounding the England captain.

There was another nerve-wracking finish at Southgate where Middlesex's last pair, Johann Louw and Chris Silverwood, held out to deny Sussex the victory which would have put them 23 points clear at the top of the table. As it was, Chris Adams' side had to settle for eight points more than Lancashire had gleaned from their Canterbury visit. The Sussex captain was left cursing the fact that rain had taken 24 overs from the final day and that he could not quite get maximum reward for the negotiations with his Middlesex counterpart Scott Styris during a third afternoon drinks break which had resulted in the home team serving up some deliberate dross so that they could chase an eventual 421 in 96 overs. Murray Goodwin was the chief beneficiary of the tasty assortments offered by the likes of Ed Smith and Ed Joyce, reaching a 32-ball hundred ineligible for the Walter Lawrence Award because it had been completed under contrived conditions. Before Goodwin's onslaught had come some fine batting performances from both sides, with Adams marking his 300th first-class match with a century.

Division Two

Matt Mason was the hero at New Road as Worcestershire won a thrilling, low-scoring match with Gloucestershire by 58 runs. First the Australian-born seamer batted bravely from No. 11 to score an unbeaten 29 and help century-maker Ben Smith add a crucial 72 for Worcestershire's final second-innings wicket. And then, revelling in the conditions, he almost single-handedly bowled out Gloucestershire for 169 on the final day – after they had reached 68 for 1 overnight – with superb figures of 8 for 45 from 22.2 overs. Seemingly tireless, at one stage he took 4 for 6 in 20 balls just after lunch to hasten Gloucestershire's decline still further. The opening day, meanwhile, had seen Jon Lewis become the first fast bowler to reach 50 first-class wickets for the season and Zaheer Khan the second. But Hamish Marshall had already moved to 56 not out by the end of that first day, at which point Gloucestershire were 115 for 2, and the New Zealander completed a fine hundred the following day to ensure a small lead for the visitors. Ultimately, however, it was Smith's fighting 106, from 174 balls and with 17 fours, and Mason's all-round heroics that tipped the delicate balance of the contest Worcestershire's way.

A county record tumbled at Guildford, on a pitch almost embarrassingly in favour of batting, as Australian Test opener Justin Langer – to the dismay of many Somerset fans – eclipsed the 322 which the great Viv Richards had scored for the West Countrymen at Taunton in 1985. Langer, who had accepted an invitation to play for Somerset for a short spell to keep his game in trim for battles ahead, could not quite believe his luck in finding such a placid Woodbridge Road strip. He was on 234 not out at the end of day one, with Somerset 442 for 2 as both Neil Edwards and Arul Suppiah also contributed seventies to stands with Langer of 227 and 162, and by the time he made his first mistake he had made 342 from 416 balls with 43 fours and two sixes. The run orgy had not finished after Somerset declared on 688 for 8, however. With Mark Ramprakash needing no second invitation to ease to 167 from 287 balls, with 21 fours and two sixes of his own, Rikki Clarke celebrating on his home club ground by completing a career-best 214 off 258 balls, with 30 fours and three sixes, and both Mark Butcher and Azhar Mahmood also having fun, Surrey themselves totalled 717 before bad weather mercifully prevented no more than 22 overs on the final day.

The bat was also on top of ball at Chelmsford where Glamorgan's Michael Powell chalked up the second double-hundred of his career in eight hours at the crease. But Essex captain Ronnie Irani, dropped on 19 by David Hemp at slip, replied with 145 and added 181 with Grant Flower – who made 101 – for the fifth wicket. James Foster also contributed a composed 64 as Essex finished just 12 runs adrift of Glamorgan's 474. On the rain-shortened last day, as the game petered out into a draw, there was time for Mark Wallace to complete his second half-century of the match and for Kiwis Brendon McCullum and James Franklin also to pass fifty.

Rain cut short final day proceedings at Grace Road too, allowing only 25 overs' play, although Derbyshire were already well on the way to saving the game against Leicestershire. Michael Di Venuto, who resumed on 131 in an overnight second-innings score of 202 for 1, added another 30 runs and was still providing a commanding presence at the crease when the weather closed in. Up to that point, it was the all-round talents of Stuart Broad which had most caught the eye, despite the fine strokeplay of Marcus North, Hassan Adnan and Jamie Pipe which had taken Derbyshire to 355 for 8 by the close of the opening day. Broad had picked up four wickets by then, adding another the next morning to finish with 5 for 89, and on day three he revealed his fast-improving batting ability to hit an unbeaten 65 from 81 balls as Leicestershire – boosted earlier by half-centuries from John Maunders and Hylton Ackerman and a jaunty 90 from skipper Jeremy Snape – went past 500.

Round Twelve: 18–23 July 2006 Division Two

WORCESTERSHIRE v. GLOUCESTERSHIRE – at Worcester

WORCS	First Innings		Second Innings	
L Vincent	c Harvey b Lewis	0	(2) c Harvey b Lewis	0
SC Moore	c Kadeer Ali b Lewis	20	(1) c Kadeer Ali b Lewis	0
VS Solanki (capt)	b Kirby	60	lbw b Lewis	6
BF Smith	lbw b Lewis	19	lbw b Ball	106
GA Hick	c Ball b Kirby	40	c Adshead b Lewis	8
*SM Davies	b Lewis	14	c Marshall b Kirby	12
GJ Batty	c Adshead b Lewis	36	b Kirby	0
RJ Sillence	c Ball b Gidman	40	c Kadeer Ali b Ball	51
Z Khan	c Spearman b Lewis	2	b Ball	8
RW Price	b Greenidge	6	b Kirby	0
MS Mason	not out	7	not out	29
Extras	lb 5, nb 22	27	lb 2, nb 10	12
	(all out 64 overs)	271	(all out 62 overs)	232

Bowling
Lewis 19-5-77-6. Kirby 19-2-64-2. Greenidge 9-1-58-1. Harvey 11-3-37-0.
Gidman 5-1-29-1. Ball 1-0-1-0.
Lewis 20.3-1-93-4. Kirby 18-3-72-3. Greenidge 1.3-0-17-0. Gidman 4-0-19-0.
Harvey 4-3-5-0. Ball 14-2-24-3.
Fall of Wickets: 1-0, 2-57, 3-88, 4-127, 5-156, 6-168, 7-236, 8-251, 9-252
1-0, 2-7, 3-18, 4-26, 5-47, 6-47, 7-151, 8-159, 9-160

GLOS	First Innings		Second Innings	
WPC Weston	b Khan	44	(2) lbw b Khan	29
CM Spearman	c Davies b Khan	15	(1) c Smith b Khan	24
HJH Marshall	c Hick b Price	112	lbw b Mason	20
Kadeer Ali	c & b Batty	6	c Davies b Mason	8
APR Gidman	b Batty	25	c Price b Mason	27
IJ Harvey	c Davies b Khan	14	c Vincent b Mason	5
*SJ Adshead	c Batty b Khan	20	not out	22
MCJ Ball	b Khan	0	b Mason	14
J Lewis (capt)	c Vincent b Mason	15	b Mason	0
CG Greenidge	c Price b Mason	20	(11) c Davies b Mason	3
SP Kirby	not out	0	(10) c Vincent b Mason	4
Extras	lb 5	5	b 4, lb 6, nb 3	13
	(all out 102.1 overs)	276	(all out 64.2 overs)	169

Bowling
Khan 23.1-6-74-5. Mason 25-6-72-2. Sillence 10-2-24-0. Vincent 6-1-19-0.
Batty 23-3-38-2. Price 15-2-44-1.
Khan 23-7-60-2. Mason 22.2-6-45-8. Batty 7-2-25-0. Price 4-1-8-0.
Sillence 4-0-11-0. Vincent 4-0-10-0.
Fall of Wickets: 1-19, 2-115, 3-137, 4-203, 5-207, 6-235, 7-235, 8-250, 9-276
1-38, 2-68, 3-85, 4-94, 5-116, 6-127, 7-149, 8-149, 9-165

Worcestershire won by 58 runs –
Worcestershire (19 pts), Gloucestershire (5 pts)

SURREY v. SOMERSET – at Guildford

SOMERSET	First Innings	
JL Langer	c Saker b Salisbury	342
NJ Edwards	c Azhar Mahmood b Salisbury	77
AV Suppiah	c Azhar Mahmood b Kumble	71
MJ Wood	b Clarke	54
CL White (capt)	run out	14
JD Francis	b Brown	41
PD Trego	c Newman b Brown	0
*CM Gazzard	not out	34
AR Caddick	c Akram b Brown	7
MK Munday		
CM Willoughby		
Extras	b 10, lb 4, w 4, nb 30	48
	(8 wkts dec 162.5 overs)	688

Bowling
Akram 21-3-79-0. Azhar Mahmood 17-0-101-0. Saker 16-2-73-0. Kumble 36-3-127-1.
Clarke 24-3-88-1. Salisbury 40-1-181-2. Brown 8.5-1-25-3.
Fall of Wickets: 1-227, 2-389, 3-504, 4-525, 5-625, 6-625, 7-671, 8-688

SURREY	First Innings	
SA Newman	c Gazzard b Willoughby	32
*JN Batty	c Wood b Trego	17
MR Ramprakash	lbw b Willoughby	167
MA Butcher (capt)	c Gazzard b White	84
AD Brown	b White	13
R Clarke	lbw b Trego	214
Azhar Mahmood	c Trego b White	98
IDK Salisbury	lbw b White	50
A Kumble	not out	6
NC Saker	lbw b White	0
Mohammad Akram	lbw b Trego	3
Extras	lb 7, w 1, nb 25	33
	(all out 168.5 overs)	717

Bowling
Caddick 35-5-166-0. Willoughby 33-5-107-2. Trego 23.5-1-87-3. Munday 27-0-126-0.
White 34-2-148-5. Salisbury 14-0-64-0. Edwards 2-0-12-0.
Fall of Wickets: 1-44, 2-64, 3-269, 4-287, 5-392, 6-573, 7-708, 8-712, 9-712

Match drawn – Surrey (10 pts),
Somerset (10 pts)

ESSEX v. GLAMORGAN – at Chelmsford

GLAMORGAN	First Innings		Second Innings	
RE Watkins	c Foster b Bichel	6	(7) not out	7
BB McCullum	c Foster b Bichel	13	(1) c sub b Middlebrook	63
DL Hemp	c Foster b Gough	14	c Middlebrook b Flower GW	21
MJ Powell	b Middlebrook	202	c Bopara b Flower GW	0
RN Grant	b Tudor	44		
JEC Franklin	c Flower A b Middlebrook	7	(5) not out	53
*MA Wallace	b Gough	64	(2) c sub b Flower GW	72
RDB Croft (capt)	c sub b Tudor	14	(6) c Flower GW b Flower A	22
DS Harrison	b Gough	64		
DA Cosker	not out	11		
AJ Harrison	b Gough	3		
Extras	b 4, lb 12, w 2, nb 14	32	b 8, lb 3, w 2	13
	(all out 139 overs)	474	(5 wkts 76 overs)	251

Bowling
Gough 29-3-104-4. Bichel 33-8-95-2. Tudor 22-2-117-2. Bopara 11-3-27-0.
Middlebrook 39-10-88-2. Flower GW 5-0-27-0.
Gough 4-0-11-0. Bichel 6-3-13-0. Tudor 7-2-13-0. Middlebrook 31-9-95-1.
Flower GW 14-3-58-3. Bopara 7-1-30-0. Flower A 7-2-20-1.
Fall of Wickets: 1-13, 2-24, 3-40, 4-177, 5-208, 6-338, 7-365, 8-444, 9-462
1-107, 2-152, 3-157, 4-178, 5-215

ESSEX	First Innings	
WI Jefferson	c Hemp b Franklin	5
ML Pettini	c Hemp b Cosker	29
RS Bopara	c Hemp b Croft	37
A Flower	b Franklin	3
RC Irani (capt)	c Cosker b Croft	145
GW Flower	b Wallace b Croft	101
*JS Foster	c Cosker b Harrison AJ	64
JD Middlebrook	c Croft b Grant	15
AJ Bichel	c McCullum b Croft	25
AJ Tudor	c Croft b Cosker	7
D Gough	not out	9
Extras	b 8, lb 9, w 3, nb 2	22
	(all out 173.2 overs)	462

Bowling
Harrison D.S. 22-9-43-0. Franklin 25-7-59-2. Harrison AJ 21-3-81-1.
Watkins 19-3-44-0. Cosker 37.2-11-105-2. Croft 45-9-104-4. Grant 4-1-9-1.
Fall of Wickets: 1-5, 2-55, 3-76, 4-76, 5-257, 6-380, 7-405, 8-435, 9-452

Match drawn – Essex (9 pts), Glamorgan (10 pts)

LEICESTERSHIRE v. DERBYSHIRE – at Leicester

DERBYSHIRE	First Innings		Second Innings	
MJ Di Venuto	c Nixon b Broad	6	(2) not out	161
SD Stubbings	c Ackerman b Walker	24	(1) b Broad	50
CR Taylor	lbw b Broad	0	(4) c Nixon b Snape	4
MJ North	lbw b Broad	80	(5) not out	0
Hassan Adnan	c Nixon b Broad	117		
G Welch (capt)	lbw b Walker	5		
*DJ Pipe	c & b Broad	89		
GG Wagg	lbw b Griffith	0		
AKD Gray	c Nixon b Masters	4	(3) lbw b Snape	24
PS Jones	lbw b Broad	27		
ID Hunter	not out	9		
Extras	lb 13, w 4, nb 8	25	b 10, lb 7, w 1, nb 6	24
	(all out 112.4 overs)	386	(3 wkts 85 overs)	263

Bowling
Broad 24.5-5-89-5. Griffith 25.4-3-95-2. Walker 17-3-74-2. Masters 24-6-53-1.
Mongia 16-4-33-0. Maunders 1-0-6-0. Snape 5-0-23-0.
Griffith 17-7-39-0. Broad 19.4-7-71-1. Masters 10-2-17-0. Mongia 20-10-44-0.
Walker 12-2-48-0. Snape 7-1-27-2.
Fall of Wickets: 1-6, 2-10, 3-67, 4-155, 5-164, 6-324, 7-325, 8-332, 9-360
1-172, 2-259, 3-263

LEICESTERSHIRE	First Innings	
DDJ Robinson	c North b Hunter	21
JK Maunders	c Pipe b Welch	64
HD Ackerman	c North b Wagg	79
D Mongia	c North b Jones	1
JL Sadler	c Taylor b North	36
JN Snape (capt)	st Pipe b Gray	90
*PA Nixon	c Pipe b Jones	7
DD Masters	c Pipe b Wagg	52
NGE Walker	b Wagg	0
SCJ Broad	not out	65
AR Griffith	c Di Venuto b Welch	34
Extras	b 19, lb 10, w 1, nb 36	66
	(all out 134.2 overs)	515

Bowling
Welch 26.2-8-88-2. Jones 30-7-112-2. Hunter 24-4-93-1. Wagg 18-1-105-3.
Gray 12-3-45-1. North 24-7-43-1.
Fall of Wickets: 1-46, 2-135, 3-146, 4-199, 5-261, 6-283, 7-387, 8-387, 9-450

Match drawn – Leicestershire (12 pts), Derbyshire (11 pts)

Coming man: Stuart Broad bowls for Leicestershire against Derbyshire in a season which saw his stock rise significantly and which later brought England recognition and the Cricket Writers' Club's Young Cricketer of the Year award.

Round Thirteen: 26–30 July 2006

Division One

There was a significant change at the head of the Championship table when, 24 hours after Lancashire's superb five-wicket victory at Trent Bridge against champions Nottinghamshire put them top, Sussex collapsed to a dramatic 13-run defeat at Edgbaston.

At 238 for 6 in their second innings, chasing 270, and with Yasir Arafat and Robin Martin-Jenkins both established at the crease, it seemed as if Sussex would complete the sort of gutsy comeback win that Lancashire had pulled off in Nottingham. But in the end the pressure told on the 2003 champions and, with South African slow left-armer Paul Harris taking 5 for 73, Sussex slipped disappointingly to 256 all out. Their defeat wasted their fine fightback on the third

day when Warwickshire, 88 for 3 overnight, folded themselves to 140 all out as Mushtaq Ahmed picked up 5 for 39 and Arafat 3 for 38. That gave Sussex a real chance, especially when Richard Montgomerie and Mike Yardy combined to put on 138 for the second wicket and leave their side on 190 for 4 at the close. It was a transformation from the first two days when Warwickshire, boosted by an excellent century by Nick Knight, further good batting from Tim Ambrose and a six-wicket haul from Neil Carter in Sussex's first innings, seemed in complete control.

Similarly, after a day and a half at Trent Bridge it looked as if Lancashire were heading for a heavy defeat. A brilliant 150 off 177 balls from David Hussey, plus innings of 53 by Stephen Fleming and 83 by Mark Ealham, had taken Nottinghamshire to 397 all out – a total which then earned them a sizeable lead as Lancashire struggled to 200 in reply.

OF NOTTINGHAMSHIRE

The 2005 County Championship title, won under New Zealand captain Stephen Fleming, was an achievement to rank alongside those of the team of the 1980s which, under Clive Rice and with Sir Richard Hadlee as another considerable inspiration, was one of the strongest in the county's proud history.

The Rice-Hadlee era ended with the great double triumph of Championship and NatWest Trophy in 1987, and they had also inspired the county to its 1981 Championship success. With other players of the calibre of Chris Broad, Tim Robinson, Derek Randall, Bruce French, Paul Johnson, Eddie Hemmings and Kevin Cooper influential at that time, it was no surprise either that the immediate legacy of the Rice-Hadlee years was further trophies in 1989 and 1991, when the Benson and Hedges Cup and Sunday League were taken. The club could have had yet more success in the mid-1980s too, reaching the final both of the Benson and Hedges Cup in 1982 and the NatWest Trophy in 1985, where they lost to Somerset and Essex.

But, before the 2005 triumph, Nottinghamshire fell into something of a trough. As the club's wonderfully evocative Trent Bridge ground was modernised and improved with wisdom and care, on-field success proved elusive.

The New Zealand connection was maintained by the signing of all-rounder Chris Cairns, and good young players like Paul Franks, Usman Afzaal and Chris Read emerged in the late 1990s. But the likes of Afzaal and Bilal Shafayat left for pastures new and it took a raft of canny signings – such as Ryan Sidebottom from Yorkshire, Darren Bicknell from Surrey, Jason Gallian from Lancashire, Andrew Harris from Derbyshire, Mark Ealham from Kent and Graeme Swann from Northamptonshire – for Notts to get their team balance right and get among the trophies again.

Fleming and David Hussey, the Australian, scored heavily in support of veteran openers Bicknell and Gallian, Read also averaged almost 45 in the lower middle-order and Swann's off breaks supported a highly effective four-pronged pace attack of Sidebottom, Harris, Ealham and Greg Smith. Injuries to key players in 2006, however, threw Nottinghamshire completely off course and illustrated yet again just how delicate and fragile a thing the make-up of a team can be.

The twin architects of Nottinghamshire's double Championship triumph of the 1980s, Clive Rice (left) and Richard Hadlee, show off the 1987 NatWest Trophy.

But, just as the Notts seamers had found conditions to their liking, so did Lancashire's Glen Chapple and Dominic Cork. By the close of day two the home side were wobbling at 94 for 5 in their second innings and, with Chapple going on to take 6 for 35 and Cork 3 for 38, Notts were bundled out for just 114 the following morning. Lancashire were back in it, and for the rest of the third day it was the batsmen who flourished. Iain Sutcliffe led the way, reaching the close on 107 not out, and he added 106 for the first wicket with Mark Chilton before the Lancashire captain was dismissed for 50. Better was to come, though, as Mal Loye kept Sutcliffe company until stumps when he was 73 not out and the visitors were in sight of victory at 236 for 1. Loye completed his own hundred on the final morning, adding 199 in all with the tenacious Sutcliffe, who finished unbeaten on a six-and-a-half-hour 139 as Lancashire ran out five-wicket winners.

Hampshire, meanwhile, did their best to keep pace with the division leaders by going third with a ten-wicket dismantling of Yorkshire at the Rose Bowl. Dimitri Mascarenhas, supported by Chris Tremlett, did the initial damage by taking 6 for 65 as Yorkshire were bundled out for 195 on day one. By the close Michael Carberry had already reached 81 not out, in a reply of 131 for 1, and although the left-handed opener was distraught to fall one short of his hundred the following morning it was only a small setback for a Hampshire team determined to ram home their advantage. No one was more determined than John Crawley, who passed 1,000 runs for the season for the 10th time in his career as he completed his 50th first-class hundred and then motored on to 173. Yorkshire's 20-year-old leg spinner Mark Lawson did

Round Thirteen: 26–30 July 2006 Division One

WARWICKSHIRE v. SUSSEX – at Edgbaston

WARWICKSHIRE	First Innings		Second Innings	
IJ Westwood	c M'gomerie b Martin-Jenkins	24	c Lewry b Yasir Arafat	53
MA Wagh	c Lewry b Kirtley	5	lbw b Kirtley	7
IJL Trott	c Lewry b Yasir Arafat	9	lbw b Yasir Arafat	19
NV Knight	lbw b Kirtley	123	c sub b Martin-Jenkins	19
AGR Loudon	c Adams b Mushtaq Ahmed	19	(6) c sub b Yasir Arafat	4
MJ Powell	c M Ahmed b Martin-Jenkins	42	(7) lbw b Mushtaq Ahmed	15
*TR Ambrose	b Yasir Arafat	67	(8) not out	11
JE Anyon	b Yasir Arafat	4	(5) c Hopkinson b M Ahmed	5
HH Streak (capt)	b Kirtley	5	c Hopkinson b M Ahmed	5
NM Carter	not out	18	c Hopkinson b M Ahmed	5
PL Harris	lbw b Yasir Arafat	0	lbw b Mushtaq Ahmed	0
Extras	b 22, lb 16, w 2, nb 8	48	nb 6	6
	(all out 115 overs)	375	(all out 55.3 overs)	140

Bowling:
Lewry 21-10-45-0. Kirtley 26-6-82-3. Yasir Arafat 22-4-77-4.
Martin-Jenkins 21-5-41-2. Mushtaq Ahmed 25-4-92-1.
Lewry 13-0-32-0. Kirtley 9-2-25-1. Yasir Arafat 12-2-38-3.
Mushtaq Ahmed 18.3-6-39-5. Martin-Jenkins 3-1-6-1.
Fall of Wickets: 1-10, 2-22, 3-54, 4-89, 5-215, 6-312, 7-321, 8-344, 9-360
1-20, 2-41, 3-81, 4-88, 5-103, 6-112, 7-126, 8-136, 9-140

SUSSEX	First Innings		Second Innings	
RR Montgomerie	c Harris b Anyon	45	(2) c Westwood b Harris	65
CD Hopkinson	c Trott b Carter	36	(1) c Ambrose b Streak	2
*MH Yardy	c Ambrose b Carter	3	c Powell b Harris	67
MW Goodwin	c Ambrose b Carter	8	c Trott b Harris	8
CJ Adams (capt)	c Loudon b Carter	63	b Anyon	16
RSC Martin-Jenkins	c Loudon b Carter	20	(7) b Harris	20
MJ Prior	c Powell b Harris	52	(6) c Powell b Anyon	9
Yasir Arafat	c Westwood b Carter	22	c Ambrose b Carter	23
Mushtaq Ahmed	c Ambrose b Anyon	2	b Harris	8
RJ Kirtley	not out	1	not out	6
JD Lewry	b Carter	0	b Carter	3
Extras	b 2, lb 3, w 2, nb 14	21	b 14, lb 4, w 1, nb 10	29
	(all out 58.4 overs)	246	(all out 93.1 overs)	256

Bowling:
Streak 11-1-52-0. Carter 17.4-4-63-6. Anyon 17-1-78-3. Harris 8-4-23-1.
Loudon 5-0-25-0.
Streak 11-4-38-1. Anyon 25-3-63-2. Harris 38-13-73-5. Carter 13.1-2-46-2.
Loudon 6-1-18-0.
Fall of Wickets: 1-87, 2-91, 3-93, 4-93, 5-93, 6-179, 7-227, 8-244, 9-246
1-14, 2-152, 3-153, 4-178, 5-190, 6-196, 7-238, 8-240, 9-247

Warwickshire won by 13 runs –
Warwickshire (21 pts), Sussex (4 pts)

NOTTINGHAMSHIRE v. LANCASHIRE – at Trent Bridge

NOTTS	First Innings		Second Innings	
DJ Bicknell	lbw b Cork	6	b Chapple	7
JER Gallian	c Chilton b Cork	4	lbw b Cork	8
D Alleyne	c Chilton b Smith	20	c Smith b Chapple	10
SP Fleming (capt)	lbw b Smith	53	lbw b Cork	15
DJ Hussey	c Astle b Keedy	150	c Cross b Chapple	18
*CMW Read	lbw b Newby	9	c Cross b Cork	16
MA Ealham	b Smith	83	c Cross b Chapple	10
GP Swann	c Cross b Chapple	27	c £t b Chapple	5
RJ Sidebottom	c Law b Keedy	4	c Cross b Chapple	0
AJ Harris	not out	28	run out	14
CE Shreck	lbw b Cork	1	not out	1
Extras	b 3, lb 4, w 1, nb 4	12	b 2, lb 8	10
	(all out 98.3 overs)	397	(all out 44 overs)	114

Bowling:
Cork 16.3-1-74-3. Chapple 20-7-76-1. Smith 20-2-69-3. Newby 15-0-72-1.
Keedy 22-0-80-2. Astle 4-0-14-0. Chilton 1-0-5-0.
Cork 14-5-38-3. Chapple 22-10-35-6. Smith 7-0-26-0. Newby 1-0-5-0.
Fall of Wickets: 1-6, 2-15, 3-79, 4-94, 5-107, 6-333, 7-343, 8-352, 9-390
1-17, 2-19, 3-35, 4-66, 5-72, 6-94, 7-94, 8-99, 9-100

LANCASHIRE	First Innings		Second Innings	
MJ Chilton (capt)	c Fleming b Shreck	44	(2) c Fleming b Swann	50
IJ Sutcliffe	c Read b Sidebottom	10	(1) not out	139
MB Loye	lbw b Sidebottom	35	c Fleming b Swann	108
SG Law	c £t b Shreck	0	c Sidebottom b Swann	2
NJ Astle	b Harris	29	b Swann	2
*GD Cross	c Read b Sidebottom	10		
G Chapple	c Sidebottom b Harris	39	(6) c £t b Hussey	2
DG Cork	b Ealham	22	(7) not out	4
TC Smith	b Ealham	0		
OJ Newby	b Harris	0		
G Keedy	not out	0		
Extras	b 1, lb 7, w 1, nb 2	11	b 3, lb 1, w 1, nb 4	9
	(all out 56.2 overs)	200	(5 wkts 106.4 overs)	314

Bowling:
Sidebottom 18-3-57-3. Harris 12-3-46-3. Shreck 11-1-57-2. Ealham 13.2-3-32-2.
Sidebottom 22-4-73-0. Harris 16-2-42-0. Shreck 14-4-59-0. Swann 38-15-81-4.
Ealham 11-3-35-0. Hussey 5.4-2-20-1.
Fall of Wickets: 1-22, 2-93, 3-93, 4-95, 5-115, 6-164, 7-195, 8-195, 9-200
1-106, 2-305, 3-305, 4-307, 5-310

Lancashire won by 5 wickets –
Nottinghamshire (7 pts), Lancashire (18 pts)

HAMPSHIRE v. YORKSHIRE – at the Rose Bowl

YORKSHIRE	First Innings		Second Innings	
C White (capt)	b Tremlett	4	lbw b Mascarenhas	0
JJ Sayers	c Pothas b Ervine	31	c Adams b Warne	43
A McGrath	c Crawley b Mascarenhas	1	(5) c Benham b Ervine	65
MJ Lumb	c Pothas b Mascarenhas	31	(6) c Pothas b Warne	105
DS Lehmann	c Pothas b Mascarenhas	41	(4) c Benham b Tremlett	4
AW Gale	b Mascarenhas	0	(7) c Thornely b Tremlett	1
*GL Brophy	c Adams b Mascarenhas	31	(8) c Warne b Tremlett	1
MAK Lawson	c Pothas b Mascarenhas	8	(3) c Crawley b Ervine	34
JN Gillespie	c Thornely b Tremlett	29	(3) c Benham b Tremlett	8
SA Patterson	not out	6	lbw b Warne	0
GJ Kruis	c Adams b Tremlett	2	not out	0
Extras	b 2, lb 6, w 1, nb 6	15	b 1, lb 1, nb 6	8
	(all out 60.3 overs)	195	(all out 72.3 overs)	311

Bowling:
Tremlett 9.3-3-25-3. Mascarenhas 19-5-65-6. Taylor 7-3-11-0. Ervine 14-3-45-1.
Thornely 7-2-19-0. Warne 4-0-22-0.
Mascarenhas 12-3-48-1. Tremlett 15-0-69-4. Warne 21.3-1-100-3. Taylor 10-1-35-0.
Ervine 14-1-57-2.
Fall of Wickets: 1-15, 2-20, 3-53, 4-105, 5-109, 6-126, 7-138, 8-165, 9-191
1-0, 2-33, 3-41, 4-87, 5-153, 6-205, 7-213, 8-281, 9-310

HAMPSHIRE	First Innings		Second Innings	
JHK Adams	lbw b Gillespie	29	not out	5
MA Carberry	c Sayers b Lawson	99	not out	10
JP Crawley	b Gillespie	173		
CC Benham	b Lehmann	56		
DJ Thornely	c Brophy b Lawson	27		
*N Pothas	c Patterson b McGrath	7		
SM Ervine	c Sayers b Lawson	2		
AD Mascarenhas	c Brophy b Lawson	39		
SK Warne (capt)	st Brophy b Lawson	30		
CT Tremlett	not out	2		
BV Taylor	c £t b Lawson	3		
Extras	b 4, lb 10, w 2, nb 8	24		
	(all out 141.4 overs)	493	(0 wkts 3.4 overs)	15

Bowling:
Gillespie 29-9-85-2. Kruis 25-4-96-0. Patterson 21-7-56-0. McGrath 25-6-67-1.
Lawson 34.4-1-125-6. Lehmann 7-0-25-1.
Lawson 2-0-8-0. Patterson 1.4-0-7-0.
Fall of Wickets: 1-97, 2-165, 3-288, 4-353, 5-357, 6-448, 7-452, 8-472, 9-489

Hampshire won by 10 wickets –
Hampshire (22 pts), Yorkshire (1 pt)

MIDDLESEX v. DURHAM – at Lord's

DURHAM	First Innings		Second Innings	
JP Maher	b Keegan	46	c Silverwood b Styris	35
JA Lowe	c Nash b Keegan	5	lbw b Styris	25
GJ Muchall	c Shah b Silverwood	68	c Smith b Dalrymple	41
DM B'kenstein (capt)	c Silverwood b Louw	125	c Styris b Dalrymple	47
BW Harmison	b Keegan	1	b Dalrymple	2
GR Breese	c Nash b Keegan	110	c Smith b Thorp	16
*P Mustard	c Joyce b Styris	1	c Keegan b Styris	16
OD Gibson	c Compton b Silverwood	12	not out	24
CD Thorp	b Keegan	5	not out	9
G Onions	c Styris b Silverwood	4		
ML Lewis	not out	16		
Extras	lb 7, w 3, nb 4	14	b 3, lb 4, w 1, nb 6	14
	(all out 105.1 overs)	407	(7 wkts 67.4 overs)	220

Bowling:
Silverwood 23-3-83-3. Keegan 23.1-6-90-5. Styris 18-3-65-1. Louw 20-2-85-1.
Peploe 17-3-64-0. Shah 1-0-1-0. Dalrymple 3-0-12-0.
Silverwood 19-4-67-0. Keegan 13-3-33-0. Louw 6-0-29-0. Styris 15-4-55-4.
Dalrymple 14.4-4-29-3.
Fall of Wickets: 1-8, 2-112, 3-130, 4-131, 5-353, 6-355, 7-381, 8-386, 9-391
1-59, 2-70, 3-152, 4-163, 5-166, 6-183, 7-191

MIDDLESEX	First Innings		Second Innings (following on)	
ET Smith	c Mustard b Onions	1	c Harmison B b Onions	10
NRD Compton	c Breese b Onions	56	c Maher b Thorp	190
OA Shah	c Lowe b Onions	0	c Mustard b Thorp	57
EC Joyce	c Harmison B b Thorp	16	c Lowe b Gibson	19
JWM Dalrymple	lbw b Gibson	6	c Thorp b Gibson	8
SB Styris (capt)	c Mustard b Gibson	28	c Mustard b Breese	84
EJG Morgan	c Mustard b Onions	38	lbw b Thorp	38
*DC Nash	lbw b Onions	1	not out	47
J Louw	not out	22	c Mustard b Lewis	10
CB Keegan	c Mustard b Benkenstein	1	lbw b Lewis	21
CEW Silverwood	c Mustard b Benkenstein	3	c Mustard b Lewis	0
CT Peploe†				
Extras	lb 1, w 1, nb 2	4	lb 14, w 3, nb 2	19
	(all out 55.1 overs)	176	(all out 133.5 overs)	503

Bowling:
Onions 15-6-45-5. Lewis 15-7-42-0. Thorp 11-2-37-1. Gibson 9-2-27-2.
Benkenstein 5.1-3-24-2.
Onions 24-3-91-1. Lewis 25.5-3-89-3. Gibson 27-5-90-2. Thorp 25-10-79-3.
Benkenstein 11-3-40-0. Breese 21-1-100-1.
Fall of Wickets: 1-2, 2-8, 3-29, 4-38, 5-88, 6-134, 7-150, 8-151, 9-160
1-10, 2-101, 3-138, 4-157, 5-318, 6-422, 7-435, 8-459, 9-503

† Replaced by JWM Dalrymple
Match drawn – Middlesex (7 pts), Durham (12 pts)

OF SOMERSET

Somerset had won nothing until 1979, but at the start of this last 25-year period stood as one of the best and most feared teams in the land. It had a lot to do with three players by the name of Ian Botham, Viv Richards and Joel Garner.

Five one-day titles were won between 1979 and 1983 and, indeed, the level of success could and perhaps should have been more. Besides their three superstars, Somerset were blessed in this era by a clutch of top-class, committed homegrown cricketers – such as Brian Rose, the captain from 1978 to 1983, Vic Marks, Peter Roebuck and Peter Denning.

Botham was also a Yeovil lad who grew into one of the game's legends while Richards spent a summer playing Western League cricket for Bath club Lansdown and then a whole season for Somerset, in 1974, before he graced the international stage with the West Indies.

The breakthrough year of 1979 had brought two trophies – the Gillette Cup and the Sunday League – while the seasons of 1981, 1982 and 1983 each contained one limited-overs success. Surrey and Nottinghamshire were vanquished in the 1981 and 1982 Benson and Hedges Cup finals respectively, while Marks made it two Lord's Man-of-the-Match awards in successive years by starring with the ball in the 1983 NatWest Trophy final win against Kent.

Botham, Richards and Garner all left the club under acrimonious circumstances in 1986, however, as a result of new captain Roebuck's new broom policy with regard to the overseas player situation. The two great West Indians, Richards and Garner, were not in Roebuck and the committee's future plans and Botham walked out in disgust at the decision. New Zealand Test batsman Martin Crowe was the overseas player chosen to provide inspiration post-Richards and Garner, but try as he might the magic seemed to desert Somerset cricket in the late 1980s and 1990s.

It took a completely new generation, with the likes of Marcus Trescothick and Andrew Caddick now the senior men, to achieve the county's next success. After reaching the NatWest Trophy final in 1999, where they were beaten by 50 runs by Gloucestershire in a West Country shoot-out, Somerset triumphed in the first year of the newly named C&G Trophy in 2001 when Leicestershire were defeated by 41 runs. Man of the Match on that day was Keith Parsons, a 28-year-old all-rounder from Taunton who personified the collective sense of purpose within a team devoid – unlike that of 20 years earlier – of big star names.

The Twenty20 Cup win of 2005, under the temporary but inspired leadership of South African captain Graeme Smith, is another modern highlight for a county still struggling – overall – to regain the glamour and sheer excitement of the glory years under Rose.

Somerset's glorious triumvirate – Ian Botham, Viv Richards and Joel Garner – brought previously elusive success to a county which for much of its history had been a cricketing backwater. There were other stars too – Brian Rose, Vic Marks and Peter Roebuck all played significant parts in a clutch of one-day trophy wins – but it was Beefy, the Master Blaster and Big Bird who made all the difference.

John Crawley reached 1,000 runs for the season for the tenth time in the match against Yorkshire at the Rose Bowl.

well to finish with career-best figures of 6 for 150, but Hampshire's 493 gave the visitors little hope of escape and not even a defiant 105 from Michael Lumb, who went to three figures from 112 balls with a six off Sean Ervine, could prevent defeat inside three days.

Durham left Lord's wondering how they had not managed to beat a Middlesex side they had forced to follow on 231 runs behind their own first innings 407, in which both Dale Benkenstein and Gareth Breese hit hundreds in a stand of 222. Benkenstein's 125 occupied only 142 balls, and included three sixes and 18 fours. Graham Onions then took 5 for 45 as Middlesex were skittled for 176 and, in the four overs to be bowled before the close, the rapidly-improving Onions also nipped out Ed Smith to leave the home side on 10 for 1. The third day, however, saw a magnificent Middlesex fightback as Nick Compton followed up his 56 of the day before with a superb, career-best 190 featuring 31 fours. He was out just five balls from the close, having batted all day, but by then

Middlesex were 435 for 7 – with Owais Shah and Scott Styris also having made valuable contributions – and on the final morning David Nash's further resistance took the total beyond 500 and set Durham 273 to win in the remaining 68 overs. At first they seemed to making a decent fist of the chase, but vital wickets fell and, from a position in which they wanted 110 from the last 20 overs, Durham lost their way and ultimately were forced to settle for a draw.

Division Two

An epic innings of 299 from the in-form Michael Powell, and a 13-wicket match haul by their captain Robert Croft, inspired Glamorgan to a ten-wicket victory over Gloucestershire in the first match of the Cheltenham Festival. It was a disappointing result, of course, for the home crowd but there was much good cricket to admire from both teams. In the end, the sheer excellence of Powell and Croft's efforts told, with Glamorgan's skipper returning the second-best match figures of his long career. A fine crowd of more than 2,000 saw Powell take charge on the opening day, with David Hemp also reaching three figures in a second-wicket stand of 238 following Brendon McCullum's early withdrawal, retiring hurt after being struck on the hand by Steve Kirby. Powell was on 176 by the close, having gone past his 1,000 runs for the season during his third hundred in ten days, and on day two he and Glamorgan pushed on relentlessly from their overnight 346 for 2. Eventually, however, trying to push a single into the offside to complete his triple-century, Powell was beaten by slow left-armer Ian Fisher's turn and edged behind. He was only 19 runs short too of W. G. Grace's Cheltenham record of 318 not out, set in 1876, but had batted in all for ten and three-quarter hours, hitting two sixes and 39 fours. Gloucestershire's reply was spirited, with Craig Spearman racing to 106 out of 180 and Kadeer Ali then joining Hamish Marshall in a third-wicket stand of 151 as the New Zealander went to 127 from 173 balls. But Croft, who did not take his first wicket until his 24th over, won reward for his perseverance by finishing with 6 for 120 as Gloucestershire were bowled out for 443 and immediately asked to follow on. In nine overs before the close of the third day, moreover, Spearman had fallen to Dean Cosker and Croft had also sent back the nightwatchman Martyn Ball to leave the home side on 30 for 2. Half-centuries on the final day from both Marshall and Alex Gidman could not now deny Croft, who took a further 7 for 67 to leave his team with just 41 needed for a sweet victory.

OF SURREY

Between 1996 and 2003 Surrey were the outstanding team in the country. They may not quite have reached the heights of their predecessors – who won seven consecutive Championships between 1952 and 1958 – but they were not far short. Three Championship titles were won in 1999, 2000 and 2002, while five one-day trophies were also secured during that golden eight-year period. There were Benson and Hedges Cup successes in 1997 and 2001, Sunday League and National League wins in 1996 and 2003 respectively, plus the inaugural Twenty20 Cup in 2003.

Many times during this period a Surrey XI entirely made up of internationals took to the field. The batting line-up was often awesome: at first featuring the likes of Alec Stewart, Graham Thorpe, Mark Butcher, Alistair Brown, Ian Ward, Adam Hollioake and Darren Bicknell – and then, when Bicknell left for Nottinghamshire in 2000, strengthened still further with the signing of Mark Ramprakash from Middlesex in 2001.

Hollioake and his younger brother Ben (who died tragically in a car crash in 2002) provided all-round depth and strength, with Adam also proving an inspirational captain. All good captains need good bowling attacks to be extra special, and Hollioake had at his disposal the prolific spin partnership of Saqlain Mushtaq and Ian Salisbury, who both joined in 1997. Martin Bicknell, who had made his Surrey debut as far back as 1986 – as a 17-year-old – matured into one of the most consistent and dangerous new-ball bowlers on the county circuit, while the likes of Alex Tudor and Ed Giddins also provided seam bowling of high quality until the arrival of Saqlain's fellow Pakistani Azhar Mahmood and James Ormond from Leicestershire, both in 2002.

The fact that so many of this great Surrey side were homegrown, however, added to the scale of their achievements. It had been a long 14 years between the lone NatWest Trophy success of 1982 and the Sunday League title of 1996. But it was the start of great things.

Another trophy for the all-conquering Surrey team under Adam Hollioake as they celebrate winning the County Championship in 1999.

County cricket's return to Chesterfield, after an eight-year gap, was well received by the Derbyshire public and was a resounding success. The county's players also marked the occasion by fighting hard to earn themselves a draw after conceding 146 on first innings to Worcestershire, for whom both Vikram Solanki and Steven Davies scored eye-catching centuries. Michael Di Venuto, though, launched Derbyshire's second innings with a superb 99 – ruined only by his decision to take on Solanki at mid-on when looking for the single to complete his hundred. If his run out gave Worcestershire renewed hope, it was soon extinguished as Marcus North went on to reach 161 and Ant Botha completed his own fine all-round match with a second half-century.

Northamptonshire's high-scoring draw with Essex was overshadowed by the news that Kepler Wessels, their director of cricket for three and a half seasons, had decided to leave the club by mutual consent and with immediate effect. Wessels still had 14 months left on his contract, but clashes with players and supporters over the direction he was taking the county made his exit more of a relief than a surprise to those who felt that Northants had lost much of its identity under his leadership. On the field, meanwhile, there was a career-best 178 from Stephen Peters on day one and – ten years to the day that he had made a double-hundred on his debut against Worcestershire as an

Glamorgan's Michael Powell was only one short of 300 when he edged a catch off Gloucestershire's Ian Fisher.

Round Thirteen: 26–30 July 2006 Division Two

GLOUCESTERSHIRE v. GLAMORGAN – at Cheltenham

GLAMORGAN	First Innings		Second Innings	
BB McCullum	c Spearman b Rudge	20	not out	34
GP Rees	b Kirby	1	not out	4
DL Hemp	b Gidman	102		
MJ Powell	c Adshead b Fisher	299		
RE Watkins	c sub b Ball	59		
JEC Franklin	c Ball b Fisher	94		
*MA Wallace	lbw b Ball	5		
RDB Croft (capt)	not out	14		
AG Wharf				
DS Harrison				
DA Cosker				
Extras	b 10, lb 2, w 6, nb 35	53	nb 6	6
	(7 wkts dec 184.3 overs)	647	(0 wkts 3.4 overs)	44

Bowling
Kirby 28-3-117-1. Rudge 19-0-99-1. Gidman 24-4-103-1. Ball 60-19-113-2. Fisher 44.3-3-166-2. Kadeer Ali 2-0-9-0. Lewis 7-0-28-0. Lewis 2-0-15-0. Kirby 1.4-0-29-0.
Fall of Wickets: 1-27, 2-265, 3-392, 4-422, 5-610, 6-619, 7-647.

GLOS	First Innings		Second Innings (following on)	
WPC Weston	c Watkins b Wharf	18	(2) lbw b Croft	9
CM Spearman	c Harrison b Franklin	106	(1) lbw b Cosker	7
HJH Marshall	c McCullum b Cosker	127	(4) c Watkins b Croft	53
Kadeer Ali	lbw b Croft	60	(5) c Wharf b Croft	0
CG Taylor	c Wallace b Franklin	30	(6) c Wallace b Harrison	23
APR Gidman (capt)	c Wharf b Croft	3	(7) lbw b Croft	66
*SJ Adshead	c Wallace b Croft	41	(8) c Watkins b Croft	26
ID Fisher	lbw b Croft	2	(9) not out	21
MCJ Ball	c Wallace b Croft	17	(3) c Watkins b Croft	1
J Lewis	c Hemp b Croft	6	c Watkins b Harrison	23
SP Kirby	not out	1	c Watkins b Croft	1
WD Rudge†				
Extras	b 16, lb 4, w 6, nb 6	32	b 9, lb 3, nb 2	14
	(all out 117.2 overs)	443	(all out 85.5 overs)	244

Bowling
Harrison 21-3-63-0. Franklin 17-3-89-2. Watkins 6-0-44-0. Wharf 14-4-34-1. Croft 37.2-4-120-6. Cosker 22-2-73-1.
Harrison 13.2-2-51-2. Franklin 9-1-31-0. Cosker 22.4-5-51-1. Croft 29.5-5-67-7. Wharf 11-2-32-0.
Fall of Wickets: 1-91, 2-180, 3-331, 4-373, 5-375, 6-382, 7-398, 8-434, 9-442
1-12, 2-13, 3-48, 4-48, 5-91, 6-121, 7-167, 8-214, 9-243
† Replaced by J Lewis

Glamorgan won by 10 wickets – Gloucestershire (6 pts), Glamorgan (22 pts)

DERBYSHIRE v. WORCESTERSHIRE – at Chesterfield

DERBYSHIRE	First Innings		Second Innings	
SD Stubbings	run out	11	(2) c Sillence b Mason	0
MJ Di Venuto	lbw b Mason	16	(1) run out	99
CR Taylor	st Davies b Price	40	c Smith b Batty	15
MJ North	c Sillence b Price	17	b Solanki	161
Hassan Adnan	c Hick b Mason	33	lbw b Khan	7
AG Botha	c Davies b Mason	87	lbw b Solanki	50
G Welch (capt)	c Hick b Batty	11	lbw b Khan	14
*DJ Pipe	b Mason	46	b Khan	12
GG Wagg	c Solanki b Khan	45	b Batty	14
PS Jones	not out	17	c Smith b Sillence	8
ID Hunter	c Davies b Mason	1	not out	0
Extras	lb 15, w 12	27	b 22, lb 6, w 1	29
	(all out 97.2 overs)	351	(all out 139.4 overs)	409

Bowling
Khan 17-2-57-1. Mason 20.2-5-49-5. Sillence 6-0-40-0. Vincent 2-0-12-0. Price 25-1-93-2. Batty 23-4-67-1. Solanki 4-0-18-0.
Khan 30-5-95-3. Mason 17-3-57-1. Batty 44-13-91-2. Price 34-3-94-0. Solanki 6-1-16-2. Sillence 8.4-2-28-1.
Fall of Wickets: 1-33, 2-42, 3-100, 4-121, 5-161, 6-176, 7-259, 8-330, 9-344
1-0, 2-53, 3-183, 4-200, 5-349, 6-362, 7-384, 8-387, 9-409

WORCS	First Innings		Second Innings	
L Vincent	lbw b Wagg	14	(2) not out	33
SC Moore	c Taylor b Botha	63	(1) c Pipe b Wagg	26
VS Solanki (capt)	c Botha b Jones	140	not out	22
BF Smith	c North b Botha	45		
GA Hick	c Pipe b Hunter	8		
*SM Davies	c & b Botha	107		
GJ Batty	c & b Botha	79		
RJ Sillence	lbw b Welch	0		
Z Khan	c North b Botha	7		
RW Price	not out	3		
MS Mason	st Pipe b Botha	4		
Extras	b 4, lb 10, w 1, nb 12	27	lb 1	1
	(all out 137.2 overs)	497	(1 wkt 14 overs)	82

Bowling
Jones 24-4-108-1. Hunter 11-2-60-1. Wagg 18-4-75-1. Welch 27-9-81-1. Botha 41.2-13-117-6. North 16-1-42-0.
Hunter 4-0-37-0. Wagg 7-1-33-1. Botha 3-0-11-0.
Fall of Wickets: 1-39, 2-159, 3-250, 4-272, 5-301, 6-466, 7-467, 8-484, 9-491
1-41

Match drawn – Derbyshire (10 pts), Worcestershire (12 pts)

NORTHAMPTONSHIRE v. ESSEX – at Northampton

NORTHANTS	First Innings		Second Innings	
SD Peters	c Bopara b Bichel	178	not out	26
*BM Shafayat	c Foster b Palladino	23	c Foster b Bopara	19
U Afzaal	c Flower A b Middlebrook	35	not out	20
SC Ganguly	c Phillips b Middlebrook	9		
DJG Sales (capt)	c Foster b Middlebrook	225		
L Klusener	not out	124		
RA White	not out	48		
BJ Phillips				
MJ Nicholson				
DH Wigley				
JF Brown				
Extras	lb 8, w 6, nb 4	18	lb 5, w 1, nb 6	12
	(5 wkts dec 159 overs)	660	(1 wkt 24 overs)	77

Bowling
Bichel 24.5-5-102-1. Palladino 23-2-88-1. Tudor 23-5-92-0. Bopara 11-1-49-0. Middlebrook 44-4-174-3. Phillips 34-2-147-0.
Tudor 5-1-13-0. Palladino 5-2-15-0. Bopara 3-0-18-1. Phillips 7-1-24-0. Flower G.W. 4-2-2-0.
Fall of Wickets: 1-56, 2-138, 3-154, 4-366, 5-597
1-39

ESSEX	First Innings	
GW Flower	b Phillips	3
ML Pettini	run out	8
RS Bopara	c White b Brown	38
A Flower	not out	271
RC Irani (capt)	c Shafayat b Phillips	41
JD Middlebrook	lbw b Wigley	45
*JS Foster	c Afzaal b Brown	60
TJ Phillips	c Klusener b Wigley	46
AJ Tudor	b White	74
AJ Palladino	b White	0
AP Palladino	c Sales b White	0
Extras	b 6, lb 9, w 11, nb 8	34
	(all out 172 overs)	620

Bowling
Nicholson 26-6-70-0. Phillips 19-4-64-2. Wigley 26-2-115-2. Klusener 19-4-68-0. Brown 53-9-146-3. Afzaal 13-0-61-0. White 10-0-57-2. Ganguly 6-1-24-0.
Fall of Wickets: 1-10, 2-15, 3-108, 4-166, 5-248, 6-364, 7-488, 8-611, 9-620

Match drawn – Northamptonshire (11 pts), Essex (10 pts)

18-year-old – another memorable innings of 225 on the second day by David Sales. There was also an unbeaten 124 from Lance Klusener to take Northants to a huge 660 for 5 declared, but Essex's own massive reply of 620 on a featherbed surface became a showcase for the considerable talents of Andy Flower, who ended up still unbeaten on 271 when the innings finally came to a close.

Round Fourteen: 1–6 August 2006

Division One

Mal Loye single-handedly kept Lancashire in the hunt for their first outright Championship title since 1934 with a truly magnificent fighting innings of 148 not out at Hove. Sussex, by contrast, were left to rue the fact that their match-winning leg spinner Mushtaq Ahmed was not fully fit – despite hobbling in to bowl 37 overs on the final day – and that Lancashire were finally able to scrape a draw with nine wickets down in a thrilling finale to a hard-fought match. Sussex took 11 points from a game that was always going to provide a major say in the outcome of the title race, and Lancashire nine, but Chris Adams' side would have gained a 15-point lead at the top of the division if they had clinched victory. As it was, they had to be content with just a one-point advantage.

Dominic Cork struck the first two telling blows of the match, in front of a 2,500 first day crowd, but Mike Yardy and Murray Goodwin steadied the Sussex first innings with a third-wicket partnership of 99 before Matt Prior and Robin Martin-Jenkins rallied them from 161 for 5 with fine innings of 112 and 73 respectively. A pugnacious unbeaten 51 from Luke Wright then took Sussex to 439 and maximum batting points. From 145 for 4 in reply, Lancashire were in turn boosted by Stuart Law's 130 and an aggressive 68 from 21-year-old reserve wicketkeeper Graham Cross, who featured two sixes and seven fours in his 46-ball half-century. Sussex, however, still won themselves a 107-run lead as Jason Lewry, with 6 for 68, and Yasir Arafat made up for the comparative ineffectiveness of Mushtaq. Hundreds from Richard Montgomerie and Goodwin, his fifth of the season, then set up a Sussex declaration overnight before the final day. In the end, despite Mushtaq's bravery in bowling for so long, it was Loye who held firm in a brilliant 256-ball effort. Cork, too, hung on for 14 overs for 10 after coming in at the fall of the eighth wicket because of the discomfort of a split finger. When Cork was finally removed, amid huge tension, last man Gary Keedy survived two balls from Mushtaq and Loye played out the last over.

Hampshire looked to have set up a victory drive at Canterbury by bowling out the home team for 285

Round Fourteen: 1–6 August 2006 Division One

SUSSEX v. LANCASHIRE – at Hove

SUSSEX	First Innings		Second Innings	
RR Montgomerie	lbw b Cork	4	(2) c Law b Keedy	100
CD Hopkinson	c Cross b Cork	0	(1) c Law b Keedy	14
MH Yardy	c Cork b Keedy	63	c Sutcliffe b Keedy	6
MW Goodwin	c & b Smith	40	c Smith b Law	103
CJ Adams (capt)	c Cross b Chapple	31	st Cross b Keedy	28
*MJ Prior	c Cross b Cork	112	c Cross b Marshall	6
RSC Martin-Jenkins	lbw b Keedy	73		
Yasir Arafat	c Law b Smith	27	(7) not out	15
LJ Wright	not out	51	(8) not out	13
Mushtaq Ahmed	c Chilton b Keedy	13		
JD Lewry	b Cork	0		
Extras	b 8, lb 12, w 1, nb 4	25	b 1, lb 3, w 1, nb 4	9
	(all out 146.5 overs)	439	(6 wkts dec 73 overs)	294

Bowling
Cork 22.5-5-54-4. Chapple 26-5-71-1. Smith 30-7-98-2. Marshall 13.3-4-47-0. Keedy 45-9-116-3. Astle 6.3-0-22-0. Law 3-0-11-0.
Cork 9-0-35-0. Chapple 13-3-45-0. Keedy 20-0-80-4. Smith 8-1-32-0. Marshall 16-0-68-1. Astle 2-0-6-0. Law 5-0-24-1.
Fall of Wickets: 1-4, 2-7, 3-106, 4-147, 5-161, 6-335, 7-347, 8-409, 9-438
1-37, 2-45, 3-211, 4-251, 5-264, 6-272

LANCASHIRE	First Innings		Second Innings	
MJ Chilton (capt)	c Hopkinson b Lewry	0	(2) b Lewry	29
IJ Sutcliffe	c Prior b Lewry	23	(1) c Prior b Yasir Arafat	2
MB Loye	lbw b Lewry	4	not out	148
SG Law	c Goodwin b Lewry	130	(4) c Yardy b Lewry	5
NJ Astle	b Yasir Arafat	41	lbw b Yasir Arafat	20
*GD Cross	lbw b Yasir Arafat	68	lbw b Wright	3
G Chapple	c sub b Lewry	27	c Adams b Mushtaq Ahmed	32
SJ Marshall	c Prior b Yasir Arafat	3	lbw b Wright	3
TC Smith	c Prior b Lewry	28	c Adams b Mushtaq Ahmed	4
G Keedy	c Adams b Yardy	2	(11) not out	0
DG Cork	not out	1	(10) c Montgomerie b M Ahmed	10
Extras	b 7, lb 5, w 1, nb 2	15	b 4, lb 5, w 5, nb 24	38
	(all out 87.1 overs)	342	(9 wkts 98 overs)	290

Bowling
Lewry 25.1-5-68-6. Yasir Arafat 21-2-97-3. Wright 4-0-25-0.
Mushtaq Ahmed 18.5-4-76-0. Martin-Jenkins 7.1-2-27-0. Yardy 11-2-37-1.
Lewry 24-6-61-2. Yasir Arafat 19-2-85-3. Wright 8-2-30-1. Martin-Jenkins 9-6-16-0.
Mushtaq Ahmed 37-11-84-3. Yardy 1-0-5-0.
Fall of Wickets: 1-0, 2-15, 3-71, 4-145, 5-277, 6-281, 7-288, 8-321, 9-336
1-21, 2-72, 3-78, 4-125, 5-141, 6-204, 7-215, 8-220, 9-276

Match drawn – Sussex (11 pts), Lancashire (9 pts)

KENT v. HAMPSHIRE – at Canterbury

KENT	First Innings		Second Innings	
DP Fulton	lbw b Thornely	14	not out	134
RWT Key (capt)	c Carberry b Thornely	27	not out	136
M van Jaarsveld	b Tremlett	34		
MJ Walker	c Warne b Mascarenhas	52		
DI Stevens	c Ervine b Tremlett	8		
DJJ Bravo	c Warne b Ervine	31		
*GO Jones	lbw b Warne	35		
T Henderson	c Ervine b Warne	59		
A Khan	not out	5		
MM Patel	c Ervine b Udal	5		
MJ Saggers	b Warne	0		
Extras	lb 9, w 2, nb 8	19	b 2, w 1, nb 8	11
	(all out 93.4 overs)	285	(0 wkts 103 overs)	281

Bowling
Bruce 11-4-31-0. Tremlett 16-3-56-2. Thornely 17-2-62-2. Mascarenhas 19-10-29-1. Ervine 6-2-18-1. Warne 11.4-1-26-3. Udal 13-2-54-1.
Bruce 17-3-59-0. Mascarenhas 8-2-24-0. Warne 32-13-54-0. Ervine 9-2-42-0. Thornely 8-2-20-0. Udal 15-4-39-0. Crawley 2-0-8-0. Adams 2-1-5-0. Pothas 6-2-12-0. Carberry 4-0-16-0.
Fall of Wickets: 1-38, 2-56, 3-114, 4-132, 5-173, 6-186, 7-277, 8-282, 9-285

HAMPSHIRE	First Innings		
JHK Adams	c Key b Stevens	38	
MA Carberry	lbw b Khan	0	
JP Crawley	c Jones b Khan	189	
SM Ervine	c Jones b Khan	15	
DJ Thornely	c Jones b Henderson	52	
*N Pothas	c & b van Jaarsveld	52	
AD Mascarenhas	c Stevens b Patel	131	
SK Warne (capt)	not out	44	
JTA Bruce			
CT Tremlett			
SD Udal			
Extras	b 8, lb 7, w 2, nb 16	33	
	(7 wkts dec 145.3 overs)	554	

Bowling
Khan 27-4-86-3. Henderson 24-7-84-1. Bravo 19-3-92-0. Saggers 15.2-1-59-0. Stevens 21.4-5-73-1. Patel 31.3-5-108-1. van Jaarsveld 5-1-37-1.
Fall of Wickets: 1-3, 2-148, 3-192, 4-308, 5-312, 6-486, 7-554

*Match drawn – Kent (7 pts),
Hampshire (12 pts)*

DURHAM v. NOTTINGHAMSHIRE – at the Riverside

DURHAM	First Innings		Second Innings	
JP Maher	c Fleming b Sidebottom	2	b Sidebottom	10
JA Lowe	c Alleyne b Shreck	6	b Harris	0
GJ Muchall	lbw b Ealham	5	c & b Shreck	5
DM B'enstein (capt)	c Alleyne b Shreck	0	b Harris	39
BW Harmison	b Shreck	0	c Gallian b Ealham	8
GR Breese	b Shreck	4	c Alleyne b Ealham	0
*P Mustard	c & b Shreck	81	c Alleyne b Sidebottom	8
CD Thorp	not out	68	c Ealham b Shreck	11
G Onions	c Alleyne b Sidebottom	3	c Hussey b Harris	26
N Killeen	c Ealham b Shreck	7	c Gallian b Shreck	34
ML Lewis	c Alleyne b Ealham	1	not out	5
Extras	lb 14, nb 4	18	lb 1, nb 10	11
	(all out 57 overs)	195	(all out 43.5 overs)	157

Bowling
Sidebottom 18-9-43-2. Shreck 21-6-67-6. Harris 8-2-48-0. Ealham 9-2-21-2. Swann 1-0-2-0.
Shreck 13.5-2-64-4. Sidebottom 11-4-21-2. Ealham 11-3-36-2. Harris 8-0-35-2.
Fall of Wickets: 1-8, 2-10, 3-10, 4-10, 5-22, 6-37, 7-162, 8-179, 9-194
1-5, 2-13, 3-27, 4-59, 5-59, 6-68, 7-83, 8-83, 9-151

NOTTS	First Innings		Second Innings	
DJ Bicknell	lbw b Killeen	18	b Onions	21
JER Gallian	lbw b Killeen	1	c Mustard b Lewis	1
SP Fleming (capt)	lbw b Onions	11	(5) not out	89
SR Patel	lbw b Onions	14	(6) not out	56
DJ Hussey	c Mustard b Onions	12		
*D Alleyne	c Mustard b Killeen	1	(4) run out	18
MA Ealham	b Lewis	9		
GP Swann	lbw b Killeen	11		
RJ Sidebottom	c Lowe b Lewis	33	(3) c Mustard b Lewis	18
AJ Harris	run out	1		
CE Shreck	not out	0		
Extras	b 1, lb 1, nb 4	6	b 4, lb 3, nb 4	11
	(all out 32.3 overs)	139	(4 wkts 63.3 overs)	214

Bowling
Onions 9-1-37-4. Thorp 4-0-31-0. Killeen 12-3-38-3. Lewis 7.3-0-31-2.
Onions 16-3-56-1. Lewis 14-4-43-2. Killeen 13-1-45-0. Thorp 11-2-42-0. Breese 9.3-2-21-0.
Fall of Wickets: 1-3, 2-21, 3-59, 4-80, 5-81, 6-81, 7-101, 8-101, 9-110
1-6, 2-44, 3-46, 4-86

*Nottinghamshire won by 6 wickets – Durham (3 pts),
Nottinghamshire (17 pts)*

Charlie Shreck, whose fine season continued with ten wickets against Durham at the Riverside.

on day one, despite Tyron Henderson's four sixes off Shaun Udal, and then notching up a massive lead thanks to John Crawley's fifth hundred of the campaign and a career-best 131 off 151 balls by Dimitri Mascarenhas. But David Fulton and Robert Key, resuming the final day with 29 on the board, then took the Kent second innings to 281 without loss to leave Hampshire totally frustrated. Shane Warne bowled 32 overs for just 54 runs but went as wicketless as everyone else as Fulton, with 134 not out from 310 balls, and Key, who hit 136 not out from 312 deliveries, classily batted out the day.

A remarkable match at the Riverside, which initially saw Durham recover from 37 for 6 to reach 145 for 6 in the 42.2 overs possible on day one, then exploded into even more dramatic action after a washed-out second day. All four innings of the match featured on that third day, with Nottinghamshire emerging at the end of the carnage on 17 for 1 in

their second innings as they chased 214 for victory. The day had begun with Phil Mustard and Callum Thorp taking their excellent seventh-wicket stand to 125 before Durham's first innings closed on 195, and the home team looked to have taken command as Graham Onions and Neil Killeen shared seven wickets as Notts crumbled to 139 in reply. But giant seamer Charlie Shreck followed up his six-wicket first innings haul by picking up another four as Durham's second innings fell apart. It took a gutsy ninth-wicket stand of 68 between Killeen and Onions, indeed, to leave Notts needing the highest score of the match to win but – despite an early slide to 86 for 4 – they were eased home in the end by Stephen Fleming and Samit Patel in drier conditions clearly far more comfortable for batting.

Division Two

Surrey's stranglehold on the second division grew tighter still as Mark Ramprakash scored the first triple-hundred of his glittering domestic career. With Indian leg spinner Anil Kumble then taking 8 for 100 on the last day, Surrey were ultimately able to complete a seven-wicket victory over Northamptonshire inside the final hour. The second and third days, though, were dominated by the relentless Ramprakash, who took his season's first-class run tally to 1,818 and his average to 113.62 by turning the 86th hundred of his career into a true epic. The underpowered Northants attack, in which Matt Nicholson and Ben Phillips kept going manfully, were impotent to prevent Ramprakash from adding 187 with Scott Newman, who made an attractive 143, and then a massive 353 in 85 overs with Mark Butcher, who hit 147. Ramprakash was very much the dominant partner in this stand, but Butcher's class also shone through as the two former England batsmen moved effortlessly through the gears. Ramprakash's only real period of worry came bizarrely in the 290s, probably as much through fatigue as tension at the approaching landmark. He suddenly lost fluency against Usman Afzaal's left-arm spin, propelled into the rough on and around his leg stump from over the wicket, and the stroke that brought up his triple-century was a rather flailed thickish edge towards the third man area. The innings, however, was nothing short of a triumph and Surrey immediately declared. Afzaal then made a considerable impact with the bat, he and Chris Rogers adding 208 for Northants' second wicket as the visitors looked initially to be capable of batting it out for a draw on a still excellent batting surface.

OF SUSSEX

A reputation of being merely a plucky little club who sometimes punched above their weight and won a few one-day titles here and there was consigned to the past when Sussex won the first two Championship titles in their history in 2003 and 2006.

These titles are a triumph for captain Chris Adams, who joined in 1998 after ten seasons with his native Derbyshire and immediately set about building a team that could be the best in the land. The behind-the-scenes management and coaching of Peter Moores, now the National Academy director, and his successor Mark Robinson, have also been vital to Sussex's rise – as has been a committee and administration team who have followed a 'one-for-all' policy in support of the players on the field.

Local-born talent has certainly been an important factor in the team's ambition and togetherness: James Kirtley, Jason Lewry, Robin Martin-Jenkins, Matt Prior and Mike Yardy all have strong links with Sussex clubs and schools. Yet it is the influence of 'outsiders' Adams, Murray Goodwin and in particular the Pakistani overseas stars Mushtaq Ahmed, Rana Naved-ul-Hasan and Yasir Arafat which has turned Sussex's cricket history on its head.

Mushtaq, of course, has been the spearhead. The leg spinner, supposedly all washed up when he joined Sussex in April 2003 at the age of almost 33, has been nothing short of a revelation as he has repaid the club's faith in him – and the welcoming nature which has seen his family settle so happily in Brighton – with a torrent of wickets. He took 103 in the thrilling 2003 title-winning campaign, and has also been the country's leading wicket-taker in each of the last three seasons. His 102 wickets in the summer of 2006 were also the single most important factor in Sussex's second Championship success.

It was James Kirtley, however, who was the bowling hero of Sussex's C&G Trophy final victory against chief rivals Lancashire in late August, a performance which gave the club the first half of their memorable 'double'.

Sussex have always been a county blessed with the occasional world-class cricketer – from C. B. Fry and Ranjitsinhji through to David Sheppard, Ted Dexter, John Snow and Imran Khan – but perhaps never had the collective strength and determination which the current squad now demonstrates day-in and day-out.

Imran, Garth Le Roux, Paul Parker and Dermot Reeve were the leading performers when the Sunday League was won in 1982 and a memorable NatWest Trophy victory over Lancashire was achieved in the 1986 final at Lord's, but for the golden years of Sussex cricket you need look no further than the last four seasons.

Sussex captain Chris Adams is joined in the 2006 Championship celebrations by the Pakistani bowlers (from left to right) Yasir Arafat, Rana Naved-ul-Hasan and Mushtaq Ahmed.

But, from 218 for 1, the innings fell away alarmingly against the nagging Kumble and not even a 78-run alliance for the ninth wicket by Nicholson and David Wigley could then save Northants.

Worcestershire stayed second in the division by beating Glamorgan by a decisive 311 runs in the lovely setting of Colwyn Bay. An unbeaten 134 from the 22-year-old Daryl Mitchell, who was joined in seventh- and tenth-wicket stands of 92 and 83 by Roger Sillence and Nadeem Malik, put Worcestershire into a position of strength with a total of 460 on the board. Mitchell had taken 131 balls to reach 50, but his dedication to the cause was rewarded still further when Glamorgan subsided to 162 for 6 in reply. Alex Wharf's excellent 86, with 15 fours, at least took Glamorgan past 300, but a first-wicket partnership of 168 between Phil Jaques and Stephen Moore confirmed the visitors' dominance and a fourth-wicket stand of 135 between Ben Smith and Steve Davies enabled Worcestershire to put the game beyond their opponents' reach. Matt Mason then led the destruction of Glamorgan's second innings, with only Robert Croft showing any lengthy resistance.

Essex also won in this round of games, defeating Somerset by 211 runs at Southend to stay third. Mervyn Westfield, a promising 18-year-old all-rounder, took the last day honours with 4 for 72 as only Cameron White held up Essex for long with 111 from 134 balls, with two sixes and 11 fours. But the real damage had been done on the second morning by Alex Tudor and Darren Gough. The former England fast bowlers combined to skittle Somerset's first innings for just 133, the previously injury-ravaged Tudor earning himself a first five-wicket analysis for four years. Ronnie Irani's 80,

Round Fourteen: 1–6 August 2006 Division Two

SURREY v. NORTHAMPTONSHIRE – at The Oval

NORTHANTS	First Innings		Second Innings	
SD Peters	c Clarke b Akram	15	(2) lbw b Azhar Mahmood	1
CJL Rogers	c Kumble b Doshi	59	(1)st Batty b Kumble	75
U Afzaal	c & b Kumble	13	lbw b Kumble	142
RA White	c Ramprakash b Akram	30	(5) c Batty b Doshi	9
DJG Sales (capt)	c Clarke b Kumble	1	(4) c Batty b Kumble	21
*BM Shafayat	c Clarke b Salisbury	91	c Batty b Kumble	16
L Klusener	c Newman b Kumble	31	c Newman b Kumble	0
BJ Phillips	c Salisbury b Kumble	65	c Newman b Kumble	13
MJ Nicholson	not out	19	not out	53
DH Wigley	c Newman b Salisbury	1	c & b Kumble	28
JF Brown	c Butcher b Salisbury	0	c Azhar Mahmood b Kumble	4
Extras	b 4, lb 6, nb 12	22	b 1, lb 9, nb 14	24
	(all out 97.5 overs)	347	(all out 118.2 overs)	386

Bowling
Akram 14-3-55-2. Azhar Mahmood 11-1-59-0. Clarke 2-0-15-0. Kumble 28-10-83-3. Doshi 16-4-42-2. Salisbury 26.5-2-83-3.
Akram 20-4-64-0. Azhar Mahmood 16-4-47-1. Doshi 20-4-62-1. Kumble 34.2-6-100-8. Salisbury 24-8-44-0. Clarke 2-0-9-0.
Fall of Wickets: 1-58, 2-87, 3-99, 4-104, 5-135, 6-183, 7-303, 8-332, 9-335
1-10, 2-218, 3-241, 4-250, 5-274, 6-274, 7-287, 8-302, 9-380

SURREY	First Innings		Second Innings	
SA Newman	c Phillips b Brown	143	c Sales b Brown	0
*JN Batty	lbw b Klusener	18	st Shafayat b Afzaal	19
MR Ramprakash	not out	301	c White b Brown	30
MA Butcher (capt)	run out	147	not out	8
AD Brown	b Brown	27	not out	2
R Clarke	b Afzaal	6		
Azhar Mahmood	not out	15		
IDK Salisbury				
A Kumble				
ND Doshi				
Mohammad Akram				
Extras	b 1, lb 9, w 2	12	b 4, lb 2	6
	(5 wkts dec 170.3 overs)	669	(3 wkts 14 overs)	65

Bowling
Nicholson 37-6-143-0. Phillips 20-2-63-0. Klusener 8-2-27-1. Wigley 21-0-117-0. Brown 52-4-187-2. White 15-2-51-0. Afzaal 17.3-0-71-1.
Brown 7-0-34-2. Afzaal 7-1-25-1.
Fall of Wickets: 1-62, 2-249, 3-602, 4-641, 5-650
1-0, 2-40, 3-58

Surrey won by 7 wickets – Surrey (22 pts), Northamptonshire (3 pts)

GLAMORGAN v. WORCESTERSHIRE – at Colwyn Bay

WORCS	First Innings		Second Innings	
PA Jaques	c Hemp b Harrison	33	c Harrison b Croft	92
SC Moore	b Harrison	2	c Watkins b Franklin	82
VS Solanki (capt)	run out	49	run out	36
BF Smith	c Wallace b Croft	35	not out	72
*SM Davies	lbw b Croft	27	c Wallace b Cosgrove	77
DKH Mitchell	not out	134	c Hemp b Grant	7
GJ Batty	c Hemp b Wharf	37		
RJ Sillence	c & b Franklin	63		
Z Khan	c Wharf b Franklin	13		
MS Mason	b Watkins	21		
MN Malik	lbw b Croft	35		
Extras	lb 8, nb 3	11	b 8, lb 6, nb 2	16
	(all out 123.4 overs)	460	(5 wkts dec 80.5 overs)	382

Bowling
Harrison 26-8-56-2. Franklin 24-3-102-2. Watkins 10-1-58-1. Wharf 20-1-98-1. Cosgrove 8-0-31-0. Tudge 7-1-21-0. Croft 28.4-5-86-3.
Harrison 19-1-95-0. Franklin 12-0-47-1. Cosgrove 11-0-36-1. Watkins 9-1-48-0. Croft 20-2-90-1. Tudge 6-0-37-0. Grant 3.5-0-15-1.
Fall of Wickets: 1-7, 2-46, 3-107, 4-147, 5-148, 6-223, 7-315, 8-335, 9-377
1-168, 2-186, 3-230, 4-365, 5-382

GLAMORGAN	First Innings		Second Innings	
MJ Cosgrove	lbw b Khan	0	(2) lbw b Mason	8
RE Watkins	c Smith b Mason	39	(1) b Malik	38
DL Hemp	c Smith b Malik	26	lbw b Sillence	16
MJ Powell	b Khan	12	c Davies b Mason	5
RN Grant	lbw b Batty	28	c Davies b Mason	12
JEC Franklin	b Batty	31	c Davies b Mason	9
*MA Wallace	c Davies b Malik	48	c Davies b Malik	27
AG Wharf	c Solanki b Khan	86	(9) c Smith b Sillence	8
RDB Croft (capt)	c Smith b Batty	25	(8) not out	44
DS Harrison	c Davies b Malik	27	c Jaques b Khan	3
KD Tudge	not out	3	c Smith b Sillence	4
Extras	b 5, lb 4, w 6	15	b 12, lb 3, w 2	17
	(all out 85.2 overs)	340	(all out 43.4 overs)	191

Bowling
Khan 24-2-95-3. Mason 16-2-71-1. Malik 13.2-2-49-3. Batty 22-7-71-3. Sillence 9-0-38-0. Solanki 1-0-7-0.
Khan 16-2-68-1. Mason 13-1-56-4. Malik 11-2-43-2. Sillence 3.4-0-9-3.
Fall of Wickets: 1-0, 2-65, 3-80, 4-84, 5-127, 6-162, 7-267, 8-304, 9-309
1-18, 2-67, 3-67, 4-89, 5-96, 6-149, 7-163, 8-169, 9-178

Worcestershire won by 311 runs – Glamorgan (6 pts), Worcestershire (22 pts)

ESSEX v. SOMERSET – at Southend

ESSEX	First Innings		Second Innings	
GW Flower	b Edwards b Trego	27	c Durston b Caddick	42
ML Pettini	lbw b Willoughby	37	c Wood b Caddick	23
RS Bopara	b Willoughby	4	c Gazzard b Munday	33
A Flower	lbw b Caddick	19	lbw b Willoughby	60
RC Irani (capt)	c Trego b Caddick	80	c Wood b Durston	61
*JS Foster	b Caddick	3	(7) not out	39
JD Middlebrook	c Hildreth b Willoughby	1	(8) c Durston b Munday	24
TJ Phillips	lbw b White	44	(9) c Durston b Caddick	29
AJ Tudor	lbw b Caddick	25	(10) not out	26
D Gough	b Caddick	12		
MS Westfield	not out	0	(6) c Gazzard b Munday	32
Extras	lb 6, w 1, nb 14	21	b 3, lb 6, w 2, nb 19	30
	(all out 81 overs)	252	(8 wkts dec 101 overs)	399

Bowling
Caddick 25-6-82-5. Willoughby 22-10-46-3. Trego 24-4-74-1. Munday 7-1-24-0. White 6-2-16-1.
Caddick 26.5-5-110-3. Willoughby 20-4-68-1. Trego 13-1-48-0. Munday 21-1-83-3. Durston 14-1-57-1. White 4-1-8-0. Suppiah 3-0-13-0.
Fall of Wickets: 1-55, 2-91, 3-152, 4-201, 5-277, 6-277, 7-316, 8-354
1-55, 2-91, 3-152, 4-201, 5-277, 6-277, 7-316, 8-354

SOMERSET	First Innings		Second Innings	
NJ Wood	c Foster b Gough	0	(2) lbw b Phillips	50
NJ Edwards	c Foster b Gough	44	(1) c Phillips b Middlebrook	20
AV Suppiah	c Pettini b Gough	5	b Westfield	20
JC Hildreth	c Westfield b Bopara	11	c Pettini b Middlebrook	43
CL White (capt)	b Tudor	26	lbw b Phillips	111
WJ Durston	c Gough b Tudor	10	(7) c Foster b Westfield	31
PD Trego	c Foster b Tudor	6	(8) c Foster b Westfield	0
*CM Gazzard	c Flower A b Tudor	0	(6) c Pettini b Tudor	16
AR Caddick	b Gough	21	c Foster b Phillips	1
MK Munday	c Pettini b Tudor	4	c Flower A b Phillips	0
CM Willoughby	not out	1	not out	0
Extras	lb 1, nb 10	11	b 2, lb 4, w 6, nb 14	14
	(all out 46.3 overs)	133	(all out 78.3 overs)	307

Bowling
Gough 19.3-4-41-4. Tudor 19-4-67-5. Bopara 4-1-22-1. Middlebrook 3-2-2-0. Phillips 1-1-0-0.
Gough 9-2-32-0. Tudor 11-2-47-1. Westfield 18-1-72-4. Middlebrook 22-2-97-2. Phillips 17.3-4-53-3.
Fall of Wickets: 1-2, 2-10, 3-31, 4-65, 5-81, 6-85, 7-87, 8-112, 9-119
1-57, 2-96, 3-97, 4-198, 5-230, 6-289, 7-290, 8-303, 9-307

Essex won by 211 runs – Essex (19 pts), Somerset (3 pts)

GLOUCESTERSHIRE v. LEICESTERSHIRE – at Cheltenham

GLOS	First Innings		Second Innings	
WPC Weston	c Nixon b Broad	36	(2) c Masters b Broad	4
CM Spearman	c Robinson b Broad	28	(1) c Nixon b Griffith	39
HJH Marshall	b Henderson	62	c Sadler b Broad	168
Kadeer Ali	c Snape b Griffith	10	c Ackerman b Henderson	8
APR Gidman (capt)	c Amjad b Henderson	58	c Henderson b Broad	120
IJ Harvey	c Robinson b Broad	31	not out	32
*SJ Adshead	c Sadler b Henderson	55	c Nixon b Broad	8
ID Fisher	c Henderson b Henderson	3	(9) not out	35
MCJ Ball	c Henderson b Henderson	14	(8) c Masters b Broad	0
WD Rudge†	b Broad	1		
SP Kirby	not out	4		
J Lewis				
Extras	lb 10, w 1, nb 10	21	b 8, lb 4, w 3, nb 10	25
	(all out 88.4 overs)	282	(7 wkts dec 114 overs)	439

Bowling
Griffith 14-2-52-1. Broad 20.4-8-47-4. Masters 21-7-60-0. Henderson 25-6-76-5. Amjad 8-0-37-0.
Broad 24-6-88-5. Griffith 25-2-91-1. Masters 19-2-73-0. Henderson 27-3-90-1. Amjad 16-1-65-0. Maunders 3-0-20-0.
Fall of Wickets: 1-56, 2-69, 3-95, 4-107, 5-153, 6-220, 7-226, 8-252, 9-278
1-17, 2-74, 3-112, 4-338, 5-379, 6-386, 7-394
† Replaced by J Lewis

LEICESTERSHIRE	First Innings		Second Innings	
DDJ Robinson	c Ball b Kirby	4	c Adshead b Lewis	17
JK Maunders	lbw b Kirby	180	run out	5
HD Ackerman	c Ball b Kirby	46	c Spearman b Kirby	46
JL Sadler	c & b Fisher	20	c Lewis b Ball	20
*PA Nixon	c Ball b Ball	103	not out	68
JN Snape (capt)	c Adshead b Fisher	7	(7) c Marshall b Lewis	7
Mansoor Amjad	c Harvey b Ball	27	(6) lbw b Ball	25
DD Masters	c Ball b Kirby	7		
CW Henderson	not out	41	(8) not out	42
SCJ Broad	c Weston b Fisher	4		
AR Griffith	b Ball	1		
Extras	b 4, lb 7, w 2, nb 19	32	b 1, lb 6, nb 4	11
	(all out 139.4 overs)	482	(6 wkts 42.5 overs)	241

Bowling
Kirby 32-7-117-4. Rudge 20-2-95-0. Harvey 16-4-27-0. Ball 34.4-7-84-3. Fisher 26-2-110-3. Gidman 4-0-11-0. Marshall 7-2-27-0.
Lewis 14-3-70-2. Kirby 7-2-27-1. Fisher 10.5-0-74-0. Ball 11-0-63-2.
Fall of Wickets: 1-12, 2-120, 3-170, 4-393, 5-394, 6-411, 7-419, 8-461, 9-470
1-12, 2-47, 3-82, 4-108, 5-164, 6-187

Leicestershire won by 4 wickets – Gloucestershire (4 pts), Leicestershire (22 pts)

meanwhile, had sustained Essex in the face of some hostile bowling from Andrew Caddick and Charl Willoughby on the opening day, and now the home skipper's 61 – together with a solid 60 from Andy Flower – took the match right away from Somerset in their second innings.

A thrilling fourth-innings chase by Leicestershire, culminating in a brilliant unbroken stand between Paul Nixon and Claude Henderson, saw Gloucestershire go down by four wickets at Cheltenham. Henderson smote six sixes in his 16-ball 42 not out; while Nixon's unbeaten 68 took him only 52 balls and included a six

Anil Kumble's second innings 8 for 100 won Surrey a high-scoring match against Northants at The Oval.

and eight fours. All this after Henderson and Stuart Broad had combined with the ball on day one to dismiss the home side for 282 and a career-best 180 from John Maunders, plus 103 from irrepressible Nixon, had given Leicestershire a seemingly match-winning first-innings lead of exactly 200. But Gloucestershire had then fought back superbly, despite yet more impressive pace bowling from Broad, with Hamish Marshall's 168 and Alex Gidman's equally fine 120 even enabling the home team to set Leicestershire their stiff target.

Round Fifteen: 8–11 August 2006

Division One

Lancashire were batted out of the Roses Match by Yorkshire's Craig White, Anthony McGrath and Michael Lumb, but the 12 points they took from the match at Old Trafford put them 11 points in front of Sussex at the top of the table with four games left for both counties. McGrath, who like White made a superb hundred in Yorkshire's second innings, also batted beautifully on day one, hitting two sixes and nine fours in his 65. But it was Darren Lehmann, completing his third Roses century and going on to reach 130 from 158 balls with 16 fours, who took the chief honours in Yorkshire's initial 345. Luke Sutton, whose 151 not out was the highest score ever made by a Lancashire wicketkeeper, Mal Loye, with a third hundred in successive Championship matches, and Kyle Hogg then ensured a decent lead. In the end, though, Yorkshire grit denied their closest rivals.

Nottinghamshire's poor defence of their title continued at Edgbaston where Warwickshire emerged with a 59-run win. Mark Ealham's 5 for 59 in the first four sessions could not prevent Warwickshire running up 381, thanks largely to Ian Westwood's 81 and a sixth-wicket stand of 106 between Tim Ambrose and Luke Parker, and then Nottinghamshire flopped to 208 all out as Alex Loudon's off breaks earned him 5 for 49. A Warwickshire second innings decline to 125 for 7 was arrested by Mark Wagh and Heath Streak's 103-run partnership for the eighth wicket, but when Darren Bicknell and Jason Gallian began with a century stand of their own, it seemed as if Notts might even achieve their distant win target. They did have a good stab at it, with Stephen Fleming and Paul Franks also passing fifty, but James Anyon's 5 for 83 finally closed out the match in Warwickshire's favour.

For three days at Lord's, with the bat holding sway over the ball, it looked as if the only possible outcome of Middlesex's match against Hampshire was a dull draw. Yet, although the result ultimately was indeed a draw, the very presence and attitude of Shane Warne made for an exciting and fascinating final day. Centuries from both Michael Carberry and Nic Pothas, plus a cultured 70 from the in-form John Crawley, had allowed Hampshire to make sure of maximum batting bonus points themselves in reply to a Middlesex first innings of 422 which owed much to the way Owais Shah and Ed Joyce in particular countered the threat of Warne. Ed Smith and Joyce then made the game seemingly safe for Middlesex before some declaration bowling brought it to life again. Set 330 to win from 70 overs, Hampshire floundered after an initial flurry, and at 170 for 7 were all but out of the running. Enter Warne, who came in at No. 9 with 27 overs remaining and immediately played as if he believed victory was still but a matter of time. With Pothas also hitting out productively at the other end, the requirement came down to 99 from the last 14 overs. Middlesex, to their credit, did not panic and eventually – with 61 now required from seven – even Warne decided to shut up shop.

Lancashire's Mal Loye pulls against Yorkshire on his way to a third successive Championship hundred.

Round Fifteen: 8–11 August 2006 Division One

LANCASHIRE v. YORKSHIRE – at Old Trafford

YORKSHIRE	First Innings		Second Innings	
C White (capt)	c Sutton b Hogg	9	c Loye b Keedy	116
JJ Sayers	c Smith b Chapple	48	c Law b Hogg	5
A McGrath	c Keedy b Smith	65	c Sutton b Newby	102
MJ Lumb	c Astle b Chapple	2	lbw b Keedy	68
DS Lehmann	c Loye b Hogg	130	c Loye b Newby	27
*GL Brophy	c Chilton b Smith	0	(7) c Chilton b Newby	0
JN Gillespie	c Sutton b Smith	43	(8) b Chilton	36
MAK Lawson	lbw b Keedy	7	(9) c Sutton b Keedy	1
SA Patterson	c Sutton b Chapple	2	(4) b Newby	46
GJ Kruis	not out	21	not out	4
JE Lee	b Chapple	1	not out	21
Extras	b 5, lb 10, nb 2	17	b 10, lb 13, w 1	24
	(all out 100.4 overs)	**345**	(9 wkts 160 overs)	**450**

Bowling
Chapple 22.4-5-60-4. Hogg 19-4-50-2. Smith 23-3-83-3. Keedy 18-0-68-1.
Newby 13-1-47-0. Astle 5-1-22-0.
Chapple 23-7-56-0. Hogg 19-8-51-1. Keedy 59-11-156-3. Smith 18-3-37-0.
Newby 19-4-69-4. Law 4-0-15-0. Astle 10-1-31-0. Chilton 8-2-12-1.
Fall of Wickets: 1-18, 2-127, 3-132, 4-135, 5-164, 6-267, 7-302, 8-319, 9-321
1-6, 2-189, 3-269, 4-292, 5-309, 6-309, 7-423, 8-423, 9-424

LANCASHIRE	First Innings	
MJ Chilton (capt)	b Brophy b Kruis	2
IJ Sutcliffe	c White b Patterson	23
MB Loye	c Lumb b Lehmann	100
SG Law	c McGrath b Kruis	32
NJ Astle	lbw b Gillespie	24
*LD Sutton	not out	151
G Chapple	c Lawson b Kruis	27
KW Hogg	c White b Lawson	60
TC Smith	b Kruis	3
OJ Newby	c McGrath b Kruis	0
G Keedy	c Sayers b Lawson	0
Extras	b 1, lb 10, w 2, nb 6	19
	(all out 125.4 overs)	**441**

Bowling
Kruis 28-7-97-5. Gillespie 26-4-82-1. Patterson 17-3-39-1. Lee 9-0-36-0.
Lawson 27.4-0-121-2. McGrath 5-0-22-0. Lehmann 13-0-33-1.
Fall of Wickets: 1-18, 2-30, 3-77, 4-131, 5-249, 6-305, 7-414, 8-425, 9-431

Match drawn – Lancashire (12 pts),
Yorkshire (10 pts)

WARWICKSHIRE v. NOTTINGHAMSHIRE – at Edgbaston

WARWICKSHIRE	First Innings		Second Innings	
IJ Westwood	lbw b Ealham	81	lbw b Ealham	29
MA Wagh	b Sidebottom	20	(8) c Bicknell b Patel	70
IJL Trott	c Alleyne b Ealham	46	c Gallian b Swann	15
NV Knight	b Ealham	9	(5) c Gallian b Swann	3
AGR Loudon	c Alleyne b Sidebottom	6	(6) st Alleyne b Swann	5
*TR Ambrose	lbw b Shreck	63	(7) lbw b Swann	34
LC Parker	lbw b Swann	73	(2) lbw b Sidebottom	0
HH Streak (capt)	c Fleming b Ealham	31	(9) c Patel b Franks	44
NM Carter	c Patel b Sidebottom	16	(10) not out	0
PL Harris	st Alleyne b Ealham	17		
JE Anyon	not out	2	(4) c Alleyne b Sidebottom	6
Extras	b 4, lb 8, w 1, nb 4	17	b 8, lb 14, nb 2	24
	(all out 124.1 overs)	**381**	(9 wkts 69.1 overs)	**230**

Bowling
Sidebottom 29-6-74-3. Shreck 25-4-95-1. Ealham 21.1-7-59-5. Franks 10-1-37-0.
Swann 38-9-96-1. Patel 1-0-8-0.
Sidebottom 14-6-32-2. Shreck 12-1-45-0. Ealham 8-2-23-1. Swann 25-9-54-4.
Patel 5.1-0-22-1. Franks 4-0-23-1. Hussey 1-0-9-0.
Fall of Wickets: 1-32, 2-142, 3-162, 4-165, 5-180, 6-286, 7-318, 8-345, 9-378
1-21, 2-50, 3-56, 4-66, 5-66, 6-82, 7-125, 8-228, 9-230

NOTTS	First Innings		Second Innings	
DJ Bicknell	c Ambrose b Carter	9	(2) c Et b Anyon	55
JER Gallian	c Loudon b Carter	0	(1) lbw b Loudon	54
*D Alleyne	st Ambrose b Loudon	61	b Anyon	16
SP Fleming (capt)	lbw b Loudon	55	c Trott b Loudon	60
DJ Hussey	run out	0	b Anyon	0
SR Patel	c Knight b Loudon	16	c Ambrose b Anyon	5
MA Ealham	c Streak b Loudon	6	c Ambrose b Streak	18
GP Swann	b Harris	23	b Harris	42
PJ Franks	lbw b Loudon	8	c Knight b Carter	64
RJ Sidebottom	b Carter	20	c Trott b Anyon	1
CE Shreck	not out	2	not out	5
Extras	b 2, lb 4, nb 2	8	b 11, lb 4, w 1, nb 8	24
	(all out 61 overs)	**208**	(all out 119.5 overs)	**344**

Bowling
Streak 5-0-29-0. Carter 9-1-43-3. Anyon 14-4-45-0. Harris 13-4-36-1.
Loudon 20-4-49-5.
Streak 18-5-49-1. Carter 15.5-3-58-1. Anyon 25-8-83-5. Harris 34-14-60-1.
Westwood 1-1-0-0. Loudon 26-5-79-2.
Fall of Wickets: 1-4, 2-17, 3-131, 4-131, 5-135, 6-143, 7-164, 8-184, 9-184
1-109, 2-131, 3-171, 4-171, 5-185, 6-223, 7-223, 8-298, 9-301

Warwickshire won by 59 runs –
Warwickshire (21 pts), Nottinghamshire (4 pts)

MIDDLESEX v. HAMPSHIRE – at Lord's

MIDDLESEX	First Innings		Second Innings	
ET Smith	c Pothas b Mascarenhas	24	not out	147
NRD Compton	lbw b Mascarenhas	11	c Warne b Thornely	15
OA Shah	lbw b Warne	91	c Pothas b Mascarenhas	6
EC Joyce	b Thornely	54	c Crawley b Ervine	92
JWM Dalrymple	lbw b Warne	40		
SB Styris (capt)	c Benham b Warne	63	(5) c Mascarenhas b Pothas	3
PN Weekes	not out	49	(6) not out	24
*BJM Scott	b Mascarenhas	41		
J Louw	lbw b Thornely	6		
CB Keegan	b Mascarenhas	6		
CEW Silverwood	b Warne	7		
Extras	b 8, lb 13, w 6, nb 4, p 5	36	b 2, lb 9, w 5, nb 4	20
	(all out 131.4 overs)	**422**	(4 wkts dec 75.1 overs)	**309**

Bowling
Bruce 22-5-79-0. Ervine 23-9-72-0. Mascarenhas 26-9-53-4. Adams 1-0-7-0.
Thornely 19-5-60-2. Warne 29.4-2-88-4. Udal 11-0-37-0.
Ervine 9-1-37-1. Bruce 5-1-23-0. Thornely 11-3-26-1. Mascarenhas 12-2-47-1.
Warne 16-0-43-0. Udal 7-0-20-0. Crawley 3-0-21-0. Benham 4-0-30-0.
Pothas 5-0-16-1. Carberry 2-0-9-0. Adams 1.1-0-26-0.
Fall of Wickets: 1-33, 2-49, 3-152, 4-218, 5-310, 6-311, 7-385, 8-386, 9-406
1-42, 2-57, 3-224, 4-237

HAMPSHIRE	First Innings		Second Innings	
JHK Adams	c Shah b Silverwood	7	c Joyce b Styris	29
MA Carberry	c Shah b Styris	104	c Scott b Keegan	1
JP Crawley	c Scott b Styris	70	c Smith b Silverwood	13
CC Benham	lbw b Silverwood	1	lbw b Styris	39
DJ Thornely	c Scott b Keegan	5	c Styris b Silverwood	45
*N Pothas	not out	102	not out	74
SM Ervine	c Styris b Silverwood	42	c Styris b Weekes	6
AD Mascarenhas	c Joyce b Keegan	34	c Smith b Silverwood	0
SK Warne (capt)	not out	14	not out	61
JTA Bruce				
SD Udal				
Extras	b 4, lb 5, w 2, nb 6	17	b 4, lb 6, nb 5	15
	(7 wkts dec 119.1 overs)	**402**	(7 wkts 67.5 overs)	**283**

Bowling
Silverwood 26-8-70-3. Keegan 28.1-4-111-2. Louw 20-2-82-0. Styris 20-6-57-1.
Dalrymple 17-2-56-1. Weekes 8-0-17-0.
Silverwood 18-6-41-3. Keegan 15-3-69-1. Styris 10-1-45-2. Louw 12.5-0-65-0.
Weekes 12-2-53-1.
Fall of Wickets: 1-24, 2-158, 3-161, 4-176, 5-223, 6-299, 7-376
1-2, 2-27, 3-86, 4-87, 5-160, 6-167, 7-170

Match drawn – Middlesex (11 pts), Hampshire (12 pts)

OF WARWICKSHIRE

The 1994 Warwickshire team will go down in the history books as one of the strongest county sides of all time. Led on the field by Dermot Reeve and Tim Munton, and off it by coach Bob Woolmer, and containing in Brian Lara the world's greatest and most exciting batsman of that era, Warwickshire won the unprecedented and still unmatched treble that summer of Championship, Sunday League and Benson and Hedges Cup. They also reached the final of the NatWest Trophy in a remarkable season, losing to Worcestershire.

In 1995, moreover, they followed it all up by winning the Championship again and this time adding another NatWest Trophy success to their incredible victory in the competition in 1993 when they had chased down Sussex's 321 for 6 to win off the final ball.

Lara's world record 501 not out, against Durham at Edgbaston, was another standout feature of the 1994 season. In all, he scored 2,066 Championship runs that summer, at an average of 89.82, and reached three figures on nine occasions. Roger Twose and Andy Moles also averaged more than 50 with the bat, while Munton's 81 wickets represented another heroic effort.

Like the Sussex team of recent years, though, this great Warwickshire side had more than just a star performer and fine supporting cast. It had an aura about it, very much created from the top by Reeve and Woolmer, and also a very influential longer-term overseas player in Allan Donald. Players like Twose, Moles, Dougie Brown, Dominic Ostler, Asif Din, Neil Smith, Keith Piper, Trevor Penney and Gladstone Small blended together into a collective unit so effectively that the sum of the Warwickshire XI that took to the field was very much bigger than its individual parts.

Lara is surrounded by his Warwickshire team-mates as the Edgbaston scoreboard records his historic feat – a world-record innings of 501 not out at Edgbaston in 1994.

Warwickshire, overall, have won ten titles in the past 25 years. There was another Championship in 2004, when Nick Knight led a canny campaign, a first success for Reeve's Warwickshire in the 1989 NatWest Trophy, another Sunday League win in 1997 and a victory in the very last Benson and Hedges Cup final, in 2002, when Ian Bell led the county home by five wickets against Essex. But it was those six wins in 1993–95 that will stand the test of time and represent one of the strongest 'streaks' of success ever enjoyed by a county team.

Division Two

Derbyshire won at their Derby headquarters for the first time since June 2002 – a span of 34 matches – but only after Somerset captain Cameron White had threatened to gatecrash the party in the most sensational manner. White reacted to his side being set an almost impossible 579 in 172 overs – largely as a result of being rolled over for a mere 151 in their first innings – by taking the attack back to Derbyshire with one of the innings of the summer. He was joined by Wes Durston, who made 73, in a fifth-wicket stand of 213 and by the end of day three he was unbeaten on 197 with Somerset on 400 for 7. The next morning, too, White continued to bat with huge power and freedom and with tail-ender Simon Francis hanging on, a further 113 was added for the eighth wicket. In the end, though, White was left on a magnificent 260 not out as Somerset's innings was brought to a close at 498. The young Australian had faced just 246 balls for his runs, hitting three sixes and 40 fours. Michael Di Venuto, passing 1,000 runs for the season during his second innings 118, Steve Stubbings, Travis Birt and Jamie Pipe all batted well for Derbyshire during the match, while it was the seam partnership of Steffan Jones and Ian Hunter which put the skids under Somerset's first innings. 'It's just good to get the monkey off our backs

because it was beginning to play on our nerves,' said Derbyshire captain Graeme Welch about the lifting of the Derby 'jinx' afterwards, as his no doubt relieved players celebrated with champagne.

Chris Rogers, the left-handed Western Australian, hit 319 to fall just 12 runs short of his fellow Aussie Mike Hussey's county individual record score, but Northamptonshire could still not see off Gloucestershire at Wantage Road. Rogers, who was on 242 not out at stumps on day one, hit two sixes and 50 fours overall. After following on, despite a brilliant 140 from Craig Spearman, Gloucestershire responded with some more heavy collective scoring of their own as fast bowler Matt Nicholson – the scourge of their first innings – understandably grew weary. Spearman notched up his second hundred of the match, putting on 229 for the opening wicket with Phil Weston, and Kadeer Ali then hit a maiden first-class century while Hamish Marshall also made 133 in a third-wicket partnership of 254.

Surrey, meanwhile, breezed 34 points clear at the top of the division table by thumping nearest rivals Worcestershire by an innings and 107 runs at New Road. Phil Jaques and Stephen Moore gave the home side a decent enough start, but then the Surrey leg spinning pair of Anil Kumble and Ian Salisbury combined to allow them no further than 304 all out. Daryl Mitchell batted well for his

Round Fifteen: 8–11 August 2006 Division Two

DERBYSHIRE v. SOMERSET – at Derby

DERBYSHIRE	First Innings		Second Innings	
MJ Di Venuto	b Trego	48	(2) lbw b Durston	118
SD Stubbings	b Willoughby	97	(1) c Caddick b Willoughby	7
Hassan Adnan	c Gazzard b Francis	3	c Durston b Caddick	18
TR Birt	c Francis b Caddick	50	c Trego b Caddick	51
GM Smith	lbw b White	23	lbw b Trego	17
AG Botha	b Willoughby	5	lbw b Willoughby	41
G Welch (capt)	c ⅋ b Willoughby	9	b Trego	11
*DJ Pipe	not out	35	not out	84
GG Wagg	lbw b White	17	b Suppiah	46
PS Jones	lbw b White	1		
ID Hunter	b Trego	0		
Extras	b 4, lb 10, nb 14	28	b 4, w 2, nb 14	20
	(all out 89.4 overs)	316	(8 wkts dec 79.2 overs)	413

Bowling
Willoughby 22-10-48-3. Caddick 24-4-87-1. Trego 8.4-0-53-2. Francis 14-2-57-1. White 21-2-57-3.
Caddick 20-2-89-2. Willoughby 15-1-85-2. Trego 17-2-101-2. Francis 3-0-44-0. Durston 19-5-56-1. Suppiah 2.2-1-13-1. White 3-0-21-0.
Fall of Wickets: 1-84, 2-100, 3-167, 4-222, 5-228, 6-251, 7-258, 8-301, 9-307 1-7, 2-71, 3-201, 4-205, 5-248, 6-266, 7-305, 8-413

SOMERSET	First Innings		Second Innings	
MJ Wood	lbw b Jones	5	(2) lbw b Jones	5
NJ Edwards	c ⅋ b Hunter	75	(1) run out	2
*CM Gazzard	c Smith b Hunter	4	(3) c Pipe b Wagg	30
AV Suppiah	b Wagg	16	(4) c Pipe b Jones	40
JC Hildreth	c Hassan Adnan b Wagg	4	(5) not out	260
CL White (capt)	c Pipe b Welch	15		
WJ Durston	c Pipe b Jones	4	(6) b Welch	73
PD Trego	c Birt b Jones	4	(7) c Di Venuto b Wagg	11
SRG Francis	not out	4	b Hunter	38
AR Caddick	lbw b Hunter	0	c Hunter b Jones	10
CM Willoughby	b Jones	1	run out	0
Extras	lb 11, nb 4	15	b 6, lb 11, nb 12	29
	(all out 52.1 overs)	151	(all out 106.1 overs)	498

Bowling
Jones 18.1-2-45-4. Welch 13-3-28-1. Hunter 13-4-28-3. Wagg 8-1-39-2.
Jones 28.1-3-119-4. Hunter 26-2-131-1. Welch 27.3-3-109-1. Wagg 13.3-2-88-2. Botha 9-2-43-0. Smith 2-0-11-0.
Fall of Wickets: 1-8, 2-12, 3-75, 4-90, 5-303, 6-349, 7-349, 8-462, 9-479
1-8, 2-12, 3-75, 4-90, 5-303, 6-349, 7-349, 8-462, 9-479

Derbyshire won by 80 runs – Derbyshire (20 pts), Somerset (3 pts)

NORTHAMPTONSHIRE v. GLOUCESTERSHIRE – at Northampton

NORTHANTS	First Innings		Second Innings	
SD Peters	c Adshead b Kirby	76	not out	20
CJL Rogers	st Adshead b Taylor	319		
U Afzaal	c Taylor b Rudge	51	(2) not out	15
DJG Sales (capt)	c Spearman b Kirby	10		
DH Wigley	c Spearman b Lewis	2		
RA White	b Kirby	8		
*BM Shafayat	lbw b Kirby	0		
L Klusener	b Taylor	44		
MJ Nicholson	lbw b Fisher	11		
SP Crook	c ⅋ b Kirby	41		
JF Brown	not out	20		
Extras	b 6, lb 29, w 1, nb 10	46		0
	(all out 150.3 overs)	628	(0 wkts 21 overs)	35

Bowling
Lewis 29-7-109-1. Kirby 32.3-5-99-5. Rudge 20-0-117-1. Gidman 19-4-63-0.
Fisher 31-5-108-1. Taylor 15-0-75-2. Kadeer Ali 4-1-22-0.
Marshall 11-3-16-0. Taylor 10-4-19-0.
Fall of Wickets: 1-179, 2-382, 3-404, 4-407, 5-465, 6-465, 7-552, 8-565, 9-585

GLOS	First Innings		Second Innings (following on)	
CM Spearman	c Shafayat b Nicholson	140	(2) lbw b Nicholson	137
WPC Weston	c ⅋ b Wigley	7	(1) c Shafayat b Nicholson	87
HJH Marshall	c Peters b Nicholson	1	(4) c Klusener b Afzaal	133
Kadeer Ali	lbw b Nicholson	32	(3) c Shafayat b Wigley	145
CG Taylor	b Nicholson	0	c White b Afzaal	37
APR Gidman	c sub b Nicholson	63	not out	17
*SJ Adshead	lbw b Crook	24	c Sales b Afzaal	14
ID Fisher	c Klusener b Nicholson	39		
J Lewis (capt)	c Crook b Nicholson	6	(8) not out	8
WD Rudge	not out	8		
SP Kirby	c Shafayat b Wigley	8		
Extras	lb 3, w 1, nb 18	22	b 6, lb 2, w 7, nb 10	25
	(all out 85.3 overs)	350	(6 wkts dec 146 overs)	596

Bowling
Nicholson 23-4-62-7. Wigley 19.3-1-104-2. Brown 22-1-77-0. Crook 16-0-89-1. White 5-0-15-0.
Nicholson 23-2-84-2. Wigley 19-4-103-1. Brown 49-12-143-0. Crook 19-1-95-0. White 7-1-44-0. Rudge 1-0-1-0. Afzaal 15-2-75-3.
Fall of Wickets: 1-22, 2-39, 3-150, 4-152, 5-245, 6-266, 7-316, 8-333, 9-338 1-229, 2-244, 3-498, 4-553, 5-564, 6-593

Match drawn – Northamptonshire (12 pts), Gloucestershire (10 pts)

WORCESTERSHIRE v. SURREY – at Worcester

WORCS	First Innings		Second Innings	
PA Jaques	lbw b Salisbury	95	c Clarke b Azhar Mahmood	7
SC Moore	c Moore b Batty	44	b Akram	0
VS Solanki (capt)	c ⅋ b Kumble	17	c Azhar Mahmood b Salisbury	56
BF Smith	st Batty b Salisbury	0	c Batty b Azhar Mahmood	28
*SM Davies	lbw b Kumble	23	c Batty b Azhar Mahmood	0
DKH Mitchell	not out	54	c Butcher b Azhar Mahmood	17
GJ Batty	c Salisbury b Azhar Mahmood	10	not out	37
RJ Sillence	c Newman b Salisbury	27	b Salisbury	0
Z Khan	lbw b Kumble	4	c Ramprakash b Salisbury	9
MS Mason	lbw b Kumble	0	b Kumble	4
MN Malik	b Kumble	17	b Kumble	4
Extras	b 4, lb 5, nb 4	13	b 5, nb 2	7
	(all out 90 overs)	304	(all out 47.3 overs)	165

Bowling
Akram 8-1-32-0. Azhar Mahmood 12-3-56-1. Clarke 4-0-29-0. Kumble 33-8-80-5. Salisbury 31-7-89-4. Brown 2-0-9-0.
Akram 10-0-42-1. Azhar Mahmood 15-3-53-4. Salisbury 14-3-37-3. Kumble 8.3-0-28-2.
Fall of Wickets: 1-97, 2-138, 3-139, 4-190, 5-192, 6-225, 7-259, 8-266, 9-282 1-3, 2-7, 3-52, 4-52, 5-80, 6-130, 7-134, 8-148, 9-149

SURREY	First Innings			
SA Newman	c Moore b Batty	64		
*JN Batty	c Smith b Sillence	104		
MR Ramprakash	c Smith b Batty	196		
MA Butcher (capt)	c Davies b Khan	0		
AD Brown	c Davies b Sillence	112		
JGE Benning	c Mitchell b Sillence	12		
Azhar Mahmood	c Davies b Khan	6		
IDK Salisbury	hit wkt b Khan	6		
R Clarke	not out	40		
A Kumble	c Batty b Malik	8		
Mohammad Akram	lbw b Mason	6		
Extras	b 7, lb 12, w 1, nb 8	28		
	(all out 139 overs)	576		

Bowling
Khan 36-6-142-3. Mason 20-3-100-1. Batty 28-3-119-2. Malik 19-4-67-1. Sillence 26-6-95-3. Solanki 10-2-34-0.
Fall of Wickets: 1-109, 2-266, 3-267, 4-496, 5-513, 6-513, 7-513, 8-530, 9-541

Surrey won by an innings and 107 runs – Worcestershire (5 pts), Surrey (22 pts)

OF WORCESTERSHIRE

I f Warwickshire had a golden spell in the early to mid-1990s then it merely followed a fine run of success by their West Midlands rivals in the late 1980s and early 1990s. From 1987 to 1991 Worcestershire won five trophies, including two Championships in 1988 and 1989, and it was the last success of many players in that great team when they overcame Warwickshire in the 1994 NatWest Trophy final to avenge the loss against them in the Benson and Hedges Cup final of two months earlier.

The catalyst for this unprecedented run of silverware was the signings of Ian Botham from Somerset and Graham Dilley from Kent in the Ashes winter of 1986–87. Worcestershire's hierarchy, led by Mike Jones and Duncan Fearnley, were hungry for success and in players like Graeme Hick, Neal Radford, Phil Newport, Tim Curtis, Steve Rhodes and Richard Illingworth they already had the core of a fine team. There was also a tough, experienced and much-respected captain in Phil Neale, and it was his dedication and selflessness that enabled the bigger-name stars to concentrate on simply enjoying their cricket.

The Sunday League was taken in 1987 and again in the 'double' year of 1988, while the Benson and Hedges Cup of 1991 was the Lord's cup final success which Neale in particular coveted following the disappointment of defeats in both the 1988 NatWest Trophy final and the 1990 Benson and Hedges final.

The 1994 cup win, meanwhile, was achieved under Neale's successor Curtis but despite the continued influence of Hick, Tom Moody, Rhodes, Illingworth, Newport and Radford it was the loss of Botham's joie de vivre and Dilley's cutting edge which Worcestershire missed badly and failed to replace.

In recent years, first under Moody's guidance as head coach and

latterly under Rhodes, Worcestershire have often threatened to rise again. Vikram Solanki, Gareth Batty and Kabir Ali have won England recognition, while Hick has continued to score heavily as his remarkable career draws to a close and Steven Davies has emerged as perhaps the best young English wicketkeeper of his generation.

This past summer, under Solanki's leadership, Worcestershire have won a double promotion in both Championship and one-day league cricket, but much still remains to be done if they are to reclaim the ground won during their glory days between 1987 and 1994.

Hick's run making still astonishes, however, into his 41st year. He first played for the county in 1984, as an overseas player, after touring England with the Zimbabwe World Cup squad of 1983. His seven-year qualification for England ended in 1991 when he played the first of 65 Tests for his adopted country, but Hick's greatest individual moment will perhaps always be his unbeaten 405 against Somerset at Taunton in 1988.

A youthful Graeme Hick plays to leg during his famous innings of 405 not out against Somerset at Taunton in 1988.

Mark Ramprakash, on 64, looks to have given a bat-pad catch to Worcestershire's Phil Jaques, but the Surrey batsman went on to score 196 as his prolific season continued in Surrey's victory at New Road.

unbeaten 54, but Kumble finished with 5 for 80 and Salisbury reached 50 wickets in a season for the first time since 2000 as he picked up 4 for 89. Surrey's batsmen then needed no second invitation to rack up a match-winning lead, with Mark Ramprakash yet again to the fore. Ramprakash hit 196, from 256 balls and with 27 fours, to become the first Englishman to reach 2,000 first-class runs since the split of the County Championship into two divisions. It was also, remarkably, his fifth score of more than 150 in five consecutive matches. Jon Batty and Alistair Brown also scored centuries; with Rikki Clarke hitting an unbeaten 40 late on to rub salt into Worcestershire wounds and also pass his own 1,000 runs for the season for the first time in his career. Battered and bruised by now, Worcestershire meekly subsided to 165 all out on the third afternoon, with only Vikram Solanki and Gareth Batty showing the necessary fight and technique against a rampant attack of Azhar Mahmood, Salisbury and Kumble.

Round Sixteen: 15–20 August 2006

Division One

A magnificent finish at the Rose Bowl saw Warwickshire pull off a remarkable two-wicket, last-ball victory and Hampshire get tantalisingly close to winning a match in which they had been forced to follow on. And all this is the absence of Hampshire captain Shane Warne, a reportedly less-than-amused participant in Australia's pre-Ashes 'boot camp' in the Queensland jungle. In the end, the sheer frustration of conceding 14 runs in the final over, after earlier taking five wickets to bowl his side to the brink of a spectacular success, was too much for Dimitri Mascarenhas who uprooted two stumps because he needed to kick something. Warwickshire's hero, at the death, was Neil Carter, who was batting with a runner due to a hamstring problem but who still had the flexibility to hammer Mascarenhas for a six and a four in that dramatic last over. Carter finished 18 not out, while Ian Westwood picked up the most important 2 not out of his young career after coming in as low as No. 10 (he had needed a hospital check-up because he was struck on the head while fielding). Earlier in the day Heath Streak's 6 for 73 had finally undone

Round Sixteen: 15–20 August 2006 Division One

HAMPSHIRE v. WARWICKSHIRE – at the Rose Bowl

WARWICKSHIRE	First Innings		Second Innings	
IJ Westwood	b Tremlett	0	(10) not out	2
MA Wagh	c Benham b Thornely	128	c Burrows b Mascarenhas	47
IJL Trott	b Tremlett	4	c Crawley b Mascarenhas	17
NV Knight	lbw b Tremlett	78	(1) c Adams b Bruce	19
AGR Loudon	c Burrows b Tremlett	10	(4) c Burrows b Mascarenhas	0
*TR Ambrose	c Udal b Thornely	36	(5) lbw b Mascarenhas	0
LC Parker	lbw b Udal	28	(6) c Burrows b Mascarenhas	0
HH Streak (capt)	c Burrows b Tremlett	16	(7) b Udal	11
NM Carter	c Adams b Tremlett	36	(8) not out	18
TD Groenewald	not out	16	(9) run out	2
PL Harris	c Crawley b Udal	16		
Extras	lb 3, w 2, nb 28	33	lb 2, w 1, nb 2	5
	(all out 114.3 overs)	401	(8 wkts 25 overs)	121

Bowling
Tremlett 26-4-89-6. Bruce 16-2-86-0. Mascarenhas 25-6-60-0. Ervine 9-1-48-0. Thornely 16-2-42-2. Udal 22.3-5-73-2.
Tremlett 6-0-29-0. Bruce 5-1-26-1. Mascarenhas 8-0-39-5. Ervine 4-0-11-0. Udal 5-0-14-1.
Fall of Wickets: 1-0, 2-6, 3-179, 4-193, 5-281, 6-296, 7-323, 8-361, 9-374
1-39, 2-77, 3-77, 4-77, 5-79, 6-90, 7-98, 8-101

HAMPSHIRE	First Innings		Second Innings (following on)	
JHK Adams	c Ambrose b Harris	94	c Ambrose b Streak	23
MA Carberry	st Ambrose b Harris	29	c Ambrose b Streak	6
JP Crawley	c Ambrose b Carter	29	run out	18
CC Benham	c Parker b Harris	5	b Streak	95
DJ Thornely	b Harris	19	lbw b Streak	65
SM Ervine	c Streak b Loudon	23	c Ambrose b Streak	10
AD Mascarenhas	run out	2	b Streak	2
*TG Burrows	c Westwood b Harris	11	b Groenewald	18
SD Udal (capt)	c Knight b Loudon	14	b Harris	28
CT Tremlett	lbw b Harris	18	b Streak	9
JTA Bruce	not out	0	not out	0
Extras	b 2, lb 2, w 8, nb 2	14	b 7, lb 3, nb 2	12
	(all out 91.1 overs)	235	(all out 73.3 overs)	286

Bowling
Streak 16-8-32-0. Carter 10-1-40-1. Harris 40.1-14-80-6. Groenewald 7-1-26-0. Loudon 18-1-53-2.
Streak 20-4-73-6. Groenewald 14-1-66-1. Harris 25.3-2-87-1. Loudon 14-4-50-1.
Fall of Wickets: 1-50, 2-96, 3-107, 4-147, 5-154, 6-175, 7-200, 8-201, 9-235
1-27, 2-52, 3-58, 4-217, 5-224, 6-229, 7-249, 8-249, 9-286

Warwickshire won by 2 wickets –
Hampshire (4 pts), Warwickshire (22 pts)

Hampshire's second-innings resistance, in which Chris Benham's 95 and Dominic Thornely's 65 stood out. That left Warwickshire requiring 121 from 25 remaining overs, and at 77 for 1 they seemed to be cruising. Mascarenhas, however, then spread panic by dismissing Alex Loudon, Tim Ambrose and Luke Parker all for ducks in an initially irresistible spell. Paul Harris, the 27-year-old left-arm spinner from South Africa signed as a replacement overseas player for the injured Daniel Vettori, added to his growing reputation with a first innings 6 for 80 as Hampshire were dismissed first time around for 235. This conceded a deficit of 166 to Warwickshire, who despite Chris Tremlett's six-wicket return, had taken control on the opening day through Mark Wagh and Nick Knight, who added 173 for the third wicket.

Mushtaq Ahmed, clearly refreshed in body and soul after returning to Pakistan for a week to rest his neck and groin ailments and to witness the birth of his fourth child, spun Durham to a heavy innings and 133-run defeat at Hove. But Sussex's much-needed win was also due to an impressive batting effort – led from the front as ever by captain Chris Adams – and some testing seam and swing bowling from Jason Lewry and Yasir Arafat. Phil Mustard resisted bravely and aggressively for Durham, hitting 58 in their first innings slide to 150 all out and then adding a second first-class hundred before being last out second time around, but it was Mushtaq who took most of the headlines again with 5 for 64 on the second day and then a further three wickets as

SUSSEX v. DURHAM – at Hove

SUSSEX	First Innings	
RR Montgomerie	c Harmison B b Lewis	69
CD Hopkinson	b Benkenstein	64
MH Yardy	b Lewis	2
MW Goodwin	c Sutcliffe b Chapple	88
CJ Adams (capt)	c Onions b Breese	155
*MJ Prior	c E b Thorp	41
RSC Martin-Jenkins	not out	45
Yasir Arafat	not out	40
Mushtaq Ahmed		
OP Rayner		
JD Lewry		
Extras	b 9, lb 6, w 1, nb 10	26
	(6 wkts dec 142 overs)	530

Bowling
Lewis 22-5-78-2. Onions 26-7-76-0. Thorp 22-7-49-1. Benkenstein 15-4-47-1. Breese 36-5-133-2. Iqbal 21-1-132-0.
Fall of Wickets: 1-140, 2-142, 3-180, 4-306, 5-382, 6-482

DURHAM	First Innings		Second Innings (following on)	
JP Maher	c Adams b Mushtaq Ahmed	35	c Montgomerie b Yasir Arafat	33
JA Lowe	b Yasir Arafat	0	lbw b Yasir Arafat	1
GJ Muchall	b Mushtaq Ahmed	17	lbw b Mushtaq Ahmed	13
DM B'kenstein (capt)	lbw b Mushtaq Ahmed	2	lbw b Mushtaq Ahmed	24
BW Harmison	st Prior b Mushtaq Ahmed	4	b Lewry	29
GR Breese	b Lewry	2	b Mushtaq Ahmed	2
*P Mustard	c Martin-Jenkins b Lewry	58	b Yasir Arafat	103
CD Thorp	b Lewry	0	c Prior b Lewry	0
G Onions	c Yardy b Mushtaq Ahmed	4	c Prior b Lewry	13
MM Iqbal	c Rayner b Lewry	19	c Rayner b Yasir Arafat	5
ML Lewis	not out	6	not out	9
Extras	lb 3	3	b 2, lb 5, nb 8	15
	(all out 49.2 overs)	150	(all out 54.2 overs)	247

Bowling
Lewry 16.2-4-55-4. Yasir Arafat 8-4-21-1. Mushtaq Ahmed 17-4-64-5. Martin-Jenkins 8-0-31-0. Iqbal 21-1-132-0.
Lewry 17-2-73-3. Yasir Arafat 16.2-3-64-4. Martin-Jenkins 4-2-6-0. Mushtaq Ahmed 12-1-57-3. Rayner 4-0-32-0. Yardy 8-1-24-0.
Fall of Wickets: 1-2, 2-55, 3-56, 4-57, 5-62, 6-80, 7-80, 8-85, 9-141
1-20, 2-42, 3-65, 4-77, 5-79, 6-161, 7-161, 8-215, 9-220

Sussex won by an innings and 133 runs – Sussex (22 pts), Durham (1 pt)

LANCASHIRE v. MIDDLESEX – at Old Trafford

MIDDLESEX	First Innings	
ET Smith	lbw b Hogg	10
NRD Compton	lbw b Hogg	21
OA Shah	c Law b Keedy	103
EC Joyce	c Sutcliffe b Chapple	32
SB Styris (capt)	lbw b Keedy	39
EJG Morgan	b Smith	8
PN Weekes	c Chilton b Keedy	36
*DC Nash	not out	68
CT Peploe	b Astle	16
CB Keegan	st Sutton b Keedy	5
J Louw	not out	2
Extras	b 6, lb 1, w 3	10
	(9 wkts dec 127.4 overs)	350

Bowling
Cork 24-5-42-0. Hogg 21-5-52-2. Smith 20-6-58-1. Chapple 13-3-30-1. Keedy 36.4-6-126-4. Astle 13-4-35-1.
Fall of Wickets: 1-13, 2-65, 3-123, 4-199, 5-214, 6-218, 7-294, 8-331, 9-348

LANCASHIRE	First Innings	
MJ Chilton (capt)	lbw b Styris	35
IJ Sutcliffe	c Nash b Keegan	1
MB Loye	st Nash b Peploe	107
SG Law	not out	64
NJ Astle	c E b Louw	44
*LD Sutton	c Nash b Louw	27
G Chapple	c Nash b Louw	0
KW Hogg	lbw b Weekes	24
TC Smith	c Styris b Peploe	26
DG Cork	c Compton b Peploe	21
G Keedy	b Keegan	0
Extras	b 6, lb 7	13
	(all out 75.2 overs)	362

Bowling
Louw 16-0-89-3. Keegan 15.2-0-76-2. Styris 9-0-33-1. Peploe 26-3-109-3. Joyce 4-0-21-0. Weekes 5-0-21-1.
Fall of Wickets: 1-24, 2-48, 3-215, 4-252, 5-258, 6-277, 7-300, 8-326, 9-356

Match drawn – Lancashire (11 pts),
Middlesex (11 pts)

YORKSHIRE v. KENT – at Headingley

YORKSHIRE	First Innings	
C White (capt)	b Khan	3
JJ Sayers	c Stevens b Khan	9
A McGrath	c van Jaarsveld b Bravo	41
MJ Lumb	c Walker b Cook	15
DS Lehmann	c Fulton b Patel	172
A Rashid	lbw b Cook	10
*SM Guy	c Jones b Cook	4
JN Gillespie	c Walker b Patel	4
MAK Lawson	c van Jaarsveld b Cook	21
SA Patterson	c van Jaarsveld b Cook	0
GJ Kruis	not out	9
Extras	b 2, lb 1, w 5, nb 14	22
	(all out 92.5 overs)	310

Bowling
Khan 17-1-50-2. Henderson 21-1-118-0. Cook 20-5-36-5. Bravo 8-0-40-1. Patel 18.5-3-38-2. Stevens 8-0-25-0.
Fall of Wickets: 1-10, 2-25, 3-64, 4-92, 5-128, 6-136, 7-166, 8-228, 9-244

KENT	First Innings	
DP Fulton	c McGrath b Kruis	6
RWT Key (capt)	b McGrath	40
SJ Cook	c Guy b Kruis	71
M van Jaarsveld	not out	61
MJ Walker	c McGrath b Kruis	6
DI Stevens	lbw b Rashid	31
DJJ Bravo	lbw b Rashid	8
*GO Jones	not out	8
T Henderson		
A Khan		
MM Patel		
Extras	lb 5, nb 2	7
	(6 wkts 68 overs)	230

Bowling
Gillespie 18-6-48-0. Kruis 17-5-39-3. Rashid 11-1-46-2. Patterson 3-0-21-0. McGrath 12-1-45-1. Lawson 4-0-24-0.
Fall of Wickets: 1-13, 2-93, 3-136, 4-151, 5-213, 6-213

Match drawn – Yorkshire (9 pts),
Kent (8 pts)

Dimitri Mascarenhas did his best to stop Warwickshire's run chase at the Rose Bowl but ended up frustrated.

the match was wrapped up 30 minutes after lunch on day three. 'We are a very good side, with both Lewry and Arafat bowling exceptionally well at the moment to help to take the weight off the shoulders of Mushtaq,' said Mark Robinson, the Sussex director of cricket. 'But it doesn't half help you when you get your international-class leg spinner back bowling with a smile on his face again.'

Lancashire, meanwhile, were foiled by the weather at Old Trafford – and Owais Shah's second hundred of the season – and had to settle for a Mal Loye-led charge for batting points in reply to a Middlesex first innings of 350 for 9 declared that lasted until 22.4 overs had been bowled on the final day. Loye's 107 was his fourth century in successive matches, while Stuart Law re-emerged after earlier retiring hurt with a twisted knee to help Lancashire get the fourth batting point they required to move level on points at the top of the table with Sussex.

The weather was even more intrusive at Headingley, meanwhile, with the third day of Yorkshire's match against Kent being washed out completely and only one over being possible on the final day. Darren Lehmann's superb 172 – he hit 19 fours, faced 189 balls and was last out – was the undoubted highlight, although Simon Cook had an inspired time of it with both bat and ball and Martin van Jaarsveld was his usual reliable self.

Division Two

Surrey were hit by injuries in the run-up to their match against Essex at Colchester, while Mark Ramprakash was also missing due to family reasons, and it certainly told as the home side stepped up their own promotion bid with a crushing innings and two-run victory. Ravi Bopara was in the thick of the action at first, taking five wickets as Surrey were dismissed relatively cheaply despite late resistance from Ian Salisbury and Neil Saker, and then hitting 94 from 138 balls, with a six and 12 fours, while adding 170 for the third wicket with Mark Pettini. Both fell disappointingly short of a century, but James Middlebrook did not make the same mistake in a lovely innings of 113. James Foster also played some eye-catching drives in his 74 and, with Tim Phillips chipping in at the end, Essex were suddenly going past 500. Surrey's second innings was a limp affair, with Middlebrook and Andy Bichel picking up three wickets apiece and only Alistair Brown threatening, although Varun Chopra's brilliant run out of Surrey captain Mark Butcher was a key moment in a decline which culminated in Essex claiming the extra half-hour on the third evening to complete their win.

Worcestershire tripped up at Grace Road, meanwhile, when captain Vikram Solanki – mindful of Essex's maximum-point success – gambled on being able to bowl out Leicestershire on the last day of a match much interrupted by the weather. Worcestershire, who had earlier taken complete control with Steven Davies hitting a fine 140 and both Stephen Moore and Gareth Batty only narrowly missing out on hundreds too, forfeited their second innings to set up a Leicestershire chase of 356 in 88 overs. At first, everything seemed to be going Worcestershire's way, but John Sadler and Darren Maddy changed the mood by adding 140 in 32 overs. Sadler hit a six and ten fours in his 81, but it was Maddy who really did the damage by striking two sixes and ten fours of his own in a 103-ball 83 that put Leicestershire back on course. The feisty Paul Nixon was also up for the challenge, and he was joined during his 77-ball fifty by Claude Henderson, whose 36 from 44 balls set the seal on Solanki's misery.

OF YORKSHIRE

This past quarter-century began with Raymond Illingworth coming out of retirement at the age of 50 to lead his native county to a remarkable Sunday League triumph in 1983 – 32 years on from when he made his debut for Yorkshire. There was also the narrowest of Benson and Hedges Cup final wins in 1987, when the scores had actually finished tied in the match against Northamptonshire, the uplifting 2001 Championship success under David Byas – the club's first since 1968 – and victory in the 2002 C&G Trophy final against Somerset at Lord's when Australian left-hander Matthew Elliott made a brilliant unbeaten hundred.

Yorkshire have also provided England with an Ashes-winning captain in Michael Vaughan and any number of other players from the days of Chris Old, David Bairstow and Graham Stevenson through to Martyn Moxon and Darren Gough and on to Matthew Hoggard, Craig White and Vaughan.

It has not been a vintage era, however, for traditionally the powerhouse of English cricket. This, after all, is the county that since 1890 has won 30 Championships and which, with legends like Illingworth, Brian Close, Fred Trueman and Geoff Boycott to the fore, won seven county titles in ten seasons between 1959 and 1968, plus Gillette Cups in 1965 and 1969. Internal strife has badly affected Yorkshire's progress in the modern era, starting with the rumpus that surrounded Boycott's captaincy in the early 1980s. It took the strong-minded (and physically imposing) Byas to achieve the significant success of the past 25 years, and the Championship triumph in 2001 was the culmination of his six years in charge.

Australian Darren Lehmann, who subsequently took over the captaincy and who until his retirement at the end of the summer of 2006 has been a batting rock in the top order, averaged 83.29 in the 2001 season and scored 1,416 Championship runs. Vaughan also batted beautifully when free from England calls, while White and Hoggard were again influential when available. Matthew Wood, and Byas, provided the other main batting support to Lehmann, while Steve Kirby arrived like a meteor to take 47 wickets with his fiery fast bowling and spearhead a strong seam attack, which also included the likes of Chris Silverwood, Ryan Sidebottom, Gavin Hamilton, White and Hoggard. Richard Dawson's off-breaks, meanwhile, brought him 30 wickets and an England winter tour call-up, but after a highly promising couple of years he has since struggled to make much of an impact.

Perhaps nothing more exciting has happened to Yorkshire cricket in the last 25 years – barring that 2001 Championship triumph, of course – than the emergence in the 2006 summer of two match-winning young leg spinners in Adil Rashid – still just 18 – and 20-year-old Mark Lawson. Tim Bresnan, still 21, won England ODI honours and both Andrew Gale and Joe Sayers won plaudits at 22 for their maturity at the crease. It is this emergence of youth that instils the hope in the county's supporters that Yorkshire, maybe, can become a serious force once more.

Yorkshire's Championship-winning class of 2001 pose for the cameras.

Rain utterly ruined Somerset's match against Glamorgan at Taunton, with both the third and fourth days being washed away. Before that, there had been some interesting cricket with Robin Lett, a 19-year-old from the Somerset Academy, marking his first-class debut with an innings of 50 and Huw Waters, the 19-year-old Glamorgan fast bowler, relishing the extra responsibility on his shoulders following an early muscle injury to David Harrison, taking 5 for 86. Andrew Caddick, too, demanded his share of the spotlight by thrashing 68 from No. 10. In Glamorgan's reply, there were some thumping strokes from Mark Cosgrove for the spectators to enjoy before the rain arrived.

An electrical storm arrived at Derby just before lunch on day one – at which point Gloucestershire were 78 for 3 – and stayed around with such ferocity that no more play was possible for the rest of the day, despite bright sunshine breaking out by late afternoon. The weather also had too much of a say in the rest of the match, allowing only 60 overs on the second day and washing away the morning session on the last. In the circumstances, Derbyshire were happy enough to have the best of the exchanges that did take place; indeed, when Steffan Jones removed both Gloucestershire openers for ducks at the start of their second innings, there were home hopes of an innings win. But Jones was suffering from blisters, Graham Wagg was also injured falling heavily in the outfield and Graeme

Welch, the Derbyshire captain, could not bowl because of an inflamed Achilles tendon. Soon, then, the game was drifting to a draw with Kadeer Ali and Chris Taylor able to concentrate on improving their averages.

Round Sixteen: 15–20 August 2006 Division Two

ESSEX v. SURREY – at Chelmsford

SURREY	First Innings		Second Innings	
SA Newman	c Foster b Bopara	41	c Flower b Phillips	25
*JN Batty	c Chopra b Tudor	4	b Bichel	12
SJ Walters	c Foster b Bichel	41	c Foster b Tudor	4
MA Butcher (capt)	c Foster b Bopara	6	run out	6
AD Brown	lbw b Bichel	36	c Flower b Westfield	63
Azhar Mahmood	c Phillips b Bichel	5	(7) c Pettini b Middlebrook	26
IDK Salisbury	c Pettini b Middlebrook	74	(8) b Middlebrook	14
RS Clinton	c Middlebrook b Bopara	11	(6) lbw b Bichel	12
NC Saker	not out	58	c Bopara b Middlebrook	9
ND Doshi	c Flower b Bopara	32	c Foster b Bichel	2
Mohammad Akram	c Foster b Bopara	6	not out	8
Extras	b 4, w 6, nb 6	16	b 9, lb 7, w 1	17
	(all out 91.5 overs)	330	(all out 72.4 overs)	198

Bowling
Bichel 22-5-80-3. Tudor 15-4-66-1. Westfield 10-2-47-0. Bopara 21.5-4-75-5. Phillips 12-4-34-0. Middlebrook 11-1-24-1.
Bichel 14.4-1-53-3. Tudor 10-4-16-1. Middlebrook 24-5-51-3. Phillips 18-3-47-1. Westfield 6-1-15-1.
Fall of Wickets: 1-17, 2-66, 3-88, 4-128, 5-134, 6-147, 7-204, 8-259, 9-314
1-29, 2-39, 3-57, 4-63, 5-100, 6-154, 7-170, 8-187, 9-188

ESSEX	First Innings	
V Chopra	c Batty b Azhar Mahmood	14
ML Pettini	c Saker b Akram	97
MS Westfield	b Azhar Mahmood	0
RS Bopara	lbw b Walters	94
A Flower	c sub b Saker	24
RC Irani (capt)	c Walters b Doshi	38
*JS Foster	c Walters b Azhar Mahmood	74
JD Middlebrook	st Batty b Doshi	113
AJ Bichel	c Saker b Doshi	14
TJ Phillips	not out	38
AJ Tudor	c Brown b Doshi	0
Extras	b 3, lb 13, nb 8	24
	(all out 148.5 overs)	530

Bowling
Akram 28-2-98-1. Azhar Mahmood 28-6-72-3. Saker 22-1-101-1. Doshi 38.5-4-135-4. Salisbury 13-2-56-0. Walters 7-3-21-1. Brown 12-1-31-0.
Fall of Wickets: 1-23, 2-23, 3-193, 4-232, 5-246, 6-310, 7-404, 8-435, 9-530

Essex won by an innings and 2 runs – Essex (22 pts), Surrey (5 pts)

LEICESTERSHIRE v. WORCESTERSHIRE – at Leicester

WORCS	First Innings		Second Innings – Forfeited	
SC Moore	b Henderson	97		
L Vincent	c Naik b Griffith	5		
VS Solanki (capt)	b Broad	0		
BF Smith	run out	21		
GA Hick	c Naik b Henderson	33		
*SM Davies	b Broad	140		
GJ Batty	c Henderson b Griffith	98		
Kabir Ali	c Broad b Maddy	31		
Z Khan	not out	7		
RW Price				
MS Mason				
Extras	b 4, lb 9, w 5, nb 6	24		
	(8 wkts dec 106.3 overs)	456		

Bowling
Broad 20-4-96-2. Griffith 24.5-5-98-2. Cummins 16-0-61-0. Maddy 10.3-1-51-1. Maunders 6-0-29-0. Henderson 19-4-57-2. Naik 11-3-51-0.
Fall of Wickets: 1-20, 2-29, 3-64, 4-121, 5-200, 6-412, 7-424, 8-456

LEICESTERSHIRE	First Innings		Second Innings	
DDJ Robinson (capt)	not out	40	b Mason	34
JK Maunders	b Khan	25	c Davies b Khan	18
HD Ackerman	c Vincent b Khan	3	c Smith b Price	17
JL Sadler	not out	30	b Price	81
DL Maddy			lbw b Vincent	83
*PA Nixon			st Davies b Price	50
CW Henderson			c Solanki b Price	36
SCJ Broad			not out	9
AR Griffith			not out	1
RAG Cummins				
JHK Naik				
Extras	lb 3	3	lb 5, w 1, nb 22	28
	(2 wkts dec 26.5 overs)	101	(7 wkts 86.4 overs)	357

Bowling
Khan 12-2-63-2. Kabir Ali 3-1-10-0. Mason 7-4-13-0. Batty 3.5-1-12-0. Vincent 1-1-0-0.
Khan 18-4-80-1. Mason 11-1-54-1. Kabir Ali 11-1-66-0. Batty 16-2-51-0. Price 27.4-3-89-4. Vincent 3-0-12-1.
Fall of Wickets: 1-48, 2-56
1-47, 2-69, 3-88, 4-228, 5-259, 6-345, 7-352

Leicestershire won by 3 wickets – Leicestershire (16 pts), Worcestershire (5 pts)

SOMERSET v. GLAMORGAN – at Taunton

SOMERSET	First Innings	
MJ Wood	lbw b Watkins	20
NJ Edwards	c Wallace b Watkins	8
AV Suppiah	c Cosgrove b Waters	1
JC Hildreth	c Wallace b Waters	41
RJ Lett	c Cosker b Waters	50
KA Parsons	c Wallace b Waters	45
WJ Durston	lbw b Croft	46
*CM Gazzard	c Rees b Waters	28
SRG Francis	b Croft	3
AR Caddick (capt)	c Croft b Croft	68
CM Willoughby	not out	12
Extras	b 4, lb 1, w 1, nb 2	8
	(all out 91.3 overs)	330

Bowling
Harrison 2.1-1-2-0. Waters 29-7-86-5. Watkins 25.5-5-115-2. Grant 3-1-14-0. Cosgrove 3-0-10-0. Cosker 9-2-35-0. Croft 19.3-5-63-3.
Fall of Wickets: 1-28, 2-29, 3-47, 4-106, 5-125, 6-214, 7-216, 8-227, 9-263

GLAMORGAN	First Innings	
MJ Cosgrove	c Parsons b Willoughby	77
GP Rees	c Gazzard b Willoughby	20
DL Hemp	c Durston b Caddick	43
MJ Powell	c Caddick b Parsons	34
RN Grant	c Durston b Willoughby	8
RE Watkins	not out	37
*MA Wallace	not out	15
RDB Croft (capt)		
DS Harrison		
DA Cosker		
HT Waters		
Extras	lb 2, nb 4	6
	(5 wkts 49 overs)	240

Bowling
Caddick 21-5-87-1. Willoughby 17-3-84-3. Francis 6-2-43-0. Parsons 5-0-24-1.
Fall of Wickets: 1-101, 2-116, 3-179, 4-179, 5-204

Match drawn – Somerset (8 pts), Glamorgan (8 pts)

DERBYSHIRE v. GLOUCESTERSHIRE – at Derby

GLOS	First Innings		Second Innings	
WPC Weston	c Stubbings b Jones	46	(2) lbw b Jones	0
CM Spearman	c & b Jones	0	(1) c Botha b Jones	0
HJH Marshall	b Hunter	1	c Goddard b Botha	70
Kadeer Ali	c Birt b Wagg	33	not out	76
CG Taylor	c Wagg b Jones	17	b Hassan Adnan	56
APR Gidman (capt)	c Botha b Wagg	35	not out	0
*SJ Adshead	c Goddard b Hunter	21		
ID Fisher	lbw b Wagg	19		
J Lewis	b Jones	7		
JMM Averis	c Smith b Botha	33		
SP Kirby	not out	13		
MA Hardinge†				
Extras	lb 5, w 1, nb 20	26	b 4, nb 2	6
	(all out 78.3 overs)	240	(4 wkts 57 overs)	208

Bowling
Jones 25-8-76-4. Hunter 17-4-52-2. Wagg 22-5-74-3. Welch 10-5-24-0. Botha 4.3-1-9-1.
Jones 4-1-6-2. Hunter 7-0-25-0. Wagg 4-0-30-0. Botha 21-5-53-1. Birt 7-1-35-0. Smith 12-3-49-0. Stubbings 1-0-2-0. Hassan Adnan 1-0-4-1.
Fall of Wickets: 1-1, 2-5, 3-75, 4-97, 5-125, 6-146, 7-146, 8-185, 9-199
1-0, 2-7, 3-110, 4-208

DERBYSHIRE	First Innings	
SD Stubbings	c Marshall b Lewis	8
MJ Di Venuto	c Weston b Kirby	104
Hassan Adnan	c Adshead b Fisher	15
TR Birt	lbw b Kirby	34
GM Smith	c Lewis b Fisher	86
AG Botha	c Taylor b Gidman	59
*LJ Goddard	not out	35
G Welch (capt)	not out	16
GG Wagg		
PS Jones		
ID Hunter		
Extras	b 1, lb 10, w 2, nb 30	43
	(6 wkts dec 114 overs)	400

Bowling
Lewis 16-2-69-1. Kirby 18.4-2-74-2. Fisher 33-4-87-2. Averis 17-3-75-0. Taylor 21-3-43-0. Gidman 8.2-1-41-1.
Fall of Wickets: 1-8, 2-51, 3-175, 4-192, 5-323, 6-354
† Replaced by J Lewis

Match drawn – Derbyshire (12 pts), Gloucestershire (7 pts)

Round Seventeen: 22–25 August 2006

Division One

Five wickets from Neil Killeen, a brilliant unbeaten hundred from Jimmy Maher, and a second half-century of the match from the promising Ben Harmison turned the tables on Warwickshire on the third day at the Riverside and brought Durham a vital seven-wicket win. Harmison's 65 and Dale Benkenstein's 79 had kept the county in the game the previous day, despite Paul Harris' latest six-wicket haul, and when Killeen broke a stand of 96 between Jonathan Trott and Alex Loudon it suddenly put Durham in command. Maher's 101 not out took him just 126 balls, and included 14 fours, while Harmison kept him company until the end with an unbeaten 61.

Mark Ealham's departure from Kent at the end of the 2003 season has always been a bone of contention within the club, and the former England all-rounder reserved yet another significant performance for a match against his old county as Nottinghamshire crushed them by an innings and 85 runs at Trent Bridge. Remarkably, the match was all over inside two days after Notts had racked up 496 with Ealham adding a typically powerful 92 to the hundreds made by David

Mark Ealham, who enjoyed scoring a beefy 92 against his former county Kent at Trent Bridge.

Hussey and Stephen Fleming. Dwayne Bravo's six wickets were almost irrelevant, but Ealham's three first-innings scalps weren't as Kent lost David Fulton early on the second day and declined fast from their overnight 115 for 2 despite Matthew Walker's 65. Following on, Kent then collapsed totally against the swing of Ryan Sidebottom, who added five more wickets to the four he had claimed in the first innings. Andrew Harris and Charlie Shreck then mopped up during the extra half hour.

Round Seventeen: 22–25 August 2006 Division One

DURHAM v. WARWICKSHIRE – at the Riverside

WARWICKSHIRE First Innings

			Second Innings	
NV Knight	c Benkenstein b Thorp	33	c Mustard b Onions	0
MA Wagh	lbw b Thorp	18	c Maher b Lewis	0
MM Ali	c Muchall b Lewis	68	lbw b Lewis	4
IJL Trott	b Killeen	18	c Breese b Killeen	69
*TR Ambrose	c Muchall b Thorp	0	b Lewis	4
AGR Loudon	b Scott	18	lbw b Killeen	55
HH Streak (capt)	c Maher b Benkenstein	19	(8) b Thorp	2
DR Brown	b Scott	18	(7) c Breese b Killeen	2
TD Groenewald	c Muchall b Thorp	76	b Killeen	7
PL Harris	b Onions	27	c Harmison B b Killeen	19
LM Daggett	not out	0	not out	1
Extras	b 4, lb 8, nb 12	24	lb 1	1
	(all out 84 overs)	**314**	(all out 40.4 overs)	**164**

Bowling
Onions 17-4-58-1. Lewis 18-4-68-1. Thorp 18-5-57-4. Killeen 14-7-24-1. Benkenstein 9-0-54-1. Breese 1-0-2-0. Scott 7-2-39-2.
Onions 8-3-50-1. Lewis 10-2-52-3. Thorp 11-2-32-1. Killeen 11.4-4-29-5.
Fall of Wickets: 1-37, 2-109, 3-139, 4-146, 5-161, 6-188, 7-206, 8-215, 9-306
1-0, 2-4, 3-4, 4-25, 5-121, 6-131, 7-134, 8-138, 9-153

DURHAM First Innings

			Second Innings	
JP Maher	c Harris b Daggett	6	not out	101
GM Scott	c Ambrose b Harris	4	lbw b Daggett	0
GJ Muchall	lbw b Brown	17	c Ambrose b Daggett	0
N Killeen	c Knight b Harris	1		
DM B'kenstein (capt)	c sub b Harris	79	(4) c Ambrose b Brown	31
BW Harmison	c Brown b Harris	65	(5) not out	61
GR Breese	lbw b Brown	29		
*P Mustard	c Daggett b Harris	31		
CD Thorp	c sub b Brown	4		
G Onions	not out	7		
ML Lewis	c Ambrose b Harris	0		
Extras	b 1, lb 9, w 1	11	lb 3	3
	(all out 89.4 overs)	**284**	(3 wkts 41.5 overs)	**196**

Bowling
Streak 5-3-13-0. Daggett 10-0-36-1. Brown 20-5-56-3. Groenewald 4-0-17-0.
Harris 34.4-11-94-6. Loudon 4-0-14-0. Ali 12-1-44-0.
Daggett 9-1-54-2. Brown 11-3-36-1. Harris 8-0-28-0. Groenewald 6-0-29-0.
Loudon 3-0-11-0. Ali 4.5-0-35-0.
Fall of Wickets: 1-9, 2-48, 3-53, 4-82, 5-200, 6-225, 7-267, 8-273, 9-283
1-7, 2-7, 3-62

Durham won by 7 wickets – Durham (19 pts), Warwickshire (6 pts)

NOTTINGHAMSHIRE v. KENT – at Trent Bridge

NOTTS First Innings

DJ Bicknell	c Jones b Bravo	19
WR Smith	lbw b Henderson	3
*D Alleyne	lbw b Cook	8
SP Fleming (capt)	c van Jaarsveld b Bravo	101
DJ Hussey	c van Jaarsveld b Cook	164
SR Patel	c & b Stevens	27
MA Ealham	c Stevens b Bravo	92
GP Swann	c Stevens b Bravo	15
RJ Sidebottom	c Jones b Bravo	7
AJ Harris	c Key b Bravo	14
CE Shreck	not out	1
Extras	b 5, lb 9, w 5, nb 26	45
	(all out 130.1 overs)	**496**

Bowling
Henderson 30-7-100-1. Cook 28-4-101-2. Joseph 17-0-80-0. Bravo 24.1-4-112-6.
Stevens 13-4-25-1. Patel 17-1-64-0. Walker 1-1-0-0.
Fall of Wickets: 1-11, 2-22, 3-61, 4-225, 5-298, 6-396, 7-426, 8-444, 9-478

KENT First Innings

			Second Innings (following on)	
DP Fulton	b Harris	57	c Alleyne b Harris	14
RWT Key (capt)	lbw b Sidebottom	20	c Alleyne b Sidebottom	31
M van Jaarsveld	c Alleyne b Sidebottom	2	lbw b Sidebottom	10
MJ Walker	c Swann b Shreck	65	lbw b Sidebottom	17
DI Stevens	c Hussey b Ealham	15	c Hussey b Sidebottom	2
*GO Jones	c Fleming b Shreck	4	lbw b Shreck	4
DJJ Bravo	c Hussey b Ealham	8	c Fleming b Harris	33
T Henderson	c Smith b Sidebottom	17	b Sidebottom	8
SJ Cook	b Ealham	30	c Ealham b Shreck	0
MM Patel	c Ealham b Sidebottom	6	b Harris	17
RH Joseph	not out	12	not out	0
Extras	lb 7, nb 8	15	b 5, lb 1, nb 18	24
	(all out 88.1 overs)	**251**	(all out 51.3 overs)	**160**

Bowling
Sidebottom 25-9-53-4. Shreck 24-6-70-2. Harris 16-4-50-1. Ealham 17.1-4-54-3.
Swann 2-0-6-0. Patel 4-1-11-0.
Sidebottom 16-7-22-5. Shreck 13-1-70-2. Ealham 10-2-22-0. Harris 12.3-3-40-3.
Fall of Wickets: 1-27, 2-43, 3-115, 4-150, 5-163, 6-180, 7-180, 8-209, 9-224
1-33, 2-56, 3-77, 4-83, 5-90, 6-100, 7-109, 8-114, 9-151

Nottinghamshire won by an innings and 85 runs – Nottinghamshire (22 pts), Kent (5 pts)

Division Two

Somerset's forgettable season suddenly took a turn for the better at Taunton as they won the West Country derby against Gloucestershire by an innings and 76 runs. Charl Willoughby took a career-best 7 for 44 in Gloucestershire's first innings fall from the comparative grace of 106 for 1, after Richard Johnson had earned the crucial wicket of Hamish Marshall. Johnson himself then blew away the visitors second time around – after Willoughby and Andrew Caddick had done the early damage – to pick up his first five-wicket haul of the season. Somerset's first innings of 409 had included uplifting performances from four homegrown players: Matthew Wood and James Hildreth returned to form with 60 and 71, Wes Durston battled to an unbeaten 60 and 19-year-old wicketkeeper Sam Spurway, from Ilminster, produced some memorable shots in his debut 46.

Northamptonshire looked to be winning their chase for victory, following Leicestershire's imaginative declaration, until a combination of Stuart Broad and the weather thwarted them. Only 126 runs were needed from the last 20 overs, with Usman Afzaal and Bilal Shafayat racing along, when Broad returned to dismiss both of them hooking. He also had Ben Phillips caught at third man but, with 79 still required from the final 10.3 overs and four

wickets remaining, a potentially exciting finish was ruined when rain arrived. Earlier in the game, Hylton Ackerman had hit a classy 216 for Leicestershire, and Paul Nixon had included a reverse sweep for six off Monty Panesar in his career-best 144 not out. Northants, though, had batted well themselves in reply, with Stephen Peters leading the way.

Round Eighteen: 30 August–5 September 2006

Division One

Lancashire were left cursing the rain at Blackpool as the final day of a match against Warwickshire that they were well placed to win was washed away. It was heartbreaking, too, for the Stanley Road groundstaff who 24 hours earlier had worked something of a miracle to get the third day's play started on time following such heavy overnight rain that almost 1,500 gallons of water were taken off the outfield during a feverish morning's mopping up. Warwickshire were forced to follow on at the end of that day, after being bowled out for 231 by a fine collective effort. Only Ian Westwood, who battled four and a half hours for 67, held Lancashire up. Tahir Naqqash had earlier completed a career-best 7 for 107, but the first half of the match had also been dominated by Lancashire, who ran up a total of 456 for 9 declared – at least earning themselves maximum batting points – on the back of a determined and dedicated 159 from Iain Sutcliffe and excellent half-centuries from Stuart Law and Nathan Astle.

Yorkshire may have been denied the chance to beat Middlesex in a relegation scrap at Scarborough, as a result of the final day being washed out, but the match will be long remembered as the one where a brighter future for the White Rose county suddenly shone like a truly silver lining to the dirty black clouds which cut short proceedings. First there was 22-year-old opener Joe Sayers keeping Yorkshire in the game by batting seven hours for 122 not out to become the first batsman since Geoff Boycott and only the

Round Seventeen: 22–25 August 2006 Division Two

SOMERSET v. GLOUCESTERSHIRE – at Taunton

SOMERSET	First Innings	
MJ Wood	b Lewis	60
NJ Edwards	c Adshead b Hardinges	32
AV Suppiah	c Adshead b Gidman	46
JC Hildreth	c Taylor b Lewis	71
RJ Lett	c Taylor b Gidman	8
KA Parsons	run out	47
WJ Durston	not out	60
*SHP Spurway	c Adshead b Averis	46
RL Johnson	b Averis	6
AR Caddick (capt)	b Averis	5
CM Willoughby	b Averis	0
Extras	lb 2, w 2, nb 24	28
	(all out 120.4 overs)	409

Bowling
Lewis 29-6-104-2. Averis 24.4-5-79-4. Hardinges 26-6-106-1. Banerjee 24-5-76-0. Gidman 16-3-38-2. Taylor 1-0-4-0.
Fall of Wickets: 1-66, 2-120, 3-157, 4-191, 5-239, 6-306, 7-391, 8-401, 9-407

GLOS	First Innings		Second Innings (following on)	
WPC Weston	b Willoughby	69	(2) lbw b Johnson	11
CM Spearman	c Suppiah b Willoughby	18	(1) c Durston b Caddick	16
HJH Marshall	c Parsons b Johnson	31	c Spurway b Caddick	0
Kadeer Ali	c & b Johnson	4	c Spurway b Willoughby	24
CG Taylor	b Parsons	5	b Willoughby	3
APR Gidman	c Edwards b Willoughby	11	b Johnson	17
*SJ Adshead	b Willoughby	1	lbw b Parsons	10
MA Hardinges	not out	6	c Spurway b Johnson	50
J Lewis (capt)	c Suppiah b Willoughby	4	b Johnson	23
JMM Averis	c Suppiah b Willoughby	0	b Johnson	7
V Banerjee	lbw b Willoughby	0	not out	0
Extras	nb 12	12	b 1, lb 2, w 2, nb 6	11
	(all out 46 overs)	161	(all out 44 overs)	172

Bowling
Caddick 16-4-60-0. Willoughby 15-5-44-7. Johnson 7-0-30-2. Parsons 7-1-27-1. Suppiah 1-1-0-0.
Caddick 12-0-49-2. Johnson 13-4-37-5. Willoughby 9-1-40-2. Parsons 7-1-34-1. Suppiah 3-0-9-0.
Fall of Wickets: 1-30, 2-106, 3-112, 4-117, 5-146, 6-150, 7-153, 8-159, 9-161
1-24, 2-28, 3-28, 4-40, 5-57, 6-79, 7-97, 8-137, 9-151

Somerset won by an innings and 76 runs –
Somerset (22 pts), Gloucestershire (3 pts)

NORTHAMPTONSHIRE v. LEICESTERSHIRE – at Northampton

LEICESTERSHIRE	First Innings		Second Innings	
DDJ Robinson (capt)	lbw b Phillips	15	c Afzaal b Crook	19
JK Maunders	run out	11	lbw b Panesar	20
HD Ackerman	c Crook b Nicholson	216	(4) b Crook	50
JL Sadler	c Nicholson b Panesar	69	(5) b Panesar	13
DL Maddy	c Shafayat b Panesar	0	(6) c Afzaal b Crook	12
*PA Nixon	not out	144	(7) not out	22
CW Henderson	c Klusener b Crook	13	(8) not out	23
SCJ Broad	c Peters b Rogers	12	(3) c Rogers b Panesar	5
JHK Naik	c Peters b Crook	1		
RAG Cummins	not out	0		
CJ Liddle				
Extras	b 10, lb 21, w 3	34	b 1, lb 8, w 2	11
	(8 wkts dec 137 overs)	515	(6 wkts dec 41 overs)	175

Bowling
Nicholson 30-6-84-1. Phillips 28-5-80-1. Klusener 13-2-48-0. Crook 21-1-105-2. Panesar 41-6-151-2. Rogers 4-0-16-1.
Nicholson 10-3-38-0. Phillips 3-0-17-0. Panesar 12-3-31-3. Crook 11-1-46-3. Afzaal 5-1-34-0.
Fall of Wickets: 1-35, 2-46, 3-228, 4-228, 5-439, 6-477, 7-499, 8-510
1-38, 2-44, 3-70, 4-89, 5-121, 6-133

NORTHANTS	First Innings		Second Innings	
SD Peters	c Nixon b Henderson	104	c Maddy b Henderson	44
CJL Rogers	b Sadler b Henderson	53	b Broad	17
U Afzaal	c Sadler b Panesar	44	c & b Broad	82
DJG Sales (capt)	c Nixon b Liddle	67	c Broad b Henderson	25
MS Klusener	not out	58	c Cummins b Broad	67
L Klusener			c & b Broad	67
BJ Phillips			c Liddle b Broad	16
SP Crook			not out	4
MJ Nicholson				
MS Panesar				
JF Brown				
Extras	b 4, lb 10, w 3, nb 6	23	lb 3, w 1	4
	(4 wkts dec 92.5 overs)	353	(6 wkts 53.3 overs)	259

Bowling
Broad 15.5-4-62-0. Liddle 18-3-60-1. Cummins 11-1-51-0. Maddy 13-5-38-0. Maunders 13-0-9-0. Henderson 29-6-110-3. Naik 3-0-9-0.
Broad 13-0-63-4. Liddle 5-1-25-0. Henderson 21.3-2-90-2. Cummins 7-2-26-0. Naik 7-0-52-0.
Fall of Wickets: 1-109, 2-215, 3-220, 4-345
1-41, 2-86, 3-142, 4-226, 5-241, 6-243

Match drawn – Northamptonshire (10 pts), Leicestershire (10 pts)

Tahir Naqqash bowled well to claim career-best figures of 7 for 107 for Warwickshire against Lancashire at Blackpool.

13th Yorkshireman since 1865 to carry his bat through a first-class innings. And then, bowling Yorkshire into a winning position on day three, were two homegrown leg spinners – Mark Lawson, aged 20 and in his 12th Championship match, and Adil Rashid, still just 18 and in only his third Championship appearance. Lawson took 6 for 88 as Middlesex were dismissed for 224, while at the other end Rashid snapped up the other four wickets. Only Ben Hutton's fighting 105, in the Middlesex captain's first match back after his bout of shingles, prevented an even sorrier slide against the two young leg-spinning maestros. Yorkshire ended the third day on 39 without loss in their second innings, in pursuit of a gettable 275, but then the weather ruined the prospect of a fascinating final day. Deon Kruis and Chris Silverwood, against his former county, had earlier taken the other bowling honours while Paul Weekes questioned the wisdom of why Middlesex had omitted him from their side for much of the summer – and even advertised him on the circuit as a possible loan signing – by frustrating both Yorkshire's attack and the majority of a 4,000 first-day crowd with a tenacious unbeaten century.

Bad weather also wrecked a potentially titanic struggle at Hove where, in a match billed as Mushtaq Ahmed v Shane Warne, the entire Sussex and Hampshire teams had for two initially rain-free days

Round Eighteen: 30 August–5 September 2006 Division One

LANCASHIRE v. WARWICKSHIRE – at Blackpool

LANCASHIRE	First Innings	
MJ Chilton (capt)	c Ambrose b Harris	18
IJ Sutcliffe	c Trott b Tahir	159
MB Loye	c Ambrose b Tahir	10
SG Law	c Knight b Tahir	61
NJ Astle	c Ali b Tahir	64
*LD Sutton	c Ambrose b Tahir	45
G Chapple	c Knight b Daggett	22
KW Hogg	b Tahir	20
DG Cork	c Harris b Tahir	10
TC Smith	not out	2
M Kartik	not out	2
Extras	b 4, lb 15, w 2, nb 22	43
	(9 wkts dec 117 overs)	456

Bowling
Daggett 25-4-92-1. Tahir 32-8-107-7. Carter 27-2-146-0. Harris 21-6-52-1. Loudon 10-0-36-0. Ali 2-1-4-0.
Fall of Wickets: 1-66, 2-91, 3-199, 4-336, 5-354, 6-409, 7-434, 8-452, 9-452.

WARWICKSHIRE	First Innings		Second Innings (following on)	
IJ Westwood	c Sutton b Chapple	67	not out	0
MA Wagh	c Kartik b Smith	15	not out	0
MM Ali	c Sutton b Hogg	11		
IJL Trott	c Sutton b Kartik	0		
NV Knight (capt)	c Sutton b Smith	32		
*TR Ambrose	b Cork	0		
AGR Loudon	lbw b Astle	31		
NM Carter	c Law b Kartik	11		
N Tahir	c Chilton b Hogg	21		
PL Harris	c Sutton b Cork	20		
LM Daggett	not out	12		
Extras	lb 7, nb 4	11		0
	(all out 92.5 overs)	231	(0 wkts 2 overs)	0

Bowling
Chapple 18-6-32-1. Cork 16.5-6-35-2. Smith 13-7-40-2. Hogg 14-6-38-2. Kartik 25-5-60-2. Astle 6-3-19-1.
Chapple 1-1-0-0. Cork 1-1-0-0.
Fall of Wickets: 1-40, 2-57, 3-58, 4-110, 5-111, 6-142, 7-153, 8-194, 9-194.

Match drawn – Lancashire (12 pts), Warwickshire (8 pts)

YORKSHIRE v. MIDDLESEX – at Scarborough

MIDDLESEX	First Innings		Second Innings	
BL Hutton (capt)	c Guy b Kruis	11	c McGrath b Lawson	105
NRD Compton	b Kruis	1	st Guy b Lawson	17
OA Shah	lbw b Kruis	0	lbw b Lawson	22
ET Smith	c Guy b Kruis	56	lbw b Rashid	5
SB Styris	c McGrath b Hoggard	64	(7) c McGrath b Rashid	5
PN Weekes	not out	128	(5) lbw b Rashid	5
*DC Nash	b Kruis	19	(6) c McGrath b Lawson	14
CT Peploe	c McGrath b Rashid	5	not out	20
CB Keegan	c Guy b Lawson	25	(10) lbw b Lawson	0
J Louw	c Lumb b Hoggard	16	(9) b Lawson	7
CEW Silverwood	lbw b Hoggard	20	st Guy b Rashid	7
Extras	b 7, lb 15, w 1, nb 8	31	b 2, lb 3, nb 2	7
	(all out 108 overs)	376	(all out 60.4 overs)	224

Bowling
Hoggard 26-2-92-3. Kruis 27-4-67-5. Shahzad 12-1-45-0. McGrath 11-1-30-0. Rashid 20-3-59-1. Lawson 12-0-61-1.
Hoggard 4-0-16-0. Kruis 8-1-19-0. Rashid 26.4-3-96-4. Lawson 22-0-88-6.
Fall of Wickets: 1-4, 2-10, 3-39, 4-115, 5-186, 6-231, 7-246, 8-301, 9-348
1-38, 2-104, 3-137, 4-159, 5-182, 6-189, 7-191, 8-203, 9-203

YORKSHIRE	First Innings		Second Innings	
C White (capt)	lbw b Silverwood	10	not out	17
JJ Sayers	not out	122	not out	15
A McGrath	lbw b Louw	49		
MJ Lumb	c Nash b Styris	17		
DS Lehmann	lbw b Weekes	43		
A Rashid	c sub b Louw	1		
*SM Guy	lbw b Louw	33		
A Shahzad	c Hutton b Silverwood	2		
MAK Lawson	c Compton b Silverwood	10		
MJ Hoggard	c Hutton b Silverwood	7		
GJ Kruis	c Nash b Silverwood	2		
Extras	b 1, lb 7, w 2, nb 20	30	lb 3, nb 4	7
	(all out 104.1 overs)	326	(0 wkts 23 overs)	39

Bowling
Silverwood 21.1-2-63-5. Keegan 16-5-53-0. Styris 14-2-38-1. Louw 25-5-76-3. Peploe 11-2-41-0. Weekes 15-3-39-1. Hutton 2-0-8-0.
Louw 9-6-6-0. Silverwood 7-4-12-0. Hutton 2-0-11-0. Peploe 5-1-7-0.
Fall of Wickets: 1-20, 2-114, 3-145, 4-212, 5-213, 6-280, 7-287, 8-305, 9-318

Match drawn – Yorkshire (10 pts), Middlesex (11 pts)

SUSSEX v. HAMPSHIRE – at Hove

HAMPSHIRE	First Innings		Second Innings	
JHK Adams	c Prior b Lewry	4	c Prior b Lewry	11
MA Carberry	c Montgomerie b Lewry	7	c Prior b Lewry	62
JP Crawley	lbw b Yasir Arafat	39	c Lewry b Martin-Jenkins	45
CC Benham	lbw b Mushtaq Ahmed	62	c Prior b Yasir Arafat	0
DJ Thornely	c Prior b Mushtaq Ahmed	5	b Martin-Jenkins	1
*N Pothas	not out	122	not out	48
SM Ervine	lbw b Mushtaq Ahmed	25	not out	50
AD Mascarenhas	lbw b Kirtley	10		
SK Warne (capt)	c Montgomerie b Yasir Arafat	53		
SD Udal	c Adams b Yasir Arafat	3		
CT Tremlett	c Adams b Yasir Arafat	1		
Extras	b 4, lb 6, nb 6	16	b 9, lb 2, w 1, nb 6	18
	(all out 90.5 overs)	347	(5 wkts 88 overs)	235

Bowling
Lewry 13.5-2-48-3. Kirtley 13-2-45-1. Martin-Jenkins 10-2-48-0. Yasir Arafat 20-2-96-3. Mushtaq Ahmed 34-4-98-3. Nash 1-0-2-0. Lewry 14-5-24-2. Kirtley 23-9-54-0. Yasir Arafat 19-6-33-1. Martin-Jenkins 12-1-42-2. Mushtaq Ahmed 12-2-46-0. Nash 5-2-13-0. Hopkinson 3-1-12-0.
Fall of Wickets: 1-9, 2-22, 3-109, 4-117, 5-117, 6-178, 7-197, 8-314, 9-329
1-16, 2-102, 3-117, 4-120, 5-146

SUSSEX	First Innings	
RR Montgomerie	c Adams b Ervine	27
CD Hopkinson	c Pothas b Ervine	15
CD Nash	c Warne b Udal	67
MW Goodwin	c Pothas b Warne	107
CJ Adams (capt)	c Pothas b Tremlett	75
*MJ Prior	c Pothas b Warne	36
RSC Martin-Jenkins	lbw b Warne	28
Yasir Arafat	st Pothas b Warne	34
Mushtaq Ahmed	c Pothas b Warne	2
RJ Kirtley	not out	16
JD Lewry	b Warne	1
Extras	b 11, lb 9, w 4, nb 16	40
	(all out 122.3 overs)	448

Bowling
Mascarenhas 11-3-19-0. Tremlett 24-1-100-1. Warne 42.3-7-136-6. Udal 25-3-82-1. Ervine 12-1-52-2. Thornely 6-1-22-0. Adams 2-0-17-0.
Fall of Wickets: 1-46, 2-57, 3-189, 4-309, 5-323, 6-372, 7-411, 8-415, 9-446

Match drawn – Sussex (12 pts), Hampshire (10 pts)

served up a magnificent contest between keen rivals and title-chasers. Sussex had edged ahead by the time the weather took half a day out of both the third and fourth days, but Warne had typically done all in his considerable power to keep his Hampshire team in touch. First, he had emerged at 197 for 7 on day one to defy Mushtaq, Jason Lewry and Yasir Arafat by helping the equally combative Nic Pothas to add 117 for the eighth wicket. Pothas went on to finish unbeaten on 122 but Warne then followed up his 53 by taking 6 for 136 to keep Sussex's lead to 101. Murray Goodwin's sixth hundred of the season, and 29th for the county, had threatened to take the game away from Warne – especially as both Chris Nash and Chris Adams batted well in support – but Hampshire ended the truncated third day on 70 for 1 and almost back to parity after Warne had determinedly worked his way through the Sussex batting. The final day's play was tense for a while, when Hampshire wobbled on 146 for 5, but Pothas again – this time with Sean Ervine – came to his team's aid.

Division Two

Mark Butcher emulated his father Alan's feat in 1984 by making two hundreds in a match against Glamorgan. Azhar Mahmood and Alistair Brown also reached three figures, and Mark Ramprakash completed another match haul of more than 100 runs – if not a century itself – as Surrey

overwhelmed their opponents despite not choosing to enforce the follow-on. Surrey captain Butcher included two sixes and 17 fours in his first innings 151, adding 192 for the sixth wicket with Azhar,

Round Eighteen: 30 August–5 September 2006
Division Two

SURREY v. GLAMORGAN – at The Oval

SURREY	First Innings		Second Innings	
SA Newman	c Watkins b Waters	35	c Watkins b Cosker	13
*JN Batty	b Franklin	5	c Franklin b Harrison	0
MR Ramprakash	b Franklin	77	b Harrison	31
MA Butcher (capt)	st Wallace b Croft	151	(5) c Wallace b Harrison	108
AD Brown	lbw b Franklin	2	(6) not out	107
CP Schofield	b Franklin	3		
Azhar Mahmood	b Harrison	101	not out	32
IDK Salisbury	b Harrison	7		
NC Saker	c Cosker b Franklin	22	(4) run out	13
ND Doshi	c Hemp b Croft	14		
Mohammad Akram	not out	0		
Extras	b 4, lb 10, nb 2	16	b 2, lb 2, w 1	5
	(all out 113.1 overs)	433	(5 wkts dec 61 overs)	309

Bowling
Harrison 23-4-86-2. Franklin 24.1-5-68-5. Waters 17-2-74-1. Watkins 9-1-47-0. Croft 21-3-90-2. Cosker 17-3-46-0. Grant 2-0-8-0.
Harrison 16-1-74-3. Franklin 15-1-72-0. Cosker 15-0-61-1. Waters 4-1-23-0. Croft 11-2-75-0.
Fall of Wickets: 1-18, 2-66, 3-190, 4-192, 5-198, 6-390, 7-390, 8-397, 9-433
1-1, 2-43, 3-45, 4-110, 5-247

GLAMORGAN	First Innings		Second Innings	
MJ Cosgrove	c Salisbury b Akram	5	(2) c Brown b Azhar Mahmood	16
RE Watkins	lbw b Saker	21	(1) c Ramprakash b Akram	9
DL Hemp	lbw b Azhar Mahmood	0	c Ramprakash b Salisbury	155
MJ Powell	c Butcher b Azhar Mahmood	18	c Akram b Saker	43
RN Grant	c Azhar Mahmood b Schofield	9	c Saker b Schofield	3
JEC Franklin	c Batty b Akram	26	c Butcher b Schofield	1
*MA Wallace	c Batty b Saker	22	c Batty b Schofield	0
RDB Croft (capt)	not out	71	c Butcher b Doshi	7
DS Harrison	lbw b Doshi	40	c sub b Doshi	5
DA Cosker	c Azhar Mahmood b Salisbury	39	not out	9
HT Waters	run out	0	c Schofield b Salisbury	0
Extras	b 6, lb 2, nb 10	18	lb 1, nb 6	7
	(all out 78 overs)	269	(all out 64 overs)	255

Bowling
Akram 15-6-46-2. Azhar Mahmood 11-0-49-2. Saker 8-2-31-2. Schofield 21-6-63-1. Doshi 11-3-30-1. Salisbury 12-3-42-1.
Akram 6-0-30-1. Azhar Mahmood 9-4-37-1. Schofield 16-1-82-3. Doshi 18-5-42-2. Salisbury 12-2-49-2. Saker 3-0-14-1.
Fall of Wickets: 1-10, 2-11, 3-44, 4-48, 5-85, 6-85, 7-130, 8-189, 9-259
1-22, 2-38, 3-148, 4-166, 5-168, 6-168, 7-193, 8-213, 9-255

Surrey won by 218 runs – Surrey (22 pts), Glamorgan (5 pts)

LEICESTERSHIRE v. SOMERSET – at Leicester

LEICESTERSHIRE	First Innings		Second Innings	
DDJ Robinson (capt)	b Caddick	2	c Spurway b Caddick	22
JK Maunders	c Durston b Willoughby	0	c Spurway b Caddick	3
HD Ackerman	lbw b Parsons	53	c Spurway b Caddick	82
JL Sadler	c Durston b Caddick	2	c & b Durston	58
DL Maddy	b Willoughby	4	not out	86
*PA Nixon	lbw b Caddick	15	c Parsons b Johnson	21
CW Henderson	c Spurway b Caddick	4	not out	62
DD Masters	c Edwards b Johnson	43		
NGE Walker	b Caddick	21		
RAG Cummins	b Johnson	6		
CJ Liddle	not out	1		
Extras	b 4, lb 3, w 6, nb 6	19	b 4, lb 8, w 2, nb 12	26
	(all out 53 overs)	170	(5 wkts dec 88 overs)	360

Bowling
Caddick 18-5-46-5. Willoughby 13-2-47-2. Johnson 14-5-38-2. Parsons 8-1-32-1.
Caddick 28-8-91-3. Willoughby 14-1-40-0. Johnson 16-4-48-1. Parsons 10-1-31-0. Munday 4-0-29-0. Durston 9-1-41-1.
Fall of Wickets: 1-0, 2-6, 3-8, 4-32, 5-52, 6-58, 7-108, 8-147, 9-161
1-9, 2-55, 3-159, 4-185, 5-240

SOMERSET	First Innings		Second Innings	
NJ Edwards	lbw b Walker	35	b Cummins	35
MJ Wood	c Maddy b Walker	73	lbw b Masters	0
WJ Durston	c Sadler b Walker	0	lbw b Masters	1
JC Hildreth	c Robinson b Walker	33	lbw b Masters	16
KA Parsons	b Walker	4	c Ackerman b Henderson	30
RJ Lett	b Masters	1	c Ackerman b Cummins	6
*SHP Spurway	c Nixon b Liddle	22	c Sadler b Cummins	13
RL Johnson	c Sadler b Liddle	39	c Masters b Liddle	16
AR Caddick (capt)	c Masters b Cummins	2	st Nixon b Henderson	23
MK Munday	lbw b Liddle	0	not out	5
CM Willoughby	not out	0	b Henderson	0
Extras	lb 5	5	lb 2, w 1	3
	(all out 70.4 overs)	192	(all out 49.3 overs)	148

Bowling
Walker 24-8-59-5. Cummins 10-3-32-1. Maddy 4-1-18-0. Liddle 11.4-3-42-3. Henderson 3-2-4-0. Masters 18-6-32-1.
Walker 8-2-22-0. Masters 13-7-23-3. Liddle 8-0-40-1. Henderson 9.3-2-25-3. Cummins 11-3-36-3.
Fall of Wickets: 1-12, 2-32, 3-90, 4-108, 5-113, 6-137, 7-158, 8-187, 9-192
1-1, 2-5, 3-49, 4-63, 5-77, 6-97, 7-113, 8-124, 9-144

Leicestershire won by 190 runs – Leicestershire (17 pts), Somerset (3 pts)

WORCESTERSHIRE v. ESSEX – at Worcester

WORCS	First Innings		Second Innings	
L Vincent	c Flower b Tudor	114	b Bichel	32
SC Moore	lbw b Bichel	16	b Foster b Tudor	3
VS Solanki (capt)	c Chopra b Phillips	122	c Foster b Middlebrook	30
BF Smith	c Foster b Bichel	19	lbw b Westfield	42
GA Hick	c Foster b Middlebrook	104	not out	105
*SM Davies	c Middlebrook b Bichel	46	st Foster b Phillips	33
GJ Batty	not out	16	not out	46
RJ Sillence	not out	1		
Kabir Ali				
Z Khan				
MN Malik				
Extras	lb 12, w 1, nb 22	35	b 8, lb 17, w 3, nb 12	40
	(6 wkts dec 98.3 overs)	473	(5 wkts dec 75 overs)	331

Bowling
Bichel 21.3-0-111-3. Tudor 15-1-72-1. Westfield 6-1-28-0. Bopara 12-2-63-0. Phillips 28-2-110-1. Middlebrook 16-2-77-1.
Bichel 19-4-77-1. Tudor 9-0-47-1. Phillips 13-0-49-1. Middlebrook 24-8-71-1. Westfield 3-0-18-1. Bopara 7-0-44-0.
Fall of Wickets: 1-61, 2-187, 3-234, 4-386, 5-410, 6-469
1-27, 2-59, 3-94, 4-154, 5-219

ESSEX	First Innings		Second Innings	
V Chopra	c Smith b Malik	70	lbw b Malik	5
ML Pettini	c Davies b Khan	6	c Hick b Khan	26
RS Bopara	c Hick b Malik	12	(4) not out	29
A Flower	b Kabir Ali	12	(5) lbw b Batty	29
RC Irani (capt)	c Davies b Solanki	66	(6) not out	8
*JS Foster	st Davies b Batty	80		
JD Middlebrook	b Khan	13		
TJ Phillips	c Davies b Kabir Ali	20		
AJ Bichel	c Kabir Ali b Khan	9	(3) c Smith b Kabir Ali	6
AJ Tudor	b Batty	12		
MS Westfield	not out	9		
Extras	b 12, lb 10, w 2, nb 4	28	b 8, lb 4, nb 2	14
	(all out 111 overs)	330	(all out 44.5 overs)	116

Bowling
Khan 26-4-95-3. Kabir Ali 24-7-49-2. Sillence 16-1-45-0. Malik 19-6-41-2. Batty 17-3-58-2. Vincent 2-0-5-0. Solanki 7-0-15-1.
Khan 13.5-3-35-1. Kabir Ali 12-1-36-1. Malik 3-1-10-1. Batty 10-6-10-1. Solanki 6-1-13-0.
Fall of Wickets: 1-39, 2-56, 3-88, 4-129, 5-266, 6-268, 7-286, 8-304, 9-314
1-15, 2-29, 3-55, 4-98

Match drawn – Worcestershire (12 pts), Essex (9 pts)

DERBYSHIRE v. NORTHAMPTONSHIRE – at Derby

DERBYSHIRE	First Innings		Second Innings	
SD Stubbings (capt)	lbw b Nicholson	0	lbw b Afzaal	64
Hassan Adnan	lbw b Wigley	12	c Crook b Phillips	8
CR Taylor	c Shafayat b Nicholson	41	c Panesar b Wigley	103
TR Birt	b Panesar	63	not out	32
GM Smith	b Nicholson	0	not out	31
*LJ Goddard	lbw b Panesar	3		
AG Botha	lbw b Panesar	3		
GG Wagg	b Phillips	16		
PS Jones	b Phillips	9		
ID Hunter	not out	6		
KJ Dean	c Shafayat b Phillips	0		
Extras	lb 15, w 2	17	b 22, lb 6, w 4, nb 16	48
	(all out 58.3 overs)	167	(3 wkts dec 92 overs)	286

Bowling
Nicholson 12-9-12-4. Phillips 8.3-3-10-3. Wigley 10-1-45-1. Crook 9-2-32-0. Klusener 5-2-12-0. Panesar 14-3-41-2.
Nicholson 17-2-59-0. Phillips 11-4-28-1. Wigley 15-4-49-1. Crook 8-0-48-0. Panesar 27-12-39-1. Klusener 4-2-15-0. Afzaal 9-3-19-1. Sales 1-0-1-0.
Fall of Wickets: 1-0, 2-36, 3-79, 4-79, 5-79, 6-131, 7-136, 8-155, 9-167
1-22, 2-213, 3-217

NORTHANTS	First Innings		
SD Peters	c Goddard b Jones	12	
CJL Rogers	run out	112	
U Afzaal	lbw b Wagg	27	
DJG Sales (capt)	lbw b Dean	27	
*BM Shafayat	c Wagg b Hunter	6	
L Klusener	c sub b Botha	128	
BJ Phillips	b Botha	1	
SP Crook	c Smith b Botha	44	
MJ Nicholson	c Goddard b Botha	25	
MS Panesar	c Stubbings b Smith	2	
DH Wigley	not out	0	
Extras	b 12, lb 5, w 3, nb 16	36	
	(all out 98.5 overs)	424	

Bowling
Jones 20-1-88-1. Wagg 16-2-58-1. Wagg 13-2-57-1. Dean 15-0-81-1. Botha 26-4-96-4. Smith 8.5-0-27-1.
Fall of Wickets: 1-16, 2-55, 3-123, 4-145, 5-247, 6-272, 7-362, 8-415, 9-420

Match drawn – Derbyshire (7 pts), Northamptonshire (12 pts)

Clubbing king: Lance Klusener swings another powerful stroke away during his fifth century of the season, against Derbyshire.

whose 101 took just 132 balls with 15 boundaries, and during his second innings 108 was joined in a fifth-wicket partnership of 137 by Brown, whose own hundred was reached with a 26-ball second fifty and 86 deliveries overall. For Glamorgan, skipper Robert Croft battled hard to revive his side from the depths of 85 for 6 on the second day, assisted by gutsy efforts from both David Harrison and Dean Cosker, while David Hemp batted magnificently for 155 – with 22 fours and a six – as wickets tumbled around him in the second innings.

A bouncy pitch at Grace Road saw Leicestershire outgun Somerset despite being bowled out for 170 on the opening day by the ageless Andrew Caddick. Somerset, however, could only make 192 themselves in reply, with Matthew Wood alone looking comfortable as Nick Walker took 5 for 59 by swinging it away and hitting the seam consistently. Hylton Ackerman then batted classily for the second time in the game, before John Sadler, Darren Maddy and Claude Henderson took the contest out of

Somerset's reach. David Masters then removed three of the visitors' top four and Leicestershire were soon celebrating a 190-run victory.

Poor weather on the final day at New Road helped Essex to escape with a draw and remain just ahead of Worcestershire in second place. For the home side, the only consolation was that they had closed the gap from five points to two as a result of dominating proceedings for the entire four days. Graeme Hick took his career tally of first-class hundreds to 132 (48 of them at his beloved Worcester) by scoring two in a match for the fifth time, and there were first-day centuries too for Lou Vincent, who became the first Worcestershire batsman since Glenn Turner in 1982 to hit a hundred before lunch, and skipper Vikram Solanki, who went past 1,000 runs for the season during his 122. Varun Chopra, Ronnie Irani and the particularly impressive James Foster tried their best to keep Essex afloat in reply, but when Worcestershire followed up Hick's second hundred by nipping out Chopra just before the close of the third day, the visitors were staring down the barrel. In the 33.5 overs possible on the final day they lost three more wickets but, fortunately for them, that was all the play there was.

Derbyshire may have been saved by the rain against Northamptonshire, as the whole final day was lost at Derby, but at least by then they were making a decent fist of fighting back after conceding a first-innings deficit of 257. Matt Nicholson and Ben Phillips had sent them tumbling to 167 all out on the opening day, after Derbyshire lost the gamble of preparing a green-tinged pitch by then seeing Northants captain David Sales win the toss, and in fast-improving conditions Chris Rogers, with 112 on his 29th birthday, and Lance Klusener – with a fifth century of the season – had taken the visitors beyond 400. But Steve Stubbings was joined by Chris Taylor in a second-wicket stand of 191, and at 286 for 3 Derbyshire were by no means out of things when the weather closed in.

Round Nineteen: 5–11 September 2006

Division One

Nottinghamshire thrashed Middlesex in a basement battle at Lord's, their innings and 25-run victory boosting the 2005 champions' hopes of avoiding relegation. A Charlie Shreck hat-trick on the opening day was an early highlight of a game in which they completely dominated their lacklustre opponents, and

Shreck went on to take four wickets in six balls with David Nash following the hat-trick victims Ed Smith, Eoin Morgan and Paul Weekes. Nick Compton, with 105 not out, was the only Middlesex batsman to show any resolve and he went past his 1,000 runs for the season while carrying his bat. Nottinghamshire then set about building a match-winning lead in determined fashion, with Will Smith and Stephen Fleming adding 288 in 77 overs for the third wicket. Smith made 141 and Fleming's 192 occupied 295 balls and, groundwork done, Samit Patel emerged to plunder the Middlesex attack to the tune of 156 which included eight sixes. Patel's third fifty took him a mere 17 balls and, like Smith, this was his maiden Championship hundred. Paul Franks weighed in with 64 and, after Notts had declared with a massive 412-run lead, only Ed Smith – with a fine 147 – held up the visitors for long.

Hampshire overwhelmed Durham at the Riverside, with Shane Warne declining to enforce the follow-on but wrapping up a 174-run victory himself on the third day by taking 5 for 135. From 15 for 2 early on, John Crawley and Chris Benham established a position of strength for Hampshire which they never relinquished. Crawley's 150 was a classy effort, while the 23-year-old Benham made 91. Durham lost two wickets in the eight overs they had to face on the first evening and were skittled out for 195 on day two.

Jimmy Adams and Michael Carberry then added 191 for Hampshire's first wicket in their second innings, and only a promising 75 from Ben Harmison and bright 40s from Gareth Breese and Phil Mustard delayed the end thereafter.

There were another 13 wickets for Mushtaq Ahmed as Sussex just about managed to see off Kent's challenge in a strange, nerve-ridden match at Canterbury. Mushtaq's first innings 6 for 58 gave Sussex the initial advantage, but their batsmen threw away several positions of potential strength – despite excellent innings from Murray Goodwin and Chris Adams – and allowed Robbie Joseph and James Tredwell to bowl Kent back into the match. Another haul of 7 for 74 then kept Kent on the back foot, but Sussex proceeded to make hard work of a win target of 161 as Tredwell took full advantage of the tense atmosphere to return career-best figures of 6 for 81. In the end, Mushtaq went down on his knees pitch-side in prayerful thanks after he and James Kirtley had edged Sussex over the finishing line for a vital win.

Division Two

Essex moved four points clear of Worcestershire in the continuing battle for second place in the division, answering their close rivals' defeat of Leicestershire 24 hours earlier with an even more comprehensive

Round Nineteen: 5–11 September 2006 Division One

MIDDLESEX v. NOTTINGHAMSHIRE – at Lord's

MIDDLESEX	First Innings		Second Innings	
BL Hutton (capt)	c Patel b Sidebottom	0	c Fleming b Harris	27
NRD Compton	not out	105	lbw b Sidebottom	2
OA Shah	lbw b Franks	26	lbw b Harris	35
ET Smith	c Ealham b Shreck	28	lbw b Sidebottom	147
EJG Morgan	c Alleyne b Shreck	4	c Alleyne b Harris	10
PN Weekes	b Shreck	0	lbw b Harris	38
*DC Nash	b Hussey b Shreck	0	lbw b Sidebottom	11
CT Peploe	c Hussey b Harris	34	c Bicknell b Shreck	16
J Louw	c Ealham b Harris	3	b Hussey	42
CJC Wright	c Fleming b Franks	4	not out	25
CEW Silverwood	c Smith b Shreck	23	c Shreck b Hussey	16
Extras	b 1, lb 3, w 1, nb 2	7	b 8, lb 9, w 1	18
	(all out 66 overs)	230	(all out 120.2 overs)	387

Bowling
Sidebottom 16-5-54-1. Shreck 22-5-79-5. Harris 15-1-53-2. Franks 13-3-40-2.
Sidebottom 27-9-62-3. Shreck 30-5-84-1. Franks 16-4-69-1. Harris 23-7-73-3.
Patel 12-7-16-0. Hussey 12.2-0-66-2.
Fall of Wickets: 1-1, 2-55, 3-88, 4-92, 5-92, 6-92, 7-145, 8-163, 9-174
1-9, 2-108, 3-128, 4-170, 5-267, 6-274, 7-286, 8-316, 9-359

NOTTS	First Innings	
DJ Bicknell	lbw b Silverwood	1
WR Smith	run out	141
*D Alleyne	c Nash b Silverwood	15
SP Fleming (capt)	c Smith b Wright	192
DJ Hussey	b Louw	19
SR Patel	c Peploe b Silverwood	156
MA Ealham	lbw b Wright	15
PJ Franks	b Louw	64
RJ Sidebottom	not out	2
AJ Harris	lbw b Louw	0
CE Shreck		
Extras	b 1, lb 6, nb 30	37
	(9 wkts dec 144 overs)	642

Bowling
Silverwood 25-4-91-3. Louw 34-4-132-3. Wright 25-2-144-2. Peploe 30-3-120-0.
Weekes 21-1-73-0. Hutton 8-0-49-0. Shah 1-0-26-0.
Fall of Wickets: 1-4, 2-42, 3-330, 4-357, 5-425, 6-475, 7-628, 8-642, 9-642

Nottinghamshire won by an innings and 25 runs –
Middlesex (3 pts), Nottinghamshire (22 pts)

DURHAM v. HAMPSHIRE – at the Riverside

HAMPSHIRE	First Innings		Second Innings	
JHK Adams	run out	4	c Lewis b Gibson	84
MA Carberry	c Mustard b Lewis	2	c Lewis b Breese	98
JP Crawley	c Lewis b Thorp	150	b Breese	29
CC Benham	c Mustard b Gibson	91	b Lewis	30
DJ Thornely	c Lewis b Gibson	10		
*N Pothas	lbw b Killeen	54	not out	5
SM Ervine	b Lewis	49		
AD Mascarenhas	c Benkenstein b Killeen	28	(5) c Killeen b Breese	0
SK Warne (capt)	b Lewis	5	(7) not out	14
CT Tremlett	b Lewis	0		
JTA Bruce	not out	0		
Extras	lb 9, nb 22	31	b 5, lb 1, nb 12	18
	(all out 97.1 overs)	425	(5 wkts dec 69 overs)	278

Bowling
Lewis 18-2-69-4. Killeen 23.1-7-45-2. Thorp 16-2-87-1. Gibson 14-0-101-2.
Benkenstein 10-1-54-0. Breese 10-1-36-0. Scott 6-2-24-0.
Killeen 11-3-38-0. Lewis 14-4-50-1. Breese 22-4-85-3. Thorp 5-3-12-0.
Scott 5-1-23-0. Gibson 11-1-60-1. Benkenstein 1-0-4-0.
Fall of Wickets: 1-8, 2-15, 3-183, 4-209, 5-322, 6-367, 7-417, 8-423, 9-425
1-191, 2-195, 3-241, 4-255, 5-264

DURHAM	First Innings		Second Innings	
JP Maher	c Pothas b Tremlett	0	c Pothas b Bruce	29
GM Scott	lbw b Warne	40	c Adams b Bruce	2
N Killeen	c Pothas b Bruce	2	(10) c Benham b Warne	8
GJ Muchall	c Crawley b Mascarenhas	19	(3) b Bruce	13
DM B'kenstein (capt)	lbw b Tremlett	31	(4) c sub b Warne	6
BW Harmison	c Pothas b Bruce	9	(5) st Pothas b Carberry	75
GR Breese	c Warne b Tremlett	15	(6) b Carberry	47
*P Mustard	c Thornely b Warne	15	(7) c Thornely b Warne	46
OD Gibson	c Adams b Warne	24	(8) not out	21
CD Thorp	run out	2	(9) c & b Warne	27
ML Lewis	not out	19	c Carberry b Warne	38
Extras	lb 4, lb 1, nb 14	19	b 2, lb 5, w 1, nb 14	22
	(all out 58.2 overs)	195	(all out 69.3 overs)	334

Bowling
Tremlett 16-5-51-3. Bruce 10-0-60-2. Mascarenhas 12-4-22-1. Ervine 8.4-3-24-1.
Warne 8.2-1-21-2. Thornely 3.2-0-12-0.
Tremlett 9-2-33-0. Bruce 11-3-78-3. Mascarenhas 6-1-19-0. Warne 23.3-1-135-5.
Pothas 5-0-22-0. Carberry 15-0-85-2.
Fall of Wickets: 1-6, 2-9, 3-50, 4-82, 5-113, 6-113, 7-147, 8-147, 9-151
1-10, 2-52, 3-53, 4-70, 5-170, 6-237, 7-241, 8-280, 9-290

Hampshire won by 174 runs –Durham (3 pts), Hampshire (22 pts)

KENT v. SUSSEX – at Canterbury

KENT	First Innings		Second Innings	
DP Fulton	lbw b Lewry	4	c Adams b Kirtley	6
RWT Key (capt)	lbw b Lewry	15	c Prior b Kirtley	0
M van Jaarsveld	c Goodwin b Mushtaq Ahmed	116	st Prior b Mushtaq Ahmed	9
MJ Walker	st Prior b Mushtaq Ahmed	48	st Prior b Mushtaq Ahmed	66
DI Stevens	c Adams b Mushtaq Ahmed	24	st Prior b Mushtaq Ahmed	54
*GO Jones	lbw b Mushtaq Ahmed	1	(7) lbw b Mushtaq Ahmed	15
NJ Dexter	b Yasir Arafat	0	(8) not out	30
JC Tredwell	not out	2	(7) lbw b Mushtaq Ahmed	15
T Henderson	b Mushtaq Ahmed	2	(11) b Lewry	1
SJ Cook	c Adams b Mushtaq Ahmed	2	(9) c Lewry b Mushtaq Ahmed	7
RH Joseph	lbw b Yasir Arafat	1	(10) c M'gomerie b M Ahmed	7
Extras	b 4, lb 1, w 1, nb 20	26	b 5, lb 8, w 1	14
	(all out 69.1 overs)	241	(all out 73 overs)	208

Bowling
Lewry 15-1-38-2. Kirtley 15.1-1-43-0. Yasir Arafat 15.1-1-85-2. Martin-Jenkins 6-2-12-0.
Mushtaq Ahmed 22-6-58-6.
Lewry 19-1-39-1. Kirtley 12-3-24-2. Mushtaq Ahmed 27-2-74-7.
Martin-Jenkins 1-0-9-0. Yasir Arafat 13-2-40-0. Nash 1-0-9-0.
Fall of Wickets: 1-10, 2-27, 3-176, 4-215, 5-221, 6-222, 7-230, 8-234, 9-240
1-5, 2-15, 3-29, 4-111, 5-119, 6-154, 7-180, 8-182, 9-203

SUSSEX	First Innings		Second Innings	
RR Montgomerie	lbw b Joseph	1	(2) c van Jaarsveld b Cook	4
CD Hopkinson	lbw b Joseph	3	(1) b Tredwell	9
CD Nash	lbw b Joseph	42	c Jones b Tredwell	28
MW Goodwin	c Jones b Cook	51	c van Jaarsveld b Tredwell	64
CJ Adams (capt)	c Jones b Joseph	75	c Walker b Cook	38
*MJ Prior	c Stevens b Tredwell	30	c & b Tredwell	19
RSC Martin-Jenkins	c Walker b Tredwell	0	c Stevens b Tredwell	5
Yasir Arafat	lbw b Tredwell	18	c Fulton b Tredwell	22
Mushtaq Ahmed	not out	25	not out	13
RJ Kirtley	c Fulton b Tredwell	0	not out	3
JD Lewry	b Joseph	2		
Extras	b 7, lb 8, w 3, nb 24	42	lb 3, w 1	4
	(all out 72.2 overs)	289	(8 wkts 48.2 overs)	161

Bowling
Cook 18-4-60-1. Joseph 17.2-4-57-5. Dexter 6-0-25-0. Stevens 15-1-48-0. Tredwell 16-0-84-4.
Cook 14.2-5-35-2. Joseph 6-0-26-0. Tredwell 20-3-81-6. Stevens 8-2-16-0.
Fall of Wickets: 1-10, 2-3, 3-116, 4-116, 5-201, 6-216, 7-253, 8-265, 9-270
1-7, 2-17, 3-53, 4-74, 5-105, 6-119, 7-144, 8-145

Sussex won by 2 wickets – Kent (4 pts), Sussex (19 pts)

victory of their own against Derbyshire at Chelmsford. Slow left-arm Tim Phillips was the Essex hero of the first day, his 5 for 41 bowling out Derbyshire cheaply and allowing Varun Chopra and Mark Pettini to move the side into a powerful position with an opening

stand of 111. On the second day it was all Essex again as Pettini and nightwatchman Alex Tudor, who once scored 99 not out for England in the role, added 230 for the second wicket. Tudor battered seven sixes in a career-best 144 while Pettini was content to anchor an innings which, with Andy Flower flying to an 85-ball hundred, soon assumed major proportions. Pettini finished up on a chanceless, career-best 208 not out, with his 416-ball knock amply celebrating the award of his county cap, while Flower contributed an unbeaten 136 to their unbroken fourth-wicket stand of 221. Tudor then shone with the ball, too, while spinners Phillips and James Middlebrook were also effective as Derbyshire were dismissed for just 218.

Five wickets in 28 balls from Kabir Ali, as tea approached on the final day, settled the match in Worcestershire's favour at New Road after John Maunders and Hylton Ackerman, for the second time in three days, had threatened to frustrate them. The batting of Lou Vincent, with a 68-ball 78 in the first innings and a more studious 141 second time around, had enabled Worcestershire to call the early shots despite Ackerman's unbeaten 111 on the second day. But it still needed Kabir's burst, plus three wickets for Matt Mason, to break Leicestershire's resistance.

Monty Panesar underlined his growing stature by spinning Northamptonshire to a welcome nine-wicket win against Glamorgan at Cardiff. Supported by Jason Brown, he outshone Glamorgan's Robert

Round Nineteen: 5–11 September 2006
Division Two

ESSEX v. DERBYSHIRE – at Chelmsford

DERBYSHIRE	First Innings		Second Innings	
SD Stubbings (capt)	c Foster b Adams	42	(2) c Phillips b Bichel	0
CR Taylor	lbw b Adams	22	(1) c Flower b Phillips	19
Hassan Adnan	c & b Phillips	60	c Bopara b Adams	32
TR Birt	c Foster b Bichel	24	c Adams b Middlebrook	1
GM Smith	c Foster b Phillips	2	(6) c Foster b Tudor	29
AG Botha	lbw b Bichel	11	(7) lbw b Tudor	10
*LJ Goddard	c Foster b Phillips	0	(8) lbw b Middlebrook	37
GG Wagg	c Adams b Phillips	0	(9) c Phillips b Middlebrook	36
J Needham	c Foster b Phillips	3	(5) c Foster b Tudor	29
PS Jones	b Bichel	4	c Tudor b Phillips	12
KJ Dean	not out	0	not out	1
Extras	b 2, lb 4, w 2, nb 11	19	lb 6, nb 6	12
	(all out 60 overs)	184	(all out 55.1 overs)	218

Bowling
Bichel 18-3-54-3. Tudor 12-2-35-0. Adams 14-4-30-2. Middlebrook 6-0-25-0. Phillips 11-1-41-5. Bopara 1-0-2-0.
Bichel 13-1-37-1. Tudor 10-2-37-3. Phillips 10.1-2-49-2. Middlebrook 15-4-63-3. Adams 7-2-26-1.
Fall of Wickets: 1-36, 2-108, 3-155, 4-159, 5-169, 6-176, 7-180, 8-180, 9-182
1-1, 2-29, 3-34, 4-58, 5-105, 6-122, 7-127, 8-183, 9-212

ESSEX	First Innings	
V Chopra	c Goddard b Wagg	42
ML Pettini	not out	208
AJ Tudor	c Goddard b Jones	144
RS Bopara	lbw b Jones	10
A Flower	not out	136
RC Irani (capt)		
*JS Foster		
JD Middlebrook		
TJ Phillips		
AJ Bichel		
AR Adams		
Extras	lb 25, w 3, nb 12	40
	(3 wkts dec 129 overs)	580

Bowling
Jones 25-5-80-2. Wagg 24-7-96-1. Dean 27-9-115-0. Botha 21-3-106-0. Needham 15-1-88-0. Smith 16-2-60-0. Birt 1-0-10-0.
Fall of Wickets: 1-111, 2-341, 3-359

Essex won by an innings and 178 runs –
Essex (22 pts), Derbyshire (1 pt)

WORCESTERSHIRE v. LEICESTERSHIRE – at Worcester

WORCS	First Innings		Second Innings	
L Vincent	c Ackerman b Liddle	78	c Nixon b Henderson	141
SC Moore	b Masters	26	c Nixon b Maddy	6
VS Solanki (capt)	c Robinson b Maddy	72	c Maunders b Maddy	16
BF Smith	b Masters	36	b Walker	7
GA Hick	c Nixon b Walker	11	c Ackerman b Maddy	72
*SM Davies	c Nixon b Masters	28	c Ackerman b Cummins	28
GJ Batty	c Masters b Maunders	35	not out	33
RJ Sillence	c Walker b Maunders	31	st Nixon b Henderson	4
Kabir Ali	c Maddy b Liddle	5	c Walker b Liddle	1
Z Khan	c Nixon b Maunders	4	not out	6
MS Mason	not out	0		
Extras	lb 2, nb 6	8	lb 11, w 3, nb 6	20
	(all out 88.2 overs)	331	(8 wkts dec 104 overs)	378

Bowling
Walker 15-2-71-1. Masters 22-7-73-2. Henderson 8-0-35-0. Cummins 7-1-45-0. Liddle 12-1-45-2. Maddy 15-5-45-1. Maunders 9.2-4-15-4.
Walker 18.1-3-49-1. Masters 10.5-2-42-0. Maddy 25-8-70-3. Maunders 10-2-21-0. Cummins 11-0-67-1. Liddle 11-1-49-1. Henderson 18-0-69-2.
Fall of Wickets: 1-14, 2-113, 3-189, 4-189, 5-213, 6-274, 7-322, 8-325, 9-331
1-40, 2-76, 3-84, 4-228, 5-282, 6-304, 7-362, 8-367

LEICESTERSHIRE	First Innings		Second Innings	
DDJ Robinson (capt)	c Solanki b Batty	28	c Batty b Mason	47
JK Maunders	b Smith b Mason	30	c & b Batty	74
HD Ackerman	not out	111	c Sillence b Kabir Ali	19
JL Sadler	c Davies b Sillence	9	b Batty b Kabir Ali	19
DL Maddy	c Davies b Kabir Ali	11	c Davies b Kabir Ali	6
*PA Nixon	c Hick b Batty	7	c sub b Batty	4
CW Henderson	c Davies b Mason	25	c Moore b Mason	6
DD Masters	c Davies b Khan	8	b Kabir Ali	0
NGE Walker	c Davies b Mason	2	c Vincent b Kabir Ali	15
RAG Cummins	c Davies b Kabir Ali	13	not out	5
CJ Liddle	b Batty b Khan	1	c Solanki b Mason	0
Extras	b 6, lb 4, w 6	16	b 4, lb 5, nb 10	19
	(all out 80.3 overs)	259	(all out 88.4 overs)	258

Bowling
Khan 20.3-5-54-3. Kabir Ali 16-3-69-2. Mason 19-3-47-2. Sillence 7-1-22-1. Batty 11-3-30-2. Vincent 3-0-10-0. Solanki 4-1-17-0.
Khan 19-5-62-0. Kabir Ali 21-2-94-5. Mason 19.4-7-35-3. Batty 24-9-50-2. Sillence 5-2-8-0.
Fall of Wickets: 1-60, 2-62, 3-99, 4-122, 5-179, 6-218, 7-232, 8-232, 9-253
1-80, 2-180, 3-213, 4-228, 5-235, 6-235, 7-235, 8-243, 9-258

Worcestershire won by 192 runs –
Worcestershire (20 pts), Leicestershire (5 pts)

GLAMORGAN v. NORTHAMPTONSHIRE – at Cardiff

GLAMORGAN	First Innings		Second Innings	
DD Cherry	b Nicholson	71	lbw b Nicholson	3
GP Rees	c Nicholson b Phillips	2	c Peters b Panesar	57
DL Hemp	b Phillips	0	lbw b Panesar	22
MJ Powell	b Panesar	27	lbw b Panesar	19
RE Watkins	st Shafayat b Panesar	30	c Sales b Nicholson	0
JEC Franklin	lbw b Panesar	2	st Shafayat b Brown	16
*MA Wallace	lbw b Panesar	9	c Shafayat b Brown	9
RDB Croft (capt)	c Shafayat b Nicholson	21	b Brown	47
DS Harrison	c Afzaal b Panesar	13	c Shafayat b Panesar	31
DA Cosker	lbw b Crook	8	b Crook	21
HT Waters	not out	5	not out	0
Extras	b 4, lb 10, nb 2	16	b 10, nb 6	16
	(all out 77.1 overs)	204	(all out 108.5 overs)	248

Bowling
Nicholson 19-10-41-2. Phillips 13-7-21-2. Crook 6.1-0-25-1. Panesar 25-11-67-5. Klusener 3-0-17-0. Brown 11-3-19-0.
Nicholson 21-5-68-2. Phillips 7-1-25-0. Panesar 43-15-73-4. Brown 28.5-10-46-3. Afzaal 5-2-13-0. Crook 4-0-13-1.
Fall of Wickets: 1-12, 2-16, 3-88, 4-138, 5-147, 6-148, 7-167, 8-179, 9-191
1-8, 2-39, 3-69, 4-74, 5-98, 6-118, 7-134, 8-182, 9-238

NORTHANTS	First Innings		Second Innings	
SD Peters	c Wallace b Franklin	13	(2) c Hemp b Harrison	31
CJL Rogers	c Wallace b Franklin	77	(1) not out	33
U Afzaal	c Hemp b Franklin	16		
DJG Sales (capt)	c Wallace b Waters	42		
*BM Shafayat	c & b Cosker	14	(3) not out	19
L Klusener	c & b Waters	131		
SP Crook	lbw b Cosker	11		
BJ Phillips	b Croft	29		
MJ Nicholson	b Waters	18		
MS Panesar	not out	0		
JF Brown	b Waters	0		
Extras	b 1, lb 8, w 1, nb 8	18	b 1	1
	(all out 90.3 overs)	369	(1 wkt 16.4 overs)	84

Bowling
Harrison 17-3-73-0. Franklin 13-1-82-3. Waters 14.3-4-33-4. Cosker 20-4-73-2. Croft 22-1-86-1. Watkins 4-1-13-0.
Harrison 8-0-33-1. Franklin 2-0-14-0. Cosker 0.2-0-2-0. Croft 5.4-2-30-0. Cherry 0.4-0-4-0.
Fall of Wickets: 1-37, 2-58, 3-161, 4-163, 5-205, 6-227, 7-321, 8-362, 9-369
1-53

Northamptonshire won by 9 wickets –
Glamorgan (4 pts), Northamptonshire (21 pts)

GLOUCESTERSHIRE v. SURREY – at Bristol

GLOS	First Innings		Second Innings	
WPC Weston	b Doshi	130	(2) c Batty b Dernbach	0
CM Spearman	lbw b Doshi	100	(1) c sub b Butcher	45
HJH Marshall	c Batty b Saker	56	b Schofield b Doshi	76
Kadeer Ali	b Azhar Mahmood	32	b Dernbach	36
CG Taylor	b Saker	14	lbw b Dernbach	4
APR Gidman (capt)	b Doshi b Schofield	52	b Doshi	20
*SJ Adshead	b Doshi	0	not out	79
MA Hardinges	c Ramprakash b Schofield	13	c Newman b Schofield	38
JMM Averis	c Batty b Doshi	53	st Batty b Doshi	6
SP Kirby	not out	3	not out	10
V Banerjee	b Schofield	0		
Extras	lb 2, nb 4	6	b 2, lb 6, w 1, nb 6	15
	(all out 123.2 overs)	459	(8 wkts dec 84 overs)	329

Bowling
Azhar Mahmood 30-10-79-1. Saker 20-4-107-2. Walters 4-0-21-0. Dernbach 9-2-55-0. Doshi 36-11-117-4. Schofield 24.2-3-78-3. Saker 12-1-63-0. Dernbach 18-2-67-3. Walters 7-2-18-0. Butcher 5-0-8-1. Doshi 30-3-92-3. Schofield 12-0-73-1.
Fall of Wickets: 1-154, 2-230, 3-316, 4-334, 5-338, 6-339, 7-364, 8-433, 9-459
1-8, 2-94, 3-160, 4-170, 5-173, 6-212, 7-275, 8-287

SURREY	First Innings		Second Innings	
SA Newman	c Batty b Averis	44	b Kirby	4
*JN Batty	c Adshead b Averis	5	c Adshead b Hardinges	50
MR Ramprakash	b Banerjee	75	c & b Kirby	51
MA Butcher (capt)	b Banerjee	6	c & b Banerjee	35
AD Brown	c Weston b Averis	14	c Spearman b Averis	43
SJ Walters	c Adshead b Kirby	7	c Kirby b Averis	67
Azhar Mahmood	b Kirby	40	c Kadeer Ali b Hardinges	22
CP Schofield	st Adshead b Banerjee	16	c Taylor b Banerjee	95
NC Saker	c Taylor b Hardinges	0	b Banerjee	47
ND Doshi	c Taylor b Hardinges	9	not out	2
JW Dernbach	lbw b Averis	9	not out	4
Extras	b 9, lb 7, w 1, nb 8	25	b 7, lb 15, w 2, nb 26	50
	(all out 86 overs)	288	(9 wkts 112 overs)	470

Bowling
Kirby 20-4-45-2. Averis 18-2-75-4. Hardinges 19-5-67-1. Banerjee 15-3-45-2. Gidman 14-3-40-1.
Kirby 28-6-95-2. Averis 24-1-133-2. Banerjee 31-6-129-3. Hardinges 16-2-61-2. Taylor 8-2-25-0. Gidman 3-2-1-0. Marshall 2-1-4-0.
Fall of Wickets: 1-14, 2-88, 3-183, 4-206, 5-222, 6-232, 7-250, 8-257, 9-265
1-9, 2-107, 3-124, 4-182, 5-210, 6-244, 7-395, 8-463, 9-466

Match drawn – Gloucestershire (12 pts), Surrey (9 pts)

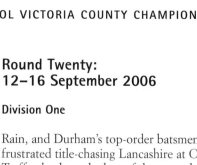

Round Twenty:
12–16 September 2006

Division One

Rain, and Durham's top-order batsmen, frustrated title-chasing Lancashire at Old Trafford, where the loss of the second day virtually ensured that the game would end in a draw. It was a vital ten points for Durham, seeking to avoid the drop, but Lancashire only made it to the consolation of a draw's maximum 12-point haul as a result of Dominic Cork's remarkable innings of 154 on the final day. Cork hit four sixes and 16 fours in his eighth first-class century, and it was a typically combative effort to resurrect a Lancashire innings which had seemed destined to dip below the 400 mark needed for a full five bonus points. Cork faced 183 balls and was joined by the promising Tom Smith in an eighth-wicket stand of 131. On the previous evening, which ended with Lancashire struggling somewhat at 210 for 5 despite half-centuries from Mark Chilton, Mal Loye and Stuart Law, the home side had even been happy to go off 11 overs from the scheduled close because of the problems caused by a low sun at the western end of the ground! Lancashire, however, had every right to complain about their more severe troubles with regards to bad weather: the second day washout took their number of Championship overs lost beyond 1,000.

Yorkshire, meanwhile, offset the loss of all but 15 overs to rain on the second day of their match with Nottinghamshire across the Pennines at Headingley to complete a crucial victory. Only 4.2 overs remained when young leg spinners Mark Lawson and Adil Rashid completed Nottinghamshire's slide to 213 all out in their second innings and a Yorkshire win by 68 runs. It was not enough to lift Yorkshire out of their second-from-bottom position, but they were now just half a point behind Durham and nine points adrift of Notts themselves. Craig White, the captain, almost single-handedly kept Yorkshire in the game on day one – batting throughout the 104 overs for 141 not out. But he was also joined in a fourth-wicket stand of 130 by the precocious 18-year-old Rashid, whose 63 was his maiden first-class fifty. White was last out for 147 the following morning, after guiding Yorkshire to their third batting point, and the home side sensed

Nine more wickets came Monty Panesar's way as he spun Northants to a comfortable victory against Glamorgan.

Croft and Dean Cosker to take 5 for 67 in the first innings and 4 for 73 from 43 overs in a second innings in which young opener Gareth Rees fought bravely through 246 balls for his 57. In between, Lance Klusener's sixth hundred of the season, with 15 fours and two sixes, and 77 from Chris Rogers kept Northants well on top.

Surrey held on for a draw at Bristol, reaching a splendid 470 for 9 after being set to score 501 in 112 overs. Chris Schofield's 95 spearheaded their late push for an unlikely victory, and their last-day heroics made up for a sloppy first innings batting effort in which they fell away alarmingly from 183 for 2 to 288 all out after Alex Gidman had yorked Mark Ramprakash for 75. The match had begun with Craig Spearman and Phil Weston adding 154 for the first Gloucestershire wicket, both scoring hundreds, but Surrey gained the two bowling points they required to make sure of the second division title on an otherwise chastening first day. James Averis, with bat and ball, helped to keep Gloucestershire in control, but in the end, the home side were not good enough to close out the match.

the chance of victory once Lawson and Rashid had shared seven first-innings wickets to dismiss Notts for 263 in reply, despite a superb 117 from David Hussey. Darren Lehmann, with a 41-ball 48, and Michael Lumb, with an unbeaten 84, then pushed on towards the declaration which allowed Lawson and Rashid to put in a repeat seven-wicket performance. Again, Hussey stood firm, but he could find no one to stay with him as Yorkshire wrapped up a magnificent win.

No play on the second day at Edgbaston, meanwhile, condemned Warwickshire's meeting with Kent to a dull draw enlivened on the final day only by an act of compassion from visiting skipper Rob Key that allowed Nick Knight the opportunity to score the unbeaten 15 runs he required to finish his first-class career with a Warwickshire average of 50. An innings of 86 from the 20-year-old Joe Denly, preferred to the omitted David Fulton, was a highlight of the opening day and Knight was then at the forefront of a Warwickshire revival in reply, following an initial slump to 15 for 3. Simon Cook bowled well for his 6 for 74, while Matthew Walker's excellent season continued with a second-innings 103 not out for Kent.

Dominic Cork hit four sixes and 16 fours in a buccaneering innings of 154 against Durham at Old Trafford.

Round Twenty: 12–16 September 2006 Division One

LANCASHIRE v. DURHAM – at Old Trafford

DURHAM	First Innings		Second Innings	
JP Maher	c Sutton b Chapple	95	not out	28
GM Scott	lbw b Keedy	53	c Law b Cork	0
GT Park	c Cork b Smith	45	not out	34
DM B'kenstein (capt)	c Keedy b Kartik	33		
BW Harmison	b Kartik	48		
GR Breese	b Cork	43		
*P Mustard	not out	11		
OD Gibson	lbw b Cork	0		
PJ Wiseman	lbw b Cork	4		
G Onions	c Chilton b Smith	0		
N Killeen	c Keedy b Kartik	6		
Extras	b 5, lb 16, w 1, nb 12	34	lb 4, lb 3	7
	(all out 134.3 overs)	372	(1 wkt 27 overs)	69

Bowling
Chapple 25-6-64-1. Cork 23-7-52-3. Smith 22-5-71-2. Kartik 35.3-7-89-3. Keedy 28-8-72-1. Astle 1-0-3-0.
Chapple 2-0-5-0. Cork 5-1-14-1. Kartik 8-3-12-0. Keedy 8-4-27-0. Smith 2-4-0.
Fall of Wickets: 1-109, 2-184, 3-229, 4-243, 5-323, 6-345, 7-345, 8-351, 9-352
1-12

LANCASHIRE	First Innings	
MJ Chilton (capt)	c Killeen b Breese	69
IJ Sutcliffe	c Mustard b Gibson	1
MB Loye	c Scott b Breese	78
SG Law	lbw b Breese	50
NJ Astle	lbw b Gibson	2
*LD Sutton	c Gibson b Onions	36
G Chapple	c Maher b Breese	29
DG Cork	c & b Scott	154
TC Smith	not out	40
G Keedy		
M Kartik		
Extras	b 8, lb 7, nb 8	23
	(8 wkts dec 132.1 overs)	482

Bowling
Onions 19-1-80-1. Gibson 27-6-75-2. Killeen 8-3-17-0. Wiseman 26-5-103-0. Scott 8.1-1-30-1. Breese 44-8-162-4.
Fall of Wickets: 1-2, 2-136, 3-197, 4-202, 5-206, 6-246, 7-351, 8-482

Match drawn – Lancashire (11 pts),
Durham (10 pts)

YORKSHIRE v. NOTTINGHAMSHIRE – at Headingley

YORKSHIRE	First Innings		Second Innings	
C White (capt)	c Swann b Shreck	147	c Fleming b Sidebottom	16
JJ Sayers	lbw b Shreck	2	c Smith b Sidebottom	37
DS Lehmann	b Sidebottom	4	run out	48
MJ Lumb	c Sidebottom b Harris	10	not out	84
A Rashid	c Ealham b Swann	63	(6) c Sidebottom b Swann	7
AW Gale	st Alleyne b Swann	11	(5) c Smith b Sidebottom	16
*SM Guy	c Fleming b Sidebottom	2	not out	19
JN Gillespie	lbw b Sidebottom	15		
MAK Lawson	b Shreck	15		
SA Patterson	c Alleyne b Shreck	17		
GJ Kruis	not out	0		
Extras	lb 7, w 1, nb 12	20	b 1, lb 1, w 1, nb 8	11
	(all out 111.2 overs)	306	(5 wkts dec 69 overs)	238

Bowling
Sidebottom 31-6-70-3. Shreck 23.2-8-63-4. Harris 21-2-75-1. Franks 17-2-58-0. Swann 17-5-28-2. Patel 2-0-5-0.
Sidebottom 21-5-55-3. Shreck 14-3-59-0. Swann 22-4-78-1. Harris 8-1-38-0. Franks 4-1-6-0.
Fall of Wickets: 1-2, 2-13, 3-42, 4-172, 5-202, 6-205, 7-237, 8-256, 9-305
1-28, 2-91, 3-132, 4-162, 5-198

NOTTS	First Innings		Second Innings	
WR Smith	c Lehmann b Lawson	41	lbw b Gillespie	0
*D Alleyne	b Gillespie	7	st Guy b Lawson	54
SP Fleming (capt)	lbw b Rashid	25	lbw b Lawson	29
SR Patel	lbw b Gillespie	8	c & b Lawson	16
DJ Hussey	b Lawson	117	not out	86
MA Ealham	c Sayers b Rashid	2	(7) b Kruis	0
GP Swann	b Kruis	24	(6) b Kruis	23
PJ Franks	c Lawson b Rashid	20	lbw b Rashid	0
RJ Sidebottom	c Sayers b Lawson	1	b Rashid	0
AJ Harris	c Lumb b Lawson	0	c White b Rashid	0
CE Shreck	not out	0	st Guy b Lawson	0
Extras	b 4, lb 5, w 1, nb 8	18	nb 4	4
	(all out 66.5 overs)	263	(all out 66.4 overs)	213

Bowling
Gillespie 14-2-47-2. Kruis 15-4-60-1. Rashid 20-1-76-3. Patterson 6-2-29-0. Lawson 11.5-0-42-4.
Gillespie 8-1-22-1. Kruis 10-1-31-2. Rashid 23-5-74-3. Lawson 22.4-0-85-4. Lehmann 1-0-1-0.
Fall of Wickets: 1-33, 2-82, 3-82, 4-111, 5-118, 6-165, 7-220, 8-235, 9-252
1-0, 2-52, 3-82, 4-119, 5-172, 6-172, 7-178, 8-190, 9-196

Yorkshire won by 68 runs –
Yorkshire (20 pts), Nottinghamshire (5 pts)

WARWICKSHIRE v. KENT – at Edgbaston

KENT	First Innings		Second Innings	
JL Denly	c Tahir b Carter	86	c Trott b Streak	13
RWT Key (capt)	b Carter	25	c Knight b Westwood	49
M van Jaarsveld	c Ambrose b Tahir	79	c Knight b Westwood	61
MJ Walker	lbw b Loudon	19	not out	103
DI Stevens	c & b Streak	61	not out	61
*GO Jones	c Ambrose b Carter	50		
NJ Dexter	b Tahir	0		
JC Tredwell	c Ambrose b Carter	21		
SJ Cook	c Trott b Streak	28		
MM Patel	c Loudon b Tahir	25		
RH Joseph	not out	4		
Extras	b 4, lb 8, w 5, nb 6	23	b 4, lb 7, w 7, nb 6	24
	(all out 119.5 overs)	421	(3 wkts dec 71 overs)	311

Bowling
Tahir 20.5-1-98-3. Streak 30-6-84-2. Carter 32-5-130-4. Harris 22-4-52-0. Loudon 13-0-37-1. Ali 2-1-8-0.
Tahir 13-2-51-0. Carter 5-0-36-0. Streak 4-1-15-1. Ali 18-2-91-0. Westwood 18-2-46-2. Knight 9-0-41-0. Wagh 3-0-14-0. Trott 1-0-6-0.
Fall of Wickets: 1-56, 2-188, 3-209, 4-249, 5-306, 6-318, 7-358, 8-371, 9-399
1-48, 2-88, 3-191

WARWICKSHIRE	First Innings		Second Innings	
IJ Westwood	c Patel b Cook	0		
MA Wagh	lbw b Joseph	3	not out	3
MM Ali	c van Jaarsveld b Cook	7		
IJL Trott	c Cook b Tredwell	75		
NV Knight	c Walker b Patel	52	(1) not out	15
*TR Ambrose	c van Jaarsveld b Cook	77		
AGR Loudon	lbw b Patel	3		
HH Streak (capt)	c van Jaarsveld b Cook	56		
NM Carter	c Stevens b Cook	13		
N Tahir	c van Jaarsveld b Cook	7		
PL Harris	not out	9		
Extras	lb 3, w 1, nb 12	16	w 1	1
	(all out 92.4 overs)	318	(0 wkts 3.3 overs)	19

Bowling
Cook 19.4-2-74-6. Joseph 11-6-67-1. Stevens 3-1-18-0. Tredwell 30-6-82-1. Patel 18-2-55-2. Denly 6-0-19-0.
Cook 2-0-9-0. Joseph 1.3-0-10-0.
Fall of Wickets: 1-1, 2-5, 3-15, 4-127, 5-163, 6-178, 7-275, 8-297, 9-307

Match drawn – Warwickshire (10 pts),
Kent (12 pts)

Back in the saddle: James Hildreth put a previously miserable season behind him with a brilliant 227 not out at Taunton.

Division Two

Runs flowed at Taunton as James Hildreth banished his season's previous struggles with a brilliant career-best 227 not out and Chris Rogers became the first Northamptonshire batsman since Allan Lamb in 1992 to score a century and double-century in the same match. The result of all this runmaking, however, plus a third day shortened to 63 overs by poor weather, was an inevitable draw. Hildreth batted 269 balls, hitting three sixes and 31 fours, and Somerset supporters were also delighted to see excellent scores from three other young locally-raised players in Arul Suppiah and Sam Spurway, who added 180 for the third wicket, and Wes Durston, who put on 173 with Hildreth for the seventh wicket. The only bowler to make much of an impact in the friendly conditions was the dependable Andrew Caddick, whose first day 4 for 76 contributed to Northants' inexplicable decline from 219 for 1 to 326 all out.

Round Twenty-One: 20–23 September 2006

Division One

Sussex wrapped up their second Championship title in four years by hammering a sorry Nottinghamshire side so comprehensively at Trent Bridge that the home team could not even secure the second bonus point that they required to avoid relegation. As it was, however, Durham's ten-point draw at Yorkshire kept them up and sent Notts down.

For Sussex it was glory all the way as – once again – Mushtaq Ahmed confounded his opponents quite utterly with his leg-spinning skills. Following up his first innings 4 for 60 with a remarkable haul of 9 for 48, Mushtaq decimated the Notts batting to give Sussex the victory they so desired in little more than two days. The first morning, by contrast, had been a tense affair as Sussex's second-wicket pair of Richard Montgomerie and Mike Yardy fought to keep out a Notts seam attack led superbly by Ryan Sidebottom. By the time they had put on 144, though, and Montgomerie had departed for a gutsy 82, any nerves had been settled. Yardy went on to reach 119, adding a further 110 with Murray Goodwin, who himself then put on 122 for the

Round Twenty: 12–16 September 2006
Division Two

SOMERSET v. NORTHAMPTONSHIRE – at Taunton

NORTHANTS	First Innings			Second Innings	
SD Peters	b Blackwell		63	lbw b Caddick	69
CJL Rogers	b Blackwell		128	not out	222
U Afzaal	not out		49	b Blackwell	0
DJG Sales (capt)	c Suppiah b Durston		35	c Caddick b Durston	93
*BM Shafayat	c Hildreth b Caddick		1	c sub b Durston	14
L Klusener	b Willoughby		0	not out	33
RA White	lbw b Willoughby		0		
BJ Phillips	c Hildreth b Caddick		0		
SP Crook	lbw b Caddick		0		
MJ Nicholson	c Edwards b Caddick		23		
JF Brown	c Hildreth b Johnson		8		
Extras	b 9, lb 8, nb 2		19	b 12, lb 3, w 3, nb 4	22
	(all out 87.1 overs)		**326**	(4 wkts 105 overs)	**453**

Bowling
Caddick 22-4-76-4. Willoughby 19-3-92-2. Johnson 8.1-0-28-1. Parsons 7-3-17-0. Blackwell 21-2-63-2. Durston 10-1-33-1.
Caddick 19-0-97-1. Willoughby 9-1-45-0. Durston 33-4-116-2. Suppiah 12-1-58-0. Johnson 6-0-37-0. Blackwell 19-4-59-1. Parsons 6-0-26-0. Edwards 1-1-0-0.
Fall of Wickets: 1-153, 2-219, 3-260, 4-269, 5-270, 6-270, 7-271, 8-271, 9-299
1-151, 2-156, 3-364, 4-400

SOMERSET	First Innings	
NJ Edwards	c Shafayat b Phillips	12
MJ Wood	c Shafayat b Nicholson	5
AV Suppiah	run out	98
*SHP Spurway	c Crook b White	83
JC Hildreth	not out	227
KA Parsons	c Rogers b Brown	10
ID Blackwell	b Crook	43
WJ Durston	c Rogers b Crook	73
RL Johnson	c Brown b Crook	3
AR Caddick (capt)	not out	28
CM Willoughby		
Extras	b 9, lb 19, w 13, nb 2	43
	(8 wkts dec 166 overs)	**625**

Bowling
Nicholson 26-4-93-1. Phillips 24-6-78-1. Brown 41-8-160-1. Crook 25-0-113-3. Klusener 7-3-15-0. Afzaal 32-6-93-0. White 8-0-34-1. Rogers 3-1-11-0.
Fall of Wickets: 1-5, 2-21, 3-201, 4-250, 5-284, 6-378, 7-551, 8-559

*Match drawn – Somerset (12 pts),
Northamptonshire (9 pts)*

fourth wicket with an aggressive Chris Adams before falling for 99 to the last ball of the day. At 420 for 5 overnight, Sussex were in complete control and another 140 runs were added the following morning as both Matt Prior and Robin Martin-Jenkins played their strokes. The declaration

condemned Notts to just the single bowling point, too, and the writing was on the wall for them once Jason Lewry and Martin-Jenkins had taken two important wickets apiece in support of Mushtaq's array of wares. Dismissed for 165, and forced to follow on, Notts found themselves almost immediately confronted again by Mushtaq in fading light. The Pakistani sorcerer only bowled three overs on the second evening, but it was enough for him to reduce Notts to 50 for 4 with a spell of 4 for 6. The next morning belonged to Mushtaq again, and only James Kirtley's dismissal of Paul Franks prevented him from taking all ten wickets. Sussex, winners by an innings and 245 runs, were soon celebrating just the second Championship success in the club's history and skipper Adams was contemplating whether or not to stay in the job for a tenth season in 2007.

'At the moment I feel like a marathon runner near collapse at the line. But if this is the time to step down, I will be completely fulfilled,' he said.

Durham's survival, meanwhile, was almost a miraculous affair at Headingley – especially after Darren Lehmann, in his last game for Yorkshire, had hit them for an epic 339 in a total of 677 for 7 declared. By the close of day two, indeed, Durham were looking down and out at 203 for 6 in reply, despite a spirited second-wicket stand of 150 between youngsters Gary Scott and Garry Park. But then, in the 48 overs of play possible before rain arrived to cut short the third day, the miracle happened. Dale Benkenstein, the Durham captain, resumed in

Round Twenty-One: 20–23 September 2006
Division One

NOTTINGHAMSHIRE v. SUSSEX – at Trent Bridge

SUSSEX — First Innings

RR Montgomerie	c Ealham b Harris	82
CD Hopkinson	run out	0
MH Yardy	lbw b Patel	119
MW Goodwin	b Shreck	99
CJ Adams (capt)	c sub b Shreck	72
*MJ Prior	not out	77
RSC Martin-Jenkins	not out	84
Naved-ul-Hasan		
Mushtaq Ahmed		
RJ Kirtley		
JD Lewry		
Extras	lb 6, nb 21	27
	(5 wkts dec 127 overs)	**560**

Bowling
Sidebottom 30-8-90-0. Shreck 24-3-141-2. Harris 27-8-103-1. Franks 20-1-121-0. Patel 20-3-67-1. Hussey 6-0-32-0.
Fall of Wickets: 1-5, 2-149, 3-259, 4-381, 5-420

NOTTS	First Innings		Second Innings (following on)	
DJ Bicknell	lbw b Kirtley	20	c Hopkinson b M Ahmed	28
WR Smith	c Prior b Lewry	28	lbw b Mushtaq Ahmed	6
*D Alleyne	b Mushtaq Ahmed	11	c Hopkinson b M Ahmed	0
SR Patel	c Yardy b Martin-Jenkins	35	(6) b Mushtaq Ahmed	24
DJ Hussey	c M'gomerie b Martin-Jenkins	31	b Mushtaq Ahmed	10
MA Ealham	b Mushtaq Ahmed	1	(7) lbw b Mushtaq Ahmed	39
SP Fleming (capt)	c Adams b Mushtaq Ahmed	0	(4) c Adams b Mushtaq Ahmed	4
PJ Franks	c Adams b Mushtaq Ahmed	10	lbw b Kirtley	16
RJ Sidebottom	lbw b Lewry	5	b Mushtaq Ahmed	3
AJ Harris	b Naved-ul-Hasan	2	lbw b Mushtaq Ahmed	0
CE Shreck	not out	0	not out	0
Extras	b 3, lb 8, w 1, nb 10	22	b 4, lb 1, w 1, nb 6	12
	(all out 54.2 overs)	**165**	(all out 27.3 overs)	**150**

Bowling
Lewry 14-2-42-2. Naved-ul-Hasan 11-0-36-1. Kirtley 6-2-12-1. Mushtaq Ahmed 19.2-4-60-4. Martin-Jenkins 4-1-4-2.
Naved-ul-Hasan 3-0-29-0. Kirtley 10-2-56-1. Mushtaq Ahmed 11.3-2-48-9. Yardy 3-0-12-0.
Fall of Wickets: 1-38, 2-58, 3-84, 4-143, 5-144, 6-144, 7-144, 8-157, 9-165
1-32, 2-36, 3-45, 4-46, 5-81, 6-82, 7-107, 8-128, 9-149

Sussex won by an innings and 245 runs –
Nottinghamshire (1 pt), Sussex (22 pts)

YORKSHIRE v. DURHAM – at Headingley

YORKSHIRE	First Innings	
C White (capt)	run out	22
JJ Sayers	c Maher b Onions	5
A McGrath	b Onions	62
DS Lehmann	b Wiseman	339
MJ Lumb	c Maher b Gibson	98
A Rashid	c Onions b Breese	24
TT Bresnan	b Killeen	3
*SM Guy	not out	52
MAK Lawson	not out	19
JN Gillespie		
GJ Kruis		
Extras	b 9, lb 7, w 1, nb 36	53
	(7 wkts dec 149 overs)	**677**

Bowling
Gibson 27-2-150-1. Onions 31-5-151-2. Killeen 20-2-103-1. Scott 5-0-35-0.
Wiseman 30-6-127-1. Breese 36-8-95-1.
Fall of Wickets: 1-24, 2-43, 3-174, 4-532, 5-583, 6-594, 7-610

DURHAM	First Innings		Second Innings (following on)	
JP Maher	c Guy b Gillespie	2	lbw b Kruis	7
GM Scott	c Guy b Kruis	77	lbw b Kruis	7
GT Park	lbw b Gillespie	77	not out	100
DM B'kenstein (capt)	c Guy b Lawson	151	c McGrath b Rashid	26
*P Mustard	lbw b Kruis	0		
BW Harmison	c Guy b Kruis	0	(5) not out	33
GR Breese	b Rashid	6		
OD Gibson	b Rashid	155		
PJ Wiseman	not out	6		
N Killeen	lbw b Rashid	0		
G Onions	b Rashid	3		
Extras	b 2, lb 18, w 1, nb 20	41	b 4, nb 4	8
	(all out 132.2 overs)	**518**	(3 wkts 39.5 overs)	**181**

Bowling
Gillespie 21-4-63-2. Kruis 24-5-92-3. Lawson 38-0-148-1. Rashid 34.2-2-144-4.
Bresnan 12-2-43-0. Lehmann 3-1-8-0.
Gillespie 5-2-8-0. Kruis 5-1-20-2. Rashid 14-2-59-1. Lawson 10.5-1-70-0.
Lehmann 5-0-20-0.
Fall of Wickets: 1-2, 2-152, 3-176, 4-176, 5-176, 6-191, 7-506, 8-510, 9-514
1-9, 2-16, 3-83

Match drawn – Yorkshire (11 pts), Durham (10 pts)

HAMPSHIRE v. LANCASHIRE – at the Rose Bowl

LANCASHIRE	First Innings		Second Innings	
MJ Chilton (capt)	c Pothas b Bruce	38	(2) b Tomlinson	1
LJ Sutcliffe	c Pothas b Mascarenhas	27	(1) b Bruce	11
MB Loye	b Lamb	67	(4) c Brown b Warne	55
SG Law	c Ervine b Lamb	79	(5) c Pothas b Tomlinson	24
NJ Astle	c Warne b Bruce	26	(6) c Brown b Adams	86
*LD Sutton	lbw b Bruce	46	(7) not out	111
G Chapple	b Bruce	42	(8) not out	18
DG Cork	b Mascarenhas	9		
TC Smith	c Warne b Tomlinson	49	(3) c Adams b Bruce	12
M Kartik	c Benham b Tomlinson	40		
JM Anderson	not out	7		
Extras	b 1, lb 5, nb 2	8	b 1, lb 4, w 2, nb 14	21
	(all out 126 overs)	**438**	(6 wkts 97 overs)	**339**

Bowling
Bruce 24-5-85-4. Tomlinson 17-4-64-2. Mascarenhas 24-5-64-2. Adams 4-1-19-0.
Warne 35-6-105-0. Lamb 22-0-95-2.
Bruce 13-4-21-2. Tomlinson 15-4-54-2. Mascarenhas 15-3-45-0. Ervine 16-0-76-0.
Lamb 10-1-27-0. Warne 15-3-50-1. Pothas 3-1-8-0. Benham 1-0-7-0.
Adams 9-2-46-1.
Fall of Wickets: 1-63, 2-84, 3-183, 4-219, 5-253, 6-316, 7-325, 8-339, 9-427
1-8, 2-12, 3-55, 4-92, 5-119, 6-302

HAMPSHIRE	First Innings	
JHK Adams	b Smith	32
MJ Brown	lbw b Kartik	13
JP Crawley	c Astle b Cork	63
CC Benham	b Astle	28
SM Ervine	c Anderson b Cork	7
*N Pothas	c Sutton b Cork	4
GA Lamb	lbw b Cork	0
AD Mascarenhas	lbw b Smith	17
SK Warne (capt)	not out	30
JTA Bruce	c Sutton b Smith	4
JA Tomlinson	run out	0
Extras	lb 5, nb 12	17
	(all out 69.3 overs)	**215**

Bowling
Anderson 10-2-38-0. Cork 17-4-47-4. Chapple 9-3-23-0. Kartik 23.3-7-73-1. Smith 7-3-20-3. Astle 3-2-9-1.
Fall of Wickets: 1-46, 2-52, 3-122, 4-144, 5-154, 6-154, 7-157, 8-210, 9-214

Match drawn – Hampshire (8 pts), Lancashire (12 pts)

KENT v. MIDDLESEX – at Canterbury

KENT	First Innings	
DP Fulton	c Peploe b Silverwood	155
JL Denly	c Peploe b Peploe	66
M v Jaarsveld (capt)	c Joyce b Peploe	2
MJ Walker	c Nash b Silverwood	104
RS Ferley	c Hutton b Peploe	22
DI Stevens	not out	126
*GO Jones	lbw b Joyce	59
NJ Dexter	not out	35
JC Tredwell		
SJ Cook		
RH Joseph		
Extras	b 3, lb 13, w 2, nb 16	34
	(6 wkts dec 164 overs)	**603**

Bowling
Silverwood 34-7-90-3. Louw 24-3-66-0. Peploe 50-4-205-2. Wright 23-1-113-0.
Hutton 4-0-25-0. Weekes 24-2-67-0. Joyce 5-0-21-1.
Fall of Wickets: 1-123, 2-138, 3-334, 4-357, 5-417, 6-538

MIDDLESEX	First Innings		Second Innings (following on)	
BL Hutton (capt)	b Ferley	20	c Tredwell b Ferley	26
NRD Compton	lbw b Joseph	1	st Jones b Ferley	100
OA Shah	b Ferley	43	c Fulton b Tredwell	52
EC Joyce	c van Jaarsveld b Tredwell	99	(5) c Tredwell b Ferley	10
ET Smith	c Denly b Ferley	7	(4) run out	16
PN Weekes	c Tredwell b Joseph	35	(7) not out	4
*DC Nash	lbw b Denly	64	(6) not out	22
CT Peploe	c Dexter b Ferley	6		
J Louw	c sub b Ferley	12		
CJC Wright	not out	34		
CEW Silverwood	b Ferley	43		
Extras	b 4, lb 5, w 2, nb 14	25	b 9, lb 1, w 8, nb 16	34
	(all out 97.2 overs)	**413**	(5 wkts 80 overs)	**264**

Bowling
Cook 13-2-56-0. Joseph 13-3-49-2. Tredwell 33-5-143-1. Ferley 31.2-3-136-6.
Stevens 4-1-12-0. Denly 3-1-8-1.
Cook 4-2-8-0. Joseph 13-1-58-0. Dexter 15-0-87-0. Tredwell 26-2-85-1.
Ferley 25-2-70-3. Stevens 4-1-7-0. Denly 7-1-17-0.
Fall of Wickets: 1-41, 2-91, 3-124, 4-136, 5-197, 6-304, 7-324, 8-324, 9-340
1-97, 2-196, 3-228, 4-228, 5-243

Match drawn – Kent (12 pts), Middlesex (10 pts)

They knew it was all but over ... and it is now, as Mushtaq Ahmed completes his demolition job on previous champions Nottinghamshire by trapping Andrew Harris lbw to clinch the 2006 Liverpool Victoria Championship title for Sussex.

partnership with Ottis Gibson, the veteran fast bowler, and they batted so well that by the time of the weather interruption they had both reached three figures and – most importantly – had taken Durham past the 400 mark. That meant that, if they went on to draw the game and thus secure another four points, Durham would go above Nottinghamshire by a mere half-point and stay in the first division. When Gibson had swung a ball from Adil Rashid high over the midwicket boundary for the six which brought up Durham's 400, the rest of the Durham team had erupted with joy on the dressing-room balcony. Then, when the rain began to fall hard enough to wash out the rest of the day, their happiness was even more complete. Benkenstein and Gibson went on to add a county record 315 for the seventh wicket, scoring a heroic 151 and 155 respectively. Benkenstein batted for 425 minutes, hitting 16 fours and a six from 223 balls, while Gibson faced 251 balls in 386 minutes,

striking four sixes and 15 fours. Durham, following on after being eventually dismissed for 518, then had little trouble in batting out time on the final afternoon with Park hitting a maiden hundred.

Shane Warne was not best pleased at the Rose Bowl, meanwhile, after Lancashire captain Mark Chilton had refused to set Hampshire a target on what became a meaningless final day. Lancashire had enjoyed much the better of the first two days, bowling out the home side for just 215 after topping 400 comfortably themselves at a time when – before Sussex's win at Trent Bridge was confirmed – they still retained outside hopes of taking the title. But rain washed away all except five overs of the third day and Warne arrived the next morning expecting a proper contest between the two next best sides in the Championship. Chilton, however, was having none of it – although later, on hearing of Warne's criticism, he did admit he should have made a game of it. Luke Sutton and Nathan Astle put on 183 for the sixth wicket, with Warne sending down a stream of bouncers at one stage to register his disgust. Hampshire's captain said afterwards, 'We thought we were going to have a game. It was ridiculous. They missed a trick and, to be honest, lost the spirit of the game'.

David Fulton marked what was likely to be his 200th and last first-class match for Kent with a determined 155 against Middlesex at Canterbury. It was undoubtedly the highlight of an otherwise colourless match, which lost 59 overs to rain on the third day, and which ultimately ended in a draw as Nick Compton's second-innings century denied Kent the chance of an innings victory. Matthew Walker and Darren Stevens also took hundreds off a hapless Middlesex attack as Kent eased past 600, while Joe Denly and Geraint Jones contributed attractive half-centuries, and left-arm spinner Rob Ferley then wheeled away patiently to take 6 for 136 in a Middlesex reply boosted by some late hitting from No. 11 Chris Silverwood, whose 25-ball 43 included three sixes and three fours. Ed Joyce was the pick of the Middlesex batting in their first innings, before being well held by a diving Martin van Jaarsveld at slip just one run short of a deserved hundred.

Division Two

Worcestershire nicked the second and final promotion spot by beating a spineless Northamptonshire by five wickets at Wantage Road, much to the displeasure of Essex, who themselves were forced to gamble in search of victory against Leicestershire at Grace Road – and lost.

What upset Essex as much as seeing Leicestershire's batsmen romp to their win target of 301 with only five wickets down was the news that Northants, following a complete third day washout, had collapsed from 100 for 1 to 143 all out after holding their end-of-season dinner in Northampton the night before. That left Worcestershire, who had begun the season's final day very much as second favourites to go up behind Essex, needing only 205 for the victory that would guarantee them promotion if their rivals lost or drew at Leicester. On a pitch by now taking spin – as Gareth Batty and Ray Price had illustrated earlier in the day – Worcestershire's batsmen decided to go on the offensive straight away against Monty Panesar, in an effort to hit the Northants dangerman out of the attack. Panesar, of course, was too good to be collared totally, and picked up all five visiting wickets to fall, but at least both Stephen Moore and Vikram Solanki had created

some forward momentum before they perished. In the end, with tension mounting and word of Leicestershire's successful chase beginning to filter through, it took all the experience and skill of Graeme Hick – supported doggedly by Batty – to get Worcestershire over the finishing line against Panesar. Hick, in particular, played him well in his 59-ball 30 not out – as he had in the first innings too while making 70 as England's new spin star had collected 5 for 101 from 37.3 beguiling overs. Hick and Roger Sillence, in fact, had kept Worcestershire in the game on day two after David Sales and Ben Phillips – with three sixes apiece – had taken Northants, with a little help too from Panesar the batsman, to a first innings 342. Sales, after being dismissed four short of his hundred, then had the considerable consolation of being able to dash from the ground to Northampton General Hospital to witness the birth of his third son.

Essex had begun their match at Leicester in fine fettle, with Alastair Cook making 132 in only his third Championship appearance of the season and James Foster also reaching three figures. Andy Bichel then

Gareth Batty turned in an excellent all-round performance as Worcestershire clinched promotion with a five-wicket win over Northants at Wantage Road.

thumped an unbeaten 75, in a last-wicket stand of 81 with Alex Tudor that took Essex to a commanding 486, but Leicestershire's batsmen were just as prolific in reply. The third day saw only 18 overs being bowled, moreover, and as John Sadler and James Allenby completed fine hundreds, each hitting three sixes, Essex captain Ronnie Irani was left with no option but to agree a final day deal with his opposite number Darren Robinson. A home first innings declaration was then followed by 9.4 overs of tripe from Paul Nixon and Robinson himself, in which Mark Pettini reached a 29-ball 114 not out with 12 fours and 11 sixes while Cook hit 66 not out from just 22 balls. This gave Leicestershire their agreed target, and ended Essex's promotion dream as Allenby's 47-ball 68 not out completed an excellent team chase.

Several young Derbyshire players caught the eye against Surrey at Derby, but it was the second division champions who eventually emerged as five-wicket winners as Scott Newman and Mark Butcher perfectly orchestrated a headlong pursuit of a 273-run target. Newman's 76-ball 83 included 11 fours and two sixes, while Butcher's unbeaten 59 came at exactly a run a ball. Both Surrey left-handers had also posted first innings half-centuries, although 21-year-old seamer Wayne White impressed with his 4 for 35. Earlier, from the depths of 124 for 6, the home team had rallied through a 181-run seventh-wicket partnership between reserve wicketkeeper Lee Goddard and all-rounder Graham Wagg.

There was hope for the future for Glamorgan at Cardiff, too, as David Hemp took over the captaincy from Robert Croft and scored 132 with three sixes and 17 fours following a brilliant 72 on debut from

Round Twenty-One: 20–23 September 2006
Division Two

NORTHANTS v. WORCESTERSHIRE – at Northampton

NORTHANTS	First Innings		Second Innings	
SD Peters	b Batty	38	c Solanki b Batty	27
CJL Rogers	b Batty	28	c Hick b Kabir Ali	19
U Afzaal	c Davies b Batty	0	c Hick b Price	51
DJG Sales (capt)	c Khan b Sillence	96	(5) b Price	4
*BM Shafayat	c Hick b Batty	18	(4) c Batty b Price	20
L Klusener	c & b Solanki	16	b Batty	8
BJ Phillips	c Davies b Khan	75	not out	14
SP Crook	b Sillence	0	lbw b Price	14
MS Panesar	c Davies b Sillence	34	c Davies b Batty	1
DH Wigley	b Khan	0	c Moore b Batty	0
JF Brown	not out	20	c Hick b Solanki	0
Extras	b 8, lb 6, w 1, nb 2	17	b 2, lb 1	3
	(all out 107 overs)	342	(all out 46 overs)	143

Bowling
Khan 21-3-81-2. Kabir Ali 17-4-41-0. Sillence 11-4-28-3. Price 26-11-44-0. Batty 28-3-109-4. Solanki 3-0-17-1. Vincent 1-0-8-0.
Khan 9-1-34-0. Kabir Ali 7-1-25-1. Batty 14-4-43-4. Price 15.3-5-38-4. Solanki 0.3-0-0-1.
Fall of Wickets: 1-46, 2-46, 3-101, 4-131, 5-148, 6-269, 7-269, 8-297, 9-297 1-28, 2-100, 3-102, 4-102, 5-114, 6-114, 7-141, 8-142, 9-142

WORCS	First Innings		Second Innings	
L Vincent	b Brown	36	c Crook b Panesar	16
SC Moore	lbw b Brown	30	b Panesar	59
VS Solanki (capt)	lbw b Panesar	14	c Rogers b Panesar	50
BF Smith	c sub b Panesar	7	c Rogers b Panesar	9
GA Hick	b Crook	70	not out	30
*SM Davies	b Panesar	11	c Klusener b Panesar	2
GJ Batty	c sub b Brown	37	not out	25
RJ Sillence	c Brown b Panesar	64		
Kabir Ali	b Crook	1		
Z Khan	b Panesar	1		
RW Price	not out	1		
Extras	b 5, lb 3, w 1	9	b 10, lb 4	14
	(all out 100.3 overs)	281	(5 wkts 50.4 overs)	205

Bowling
Wigley 5-1-17-0. Phillips 3-1-8-0. Crook 9-1-26-2. Panesar 37.3-6-101-5.
Brown 37-12-92-3. Klusener 5-1-14-0. Afzaal 4-1-15-0.
Brown 20-0-75-0. Phillips 3-0-16-0. Panesar 21.4-3-76-5. Klusener 1-0-1-0. Crook 2-0-18-0. Afzaal 3-0-5-0.
Fall of Wickets: 1-57, 2-72, 3-89, 4-96, 5-114, 6-191, 7-251, 8-265, 9-266 1-45, 2-114, 3-134, 4-149, 5-157

*Worcestershire won by 5 wickets –
Northamptonshire (6 pts), Worcestershire (19 pts)*

LEICESTERSHIRE v. ESSEX – at Leicester

ESSEX	First Innings		Second Innings	
AN Cook	c Robinson b Maddy	132	not out	66
ML Pettini	c Maddy b Liddle	11	not out	114
RS Bopara	b Masters	11		
A Flower	c Masters b Maunders	5		
RC Irani (capt)	lbw b Masters	7		
*JS Foster	lbw b Walker	103		
RN ten Doeschate	b Masters	45		
JD Middlebrook	c Liddle b Henderson	44		
TJ Phillips	b Walker	4		
AJ Bichel	b Walker	75		
AJ Tudor	b Henderson	22		
Extras	b 8, lb 18, w 1	27	nb 6	6
	(all out 146.5 overs)	486	(0 wkts dec 9.4 overs)	186

Bowling
Masters 32-13-58-3. Walker 27-5-83-2. Liddle 24-6-105-1. Maddy 19-6-52-1.
Maunders 7-0-25-1. Allenby 8-2-23-0. Henderson 29.5-5-114-2.
Nixon 5-0-69-0. Robinson 4.4-0-117-0.
Fall of Wickets: 1-42, 2-64, 3-75, 4-82, 5-237, 6-322, 7-335, 8-339, 9-405

LEICESTERSHIRE	First Innings		Second Innings	
DDJ Robinson (capt)	lbw b Bopara	80	c Foster b Bichel	7
JK Maunders	lbw b Bichel	7	c Cook b Middlebrook	49
*TJ New	lbw b Bichel	0	Phillips	51
JL Sadler	not out	128	run out	38
DL Maddy	c ten Doeschate b Bopara	39	b ten Doeschate	39
J Allenby	not out	103	(7) not out	68
PA Nixon			(6) not out	38
CW Henderson				
DD Masters				
CJ Liddle				
NGE Walker				
Extras	b 7, lb 16, w 1, nb 30	54	b 4, lb 3, w 2, nb 2	11
	(4 wkts dec 93.5 overs)	372	(5 wkts 70.1 overs)	301

Bowling
Bichel 21-4-86-2. Tudor 11.5-3-69-0. Phillips 18-3-54-0. Bopara 21-8-61-2.
Middlebrook 8-1-36-0. ten Doeschate 14-4-43-0.
Bichel 13-4-49-1. Tudor 5-1-18-0. Bopara 7-0-25-0. ten Doeschate 13.1-1-72-1.
Middlebrook 16-1-55-1. Phillips 14-2-71-1. Cook 2-1-4-0.
Fall of Wickets: 1-21, 2-21, 3-129, 4-129 1-25, 2-111, 3-117, 4-189, 5-199

*Leicestershire won by 5 wickets –
Leicestershire (21 pts), Essex (6 pts)*

DERBYSHIRE v. SURREY – at Derby

DERBYSHIRE	First Innings		Second Innings	
SD Stubbings (capt)	b Murtagh	2	(2) lbw b Murtagh	0
PM Borrington	c Salisbury b Saker	18	(1) c Batty b Salisbury	38
CR Taylor	c Salisbury b Murtagh	20	c sub b Murtagh	6
Hassan Adnan	c Butcher b Saker	23	c Brown b Salisbury	30
GM Smith	c Batty b Dernbach	39	lbw b Salisbury	0
AG Botha	c Benning b Walters	2	c sub b Doshi	0
*LJ Goddard	c sub b Saker	91	not out	43
GG Wagg	c Brown b Salisbury	94	c Walters b Doshi	6
PS Jones	b Doshi	28	c sub b Salisbury	2
WA White	not out	18	not out	19
KJ Dean	c Newman b Salisbury	18		
Extras	b 5, lb 10, w 2, nb 10, p 5	32	b 3, lb 5, nb 10	18
	(all out 134.3 overs)	385	(8 wkts dec 54 overs)	162

Bowling
Murtagh 25-6-82-2. Dernbach 17.2-5-43-1. Saker 22.4-2-73-3. Walters 8-2-9-1.
Salisbury 28.3-7-88-2. Benning 3-0-12-0. Doshi 18-3-58-1.
Murtagh 6-1-16-2. Saker 8-1-41-0. Doshi 21-2-44-2. Salisbury 19-7-53-4.
Fall of Wickets: 1-2, 2-32, 3-126, 4-145, 5-168, 6-201, 7-271, 8-275 1-1, 2-17, 3-74, 4-74, 5-75, 6-93, 7-110, 8-121

SURREY	First Innings		Second Innings	
SA Newman	lbw b Dean	67	c sub b Smith	83
*JN Batty	lbw b White	0	(6) c Smith b White	3
SJ Walters	lbw b White	6	(4) c Goddard b White	41
MA Butcher (capt)	retired hurt	51	(5) not out	59
AD Brown	lbw b Botha	14	(3) b Botha	8
JGE Benning	c Jones b Botha	22	(2) c Botha b Wagg	26
IDK Salisbury	c Goddard b Botha	16	not out	21
TJ Murtagh	not out	41		
NC Saker	c Taylor b White	30		
ND Doshi	c Botha b White	0		
JW Dernbach	not out	0		
Extras	b 5, lb 9, w 4, nb 10	28	b 15, lb 12, w 5	32
	(8 wkts dec 93.5 overs)	275	(5 wkts 40 overs)	273

Bowling
Jones 25-6-76-0. White 14-4-35-4. Wagg 18.5-2-70-0. Dean 10-2-31-1.
Smith 5-0-17-0. Botha 19-4-39-3.
Jones 5-1-38-0. White 7-0-48-2. Wagg 10-0-52-1. Dean 1-0-4-0. Botha 14-0-86-1. Smith 3-1-18-1.
Fall of Wickets: 1-2, 2-32, 3-58, 4-95, 5-102, 6-124, 7-305, 8-322, 9-358 1-62, 2-89, 3-146, 4-206, 5-222

Surrey won by 5 wickets – Derbyshire (6 pts), Surrey (19 pts)

GLAMORGAN v. GLOUCESTERSHIRE – at Cardiff

GLOS	First Innings		Second Innings	
CM Spearman	c Wright b Harrison	26	b Harrison	4
Kadeer Ali	b Harrison	18	c Wallace b Harrison	23
HJH Marshall	run out	79	c Harrison b Cosker	73
CG Taylor	b Franklin	54	c Wallace b Franklin	28
APR Gidman (capt)	b Franklin	92	c Hemp b Croft	118
*SJ Adshead	st Wallace b Cosker	29	c Hemp b Croft	11
DO Brown	b Harrison	34	lbw b Croft	22
MA Hardinges	c Croft b Watkins	101	c Wallace b Harrison	0
SP Kirby	lbw b Franklin	2	not out	17
DA Burton	not out	52	c Wright b Harrison	1
V Banerjee	b Franklin	7	not out	5
Extras	b 6, lb 17, w 2, nb 6	31	lb 5, w 1	6
	(all out 133.3 overs)	525	(9 wkts 84 overs)	308

Bowling
Harrison 29-8-95-4. Franklin 23.3-6-67-3. Watkins 17-3-55-1. Waters 17-2-87-0.
Croft 26-2-98-0. Cosker 21-2-100-1.
Harrison 23-8-88-4. Croft 29-4-88-3. Cosker 12-3-37-1. Franklin 13-3-56-1.
Watkins 3-0-24-0. Waters 4-1-10-0.
Fall of Wickets: 1-29, 2-70, 3-186, 4-220, 5-305, 6-347, 7-365, 8-384, 9-512 1-12, 2-123, 3-128, 4-211, 5-254, 6-273, 7-275, 8-285, 9-286

GLAMORGAN	First Innings			
DD Cherry	b Banerjee	121		
*MA Wallace	c Adshead b Kirby	64		
BJ Wright	b Marshall	72		
MJ Powell	c Adshead b Hardinges	12		
DL Hemp (capt)	lbw b Banerjee	132		
JEC Franklin	c Marshall b Hardinges	21		
RE Watkins	b Banerjee	36		
RDB Croft	not out	40		
DS Harrison	c Marshall b Kirby	20		
DA Cosker	c Kadeer Ali b Banerjee	1		
HT Waters	b Kirby	0		
Extras	b 10, lb 21, w 5, nb 42	78		
	(all out 153.2 overs)	597		

Bowling
Kirby 32.2-4-125-3. Burton 20-1-129-0. Hardinges 21-4-55-2. Banerjee 42-10-150-4.
Gidman 18-5-36-0. Taylor 5-0-25-0. Brown 9-2-30-0. Marshall 6-1-16-1.
Fall of Wickets: 1-147, 2-291, 3-306, 4-480, 5-424, 6-522, 7-534, 8-573, 9-594

Match drawn – Glamorgan (11 pts), Gloucestershire (10 pts)

18-year-old Ben Wright. With Dan Cherry also scoring his third career hundred, and Mark Wallace a jaunty 64, Glamorgan were able to surpass even Gloucestershire's mammoth 525 in a game that, predictably, finished in a draw. Hamish Marshall and Alex Gidman were in particularly fine form for the visitors, hitting 79 and 73 and 92 and 118 respectively, while Mark Hardinges included four sixes and ten fours in his 117-ball 101.

Division One Final Positions

	P	W	L	D	Bat	Bowl	Pts
Sussex	16	9	2	5	49	47	242.00
Lancashire	16	6	1	9	58	46	224.00
Hampshire	16	6	3	7	48	48	207.00
Warwickshire	16	6	5	5	42	43	189.00
Kent	16	4	4	8	43	44	175.00
Yorkshire	16	3	6	7	43	41	154.00
Durham	16	4	8	4	39	43	153.50
Nottinghamshire	16	4	7	5	40	37	153.00
Middlesex	16	1	7	8	47	42	133.50

Slow Over Rate Deductions

Hampshire	1.00	v. Warwicks	(the Rose Bowl, 16 Aug)
Durham	0.50	v. Sussex	(the Riverside, 23 May)
Middlesex	1.50	v. Hampshire	(Lord's, 8 August)

Division Two Final Positions

	P	W	L	D	Bat	Bowl	Pts
Surrey	16	10	2	4	62	44	262.00
Worcestershire	16	8	4	4	58	43	229.00
Essex	16	7	4	5	62	40	220.00
Leicestershire	16	5	4	7	47	41	185.50
Derbyshire	16	4	4	8	51	41	178.50
Northamptonshire	16	3	5	8	52	37	163.00
Gloucestershire	16	3	6	7	51	36	155.50
Glamorgan	16	2	7	7	51	41	146.50
Somerset	16	3	9	4	43	40	140.00

Slow Over Rate Deductions

Leicestershire	0.50	v. Derbyshire	(Derby, 17 May)
Derbyshire	1.00	v. Somerset	(Derby, 8 August)
Derbyshire	0.50	v. Somerset	(Taunton, 14 July)
Gloucestershire	1.00	v. Northants	(Bristol, 10 May)
Gloucestershire	0.50	v. Worcs	(Worcester, 20 July)
Glamorgan	0.50	v. Essex	(Cardiff, 26 April)
Glamorgan	1.00	v. Worcs	(Worcester, 23 May)
Somerset	0.50	v. Glos	(Bristol, 18 April)
Somerset	0.50	v. Leics	(Leicester, 1 September)

COUNTY CHAMPIONSHIP FEATURES 2006

INDIVIDUAL SCORES OVER 200

JL Langer	342	Somerset v. Surrey	at Guildford
DS Lehmann	339	Yorkshire v. Durham	at Headingley
CJL Rogers	319	Northamptonshire v. Gloucestershire	at Northampton
HD Ackerman	309*	Leicestershire v. Glamorgan	at Cardiff
MR Ramprakash	301*	Surrey v. Northamptonshire	at The Oval
MJ Powell	299	Glamorgan v. Gloucestershire	at Cheltenham
MR Ramprakash	292	Surrey v. Gloucestershire	at The Oval
A Flower	271*	Essex v. Northamptonshire	at Northampton
JHK Adams	262*	Hampshire v. Nottinghamshire	at Trent Bridge
CL White	260*	Somerset v. Derbyshire	at Derby
PA Jaques	244	Worcestershire v. Essex	at Chelmsford
MW Goodwin	235	Sussex v. Yorkshire	at Arundel Castle
MJ Cosgrove	233	Glamorgan v. Derbyshire	at Derby
JC Hildreth	227*	Somerset v. Northamptonshire	at Taunton
DJG Sales	225	Northamptonshire v. Essex	at Northampton
CJL Rogers	222*	Northamptonshire v. Somerset	at Taunton
VS Solanki	222	Worcestershire v. Gloucestershire	at Bristol
GJ Muchall	219	Durham v. Kent	at Canterbury
HD Ackerman	216	Leicestershire v. Northamptonshire	at Northampton
AD Brown	215	Surrey v. Leicestershire	at The Oval
MW Goodwin	214*	Sussex v. Warwickshire	at Hove
R Clarke	214	Surrey v. Somerset	at Guildford
EC Joyce	211	Middlesex v. Warwickshire	at Edgbaston
ML Pettini	208*	Essex v. Derbyshire	at Chelmsford
BF Smith	203	Worcestershire v. Somerset	at Taunton
PA Jaques	202	Worcestershire v. Northamptonshire	at Worcester
MJ Powell	202	Glamorgan v. Essex	at Chelmsford

BEST INNINGS BOWLING (6 WICKETS OR MORE)

Mushtaq Ahmed	9/48	Sussex v. Nottinghamshire	at Trent Bridge
Z Khan	9/138	Worcestershire v. Essex	at Chelmsford
CE Shreck	8/31	Nottinghamshire v. Middlesex	at Trent Bridge
MS Mason	8/45	Worcestershire v. Gloucestershire	at Worcester
A Kumble	8/100	Surrey v. Northamptonshire	at The Oval
J Lewis	7/38	Gloucestershire v. Somerset	at Bristol
Kabir Ali	7/43	Worcestershire v. Derbyshire	at Worcester
CM Willoughby	7/44	Somerset v. Gloucestershire	at Taunton
Naved-ul-Hasan	7/62	Sussex v. Yorkshire	at Headingley
MJ Nicholson	7/62	Northamptonshire v. Gloucestershire	at Northampton
Mushtaq Ahmed	7/64	Sussex v. Hampshire	at the Rose Bowl
RDB Croft	7/67	Glamorgan v. Gloucestershire	at Cheltenham
Mushtaq Ahmed	7/74	Sussex v. Kent	at Canterbury
RJ Sillence	7/96	Worcestershire v. Somerset	at Taunton
SK Warne	7/99	Hampshire v. Middlesex	at the Rose Bowl
N Tahir	7/107	Warwickshire v. Lancashire	at Blackpool
MJ Nicholson	6/23	Northamptonshire v. Glamorgan	at Northampton
PS Jones	6/25	Derbyshire v. Glamorgan	at Cardiff
LM Daggett	6/30	Warwickshire v. Durham	at Edgbaston
BV Taylor	6/32	Hampshire v. Middlesex	at the Rose Bowl

BEST MATCH BOWLING

Mushtaq Ahmed	13/108	Sussex v. Nottinghamshire	at Trent Bridge
Mushtaq Ahmed	13/132	Sussex v. Kent	at Canterbury
RDB Croft	13/187	Glamorgan v. Gloucestershire	at Cheltenham
CE Shreck	12/129	Nottinghamshire v. Middlesex	at Trent Bridge
CD Thorp	11/97	Durham v. Hampshire	at the Rose Bowl
Naved-ul-Hasan	11/148	Sussex v. Yorkshire	at Headingley
A Kumble	11/183	Surrey v. Northamptonshire	at The Oval
Z Khan	11/260	Worcestershire v. Essex	at Chelmsford
Mushtaq Ahmed	10/37	Sussex v. Durham	at the Riverside
J Lewis	10/75	Gloucestershire v. Somerset	at Bristol

COUNTY CHAMPIONSHIP FEATURES 2006

BEST MATCH BOWLING (continued)

MS Mason	10/117	Worcestershire v. Gloucestershire	at Worcester
CE Shreck	10/131	Nottinghamshire v. Durham	at the Riverside
Z Khan	10/140	Worcestershire v. Somerset	at Worcester
ND Doshi	10/159	Surrey v. Worcestershire	at The Oval
JC Tredwell	10/165	Kent v. Sussex	at Canterbury
J Lewis	10/170	Gloucestershire v. Worcestershire	at Worcester
MS Panesar	10/177	Northamptonshire v. Worcestershire	at Northampton
Mushtaq Ahmed	10/202	Sussex v. Middlesex	at Horsham
AR Caddick	9/65	Somerset v. Worcestershire	at Worcester
Naved-ul-Hasan	9/70	Sussex v. Durham	at Riverside

HIGHEST TEAM TOTALS

717	Surrey v. Somerset	at Guildford
688 for 8d	Somerset v. Surrey	at Guildford
677 for 7d	Yorkshire v. Durham	at Headingley
669 for 5d	Surrey v. Northamptonshire	at The Oval
668 for 7d	Surrey v. Leicestershire	at The Oval
660 for 5d	Northamptonshire v. Essex	at Northampton
650 for 7d	Worcestershire v. Essex	at Chelmsford
647 for 7d	Glamorgan v. Gloucestershire	at Cheltenham
642 for 9d	Nottinghamshire v. Middlesex	at Lord's
639 for 8d	Essex v. Glamorgan	at Cardiff
639 for 8d	Surrey v. Gloucestershire	at The Oval
628	Northamptonshire v. Gloucestershire	at Northampton
625 for 8d	Somerset v. Northamptonshire	at Taunton
620	Essex v. Northamptonshire	at Northampton
618	Worcestershire v. Somerset	at Taunton
603 for 6d	Kent v. Middlesex	at Canterbury
600 for 6d	Kent v. Nottinghamshire	at Canterbury
597	Glamorgan v. Gloucestershire	at Cardiff
596 for 6d	Gloucestershire v. Northamptonshire	at Northampton
587 for 8d	Worcestershire v. Gloucestershire	at Bristol

LOWEST TEAM TOTALS

49	Middlesex v. Nottinghamshire	at Trent Bridge
56	Glamorgan v. Northamptonshire	at Northampton
67	Northamptonshire v. Worcestershire	at Worcester
80	Durham v. Sussex	at the Riverside
98	Middlesex v. Hampshire	at the Rose Bowl
103	Glamorgan v. Somerset	at Swansea
104	Hampshire v. Durham	at the Rose Bowl
110	Durham v. Sussex	at the Riverside
114	Northamptonshire v. Gloucestershire	at Bristol
114	Nottinghamshire v. Lancashire	at Trent Bridge
120	Somerset v. Worcestershire	at Worcester
120	Nottinghamshire v. Sussex	at Hove
124	Kent v. Lancashire	at Old Trafford
127	Somerset v. Derbyshire	at Taunton
130	Yorkshire v. Middlesex	at Southgate
133	Somerset v. Essex	at Southend
135	Gloucestershire v. Surrey	at The Oval
138	Worcestershire v. Somerset	at Worcester
139	Nottinghamshire v. Durham	at the Riverside
140	Warwickshire v. Sussex	at Edgbaston

COUNTY CHAMPIONSHIP FEATURES 2006

LEADING RUN SCORERS

Player	Runs	Matches
MR Ramprakash (Surrey)	2211	14
HD Ackerman (Leicestershire)	1804	14
JP Crawley (Hampshire)	1737	16
DS Lehmann (Yorkshire)	1706	15
MW Goodwin (Sussex)	1649	16
DM Benkenstein (Durham)	1427	16
A Flower (Essex)	1424	16
MJ Walker (Kent)	1419	16
MA Butcher (Surrey)	1418	16
CM Spearman (Gloucestershire)	1370	16
CJL Rogers (Northamptonshire)	1352	13
MJ Powell (Glamorgan)	1327	16
MB Loye (Lancashire)	1296	16
A McGrath (Yorkshire)	1293	15
VS Solanki (Worcestershire)	1252	16
L Klusener (Northamptonshire)	1251	16
APR Gidman (Gloucestershire)	1244	16
HJH Marshall (Gloucestershire)	1218	11
CJ Adams (Sussex)	1218	16
M van Jaarsveld (Kent)	1217	16

MOST SIXES

Player	Sixes	Matches
DJG Sales (Northamptonshire)	25	16
R Clarke (Surrey)	21	11
MR Ramprakash (Surrey)	20	14
AD Brown (Surrey)	20	15
RC Irani (Essex)	16	16
MW Goodwin (Sussex)	16	16
DS Lehmann (Yorkshire)	15	15
OD Gibson (Durham)	14	13
ML Pettini (Essex)	14	16
JL Sadler (Leicestershire)	13	14
TR Birt (Derbyshire)	12	12
PA Jaques (Worcestershire)	11	8
NM Carter (Warwickshire)	11	12
SP Fleming (Nottinghamshire)	11	13
CJ Adams (Sussex)	11	16
A Flower (Essex)	11	16
APR Gidman (Gloucestershire)	11	16
MJ Cosgrove (Glamorgan)	10	10
Azhar Mahmood (Surrey)	10	13
RJ Sillence (Worcestershire)	10	13

COUNTY CHAMPIONSHIP FEATURES 2006

MOST FOURS

Player	Fours	Matches
MR Ramprakash (Surrey)	307	14
HD Ackerman (Leicestershire)	247	14
DS Lehmann (Yorkshire)	211	15
MW Goodwin (Sussex)	207	16
CM Spearman (Gloucestershire)	207	16
JP Crawley (Hampshire)	206	16
VS Solanki (Worcestershire)	206	16
MA Butcher (Surrey)	182	16
SA Newman (Surrey)	180	16
DM Benkenstein (Durham)	179	16
A Flower (Essex)	176	16
MJ Powell (Glamorgan)	176	16
MJ Walker (Kent)	173	16
MB Loye (Lancashire)	168	16
CJL Rogers (Northamptonshire)	167	13
M van Jaarsveld (Kent)	161	16
SC Moore (Worcestershire)	160	16
ET Smith (Middlesex)	156	16
CJ Adams (Sussex)	155	16
PA Jaques (Worcestershire)	154	8

LEADING WICKET-TAKERS

Player	Wickets	Matches
Mushtaq Ahmed (Sussex)	102	15
Z Khan (Worcestershire)	78	16
CM Willoughby (Somerset)	66	15
RDB Croft (Glamorgan)	66	16
AR Caddick (Somerset)	63	16
CEW Silverwood (Middlesex)	61	15
IDK Salisbury (Surrey)	59	15
SK Warne (Hampshire)	58	13
JD Lewry (Sussex)	57	16
PS Jones (Derbyshire)	56	16
CE Shreck (Nottinghamshire)	54	11
G Keedy (Lancashire)	54	14
ND Doshi (Surrey)	50	13
G Onions (Durham)	50	15
OD Gibson (Durham)	49	13
SP Kirby (Gloucestershire)	49	15
J Lewis (Gloucestershire)	48	11
MJ Nicholson (Northamptonshire)	46	15
SCJ Broad (Leicestershire)	44	12
CW Henderson (Leicestershire)	44	15

COUNTY CHAMPIONSHIP FEATURES 2006

LEADING CATCHES (EXCLUDING WICKETKEEPERS)

Player	Catches	Matches
GA Hick (Worcestershire)	36	14
M van Jaarsveld (Kent)	36	16
CJ Adams (Sussex)	28	16
BF Smith (Worcestershire)	23	16
NV Knight (Warwickshire)	21	16
IJL Trott (Warwickshire)	20	16
Azhar Mahmood (Surrey)	18	13
MJ Di Venuto (Derbyshire)	18	13
A McGrath (Yorkshire)	18	15
DL Hemp (Glamorgan)	18	16
JHK Adams (Hampshire)	18	16
CM Spearman (Gloucestershire)	18	16
SP Fleming (Nottinghamshire)	17	13
RR Montgomerie (Sussex)	17	16
MA Butcher (Surrey)	17	16
A Flower (Essex)	17	16
DI Stevens (Kent)	17	16
MCJ Ball (Gloucestershire)	16	10
BL Hutton (Middlesex)	16	10
JER Gallian (Nottinghamshire)	16	12

LEADING DISMISSALS (WICKETKEEPERS)

Player	Dismissals	Matches
JS Foster (Essex)	68	16
SM Davies (Worcestershire)	63	16
N Pothas (Hampshire)	58	15
P Mustard (Durham)	54	16
JN Batty (Surrey)	53	16
SJ Adshead (Gloucestershire)	49	16
PA Nixon (Leicestershire)	46	15
DJ Pipe (Derbyshire)	45	12
MJ Prior (Sussex)	45	13
MA Wallace (Glamorgan)	44	16
LD Sutton (Lancashire)	41	13
TR Ambrose (Warwickshire)	34	9
CM Gazzard (Somerset)	32	13
D Alleyne (Nottinghamshire)	29	7
GL Brophy (Yorkshire)	29	10
CMW Read (Nottinghamshire)	27	9
NJ O'Brien (Kent)	27	9
MH Wessels (Northamptonshire)	24	8
BJM Scott (Middlesex)	23	8
SM Guy (Yorkshire)	20	6

COUNTY CHAMPIONSHIP FEATURES 2006

MOST HUNDREDS

Player	Hundreds	Matches
MR Ramprakash (Surrey)	8	14
DS Lehmann (Yorkshire)	6	15
JP Crawley (Hampshire)	6	16
MB Loye (Lancashire)	6	16
A Flower (Essex)	6	16
L Klusener (Northamptonshire)	6	16
MW Goodwin (Sussex)	6	16
CM Spearman (Gloucestershire)	6	16
HJH Marshall (Gloucestershire)	5	11
CL White (Somerset)	5	12
AD Brown (Surrey)	5	15
MA Butcher (Surrey)	5	16
MJ Walker (Kent)	5	16
DJ Hussey (Nottinghamshire)	5	16
NRD Compton (Middlesex)	5	16
CJL Rogers (Northamptonshire)	4	13
GA Hick (Worcestershire)	4	14
HD Ackerman (Leicestershire)	4	14
A McGrath (Yorkshire)	4	15
N Pothas (Hampshire)	4	15

MOST FIFTIES (INCLUDING HUNDREDS)

Player	Fifties	Matches
HD Ackerman (Leicestershire)	18	14
MR Ramprakash (Surrey)	16	14
A McGrath (Yorkshire)	13	15
JP Crawley (Hampshire)	13	16
MA Butcher (Surrey)	13	16
MJ Walker (Kent)	13	16
MW Goodwin (Sussex)	13	16
M van Jaarsveld (Kent)	13	16
HJH Marshall (Gloucestershire)	12	11
MB Loye (Lancashire)	12	16
APR Gidman (Gloucestershire)	11	16
PA Jaques (Worcestershire)	10	8
SP Fleming (Nottinghamshire)	10	13
CJ Adams (Sussex)	10	16
SG Law (Lancashire)	10	16
DM Benkenstein (Durham)	10	16
SA Newman (Surrey)	10	16
MJ Di Venuto (Derbyshire)	9	13
CJL Rogers (Northamptonshire)	9	13
DS Lehmann (Yorkshire)	9	15

COUNTY CHAMPIONSHIP FEATURES 2006

LEADING DUCK-MAKERS

Player	Ducks	Matches
JF Brown (Northamptonshire)	6	13
CD Thorp (Durham)	5	11
CM Willoughby (Somerset)	5	15
BM Shafayat (Northamptonshire)	5	16
HT Waters (Glamorgan)	4	5
RA White (Northamptonshire)	4	7
PL Harris (Warwickshire)	4	8
AG Botha (Derbyshire)	4	10
Kabir Ali (Worcestershire)	4	11
AJ Harris (Nottinghamshire)	4	12
NV Knight (Warwickshire)	4	16
AR Caddick (Somerset)	4	16
DL Hemp (Glamorgan)	4	16
JD Lewry (Sussex)	4	16
ET Smith (Middlesex)	4	16
L Klusener (Northamptonshire)	4	16
AD Mascarenhas (Hampshire)	4	16
SD Stubbings (Derbyshire)	4	16
J Louw (Middlesex)	4	16
LC Parker (Warwickshire)	3	3

HUNDREDS IN EACH INNINGS

Name	For	Against	Venue	Date	1st	2nd
JP Crawley	Hampshire	Notts	the Rose Bowl	7 June	106	116
CM Spearman	Glos	Northants	Northampton	8 August	140	137
MA Butcher	Surrey	Glamorgan	The Oval	30 August	151	108
GA Hick	Worcs	Essex	Worcester	30 August	104	105*
CJL Rogers	Northants	Somerset	Taunton	12 Sept	128	222*

FASTEST COUNTY CHAMPIONSHIP HUNDREDS

ML Pettini	27 balls	Essex v. Leicestershire	at Grace Road	24 September
MW Goodwin	32 balls	Sussex v. Middlesex	at Southgate	21 July
PA Jaques	64 balls	Worcs v. Surrey	at The Oval	20 May
CL White	68 balls	Somerset v. Derbyshire	at Derby	10 August

NATWEST PRO40 LEAGUE
By Mark Baldwin

18 July 2006: Division One
at Chelmsford
Essex 280 for 6 (40 overs) (ML Pettini 61, RC Irani 59, RS Bopara 58*)
Northamptonshire 171 all out (36.2 overs)
Essex (2 pts) won by 109 runs

Essex, champions of the ECB's 45-over league in 2005, began their campaign in the new-look Pro40 by doing what they know best in this type of cricket: winning. Ronnie Irani's side only lost one match on their way to the totesport League title ten months earlier, and here they thumped Northamptonshire by 109 runs. Mark Pettini and Irani himself gave Essex a sound start, putting on 95 for the first wicket, and then Ravi Bopara and James Middlebrook ensured a highly challenging total with an unbroken seventh-wicket stand of 73.

19 July 2006: Divison Two
at Worcester
Gloucestershire 245 for 6 (40 overs) (CG Taylor 93, SJ Adshead 69*)
Worcestershire 233 for 9 (40 overs) (L Vincent 56, MCJ Ball 4 for 47)
Gloucestershire (2 pts) won by 12 runs

Chris Taylor equalled his best one-day score with a 93 that included nine fours, while Stephen Adshead's 48-ball 69 not out gave Gloucestershire a total just big enough to defend as Worcestershire's reply kept losing wickets at regular intervals despite the fine start given them by Lou Vincent's 34-ball half-century.

22 July 2006: Division One
at Trent Bridge
Lancashire 95 for 2 (21 overs)
Nottinghamshire
Match abandoned (1 pt each)

23 July 2006: Division One
at Southgate
Middlesex 209 for 7 (40 overs) (JWM Dalrymple 82)
Glamorgan 213 for 7 (40 overs) (MJ Powell 81)
Glamorgan (2 pts) won by 3 wickets

The 19-year-old debutant, Michael O'Shea, came in at No. 9 with Glamorgan still needing eight runs off four balls to beat Middlesex at Southgate. His first delivery from Chad Keegan was a yorker, which he could only dig out, but he then glanced a leg-side full

Gloucestershire batsman Chris Taylor hits out during his 93 against Worcestershire at New Road.

toss to the fine leg boundary and pulled the next ball for three to bring the scores level. From the last ball, James Franklin drove a straight four and Glamorgan, for whom Michael Powell's 81 had cancelled out Jamie Dalrymple's earlier 82 for Middlesex, were home by three wickets.

Division Two
at Guildford
Kent 229 for 9 (40 overs) (DI Stevens 81)
Surrey 232 for 4 (37 overs) (JGE Benning 71, MA Butcher 52*)
Surrey (2 pts) won by 6 wickets

at Scarborough
Leicestershire 263 for 7 (40 overs) (PA Nixon 69, PW Harrison 61)
Yorkshire 96 all out (26.3 overs)
Leicestershire (2 pts) won by 167 runs

James Benning followed up a 54-ball 88 in the Twenty20 Cup against Kent by hammering the same attack for 71 from 51 balls as Surrey eased to a six-wicket victory at Guildford. A full house of 3,250 at Woodbridge Road saw Darren Stevens hit a polished 81 from 92 balls for Kent, but then 23-year-old Benning got his side off to a flier in reply before leaving the stage free for Mark Butcher to guide Surrey to their target.

Half-centuries from the veteran Paul Nixon and the 22-year-old Paul Harrison took Leicestershire to a total that proved way beyond a Yorkshire side who crumbled embarrassingly in reply to 96 all out in front of a disappointed Scarborough crowd.

25 July 2006: Division One
at Hove
Sussex 238 for 6 (40 overs) (CD Nash 82)
Warwickshire 201 all out (38.3 overs)
Sussex (2 pts) won by 37 runs

Chris Nash hit 82 from 101 balls before Robin Martin-Jenkins and Yasir Arafat plundered 43 runs from the last four overs to take Sussex to a match-winning total against Warwickshire under the Hove lights.

26 July 2006: Division Two
at Taunton
Kent 213 for 8 (40 overs)
Somerset 104 all out (25 overs) (T Henderson 5 for 28)
Kent (2 pts) won by 109 runs

Justin Langer was involved in a heated exchange with Somerset supporters on the boundary edge before falling cheaply in an unhappy last match for the county. Kent's 213 for 8 did not look anything more than a workaday total on a dry, dusting pitch, but Min Patel and James Tredwell cleaned up the Somerset tail with maximum efficiency after Tyron Henderson had cut a swathe through the top order – helped, it must be said, by a number of poor strokes.

30 July 2006: Division One
at Lord's
Middlesex 258 for 3 (40 overs) (OA Shah 122*, SB Styris 74*)
Durham 245 for 8 (40 overs)
Middlesex (2 pts) won by 13 runs

at Northampton
Northamptonshire 271 for 6 (40 overs) (RA White 77, U Afzaal 66)

James Benning and Alistair Brown walk out to open Surrey's batting at Guildford.

Nottinghamshire 248 all out (39.5 overs) (CMW Read 72, WR Smith 51, L Klusener 4 for 54)
Northamptonshire (2 pts) won by 23 runs

A magnificent 98-ball hundred by Owais Shah, who went on to finish on 122 not out and add an unbroken 145 with Scott Styris, put Middlesex's total out of reach of Durham, despite their lower order rally from 99 for 5 which eventually got the equation down to 38 from the last three overs.

In another high-scoring affair at Wantage Road, it was a Northamptonshire side beginning a new era following the departure of director of cricket Kepler Wessels who prevailed. Usman Afzaal and Rob White, who made a 78-ball 77, put on 90 for the second wicket and captain David Sales contributed a quickfire 32 to maintain this early momentum. Chris Read's 72 off just 56 balls kept Notts in the game in reply.

Division Two
at the Rose Bowl
Hampshire 156 all out (38.4 overs) (DJ Thornely 66)
Somerset 157 for 4 (39.3 overs) (MJ Wood 77*)
Somerset (2 pts) won by 6 wickets

at Cheltenham
Yorkshire 154 for 9 (40 overs) (C White 69*)
Gloucestershire 155 for 2 (23.5 overs) (HJH Marshall 62*, CG Taylor 55*)
Gloucestershire (2 pts) won by 8 wickets

at Chesterfield
Derbyshire 207 all out (39.4 overs) (ND Doshi 5 for 30)
Surrey 211 for 2 (27.2 overs) (AD Brown 106,
JGE Benning 66)
Surrey (2 pts) won by 8 wickets

Matthew Wood, dropped on 5 by Shane Warne
off Billy Taylor, went on to score 77 not out from 107
balls to guide Somerset to a six-wicket win against
Hampshire, with just three balls to spare, at the Rose
Bowl. That Hampshire got as many as 156 was down
to Dominic Thornely, who overcame a sticky start to
hit 66 and dominate a last-wicket stand of 50 with
No. 11 Taylor, who finished on 3 not out.

Gloucestershire made it two wins out of two by
outplaying Yorkshire at Cheltenham and strolling to
an eight-wicket victory on the back of a fine collective
bowling performance and then an unbroken stand
of 104 between Hamish Marshall and Chris Taylor.
Only Craig White, who carried his bat for 69, resisted
for Yorkshire.

Derbyshire were routed at Chesterfield by the
left-arm spin of Surrey's Nayan Doshi, who
followed up being the leading wicket-taker in the
Twenty20 Cup by taking 5 for 30. A thunderous
65-ball century by Alistair Brown, who dominated
an opening stand of 155 with James Benning, then
saw Surrey coast past Derbyshire's 207 with 12.4
overs to spare. Brown struck eight sixes and eight
fours in his 18th one-day hundred.

31 July 2006: Division One
at Cardiff
Glamorgan v. **Essex**
Match abandoned (1 pt each)

1 August 2006: Division One
at Edgbaston
Warwickshire 228 for 6 (40 overs) (NV Knight 95)
Middlesex 162 all out (33.1 overs)
*Warwickshire (2 pts) won by 65 runs – DL Method:
target 228 from 39 overs*

Nick Knight's 95 from 103 balls, with two sixes and
seven fours, provided the only splashes of real colour
in an otherwise turgid day-night affair at Edgbaston.
In reply to Warwickshire's 228 for 6, Middlesex lost
half their side for just 46 and were never in the hunt
thereafter.

Division Two
at Cheltenham
Leicestershire 225 for 8 (40 overs) (MCJ Ball 4 for 29)

Gloucestershire 227 for 8 (37.5 overs)
Gloucestershire (2 pts) won by 2 wickets

A tight finish in front of a big festival crowd finally
went Gloucestershire's way at Cheltenham as Jon
Lewis and Ian Fisher came together to thrash 39
from 26 balls and leave Leicestershire wondering
how they had managed to lose after restricting the
home side to 188 for 8. David Masters and Claude
Henderson had earlier thumped three sixes apiece
as 41 runs were scored in the last three overs of the
Leicestershire innings.

2 August 2006: Division Two
at Derby
Derbyshire v. **Yorkshire**
Match abandoned (1 pt each)

6 August 2006: Division One
at Southend
Middlesex 144 all out (36.4 overs) (SB Styris 50)
Essex 148 for 1 (18.3 overs) (ML Pettini 60*, D Gough 53*)
Essex (2 pts) won by 9 wickets

at Hove
Lancashire 277 for 4 (40 overs) (MJ Chilton 76*,
SG Law 59, SJ Croft 56, MB Loye 51)
Sussex 279 for 8 (39.4 overs) (CJ Adams 132*,
OP Rayner 61, SJ Croft 4 for 59)
Sussex (2 pts) won by 2 wickets

at Northampton
Northamptonshire 212 for 4 (40 overs) (U Afzaal 108*,
L Klusener 59*)
Durham 215 for 6 (38.2 overs) (DM Benkenstein 81,
GM Scott 57)
Durham (2 pts) won by 4 wickets

at Colwyn Bay
Warwickshire 120 for 6 (29 overs)
Glamorgan
Match abandoned (1 pt each)

Darren Gough's all-round skills shone through at
Southend as Essex thumped Middlesex by nine
wickets. First Gough took 3 for 16, including the
wicket of Middlesex captain Scott Styris for 50, and
then strode in at No. 3 to swing 53 not out from 49
balls and add an unbroken 117 with Mark Pettini.

Sussex's pursuit of a treble was boosted as they
won their second Pro40 match, against Lancashire at
Hove, to maintain their 100 per cent record and
move into second place in the first division table

behind Essex. Chris Adams hit three sixes off Oliver Newby, in the 29th over, during a century that took him just 77 balls. Adams was helped in a third-wicket stand of 124 by Ollie Rayner, who struck a maiden one-day fifty, and went on to finish up 132 not out as victory arrived with two balls remaining.

Durham's first win in the competition came despite a late wobble against Northamptonshire, who had earlier totalled 212 for 4 thanks to Usman Afzaal's unbeaten 108 and his unbroken fifth-wicket partnership of 100 with Lance Klusener. Dale Benkenstein hit 81 from 69 balls but he and Gary Scott fell in the same over from Chris Rogers after adding 133.

Division Two
at Canterbury
Hampshire 200 for 8 (40 overs) (N Pothas 55)
Kent 182 all out (37.3 overs) (SK Warne 4 for 14)
Hampshire (2 pts) won by 18 runs

at Cheltenham
Somerset 244 for 7 (40 overs) (MJ Wood 61,
WJ Durston 54, JC Hildreth 51)
Gloucestershire 245 for 6 (33.1 overs) (CG Taylor 72)
Gloucestershire (2 pts) won by 4 wickets

at The Oval
Surrey 275 for 7 (40 overs) (MA Butcher 88*,
JGE Benning 70)
Leicestershire 242 all out (36 overs) (DL Maddy 152,
ND Doshi 4 for 63)
Surrey (2 pts) won by 33 runs

Geraint Jones's wicketkeeping caught the eye of Alan Knott despite Kent's 18-run defeat to a Shane Warne-inspired Hampshire at Canterbury. Knott, visiting festival week from his home in Cyprus, said Jones's diving left-handed effort to remove Sean Ervine for 44 in Hampshire's 200 for 8 was, 'a catch that any keeper anywhere would be proud of'.

Second division leaders Gloucestershire stretched their 100 per cent record into a fourth match, with Chris Taylor's superb 59-ball 72 spearheading their emphatic chasing-down of Somerset's 244 for 7 in the West Country derby at Cheltenham. Taylor and Alex Gidman put on 102 in 12 overs for the fourth wicket.

Darren Maddy, meanwhile, played one of the great limited-overs innings of the season at The Oval – but still ended up on the losing side. Maddy struck a heroic 152 from a mere 110 balls, including five sixes and 18 fours, but sank to his knees in despair after being bowled by Nayan Doshi. No one else in the Leicestershire team had managed to stay with Maddy

for long, leaving the opener to wage a one-man chase of a Surrey total of 275 for 7 that had been based on fine knocks from James Benning and Mark Butcher.

9 August 2006: Division Two
at Canterbury
Kent 198 for 7 (40 overs) (DI Stevens 74)
Leicestershire 157 all out (37 overs) (PA Nixon 50)
Kent (2 pts) won by 41 runs

A sluggish pitch at Canterbury produced an uninspiring advertisement for the 40-over format. Darren Stevens played a well-judged innings of 74 at the top of the Kent order, and Geraint Jones's 34-ball 40 not out, including one straight six, was the nearest anyone came to batting with fluency. Leicestershire never looked like getting close in reply, despite Paul Nixon's 51-ball 50.

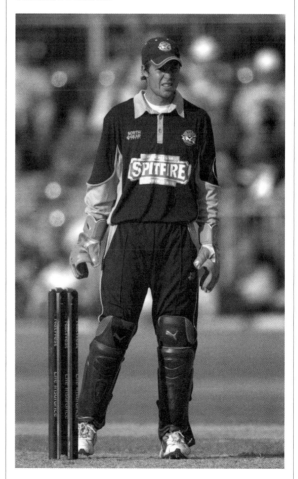

Geraint Jones caught the eye of Kent wicketkeeping great Alan Knott during the Canterbury defeat to Hampshire.

10 August 2006: Division One
at Cardiff
Durham 223 for 9 (40 overs) (DM Benkenstein 84)
Glamorgan 223 for 8 (40 overs) (JEC Franklin 68*,
MJ Powell 56)
Match tied (1 pt each)

Gary Pratt, who made his name as a substitute fielder
in the 2005 Ashes series when he ran out Australian
captain Ricky Ponting, was at it again for Durham in a
dramatic tie with Glamorgan. The Welsh county looked
home and dry in a tense finish, but then lost wickets
from the last two balls. Robert Croft was run out going
for the winning run and then Ryan Watkins was caught
by Pratt. The result was tough on James Franklin, who
remained 68 not out to guide Glamorgan all but over
the line after Dale Benkenstein's excellent 84 from 59
balls had propelled Durham to 223 for 9.

13 August 2006: Division One
at the Riverside
Durham v. **Lancashire**
Match abandoned (1 pt each)

at Edgbaston
Warwickshire 127 for 4 (28.4 overs) (MM Ali 64)
Northamptonshire 158 for 6 (27 overs)
Northamptonshire (2 pts) won by 4 wickets –
DL Method: target 158 from 28 overs

A revised Duckworth-Lewis target of 158 in 28 overs
provided an exciting finish to a weather-interrupted
match at Edgbaston. In poor light, Lance Klusener
and Rob White proved equal to the task of scoring
50 from the last six overs to take Northamptonshire
to a four-wicket victory. Moeen Ali's maiden one-day
half-century had been the highlight earlier of
Warwickshire's unfinished innings.

Division Two
at the Rose Bowl
Derbyshire 238 for 6 (40 overs) (GS Balance 73,
SD Stubbings 72)
Hampshire 241 for 9 (40 overs) (JP Crawley 100,
MA Carberry 53, GG Wagg 4 for 66)
Hampshire (2 pts) won by 1 wicket

at Taunton
Yorkshire 284 for 3 (40 overs) (A McGrath 148,
DS Lehmann 74*, C White 53)
Somerset 268 for 5 (40 overs) (NJ Edwards 65,
WJ Durston 62*, JC Hildreth 53)
Yorkshire (2 pts) won by 16 runs

Billy Taylor drove the final ball of the match from
Graham Wagg for four to clinch a thrilling one-wicket
win for Hampshire, for whom John Crawley had made
a wonderful century, but spectators left the Rose Bowl
talking more about the 73 which 16-year-old schoolboy
Gary Balance had made for Derbyshire. Balance, the
nephew of Derbyshire's director of cricket, and former
Zimbabwe captain David Houghton, did not have to
face Shane Warne because the Hampshire skipper was
laid low with a virus. But he impressed mightily
against the rest of the home attack on his debut in this
competition, figuring in a 124-run stand for the
second wicket with Steve Stubbings and hitting seven
fours in his 85-ball stay. Houghton said, 'He came over
here in April from Zimbabwe, for whom he played in
last winter's Under 19 World Cup, and has decided to
emigrate and spend the next three years qualifying for
England after winning a scholarship to attend Harrow
School. I think he's good enough to go all the way.'

A career-best one-day 148 by Anthony McGrath,
including six sixes and 11 fours, allowed Yorkshire to
see off Somerset by 16 runs in a high-scoring match at
Taunton. McGrath was joined by Darren Lehmann in
a savage late assault after Yorkshire had passed the
200 mark in the 34th over, and Somerset were always
just behind the clock despite reaching 163 for 2 at one
stage. Neil Edwards and James Hildreth batted well
for 65 and 53 respectively, while Wes Durston saw his
brilliant late 62 not out ultimately come to no avail.

14 August 2006: Division One
at Hove
Essex 269 for 4 (40 overs) (RC Irani 100, RS Bopara 54*)
Sussex 239 all out (37.5 overs) (MJ Prior 82, CD
Hopkinson 68, D Gough 4 for 39)
Essex (2 pts) won by 30 runs

Essex outmuscled Sussex under the Hove lights to
tighten their grip at the top of the first division, with
skipper Ronnie Irani in particularly strongarmed
mood at the top of the order. Irani's 100, with support
from Andy Flower and Ravi Bopara, took Essex to a
challenging 269 for 4, and it proved too hot a total for
Sussex to handle despite a fine recovery from 60 for 4
orchestrated by Matt Prior, who hit 82. Darren Gough
finished with four wickets, including that of Carl
Hopkinson who resisted late on to reach 68.

Division Two
at Leicester
Leicestershire 200 for 6 (40 overs) (HD Ackerman 86)
Worcestershire 201 for 2 (31.3 overs) (SC Moore 105*)
Worcestershire (2 pts) won by 8 wickets

Ronnie Irani led from the front with a powerful century as Essex's title challenge was stepped up at Hove.

A career-best one-day score by Stephen Moore, who finished on 105 not out, enabled Worcestershire to romp to their target of 201 and consign Leicestershire to their fourth defeat in five Pro40 matches. Hylton Ackerman hit 86 for the home side, but fine new ball bowling by Zaheer Khan and Matt Mason, whose eight overs cost only 13 runs, gave Worcestershire an early control they never relinquished.

15 August 2006: Division Two
at Derby
Gloucestershire 285 for 6 (40 overs) (APR Gidman 84, CG Taylor 50)
Derbyshire 248 for 9 (37.5 overs) (TR Birt 84)
Gloucestershire (2 pts) won by 37 runs

Alex Gidman's excellent 84 from 60 balls at Derby stretched Gloucestershire's unbeaten record in the competition to five matches and left Derbyshire still searching for a first win. Chris Taylor also scored his fourth half-century in five innings, while Gidman struck three sixes and seven fours as Gloucestershire reached an impressive 285 for 6. Travis Birt batted well in reply, scoring 84 before being fourth out, and Derbyshire were never in the hunt after that.

16 August 2006: Division One
at Old Trafford
Middlesex 244 for 6 (40 overs) (OA Shah 125*)
Lancashire 84 all out (12 overs)
Middlesex (2 pts) won by 12 runs – DL Method: target 97 from 12 overs

Middlesex chiefly had the brilliance of Owais Shah to thank for getting enough runs in the bank before the rain came at Old Trafford to insure them against Lancashire's shortened reply calculated under the Duckworth-Lewis formula. Shah's unbeaten 125 took Middlesex to a 40-over total of 244 for 6, but Lancashire lost wickets steadily as they tried to chase 97 from 12 overs.

20 August 2006: Division One
at Colchester
Nottinghamshire 252 for 9 (40 overs) (DJ Hussey 81, WR Smith 64, AJ Bichel 5 for 44)
Essex 235 for 9 (40 overs) (A Flower 57)
Nottinghamshire (2 pts) won by 17 runs

at Hove
Glamorgan 193 for 6 (33 overs)
Sussex 197 for 1 (25 overs) (MJ Prior 141, RR Montgomerie 51*)
Sussex (2 pts) won by 9 wickets – DL Method: target 197 from 33 overs

Essex, badly missing the injured Darren Gough and paying a price for omitting Grant Flower's useful slow left-arm spin on a turning pitch, were beaten for the first time after Nottinghamshire ran up a testing 252 for 9. David Hussey, kept in check only by Tim Phillips, smashed five sixes in his 54-ball 81 and Essex slid to 97 for 5 in reply before Andy Flower, with a 51-ball fifty, added 82 in ten overs with James Foster. In the end, though, they finished 17 runs short.

Sussex, meanwhile, moved into second place as Matt Prior produced a withering assault on the Glamorgan bowlers that brought him an irresistible 141 from a mere 86 balls at Hove. Glamorgan had themselves been in second position before the game began, but Prior blew them away as he smote six sixes and 20 fours while completely dominating an opening stand of 195 with Richard Montgomerie that propelled Sussex to within touching distance of their nine-wicket victory. With just two runs needed, and eight overs still remaining, Prior aimed one reverse sweep too many and was caught.

Division Two
at Worcester
Worcestershire 226 all out (39.5 overs) (L Vincent 61)
Kent 221 for 7 (40 overs) (M van Jaarsveld 73,
DI Stevens 66, Z Khan 4 for 29)
Worcestershire (2 pts) won by 5 runs

Zaheer Khan turned in a match-winning all-round performance at New Road, following his 43-ball 42 with figures of 4 for 29 as Kent failed by five runs to match Worcestershire's 226. Lou Vincent's 61 laid the foundations for the home total, but Kent seemed well placed at 184 for 2 after Darren Stevens and Martin van Jaarsveld added 97 for the second wicket and van Jaarsveld and Rob Key another 49 for the third, but 36 runs from the last four overs ultimately proved beyond the visitors.

22 August 2006: Division Two
at Headingley
Yorkshire 192 for 9 (40 overs)
Worcestershire 196 for 6 (38.1 overs) (L Vincent 72)
Worcestershire (2 pts) won by 4 wickets

New Zealand Test batsman Lou Vincent led a successful Worcestershire run chase at Headingley with 72 from 74 balls, while Vikram Solanki had an unusual reprieve during the 43 he scored in a second-wicket partnership of 91 in 15 overs with Vincent when umpire George Sharp changed his mind after initially upholding an lbw appeal. Matt Mason's 3 for 26 had earlier put Yorkshire on the back foot at 52 for 4, but the home side at least battled hard to set their opponents a decent target.

23 August 2006: Division Two
at the Rose Bowl
Hampshire v. **Surrey**
Match abandoned (1 pt each)

27 August 2006: Division One
at Edgbaston
Essex 197 for 9 (40 overs)
Warwickshire 130 all out (34.4 overs) (TJ Phillips 4 for 25)
Essex (2 pts) won by 67 runs

Zaheer Khan got wickets and runs for Worcestershire in their win against Kent.

at Trent Bridge
Nottinghamshire 131 all out (33.2 overs) (SR Patel 81)
Glamorgan 132 for 5 (28 overs) (AJ Harris 4 for 30)
Glamorgan (2 pts) won by 5 wickets

Glamorgan kept up their hopes of challenging Essex for the Pro40 title by outplaying a sorry Nottinghamshire side at Trent Bridge and winning, in the end, by five wickets with 12 overs to spare. Samit Patel was the honourable exception to a succession of rash strokes, as Notts crumbled to 38 for 5 and then 56 for 7, making a commanding 81 from 78 balls with a six and six fours as wickets fell all about him. Andrew Harris did trouble the Glamorgan top order, in turn, by snatching 4 for 30 in his eight-over spell, but James Franklin's composed, unbeaten 41 settled the issue.

Leaders Essex, meanwhile, made it four wins from six matches by playing much the best cricket on an unworthy one-day pitch at Edgbaston. Ryan ten Doeschate's 48 from 63 balls boosted a flagging Essex innings, and then Tim Phillips's slow left-arm spinners, in helpful conditions, brought him 4 for 25 as the Warwickshire reply all but ground to a halt.

Division Two
at Canterbury
Derbyshire 162 for 8 (40 overs) (SD Stubbings 57)
Kent 164 for 3 (33.5 overs) (RWT Key 58*)
Kent (2 pts) won by 7 wickets

at The Oval
Surrey 277 for 4 (40 overs) (MR Ramprakash 106*)
Yorkshire 202 for 9 (40 overs)
Surrey (2 pts) won by 75 runs

at Leicester
Hampshire 239 for 5 (40 overs) (MA Carberry 74, CC Benham 63)
Leicestershire 194 all out (36.4 overs) (JL Sadler 68, CT Tremlett 4 for 35)
Hampshire (2 pts) won by 45 runs

at Taunton
Worcestershire 268 for 6 (40 overs) (L Vincent 106)
Somerset 108 all out (28.2 overs) (VS Solanki 4 for 14)
Worcestershire (2 pts) won by 160 runs

Geraint Jones and Rob Key, coming together with Kent on 5 for 2 in reply to Derbyshire's laboured 162 for 8 on an untypical, turgid Canterbury pitch, reacted with a fluent stand of 87 which decided the game. Jones made 49 from 41 balls, including eight fours, while Key stayed to anchor the innings with 58 not out. Then Matthew Walker arrived to offer some more attractive strokes in an eventual seven-wicket win.

The prolific Mark Ramprakash, already with eight first-class hundreds to his name and a three-figure average in Surrey's Championship campaign at this stage of the season, scored his first one-day century for three years as Yorkshire were overpowered at The Oval. His 106 not out from 101 balls, counterpointed by some big hitting by the likes of Azhar Mahmood at the other end, steered Surrey to 277 for 4 from their 40 overs – a total predictably out of Yorkshire's range once they had subsided to 15 for 3.

Twenty20 Cup champions Leicestershire slumped to their fifth consecutive defeat, their batting caving in against Chris Tremlett and Dimitri Mascarenhas, after a second-wicket stand of 132 between Michael Carberry and Chris Benham had set Hampshire on the way to 239 for 5.

Somerset, their batting display simply inept, were slaughtered by 160 runs on their home turf at Taunton.

Lou Vincent led the way for Worcestershire with a superb 80-ball hundred, before Graeme Hick and Roger Sillence signed off with an unbroken stand of 76 which included the plundering of 69 from the last six overs.

28 August 2006: Division One
at the Riverside
Durham 154 for 8 (40 overs) (GR Breese 50)
Sussex 155 for 3 (26.2 overs) (RR Montgomerie 71)
Sussex (2 pts) won by 7 wickets

Fresh from their triumph in the C&G Trophy final two days earlier, Sussex crushed Durham by seven wickets at the Riverside to step up their treble chase. The Sussex seamers all bowled well on a slow pitch, while 19-year-old slow left-armer Tom Smith picked up two wickets. Then, when Sussex batted after restricting Durham to just 154 for 8, Richard Montgomerie's 71 made the target look even more inadequate than it first seemed.

29 August 2006: Division One
at Northampton
Northamptonshire 148 for 9 (36 overs) (Mushtaq Ahmed 5 for 25)
Sussex 110 (26 overs) (SP Crook 4 for 20)
Northamptonshire (2 pts) won by 33 runs – DL Method: target 144 from 34 overs

Twenty-four hours later, however, it was a different story for Sussex as Northamptonshire's seamers jumped on them at Wantage Road. At first it looked as if Sussex were calling all the shots, especially with Mushtaq Ahmed picking up 5 for 25, all claimed with googlies. But, after a brief floodlight failure had left Sussex to chase 144 from 34 overs, the visitors suddenly began to stumble – and fall. Steven Crook finished with 4 for 20 and, from 42 for 1, Sussex lost five wickets while adding only 22 more runs. There was no way back from that.

31 August 2006: Division Two
at Leicester
Leicestershire 173 for 8 (40 overs) (HD Ackerman 51)
Somerset 137 all out (36.3 overs) (NGE Walker 4 for 26)
Leicestershire (2 pts) won by 36 runs

Former Derbyshire swing bowler Nick Walker, still only 22, took one-day best figures of 4 for 26 to propel Leicestershire to a comfortable 36-run win over Somerset at Grace Road. Batting was never easy in gloomy conditions, but Hylton Ackerman impressed with 51 from 62 balls for the home side while youngsters Sam Spurway and Gareth Andrew featured in a plucky alliance worth 57 after Somerset had initially plunged to 67 for 7.

1 September 2006: Division One
at the Riverside
Nottinghamshire 186 all out (39.5 overs)
Durham 173 all out (38.5 overs) (BW Harmison 57)
Nottinghamshire (2 pts) won by 13 runs

A close-fought encounter at the Riverside ultimately went Nottinghamshire's way after Samit Patel's left-arm spin sent back both Ben Harmison and Dale Benkenstein in one match-turning over after the Durham pair had put on 80 for the fourth wicket.

3 September 2006: Division One
at Old Trafford
Lancashire v. **Northamptonshire**
Match abandoned (1 pt each)

at Edgbaston
Durham 213 all out (39.2 overs) (GM Scott 50, NM Carter 4 for 39)
Warwickshire 214 for 8 (39.1 overs) (MM Ali 57)
Warwickshire (2 pts) won by 2 wickets

A classily constructed 57 by the 19-year-old Moeen Ali, who reached his half-century in just 32 balls without ever seeming to be forcing the pace and who was joined in a third-wicket stand of 66 by Jonathan Trott, tipped the balance of a tight match Warwickshire's way at Edgbaston. Heath Streak, with an unbeaten 37, finished things off by square-driving the first ball of the final over for four, and he had been given some excellent late support by Neil Carter, who earlier had taken four wickets in Durham's 213. From 194 for 4, though, this looked a below-par final total – and so it proved.

Division Two
at Worcester
Worcestershire 223 for 9 (40 overs)
(SC Moore 53, SM Davies 52)
Derbyshire 147 all out (31.5 overs)
Worcestershire (2 pts) won by 76 runs

at Scarborough
Kent 246 for 6 (40 overs) (MJ Walker 74*, DJ Bravo 50)

A maiden one-day hundred from James Hildreth was not enough to prevent a Somerset defeat at Derby.

Yorkshire 184 all out (35.5 overs) (MJ Lumb 51, RS Ferley 4 for 33)
Kent (2 pts) won by 62 runs

An outstanding performance by Worcestershire in the field, spearheaded with the ball by Kabir Ali's 3 for 8 from 4.5 overs, ensured that a depleted Derbyshire side – which included 16-year-old debutant Daniel Redfern – were never going to get close to the home team's 223 for 9 at New Road. Stephen Moore anchored things for Worcestershire with a 70-ball fifty while Vikram Solanki produced a buccaneering 49 from 36 balls and Steven Davies hit a maiden one-day fifty.

Dwayne Bravo treated the last day of the Scarborough festival as if it was carnival time in his native Trinidad, first hitting three sixes and five fours in a 22-ball 50 and then picking up two late Yorkshire wickets to put the finishing touches to an emphatic 62-run win for Kent. Slow left-armer Rob Ferley had by then taken four wickets of his own as Yorkshire found Kent's eventual Bravo-boosted total of 246 for 6 too much for them. Matthew Walker also struck a finely paced 74 not out from 70 balls, with three sixes and four fours, as he and Bravo took 74 from the last seven overs of the innings.

4 September 2006: Division Two
at Bristol
Hampshire 226 for 6 (33 overs) (DJ Thornely 60*, CC Benham 51)
Gloucestershire 114 all out (22.5 overs)
(JTA Bruce 4 for 29)
Hampshire (2 pts) won by 90 runs – DL Method: target 205 from 28 overs

James Foster: important runs with the bat, and a flawless display behind the stumps as Essex beat Lancashire.

Missing key bowlers Jon Lewis and Ian Harvey proved too heavy a handicap for Gloucestershire, who surrendered their 100 per cent record in the competition to Hampshire under the Bristol lights. With no Lewis or Harvey to call upon, acting captain Alex Gidman was powerless to prevent Dimitri Mascarenhas and Dominic Thornely from pillaging 83 from the last six overs in an innings already reduced by rain to 33 overs' duration. James Bruce's 4 for 29 then left Gloucestershire with far too much to do with the bat, and a heavy defeat was assured long before the end.

5 September 2006: Division One
at Lord's
Nottinghamshire 228 for 7 (40 overs) (WR Smith 53)
Middlesex 204 all out (39.3 overs) (EJG Morgan 56)
Nottinghamshire (2 pts) won by 24 runs

Dropped catches let Middlesex down badly at Lord's, where defeat to Nottinghamshire meant they slipped further into relegation contention. Will Smith and Samit Patel made 53 and 46 respectively in the first half of the Notts innings, but the 53 runs that David Hussey and David Alleyne plundered from the final five overs and Middlesex's painfully slow start – just 14 came from the initial seven overs – ultimately proved decisive, despite a little gem of 56 from 35 balls from Eoin Morgan before he was needlessly run out.

6 September 2006: Division One
at Cardiff
Glamorgan 158 for 8 (36 overs) (RDB Croft 54)
Northamptonshire 165 for 2 (32.1 overs) (SD Peters 84*)
Northamptonshire (2 pts) won by 8 wickets –
DL Method: target 165 from 36 overs

A match reduced to 36 overs per side because of rain saw Northamptonshire make light work of Glamorgan under the Cardiff lights and move themselves into title contention at the expense of their Welsh hosts. Monty Panesar bowled a tight and telling six-over spell costing 24 runs, in which he also dismissed both Glamorgan's top scorer Robert Croft for an 88-ball 54 and the left-handed Dan Cherry, while Stephen Peters's fluent unbeaten 84, from 109 balls, steered Northants home in an unbroken alliance of 113 runs with Usman Afzaal.

Division Two
at Derby
Somerset 277 for 3 (40 overs) (JC Hildreth 122)
Derbyshire 278 for 3 (38.4 overs) (TR Birt 108, CR Taylor 60*, MJ Di Venuto 58)
Derbyshire (2 pts) won by 7 wickets

Travis Birt's first one-day century for Derbyshire, from 101 balls and featuring eight fours and three sixes, trumped an earlier maiden one-day hundred from Somerset's James Hildreth in a high-scoring contest at Derby. Hildreth's 122 propelled Somerset to 277 for 3, but it was not enough to stop them from going bottom of the second division table as Derbyshire leap-frogged above them as Birt added 124 with Michael Di Venuto and 95 with Chris Taylor, who finished 60 not out.

7 September 2006: Division One

at Chelmsford
Essex 233 for 7 (40 overs) (JS Foster 67)
Lancashire 202 all out (37.3 overs) (MB Loye 71, TJ Phillips 5 for 34)
Essex (2 pts) won by 31 runs

Essex overcame the loss of both openers with only five runs on the board to beat Lancashire by 31 runs in an all-round performance that kept them on course for a second successive one-day league title. Andy Bichel, promoted to No. 3, steadied the ship with Ravi Bopara and later took three wickets after a fine 67 from James Foster had boosted the Essex total to 233 for 7. Foster then turned in a superb display of wicketkeeping, including two stumpings, as slow left-armer Tim Phillips returned one-day best figures of 5 for 34 – the most important wicket of which was that of Mal Loye for 71.

9 September 2006: Division One
at Old Trafford
Warwickshire 208 for 7 (40 overs) (JO Troughton 57, NV Knight 52)
Lancashire 209 for 2 (38.4 overs) (NJ Astle 71*, MJ Chilton 67*)
Lancashire (2 pts) won by 8 wickets

Lancashire moved out of the relegation places by trouncing Warwickshire by eight wickets at Old Trafford. Half-centuries from Jim Troughton and Nick Knight helped Warwickshire beyond 200, but a fine unbroken third-wicket stand between Nathan Astle and Mark Chilton, following an aggressive 46 from Mal Loye, hastened the home side to their target.

10 September 2006: Division One
at Lord's
Middlesex 185 all out (39.4 overs) (ET Smith 87, Yasir Arafat 4 for 29)
Sussex 187 for 6 (39.3 overs) (MW Goodwin 92)
Sussex (2 pts) won by 4 wickets

Yasir Arafat put the skids under Middlesex, taking four wickets in 12 balls just when they looked capable of posting a big total following Ed Smith's accomplished 87 and Ben Hutton's 58-ball 40. But Sussex still gave their supporters some uneasy moments, even with Murray Goodwin leading what seemed to be a routine chase with an excellent 92. When Goodwin was yorked in the final over, Arafat came in to straight drive his first ball for four and wrap up the victory that Sussex needed to stay in contention for a treble.

11 September 2006: Division One
at Trent Bridge
Nottinghamshire 191 for 9 (40 overs) (DJ Hussey 73)
Warwickshire 123 for 5 (19.5 overs)
Warwickshire (2 pts) won by 5 wickets – DL Method: target 122 from 21 overs

A dramatic floodlit night of stormy weather ended with Warwickshire successfully chasing down a revised target of 122 in 21 overs. Play had been interrupted after 9.1 overs of their reply – initially because the floodlights had to be lowered while electric storms passed by the ground, and then due to heavy drizzle. A stand of 50 in seven overs between Tim Ambrose and Alex Loudon settled things, much to the frustration of David Hussey who had earlier rescued Notts from 86 for 5 with a belligerent 73 off 85 balls.

12 September 2006: Division Two
at The Oval
Surrey 278 for 6 (40 overs) (MR Ramprakash 58, SA Newman 53, JN Batty 53, JGE Benning 52)
Gloucestershire 282 for 5 (38.1 overs) (HJH Marshall 105*, IJ Harvey 91)
Gloucestershire (2 pts) won by 5 wickets

Hamish Marshall, with 105 not out, and Ian Harvey, who made a blistering 91 off just 69 balls, led a brilliant Gloucestershire pursuit of Surrey's 278 for 6 under the Oval lights. Winning, in the end, with 11 balls to spare – after Marshall and Harvey had put on 160 in 21 overs for the third wicket – meant that Gloucestershire made themselves virtually certain of promotion to the first division.

13 September 2006: Division Two
at the Rose Bowl
Hampshire 131 all out (36.1 overs) (DJ Thornely 60)
Worcestershire 72 for 3 (14.4 overs)
Worcestershire (2 pts) won by 24 runs – DL Method: target 49 from 14.4 overs

Shane Warne had a 37th birthday he will never forget as Hampshire lost out to Worcestershire in a match decided on the Duckworth-Lewis formula when heavy rain descended upon the Rose Bowl. Before the game, in warm sunshine, Warne was all decked out in robes and hat when, in front of the pavilion, he was awarded an honorary doctorate from Solent University for his services to cricket. But then, when Hampshire were put in on a tricky pitch, Warne promoted himself up to No. 3 and was hit a nasty blow attempting to hook a ball from Matt Mason, his fellow Australian. The ball wedged between his helmet peak and grille, cutting the skin above his right eye, and he was forced to leave the field for stitches as blood flowed from the wound. He later resumed his innings, as Hampshire subsided to 121 for 8 despite Dominic Thornely's best efforts, but was out to the first ball he received from Indian fast bowler Zaheer Khan. Warne then did not field at first, complaining of blurred vision in his right eye, but two overs before the rain came he bravely emerged from the pavilion again to reassume command of his team in a match situation which was already slipping away.

16 September 2006: Division Two
at Worcester
Surrey 220 for 6 (40 overs) (MA Butcher 79)
Worcestershire 207 for 9 (40 overs) (BF Smith 76, VS Solanki 54)
Surrey (2 pts) won by 13 runs

Entertainment value is always high when Ian Harvey bats, as his 91 off 69 balls against Surrey underlined.

Despite reaching 179 for 3, in pursuit of Surrey's 220 for 6, Worcestershire fell apart against the spin of Chris Schofield and Nayan Doshi, and ended up 13 runs short. Vikram Solanki and Ben Smith had rallied the innings with a stand of 89, before Smith and Graeme Hick maintained the momentum. But then Smith fell for 76 and Hick speared a catch to wide long off. Earlier Mark Butcher played a captain's innings of 79 on what was a sluggish pitch.

17 September 2006: Division One
at the Riverside
Essex 201 for 8 (40 overs) (A Flower 81)
Durham 205 for 4 (39 overs) (P Mustard 84, JP Maher 70)
Durham (2 pts) won by 6 wickets

at Trent Bridge
Sussex 110 all out (33.2 overs) (GD Clough 6 for 25)
Nottinghamshire 111 for 2 (29.3 overs) (DJ Bicknell 53*)
Nottinghamshire (2 pts) won by 8 wickets

at Old Trafford
Lancashire 256 for 7 (40 overs) (NJ Astle 78)
Glamorgan 147 all out (31.1 overs)
Lancashire (2 pts) won by 109 runs

at Northampton
Northamptonshire 198 for 6 (40 overs) (CJL Rogers 70)
Middlesex 170 all out (38 overs) (OA Shah 63, JWM Dalrymple 57, L Klusener 5 for 33)
Northamptonshire (2 pts) won by 28 runs

Gareth Clough, Jimmy Maher and Phil Mustard produced the telling performances of a day on which Essex were confirmed as Pro40 champions despite losing to Durham, and Sussex blew their chance of a treble by collapsing to emphatic defeat at Nottinghamshire.

Clough's 6 for 25 at Trent Bridge – not bad for a man almost out of contract – enabled Notts to blow away the Sussex batting, leaving Darren Bicknell to lead the straightforward process of chasing down a mere 111 to win. Meanwhile, at the Riverside, Ronnie Irani's Essex were mightily relieved to hear of their rivals' swift demise. Batting first, they had themselves struggled initially, slipping to 12 for 3 and then 39 for 4 before Andy Flower made an invaluable 81 and was well supported by both Andre Adams and James Foster in stands of 54 and 60. Yet Essex's eventual total of 201 for 8 was soon made to look hopelessly inadequate as Maher, with 70, and Mustard, mixing old-fashioned slogs with some lovely deft touches in his 84, added 152 for the Durham first wicket. Essex captain Irani said, 'It's been a strange day, and we were a bit flat out there, but we knew what had happened at Nottingham and – overall in this competition – I think we have deserved to take the silverware'.

Jimmy Anderson made a successful comeback at Old Trafford, taking 2 for 31 in his first match since 15 April to show that he was on the road to recovery following a stress fracture of the back. 'I felt really good,' said Anderson, after taking the wickets of Robert Croft and Dan Cherry. 'I've been waiting for this for a long time'. Anderson's wickets helped Lancashire to bowl out Glamorgan for 147, in reply to their own impressive 256 for 7, and thus avoid the drop to Division Two. Nathan Astle made 78 from 71 balls, and Glamorgan were condemned to a relegation play-off match against Hampshire as a result of this defeat.

Lance Klusener's all-round excellence, meanwhile, helped Northamptonshire to £22,000 of prize money for finishing second as they beat Middlesex by 28 runs at Wantage Road. There was even the rare sight at

Northampton of a pitch invasion by several hundred happy home fans after Klusener had taken his fifth wicket to finish off the Middlesex innings for 170. A fourth-wicket stand of 127 between Owais Shah and Jamie Dalrymple had threatened to take the game away from Northants, after Matt Nicholson had reduced the visitors to 17 for 3 with a wicket in each of his first three overs with the new ball. But Monty Panesar bowled Shah and caught Dalrymple off his own bowling. Klusener, who earlier had hit 45 not out in an unbroken stand of 81 with Ben Phillips, rallied Northants after a fine innings of 70 by Chris Rogers had looked like being wasted, then wrapped things up in style.

Division Two
at Canterbury
Kent 176 for 9 (40 overs)
Gloucestershire 134 all out (32.5 overs)
Kent (2 pts) won by 42 runs

at Taunton
Surrey 177 for 9 (40 overs)
Somerset 179 for 3 (20.3 overs) (AV Suppiah 51)
Somerset (2 pts) won by 7 wickets

at Headingley
Hampshire 220 for 9 (40 overs) (GA Lamb 64, DJ Thornely 60)
Yorkshire 215 all out (39.4 overs) (C White 50, GA Lamb 4 for 38)
Hampshire (2 pts) won by 5 runs

at Leicester
Derbyshire 222 for 7 (40 overs)
Leicestershire 223 for 6 (38.4 overs) (DL Maddy 74)
Leicestershire (2 pts) won by 4 wickets

There was a similar tale of anticlimax at the top of the second division, as Gloucestershire limped to the title – and the £15,000 cheque that went with it – despite losing comfortably to Kent at Canterbury. Surrey's defeat by Somerset at Taunton saved Alex Gidman's side, who always struggled to match Kent's score of 176 for 9 on a painfully turgid surface and slipped to 134 all out.

Surrey's surprise loss also let in Hampshire to claim the play-off spot and came after an uncharacteristically uncertain batting display, which produced an inadequate 177 for 9. Arul Suppiah then anchored Somerset to a seven-wicket win, following a quick-fire 37 from Matthew Wood at the top of the order. Suppiah hit 51 and put on 77 for the second wicket with James Hildreth to all but settle matters.

The news from Taunton that Somerset's remarkable victory, achieved with 19.3 overs to spare, had suddenly slashed Surrey's net run rate from 0.91 to 0.33 had the result of energising Hampshire at Headingley. Greg Lamb and Dominic Thornely had respectively hit 64 and 60 to add 103 for the fourth wicket, but Yorkshire still looked like chasing down Hampshire's 220 for 9 as Craig White's 50 kicked things off well. But Shane Warne, sitting out the match with a face injury, then came on to the field as a substitute to take a stinging catch at midwicket, run out Mark Lawson and persuade acting captain Shaun Udal to continue with Lamb's off spin. The result? Lamb finished with a one-day best 4 for 38 and Yorkshire were bowled out for 215.

A loss of momentum in their batting in the final ten overs, when only 63 runs were scored, cost Derbyshire the match at Grace Road. Leicestershire, given a fine start by Darren Maddy's 80-ball 74, made no such mistake as Paul Nixon thrashed an unbeaten 38 from 23 balls, and victory arrived with eight balls to spare.

FINAL LEAGUE TABLES

NatWest Pro40 Division One

	P	W	L	T	NR	RR	Pts
Essex	8	5	2	0	1	1.23	11
Northants	8	5	2	0	1	-0.04	11
Sussex	8	5	3	0	0	0.14	10
Nottinghamshire	8	4	3	0	1	0.07	9
Warwickshire	8	3	4	0	1	-0.17	7
Lancashire	8	2	3	0	3	0.41	7
Glamorgan	8	2	3	1	2	-0.48	7
Durham	8	2	4	1	1	-0.31	6
Middlesex	8	2	6	0	0	-0.78	4

NatWest Pro40 Division Two

	P	W	L	T	NR	RR	Pts
Gloucestershire	8	6	2	0	0	0.28	12
Worcestershire	8	6	2	0	0	1.03	12
Hampshire	8	5	2	0	1	0.55	11
Surrey	8	5	2	0	1	0.33	11
Kent	8	5	3	0	0	0.78	10
Leicestershire	8	3	5	0	0	0.11	6
Somerset	8	2	6	0	0	-0.84	4
Derbyshire	8	1	6	0	1	-0.86	3
Yorkshire	8	1	6	0	1	-1.46	3

PLAY-OFF MATCH

24 September 2006:
at the Rose Bowl
Hampshire 265 for 9 (40 overs) (CC Benham 158)
Glamorgan 114 (25.2 overs) (SM Ervine 4 for 24)
Hampshire won by 151 runs

Hampshire and Glamorgan swapped divisions as a result of this last match of the 2006 summer. And the day belonged to Chris Benham, the 23-year-old Hampshire batsman, who tore the Glamorgan attack apart with a coruscating 158. Benham flashed to his hundred in 79 balls, and then throttled back to provide an equally impressive anchor role. The next best score in the whole game was Dimitri Mascarenhas's 30, and after James Bruce and Sean Ervine had shared seven wickets to wreck Glamorgan's reply, it was left to Shane Warne to enjoy having the last word with the wickets of Robert Croft and No. 11 Dean Cosker.

Opposite: Essex emerged as inaugural Division One winners of the NatWest Pro40 League, despite losing to Durham at Chester-le-Street on the last day of the competition.

FEATURES OF NATWEST PRO40 LEAGUE 2006

HIGHEST TOTAL

285 for 6 (40 overs)	Gloucestershire v. Derbyshire at Derby	15 August

HIGHEST TOTAL BATTING SECOND

282 for 5 (38.1 overs)	Gloucestershire v. Surrey at The Oval	12 September

LOWEST TOTAL

84 (26.3 overs)	Lancashire v. Middlesex at Old Trafford	23 July

BEST INDIVIDUAL SCORE

158	CC Benham	Hampshire v. Glamorgan at the Rose Bowl	24 September

SIX WICKETS IN AN INNINGS

6/25	GD Clough	Nottinghamshire v. Sussex at Trent Bridge	17 September

TIED MATCHES

Glamorgan tied with Durham at Cardiff	10 August

WINNING BY ONE WICKET

Hampshire beat Derbyshire at the Rose Bowl	13 August

WINNING BY MORE THAN 150 RUNS

167	Leicestershire beat Yorkshire at Scarborough	23 July
160	Worcestershire beat Somerset at Taunton	27 August
151	Hampshire beat Glamorgan at the Rose Bowl	24 September

WINNING BY ONE RUN

No team won by one run

NO PLAY POSSIBLE

Glamorgan v. Essex at Cardiff	31 July
Derbyshire v. Yorkshire at Derby	2 August
Durham v. Lancashire at the Riverside	13 August
Hampshire v. Surrey at the Rose Bowl	23 August
Lancashire v. Northamptonshire at Old Trafford	3 September

NATWEST PRO40: DIVISION ONE FEATURES 2006

BATTING: LEADING AVERAGES

	M	Inns	NO	Runs	HS	Av	100	50
U Afzaal (Northants)	7	7	2	319	108*	63.80	1	1
OA Shah (Middx)	8	8	2	360	125*	60.00	2	1
A Flower (Essex)	6	5	0	244	81	48.80	-	2
DJ Hussey (Notts)	8	6	1	230	81	46.00	-	2
GM Scott (Durham)	7	7	2	216	57	43.20	-	2
DM B'kenstein (Durham)	7	7	1	255	84	42.50	-	2
MJ Powell (Glam)	7	6	0	230	81	38.33	-	2
SR Patel (Notts)	8	7	1	224	81	37.33	-	2
MJ Prior (Sussex)	8	8	0	286	141	35.75	1	1
MB Loye (Lancs)	6	6	0	208	71	34.66	-	2
JWM Dalrymple (Middx)	5	5	0	170	82	34.00	-	2
MW Goodwin (Sussex)	8	8	2	193	92	32.16	-	1
GR Breese (Durham)	7	6	1	157	50	31.40	-	1
MM Ali (Warwicks)	6	6	1	157	64	31.40	-	2
CD Nash (Sussex)	5	5	0	153	82	30.60	-	1
JS Foster (Essex)	7	5	0	147	67	29.40	-	1
WR Smith (Notts)	8	7	0	205	64	29.28	-	3
NV Knight (Warwicks)	8	8	0	233	95	29.12	-	2
RC Irani (Essex)	7	7	0	198	100	28.28	1	1
ML Pettini (Essex)	7	7	1	168	61	28.00	-	2
P Mustard (Durham)	7	7	1	165	84	27.50	-	1
RR M'gomerie (Sussex)	7	7	1	155	71	25.83	-	2
CD Hopkinson (Sussex)	8	7	1	154	68	25.66	-	1

Qualification: averages 25 or above (minimum of five innings)

LEADING RUN SCORERS – TOP 20

Player	Runs	Inns
OA Shah (Middx)	360	8
U Afzaal (Northants)	319	7
MJ Prior (Sussex)	286	8
MJ Chilton (Lancs)	260	6
DM Benkenstein (Durham)	255	7
A Flower (Essex)	244	5
NV Knight (Warwicks)	233	8
MJ Powell (Glam)	230	7
DJ Hussey (Notts)	230	6
NJ Astle (Lancs)	228	6
SR Patel (Notts)	224	7
GM Scott (Durham)	216	7
MB Loye (Lancs)	208	6
WR Smith (Notts)	205	7
RC Irani (Essex)	198	7
MW Goodwin (Sussex)	193	8
CJ Adams (Sussex)	183	5
SB Styris (Middx)	182	6
JWM Dalrymple (Middx)	170	5
ML Pettini (Essex)	168	7

BOWLING: LEADING AVERAGES

Bowling	O	M	Runs	W	Av	Best	4i	Econ
D Gough (Essex)	17.3	0	67	7	9.57	4-39	1	3.82
GD Clough (Notts)	18	1	99	9	11.00	6-25	1	5.50
AJ Bichel (Essex)	44.3	2	211	17	12.41	5-44	1	4.74
L Klusener (Northants)	43.3	1	231	16	14.43	5-33	2	5.31
TJ Phillips (Essex)	43.4	2	175	12	14.58	5-34	2	4.00
MS Panesar (Northants)	17	0	76	5	15.20	2-24	-	4.47
Mushtaq Ahmed (Sussex)	27	0	111	7	15.85	5-25	1	4.11
AJ Harris (Notts)	53	5	220	12	18.33	4-30	1	4.15
M Kartik (Lancs)	24	0	110	6	18.33	3-24	-	4.58
DG Cork (Lancs)	26	2	129	7	18.42	3-24	-	4.96
CT Peploe (Middx)	31	0	133	7	19.00	3-35	-	4.29
PL Harris (Notts)	54	2	232	12	19.33	3-33	-	4.29
KW Hogg (Lancs)	29	4	117	6	19.50	2-20	-	4.03
RJ Kirtley (Sussex)	54.4	5	254	13	19.53	3-27	-	4.64
DS Harrison (Glam)	36	6	151	7	21.57	2-23	-	4.19
NM Carter (Warwicks)	49	2	260	12	21.66	4-39	1	5.30
SB Styris (Middx)	23	0	132	6	22.00	3-24	-	5.73
SJ Croft (Lancs)	18.1	0	145	6	24.16	4-59	1	7.98
AP Davies (Glam)	34	4	173	7	24.71	3-27	-	5.08
Yasir Arafat (Sussex)	49.3	2	248	10	24.80	4-29	1	5.01
SR Patel (Notts)	26.5	0	177	7	25.28	3-40	-	6.59
HH Streak (Warwicks)	39.2	2	206	8	25.75	3-13	-	5.23
JF Brown (Northants)	42	0	181	7	25.85	2-32	-	4.30
GR Breese (Durham)	46	1	239	9	26.55	3-42	-	5.19
J Louw (Middx)	52.3	2	294	11	26.72	2-19	-	5.60
MA Ealham (Notts)	29	2	135	5	27.00	2-26	-	4.65
JWM Dalrymple (Middx)	37.3	2	199	7	28.42	3-61	-	5.30
SP Crook (Northants)	33	1	144	5	28.80	4-29	1	4.36
RJ Sidebottom (Notts)	36.5	3	146	5	29.20	2-15	-	3.96
RS Bopara (Essex)	36.2	1	214	7	30.57	3-28	-	5.88
GP Swann (Notts)	23.2	0	153	5	30.60	2-56	-	6.55
CB Keegan (Middx)	25	1	155	5	31.00	2-25	-	6.20
RDB Croft (Glam)	40.2	1	204	6	34.00	2-19	-	5.05
DA Cosker (Glam)	42	4	209	6	34.83	3-37	-	4.97
CEW Silverwood (Middx)	36	1	183	5	36.60	2-36	-	5.08
BJ Phillips (Northants)	39	2	184	5	36.80	3-52	-	4.71
MH Yardy (Sussex)	28	2	187	5	37.40	3-35	-	6.67

Qualification: averages 38 or less (minimum of five wickets)

LEADING WICKET-TAKERS – TOP 20

Player	W	O
AJ Bichel (Essex)	17	44.3
L Klusener (Northants)	16	43.4
RJ Kirtley (Sussex)	13	54.4
TJ Phillips (Essex)	12	43.4
AJ Harris (Notts)	12	54
NM Carter (Warwicks)	12	49
PL Harris (Warwicks)	12	54
J Louw (Middx)	11	52.3
Yasir Arafat (Sussex)	10	49.3
GD Clough (Notts)	9	18
GR Breese (Durham)	9	46
HH Streak (Warwicks)	8	39.2
D Gough (Essex)	7	17.3
Mushtaq Ahmed (Sussex)	7	27
DG Cork (Lancs)	7	26
AP Davies (Glam)	7	34
DS Harrison (Glam)	7	36
JWM Dalrymple (Middx)	7	37.3
CT Peploe (Middx)	7	31
JF Brown (Northants)	7	42

FIELDING: LEADING DISMISSALS – TOP 20

TR Ambrose (Warwicks) – 13 (10ct, 3st); JS Foster (Essex) – 11 (7ct, 4st); LD Sutton (Lancs) – 9 (7ct, 2st); D Alleyne (Notts) – 8 (7ct, 1st); P Mustard (Durham) – 8 (6ct, 2st); IJL Trott (Warwicks) – 8 (8ct); BM Shafayat (Northants) – 7 (6ct, 1st); MJ Prior (Sussex) – 7 (5ct, 2st); CJL Rogers (Northants) – 7 (7ct); OA Shah (Middx) – 7 (7ct); DJ Hussey (Notts) – 7 (7ct); MA Wallace (Glam)– 6 (5ct, 1st); SP Fleming (Notts) – 6 (6ct); BJM Scott (Middx) – 5 (3ct, 2st); SJ Croft (Lancs) – 5 (5ct); DJG Sales (Northants) – 5 (5ct); DA Cosker (Glam) – 5 (5ct); ML Pettini (Essex) – 5 (5 ct); JP Maher (Durham) – 5 (5ct); NRD Compton (Middx) – 5 (5ct)

NATWEST PRO40: DIVISION TWO FEATURES 2006

BATTING: LEADING AVERAGES

	M	Inns	NO	Runs	HS	Av	100	50
DJ Thornely (Hants)	7	7	2	309	66	61.80	–	4
MR Ramprakash (Surrey)	7	7	2	284	106*	56.80	1	1
CG Taylor (Glos)	8	8	1	354	93	50.57	–	4
L Vincent (Worcs)	7	7	0	344	106	49.14	1	3
HJH Marshall (Glos)	8	8	2	266	105*	44.33	1	1
BF Smith (Worcs)	7	7	2	215	76	43.00	–	1
JC Hildreth (Somerset)	8	8	0	326	122	40.75	1	2
DL Maddy (Leics)	8	8	0	324	152	40.50	1	1
C White (Yorks)	6	6	1	201	69*	40.20	–	3
GO Jones (Kent)	7	7	2	197	49	39.40	–	–
IJ Harvey (Glos)	5	5	0	191	91	38.20	–	1
SD Stubbings (Derbys)	7	7	0	254	72	36.28	–	2
TR Birt (Derbys)	6	6	0	211	108	35.16	1	1
MJ Wood (Yorks)	8	8	1	242	77*	34.57	–	2
MJ Walker (Kent)	8	8	2	194	74*	32.33	–	1
A McGrath (Yorks)	6	6	0	193	148	32.16	1	–
AD Brown (Surrey)	7	7	0	213	106	30.42	1	–
APR Gidman (Glos)	8	7	0	212	84	30.28	–	1
SC Moore (Worcs)	8	8	1	211	105*	30.14	1	1
VS Solanki (Worcs)	8	8	0	240	54	30.00	–	1
DI Stevens (Kent)	8	8	0	240	81	30.00	–	3
M van Jaarsveld (Kent)	8	8	0	238	73	29.75	–	1
AD Mascarenhas (Hants)	7	7	2	146	47*	29.20	–	–
AW Gale (Yorks)	6	5	0	146	46	29.20	–	–
JP Crawley (Hants)	6	6	0	173	100	28.83	1	–
RWT Key (Kent)	8	8	1	196	58*	28.00	–	1
PA Nixon (Leics)	8	8	1	191	69	27.28	–	2
HD Ackerman (Leics)	7	7	0	191	86	27.28	–	2
Hassan Adnan (Derbys)	6	5	0	135	36	27.00	–	–
DJ Bravo (Kent)	7	6	1	129	50	25.80	–	1
GA Hick (Worcs)	7	7	2	126	44*	25.20	–	–

Qualification: averages 25 or above (minimum of five innings)

LEADING RUN SCORERS – TOP 20

Player	Runs	Inns
CG Taylor (Glos)	354	8
L Vincent (Worcs)	344	7
JC Hildreth (Somerset)	326	8
DL Maddy (Leics)	324	8
DJ Thornely (Hants)	309	7
MA Butcher (Surrey)	299	7
MR Ramprakash (Surrey)	284	7
HJH Marshall (Glos)	266	8
JGE Benning (Surrey)	259	4
SD Stubbings (Derbys)	254	7
MJ Wood (Somerset)	242	8
VS Solanki (Worcs)	240	8
DI Stevens (Kent)	240	8
M van Jaarsveld (Kent)	238	8
BF Smith (Worcs)	215	7
AD Brown (Surrey)	213	7
APR Gidman (Glos)	212	7
TR Birt (Derbys)	211	6
SC Moore (Worcs)	211	8
C White (Yorks)	201	6

BOWLING: LEADING AVERAGES

Bowling	O	M	Runs	W	Av	Best	4i	Econ
SK Warne (Hants)	17.3	2	55	6	9.16	4-14	1	3.14
RS Ferley (Kent)	18.5	0	92	9	10.22	4-33	1	4.88
JTA Bruce (Hants)	24	4	99	8	12.37	4-29	1	4.12
Z Khan (Worcs)	47.1	5	199	16	12.43	4-29	1	4.21
NJ Dexter (Kent)	19	0	92	7	13.14	3-17	–	4.84
VS Solanki (Worcs)	16.2	0	96	6	16.00	4-14	1	5.87
CT Tremlett (Hants)	21.4	1	116	7	16.57	4-35	1	5.35
ND Doshi (Surrey)	52.4	0	331	19	17.42	5-30	2	6.28
NGE Walker (Leics)	25	1	122	7	17.42	4-26	1	4.88
Kabir Ali (Worcs)	33.5	2	188	10	18.80	3-8	–	5.55
RAG Cummins (Leics)	22	3	113	6	18.83	2-20	–	5.13
APR Gidman (Glos)	31	1	170	8	21.25	3-21	–	5.48
DD Masters (Leics)	34	4	154	7	22.00	2-20	–	4.52
MCJ Ball (Glos)	51	1	248	11	22.54	4-29	2	4.86
GA Lamb (Hants)	19.4	1	114	5	22.80	4-38	1	5.79
DJ Bravo (Kent)	37.5	1	183	8	22.87	2-33	–	4.83
T Henderson (Kent)	53	7	231	10	23.10	5-28	1	4.35
SD Udal (Hants)	39	0	191	8	23.87	2-32	–	4.89
CP Schofield (Surrey)	25	0	144	6	24.00	3-34	–	5.76
CW Henderson (Leics)	56	1	245	10	24.50	4-36	–	4.37
JN Snape (Leics)	37.3	0	174	7	24.85	3-28	–	4.64
AV Suppiah (Somerset)	35.1	0	200	8	25.00	3-43	–	5.68
MS Mason (Worcs)	42	5	150	6	25.00	3-26	–	3.57
JC Tredwell (Kent)	53	1	254	10	25.40	3-35	–	4.79
WJ Durston (Somerset)	35	0	205	8	25.62	3-44	–	5.85
SM Ervine (Hants)	24.5	0	155	6	25.83	3-22	–	6.24
GJ Batty (Worcs)	62	2	275	10	27.50	3-17	–	4.43
AD Mascarenhas (Hants)	35.4	5	171	6	28.50	3-41	–	4.79
IJ Harvey (Glos)	33	3	171	6	28.50	2-26	–	5.18
SJ Cook (Kent)	34	2	144	5	28.80	2-39	–	4.23
ID Fisher (Glos)	51	1	231	7	33.00	3-41	–	4.52
CM Willoughby (Somerset)	60	5	331	10	33.10	2-26	–	5.51
GJ Kruis (Yorks)	38	2	208	6	34.66	2-38	–	5.47
RW Price (Worcs)	59	2	243	7	34.71	2-20	–	4.11
A Khan (Kent)	31.5	3	177	5	35.40	2-25	–	5.56
JMM Averis (Glos)	61	4	393	11	35.72	3-58	–	6.44
JW Dernbach (Surrey)	20	1	180	5	36.00	3-44	–	9.00
AR Caddick (Somerset)	52	4	294	8	36.75	2-37	–	5.65
M Akram (Surrey)	30.3	1	184	5	36.80	3-37	–	6.03
SA Patterson (Yorks)	50	3	297	8	37.12	3-59	–	5.94
SP Kirby (Glos)	27	1	187	5	37.40	3-56	–	6.92
GG Wagg (Derbys)	40	0	300	8	37.50	4-66	1	7.50

Qualification: averages 38 or less (minimum of five wickets)

LEADING WICKET-TAKERS – TOP 20

Player	W	O
ND Doshi (Surrey)	19	52.4
Z Khan (Worcs)	16	47.1
MCJ Ball (Glos)	11	51
JMM Averis (Glos)	11	61
Kabir Ali (Worcs)	10	33.5
T Henderson (Kent)	10	53
GJ Batty (Worcs)	10	62
CW Henderson (Leics)	10	56
JC Tredwell (Kent)	10	53
CM Willoughby (Somerset)	10	60
RS Ferley (Kent)	9	18.5
JTA Bruce (Hants)	8	24
GG Wagg (Derbys)	8	40
SD Udal (Hants)	8	39
AR Caddick (Somerset)	8	52
DJ Bravo (Kent)	8	37.5
SA Patterson (Yorks)	8	50
WJ Durston (Somerset)	8	35
AV Suppiah (Somerset)	8	35.1
APR Gidman (Glos)	8	31

FIELDING: LEADING DISMISSALS – TOP 20

GO Jones (Kent) – 16 (13ct, 3st); SM Davies (Worcs) – 12 (9ct, 3st); SJ Adshead (Glos) – 12 (7ct, 5st); PA Nixon (Leics) – 10 (7ct, 3st); BF Smith (Worcs) – 9 (9ct); MCJ Ball (Glos) – 7 (7ct); SHP Spurway (Somerset) – 6 (4ct, 2st); JN Snape (Leics) – 6 (6ct); M van Jaarsveld (Kent) – 6 (6ct); HJH Marshall (Glos) – 6 (6ct); SM Guy (Yorks) – 5 (3ct, 2st); JN Batty (Surrey) – 5 (2ct, 3st); TJ Murtagh (Surrey) – 5 (5ct); JC Tredwell (Kent) – 5 (5ct); CM Gazzard (Somerset) – 4 (4ct); GL Brophy (Yorks) – 4 (3ct, 1st); N Pothas (Hants) – 4 (4ct); MGN Windows (Glos) – 4 (4ct); JW Dernbach (Surrey) – 4 (4ct); CR Taylor (Derbys) – 4 (4ct)

NATWEST PRO40 LEAGUE COUNTY COLOURS: DIVISION ONE

For full county details, please refer to the form charts at the back of the book.

NATWEST PRO40 LEAGUE COUNTY COLOURS: DIVISION TWO

DERBYSHIRE CCC
League nickname:
DERBYSHIRE SCORPIONS

GLOUCESTERSHIRE CCC
League nickname:
GLOUCESTERSHIRE GLADIATORS

HAMPSHIRE CCC
League nickname:
HAMPSHIRE HAWKS

KENT CCC
League nickname:
KENT SPITFIRES

LEICESTERSHIRE CCC
League nickname:
LEICESTERSHIRE FOXES

SOMERSET CCC
League nickname:
SOMERSET SABRES

SURREY CCC
League nickname:
SURREY LIONS

WORCESTERSHIRE CCC
League nickname:
WORCESTERSHIRE ROYALS

YORKSHIRE CCC
League nickname:
YORKSHIRE PHOENIX

For full county details, please refer to the form charts at the back of the book.

TWENTY20 CUP
By Mark Baldwin

The fourth year of Twenty20 Cup cricket saw the short-form of the county game bring in yet more admirers and yet more supporters. It also had a Finals Day, at Trent Bridge on 12 August, packed with the thrills, spills and high drama that have quickly come to be associated with Twenty20. Sid the Shark, winning the traditional mascots race to grab a share of the glory of the day for Sussex, was never really troubled as he romped to the finishing line. Leicestershire, by contrast, had to battle every inch of the way … and, even in the last stride, their ultimate victory was accompanied by a certain controversy.

The record books show that Leicestershire beat Nottinghamshire by four runs to become the first county to win the Twenty20 Cup twice. It is not even half the story. One of the most intense, full-on games of cricket that can have been played – in any format – ended with both teams ignoring heavy drizzle to produce a pulsating finish under the lights at a packed Trent Bridge.

Leicestershire, who had seen off Essex's flawed challenge by 23 runs in the first semi-final earlier in the day, were spearheaded by Darren Maddy and Jim Allenby in their charge to 177 for 2. Nottinghamshire, fresh from thrashing a sadly off-key Surrey by 37 runs in the second semi-final, set about the chase with purpose and, when Stephen Fleming and David Hussey were adding 57 for the second wicket in double quick time, they looked favourites.

But, whereas Maddy had earlier batted right through the innings to hit a brilliantly-paced 86 not out – with six fours and four sixes – and the unheralded Allenby had played with equal skill and intelligence to score 64 in a stand of 133 from just 14 overs, neither Fleming nor Hussey could see their side all the way to the finishing post. Fleming fell for 53 to an excellent diving catch at deep square leg by Ryan Cummins off the canny Jeremy Snape, Leicestershire's captain, and in the next over Hussey holed out to extra cover off the superb Stuart Broad – recalled for his fourth and final over at just the right time by Snape.

Yet, in a twist that had the crowd hardly daring to take their eyes off the unfolding drama, Samit Patel and Mark Ealham somehow made an equation that had stood at 52 from the last four overs seem possible. Their clean and – in the worsening conditions – astonishing hitting left Notts requiring 18 from the last six balls. But Allenby, bowling the final over with his medium pace, allowed just seven runs from the first five balls and that seemed to be that.

Yet, when he let slip a high full toss, Will Smith – who in the semi-final had leapt to claim one of the most breathtaking boundary-edge catches ever seen – clubbed it over the long-on boundary for six. The Notts players, thinking that the delivery would also be called a no-ball, suddenly believed that an extra ball would now give them an unexpected chance of victory. With two penalty runs for the no-ball to be added on, Smith's magnificent blow would have seen eight runs being entered into the scorebook … and therefore leave only three more runs to be scored from the extra ball now required to be bowled. The umpires, however, ruled that the ball had not been 'dangerous and unfair' – and Leicestershire's players were able to continue their celebrations.

Television replays suggested that Notts had every right to be aggrieved. And yet it was hard, too, not to feel that Leicestershire fully deserved their second Twenty20 Cup victory in the four years of the competition. Maddy, in particular, was superb, adding enthusiastic fielding to his all-round influence. The first batsman to reach 1,000 runs in the Twenty20 Cup, he is not known for nothing in his home county as 'Mr Twenty20'.

On the concept of Finals Day itself, as well as the expertise of Leicestershire's approach, Maddy said, 'This is the most exciting day of the season. Even though many people still look upon us as underdogs, I was confident we would win the Cup again. Twenty20 seems to suit the way we play and a significant reason for our success has been our good game plans.'

Along with the mascots' race, part of the traditional non-cricket entertainment of Finals Day has been an appearance of a female pop group following the second semi-final. This year, it was Sugababes – in succession to Atomic Kitten (2003), Liberty X (2004) and Girls Aloud (2005).

Yet, overall, the first four years of the Twenty20 Cup revolution has proved beyond doubt that it is the format of the cricket, and not the extra-curricular activities, which has drawn in the crowds. For the second year running, indeed, the whole Twenty20 Cup competition attracted an aggregate attendance of around the half-million mark.

There was even a fascinating sub-plot early on Finals Day, meanwhile, with the Essex v. Leicestershire semi-final throwing up a 'confrontation' between English fast bowlers young and old in Stuart Broad and Darren Gough. It was a contest that the 20-year-old Broad – then yet to be selected by his country – won hands down, although the real element of confrontation came between Leicestershire's tyro and the veteran Essex captain Ronnie Irani.

Irani made 0, caught behind off Broad as he fenced outside off stump, but he could easily have been lbw in the previous over and was in just long enough to get a good working over from the bowler soon to be chosen – alongside Gough, ironically – in England's NatWest Series squad against Pakistan.

Broad went on to be one of the stars of the day, and to pick up a £1,500 prize for being the most economical bowler in the whole tournament, and Irani said, 'He's a real goer. He nipped the ball both ways off the seam a bit like Glenn McGrath.'

North Division

27 June 2006
at Headingley
Durham 121 for 8 (20 overs)
Yorkshire 123 for 2 (16.2 overs)
Yorkshire (2 pts) won by 8 wickets

at Leicester
Leicestershire 137 for 6 (20 overs)
Nottinghamshire 123 for 8 (20 overs)
Leicestershire (2 pts) won by 14 runs

at Derby
Lancashire 114 all out (19.1 overs)
Derbyshire 118 for 5 (19.3 overs) (SD Stubbings 51)
Derbyshire (2 pts) won by 5 wickets

28 June 2006
at Trent Bridge
Nottinghamshire 175 for 7 (20 overs)
Durham 123 all out (19.1 overs)
Nottinghamshire (2 pts) won by 52 runs

29 June 2006
at Leicester
Leicestershire 160 for 6 (20 overs)
Lancashire 164 for 5 (20 overs) (SG Law 58)
Lancashire (2 pts) won by 5 wickets

30 June 2006
at Trent Bridge
Nottinghamshire 195 for 4 (20 overs) (DJ Hussey 58)
Yorkshire 174 for 6 (20 overs)
Nottinghamshire (2 pts) won by 21 runs

at the Riverside
Lancashire 135 for 9 (20 overs)
Durham 139 for 4 (19.2 overs) (DM Benkenstein 56*)
Durham (2 pts) won by 6 wickets

at Derby
Leicestershire 204 for 6 (20 overs) (DL Maddy 50)
Derbyshire 118 all out (17 overs)
Leicestershire (2 pts) won by 86 runs

3 July 2006
at Old Trafford
Lancashire 173 for 5 (20 overs)
Derbyshire 125 all out (18.5 overs) (SJ Marshall 4 for 20)
Lancashire (2 pts) won by 48 runs

at the Riverside
Yorkshire 149 for 6 (20 overs)
Durham 98 all out (17.2 overs)
Yorkshire (2 pts) won by 51 runs

4 July 2006
at Trent Bridge
Leicestershire 136 for 8 (20 overs)
Nottinghamshire 137 for 5 (18.1 overs)
Nottinghamshire (2 pts) won by 5 wickets

5 July 2006
at Headingley
Yorkshire 159 for 6 (20 overs) (AW Gale 50)
Nottinghamshire 160 for 3 (19.1 overs)
(SP Fleming 60)
Nottinghamshire (2 pts) won by 7 wickets

at Leicester
Leicestershire 161 for 6 (20 overs)
(HD Ackerman 53)
Derbyshire 143 for 6 (20 overs) (SD Stubbings 57)
Leicestershire (2 pts) won by 18 runs

6 July 2006
at Old Trafford
Lancashire 117 for 8 (20 overs)
(ML Lewis 4 for 19)
Durham 118 for 5 (20 overs) (JP Maher 51*)
Durham (2 pts) won by 5 wickets

7 July 2006
at Old Trafford
Yorkshire 156 for 7 (20 overs) (A McGrath 52)
Lancashire 141 for 9 (20 overs)
Yorkshire (2 pts) won by 15 runs

at Leicester
Leicestershire 144 for 5 (20 overs)
(HD Ackerman 60)
Durham 112 all out (19.4 overs)
Leicestershire (2 pts) won by 32 runs

at Derby
Derbyshire 128 all out (19.2 overs)
Nottinghamshire 132 for 3 (19.2 overs)
Nottinghamshire (2 pts) won by 7 wickets

8 July 2006
at Headingley
Leicestershire 155 for 8 (20 overs) (PA Nixon 52)
Yorkshire 134 all out (19.3 overs) (MJ Lumb 66)
Leicestershire (2 pts) won by 21 runs

at the Riverside
Derbyshire 172 for 4 (20 overs) (Hassan Adnan 54*)
Durham 170 for 8 (20 overs) (P Mustard 67*)
Derbyshire (2 pts) won by 2 runs

9 July 2006
at Old Trafford
Nottinghamshire 91 all out (19 overs) (DG Cork 4 for 16)
Lancashire 93 for 3 (15.2 overs) (SG Law 62*)
Lancashire (2 pts) won by 7 wickets

10 July 2006
at Derby
Yorkshire 210 for 3 (20 overs) (A McGrath 58*,
GL Brophy 57, C White 54)
Derbyshire 34 for 0 (2.1 overs)
Match abandoned (1 pt each)

11 July 2006
at Headingley
Lancashire 131 for 9 (20 overs)
Yorkshire 137 for 3 (13.4 overs) (MJ Lumb 84*)
Yorkshire (2 pts) won by 7 wickets

at Trent Bridge
Derbyshire 141 for 6 (20 overs) (MJ Di Venuto 53)
Nottinghamshire 142 for 1 (15.5 overs)
(SP Fleming 64*, SR Patel 53*)
Nottinghamshire (2 pts) won by 9 wickets

at the Riverside
Leicestershire 183 for 7 (20 overs) (HD Ackerman 87)
Durham 104 for 8 (20 overs) (JP Maher 55*)
Leicestershire (2 pts) won by 79 runs

South Division

27 June 2006
at Beckenham
Kent 186 for 6 (20 overs)
Essex 147 all out (18.4 overs) (RC Irani 61)
Kent (2 pts) won by 39 runs

at Lord's
Surrey 218 for 7 (20 overs) (AD Brown 83,
JGE Benning 57)
Middlesex 178 for 7 (20 overs) (EJG Morgan 66,
SB Styris 56)
Surrey (2 pts) won by 40 runs

at Arundel Castle
Hampshire 152 for 6 (20 overs) (GA Lamb 55*,
Mushtaq Ahmed 4 for 30)
Sussex 153 for 6 (19.1 overs)
Sussex (2 pts) won by 4 wickets

28 June 2006
at The Oval
Surrey 198 for 6 (20 overs) (JGE Benning 88,
MR Ramprakash 58)
Kent 91 all out (11.4 overs)
Surrey (2 pts) won by 107 runs

at Chelmsford
Essex 196 for 6 (20 overs)
Sussex 109 all out (13.3 overs) (AJ Bichel 4 for 23)
Essex (2 pts) won by 87 runs

29 June 2006
at the Rose Bowl
Hampshire 225 for 2 (20 overs) (MA Carberry 90,
MST Stokes 62, DJ Thornely 50*)
Middlesex 166 for 9 (20 overs)
Hampshire (2 pts) won by 59 runs

30 June 2006
at Lord's
Kent 182 for 5 (20 overs) (DI Stevens 69)
Middlesex 165 for 7 (20 overs) (SB Styris 54,
MM Patel 4 for 26)
Kent (2 pts) won by 17 runs

at Chelmsford
Hampshire 158 for 7 (20 overs) (CC Benham 59)
Essex 162 for 3 (16.4 overs) (RC Irani 81*)
Essex (2 pts) won by 7 wickets

at Hove
Surrey 123 all out (19.5 overs) (Yasir Arafat 4 for 21)
Sussex 126 for 5 (18.2 overs)
Sussex (2 pts) won by 5 wickets

1 July 2006
at The Oval
Surrey 188 for 7 (20 overs) (JN Batty 59,
MR Ramprakash 54)

Essex 189 for 6 (18.2 overs) (RS Bopara 83)
Essex (2 pts) won by 4 wickets

2 July 2006
at Richmond
Middlesex 108 all out (18 overs)
Sussex 111 for 1 (12.4 overs) (MW Goodwin 67*)
Sussex (2 pts) won by 9 wickets

at Beckenham
Kent 134 for 9 (20 overs) (T Henderson 63,
DJ Thornely 4 for 22)
Hampshire 119 all out (19.5 overs)
Kent (2 pts) won by 15 runs

3 July 2006
at the Rose Bowl
Hampshire 151 for 4 (20 overs) (MA Carberry 53)
Essex 115 all out (16.2 overs)
Hampshire (2 pts) won by 36 runs

4 July 2006
at Beckenham
Kent 178 for 5 (20 overs) (MJ Walker 58*)
Middlesex 126 all out (17.4 overs) (JC Tredwell 4 for 21)
Kent (2 pts) won by 52 runs

at The Oval
Surrey 131 all out (19.5 overs) (Yasir Arafat 4 for 31)
Sussex 135 for 5 (18.1 overs) (MH Yardy 68*)
Sussex (2 pts) won by 5 wickets

6 July 2006
at the Rose Bowl
Surrey 141 for 5 (20 overs)
(Azhar Mahmood 65*)
Hampshire 131 all out (19.1 overs) (ND Doshi 4 for 30)
Surrey (2 pts) won by 10 runs

at Chelmsford
Middlesex 177 for 6 (20 overs)
Essex 178 for 7 (19.2 overs)
(WI Jefferson 51)
Essex (2 pts) won by 3 wickets

at Hove
Kent 155 for 7 (20 overs)
Sussex 145 all out (18.5 overs) (CJ Adams 63)
Kent (2 pts) won by 10 runs

7 July 2006
at The Oval
Middlesex 115 all out (18.4 overs)
(ND Doshi 4 for 22)
Surrey 116 for 3 (13.1 overs)
(JGE Benning 61*)
Surrey (2 pts) won by 7 wickets

at the Rose Bowl
Hampshire 112 for 5 (20 overs)
Sussex 97 for 9 (20 overs)
(AD Mascarenhas 4 for 23)
Hampshire (2 pts) won by 15 runs

at Chelmsford
Kent 157 all out (20 overs)
Essex 160 for 5 (18.4 overs)
(RC Irani 53)
Essex (2 pts) won by 5 wickets

James Benning was in prolific form for Surrey
during the group stages of the Twenty20 Cup.

11 July 2006
at Southgate
Hampshire 111 all out (19.3 overs) (J Louw 4 for 18)
Middlesex 116 for 1 (14 overs) (NRD Compton 50*)
Middlesex (2 pts) won by 9 wickets

at Canterbury
Surrey 217 for 4 (20 overs) (JGE Benning 66)
Kent 157 all out (18.2 overs)
Surrey (2 pts) won by 60 runs

at Hove
Sussex 173 for 5 (20 overs) (MJ Prior 73)
Essex 177 for 6 (20 overs) (RC Irani 100*)
Essex (2 pts) won by 4 wickets

Midlands/Wales/West Division

27 June 2006
at Northampton
Warwickshire 185 for 5 (20 overs)
Northamptonshire 161 all out (19.3 overs)
Warwickshire (2 pts) won by 24 runs

at Taunton
Somerset 250 for 3 (20 overs) (CL White 116*,
JL Langer 90)
Gloucestershire 133 all out (16.1 overs)
(CM Willoughby 4 for 30)
Somerset (2 pts) won by 117 runs

at Cardiff
Worcestershire 163 for 7 (20 overs)
Glamorgan 164 for 3 (19.1 overs) (BB McCullum 63,
MJ Powell 54)
Glamorgan (2 pts) won by 7 wickets

28 June 2006
at Edgbaston
Warwickshire 170 for 9 (20 overs) (MA Wagh 56,
AG Wharf 4 for 42)
Glamorgan 174 for 4 (18.2 overs) (JEC Franklin 69*,
DL Hemp 60*)
Glamorgan (2 pts) won by 6 wickets

29 June 2006
at Bristol
Gloucestershire 181 for 7 (20 overs) (CG Taylor 61)
Worcestershire 180 for 5 (20 overs) (VS Solanki 92)
Gloucestershire (2 pts) won by 1 run

at Northampton
Somerset 151 for 9 (20 overs)

Northamptonshire 151 for 6 (20 overs)
(U Afzaal 64*)
Match tied (1 pt each)

30 June 2006
at Worcester
Worcestershire 86 all out (19.3 overs)
Northamptonshire 87 for 1 (16.3 overs)
Northamptonshire (2 pts) won by 9 wickets

at Edgbaston
Gloucestershire 188 for 6 (20 overs)
(MA Hardinges 51)
Warwickshire 185 for 8 (20 overs)
Gloucestershire (2 pts) won by 3 runs

at Cardiff
Somerset 185 for 3 (20 overs) (JL Langer 76*,
CL White 52)
Glamorgan 186 for 9 (20 overs) (RN Grant 51)
Glamorgan (2 pts) won by 1 wicket

2 July 2006
at Taunton
Somerset 167 for 7 (20 overs)
Warwickshire 169 for 3 (16.2 overs)
Warwickshire (2 pts) won by 7 wickets

3 July 2006
at Northampton
Northamptonshire 190 for 3 (20 overs)
(SC Ganguly 73, RA White 66)
Worcestershire 179 for 5 (20 overs) (GA Hick 55)
Northamptonshire (2 pts) won by 11 runs

4 July 2006
at Bristol
Glamorgan 162 for 5 (17 overs)
Gloucestershire 165 for 3 (15.2 overs)
(CG Taylor 55*)
Gloucestershire (2 pts) won by 7 wickets

5 July 2006
at Taunton
Somerset 188 for 6 (20 overs) (JL Langer 97)
Northamptonshire 191 for 5 (19.3 overs)
(DJG Sales 62*)
Northamptonshire (2 pts) won by 5 wickets

at Cardiff
Glamorgan 19 for 1 (3 overs)
Warwickshire
Match abandoned (1 pt each)

6 July 2006
at Worcester
Gloucestershire 203 for 7
(19 overs) (IJ Harvey 56)
Worcestershire 179 for 7
(19 overs) (GA Hick 75)
*Gloucestershire (2 pts) won
by 24 runs*

7 July 2006
at Northampton
Northamptonshire
174 for 6 (20 overs)
(DJG Sales 51,
AG Wharf 4 for 39)
Glamorgan
160 for 6 (20 overs)
*Northamptonshire (2 pts)
won by 14 runs*

at Bristol
Gloucestershire 227 for 4
(20 overs) (CG Taylor 83,
CM Spearman 63)
Somerset 200 all out
(19.2 overs)
*Gloucestershire (2 pts) won
by 27 runs*

at Edgbaston
Worcestershire 186 for 5 (20 overs)
(BF Smith 69*)
Warwickshire 182 for 8 (20 overs) (IJL Trott 75*)
Worcestershire (2 pts) won by 4 runs

9 July 2006
at Worcester
Somerset 198 for 4 (20 overs) (CL White 141*)
Worcestershire 200 for 7 (19 overs) (GA Hick 97*)
Worcestershire (2 pts) won by 3 wickets

10 July 2006
at Edgbaston
Warwickshire 187 for 7 (20 overs)
Northamptonshire 167 for 9 (20 overs)
Warwickshire (2 pts) won by 20 runs

at Cardiff
Glamorgan 190 for 5 (20 overs) (RN Grant 77,
MJ Powell 51)
Gloucestershire 191 for 5 (19.3 overs)
(APR Gidman 52*, CM Spearman 51)
Gloucestershire (2 pts) won by 5 wickets

Hard luck story of the season? Somerset's Australian captain Cameron White thumped a remarkable unbeaten 141 against Worcestershire at New Road – a competition record – and yet still ended up on the losing side.

11 July 2006
at Bristol
Gloucestershire 154 for 7 (20 overs)
(MA Hardinges 94*)
Northamptonshire 155 for 2 (17.4 overs)
(DJG Sales 68*, RA White 62)
Northamptonshire (2 pts) won by 8 wickets

at Worcester
Warwickshire 196 for 7 (20 overs)
(IJL Trott 61)
Worcestershire 185 for 6 (20 overs)
(VS Solanki 90, AGR Loudon 4 for 20)
Warwickshire (2 pts) won by 11 runs

at Taunton
Somerset 219 for 5 (20 overs)
(JL Langer 78)
Glamorgan 206 for 6 (20 overs)
(DL Hemp 74)
Somerset (2 pts) won by 13 runs

FINAL GROUP TABLES
NORTH

	P	W	L	T	NR	RR	Pts
Leicestershire	8	6	2	0	0	1.46	12
Nottinghamshire	8	6	2	0	0	0.55	12
Yorkshire	8	4	3	0	1	0.75	9
Lancashire	8	3	5	0	0	0.03	6
Derbyshire	8	2	5	0	1	-1.33	5
Durham	8	2	6	0	0	-1.48	4

SOUTH

	P	W	L	T	NR	RR	Pts
Essex	8	6	2	0	0	0.53	12
Surrey	8	5	3	0	0	1.45	10
Kent	8	5	3	0	0	-0.30	10
Sussex	8	4	4	0	0	-0.14	8
Hampshire	8	3	5	0	0	0.01	6
Middlesex	8	1	7	0	0	-1.61	2

MIDLANDS/WEST/WALES

	P	W	L	T	NR	RR	Pts
Gloucestershire	8	6	2	0	0	-0.39	12
Northants	8	5	2	1	0	0.24	11
Warwickshire	8	4	3	0	1	0.47	9
Glamorgan	8	3	4	0	1	-0.16	7
Somerset	8	2	5	1	0	0.29	5
Worcestershire	8	2	6	0	0	-0.46	4

24 July 2006: Quarter-finals
at Bristol
Surrey 224 for 5 (20 overs) (MR Ramprakash 85, R Clarke 79*)
Gloucestershire 144 all out (18.5 overs) (ND Doshi 4 for 25)
Surrey won by 80 runs

at Leicester
Kent 153 for 5 (20 overs) (M van Jaarsveld 75)
Leicestershire 156 for 1 (18 overs) (DL Maddy 79*, HD Ackerman 50)
Leicestershire won by 9 wickets

at Trent Bridge
Nottinghamshire 213 for 6 (20 overs) (DJ Hussey 71, SR Patel 65)
Northamptonshire 150 for 6 (20 overs) (L Klusener 72*)
Nottinghamshire won by 63 runs

at Chelmsford
Yorkshire 143 for 7 (20 overs)
Essex 149 for 5 (19.2 overs)
Essex won by 5 wickets

12 August 2006: Semi-finals
at Trent Bridge
Leicestershire 173 for 4 (20 overs)
(HD Ackerman 64, PA Nixon 57*)
Essex 150 for 9 (20 overs)
(ML Pettini 57, JN Snape 4 for 22)
Leicestershire won by 23 runs

Nottinghamshire 176 for 6 (20 overs)
Surrey 139 all out (19.1 overs) (JN Batty 58*)
Nottinghamshire won by 37 runs

FINAL – LEICESTERSHIRE v. NOTTINGHAMSHIRE
12 August 2006 at Trent Bridge

LEICESTERSHIRE

HD Ackerman	b Sidebottom	11
DL Maddy	not out	86
J Allenby	run out	64
PW Harrison	not out	10
*PA Nixon		
JN Snape (capt)		
JL Sadler		
CW Henderson		
DD Masters		
SCJ Broad		
RAG Cummins		
Extras	lb 6	6
	(2 wkts 20 overs)	177

	O	M	R	W
Sidebottom	4	0	23	1
Shreck	4	0	33	0
Swann	4	0	30	0
Ealham	4	0	47	0
Clough	2	0	15	0
Franks	2	0	23	0

Fall of Wickets: 1-26, 2-159

NOTTINGHAMSHIRE

GP Swann	lbw b Maddy	14
SP Fleming (capt)	c Cummins b Snape	53
DJ Hussey	c Snape b Broad	37
*CMW Read	c Broad b Henderson	2
SR Patel	run out	27
MA Ealham	c Maddy b Allenby	16
PJ Franks	run out	11
GD Clough	c Maddy b Allenby	0
WR Smith	not out	9
RJ Sidebottom	not out	0
CE Shreck		
Extras	lb 3, w 1	4
	(8 wkts 20 overs)	173

	O	M	R	W
Broad	4	0	18	1
Cummins	3	0	40	0
Masters	2	0	18	0
Maddy	2	0	16	1
Henderson	4	0	34	1
Snape	3	0	21	1
Allenby	2	0	23	2

Fall of Wickets: 1-51, 2-108, 3-109, 4-122, 5-151, 6-160, 7-164, 8-165

Umpires: PJ Hartley & AA Jones
Toss: Leicestershire
Debut: RAG Cummins
Man of the Match: DL Maddy

Leicestershire won by 4 runs

Right: Stuart Broad appeals for lbw against Essex captain Ronnie Irani during his explosive new-ball spell at the start of the first semi-final.

Below: Darren Maddy, Leicestershire's 'Mr Twenty20', reverse pulls against Nottinghamshire in the final.

Below: Leicestershire, the first team to win two Twenty20 Cups, celebrate in champagne and rain at Trent Bridge.

CHELTENHAM & GLOUCESTER TROPHY
By Mark Baldwin

North Division

23 April 2006
at Old Trafford
Lancashire 194 for 8 (50 overs) (D Mongia 4 for 25)
Leicestershire 125 all out (40.4 overs)
Lancashire (2 pts) won by 69 runs

at Headingley
Derbyshire 251 for 6 (50 overs) (CR Taylor 100,
SD Stubbings 62)
Yorkshire 230 all out (48.4 overs) (DS Lehmann 55)
Derbyshire (2 pts) won by 21 runs

at Trent Bridge
Nottinghamshire 161 all out (41.2 overs)
Worcestershire 165 for 8 (42.3 overs)
Worcestershire (2 pts) won by 2 wickets – DL Method:
target 162 from 43 overs

30 April 2006
at Edgbaston
Warwickshire 352 for 2 (50 overs) (NM Carter 135,
NV Knight 128*, IJL Trott 52*)
Scotland 238 all out (46 overs) (CJ Richards 56)
Warwickshire (2 pts) won by 114 runs

1 May 2006
at Trent Bridge
Scotland 192 all out (50 overs) (RR Watson 84)
Nottinghamshire 196 for 1 (40.2 overs) (WR Smith 95*,
SR Patel 93*)
Nottinghamshire (2 pts) won by 9 wickets

at Worcester
Lancashire 248 for 5 (50 overs) (SG Law 70*,
MB Loye 64, DKH Mitchell 4 for 42)
Worcestershire 129 all out (42.1 overs)
Lancashire (2 pts) won by 119 runs

at Chester-le-Street
Northamptonshire 195 for 7 (36 overs) (RA White 54)
Durham 197 for 6 (35 overs) (DM Benkenstein 63*)
Durham (2 pts) won by 4 wickets

at Leicester
Warwickshire 128 for 9 (33 overs) (J Allenby 4 for 19)
Leicestershire 116 for 3 (22.4 overs) (DL Maddy 53)
Leicestershire (2 pts) won by 7 wickets – DL Method:
target 116 from 30 overs

7 May 2006
at Headingley
Yorkshire v. Nottinghamshire
Match abandoned (1 pt each)

at Northampton
Northamptonshire 172 for 9 (45 overs)
(L Klusener 63*)
Lancashire 175 for 2 (38.4 overs) (BJ Hodge 67*,
SG Law 63*)
Lancashire (2 pts) won by 8 wickets – DL Method: target
175 from 45 overs

at the Grange
Scotland 187 for 6 (25 overs) (CJ Richards 88*)
Worcestershire 179 for 5 (25 overs) (VS Solanki 61,
GA Hick 50*)
Scotland (2 pts) won by 8 runs

at Derby
Leicestershire 188 for 6 (45 overs)
Derbyshire 190 for 5 (43.4 overs) (CR Taylor 66*)
Derbyshire (2 pts) won by 5 wickets – DL Method: target
190 from 45 overs

at the Riverside
Durham 224 for 5 (36 overs) (JJB Lewis 61,
PD Collingwood 53)
Warwickshire 158 all out (30.1 overs)
(GR Breese 4 for 36)
Durham (2 pts) won by 66 runs

14 May 2006
at Old Trafford
Lancashire 307 for 5 (50 overs) (MB Loye 127,
BJ Hodge 118)
Durham 182 all out (43.4 overs)
Lancashire (2 pts) won by 125 runs

at Edgbaston
Derbyshire 206 all out (48.1 overs) (TR Birt 61,
G Welch 50, NM Carter 4 for 37,
JO Troughton 4 for 39)
Warwickshire 197 all out (49.1 overs) (IR Bell 78,
PS Jones 5 for 49)
Derbyshire (2 pts) won by 9 runs

at Leicester
Worcestershire 191 for 8 (45 overs)
(BF Smith 59)
Leicestershire 130 all out (39.1 overs) (PA Nixon 67,
GJ Batty 4 for 27)
Worcestershire (2 pts) won by 61 runs

at Northampton
Yorkshire 341 for 3 (50 overs) (DS Lehmann 118*,
C White 112)
Northamptonshire 339 for 7 (50 overs)
(DJG Sales 161, CJL Rogers 85)
Yorkshire (2 pts) won by 2 runs

21 May 2006
at Worcester
Worcestershire v. Durham
Match abandoned (1 pt each)

at Headingley
Yorkshire 14 for 0 (4 overs)
Warwickshire
Match abandoned (1 pt each)

at Trent Bridge
Nottinghamshire v. Leicestershire
Match abandoned (1 pt each)

at the Grange
Scotland 202 for 6 (36 overs) (CJ Richards 73,
RR Watson 63)
Northamptonshire 150 all out (33.2 overs)
(IA Moran 5 for 28)
Scotland (2 pts) won by 52 runs

28 May 2006
at Derby
Derbyshire 180 all out (49.4 overs)
Scotland 181 for 2 (40.2 overs) (RR Watson 108*)
Scotland (2 pts) won by 8 wickets

at Worcester
Worcestershire 256 for 6 (50 overs) (PA Jaques 112,
BF Smith 60)
Northamptonshire 206 for 9 (50 overs) (L Klusener 85*,
CJL Rogers 51, Z Khan 4 for 30)
Worcestershire (2 pts) won by 50 runs

at Headingley
Lancashire 287 for 9 (50 overs) (MB Loye 95)
Yorkshire 292 for 4 (48.4 overs) (DS Lehmann 92*,
C White 59, A McGrath 54)
Yorkshire (2 pts) won by 6 wickets

29 May 2006
at Northampton
Northamptonshire 219 for 7 (47 overs) (L Klusener 66,
CJL Rogers 57)
Warwickshire 66 for 0 (10.5 overs)
*Warwickshire (2 pts) won by 37 runs – DL Method:
target 30 from 10.5 overs*

at Derby
Worcestershire 204 for 5 (42.2 overs) (SC Moore 68,
VS Solanki 53)
Derbyshire 189 for 3 (31.1 overs) (MJ Di Venuto 93*)
*Derbyshire (2 pts) won by 7 wickets – DL Method: target
189 from 32 overs*

at the Riverside
Leicestershire 151 for 6 (39 overs)
Durham 164 for 7 (36.4 overs)
*Durham (2 pts) won by 3 wickets – DL Method: target
164 from 39 overs*

at Old Trafford
Nottinghamshire 61 for 6 (19 overs)
Lancashire 15 for 0 (2.3 overs)
Match abandoned (1 pt each)

at Headingley
Scotland 212 for 9 (50 overs) (CJO Smith 71)
Yorkshire 160 for 4 (26.5 overs) (MP Vaughan 67)
*Yorkshire (2 pts) won by 6 wickets – DL Method: target
158 from 30 overs*

2 June 2006
at Derby
Nottinghamshire 250 for 6 (50 overs) (JER Gallian 91,
WR Smith 73)
Derbyshire 194 all out (45.3 overs) (TR Birt 70)
Nottinghamshire (2 pts) won by 56 runs

Darren Lehmann in action for Yorkshire.

4 June 2006
at the Grange
Scotland 167 all out (50 overs) (G Chapple 4 for 23)
Lancashire 168 for 5 (40 overs) (SG Law 78, LD Sutton 53*)
Lancashire (2 pts) won by 5 wickets

at Oakham School
Northamptonshire 203 for 8 (50 overs)
Leicestershire 207 for 4 (47.3 overs) (DDJ Robinson 85, TJ New 68)
Leicestershire (2 pts) won by 6 wickets

at the Riverside
Yorkshire 227 for 4 (50 overs) (C White 101*)
Durham 229 for 8 (50 overs) (JP Maher 124*)
Durham (2 pts) won by 2 wickets

11 June 2006
at Old Trafford
Derbyshire 193 all out (48.2 overs) (TR Birt 76)
Lancashire 196 for 1 (43.3 overs) (MB Loye 120*)
Lancashire (2pts) won by 9 wickets

at Trent Bridge
Durham 280 for 6 (50 overs) (JP Maher 109, JJB Lewis 73, MA Ealham 4 for 53)
Nottinghamshire 252 all out (48.2 overs) (CMW Read 135, OD Gibson 4 for 63)
Durham (2 pts) won by 28 runs

at Edgbaston
Worcestershire 267 all out (49.5 overs) (SC Moore 80, VS Solanki 60)
Warwickshire 209 all out (45.2 overs) (JO Troughton 58)
Worcestershire (2 pts) won by 58 runs

16 June 2006
at Leicester
Yorkshire 185 for 7 (50 overs) (AW Gale 63*)
Leicestershire 189 for 6 (41.4 overs) (TJ New 51)
Leicestershire (2 pts) won by 4 wickets

18 June 2006
at Edgbaston
Warwickshire 186 all out (49.3 overs) (NS Poonia 59)
Nottinghamshire 189 for 3 (35 overs) (A Singh 78*)
Nottinghamshire (2 pts) won by 7 wickets

at the Grange
Scotland 161 all out (39 overs) (CD Thorp 6 for 17)
Durham 99 for 5 (17.5 overs)
Durham (2 pts) won by 5 wickets – DL Method: target 99 from 19 overs

at Northampton
Northamptonshire 257 all out (49.5 overs) (BM Shafayat 55, DJG Sales 50, GG Wagg 4 for 59)
Derbyshire 256 all out (50 overs) (SD Stubbings 110)
Northamptonshire (2 pts) won by 1 run

25 June 2006
at Worcester
Worcestershire 270 for 4 (50 overs) (L Vincent 83)
Yorkshire 220 all out (47.1 overs) (MJ Lumb 76)
Worcestershire (2 pts) won by 50 runs

at the Grange
Leicestershire 314 for 3 (50 overs) (DL Maddy 167*)
Scotland 261 all out (47.2 overs) (GM Hamilton 131, NFI McCallum 53)
Leicestershire (2 pts) won by 53 runs

at Trent Bridge
Northamptonshire 264 for 7 (50 overs) (SC Ganguly 71, BM Shafayat 53)
Nottinghamshire 267 for 8 (49.4 overs) (SP Fleming 121*, CMW Read 61)
Nottinghamshire (2 pts) won by 2 wickets

at Edgbaston
Warwickshire 249 for 5 (50 overs) (IJL Trott 76*, MA Wagh 51)
Lancashire 250 for 7 (47.2 overs) (SG Law 68, MB Loye 60)
Lancashire (2 pts) won by 3 wickets

at Derby
Durham 274 for 6 (50 overs) (JP Maher 125, DM Benkenstein 52)
Derbyshire 276 for 5 (48.4 overs) (CR Taylor 111*)
Derbyshire (2 pts) won by 5 wickets

South Division

23 April 2006
at Bristol
Middlesex 95 all out (30.5 overs) (J Lewis 4 for 14)
Gloucestershire 96 for 4 (20.2 overs)
Gloucestershire (2 pts) won by 6 wickets

at Dublin
Ireland 202 all out (49.3 overs) (JP Bray 59, JTA Bruce 4 for 31)
Hampshire 206 for 2 (33.4 overs) (JP Crawley 76*, N Pothas 69)
Hampshire (2 pts) won by 8 wickets

1 May 2006
at Taunton
Gloucestershire 328 for 8 (50 overs)
(IJ Harvey 112, CG Taylor 58, APR Gidman 53)
Somerset 199 all out (38.2 overs) (KA Parsons 65,
MCJ Ball 5 for 48)
Gloucestershire (2 pts) won by 129 runs

at Cardiff
Glamorgan 250 for 9 (50 overs) (MJ Cosgrove 75)
Ireland 235 all out (48.3 overs) (Shahid Afridi 54,
PG Gillespie 54)
Glamorgan (2 pts) won by 15 runs

at Canterbury
Surrey 223 for 5 (30 overs) (AD Brown 64, JN Batty 52)
Kent 222 for 6 (30 overs) (NJ Dexter 94,
DI Stevens 67)
Surrey (2 pts) won by 1 run

at Hove
Middlesex 200 for 6 (40 overs) (OA Shah 82,
PN Weekes 50, Naved-ul-Hasan 4 for 34)
Sussex 201 for 4 (39.4 overs) (MW Goodwin 88*,
RR Montgomerie 72)
Sussex (2 pts) won by 6 wickets

Somerset's Matthew Wood put together a string of good
scores in the C&G Trophy's South Division.

at Canterbury
Somerset 338 for 5 (50 overs) (ME Trescothick 158,
MJ Wood 72)
Kent 93 for 5 (26.2 overs)
*Somerset (2 pts) won by 112 runs – DL Method: target
206 from 26.2 overs*

at Chelmsford
Glamorgan 98 for 5 (10 overs)
Essex 102 for 0 (7.1 overs) (RC Irani 51*)
Essex (2 pts) won by 10 wickets

30 April 2006
at Bristol
Ireland 193 for 9 (50 overs) (JMM Averis 4 for 17)
Gloucestershire 146 all out (38 overs)
Ireland (2 pts) won by 47 runs

at The Oval
Surrey 272 for 9 (50 overs) (MA Butcher 57, JN Batty 53)
Sussex 274 for 5 (48.2 overs) (MH Yardy 98*,
MW Goodwin 89)
Sussex (2 pts) won by 5 wickets

at the Rose Bowl
Hampshire 257 for 9 (49 overs)
(KP Pietersen 98)
Essex 249 all out (48.3 overs) (RS Bopara 54)
Hampshire (2 pts) won by 8 runs

7 May 2006
at Uxbridge
Middlesex 254 all out (49.4 overs) (ET Smith 88,
SK Warne 4 for 48)
Hampshire 241 all out (49.1 overs) (MA Carberry 52)
Middlesex (2 pts) won by 13 runs

at The Oval
Somerset 279 for 5 (50 overs) (MJ Wood 92,
AV Suppiah 63)
Surrey 253 all out (47.5 overs) (MR Ramprakash 56,
AV Suppiah 4 for 39)
Somerset (2 pts) won by 26 runs

at Chelmsford
Ireland 192 all out (43 overs) (AC Botha 64,
RN ten Doeschate 4 for 49)
Essex 193 for 2 (37 overs) (AN Cook 91*,
GW Flower 61)
Essex (2 pts) won by 8 wickets

14 May 2006
at Taunton
Somerset 188 all out (39.4 overs) (MJ Wood 55,
JD Middlebrook 4 for 27)
Essex 189 for 2 (32.3 overs) (RS Bopara 101*)
Essex (2 pts) won by 8 wickets

at Belfast
Surrey 100 for 2 (15 overs) (JGE Benning 61*)
Ireland
Match abandoned (1 pt each)

at Cardiff
Sussex 257 for 8 (50 overs) (MH Yardy 88, CD Hopkinson 61)
Glamorgan 160 all out (38.2 overs)
Sussex (2 pts) won by 97 runs

at the Rose Bowl
Hampshire 258 for 7 (50 overs) (DJ Thornely 107*)
Kent 259 for 6 (50 overs) (RWT Key 76)
Kent (2 pts) won by 4 wickets

19 May 2006
at Cardiff
Glamorgan v. **Middlesex**
Match abandoned (1 pt each)

21 May 2006
at Bristol
Gloucestershire v. **Kent**
Match abandoned (1 pt each)

at Taunton
Hampshire 56 for 2 (6.1 overs)
Somerset
Match abandoned (1 pt each)

28 May 2006
at Lord's
Ireland 184 all out (48.3 overs)
Middlesex 185 for 1 (24.2 overs)
(EC Joyce 95, ET Smith 81*)
Middlesex (2 pts) won by 9 wickets

at Chelmsford
Essex 296 for 6 (50 overs) (RC Irani 132*,
RS Bopara 59, A Flower 53)
Sussex 298 for 5 (48.5 overs) (MW Goodwin 158*,
CD Hopkinson 64)
Sussex (2 pts) won by 5 wickets

at Bristol
Glamorgan 168 for 9 (36 overs)

Gloucestershire 170 for 5 (34.1 overs) (IJ Harvey 53)
Gloucestershire (2 pts) won by 5 wickets

29 May 2006
at The Oval
Surrey 200 all out (45 overs) (Azhar Mahmood 101*,
DS Harrison 4 for 31)
Glamorgan 132 all out (31.3 overs)
(Azhar Mahmood 4 for 17)
Surrey (2 pts) won by 68 runs

at Horsham
Somerset 158 for 7 (24 overs) (MJ Wood 59,
Mushtaq Ahmed 4 for 42)
Sussex 123 for 5 (15.2 overs)
*Sussex (2 pts) won by 5 wickets – DL Method: target
122 from 17 overs*

at the Rose Bowl
Hampshire 221 all out (50 overs) (GA Lamb 59)
Gloucestershire 147 all out (33.5 overs)
(MA Hardinges 60, JTA Bruce 4 for 18)
*Hampshire (2 pts) won by 62 runs – DL Method: target
210 from 42 overs*

at Tunbridge Wells
Kent 194 for 4 (23 overs) (DI Stevens 59, JM Kemp 57)
Ireland 95 for 7 (19.5 overs)
*Kent (2 pts) won by 83 runs – DL Method: target 179
from 19.5 overs*

No wonder he is leading Surrey off: Azhar Mahmood took 4 for 17 to add
to his unbeaten 101 against Glamorgan.

4 June 2006
at Whitgift School
Surrey 166 all out (40.2 overs) (MA Butcher 77,
SK Warne 6 for 42)
Hampshire 167 for 2 (26 overs) (MA Carberry 88)
Hampshire (2 pts) won by 8 wickets

at Tunbridge Wells
Sussex 284 for 9 (50 overs)
(RR Montgomerie 127)
Kent 290 for 4 (47 overs) (M van Jaarsveld 75*,
RWT Key 63, JM Kemp 54*)
Kent (2 pts) won by 6 wickets

at Swansea
Glamorgan 203 for 8 (50 overs) (MJ Cosgrove 51)
Somerset 207 for 7 (47 overs) (CL White 109*)
Somerset (2 pts) won by 3 wickets

at Lord's
Essex 202 for 8 (50 overs) (RC Irani 83)
Middlesex 206 for 5 (44.1 overs)
Middlesex (2 pts) won by 5 wickets

11 June 2006
at Southgate
Middlesex 257 for 9 (50 overs) (OA Shah 76,
BJM Scott 73*, NRD Compton 54)
Surrey 149 all out (33.4 overs) (AD Brown 57*)
Middlesex (2 pts) won by 108 runs

at Dublin
Ireland 216 all out (49.1 overs) (PG Gillespie 51,
LJ Wright 4 for 56)
Sussex 217 for 3 (37 overs) (RR Montgomerie 108*,
CJ Adams 65)
Sussex (2 pts) won by 7 wickets

at Chelmsford
Gloucestershire 217 all out (48 overs) (WPC Weston 54)
Essex 218 for 5 (47.3 overs) (A Flower 71*)
Essex (2 pts) won by 5 wickets

at Cardiff
Kent 332 for 2 (50 overs) (NJ Dexter 135*,
AJ Hall 100, DI Stevens 82)
Glamorgan 291 for 9 (50 overs) (DL Hemp 61)
Kent (2 pts) won by 41 runs

16 June 2006
at Hove
Hampshire 254 all out (49.3 overs) (MA Carberry 71,
RJ Kirtley 5 for 43)

Sussex 257 for 5 (49 overs) (CD Hopkinson 69*,
MJ Prior 54)
Sussex (2 pts) won by 5 wickets

18 June 2006
at Canterbury
Kent 281 for 6 (50 overs) (RWT Key 89, MJ Walker 52*)
Essex 282 for 6 (46.2 overs) (ML Pettini 80,
A Flower 61)
Essex (2 pts) won by 4 wickets

at Taunton
Middlesex 215 for 9 (50 overs) (OA Shah 63,
EJG Morgan 50*)
Somerset 212 for 9 (50 overs) (JD Francis 51,
CT Peploe 4 for 41)
Middlesex (2 pts) won by 3 runs

at Bristol
Gloucestershire 339 for 8 (50 overs) (IJ Harvey 108,
DO Brown 63*)
Surrey 337 all out (49.5 overs) (JGE Benning 189*)
Gloucestershire (2 pts) won by 2 runs

25 June 2006
at Chelmsford
Surrey 128 all out (39 overs)
Essex 131 for 4 (15.3 overs) (ML Pettini 57)
Essex (2 pts) won by 6 wickets

at the Rose Bowl
Hampshire 310 for 7 (50 overs) (MJ Brown 76,
CC Benham 73*, MA Carberry 69)
Glamorgan 145 all out (32 overs) (JA Tomlinson 4 for 47)
Hampshire (2 pts) won by 165 runs

at Belfast
Somerset 238 for 8 (50 overs)
Ireland 165 all out (41.5 overs)
Somerset (2 pts) won by 73 runs

at Arundel Castle
Gloucestershire 98 all out (36.3 overs)
Sussex 96 all out (17.5 overs) (CG Greenidge 4 for 40,
JMM Averis 4 for 54)
Gloucestershire (2 pts) won by 2 runs

at Lord's
Middlesex 284 for 5 (50 overs) (OA Shah 123*,
NRD Compton 60)
Kent 275 for 5 (50 overs) (DI Stevens 75, JL Denly 70,
M van Jaarsveld 58)
Middlesex (2 pts) won by 9 runs

SUSSEX'S CAMPAIGN

The back-to-back May Bank Holiday wins at Essex and at home to Somerset, both achieved against the odds given how the earlier part of the games went, handed Sussex total control of their own destiny in the South Division. By starting their campaign with five straight victories, Chris Adams' side could then afford a stutter or two in the remaining fixtures.

In fact, Sussex made sure of their Lord's appearance when they defeated south coast rivals Hampshire in front of a raucous floodlit crowd at Hove in their penultimate group match. The narrow defeat to Gloucestershire, to add to that suffered at Kent three weeks earlier, did not therefore matter.

Like Lancashire, their eventual opponents in the final, Sussex's qualification was earned on the back of a real team performance over the nine games. If Murray Goodwin produced the most stellar display, with his awesome unbeaten 158 against Essex, then there were many other stars shining brightly in the Sussex sky too.

Michael Yardy: a key component in Sussex's success, with both bat and ball.

Murray Goodwin: his 158 at Essex was the best one-day innings his Sussex captain had seen.

Take Michael Yardy and Richard Montgomerie. Neither would be classed as the most dynamic of limited-overs cricketers, yet Yardy consistently stood out with both bat and ball, and Montgomerie produced back-to-back centuries against Kent and Ireland (127 and 108 not out respectively). Yardy's unbeaten 98 from 105 balls in the opening game of the campaign, at The Oval, followed up his 3 for 44 with the ball to check Surrey's progress. He and Goodwin, who made 89, then added 156 in 27 overs for the fourth wicket to take Sussex sailing past Surrey's 272 for 9 with ten balls to spare. Goodwin hit a run-a-ball unbeaten 88 to steer Sussex past Middlesex's 200 for 6 with two balls in hand in a match reduced to 40 overs per side (Montgomerie made 72), before really turning on the power to win an extraordinary contest at Chelmsford.

Ronnie Irani's unbeaten 132 had spearheaded Essex's drive to 296 for 6 from their 50 overs, and at 56 for 4 Sussex were struggling in reply. But Carl Hopkinson (64) proved a stout partner in a stand eventually worth 146 for the fifth wicket, and

Goodwin stepped up his assault so magnificently that, in the end, victory came with more than an over outstanding. Goodwin's first 50 had taken 71 balls, his second 50 exactly 50 balls, and his third 50 just 28. In all, he hit five sixes and 15 fours and Chris Adams, his captain, afterwards called it, 'the best one-day innings I've ever seen'.

The next day, at Horsham, saw Robin Martin-Jenkins and Luke Wright add an unbroken 57 from just 26 balls to snatch victory against Somerset, even though Sussex had at one stage been 66 for 5 as they chased 159 in a game reduced to only 24 overs per side.

Hopkinson, who had also scored a valuable 61 against Glamorgan (putting on 126 with Yardy, who made 88), then played one of the best innings of his fledgling career to help Sussex chase down Hampshire's 254 under the Hove lights in the game which clinched the Lord's final place. Hopkinson made a gutsy and skilful 69 not out, while both Matt Prior with 54 up front and Martin-Jenkins with some cool hitting at the end also played significant parts.

James Kirtley took 5 for 43 in that vital victory, but early bowling honours went to Rana Naved-ul-Hasan, who picked up 4 for 34 against Middlesex and a destructive 5 for 30 against Glamorgan, while Mushtaq Ahmed grabbed 4 for 42 against his former county Somerset and the ever-improving Wright weighed in with 4 for 56 against Ireland.

Sussex's C&G Trophy South Division results:

30 April (The Oval): beat Surrey by 5 wickets
1 May (Hove): beat Middlesex by 6 wickets
14 May (Cardiff): beat Glamorgan by 97 runs
28 May (Chelmsford): beat Essex by 5 wickets
29 May (Horsham): beat Somerset by 5 wickets (DL Method)
4 June (Tunbridge Wells): lost to Kent by 6 wickets
11 June (Dublin): beat Ireland by 7 wickets
16 June (Hove): beat Hampshire by 5 wickets
25 June (Arundel): lost to Gloucestershire by 2 runs

Final South Division Table

		P	W	L	NR	Pts
1	Sussex	9	7	2	0	14
2	Middlesex	9	6	2	1	13
3	Essex	9	6	3	0	12
4	Hampshire	9	5	3	1	11
5	Gloucestershire	9	5	3	1	11
6	Somerset	9	4	4	1	9
7	Kent	9	4	4	1	9
8	Surrey	9	2	6	1	5
9	Glamorgan	9	1	7	1	3
10	Ireland	9	1	7	1	3

LANCASHIRE'S CAMPAIGN

Mark Chilton's team took early control of their group, and never relinquished it. Only one defeat was suffered, against Roses rivals Yorkshire, but by then they were clear in front of the chasing pack following the crushing victory over nearest challengers Durham on 14 May. For once, too, the Manchester rain aided their progress, when Nottinghamshire were denied the chance to further stall Lancashire's momentum the day after the loss to Yorkshire. A trip north of the border to Edinburgh in the next match was just what Lancashire needed to pep up their campaign again, and two more wins against Derbyshire and Warwickshire then finished off the qualifying process in some style.

Mal Loye was the undoubted star of the qualification process, becoming the first batsman in the history of the premier domestic one-day tournament to score more than 500 runs in a season. Loye's 531-run tally in the group stage, at an average of 75.85, included a 122-ball 127 as he

Lancashire's one-day opener Mal Loye was in irresistible form in the North Division, hitting two centuries and three half-centuries to become the first player to top 500 runs in a season in the competition's history.

and Brad Hodge (118) saw off Durham and a violent 44-ball 60 against Warwickshire which included four slog-swept sixes and eight fours. The opener also hit 64 against Worcestershire, 95 against Yorkshire and 120 not out against Derbyshire.

But there were other standout performances, too, in a campaign that illustrated the strength in depth of this current Lancashire squad. Tom Smith, the 20-year-old all-rounder, immediately impressed with a spell of 8-3-8-3 in the opening victory against Leicestershire, and he then followed this up by taking a further 3 for 17 from eight overs in the next match against Worcestershire. Glen Chapple had 3 for 26 against Durham and 4 for 23 against Scotland, who were bowled out for 167, while

Tom Smith: the 20-year-old Lancashire seamer made an early impression on events in the North Division.

Dominic Cork enjoyed taking 4 for 35 against his former club Derbyshire, as they were dismissed for 193, after picking up 3 for 23 at Northampton.

Andrew Flintoff had in that match removed three of the top four Northamptonshire batsmen, proving his return to fitness for England's Test series against Sri Lanka by finishing with 3 for 30 from nine overs as Northants were restricted to 172 for 9 in a contest reduced to 45 overs per side. Sajid Mahmood, Gary Keedy, Kyle Hogg and Simon Marshall all had their moments with the ball, too, and the power of Lancashire's bowling attack is reflected in the all-out totals of Leicestershire (125), Worcestershire (129), Durham (182), Scotland (167) and Derbyshire (193).

Only Warwickshire (249 for 5) and Yorkshire, for whom Darren Lehmann hit 92 not out as they overhauled Lancashire's 287 for 9, made it past 200 against the Lancashire bowlers.

Apart from Loye, runs also flowed freely from the bat of Stuart Law, who made an unbeaten 70 against Worcestershire, 63 not out against Northamptonshire, 78 against Scotland and 68 against Warwickshire. Luke Sutton contributed an important 53 not out against the Scots and the irrepressible Cork helped to guide Lancashire home in a pressure situation against Warwickshire with a combative, unbeaten 33.

Lancashire's C&G Trophy North Division results:

23 April (Old Trafford): beat Leicestershire by 69 runs
1 May (Worcester): beat Worcestershire by 119 runs
7 May (Northampton): beat Northamptonshire by 8 wickets (DL method)
14 May (Old Trafford): beat Durham by 125 runs
28 May (Headingley): lost to Yorkshire by 6 wickets
29 May (Old Trafford): no result v Nottinghamshire
4 June (Edinburgh): beat Scotland by 5 wickets
11 June (Old Trafford): beat Derbyshire by 8 wickets
25 June (Edgbaston): beat Warwickshire by 3 wickets

Final North Division Table

		P	W	L	NR	Pts
1	Lancashire	9	7	1	1	15
2	Durham	9	6	2	1	13
3	Worcestershire	9	5	3	1	11
4	Nottinghamshire	9	4	2	3	11
5	Derbyshire	9	5	4	0	10
6	Leicestershire	9	4	4	1	9
7	Yorkshire	9	3	4	2	8
8	Scotland	9	3	6	0	6
9	Warwickshire	9	2	6	1	5
10	Northamptonshire	9	1	8	0	2

C&G TROPHY FINAL
26 August 2006

A triumph for Sussex, in a low-scoring but genuinely exciting Lord's final, was also a personal triumph for James Kirtley. Lancashire, with the advantage of winning the toss, bowled out Sussex for 172 but could make only 157 themselves as Kirtley took 5 for 27 – all lbw. It was a remarkable, emotional performance from Kirtley, who had endured a struggle of a season after the trauma the previous winter of having to remodel his bowling action for the second time in his career.

Kirtley's opening burst accounted for Lancashire's three most dangerous batsmen – Mal Loye, Nathan Astle and Stuart Law – although the veteran Australian Law could feel himself extremely hard done by after getting a big inside edge on the off-cutter with which Kirtley won his appeal to umpire Jeremy Lloyds. Yet, if that was a significant moment of luck, everything else about Sussex's display – after an initial bout of nerves that saw them slide perilously to 52 for 5 on an overcast morning – spoke of courage, determination and self-belief that they could defend such a moderate total.

Richard Montgomerie was run out by a brilliant stop and throw to the bowler's end by Tom Smith from backward point, and both Chris Adams and Murray Goodwin fell to movement off the pitch. Matt Prior threatened all too briefly, to Sussex eyes, at the top of the order and Carl Hopkinson clearly let the big occasion get to him when he drove straight to Dominic Cork at mid-off and ran.

Robin Martin-Jenkins and Michael Yardy began the recovery, however, and the unflappable Yardy was then joined in a crucial seventh-wicket stand of 56 by the hard-hitting Yasir Arafat. Both players made it to 37 – Yardy's a grinding effort which occupied 96 balls – and some late blows from Luke Wright and Mushtaq Ahmed at least gave Adams and his team something to bowl at.

After Kirtley's new ball incisions, Sussex always seemed in control of their own destiny – especially when Luke Sutton mis-hit a pull to mid-on and Mark Chilton gave Mushtaq the charge and was stumped down the leg side by Prior. A jittery 67 for 5 became a distinctly uncomfortable 72 for 6 when Glen Chapple was caught off bat-and-pad at silly point pushing out tentatively at a Mushtaq googly. But the 35-year-old Cork has always relished the big stage, and he found a willing partner in Kyle Hogg as 58 runs were put together for the seventh wicket.

FINAL – LANCASHIRE v. SUSSEX
26 August 2006 at Lord's

SUSSEX

RR Montgomerie	run out	1
*MJ Prior	c Mahmood b Hogg	23
CJ Adams (capt)	c Astle b Mahmood	6
MW Goodwin	c Sutton b Chapple	7
MH Yardy	lbw b Kartik	37
CD Hopkinson	run out	1
RSC Martin-Jenkins	c Sutton b Chapple	15
Yasir Arafat	c Sutton b Mahmood	37
LJ Wright	st Sutton b Kartik	19
Mushtaq Ahmed	b Mahmood	8
RJ Kirtley	not out	4
Extras	lb 1, w 11, nb 2	14
	(all out 47.1 overs)	172

	O	M	R	W
Cork	8	0	30	0
Hogg	8	1	31	1
Mahmood	8.1	1	16	3
Chapple	9	0	36	2
Kartik	8	1	28	2
Smith	6	0	30	0

Fall of Wickets
1-4, 2-27, 3-38, 4-46, 5-52, 6-78, 7-134, 8-145, 9-164

LANCASHIRE

MB Loye	lbw b Kirtley	12
MJ Chilton (capt)	st Prior b Mushtaq Ahmed	20
NJ Astle	lbw b Kirtley	3
SG Law	lbw b Kirtley	0
*LD Sutton	c Yasir Arafat b Wright	13
G Chapple	c Montgomerie b Mushtaq Ahmed	17
KW Hogg	c Montgomerie b Wright	28
DG Cork	not out	35
TC Smith	lbw b Kirtley	10
SI Mahmood	b Yasir Arafat	2
M Kartik	lbw b Kirtley	0
Extras	lb 10, w 5, nb 2	17
	(all out 47.2 overs)	157

	O	M	R	W
Kirtley	8.2	1	27	5
Yasir Arafat	9	2	24	1
Martin-Jenkins	9	2	26	0
Wright	6	0	33	2
Mushtaq Ahmed	10	1	19	2
Yardy	5	0	18	0

Fall of Wickets
1-23, 2-27, 3-27, 4-51, 5-67, 6-72, 7-130, 8-151, 9-156

Umpires: JW Lloyds & NA Mallender
Toss: Lancashire
Man of the Match: RJ Kirtley

Sussex won by 15 runs

Stuart Law stands in disbelief at the decision, but James Kirtley is already celebrating the controversial lbw dismissal of Lancashire's star batsman.

When Hogg mis-hit to mid-on, Cork was joined by Smith with a further 43 needed from the remaining 8.1 overs. The pair got 21 of them, before young all-rounder Smith was undone by Kirtley's movement back into the right-hander when the Sussex opening bowler returned. Sajid Mahmood disappointed with the bat, especially after his fine pacy bowling of earlier in the day, by missing a wild slog at Arafat and in the end Cork was left high and dry on 35 not out as last man Murali Kartik was defeated by the first ball he faced.

As Sussex celebrated, Adams said Kirtley's display was, 'An Andrew Flintoff performance … like winning a Test for England'. He said that Kirtley, who has won four Test caps for England, should be immediately drafted into the one-day international squad.

Kirtley, referring to the remedial work he had put in throughout the winter of 2005–06, said, 'It's been tough, but this is the reward for all the support I've had from everybody at Sussex over the past nine months … I've had doubts and dark moments but I had no choice. I had to be sure that I could deliver. I couldn't always be fighting demons in my head. Now I've shown I can deliver.'

As for Lancashire, their captain Chilton summed up the mood in the beaten dressing room by saying, 'It was a game we should have won'.

As for the competition itself, such a thrilling final provided Cheltenham & Gloucester with a fitting end to their six-year sponsorship, although the eagerly awaited meeting of Sussex and Lancashire – also locked together at the front of the Championship race for the second half of the season – camouflaged a severe misjudgement by the England and Wales Cricket Board. By reorganising the competition into two qualifying groups of ten teams, from which only the top team in each went through, it ensured at a stroke that many of the

90 matches played in the Northern and Southern conferences were all but meaningless. Both Sussex and Lancashire quickly assumed control of their respective groups, although a frisson of excitement did linger around Lancashire's qualification progress right up to their final match at Warwickshire on 25 June.

Yet, while each county – plus Scotland and Ireland – benefited from being exposed to more 50-over cricket, which itself is essential for the development of one-day international cricketers, the ECB admitted its error well before the competition was won by announcing that, in 2007, there would be a semi-final stage as well.

How typical of the authorities, however, that they could not quite bring themselves into line with all the popular (and sensible) opinion urging that there be quarter-finals too. Perhaps it is still not too late for these to be added – especially if the new sponsors insist – because, for all counties, the financial benefit of a sell-out cup quarter-final or semi-final is substantial. From a playing point of view, moreover, the more English cricketers that are exposed to the particular pressures of a big cup tie the better.

So, come on ECB, let's go for the top four in each conference qualifying for the knockout stage … not just the top two. It really is very simple. And no one will think any worse of you.

The last C&G Trophy is held aloft by Sussex captain Chris Adams, and he and his players are ecstatic at winning what would prove to be the first leg of a memorable 'double' of domestic titles.

THE C&G YEARS

MARK BALDWIN looks back at C&G's six-year stewardship of English domestic cricket's premier one-day competition.

When Sussex beat Lancashire in dramatic fashion at Lord's in August 2006 they became the 44th winner of England's oldest and most prestigious limited-overs tournament, but for sponsors Cheltenham & Gloucester it was six and out. The competition, which started life in 1963 as the Gillette Cup and which, for a further 20 years, metamorphosed into the NatWest Trophy, has existed from 2001 until today as the C&G Trophy.

The past six years have seen much good cricket, as the competition continues to inspire county players dreaming of experiencing that major highlight of a career: taking part in a cup final at Lord's. Somerset were the first winners of the C&G Trophy, in 2001, and since then there have been victories for Yorkshire (2002), Gloucestershire (2003 and 2004), Hampshire (2005) and now Sussex.

It was Somerset's first trophy since the county's halcyon days of Botham, Richards and Garner in 1983, and they overpowered Leicestershire by 41 runs by dint of controlled aggression with the bat and a steadier bowling display than their opponents. The two big guns, Marcus Trescothick and Andrew Caddick, did not really fire for Somerset – Trescothick made only 18 and Caddick was wicketless although his ten overs cost just 33 runs – but both Peter Bowler and skipper Jamie Cox hit solid 40s and the ever-dependable Keith Parsons struck an unbeaten 60 as he and wicketkeeper Rob Turner boosted the eventual total to 271 for 5 by adding an unbroken 95 for the sixth wicket in little more than 13 overs.

Leicestershire's reply was given a manic start by Shahid Afridi's 20 off ten balls, and Darren Maddy then joined Trevor Ward in a stand of 85. But Man-of-the-Match Parsons bowled Ward for 54 and also removed the Foxes' captain, Vince Wells, for three as wickets began to tumble at regular intervals. Eventually, Leicestershire were all out for 230 in the 46th over.

Somerset were finalists again in 2002, but this time their total of 256 for 8, of which Bowler made 67 and Parsons 41, proved inadequate as Australian batsman Matthew Elliott rallied Yorkshire from 19 for 2 to hit a magnificent 128 not out and guide the county home by six wickets.

The first of Gloucestershire's back-to-back triumphs was the humbling of highly fancied Worcestershire in a 2003 final that was all over by 4.10 pm Worcestershire, put in, reached 64 without loss before the loss of three wickets in quick succession – including that of the talismanic Graeme Hick for a fourth-ball duck – seemed to knock all the stuffing out of them.

Gloucestershire's battery of clever seamers, led by Jon Lewis and Ian Harvey and supported by the relentless urging behind the stumps of wicketkeeper Jack Russell, who stood up most of the time to add to the pressure-cooker atmosphere, eventually strangled Worcestershire out for 149. With Harvey then smashing a brilliant 36-ball 61 and Phil Weston enjoying every moment of his 50-ball 46 against his former county, Gloucestershire were home and hosed by seven wickets in just 20.3 overs.

When the same two sides made it all the way through to the 2004 final, it was billed as 'The Rematch' – or, if you were a Worcestershire fan, 'The Revenge Mission'. In reality, it was almost Groundhog Day. This time, put in to bat, Worcestershire made a far better fist of setting Gloucestershire a target; indeed, from the depths of 8 for 3 and with Hick again out for 0, Worcestershire reached 236 for 9 with Vikram Solanki batting courageously and skilfully through the first 45 overs to reach

Somerset are confirmed as the first winners of the C&G Trophy in 2001 as Steffan Jones castles Leicestershire's Scott Boswell.

115, and the nuggety David Leatherdale hitting 66 to help him add 194 for the fourth wicket.

But it was still nowhere near enough as Weston's unbeaten 110 saw Gloucestershire to victory by eight wickets, with 6.1 overs still remaining, after an opening stand of 141 between the left-hander and Craig Spearman, who made 70.

And so to 2005, when Hampshire held their nerve to beat Warwickshire by 18 runs despite missing their inspirational captain Shane Warne, who was forced to be with the Australian squad in Chelmsford – where the then uncapped Alastair Cook hit them for a double-century and his fellow 20-year-old Ravi Bopara also romped to three figures for Essex.

Hampshire, asked to bat first as is usual on cup final morning in late August or early September, chiefly had Sean Ervine (104) and Nic Pothas (68) to thank for totalling 290. In reply, Warwickshire were moving nicely as Ian Bell joined Nick Knight in a century stand for the second wicket after some early-over fireworks from Neil Carter (32), but then Bell began to suffer from cramp and – instead of leaving the field for treatment – soldiered on initially in clear discomfort and then holed out for 54.

By then, the asking rate had increased and, despite Knight's best efforts in a fine innings of 118 from 127 balls, Warwickshire could find no one else to help him reach out for glory. With wickets having fallen like autumn leaves at the other end, Knight was finally out in the 48th over and, two overs later, Warwickshire themselves were 272 all out.

Fast bowler James Kirtley sinks to his knees at the fall of the last Lancashire wicket. Sussex are the 2006 champions.

ONE-DAY ROLL OF HONOUR: 1963–2006

Gillette Cup	NatWest Trophy	C&G Trophy
1963 Sussex	1981 Derbyshire	2001 Somerset
1964 Sussex	1982 Surrey	2002 Yorkshire
1965 Yorkshire	1983 Somerset	2003 Gloucestershire
1966 Warwickshire	1984 Middlesex	2004 Gloucestershire
1967 Kent	1985 Essex	2005 Hampshire
1968 Warwickshire	1986 Sussex	2006 Sussex
1969 Yorkshire	1987 Nottinghamshire	
1970 Lancashire	1988 Middlesex	
1971 Lancashire	1989 Warwickshire	
1972 Lancashire	1990 Lancashire	
1973 Gloucestershire	1991 Hampshire	
1974 Kent	1992 Northamptonshire	
1975 Lancashire	1993 Warwickshire	
1976 Northamptonshire	1994 Worcestershire	
1977 Middlesex	1995 Warwickshire	
1978 Sussex	1996 Lancashire	
1979 Somerset	1997 Essex	
1980 Middlesex	1998 Lancashire	
	1999 Gloucestershire	
	2000 Gloucestershire	

PAKISTAN

ENGLAND IN PAKISTAN

ENGLAND IN PAKISTAN
By Jonathan Agnew

FIRST TEST
12–16 November 2005
at Multan Cricket Stadium, Multan

This first Test match after the Ashes euphoria proved to be a chastening experience for England. Snatching defeat from the jaws of certain victory was a habit we thought had been buried long ago, but this was a spectacular effort, and certainly one worthy of comparison with some of the classics of the bad old days. Ultimately, England's thoughtless and rather arrogant attempt to score the 198 they needed to win would cost them the series – and, as this young team grew to appreciate, only very rarely are tourists presented with winning opportunities in this part of the world.

England were also without their inspirational leader, Michael Vaughan – a situation that would worsen throughout the winter. A twisted knee – the same right knee that has caused him so many difficulties – meant that he missed this Multan Test match, and the one-day series in Pakistan. More worryingly, Vaughan did not play against India after Christmas, or in the series against Sri Lanka at the start of the following summer.

His regular deputy, Marcus Trescothick, took charge at the new stadium, which is a hair-raising half-hour drive between the

bullock carts from the city of Multan, and at 161 for 1, Pakistan seemed destined for a large score. Shaun Udal who, aged 36, was the oldest England debutant since John Childs in 1988, broke the stand of 81 between Salman Butt and Younis Khan, and shortly after tea Pakistan had slumped to 183 for 5, thanks to some fine pace bowling from Steve Harmison and Andrew Flintoff. Inzamam-ul-Haq held the innings together until the close, but the collapse continued on the second morning – including Inzamam for 53 – and when Danish

Marcus Trescothick takes charge of England in the opening Test of the three-match series against Pakistan, at Multan.

Kaneria was caught by Giles for 6, Pakistan were 274 all out, having lost nine wickets for 113 runs.

The pressure was now on England's depleted and inexperienced batting line-up: Ian Bell, Kevin Pietersen and Paul Collingwood at Nos. 3, 4 and 5 respectively totalled merely 16 caps between them. Although Andrew Strauss was trapped lbw for 9, Trescothick produced an outstanding innings of 193 without which England would have been in great difficulty. He shared a stand of 180 with Bell – who would have been dropped had Vaughan played – which dominated the second afternoon, and ended when Bell was caught at short leg for a composed and patient 71.

Trescothick continued his marathon on the third morning but, Flintoff apart, had precious little support. They added 93 after Pietersen and Collingwood scored 15 between them, but Flintoff perished on 45 aiming a slog to leg off Shoaib Akhtar, and having been dropped on 181, Trescothick finally edged Shabbir Ahmed to the wicketkeeper for 193 – his third-highest Test score made from 305 deliveries. England were encouraged by the statistic that they had always won on each of the previous occasions that Trescothick scored 150 or more, but their loss of seven wickets for 165 on the third day denied them a crushing lead. Shabbir, whose action was reported to the ICC after the match, took 4 for 54 and Pakistan began their second innings 144 runs behind.

By the close of the third day, Pakistan were only 19 runs behind with eight wickets left. Again the left-handed opener Butt played solidly and he teamed up with Inzamam the following morning to add 135. England took the new ball and with the second delivery, Inzamam suffered a brainstorm and offered no stroke to a ball from Matthew Hoggard that would have hit middle stump. Inzamam had scored 72 and his demise allowed England to take control of the game. Butt edged Hoggard to Geraint Jones for 122, and although Kamran Akmal showed his promise with 33, Pakistan slipped to 341 all out to leave England requiring 198 to win on a good batting pitch. Trescothick fell before the close of the fourth day, leaving his team all of the final day to score a further 174 with nine wickets in hand.

The trouble started in the 11th over of the morning when Bell, on 31, was caught behind off Kaneria, the leg spinner who, until now, had not looked either confident or effective. Four balls later, Strauss edged Kaneria to slip for 23 and the jitters began. In the following over Collingwood was

FIRST TEST – PAKISTAN v. ENGLAND
12–16 November 2005 at Multan

PAKISTAN

	First Innings		Second Innings	
Shoaib Malik	lbw b Flintoff	39	c Trescothick b Harmison	18
Salman Butt	c Jones b Udal	74	c Jones b Hoggard	122
Younis Khan	lbw b Harmison	39	c Trescothick b Flintoff	48
Mohammad Yousuf	b Flintoff	5	(6) c Bell b Flintoff	16
Inzamam-ul-Haq (capt)	c Strauss b Flintoff	53	lbw b Hoggard	72
Hasan Raza	b Harmison	0	(7) c Trescothick b Flintoff	1
*Kamran Akmal	c Trescothick b Hoggard	28	(8) c Pietersen b Harmison	33
Mohammad Sami	c Jones b Hoggard	1	(4) c Jones b Flintoff	3
Shoaib Akhtar	not out	10	c Bell b Giles	11
Shabbir Ahmed	b Flintoff	0	c Jones b Harmison	0
Danish Kaneria	c Giles b Harmison	6	not out	1
Extras	b 1, lb 7, nb 11	19	lb 6, nb 10	16
	(all out 98.2 overs)	274	(all out 105.5 overs)	341

	First Innings				Second Innings			
	O	M	R	W	O	M	R	W
Hoggard	22	4	55	2	27	2	81	2
Harmison	16.2	5	37	3	19.5	3	52	3
Flintoff	23	6	68	4	25	3	88	4
Collingwood	4	1	15	0	-	-	-	-
Giles	16	3	44	0	22	2	67	1
Udal	17	3	47	1	12	1	47	0

Fall of Wickets
1-80, 2-161, 3-166, 4-181, 5-183, 6-238, 7-244, 8-260, 9-260
1-31, 2-124, 3-131, 4-266, 5-285, 6-291, 7-295, 8-331, 9-332

ENGLAND

	First Innings		Second Innings	
ME Trescothick (capt)	c K Akmal b Shabbir Ahmed	193	b Shabbir Ahmed	5
AJ Strauss	lbw b Mohammad Sami	9	c Hasan Raza b Danish Kaneria	23
IR Bell	c Salman Butt b Shoaib Malik	71	c Kamran Akmal b Danish Kaneria	31
PD Collingwood	c K Akmal b Shabbir Ahmed	10	lbw b Mohammad Sami	3
MJ Hoggard	c Kamran Akmal b Shoaib Akhtar	1	(10) not out	0
KP Pietersen	c Salman Butt b Danish Kaneria	5	(5) c Kamran Akmal b M Sami	19
A Flintoff	c Shoaib Malik b Shoaib Akhtar	45	(6) c Younis Khan b Danish Kaneria	11
*GO Jones	b Shabbir Ahmed	22	(7) b Shoaib Akhtar	33
AF Giles	c Hasan Raza b Shabbir Ahmed	16	(8) b Shoaib Akhtar	14
SD Udal	lbw b Shoaib Akhtar	0	(9) b Danish Kaneria	18
SJ Harmison	not out	4	c Younis Khan b Shoaib Akhtar	9
Extras	b 8, lb 11, w 1, nb 22	42	b 6, lb 1, nb 2	9
	(all out 110.4 overs)	418	(all out 52.4 overs)	175

	First Innings				Second Innings			
	O	M	R	W	O	M	R	W
Shoaib Akhtar	27	2	99	3	12.4	1	49	3
Mohammad Sami	16	1	76	1	9	0	31	2
Shabbir Ahmed	22.4	7	54	4	10	0	25	1
Danish Kaneria	27	4	106	1	20	0	62	4
Shoaib Malik	18	1	64	1	1	0	1	0

Fall of Wickets
1-18, 2-198, 3-251, 4-266, 5-271, 6-364, 7-388, 8-399, 9-400
1-7, 2-64, 3-67, 4-67, 5-93, 6-101, 7-117, 8-166, 9-166

Umpires: BF Bowden (New Zealand) & SJA Taufel (Australia)
Toss: Pakistan
Test Debut: SD Udal
Man of the Match: Salman Butt

Pakistan won by 22 runs

trapped lbw by Mohammad Sami and England, needing 131 more runs, had lost three wickets for just three runs.

Pakistan now sensed their opportunity, but Flintoff and Pietersen added 26 crucial runs before Flintoff suffered his second rush of blood in the game, and hoisted Kaneria to deep midwicket for 11. Pietersen also paid the price for needless aggression when he played a wild slash at Sami and was caught behind for 19, and England were now 101 for 6. Jones played excellently first with Ashley Giles and then Udal to take England to within 32 of victory, but he was bowled by a Shoaib thunderbolt for 33, Kaneria deceived Udal with a perfect googly, leaving Harmison to be blown away by Shoaib and become his 150th Test victim.

It was a hapless batting performance in which England's batsmen seemed determined to complete their task as quickly as possible. They vowed to learn from this experience and to get it right next time – but the opportunity never arose again.

SECOND TEST
20–24 November 2005
at Iqbal Stadium, Faisalabad

A drawn match, but there was no shortage of controversy, excitement and, surely, the most blatant example of cheating there has been in modern Test cricket. Shahid Afridi was the man so outrageously guilty of unsporting behaviour that it beggared belief, not only because of the manner in which he deliberately attempted seriously to damage the pitch by performing a pirouette on a good length, but particularly that he chose to do so when a deafening bomb-like explosion from within the stadium had stopped play. With security such an issue on this tour, the blast – from what turned out to be a gas cylinder – might have had very serious consequences. The players from both teams gathered in the middle of the ground, anxiously wondering what would follow, and it was at this moment, with everyone's attention diverted, that Afridi shamelessly scuffed the pitch. His act of folly was caught on television, and he was subsequently banned for one Test and two one-day internationals. Not nearly enough, in my view.

Another controversial moment involved the first-innings dismissal of the Pakistan captain, Inzamam, which exposed an alarming mistake by all three umpires and, yet again, highlighted the fact that technology is far from foolproof. Batting serenely on 109, and with his team well set for a commanding

score on 369 for 5, Inzamam defended a ball from Harmison, which the bowler picked up in his follow through. Then, in a deliberate attempt to intimidate the batsman, Harmison hurled the ball at the stumps, which required Inzamam to take urgent evasive action. In so doing, and when the ball hit the wicket, he was out of his ground.

Despite Law 38.2 clearly stating that the batsman has to be attempting a run in order to be run out, Simon Taufel at the bowler's end referred the decision to Darrell Hair at square leg, who passed it on to the third umpire. As the two senior Australians chatted, either of them could have stopped the process there and then before, amazingly, the third umpire despatched Inzamam to the pavilion. It was a ghastly error by all concerned, and shows again that even when cut off from the pressure in the middle and with time to think everything through calmly and deliberately, the third umpire can still make a glaring error. The incident also highlighted the growing and deeply unpleasant trend of bowlers hurling the ball at a batsman under the guise of running him out.

Afridi – batting before his misdemeanour – scored 92 at the remarkable rate of only 85 balls, including six fours and six sixes. Dropped by Vaughan on 34, Afridi added 145 with Inzamam, and another useful contribution from Akmal steered Pakistan to a total of 462, which included 13 sixes.

At the close of the second day, England were 113 for 3 having lost Strauss for 12, Vaughan for 2 and Trescothick for 48. Had Akmal not missed a stumping chance offered by Bell in the fourth over of the third morning, Pakistan would have been in control, but Bell was reprieved on 38, and went on to score 115 from 272 balls. Pietersen provided the fireworks during a stand of 154, but once again fell recklessly to the second new ball when he drove Shoaib straight to mid-on for exactly 100 from 137 balls. This provided Pakistan with another opening, and England lost Bell and then Flintoff for 1 before Jones and Giles added 51. Udal added 33 on the fourth morning to lift England's total to within 16 of Pakistan – who now needed to bat carefully through the remainder of the day to make the game safe.

But although their second innings began securely enough, England chipped away to leave Pakistan only 199 ahead at the start of the final day with just four wickets – including Inzamam's – left to fall. This was when England adopted amazingly defensive tactics. Instead of going for the kill and trying to dismiss Pakistan, they declined to take the new ball, and men were scattered in run-saving

SECOND TEST – PAKISTAN v. ENGLAND
20–24 November 2005 at Faisalabad

PAKISTAN

	First Innings		Second Innings	
Shoaib Malik	c Flintoff b Hoggard	27	c Bell b Flintoff	26
Salman Butt	c Jones b Harmison	26	lbw b Udal	50
Younis Khan	c Pietersen b Flintoff	7	lbw b Hoggard	27
Mohammad Yousuf	c & b Bell	78	b Flintoff	20
Inzamam-ul-Haq (capt)	run out	109	not out	100
Shahid Afridi	c Trescothick b Hoggard	92	b Flintoff	0
*Kamran Akmal	c Jones b Giles	41	c Jones b Harmison	9
Naved-ul-Hasan	b Harmison	25	c Jones b Harmison	1
Mohammad Sami	c & b Giles	18	(10) lbw b Hoggard	5
Shoaib Akhtar	c Flintoff b Harmison	12	(9) c Jones b Hoggard	14
Danish Kaneria	not out	4	not out	2
Extras	b 5, lb 3, nb 15	23	b 4, lb 5, w 2, nb 3	14
	(all out 115.4 overs)	**462**	(9 wkts dec 93.1 overs)	**268**

	First Innings				Second Innings			
	O	M	R	W	O	M	R	W
Hoggard	22	0	115	2	16	1	50	3
Flintoff	29	2	76	1	27.1	2	66	3
Giles	20	1	85	2	17	3	51	0
Harmison	24.4	5	85	3	19	2	61	2
Udal	13	1	60	0	14	2	31	1
Bell	7	1	33	1	–	–	–	–

Fall of Wickets
1-53, 2-63, 3-73, 4-201, 5-346, 6-369, 7-403, 8-431, 9-446
1-54, 2-104, 3-108, 4-164, 5-164, 6-183, 7-187, 8-234, 9-244

ENGLAND

	First Innings		Second Innings	
ME Trescothick	c Kamran Akmal b M Sami	48	b Shoaib Akhtar	0
AJ Strauss	b Naved-ul-Hasan	12	b Naved-ul-Hasan	0
MP Vaughan (capt)	b Naved-ul-Hasan	2	lbw b Naved-ul-Hasan	9
IR Bell	c Kamran Akmal b Shahid Afridi	115	c Kamran Akmal b Shoaib Akhtar	0
KP Pietersen	c M Yousuf b Shoaib Akhtar	100	c sub b Naved-ul-Hasan	42
A Flintoff	b Shoaib Akhtar	1	c sub b Shoaib Akhtar	56
*GO Jones	lbw b Shahid Afridi	55	not out	30
AF Giles	b Shahid Afridi	26	not out	13
SD Udal	not out	33		
MJ Hoggard	b Shahid Afridi	2		
SJ Harmison	run out	16		
Extras	b 1, lb 12, w 1, nb 22	36	b 4, lb 8, nb 2	14
	(all out 132.3 overs)	**446**	(6 wkts 48 overs)	**164**

	First Innings				Second Innings			
	O	M	R	W	O	M	R	W
Shoaib Akhtar	27	4	93	2	11	2	61	3
Naved-ul-Hasan	20	2	63	2	12	3	30	3
Mohammad Sami	19	4	51	1	6	1	18	0
Shahid Afridi	30.3	3	95	4	7	2	16	0
Danish Kaneria	32	3	102	0	12	4	27	0
Shoaib Malik	4	0	29	0	–	–	–	–

Fall of Wickets
1-33, 2-39, 3-107, 4-261, 5-272, 6-327, 7-378, 8-395, 9-399
1-1, 2-5, 3-10, 4-20, 5-100, 6-138

Umpires: DB Hair (Australia) & SJA Taufel (Australia)
Toss: Pakistan
Man of the Match: Inzamam-ul-Haq

Match drawn

Ian Bell, who scored 115 in the first innings at Faisalabad and went on to become England's most successful batsman in the series against Pakistan.

positions. Strauss, who was due immediately to leave the tour on paternity leave, might have had his mind on other things when he dropped an absolute sitter at deep midwicket to give Inzamam a life on 79. It was desperately unimaginative cricket from a team that had played so positively the previous summer, and when Inzamam finally declared, he had completed his second hundred of the match – and his 24th in all, to overhaul Javed Miandad's record for Pakistan.

England's target was now 285 from a minimum of 64 overs, but there could only be one winner when, within six overs, England were 20 for 4 having lost Strauss, Trescothick and Bell for ducks, and Vaughan for 9. Pietersen and Flintoff set about averting defeat with a stand of 80, but Naved had Pietersen caught at midwicket for 42 and Flintoff gloved the rampant Shoaib to gully for 56. There was always the likelihood of bad light rescuing England in the late afternoon, but Jones and Giles needed to battle away for 47 minutes before the umpires offered them salvation with 16 overs remaining.

THIRD TEST
29 November–3 December 2005
at Gaddafi Stadium, Lahore

Lahore, we all thought, would be a certain draw. The winter days are short in this part of the world and, by December, the evenings draw in very quickly. Bad light would knock at least an hour off each day, and morning dew would prevent the lost time from being made up. In fact, Pakistan meted out a thrashing – by an innings and 100 runs – to take the series 2-0.

With Strauss at home awaiting the birth of his first child, Vaughan returned to the position he overwhelmingly prefers at the top of the order. He won England's first toss of the series, and all seemed well when he cruised to an excellent half-century. But with the score on 101, he became the first of several England batsmen to fall to the sweep stroke – being caught at square leg for 58. In no time Bell had perished in similar style for 4 and, on 50, Trescothick was brilliantly caught by the diving Akmal. Shoaib Malik – another with a dodgy action – took all three wickets in four overs as England slipped to 115 for 3.

Paul Collingwood, restored to the team in Strauss's absence, seized his opportunity in style as, at the other end, partners came and went. Pietersen scored 34 before edging Naved down the legside, and

Pakistan's grip tightened when Flintoff hooked the same bowler to Shoaib at fine leg for 12. England were now squandering the benign batting conditions on 201 for 5, and they also lost Jones to the dreaded sweep shot before the close.

Collingwood started the second day 29 runs away from his maiden Test century, but he lost Udal to the fourth ball of the morning – Udal's first – and the battle was on to see if Collingwood could reach his landmark. Liam Plunkett, in his first Test, helped his Durham team-mate to reach 96, when Shoaib bowled a searing bouncer. Collingwood took it on, knowing it was either his century, or out – and he was caught by Kaneria on the fine leg boundary. Another five yards, and Collingwood would have been celebrating. As it was, his downfall hastened England's demise, and their total of 288 was woefully inadequate.

Hoggard nipped out Shoaib Malik and Asim Kamal within five overs, though, and Plunkett took the wicket of Butt with his 11th delivery in Test cricket. At 68 for 3, Pakistan urgently needed a substantial partnership. Inzamam and Mohammad Yousuf threatened to steer their team out of trouble, but having put on 80, Inzamam was hit on the right wrist by Harmison and was forced to retire hurt on 35. At the close of the second day, Pakistan were 103 behind with six wickets left, and Yousuf on 84.

Shoaib Akhtar, the nightwatchman, made 38 – his highest score in Tests – as Pakistan strove to establish a lead on the third day, and his dismissal enabled Kamran Akmal to join forces with Yousuf. They batted throughout the day – and into the next – establishing a record sixth-wicket stand of 269, with Akmal making his second Test century from 178 balls. On and on they went until, after a ten-hour marathon, Yousuf holed out at long on for 223 from 373 deliveries. Pakistan were 516 for 6, and led by 228 but this merely brought Inzamam back to the crease. Although, six overs later, Akmal was caught at midwicket for 154, Inzamam played with extraordinary fluency and despite eight fielders being posted on the boundary at times, he raced to 97 from only 101 balls. 190 runs were scored in 28 overs before lunch at a rate of 6.6 per over but his run out, three short of a third century in the series, brought about the declaration on 636 for 8.

Pakistan held a massive lead of 348, and England promptly lost Trescothick to the second ball of their reply. Vaughan was caught and bowled by Shoaib for 13 in the sixth over after lunch, but Bell and

Paul Collingwood needed all his Geordie grit to survive against some hostile Pakistani fast bowling, but innings of 96 and 80 at Lahore provided him with a memorable Test comeback amid the ruins of another England defeat.

Collingwood batted out the rest of the day to leave England with a fighting chance of saving the match.

When the pair were still together at lunch – and with the usual prospect of bad light intervening around teatime – England appeared to be home and dry. What followed was a staggering collapse of eight wickets for 43 in 73 balls. Collingwood's dismissal, to the fourth ball after the break, triggered the disintegration. He was caught at slip off Kaneria for 80, Pietersen fell in the leg spinner's following over for 1 and Flintoff was undone by a

brilliant googly next ball. Alarm bells were ringing loudly as panic seemed to grip the lower order, and things got speedily worse when Bell was fooled by Shoaib's slower ball and was lbw for 92 from 189 deliveries.

The end was nigh. Jones was unluckily given out lbw for 5, Udal scored 25, but the combination of Shoaib, Sami and Kaneria blew away the tail. Shoaib took 5 for 71 to complete a superb series in which, on lifeless pitches, he had claimed 17 wickets while Kaneria finished with 4 for 52.

THIRD TEST – PAKISTAN v. ENGLAND
29 November –3 December 2005 at Lahore

ENGLAND

	First Innings		Second Innings	
ME Trescothick	c K Akmal b Shoaib Malik	50	lbw b Shoaib Akhtar	0
MP Vaughan (capt)	c M Yousuf b Shoaib Malik	58	c & b Shoaib Akhtar	13
IR Bell	c M Yousuf b Shoaib Malik	4	lbw b Shoaib Akhtar	92
PD Collingwood	c Danish Kaneria b Shoaib Akhtar	96	c Hasan Raza b Danish Kaneria	80
KP Pietersen	c K Akmal b Naved-ul-Hasan	34	c Hasan Raza b Danish Kaneria	1
A Flintoff	c S Akhtar b Naved-ul-Hasan	12	b Danish Kaneria	0
*GO Jones	b Danish Kaneria	4	lbw b Shoaib Akhtar	5
SD Udal	c Asim Kamal b Danish Kaneria	10	c Salman Butt b M Sami	25
LE Plunkett	b Mohammad Sami	9	lbw b Shoaib Akhtar	0
MJ Hoggard	not out	1	b Danish Kaneria	0
SJ Harmison	c K Akmal b Mohammad Sami	0	not out	0
Extras	lb 5, nb 5	10	b 13, lb 9, w 1, nb 9	32
	(all out 94 overs)	**288**	(all out 77.1 overs)	**248**

	First Innings				Second Innings			
	O	M	R	W	O	M	R	W
Shoaib Akhtar	22	6	45	1	19	3	71	5
Naved-ul-Hasan	20	3	76	2	16	3	55	0
Mohammad Sami	18	2	57	2	16	4	39	1
Shoaib Malik	14	1	58	3	4	2	9	0
Danish Kaneria	20	2	47	2	22.1	8	52	4

Fall of Wickets
1-101, 2-114, 3-115, 4-183, 5-201, 6-225, 7-249, 8-280, 9-288
1-0, 2-30, 3-205, 4-212, 5-212, 6-212, 7-227, 8-227, 9-248

PAKISTAN

	First Innings	
Shoaib Malik	c Plunkett b Hoggard	0
Salman Butt	c Jones b Plunkett	28
Asim Kamal	lbw b Hoggard	5
Mohammad Yousuf	c Pietersen b Udal	223
Inzamam-ul-Haq (capt)	run out	97
Hasan Raza	c Flintoff b Harmison	21
Shoaib Akhtar	c Udal b Plunkett	38
*Kamran Akmal	c Vaughan b Flintoff	154
Naved-ul-Hasan	not out	42
Mohammad Sami		
Danish Kaneria		
Extras	b 5, lb 12, w 4, nb 7	28
	(8 wkts dec 156.2 overs)	**636**

	First Innings			
	O	M	R	W
Hoggard	23	4	106	2
Flintoff	36	8	111	1
Harmison	43	3	154	1
Plunkett	28.2	1	125	2
Udal	18	1	92	1
Collingwood	6	0	22	0
Bell	2	0	9	0

Fall of Wickets
1-0, 2-12, 3-68, 4-180, 5-247, 6-516, 7-546, 8-636

Umpires: DB Hair (Australia) & RE Koertzen (South Africa)
Toss: England
Man of the Match: Mohammad Yousuf
Man of the Series: Inzamam-ul-Haq

<u>Pakistan won by an innings and 100 runs</u>

SERIES AVERAGES
Pakistan v. England

PAKISTAN

Batting	M	Inns	NO	Runs	HS	Av	100	50	c/st
Inzamam-ul-Haq	3	5	1	431	109	107.75	2	3	-/-
Mohammad Yousuf	3	5	0	342	223	68.40	1	1	3/-
Salman Butt	3	5	0	300	122	60.00	1	2	3/-
Kamran Akmal	3	5	0	265	154	53.00	1	-	11/-
Shahid Afridi	2	2	0	92	92	46.00	-	1	-/-
Naved-ul-Hasan	2	3	1	68	42*	34.00	-	-	-/-
Younis Khan	2	4	0	121	48	30.25	-	-	2/-
Shoaib Malik	3	5	0	110	39	22.00	-	-	1/-
Shoaib Akhtar	3	5	1	85	38	21.25	-	-	2/-
Danish Kaneria	3	4	3	13	6	13.00	-	-	1/-
Hasan Raza	2	3	0	22	21	7.33	-	-	4/-
Mohammad Sami	3	4	0	27	18	6.75	-	-	-/-
Asim Kamal	1	1	0	5	5	5.00	-	-	1/-
Shabbir Ahmed	1	2	0	0	0	0.00	-	-	-/-

Bowling	Overs	Mds	Runs	Wkts	Av	Best	5/inn	10m
Shabbir Ahmed	32.4	7	79	5	15.80	4-54	-	-
Shoaib Akhtar	118.4	18	418	17	24.58	5-71	1	-
Shahid Afridi	37.3	5	111	4	27.75	4-95	-	-
Naved-ul-Hasan	68	11	224	7	32.00	3-30	-	-
Danish Kaneria	133.1	21	396	11	36.00	4-52	-	-
Mohammad Sami	84	12	272	7	38.85	2-31	-	-
Shoaib Malik	41	4	161	4	40.25	3-58	-	-

ENGLAND

Batting	M	Inns	NO	Runs	HS	Av	100	50	c/st
IR Bell	3	6	0	313	115	52.16	1	2	4/-
ME Trescothick	3	6	0	296	193	49.33	1	1	5/-
PD Collingwood	2	4	0	189	96	47.25	-	2	-/-
KP Pietersen	3	6	0	201	100	33.50	1	-	3/-
GO Jones	3	6	1	149	55	29.80	-	1	11/-
AF Giles	2	4	1	69	26	23.00	-	-	2/-
SD Udal	3	5	1	86	33*	21.50	-	-	1/-
A Flintoff	3	6	0	125	56	20.83	-	1	3/-
MP Vaughan	2	4	0	82	58	20.50	-	1	1/-
AJ Strauss	2	4	0	44	23	11.00	-	-	1/-
SJ Harmison	3	5	2	29	16	9.66	-	-	-/-
LE Plunkett	1	2	0	9	9	4.50	-	-	1/-
MJ Hoggard	3	5	2	4	2	1.33	-	-	-/-

Bowling	Overs	Mds	Runs	Wkts	Av	Best	5/inn	10m
A Flintoff	140.1	21	409	13	31.46	4-68	-	-
SJ Harmison	122.5	18	389	12	32.41	3-37	-	-
MJ Hoggard	110	11	407	11	37.00	3-50	-	-
IR Bell	9	1	42	1	42.00	1-33	-	-
LE Plunkett	28.2	1	125	2	62.50	2-125	-	-
AF Giles	75	9	247	3	82.33	2-85	-	-
SD Udal	74	8	277	3	92.33	1-31	-	-

Also bowled: PD Collingwood 10-1-37-0.

ONE-DAY INTERNATIONALS
v. England

Match One
10 December 2005 at Lahore
England 327 for 4 (50 overs)
(AJ Strauss 94, A Flintoff 72*,
KP Pietersen 56)
Pakistan 285 all out (46.5 overs)
(Salman Butt 67, Younis Khan 60,
Mohammad Yousuf 59, Shoaib Malik 50,
LE Plunkett 3 for 51, A Flintoff 3 for 73)
England won by 42 runs

Match Two
12 December 2005 at Lahore
England 230 all out (48.4 overs) (LE Plunkett 56,
Shoaib Akhtar 5 for 54)
Pakistan 231 for 3 (44 overs) (Kamran Akmal 102)
Pakistan won by 7 wickets

Match Three
15 December 2005 at Karachi
Pakistan 353 for 6 (50 overs) (Kamran Akmal 109,
Mohammad Yousuf 68, Abdul Razzaq 51*)
England 188 all out (42 overs) (Shoaib Malik 3 for 29)
Pakistan won by 165 runs

Kevin Pietersen drives Shoaib Malik for four during his innings of 56 in England's opening one-day international win against Pakistan at Lahore.

Match Four
19 December 2005 at Rawalpindi
Pakistan 210 all out (47.2 overs) (Inzamam-ul-Haq 81*)
England 197 all out (48.1 overs) (Shahid Afridi 3 for 34)
Pakistan won by 13 runs

Match Five
21 December 2005 at Rawalpindi
England 206 for 9 (50 overs)
Pakistan 200 for 9 (50 overs)
(Yasir Hameed 57, Mohammad Yousuf 54,
JM Anderson 4 for 48, ID Blackwell 3 for 29)
England won by 6 runs

Pakistan won the series 3–2

Although England's hopes of rare overseas success
were raised by victory in the opening match of the
series, two heavy defeats confirmed that there is still
a great deal of room for improvement.

Strauss, Pietersen and Flintoff all hit half-centuries
as England rattled up 327 for 4 in the first game in
Lahore. Although Pakistan got away to a flier,
Plunkett took three middle-order wickets to give
England victory by 42 runs. In the second match
Shoaib Akhtar claimed 5 for 54 to skittle England
out for 230. This was never going to be enough of a
target, and Kamran Akmal's 102 from 111 balls
guided Pakistan home with six overs in hand.

At the National Stadium, Karachi, England
equalled their heaviest-ever defeat in this form of
the game to put Pakistan 2-1 up in the series. Put in
to bat, the hosts reached 353-6, the most ever
conceded by England, with Akmal hitting 109,
Yousuf 68 and Abdul Razzaq 51. Shahid Afridi
blasted 31 from 14 balls and Inzamam-ul-Haq 45
from 35. England were bowled out for only 188 in
42 overs with Malik taking 3 for 29.

One more win by Pakistan would clinch the
series, and this they achieved in the fourth match, at
Rawalpindi, albeit by the relatively narrow margin of
13 runs. After another disappointing performance
by the top order, England's last-wicket pair of
Anderson and Kabir Ali came together with 47 still
needed, and they put on 33 to nudge the visitors
within sight of victory. But Younis Khan brilliantly
caught Anderson at slip with 11 balls remaining.

With the pressure off, Pakistan slipped to a
narrow six-run defeat in the final match. Chasing
only 207 to win, they were coasting at 159 for 4, but
were swept away by Anderson who finished with 4
for 48, while Blackwell took three wickets in
successive overs.

PAKISTAN REPORT
By Qamar Ahmed

Pakistan came to England in the summer of 2006
expecting to continue their fine form and end their
season on a triumphant note. Had they done so it
would have been the perfect icing on the cake for a
season in which they humbled the Ashes-winning
England team in a home series late in 2005, beat
India in the last of the three Tests at home to win
another series and followed that up with a 1-0
victory against Sri Lanka immediately afterwards.

Disappointingly for them, however, injuries to
their key bowlers Shoaib Akhtar, Rana Naved-ul-
Hasan, Mohammad Asif and Shoaib Malik just
before the start of the English tour – plus the ball-
tampering controversy during the Fourth and final
Test at The Oval – ruined a season which surely
would have appeared highly impressive.

Pakistan's most satisfying moment of the year was
undoubtedly their 2-0 win against England at the
end of 2005. England, oozing with confidence
having just regained the Ashes after 18 years, had
arrived in Pakistan with their heads high, hoping to
win another series against a top-rated team to
confirm that their victory against Australia was not
just a flash in the pan.

But they found conditions tough as they were
emphatically beaten by an impressive margin of 2-0
in a three-match Test series, losing at Multan and
Lahore. Their 3-2 defeat in the five match one-day
series was yet another setback.

Up against a fit and fast Shoaib Akhtar they were
devastated as the tearaway fast bowler controlled his
line and length superbly to finish with a haul of 17
wickets at 24.58 apiece in the series. Naved-ul-
Hasan, Shabbir Ahmed and leg spinner Danish
Kaneria assisted him expertly. In contrast, England's
batting failed to live up to expectations, while their
much-vaunted fast bowling line-up of Andrew
Flintoff, Steve Harmison and Matthew Hoggard
could not find much help from the Pakistan pitches.

For Pakistan, captain Inzamam-ul-Haq with 431
runs at 107.75 which included two hundreds and
three fifties in five innings and Mohammad Yousuf,
who hit a career-best 223 at Lahore, were a cut
above the rest. Salman Butt, the opener, and
wicketkeeper Kamran Akmal also contributed
handsomely at crucial junctures.

India, paying a return visit to Pakistan at the
beginning of 2006 to play their third series within
two years against their arch-rivals, found the hosts
in stunning form. The first two Tests, though,

Shoaib Akhtar, the 'Rawalpindi Express', is too quick for another victim as England's Liam Plunkett is sent packing in the Third Test at Lahore.

played in rather cold conditions, petered out into high-scoring draws.

Indian openers Virender Sehwag and his captain Rahul Dravid missed the all-time first-wicket record of 413, set by their own countrymen Vinoo Mankad and Pankaj Roy 50 years ago, by a whisker as the Lahore Test fizzled out in a draw. Younis Khan (199), Mohammad Yousuf (173), Shahid Afridi (103) and Kamran Akmal (102 not out) also scored centuries in the match. At Faisalabad, in another high-scoring match, there was a century each for Inzamam-ul-Haq (119), Shahid Afridi (156), Younis Khan (194), Mohammad Yousuf (126) and, for India, for Rahul Dravid (103) and Mahendra Dhoni (148).

In the Third and final Test at Karachi, however, Pakistan won by 341 runs and with it the series 1-0. Having led India by seven runs on the first innings, Pakistan scored a massive 599 in their second knock to set India an impossible 607 runs to get. They

were dismissed for 265 with some fine bowling by Mohammad Asif.

India, in consolation, hit back to win the one-day series. Younis Khan, with 553 runs at 110.60 including two near double-centuries, and Mohammad Yousuf, with 461 runs at 92.20, were the top batsmen for the Test series.

On the tour to Sri Lanka that followed, Pakistan won both the two-match Test series and the one-day series. Their one-day series success also enabled them to gain enough points to qualify for the ICC Champions Trophy in India. Mohammad Asif, who did so well in Pakistan against India, once again showed great promise and improvement by taking 11 wickets in the Second Test win at Kandy. Asif finished with 17 wickets at 10.76 in the series.

Pakistan's international season finally culminated with their participation in a tournament at Abu Dhabi where they lost to India in the final to share

OF PAKISTAN

By Qamar Ahmed

Pakistan have come a long way since becoming a full member of the ICC 54 years ago. They may have been the whipping boys of international cricket in their years of infancy but now only a few would argue their claim of being one of the best teams of the last quarter of a century.

Having achieved the status of a newly created country in 1947, after the end of colonial rule when India was partitioned, Pakistan lost no time in establishing itself as a Test-playing country too. There was, of course, a ready-made cricket culture from the years of being part of undivided India.

Whereas countries like India, New Zealand, South Africa and West Indies took 25, 45, 12 and 6 matches respectively to win their first Test, Pakistan – like Australia and England – achieved that goal in the first year as a Test-playing nation. In fact, their historic first victory came in only their second Test, against India, when they beat them at Lucknow by an innings and 43 runs in 1952.

They were well served in their early years by men like Abdul Hafeez Kardar, their first Test captain, Fazal Mahmood, Hanif Mohammad, Imtiaz Ahmed, Zaheer Abbas, Majid Khan, Sarfraz Nawaz, Wasim Bari and Asif Iqbal to name but a few.

But it was from the 1980s onwards that Pakistan started to emerge as a force through the astute leadership of all-rounder Imran Khan who, with the help of great talents like Wasim Akram, Waqar Younis, Javed Miandad, Salim Malik, Inzamam-ul-Haq, Abdul Qadir and Mushtaq Ahmed, started to win against the top nations both at home and on overseas tours.

Under Imran's leadership, Pakistan arguably had their best results both at Test and one-day level and with Imran, Wasim, Waqar, Miandad, Saeed Anwar, Aamir Sohail, Abdul Qadir, Mushtaq Ahmed, Saqlain Mushtaq and Moin Khan around this whole era might best be described as incredible.

There is no doubt, however, that Pakistan's most glorious moments in the last 25 years came when they won their first-ever Test series against England in England in 1987, when Imran led them to a 1-0 win in the series by winning at Headingley by an innings and 18 runs.

Their further wins against England in the 1992 and 1996 series, under Javed Miandad and Wasim Akram respectively, and by margins of 2-1 and 2-0, were also highly impressive.

The emergence of record-breaking fast bowlers like Wasim and Waqar, spinners of the ability of Qadir, Mushtaq and Saqlain, and batsmen of the quality of Miandad, Malik, Ijaz Ahmed, Inzamam, Anwar and Sohail were all part of that successful machine.

Pakistan's first win in a Triangular series in Australia, when they won the Carlton and United one-day series in 1996–97, was another big achievement, and on an individual level so was the triple century (329) by Inzamam against New Zealand at Lahore in 2002 and Shahid Afridi's remarkable 37-ball hundred against Sri Lanka at Nairobi in a one-day international in 1996-97.

Yet, over and above all of this, it was Pakistan's victory in the World Cup final at the MCG in 1992, against England by 22 runs, which attracted a nationwide celebration and which still remains their crowning moment of the last 25 years.

Imran Khan's great career gets its crowning glory as Pakistan win the 1992 World Cup final in Melbourne.

Pakistan's master batsman of the next five years? Mohammad Yousuf has enjoyed a prolific 2006.

the two-match one-day rubber. All-rounder Shahid Afridi's announcement of his retirement from Tests soon after this came as a huge shock – but he reversed his decision, after discussions with team management and family, and subsequently played a full part in Pakistan's tour of England.

The 2005–06 domestic season turned out to be the longest ever, only 36 days short of a year in fact, with Sialkot emerging as the Quaid-e-Azam Trophy champions for the first time. The Patron's Trophy first-class competition was won by National Bank of Pakistan. Habib Bank won the Patron's National One-Day Tournament and Sialkot Stallions dethroned Faisalabad Wolves by winning the National Twenty20 championship. Test batsman Faisal Iqbal of PIA and Karachi Harbour scored 1213 runs at 71.35, including five hundreds and six fifties, and Fawad Alam of Karachi Harbour and Pakistan Customs made 1,072 runs at 53.60. Pace bowlers Fazl-e-Akbar, with 80 wickets, and Samiullah Niazi, with 75 scalps, were the most successful bowlers of the domestic season.

FIRST TEST – PAKISTAN v. INDIA
13–17 January 2006 at Lahore

PAKISTAN

	First Innings	
Shoaib Malik	c Harbhajan Singh b Pathan	59
Salman Butt	run out	6
Younis Khan	run out	199
Mohammad Yousuf	st Dhoni b Kumble	173
Inzamam-ul-Haq (capt)	lbw b Kumble	1
Shahid Afridi	c Harbhajan Singh b Agarkar	103
*Kamran Akmal	not out	102
Naved-ul-Hasan	c Ganguly b Agarkar	9
Mohammad Sami	not out	1
Shoaib Akhtar		
Danish Kaneria		
Extras	b 4, lb 12, w 2, nb 8	26
	(7 wkts dec 143.3 overs)	679

	First Innings			
	O	M	R	W
Pathan	32	4	133	1
Agarkar	24	3	122	2
Ganguly	6	1	14	0
Harbhajan Singh	34	5	176	0
Kumble	39.3	2	178	2
Sehwag	6	0	24	0
Tendulkar	2	0	16	0

Fall of Wickets
1-12, 2-136, 3-455, 4-456, 5-477, 6-647, 7-668

INDIA

	First Innings	
V Sehwag	c K Akmal b Naved-ul-Hasan	254
R Dravid (capt)	not out	128
VVS Laxman	not out	0
SC Ganguly		
SR Tendulkar		
Yuvraj Singh		
*MS Dhoni		
IK Pathan		
AB Agarkar		
A Kumble		
Harbhajan Singh		
Extras	b 2, lb 7, w 2, nb 17	28
	(1 wkt 77.2 overs)	410

	First Innings			
	O	M	R	W
Shoaib Akhtar	16.2	6	46	0
Naved-ul-Hasan	16	1	94	1
Shahid Afridi	11	0	55	0
Mohammad Sami	12	1	67	0
Danish Kaneria	10	0	69	0
Shoaib Malik	12	1	70	0

Fall of Wickets
1-410

Umpires: DB Hair (Australia) & RE Koertzen (South Africa)
Toss: Pakistan
Man of the Match: V Sehwag

Match drawn

SECOND TEST – PAKISTAN v. INDIA
21–25 January 2006 at Faisalabad

PAKISTAN

	First Innings	R		Second Innings	R
Shoaib Malik	c Dravid b RP Singh	19			
Salman Butt	c Dhoni b Khan	37	(1) c Tendulkar b Kumble	24
Younis Khan	c Yuvraj Singh b RP Singh	83	lbw b RP Singh	194
Mohammad Yousuf	c Dhoni b RP Singh	65	run out	126
Inzamam-ul-Haq (capt)	c Dhoni b Khan	119		
Shahid Afridi	c Yuvraj Singh b Kumble	156	c Dhoni b Khan	1
Abdul Razzaq	c Dhoni b RP Singh	37	(5) c Laxman b Khan	32
*Kamran Akmal	c Sehwag b Kumble	0	(2) c Kumble b Pathan	78
Shoaib Akhtar	c Harbhajan Singh b Khan	47	(8) not out	0
Mohammad Asif	not out	6	(7) b Khan	0
Danish Kaneria	b Kumble	0	(9) b Khan	0
Extras	b 3, lb 4, w 3, nb 9	19	b 9, lb 10, w 3, nb 13	35
	(all out 136.2 overs)	588	(8 wkts dec 116.4 overs)	490

	First Innings				Second Innings			
	O	M	R	W	O	M	R	W
Pathan	19	4	106	0	22	2	80	1
RP Singh	25	3	89	4	22	3	75	1
Khan	32	7	135	3	19.4	4	61	4
Harbhajan Singh	25	1	101	0	22	2	78	0
Kumble	35.2	5	150	3	21	3	118	1
Yuvraj Singh	-	-	-	-	9	0	46	0
Dhoni	-	-	-	-	1	0	13	0

Fall of Wickets
1-49, 2-62, 3-207, 4-216, 5-467, 6-469, 7-509, 8-567, 9-584
1-52, 2-181, 3-423, 4-488, 5-490, 6-490, 7-490, 8-490

INDIA

	First Innings	R		Second Innings	R
V Sehwag	c sub b Abdul Razzaq	31		
R Dravid (capt)	run out	103	not out	5
VVS Laxman	c K Akmal b Danish Kaneria	90	(1) not out	8
SR Tendulkar	c K Akmal b Shoaib Akhtar	14		
Yuvraj Singh	c Danish Kaneria b M Asif	4		
*MS Dhoni	st K Akmal b Danish Kaneria	148		
IK Pathan	lbw b Abdul Razzaq	90		
A Kumble	c K Akmal b Danish Kaneria	15		
Harbhajan Singh	lbw b Shahid Afridi	38		
Z Khan	not out	20		
RP Singh	c & b Shahid Afridi	6		
Extras	b 3, lb 15, w 3, nb 23	44	w 6, nb 2	8
	(all out 165.4 overs)	603	(0 wkts 8 overs)	21

	First Innings				Second Innings			
	O	M	R	W	O	M	R	W
Shoaib Akhtar	25	7	100	1	-	-	-	-
Mohammad Asif	34	6	103	1	-	-	-	-
Abdul Razzaq	28	1	126	2	-	-	-	-
Danish Kaneria	54	6	165	3	-	-	-	-
Shahid Afridi	24.4	0	91	2	4	0	16	0
Younis Khan	-	-	-	-	4	0	5	0

Fall of Wickets
1-39, 2-236, 3-241, 4-258, 5-281, 6-491, 7-529, 8-553, 9-587

Umpires: RE Koertzen (South Africa) & SJA Taufel (Australia)
Toss: Pakistan
Test Debut: RP Singh
Man of the Match: RP Singh

Match drawn

THIRD TEST – PAKISTAN v. INDIA
29 January – 1 February 2006 at Karachi

PAKISTAN

	First Innings	R		Second Innings	R
Salman Butt	c Dravid b Pathan	0	lbw b Ganguly	53
Imran Farhat	c Dhoni b RP Singh	22	c Tendulkar b Pathan	57
Younis Khan (capt)	lbw b Pathan	0	lbw b Kumble	77
Mohammad Yousuf	b Pathan	0	lbw b Kumble	97
Faisal Iqbal	lbw b Khan	5	c Tendulkar b Khan	139
Shahid Afridi	b Khan	10	c Tendulkar b RP Singh	60
Abdul Razzaq	lbw b RP Singh	45	c Yuvraj Singh b Kumble	90
*Kamran Akmal	c Dhoni b Pathan	113	not out	0
Shoaib Akhtar	c Yuvraj Singh b Pathan	45		
Mohammad Asif	c Laxman b RP Singh	0		
Danish Kaneria	not out	0		
Extras	lb 2, w 2, nb 1	5	b 7, lb 7, w 1, nb 11	26
	(all out 60.1 overs)	245	(7 wkts dec 140.1 overs)	599

	First Innings				Second Innings			
	O	M	R	W	O	M	R	W
Pathan	17.1	4	61	5	25	3	106	1
Khan	15	2	75	2	28	4	103	1
RP Singh	16	1	66	3	24	1	115	1
Ganguly	2	0	9	0	16	1	68	1
Kumble	10	1	32	0	37.1	3	151	3
Sehwag	-	-	-	-	1	0	2	0
Tendulkar	-	-	-	-	9	0	40	0

Fall of Wickets
1-0, 2-0, 3-0, 4-13, 5-37, 6-39, 7-154, 8-236, 9-245
1-109, 2-122, 3-280, 4-318, 5-402, 6-598, 7-599

INDIA

	First Innings	R		Second Innings	R
VVS Laxman	b Mohammad Asif	19	(3) b Mohammad Asif	21
R Dravid (capt)	c K Akmal b Mohammad Asif	3	c Kamran Akmal b Shoaib Akhtar	2
V Sehwag	c Kamran Akmal b Shoaib Akhtar	5	(1) b Mohammad Asif	4
SR Tendulkar	b Abdul Razzaq	23	b Mohammad Asif	26
SC Ganguly	c M Asif b Abdul Razzaq	34	lbw b Abdul Razzaq	37
Yuvraj Singh	lbw b Mohammad Asif	45	c K Akmal b Abdul Razzaq	122
*MS Dhoni	c K Akmal b Abdul Razzaq	13	c Imran Farhat b Abdul Razzaq	18
IK Pathan	c M Yousuf b Shahid Afridi	40	c Faisal Iqbal b Abdul Razzaq	4
A Kumble	lbw b Shoaib Akhtar	7	c Imran Farhat b Danish Kaneria	5
Z Khan	c K Akmal b Mohammad Asif	21	b Danish Kaneria	10
RP Singh	not out	0	not out	0
Extras	b 8, lb 3, nb 17	28	b 7, w 5, nb 4	16
	(all out 54.1 overs)	238	(all out 58.4 overs)	265

	First Innings				Second Innings			
	O	M	R	W	O	M	R	W
Shoaib Akhtar	16	3	70	2	8	1	37	1
Mohammad Asif	19.1	1	78	4	12	1	48	3
Abdul Razzaq	16	3	67	3	18.4	0	88	4
Shahid Afridi	3	0	12	1	2	0	10	0
Danish Kaneria	-	-	-	-	18	0	75	2

Fall of Wickets
1-9, 2-14, 3-56, 4-56, 5-137, 6-165, 7-165, 8-181, 9-237
1-8, 2-8, 3-63, 4-74, 5-177, 6-177, 7-216, 8-231, 9-251

Umpires: DJ Harper (Australia) & SJA Taufel (Australia)
Toss: India
Man of the Match: Kamran Akmal
Man of the Series: Younis Khan

Pakistan won by 341 runs

SERIES AVERAGES
Pakistan v. India

PAKISTAN

Batting	M	Inns	NO	Runs	HS	Av	100	50	c/st
Younis Khan	3	5	0	553	199	110.60	2	2	-/-
Kamran Akmal	3	5	2	293	113	97.66	2	1	9/2
Mohammad Yousuf	3	5	0	461	173	92.20	2	2	1/-
Faisal Iqbal	1	2	0	144	139	72.00	1	-	1/-
Shahid Afridi	3	5	0	330	156	66.00	2	1	1/-
Inzamam-ul-Haq	2	2	0	120	119	60.00	1	-	-/-
Abdul Razzaq	2	4	0	204	90	51.00	-	1	-/-
Shoaib Akhtar	3	3	1	92	47	46.00	-	-	-/-
Imran Farhat	1	2	0	79	57	39.50	-	1	2/-
Shoaib Malik	2	2	0	78	59	39.00	-	1	-/-
Salman Butt	3	5	0	120	53	24.00	-	1	-/-
Naved-ul-Hasan	1	1	0	9	9	9.00	-	-	-/-
Mohammad Asif	2	3	1	6	6*	3.00	-	-	1/-
Danish Kaneria	3	3	1	0	0*	0.00	-	-	1/-
Mohammad Sami	1	1	1	1	1*	-	-	-	-/-

Bowling	Overs	Mds	Runs	Wkts	Av	Best	5/inn	10m
Mohammad Asif	65.1	8	229	8	28.62	4-78	-	-
Abdul Razzaq	62.4	4	281	9	31.22	4-88	-	-
Shahid Afridi	44.4	0	184	3	61.33	2-91	-	-
Danish Kaneria	82	6	309	5	61.80	3-165	-	-
Shoaib Akhtar	65.2	17	253	4	63.25	2-70	-	-
Naved-ul-Hasan	16	1	94	1	94.00	1-94	-	-

Also bowled: Younis Khan 4-0-5-0, Mohammad Sami 12-1-67-0, Shoaib Malik 12-1-70-0.

INDIA

Batting	M	Inns	NO	Runs	HS	Av	100	50	c/st
R Dravid	3	5	2	241	128*	80.33	2	-	2/-
V Sehwag	3	4	0	294	254	73.50	1	-	1/-
MS Dhoni	3	3	0	179	148	59.66	1	-	7/1
Yuvraj Singh	3	3	0	171	122	57.00	1	-	4/-
VVS Laxman	3	5	2	138	90	46.00	-	1	2/-
IK Pathan	3	3	0	134	90	44.66	-	1	-/-
Harbhajan Singh	2	1	0	38	38	38.00	-	-	3/-
SC Ganguly	2	2	0	71	37	35.50	-	-	1/-
Z Khan	2	3	1	51	21	25.50	-	-	-/-
SR Tendulkar	3	3	0	63	26	21.00	-	-	4/-
A Kumble	3	3	0	27	15	9.00	-	-	1/-
RP Singh	2	3	2	6	6	6.00	-	-	-/-
AB Agarkar	1	0	0	0	0	-	-	-	-/-

Bowling	Overs	Mds	Runs	Wkts	Av	Best	5/inn	10m
Z Khan	94.4	17	374	10	37.40	4-61	-	-
RP Singh	87	8	345	9	38.33	4-89	-	-
IK Pathan	115.1	17	486	8	60.75	5-61	1	-
AB Agarkar	24	3	122	2	61.00	2-122	-	-
A Kumble	143	14	629	9	69.88	3-150	-	-
SC Ganguly	24	2	91	1	91.00	1-68	-	-

Also bowled: MS Dhoni 1-0-13-0, V Sehwag 7-0-26-0, Yuvraj Singh 9-0-46-0, SR Tendulkar 11-0-56-0, Harbhajan Singh 81-8-355-0.

ONE-DAY INTERNATIONALS
v. India

Match One
6 February 2006 at Peshawar
India 328 all out (49.4 overs) (SR Tendulkar 100, MS Dhoni 68, IK Pathan 65, Naved-ul-Hasan 4 for 62, Mohammad Asif 3 for 30)
Pakistan 311 for 7 (47 overs) (Salman Butt 101, Shoaib Malik 90)
Pakistan won by 7 runs – DL Method: target 305 from 47 overs

Match Two
11 February 2006 at Rawalpindi
Pakistan 265 all out (49.2 overs) (Shoaib Malik 95, Younis Khan 81, IK Pathan 3 for 43)
India 266 for 3 (43.1 overs) (Yuvraj Singh 82*, V Sehwag 67, R Dravid 56)
India won by 7 wickets

Match Three
13 February 2006 at Lahore
Pakistan 288 for 8 (50 overs) (Shoaib Malik 108, Abdul Razzaq 64*, IK Pathan 3 for 49, RP Singh 3 for 51)
India 292 for 5 (47.4 overs) (SR Tendulkar 95, Yuvraj Singh 79*, MS Dhoni 72*)
India won by 5 wickets

Match Four
16 February 2006 at Multan
Pakistan 161 all out (41.5 overs) (RP Singh 4 for 40, IK Pathan 3 for 26)
India 162 for 5 (32.3 overs) (R Dravid 59, Mohammad Sami 3 for 42)
India won by 5 wickets

Match Five
19 February 2006 at Karachi
Pakistan 286 for 8 (50 overs) (Younis Khan 74*, Mohammad Yousuf 67, S Sreesanth 4 for 58)
India 287 for 2 (46.5 overs) (Yuvraj Singh 107*, MS Dhoni 77*, R Dravid 50)
India won by 8 wickets

India won the series 4–1

INDIA

ENGLAND IN INDIA

ENGLAND IN INDIA
By Jonathan Agnew

FIRST TEST
1–5 March 2006
at Vidarbha Cricket Association Ground, Nagpur

It is difficult to imagine a more chaotic build-up to an opening Test match of a series than this. In fact, so absurd did it become – with players flying hither and thither – that all the farce lacked was Sid James, Hattie Jacques and the rest of the *Carry On* crew. Marcus Trescothick had already returned home for 'personal reasons'. This was kept deliberately vague at the time, Trescothick having broken down after receiving a telephone call during the practice match in Indore. The vice-captain muddied the waters when, two months later, he announced that he had been suffering from a virus at the time – although this was never mentioned – and that he had not been considered fit to play. An emergency call was sent to Antigua where Essex's Alastair Cook was playing for England A. He arrived 48 hours before the start of the match, having endured a time change of nine and a half hours, and a day spent at Heathrow airport waiting for a visa.

But that was only part of the drama. Two days before the scheduled start of the Test, England embarked on a disastrous practice session that claimed a further two victims. The first was Simon Jones who, bowling quietly and without excessive effort in the nets, twisted his left knee. The news quickly spread from bad to worse, and following an MRI scan he was flown home for surgery. Michael Vaughan,

meanwhile, appeared to come through a batting session in which he clearly was not tested seriously. Nevertheless, it was still a shock when he announced that not only was he out of the match, but would also be flying back to England. The team was thus left without its captain and vice-captain, and another leading Ashes hero and senior spinner in Ashley Giles, who had remained at home recovering from a hip operation. The only two candidates for the

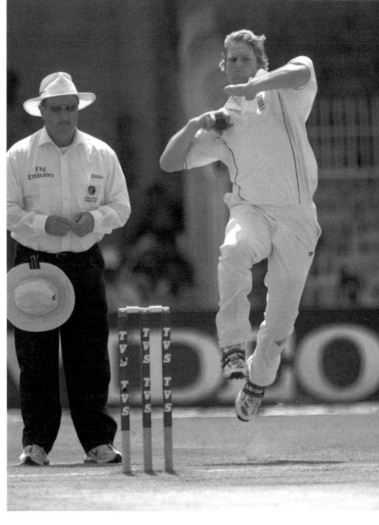

Matthew Hoggard gave England the upper hand in the Nagpur Test with a superb first innings haul of 6 for 57.

captaincy were Andrew Strauss and Andrew Flintoff who, because of the sheer volume of his workload, would be seriously overstretched. Nonetheless, Flintoff was the players' choice and, unselfish and magnanimous man that he is, he not only agreed to take it on but also cancelled his pre-arranged paternity leave that had been scheduled to rule him out of the Third Test.

Thanks to the long injury list, England named a team that, for the first time since the winter of 1999, included three debutants: the jet-lagged Alastair Cook, Ian Blackwell, and the promising left-arm spinner Monty Panesar – the first Sikh to represent England.

It must have come as a merciful relief when, on a boiling morning, Flintoff won the toss and, led admirably by Cook, England battled through the day to be 246 for 7 at the close – Cook having scored a very promising 60. The second morning was crucial, and having missed out in the previous Test at Lahore, Collingwood made sure of his first Test century as he and the tail-enders added 149 for the last three wickets. Remarkably, Collingwood was only on 79 when he was joined by the No. 11, Panesar, whose prowess with the bat is only marginally more skilful than his appalling fielding. But Panesar gritted his teeth, Collingwood flew through the 90s and when the No. 11 finally succumbed to Sreesanth for 9, Collingwood was undefeated on 134 – and the last pair had added 66.

At the close of the second day, India were ominously placed on 136 for 1, with Rahul Dravid and Wasim Jaffer apparently certain to build a lead. But Matthew Hoggard took 3 for 5 in 11 deliveries on the third morning – India lost 8 for 186 on the day – and only an obdurate partnership of 128 between Mohammad Kaif and Anil Kumble enabled India to limit England's first-innings advantage to 70. Hoggard finished with the admirable figures of 6 for 57 while Panesar's promising debut with ball in hand yielded 2 for 73 from 42 tidy overs.

England quickly built on their lead with an opening stand of 95 between Strauss and Cook who, in his second Test innings, scored 104 in six hours to join an exclusive group of England batsmen – including W. G. Grace and, most recently, Strauss himself – who have scored a century on debut. Ian Bell failed for the second time in the game, but Pietersen embarked on a lively riposte which, with Collingwood's 35, enabled Flintoff to declare before the fifth morning, setting India 368 to win in what were still excellent conditions.

FIRST TEST – INDIA v. ENGLAND
1–5 March 2006 at Nagpur

ENGLAND

	First Innings		Second Innings	
AJ Strauss	c Laxman b Sreesanth	28	c Dhoni b Pathan	46
AN Cook	b Pathan	60	not out	104
IR Bell	c Dravid b Harbhajan Singh	9	c Dhoni b Pathan	1
KP Pietersen	b Sreesanth	15	c Dravid b Kumble	87
PD Collingwood	not out	134	not out	36
A Flintoff (capt)	lbw b Kumble	43		
*GO Jones	lbw b Pathan	14		
ID Blackwell	b Pathan	4		
MJ Hoggard	c Dhoni b Sreesanth	11		
SJ Harmison	st Dhoni b Harbhajan Singh	39		
MS Panesar	lbw b Sreesanth	9		
Extras	b 7, lb 7, w 1, nb 12	27	b 12, lb 7, w 2, nb 2	23
	(all out 127.5 overs)	**393**	(3 wkts dec 87 overs)	**297**

	First Innings				Second Innings			
	O	M	R	W	O	M	R	W
Pathan	23	5	92	3	14	2	48	2
Sreesanth	28.5	6	95	4	10	2	36	0
Harbhajan Singh	34	5	93	2	30	6	79	0
Kumble	40	13	88	1	32	8	101	1
Tendulkar	2	0	11	0	-	-	-	-
Sehwag	-	-	-	-	1	0	14	0

Fall of Wickets
1-56, 2-81, 3-110, 4-136, 5-204, 6-225, 7-244, 8-267, 9-327
1-95, 2-97, 3-221

INDIA

	First Innings		Second Innings	
W Jaffer	c Flintoff b Hoggard	81	c Strauss b Flintoff	100
V Sehwag	c Pietersen b Hoggard	2	b Hoggard	0
R Dravid (capt)	lbw b Hoggard	40	b Panesar	71
SR Tendulkar	lbw b Panesar	16	(6) not out	28
VVS Laxman	lbw b Hoggard	0		
M Kaif	b Panesar	91		
*MS Dhoni	c Jones b Flintoff	5	(5) c Strauss b Harmison	16
IK Pathan	c Flintoff b Hoggard	2	(4) c Strauss b Flintoff	35
A Kumble	c Cook b Harmison	58		
Harbhajan Singh	not out	0	(7) b Harmison	7
S Sreesanth	lbw b Hoggard	1		
Extras	b 17, lb 3, w 5, nb 2	27	lb 3	3
	(all out 136.5 overs)	**323**	(6 wkts 78.2 overs)	**260**

	First Innings				Second Innings			
	O	M	R	W	O	M	R	W
Hoggard	30.5	13	57	6	16	7	29	1
Harmison	27	5	75	1	17.2	4	48	2
Flintoff	29	10	68	1	17	2	79	2
Panesar	42	19	73	2	16	2	58	1
Blackwell	7	0	28	0	12	2	43	0
Bell	1	0	2	0	-	-	-	-

Fall of Wickets
1-11, 2-140, 3-149, 4-149, 5-176, 6-183, 7-190, 8-318, 9-322
1-1, 2-168, 3-198, 4-215, 5-252, 6-260

Umpires: Aleem Dar (Pakistan) & IL Howell (South Africa)
Toss: England
Test Debuts: S Sreesanth, ID Blackwell, AN Cook, MS Panesar
Man of the Match: MJ Hoggard

Match drawn

Sehwag played a dreadfully loose drive at Hoggard and was bowled for a duck to go with his first innings 2, but that was the only time England had an opening. Jones dropped two chances – Jaffer on 61 and Dravid on 17 – but the pair defended until tea when Dravid felt confident enough to have a speculative stab at their target. The game finally woke up as 98 runs were scored from 14.2 overs, but India lost six wickets in that time, and both teams were happy to shake hands when bad light descended after three of the last 15 overs had been bowled.

SECOND TEST

9–13 March 2006
at Punjab Cricket Association Stadium, Mohali

Not even unseasonable damp and thoroughly miserable weather could prevent England from slipping to a nine-wicket defeat on the stroke of tea on the final day. Flintoff's second patient half-century of the game illustrated the benefit that the responsibility of captaincy had brought to his batting, in particular, but his was the final wicket to fall as England's lower order capitulated for the second time in the match, leaving India with the easy task of scoring 144 from 70 overs.

It seemed to have been a good toss to win and, at 117 for 2, Bell and Pietersen were moving along well in a stand of 81. But Bell was deceived by a Kumble googly, played no stroke and perished for 38. Pietersen passed 50 but then, as is becoming something of a habit, an unnecessary stroke brought about his downfall – in this case, caught and bowled by the promising young fast bowler Munaf Patel, for 64. Bad light ended play early with England on 163 for 4, after only 50 overs of play.

A truncated second day saw only 14 overs bowled and it was not until after lunch on the third that England's first innings came to an end. From 283 for 5, they lost 5 wickets for 17 with Kumble finishing with 5 for 76, and a first-innings total of 300 was a disappointment.

But England's seam bowlers plugged away in determined fashion. After Sehwag had fallen to Harmison for 11, Jaffer and Dravid added 78. Panesar ended the stand when Flintoff caught Jaffer for 31, and the captain then ripped out Tendulkar for 4 with a brutal delivery, which was caught by Strauss at second slip. Bell clung on to a magnificent catch at short extra-cover to dispose of Yuvraj for 15 and, at the close of the third day, only Dravid – on 60 – was putting up much of a fight with India still 151 runs behind.

SECOND TEST – INDIA v. ENGLAND
9–13 March 2006 at Mohali

ENGLAND

	First Innings		Second Innings	
AJ Strauss	c Dhoni b Pathan	18	c Dhoni b Kumble	13
AN Cook	lbw b Pathan	17	c Dhoni b Patel	2
IR Bell	b Kumble	38	c Dhoni b Kumble	57
KP Pietersen	c & b Patel	64	c Dravid b Harbhajan Singh	4
PD Collingwood	b Kumble	25	c Dravid b Kumble	14
A Flintoff (capt)	c & b Patel	70	c Patel b Piyush Chawla	51
*GO Jones	b Kumble	52	b Patel	5
LE Plunkett	c Dhoni b Patel	0	lbw b Patel	1
MJ Hoggard	not out	4	b Patel	4
SJ Harmison	lbw b Kumble	0	st Dhoni b Kumble	13
MS Panesar	c Dravid b Kumble	0	not out	0
Extras	lb 5, w 1, nb 6	12	lb 10, w 1, nb 6	17
	(all out 103.4 overs)	300	(all out 76.1 overs)	181

	First Innings				Second Innings			
	O	M	R	W	O	M	R	W
Pathan	28	9	71	2	6	1	16	0
Patel	25	6	72	3	13	4	25	4
Harbhajan Singh	12	0	31	0	23	5	52	1
Piyush Chawla	9	1	45	0	5.1	2	8	1
Kumble	29.4	8	76	5	29	7	70	4

Fall of Wickets
1-35, 2-36, 3-117, 4-157, 5-180, 6-283, 7-290, 8-300, 9-300
1-7, 2-50, 3-55, 4-88, 5-109, 6-116, 7-124, 8-139, 9-181

INDIA

	First Innings		Second Innings	
W Jaffer	c Flintoff b Panesar	31	lbw b Hoggard	17
V Sehwag	c Jones b Harmison	11	not out	76
R Dravid (capt)	b Flintoff	95	not out	42
SR Tendulkar	c Strauss b Flintoff	4		
Yuvraj Singh	c Bell b Hoggard	15		
*MS Dhoni	c Jones b Harmison	16		
IK Pathan	c Collingwood b Flintoff	52		
A Kumble	b Plunkett	32		
Harbhajan Singh	c Jones b Flintoff	36		
Piyush Chawla	c Collingwood b Hoggard	1		
MM Patel	not out	11		
Extras	lb 25, w 1, nb 8	34	b 4, lb 5	9
	(all out 96.2 overs)	338	(1 wkt 33 overs)	144

	First Innings				Second Innings			
	O	M	R	W	O	M	R	W
Hoggard	18	6	55	2	8	2	24	1
Harmison	28	9	60	2	4	1	10	0
Flintoff	22	3	96	4	5	0	11	0
Plunkett	9.2	1	37	1	2	0	22	0
Panesar	19	3	65	1	11	0	48	0
Collingwood	–	–	–	–	3	1	20	0

Fall of Wickets
1-18, 2-96, 3-103, 4-134, 5-153, 6-229, 7-260, 8-313, 9-321
1-39

Umpires: DB Hair (Australia) & SJA Taufel (Australia)
Toss: England
Test Debuts: MM Patel, Piyush Chawla
Man of the Match: A Kumble

India won by 9 wickets

Andrew Flintoff grew visibly in the role of England captain as the series against India went on.

crucial runs – 109 from the last four wickets, although Matt Prior, England's fielding substitute, dropped an absolute sitter to reprieve Harbhajan. Pathan scored a very good 52 from 58 balls and when Kumble was finally yorked by Plunkett for 32, the Indian tail had transformed a deficit of 71 into a lead of 38.

By the close of the fourth day, England were already facing defeat on 112 for 5 – a lead of just 74. Patel had removed Cook for 2, but it was the spinners, Kumble and Harbhajan, who did the damage on a pitch that was now giving them plenty of help. Two unfortunate dismissals did not aid England's cause. For the second time in his Test career, Strauss was caught off his boot as he swept Kumble for 13, and Pietersen was given out caught at slip for 4 when the ball came off his forearm. In contrast, Bell enjoyed a couple of slices of luck as he dug in and reached 57 from 137 balls before falling to Kumble just before the close.

Flintoff and Jones have produced a number of partnerships for England but, crucially, they were separated by only the fifth ball of the last morning when Jones played-on to Patel for 5. This provided India with just the opening they sought. Plunkett and Hoggard were swept aside by Patel, who took 3 for 4, before Harmison and Flintoff added 42. But when Flintoff was left only with Panesar for company he opened his shoulders and was caught on the deep square leg boundary for 51.

Hoggard nipped out Jaffer for 17, but Sehwag breezed to 76 from 89 balls to take India into the lead with just one Test remaining.

Much of the fourth morning was played with the floodlights on, but not even they could lift the gloom. Dravid chopped Flintoff into his stumps for 95 after Harmison had accounted for the dangerous Dhoni for 16 with the tenth ball of the day. But unlike England, the Indian lower order added

THIRD TEST
18–22 March 2006
at Wankhede Stadium, Mumbai

Not even the several hundred England supporters that arrived for the final Test of the winter gave their team a prayer of levelling the series. The filthy, decrepit Wankhede Stadium was as unappealing as England's predicament, which was compounded early on the first morning as, first, Cook withdrew through illness and then Harmison stood down with a sore right shin. This injury would also prevent him from appearing against Sri Lanka at the start of the summer. Owais Shah found himself making a startlingly unpredicted debut, and James Anderson returned to the ranks for the first time for a year. Both would enjoy an outstanding match.

Dravid won the toss for the first time in the series, and then bewildered everybody – including Flintoff – by putting England into bat. It was a staggering decision, and one that backfired spectacularly. Promoted to open the innings, Bell was caught at point for 18, carelessly driving at a wide delivery from the recalled and distinctly lively Sreesanth. This brought Shah to the crease, and he immediately looked at home. With his Middlesex team-mate, Strauss, Shah batted until tea at which point – with their stand worth 106, he was forced to retire hurt for exactly 50 with cramp in his hands. Strauss continued on his determined, gritty way to 128 from 240 balls when, having put on 72 with Pietersen, he was caught behind off Harbhajan. Twelve runs later – with England on 242 for 2 – Pietersen edged Sreesanth to be out for 39, but at the close the tourists were 272 for 3, and Dravid's decision to field first was savaged the length and breadth of the cricket-crazy country.

Dravid's position became even more uncomfortable early the following morning when Flintoff, on 29, was dropped from consecutive deliveries. Sehwag spilt the first straightforward chance at second slip and, next ball, Kumble put him down in the gully. Flintoff and Collingwood added 84, but they were dismissed in successive overs – Collingwood was caught behind off Sreesanth for 31 and, on exactly 50, Flintoff was taken by Tendulkar, running round the legside boundary off Kumble. Shah had now returned, and progressed to 88 from 163 balls before becoming the ninth wicket to fall thanks to a breathtaking slip catch by Dravid off Harbhajan. England's 400 was a good score, but having been 326 for 3, should have been better.

India were soon in trouble on 28 for 3 with Hoggard removing Sehwag and Jaffer while Anderson claimed the prized wicket of Tendulkar, caught behind for a desperately laboured 1, which took 21 balls.

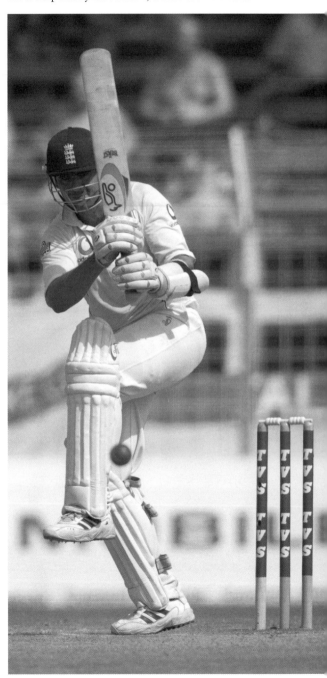

Owais Shah answered England's late call in style, scoring 88 and 38 on a memorable Test debut in Mumbai.

At the close of the second day, India had recovered to 89 for 3, but were still 311 runs behind.

England needed early wickets on the third morning if they were seriously to threaten India's lead and, with only five runs added, Yuvraj slashed a catch to Jones off Flintoff. Dravid was dropped in the gully on 52, but next over edged Anderson down the legside where Jones took a good catch. Pathan and Dhoni added 44 – Dhoni was dropped by Panesar at mid-off – before Pathan was caught off Udal for 26 and having struck three consecutive fours, Dhoni was brilliantly run out by Anderson's direct throw from mid-on for 64. Kumble's batting was a source of frustration throughout the series, and he knuckled down with Sreesanth to take the score from 217 for 8 to 272 for 9, but he fell to Panesar for 30, and Anderson's fourth wicket dismissed India for 279 giving England a handy lead of 121 with an hour of batting left on the third day.

Strauss and Bell both perished before the close, and the nightwatchman Udal survived a confident appeal for caught behind, but Shah, Collingwood and Flintoff made solid contributions on a desperately slow fourth day in which England scored at less than three runs per over. With half an hour to go, the innings ended on 191 from 92 overs, setting India 313 to win.

Pathan was promoted to open because Sehwag's back was playing up, and he dragged a full toss from Anderson into his stumps for 6, and the nightwatchman Kumble was disposed of early on the last day. Flintoff snared Jaffer lbw for 10 and it was 75 for 4 when Flintoff captured the crucial wicket of Dravid in the first over after lunch. What followed was totally unexpected and, from an Indian perspective, absolutely wretched. Tendulkar was well taken by Bell at short leg in the next over – 76 for 5 – and the incapacitated Sehwag was lbw for a 16-ball duck, only for Dhoni to play the most irresponsible innings imaginable. Dropped on 0, he then hoisted a catch to mid-off where Panesar failed by several yards even to lay hand on it. Undeterred, three balls later Dhoni attempted precisely the same shot and while his team-mates held their breath and thousands of Indian fans bayed and hooted, Panesar managed – somehow – to cling on. Dhoni's miserable innings was over and, minutes later, India's demise was complete.

From lunch, India lost seven wickets for 25 runs in 15.2 overs, with Udal benefiting from some ugly swipes to finish with 4 for 14. Against all odds, England had come back to level the series 1-1 due, in great measure, both to Flintoff's leadership and contributions with the bat.

THIRD TEST – INDIA v. ENGLAND
18–22 March 2006 at Mumbai

ENGLAND

	First Innings		Second Innings	
AJ Strauss	c Dhoni b Harbhajan Singh	128	c Dhoni b Patel	4
IR Bell	c Harbhajan Singh b Sreesanth	18	c Dhoni b Sreesanth	8
OA Shah	c Dravid b Harbhajan Singh	88	run out	38
KP Pietersen	c Dhoni b Sreesanth	39	(5) c & b Kumble	7
PD Collingwood	c Dhoni b Sreesanth	31	(6) c & b Harbhajan Singh	32
A Flintoff (capt)	c Tendulkar b Kumble	50	(7) st Dhoni b Kumble	50
*GO Jones	c Kumble b Sreesanth	1	(8) c Pathan b Harbhajan Singh	3
SD Udal	lbw b Patel	9	(4) c Jaffer b Pathan	14
MJ Hoggard	b Patel	0	lbw b Kumble	6
JM Anderson	c Yuvraj Singh b Harbhajan Singh	15	c Dravid b Kumble	6
MS Panesar	not out	3	not out	0
Extras	b 5, lb 7, w 3, nb 3	18	lb 9, w 4, nb 10	23
	(all out 133.4 overs)	400	(all out 92.4 overs)	191

	First Innings				Second Innings			
	O	M	R	W	O	M	R	W
Pathan	17	4	64	0	13	2	24	1
Sreesanth	22	5	70	4	13	3	30	1
Patel	29	4	81	2	13	2	39	1
Kumble	39	7	84	1	30.4	13	49	4
Harbhajan Singh	26.4	4	89	3	23	9	40	2

Fall of Wickets
1-52, 2-230, 3-242, 4-326, 5-328, 6-333, 7-356, 8-356, 9-385
1-9, 2-21, 3-61, 4-73, 5-85, 6-151, 7-157, 8-183, 9-188

INDIA

	First Innings		Second Innings	
W Jaffer	c Jones b Hoggard	11	lbw b Flintoff	10
V Sehwag	c Shah b Hoggard	6	(7) lbw b Anderson	0
R Dravid (capt)	c Jones b Anderson	52	(4) c Jones b Flintoff	9
SR Tendulkar	c Jones b Anderson	1	(5) c Bell b Udal	34
Yuvraj Singh	c Jones b Flintoff	37	(6) c Collingwood b Flintoff	12
*MS Dhoni	run out	64	(8) c Panesar b Udal	5
IK Pathan	c Hoggard b Udal	26	(2) b Anderson	6
A Kumble	lbw b Panesar	30	(3) lbw b Hoggard	8
Harbhajan Singh	c Jones b Anderson	2	c Hoggard b Udal	6
S Sreesanth	not out	29	not out	0
MM Patel	b Anderson	7	c Hoggard b Udal	1
Extras	b 4, lb 7, nb 3	14	b 1, lb 4, w 1, nb 3	9
	(all out 104.1 overs)	279	(all out 48.2 overs)	100

	First Innings				Second Innings			
	O	M	R	W	O	M	R	W
Hoggard	22	6	54	2	12	6	13	1
Flintoff	21	4	68	1	11	4	14	3
Anderson	19.1	8	40	4	12	2	39	2
Panesar	26	7	53	1	4	1	15	0
Udal	16	2	53	1	9.2	3	14	4

Fall of Wickets
1-9, 2-24, 3-28, 4-94, 5-142, 6-186, 7-212, 8-217, 9-272
1-6, 2-21, 3-33, 4-75, 5-76, 6-77, 7-92, 8-99, 9-99

Umpires: DB Hair (Australia) & SJA Taufel (Australia)
Toss: India
Man of the Match: A Flintoff
Man of the Series: A Flintoff

England won by 212 runs

SERIES AVERAGES
India v. England

INDIA

Batting	M	Inns	NO	Runs	HS	Av	100	50	c/st
M Kaif	1	1	0	91	91	91.00	-	1	-/-
R Dravid	3	6	1	309	95	61.80	-	3	7/-
W Jaffer	3	6	0	250	100	41.66	1	1	1/-
A Kumble	3	4	0	128	58	32.00	-	1	2/-
S Sreesanth	2	3	2	30	29*	30.00	-	-	-/-
IK Pathan	3	5	0	121	52	24.20	-	1	1/-
Yuvraj Singh	2	3	0	64	37	21.33	-	-	1/-
MS Dhoni	3	5	0	106	64	21.20	-	1	13/3
SR Tendulkar	3	5	1	83	34	20.75	-	-	1/-
V Sehwag	3	6	1	95	76*	19.00	-	1	-/-
Harbhajan Singh	3	5	1	51	36	12.75	-	-	2/-
MM Patel	2	3	1	19	11*	9.50	-	-	3/-
Piyush Chawla	1	1	0	1	1	1.00	-	-	-/-
VVS Laxman	1	1	0	0	0	0.00	-	-	1/-

Bowling	Overs	Mds	Runs	Wkts	Av	Best	5/inn	10m
MM Patel	80	16	217	10	21.70	4-25	-	-
S Sreesanth	73.5	16	231	9	25.66	4-70	-	-
A Kumble	200.2	56	468	16	29.25	5-76	1	-
IK Pathan	101	23	315	8	39.37	3-92	-	-
Harbhajan Singh	148.4	29	384	8	48.00	3-89	-	-
Piyush Chawla	14.1	3	53	1	53.00	1-8	-	-

Also bowled: SR Tendulkar 2-0-11-0, V Sehwag 1-0-14-0.

ENGLAND

Batting	M	Inns	NO	Runs	HS	Av	100	50	c/st
PD Collingwood	3	6	2	272	134*	68.00	1	-	3/-
OA Shah	1	2	0	126	88	63.00	-	1	1/-
AN Cook	2	4	1	183	104*	61.00	1	1	1/-
A Flintoff	3	5	0	264	70	52.80	-	4	3/-
AJ Strauss	3	6	0	237	128	39.50	1	-	4/-
KP Pietersen	3	6	0	216	87	36.00	-	2	1/-
IR Bell	3	6	0	131	57	21.83	-	1	2/-
SJ Harmison	2	3	0	52	39	17.33	-	-	-/-
GO Jones	3	5	0	75	52	15.00	-	1	10/-
SD Udal	1	2	0	23	14	11.50	-	-	-/-
JM Anderson	1	2	0	21	15	10.50	-	-	-/-
MJ Hoggard	3	5	1	25	11	6.25	-	-	3/-
MS Panesar	3	5	3	12	9	6.00	-	-	1/-
ID Blackwell	1	1	0	4	4	4.00	-	-	-/-
LE Plunkett	1	2	0	1	1	0.50	-	-	-/-

Bowling	Overs	Mds	Runs	Wkts	Av	Best	5/inn	10m
JM Anderson	31.1	10	79	6	13.16	4-40	-	-
SD Udal	25.2	5	67	5	13.40	4-14	-	-
MJ Hoggard	106.5	40	232	13	17.84	6-57	1	-
A Flintoff	105	23	336	11	30.54	4-96	-	-
SJ Harmison	76.2	19	193	5	38.60	2-48	-	-
LE Plunkett	11.2	1	59	1	59.00	1-37	-	-
MS Panesar	118	32	312	5	62.40	2-73	-	-

Also bowled: IR Bell 1-0-2-0, PD Collingwood 3-1-20-0, ID Blackwell 19-2-71-0.

ONE-DAY INTERNATIONALS
v. England

Match One
28 March 2006 at Delhi
India 203 all out (46.4 overs) (Kabir Ali 4 for 45)
England 164 all out (38.1 overs) (Harbhajan Singh 5 for 31)
India won by 39 runs

Match Two
31 March 2006 at Faridabad
England 226 all out (49.5 overs) (KP Pietersen 71, AJ Strauss 61)
India 230 for 6 (49 overs) (SK Raina 81*)
India won by 4 wickets

Match Three
3 April 2006 at Goa
India 294 for 6 (50 overs) (Yuvraj Singh 103, SK Raina 61)
England 245 all out (48.5 overs) (PD Collingwood 93, IK Pathan 4 for 51)
India won by 49 runs

Match Four
6 April 2006 at Kochi
England 237 all out (48.4 overs) (KP Pietersen 77)
India 238 for 6 (47.2 overs) (R Dravid 65)
India won by 4 wickets

Kevin Pietersen unfurls one of his trademark legside strokes during England's one-day series in India.

Match Five
9 April 2006 at Guwahati
India v. **England**
Match abandoned – no result

Match Six
12 April 2006 at Jamshedpur
India 223 all out (48 overs) (MS Dhoni 96, RR Powar 54)
England 227 for 5 (42.4 overs) (AJ Strauss 74*)
England won by 5 wickets

Match Seven
15 April 2006 at Indore
England 288 all out (50 overs) (KP Pietersen 64,
PD Collingwood 64, GO Jones 53, S Sreesanth 6 for 55)
India 289 for 3 (49.1 overs) (AR Uthappa 86,
R Dravid 69, Yuvraj Singh 63*, SK Raina 53)
India won by 7 wickets

India won the series 5–1

Before the inevitably lengthy one-day series kicked off, the widespread view was that England were facing a drubbing. Thankfully the absurd itinerary – devised by the recently ousted President Jagmohan Dalmiya – was revised to remove the need for England to warm up for a match in Goa with a game in the Himalayas! What remained, however, would still have tested the most intrepid explorer of the subcontinent.

Sadly, England were never in the contest. In the opening game in Delhi, they were set the not unrealistic target of 204 to win, and were moving along nicely at 117 for 3, only to collapse to 164 all out, Harbhajan taking a career-best 5 for 31 after top scoring with just 37. Kevin Pietersen (46) and Andrew Flintoff (41) put on 60 in eight overs as England recovered from 4 for 2 but both fell to expansive shots to trigger England's demise.

In Faridabad, Pietersen made 71 and passed 1,000 runs in ODI cricket in only his 21st innings, and Strauss scored 61 to set India a below-par target of 227. India got away to a blazing start before losing five wickets for 31 runs. Dhoni patiently restored India's prospects and although Flintoff removed the wicketkeeper for 24, Pathan finished the job by striking Anderson for four.

The circus then moved south to Goa, where England lost the eighth match in their last ten. Yuvraj Singh scored 103 to set England a challenging 295, and although Collingwood responded with a fine 93, Pathan took 4 for 51 as a one-sided contest ended with a 49-run victory in the 49th over.

Urgently seeking to restore some pride, England

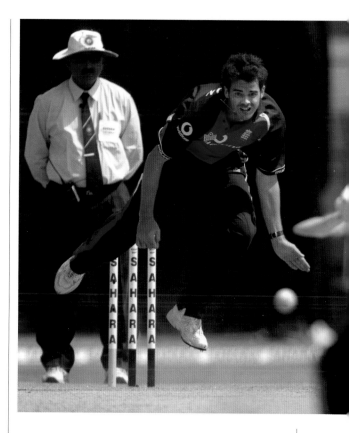

James Anderson, who had enjoyed a fine Test comeback performance at Mumbai, also impressed with the ball during the seven-match one-day series.

were comfortably beaten again in Kochi by four wickets and with more than two overs to spare. This result rendered the rest of the series rather aimless. Dravid and Pathan put India in the hunt for their small target of 238 with a second-wicket stand of 76, and Yuvraj (48) added 72 in 14 overs with Raina to complete the task. Earlier, England were bowled out for the fourth time in the series, despite Pietersen's 77.

England's losing trot finally ended in Guwahati, but this was only due to a washout, and a riot by a number of the 20,000 spectators who had been forced to sit and wait for hours with no information about the prospects of play. Tear-gas was fired when, not surprisingly, many chose to vent their frustration on the hopelessly equipped stadium having learnt that the players from both teams had been driven away under armed escort.

Three days later, under the leadership of Strauss, England actually registered a win, largely thanks to their stand-in skipper who made 74 not out and successfully chased India's small total of 223. India

OF INDIA

By Gulu Ezekiel

Ask any Indian cricket fan his favourite moment of the last 25 years and it would undoubtedly be that most improbable victory of all, the 1983 Prudential World Cup final against the West Indies at Lord's. But it was a 12-month period starting with Sachin Tendulkar's maiden Test century at the age of 17 at Old Trafford in August 1990 that really changed the face of Indian and world cricket.

Exactly a year later, after five decades of being one of the world's most protected economies, the Indian government finally decided to open up its markets and the economic reform movement had begun. That in turn led to the satellite TV boom by early 1992 and the flood of giant multinational companies all eager for a share of the huge Indian pie. Their first target was Tendulkar, and then other Indian cricketers, with the big brands lining up eagerly to sign them for endorsements. These were beamed almost continuously on the 100 plus channels that now proliferate on our TV sets.

In 1995 Tendulkar signed a five-year deal worth US$7.5 million with the late Mark Mascarenhas' WorldTel, and that changed the way cricketers in India did business.

WorldTel also bagged the rights to telecast the World Cup when it returned to the subcontinent for the second time in 1996. It was the 1983 victory that emboldened the Indian Cricket Board to bid and win the right to stage the 1987 event, breaking England's monopoly.

India took late to one-day cricket. All that changed in 1983. But it was after the financial windfall from the 1996 event that the format really took off across Asia with India, Pakistan and Sri Lanka (the surprise 1996 champions) playing a bewildering number of ODIs all over the world, including Sharjah, Toronto and Nairobi. And over the last ten years this market – in India in particular – has become the financial engine that drives world cricket.

On the field it was the batting feats of Tendulkar in particular which grabbed the headlines, though the match-fixing scandal briefly threatened the fabric of Indian cricket. Leg spinner Anil Kumble's feat of ten wickets in an innings (against Pakistan in New Delhi in 1999) is the outstanding bowling performance. The Indian team, meanwhile, under the captaincy of Sourav Ganguly and Rahul Dravid, also finally proved they could win on foreign soil.

Sachin Tendulkar, still just 17, scores his maiden Test century at Old Trafford in 1990 to save the match for India.

were reduced to 79 for 5 in the 16th over, but were rescued by a century stand between Dhoni and Powar. Dhoni made 96, including three sixes while James Anderson claimed 3 for 28. Ian Bell had batted well until undone by a Harbhajan doosra on 46, while Pietersen made a combative 33.

With nothing to play for, and England's players desperate to get home, it was not surprising that the trip should end with an emphatic Indian victory in Indore. England set India a target of 289, which they comfortably achieved by a seven-wicket margin in the final over, thanks to an opening stand of 166 between Uthappa (86) and Dravid (69). Fast bowler Sreesanth had taken 6 for 55 for India, and although Pietersen (64), Collingwood (64) and Jones (53) all made solid contributions, England's seam attack could not match his penetration.

INDIA REPORT
By Gulu Ezekiel

A season that began amidst intrigue and bitterness, threatening to undermine a new coach and captain, ended in a rare triumph on foreign soil for the Indian team. The woeful form of India's most successful captain, Sourav Ganguly, coincided with the slide in the team's fortunes after the high of 2003–04. Ganguly was barely hanging on to his place at the start of the 2005–06 season as all the progress made in the previous 12 months was rapidly being undone. His end was hastened by events that caused an earthquake of sorts in the Indian cricket set-up.

Coach John Wright's departure at the end of the disappointing 2004–05 season led to weeks of intense speculation before Australian legend Greg Chappell was appointed to the post. The tour to Zimbabwe in September was to be his first–and last–in tandem with Ganguly. Ganguly had flown to Chappell's coaching centre just before the tour to Australia in late 2003 for batting lessons in tackling the short ball. The tips seemed to pay off as he scored a barnstorming century in the First Test in Brisbane and Ganguly's subsequent backing for Chappell's appointment helped swing it in the former Australian captain's favour.

It was something of a soap-operatic twist then, that Chappell, in an email to the Board that was leaked to the media, condemned Ganguly as having undermined the team's morale in order to hang on to his place. This was just days after the captain had blurted out to the media, immediately after his painstaking century against Zimbabwe in the Bulawayo Test, that the coach had suggested on the morning of the match that he drop himself.

It was Ganguly's first century for nearly two years (the previous one being at Brisbane) and India's first series win outside Asia since beating England 2-0 in 1986. Neither landmark, of course, held much significance as the quality of the opposition was little better than club-standard.

Back home, there was a storm of protest, particularly in Kolkata, Ganguly's home patch, where protest marches against the coach were staged and his effigy repeatedly burnt. In the rest of the country, however, the feeling was that Ganguly spilling the beans in public was a serious breach of faith. In that sense he was seen as having fallen on his sword.

An elbow injury put Ganguly out of the home one-day series against Sri Lanka which followed the tour of Zimbabwe, and Rahul Dravid was appointed captain on a short-term basis. This was nothing new for Dravid who had often filled in for Ganguly during his numerous absences due to injuries and bans imposed by the ICC. However, there was a further setback to Ganguly's career, one that virtually sealed his fate even as he was hoping to get back the captaincy.

Mahendra Singh Dhoni, the charismatic wicketkeeper–batsman, has emerged as a new star of Indian cricket.

Rival captains Andrew Flintoff and Rahul Dravid share a lighter moment.

Ganguly had all along enjoyed the backing of Indian cricket's strongman Jagmohan Dalmiya, also from Kolkata. Now that support was suddenly gone. In a dramatic turnaround, Union Minister Sharad Pawar finally broke Dalmiya's vice-like grip in the BCCI elections. With a change at the top and a change in the selection committee as well, it was curtains for Ganguly. That he was dropped after scoring 40 and 39 in the Second Test against Sri Lanka in New Delhi only added poignancy to his departure. Dispassionately though, it had been long overdue. All this obscured yet another return from injury by Sachin Tendulkar and his 35th Test century in New Delhi that saw him eclipse Sunil Gavaskar's world record.

Stand-in skipper Dravid left an immediate impression as India crushed the Sri Lankans 6-1 in the ODI series and 2-0 in the Tests. Next up were the South Africans who were held 2-2 in the ODI series. Sadly, the cricket itself was overshadowed by one of the most shocking crowd displays in the history of international cricket. Furious at the absence of their favourite son, Eden Gardens in Kolkata gave Dravid and his men a torrid time in the fourth ODI, which they lost by ten wickets. 'It is nice to be back home in India,' commented one of the Indians the next day in Mumbai as they beat a hasty retreat, drawing level with an outstanding display in the decider (one was washed out).

It was another India v. Pakistan series – the third in two years – that saw the first setback for the fledgling Dravid/Chappell partnership. The first two Test matches on the featherbeds of Lahore and Faisalabad ended in high-scoring draws. But in the final Test at Karachi, the famed Indian batting crumbled in the face of hostile fast bowling, and Pakistan won in four days by a whopping 341 runs. Ganguly had made another comeback for the tour, scoring 34 and 37 in Karachi in possibly his final Test match.

The average Indian cricket fan's attention span is pretty short and a sweeping 4-1 win for the Indians in the ODI series just a couple of weeks later and all was instantly forgotten and forgiven. The stars were Yuvraj Singh and wicketkeeper Mahendra Singh Dhoni with a series of barnstorming innings.

Dhoni had within less than a year become the darling of Indian fans thanks to his audacious batting and his flamboyant personality. In November at Jaipur against the Sri Lankans he had set the world record for the highest score in an ODI by a wicketkeeper (183 not out). By the time he was chosen by MTV as India's latest youth icon, the young man from the backward state of Jharkhand had pushed even Tendulkar off the nation's TV screens with his slew of endorsements for everything from hair creams to motorbikes.

When England's Ashes heroes landed in India in February 2006, confidence at home was sky-high. And as the tourists began to lose their top players to a bewildering array of illnesses and injuries (including captain Michael Vaughan) and a mystery to boot (vice-captain Marcus Trescothick), it looked like they would simply roll over and die. Thanks to Andrew Flintoff's inspiring eleventh-hour leadership, that was hardly the case. Centuries by Paul Collingwood and debutant Alastair Cook (rushed across from England A's tour of the West Indies) saw them battle to a worthy draw in the First Test at Nagpur.

England had their chances in the Second Test at Mohali too before being undone by Anil Kumble. The awaiting dustbowl at Mumbai for the Third and final Test meant the 0-2 defeat suffered a few months earlier in Pakistan was likely to be repeated. Then came one of those inexplicable decisions that left everyone scratching their heads in disbelief. Dravid won the toss and promptly put England in to bat. It meant India would bat last and after being set 313 to win, it was the unlikely off-spin bowling of Shaun Udal that saw them crash to 100 all out. England had won a Test match in India after a gap of 21 years.

Dravid picked up the pieces to crush England 5-1 in the ODI series and that went some way to healing the wounds. That sweeping victory meant that India had won 18 out of 24 ODIs under the Dravid/Chappell partnership after drawing 1-1 with Pakistan in Abu

Dhabi and things looked hunky-dory as they left for the West Indies. Most of the occasionally bewildering experiments undertaken in the one-day side appeared to have worked wonders.

The wheels rapidly fell off, however, after a winning start, and it was back to the drawing board with Brian Lara leading his side to a shock 4-1 success. The tour though ended on a high note as India won their first Test series in the West Indies for 35 years. Veterans Dravid and Kumble dominated the series and took the side to victory by 49 runs in the Fourth and final Test at Kingston. The achievement was doubly significant as India were without the services of Tendulkar, out once again with another injury.

The tri-nation ODI series in Sri Lanka in August, involving India and South Africa, was jinxed from the start. A bomb attack in the capital Colombo saw the South Africans abandon the tournament which was then reduced to a three-match series between the hosts and India. But with persistent rain washing out the first two games, it was decided to scrap the tournament and hold it sometime after next year's World Cup.

ONE-DAY INTERNATIONALS v. Sri Lanka

Match One
25 October 2005 at Nagpur
India 350 for 6 (50 overs) (SR Tendulkar 93, R Dravid 85*, IK Pathan 83)
Sri Lanka 198 all out (35.4 overs)
(Harbhajan Singh 3 for 35, M Kartik 3 for 48)
India won by 152 runs

Match Two
28 October 2005 at Mohali
Sri Lanka 122 all out (35.4 overs) (IK Pathan 4 for 37)
India 123 for 2 (20.2 overs) (SR Tendulkar 67*)
India won by 8 wickets

Match Three
31 October 2005 at Jaipur
Sri Lanka 298 for 4 (50 overs) (KC Sangakkara 138*, DPMD Jayawardene 71)
India 303 for 4 (46.1 overs) (MS Dhoni 183*)
India won by 6 wickets

Match Four
3 November 2005 at Pune
Sri Lanka 261 all out (49.5 overs) (MS Atapattu 87, TM Dilshan 52, AB Agarkar 5 for 44)
India 262 for 6 (45.4 overs) (R Dravid 63, M Muralitharan 3 for 35)
India won by 4 wickets

Match Five
6 November 2005 at Ahmedabad
India 285 for 8 (50 overs) (G Gambhir 103, R Dravid 103*, MF Maharoof 4 for 20)
Sri Lanka 286 for 5 (47.4 overs) (TM Dilshan 81*)
Sri Lanka won by 5 wickets

Match Six
9 November 2005 at Rajkot
Sri Lanka 196 all out (42.5 overs) (TM Dilshan 59, RP Singh 4 for 35)
India 197 for 3 (34.5 overs) (Yuvraj Singh 79*)
India won by 7 wickets

Match Seven
12 November 2005 at Vadodara
Sri Lanka 244 for 9 (50 overs) (RP Arnold 68, MS Atapattu 59, RP Singh 3 for 33, IK Pathan 3 for 38)
India 245 for 5 (39.3 overs) (MS Dhoni 80)
India won by 7 wickets

India won the series 6–1

ONE-DAY INTERNATIONALS v. South Africa

Match One
16 November 2005 at Hyderabad
India 249 for 9 (50 overs) (Yuvraj Singh 103)
South Africa 252 for 5 (48.5 overs) (JH Kallis 68*)
South Africa won by 5 wickets

Match Two
19 November 2005 at Bangalore
South Africa 169 for 9 (50 overs) (IK Pathan 3 for 23)
India 171 for 4 (35.4 overs) (V Sehwag 77*)
India won by 6 wickets

Match Three
22 November 2005 at Chennai
India v. **South Africa**
Match abandoned – no result

Match Four
25 November 2005 at Kolkata
India 188 all out (45.5 overs) (Yuvraj Singh 53, SM Pollock 3 for 25, AJ Hall 3 for 36)
South Africa 189 for 0 (35.5 overs) (GC Smith 134*)
South Africa won by 10 wickets

Match Five
28 November 2005 at Mumbai
South Africa 221 for 6 (50 overs) (JH Kallis 91, IK Pathan 3 for 20)
India 224 for 5 (47.3 overs) (R Dravid 78*)
India won by 5 wickets

Series drawn

FIRST TEST – INDIA v. SRI LANKA
2–6 December 2005 at Chennai

INDIA

	First Innings			
G Gambhir	b Vaas			0
V Sehwag	c Atapattu b Vaas			36
R Dravid (capt)	c Sangakkara b Vaas			32
SR Tendulkar	lbw b Muralitharan			22
VVS Laxman	run out			5
SC Ganguly	c Dilshan b Fernando			5
*MS Dhoni	c Gunawardene b Bandara			30
IK Pathan	c & b Muralitharan			0
AB Agarkar	run out			4
A Kumble	c & b Vaas			9
Harbhajan Singh	not out			4
Extras	b 12, lb 2, nb 6			20
	(all out 73.2 overs)			**167**

	First Innings			
	O	M	R	W
Vaas	21	14	20	4
Fernando	16	4	58	1
Muralitharan	25	6	60	2
Bandara	11.2	6	15	1

Fall of Wickets
1-13, 2-45, 3-97, 4-108, 5-109, 6-117, 7-118, 8-128, 9-159

SRI LANKA

	First Innings			
DA Gunawardene	c Dhoni b Pathan			4
*KC Sangakkara	lbw b Kumble			30
DPMD Jayawardene	c Gambhir b Kumble			71
TT Samaraweera	not out			35
MS Atapattu (capt)	b Kumble			7
TM Dilshan	not out			8
WPUJC Vaas				
CM Bandara				
CRD Fernando				
M Muralitharan				
J Mubarak				
Extras	w 1, nb 7, p 5			13
	(4 wkts 43 overs)			**168**

	First Innings			
	O	M	R	W
Pathan	7	0	43	1
Agarkar	10	3	29	0
Ganguly	2	0	16	0
Harbhajan Singh	9	2	34	0
Kumble	15	3	41	3

Fall of Wickets
1-5, 2-62, 3-124, 4-158

Umpires: MR Benson (England) & DJ Harper (Australia)
Toss: India
Test Debut: MS Dhoni
Man of the Match: WPUJC Vaas

Match drawn

SECOND TEST – INDIA v. SRI LANKA
10–14 December 2005 at Delhi

INDIA

	First Innings		Second Innings	
G Gambhir	lbw b Vaas	2	lbw b Vaas	3
R Dravid (capt)	c Mubarak b Muralitharan	24	(5) run out	53
VVS Laxman	c Sangakkara b Muralitharan	69	c Sangakkara b Vaas	11
SR Tendulkar	lbw b Muralitharan	109	lbw b Bandara	16
SC Ganguly	lbw b Muralitharan	40	(6) b Muralitharan	39
Yuvraj Singh	c Mubarak b Bandara	0	(7) not out	77
*MS Dhoni	b Muralitharan	5	(8) not out	51
IK Pathan	c Mubarak b Muralitharan	0	(2) c Sangakkara b Fernando	93
AB Agarkar	not out	14		
A Kumble	b Bandara	8		
Harbhajan Singh	b Muralitharan	7		
Extras	b 4, lb 8	12	b 9, lb 16, nb 7	32
	(all out 96.4 overs)	**290**	(6 wkts dec 105 overs)	**375**

	First Innings				Second Innings			
	O	M	R	W	O	M	R	W
Vaas	22	5	77	1	21	4	65	2
Fernando	18	5	43	0	22	5	75	1
Muralitharan	38.4	8	100	7	38	5	118	1
Bandara	17	1	54	2	20	2	74	1
Dilshan	1	0	4	0	4	0	18	0

Fall of Wickets
1-2, 2-56, 3-133, 4-254, 5-255, 6-255, 7-255, 8-260, 9-271
1-12, 2-42, 3-86, 4-178, 5-190, 6-271

SRI LANKA

	First Innings		Second Innings	
DA Gunawardene	lbw b Pathan	25	lbw b Pathan	9
MS Atapattu (capt)	c Gambhir b Kumble	88	c & b Kumble	67
*KC Sangakkara	c Kumble b Pathan	3	c Dhoni b Agarkar	33
DPMD Jayawardene	lbw b Kumble	60	c Gambhir b Harbhajan Singh	67
TT Samaraweera	b Kumble	1	(6) c Dravid b Harbhajan Singh	0
TM Dilshan	lbw b Kumble	0	(8) b Kumble	32
J Mubarak	not out	29	lbw b Agarkar	3
WPUJC Vaas	c Harbhajan Singh b Kumble	2	(9) c Harbhajan Singh b Kumble	17
CM Bandara	b Pathan	1	(5) lbw b Kumble	0
M Muralitharan	b Kumble	9	c Dhoni b Harbhajan Singh	2
CRD Fernando	c Ganguly b Harbhajan Singh	0	not out	2
Extras	b 4, lb 2, nb 1, p 5	12	b 2, lb 7, nb 6	15
	(all out 83.3 overs)	**230**	(all out 91.2 overs)	**247**

	First Innings				Second Innings			
	O	M	R	W	O	M	R	W
Pathan	22	8	34	3	14	2	38	1
Agarkar	16	4	40	0	16	4	45	2
Kumble	28	6	72	6	36	7	85	4
Harbhajan Singh	15.3	0	67	1	25.2	5	70	3
Tendulkar	2	0	6	0	–	–	–	–

Fall of Wickets
1-54, 2-62, 3-175, 4-179, 5-179, 6-198, 7-200, 8-204, 9-219
1-30, 2-109, 3-119, 4-119, 5-123, 6-131, 7-199, 8-243, 9-243

Umpires: Nadeem Ghauri (Pakistan) & SJA Taufel (Australia)
Toss: India
Man of the Match: A Kumble

India won by 188 runs

THIRD TEST – INDIA v. SRI LANKA
18–22 December 2005 at Ahmedabad

INDIA

	First Innings		Second Innings	
G Gambhir	c Tharanga b Malinga	19	(2) c Sangakkara b Muralitharan	30
V Sehwag (capt)	b Malinga	20	(1) c Maharoof b Malinga	0
VVS Laxman	b Maharoof	104	c Sangakkara b Maharoof	5
SR Tendulkar	c Mubarak b Muralitharan	23	lbw b Dilshan	19
Yuvraj Singh	c Samaraweera b Muralitharan	0	c Sangakkara b Bandara	75
M Kaif	c Atapattu b Bandara	4	lbw b Bandara	9
*MS Dhoni	lbw b Muralitharan	49	lbw b Muralitharan	14
IK Pathan	lbw b Maharoof	82	b Muralitharan	27
AB Agarkar	b Malinga	26	c & b Bandara	48
A Kumble	c Jayawardene b Bandara	21	not out	29
Harbhajan Singh	not out	8	not out	40
Extras	b 15, lb 13, w 5, nb 9	42	b 7, lb 9, w 1, nb 3	20
	(all out 122.4 overs)	398	(9 wkts dec 71 overs)	316

	First Innings				Second Innings			
	O	M	R	W	O	M	R	W
Malinga	32	4	113	3	12	2	63	1
Maharoof	27	11	52	2	6	0	25	1
Muralitharan	36	4	128	3	21	5	90	3
Bandara	24.4	3	69	2	19	2	84	3
Dilshan	3	0	8	0	12	2	36	1
Mubarak	-	-	-	-	1	0	2	0

Fall of Wickets
1-31, 2-52, 3-88, 4-88, 5-97, 6-183, 7-308, 8-345, 9-384
1-0, 2-9, 3-34, 4-81, 5-100, 6-134, 7-174, 8-198, 9-247

SRI LANKA

	First Innings		Second Innings	
WU Tharanga	c Dhoni b Pathan	2	c Gambhir b Kumble	47
MS Atapattu (capt)	c Sehwag b Harbhajan Singh	40	c Kaif b Harbhajan Singh	16
*KC Sangakkara	b Harbhajan Singh	41	lbw b Kumble	17
DPMD Jayawardene	c Kaif b Harbhajan Singh	0	c & b Agarkar	57
TT Samaraweera	c Kaif b Harbhajan Singh	1	c Kaif b Kumble	5
TM Dilshan	c Kaif b Harbhajan Singh	65	c Dhoni b Pathan	65
J Mubarak	b Kumble	13	c Laxman b Harbhajan Singh	18
MF Maharoof	c & b Harbhajan Singh	4	lbw b Kumble	2
CM Bandara	not out	28	c Sehwag b Kumble	11
M Muralitharan	st Dhoni b Kumble	3	b Harbhajan Singh	3
SL Malinga	c Sehwag b Harbhajan Singh	0	not out	0
Extras	b 1, lb 2, nb 6	9	b 1, nb 7	8
	(all out 63.2 overs)	206	(all out 92.3 overs)	249

	First Innings				Second Innings			
	O	M	R	W	O	M	R	W
Pathan	10	1	36	1	9	1	31	1
Agarkar	6	2	18	0	11	3	18	1
Kumble	25	3	87	2	34.3	9	89	5
Harbhajan Singh	22.2	3	62	7	31	7	79	3
Sehwag	-	-	-	-	3	0	18	0
Tendulkar	-	-	-	-	4	0	13	0

Fall of Wickets
1-14, 2-74, 3-74, 4-82, 5-105, 6-144, 7-155, 8-198, 9-201
1-39, 2-84, 3-89, 4-96, 5-201, 6-229, 7-235, 8-235, 9-245

Umpires: BF Bowden (New Zealand) & Nadeem Ghauri (Pakistan)
Toss: India
Man of the Match: Harbhajan Singh
Man of the Series: A Kumble

India won by 259 runs

SERIES AVERAGES
India v. Sri Lanka

INDIA

Batting	M	Inns	NO	Runs	HS	Av	100	50	c/st
Harbhajan Singh	3	4	3	59	40*	59.00	-	-	3/-
Yuvraj Singh	2	4	1	152	77*	50.66	-	2	-/-
IK Pathan	3	5	0	202	93	40.40	-	2	-/-
VVS Laxman	3	5	0	194	104	38.80	1	1	1/-
SR Tendulkar	3	5	0	189	109	37.80	1	-	-/-
MS Dhoni	3	5	1	149	51*	37.25	-	1	5/1
R Dravid	2	3	0	109	53	36.33	-	1	1/-
AB Agarkar	3	4	1	92	48	30.66	-	-	1/-
SC Ganguly	2	3	0	84	40	28.00	-	-	1/-
A Kumble	3	4	1	67	29*	22.33	-	-	2/-
V Sehwag	2	3	0	56	36	18.66	-	-	3/-
G Gambhir	3	5	0	54	30	10.80	-	-	4/-
M Kaif	1	2	0	13	9	6.50	-	-	5/-

Bowling	Overs	Mds	Runs	Wkts	Av	Best	5/inn	10m
A Kumble	138.3	28	374	20	18.70	6-72	2	1
Harbhajan Singh	103.1	17	312	14	22.28	7-62	1	1
IK Pathan	62	12	182	7	26.00	3-34	-	-
AB Agarkar	59	16	150	3	50.00	2-45	-	-

Also bowled: SC Ganguly 2-0-16-0, V Sehwag 3-0-18-0, SR Tendulkar 6-0-19-0.

SRI LANKA

Batting	M	Inns	NO	Runs	HS	Av	100	50	c/st
DPMD Jayawardene	3	5	0	255	71	51.00	-	4	1/-
MS Atapattu	3	5	0	218	88	43.60	-	2	2/-
TM Dilshan	3	5	1	170	65	42.50	-	2	1/-
KC Sangakkara	3	5	0	124	41	24.80	-	-	7/-
WU Tharanga	1	2	0	49	47	24.50	-	-	1/-
J Mubarak	3	4	1	63	29*	21.00	-	-	4/-
CM Bandara	3	4	1	40	28*	13.33	-	-	1/-
DA Gunawardene	2	3	0	38	25	12.66	-	-	1/-
TT Samaraweera	3	5	1	42	35*	10.50	-	-	1/-
WPUJC Vaas	2	2	0	19	17	9.50	-	-	1/-
M Muralitharan	3	4	0	17	9	4.25	-	-	1/-
MF Maharoof	1	2	0	6	4	3.00	-	-	1/-
CRD Fernando	2	2	1	2	2*	2.00	-	-	-/-
SL Malinga	1	2	1	0	0*	0.00	-	-	-/-

Bowling	Overs	Mds	Runs	Wkts	Av	Best	5/inn	10m
WPUJC Vaas	64	23	162	7	23.14	4-20	-	-
MF Maharoof	33	11	77	3	25.66	2-52	-	-
M Muralitharan	158.4	28	496	16	31.00	7-100	1	-
CM Bandara	92	14	296	9	32.88	3-84	-	-
SL Malinga	44	6	176	4	44.00	3-113	-	-
TM Dilshan	20	2	66	1	66.00	1-36	-	-
CRD Fernando	56	14	176	2	88.00	1-58	-	-

Also bowled: J Mubarak 1-0-2-0.

AUSTRALIA

AUSTRALIA REPORT
By Jim Maxwell

The shock and humiliation of losing the Ashes brought a powerful response from Australia's chastened players. Ricky Ponting's team quickly reaffirmed their number one status with convincing wins over the best of the rest in the overrated Super Series. Combined hangovers from Ashes success and the ICC's Oscar awards dulled the stellar qualities of the Supermen, who played without conviction or inspiration, allowing the home team to redress some of the lost faith of their fans.

Only Andrew Flintoff's lively bowling at the SCG in the 'Test match' excited what might occur in the next Ashes series. A weary but determined Freddie took seven wickets in the match, dominated by the wrist spin performance of Stuart MacGill, with nine wickets in an imposing 210-run win for Australia.

Damien Martyn was the immediate casualty of the Ashes loss, losing his place to all-rounder Shane Watson. It was a harsh decision, based on the evidence of one poor series for Martyn, who had previously been one of Australia's most consistent run scorers. Martyn thought at 34 that his career was over, but he was retained in the one-day side, and was eventually recalled to the Test team in South Africa, where he showed his mettle in the Third Test with a match-influencing second-innings century.

The move to position Watson as a long-term all-rounder floundered when he succumbed to another injury, dislocating his shoulder, in Hobart, in the Second Test against the West Indies. But the selectors stuck to their plan, and re-introduced Andrew Symonds. Symonds's occasional brutal batting, and less inspiring medium pace or spin bowling contributed marginally to Australia's overall record of 11 wins in 12 Tests. He was spectacular in the one-dayers, his proudest moment coming in Sydney where a full house cheered his lambasting 151 in the second final against Sri Lanka.

The middle order was reshuffled several times with Katich and Clarke moving out to allow Michael Hussey and, for five matches, Brad Hodge, to take their chances. Hussey had subbed for the injured opener, Justin Langer, making a hundred in his second Test, and by the end of the summer had hit four centuries, averaging over 75 to establish a permanent middle-order place. Hussey's batting was a revelation, and he cherished the Boxing Day Man-of-the-Match performance, making a century and sharing a surprising last-wicket partnership of 107 with Glenn McGrath.

Hussey also scored heavily in the one-dayers, supporting the consistent brilliance of his captain Ponting. Ponting's form was emphatic, scoring eight Test centuries averaging 78, and two more in the one-dayers where he averaged almost 50. South Africa's bowlers suffered most; Ponting twice hit centuries in each innings.

Numbers don't always count, however. Ask Brad Hodge. Replacing an out-of-form Michael Clarke, Hodge made 60 on debut, and a double-century against South Africa in Perth. Averaging 58, he made way for Martyn, 'a judgement call' according to Trevor Hohns, the chairman of selectors.

Hohns resigned a month later, ending 13 years of tough decision-making, including the dropping of Ian Healy, Steve Waugh from the one-day captaincy and Mark Waugh. Hohns had been involved in 35 series wins by Australian teams, but he made way for Allan Border to succeed him on the panel alongside new chairman Andrew Hilditch, David Boon and Merv Hughes.

Emphasising their post-Ashes recovery, Australia inflicted heavy Test defeats on the West Indies, South Africa and, after a fright, Bangladesh. In the one-dayers the record was 18 victories against seven losses, and the Twenty20 frolics finished one-all.

Following a timely hundred at The Oval in the last Ashes Test, Matthew Hayden's return to form produced five Test centuries, and an eventual recall to the one-day theatre. Shane Warne's match-winning skills were undiminished, taking 62 wickets in 12 Tests, and he was well supported by a maturer, controlled Brett Lee, who blasted out 52 victims. MacGill was again under-employed, grabbing 38 wickets in seven matches. Glenn McGrath's accuracy and bounce covered a loss of pace, gleaning 24 wickets.

In McGrath's absence for the South African tour, caring for his family while his wife Jane battled illness; Stuart Clark made an impressive debut, taking 20 wickets, a performance that won the Man-of-the-

Series award. Clark's skill mirrored McGrath, pushing his claims for a regular place in the Ashes series.

In Bangladesh, Australia avoided an embarrassing defeat thanks to a rescue century from Adam Gilchrist, and another disciplined innings from Ponting to squeak home by three wickets. In the Second Test Jason Gillespie batted on the first four days of a rain-affected game to compile a remarkable nightwatchman's double-century, an innings that team-mates have been constantly reminded of with Gillespie's email address now reading 'Dizzy201'.

In the limited-overs matches Symonds's ferocious hitting produced a stunning 156 from only 127 balls against New Zealand in the Chappell-Hadlee Trophy. Australia's series win was tempered by New Zealand's record-breaking chase in the third game, eclipsing the 331-run target with an over in hand.

Three months later Australia compiled a staggering record one-day total of 434 for 4 in the deciding match against South Africa at the Wanderers, with Ponting crashing 164 from 105 balls. But the South African chase was even more remarkable, Herschelle Gibbs slamming a 111-ball 175 to launch the innings towards, and eventually beyond the target with a wicket and a ball to spare. This run-scoring orgy confirmed Bill O'Reilly's initial impression of the limited-overs game, or what he dubbed the 'pyjama game'; bowlers turn up for the batsman's pleasure.

Australia had won the tripartite series at home against South Africa and Sri Lanka, after the Sri Lankans stunned the locals with a rousing win in the first final, cueing a powerful response from Australia. They lashed an imposing 368 for 5, targeting Muralitharan who went for 99 from his ten overs. In the decider Gilchrist slammed a 67-ball century, and with the other established one-day opener Katich also scoring a hundred, Australia won by eight wickets.

In South Africa, meanwhile, Australia struggled with injuries against a reinvigorated home team, and were lucky – and plucky – to recover from a 2-0 deficit to level the series before the run orgy in the decider. Underlining Australia's depth were the contributions made by Clarke, Katich and fleetingly Jaques and Cosgrove. Certainly Clarke's consistent batting put him line for an Ashes recall.

Coach John Buchanan had his contract extended until the end of the World Cup, a decision that was at least publicly endorsed by the captain. Buchanan's fascination with technology and analysis unravelled during the 2005 Ashes loss, and he was fortunate to survive.

In domestic cricket Queensland clobbered Victoria in the Pura Cup Final, amassing 900 for 6 to win by an innings and 354 runs. Mitchell Johnson's rapid left-arm pace bowling featured impressively, taking ten wickets in the match, indicating his maturity and potential for Test selection. NSW overcame South Australia by one wicket to win the one-day final, ending a 14-year association with sponsor ING. MacGill hit the winning runs, after Man-of-the-Match Shaun Tait had ripped out five wickets to put the game in the balance. Victoria won the inaugural Twenty20 competition, thanks to Brad Hodge's thumping 54-ball hundred against NSW in the final.

Brett Lee lets fly at South Africa's Mark Boucher on the final day of the Second Test at Durban's Kingsmead Stadium.

OF AUSTRALIA

By Jim Maxwell

Australian cricket has enjoyed a boom since Mark Taylor's team regained the Frank Worrell Trophy in the Caribbean in 1995. But the genesis of this success can be traced back to the appointment of Bob Simpson as coach in 1986. Simpson's guidance reinvigorated Australia from mediocrity to number one in the world, a position they have held and consolidated in both formats of the game.

The assets that ensured this success were a clutch of exceptional players, headed by the greatest wrist-spin bowler in the game, Shane Warne. Warne's influence, alongside the consistency of top-order wicket-taker Glenn McGrath, can be measured by the following numbers: from 1981 until Warne's debut in 1991, Australia won 28 per cent of all Test matches, a figure enhanced by the emphatic 4-0 regaining of the Ashes in 1989. Since the arrival of Warne, however, Australia have won 60 per cent of all Tests – a statistic that bears comparison with Bradman's influence, as Australia won 58 per cent of matches played during the Don's illustrious career from 1928 to 1948.

The pre-eminence of Warne and McGrath has shone out spectacularly alongside even the likes of Allan Border, Mark Taylor, Steve Waugh, Mark Waugh, David Boon, Ian Healy, Jason Gillespie, Adam Gilchrist, Matthew Hayden, Justin Langer and Ricky Ponting. And, in the limited-overs arena, you can add the qualities of Michael Bevan, Dean Jones and Andrew Symonds.

Australia's renaissance began in the subcontinent in 1987 when Allan Border's team played an extraordinary tied match against India, with Dean Jones' double-century defying debilitating Madras heat. The experience toughened Border's team for the World Cup, triumphantly won at Eden Gardens over England.

Though the West Indies were still unbeatable, Terry Alderman added lbw to his name in 1989, and Australia dominated England for further Ashes wins in 1990-91 and 1993. Then Australia went close to toppling the West Indies in 1993, losing a magnificent contest at Adelaide by one run. A Steve Waugh double-century set up Australia's memorable 1995 victory at Sabina Park, captain Mark Taylor bagging the catch off Shane Warne to finish the match.

Taylor's astute leadership, and a record equalling 334 not out, figured in the first series win in Pakistan for 38 years in 1998. Taylor made way for Steve Waugh after more Ashes wins in 1997 and 1998-99, and Waugh had to overcome Lara's brilliance to draw 2-2 in the

Shane Warne is one of the greatest bowlers the game has ever seen. Since his international debut in 1992 he has taken over 670 Test wickets at an average of 25 runs – figures that have played a big part in Australia's rise to the top of the cricketing tree.

Caribbean. Waugh's batting motivated a World Cup win in England in 1999, knocking out South Africa in a tied semi-final, a victory repeated breathtakingly by Ponting's undefeated team in South Africa in 2003.

Waugh maintained the attacking approach instilled by Taylor, but lost an amazing series in 2001 after India had been forced to follow on in Kolkata. He then presided over more Ashes wins in 2001 and 2002-03, reaching an emotional hundred off the last ball of the day in the SCG Test.

In Ponting's absence through injury, Adam Gilchrist led Australia to a historic series win in India in 2004. Ponting returned to lead the side in England in 2005, a series in which Australia's pride was severely dented. But like all great teams, Australia have since fought back, and Test series wins over West Indies and South Africa among others, have reaffirmed that Australia remain the world's number one side.

FIRST TEST – AUSTRALIA v. WEST INDIES
3–6 November 2005 at Brisbane

AUSTRALIA

	First Innings		Second Innings	
ML Hayden	lbw b Collymore	37	(2) c Sarwan b Gayle	118
MEK Hussey	c Ramdin b Powell	1	(1) c Collymore b Gayle	29
RT Ponting (capt)	c Sarwan b Lawson	149	not out	104
MJ Clarke	c Ramdin b Collymore	5	not out	14
SM Katich	c Gayle b Collymore	0		
*AC Gilchrist	lbw b Collymore	44		
SR Watson	lbw b Edwards	16		
SK Warne	c Ramdin b Powell	47		
B Lee	c Collymore b Powell	47		
NW Bracken	c Sarwan b Edwards	37		
GD McGrath	not out	6		
Extras	b 5, lb 13, w 6, nb 22	46	b 6, lb 3, w 1, nb 8	18
	(all out 105.3 overs)	435	(2 wkts dec 66 overs)	283

	First Innings				Second Innings			
	O	M	R	W	O	M	R	W
Edwards	21.3	1	94	2	5	0	27	0
Powell	20	1	100	3	5	1	24	0
Collymore	26	4	72	4	11	0	56	0
Lawson	14	0	73	1	6	0	47	0
Samuels	4	0	29	0	12	1	46	0
Gayle	20	3	49	0	27	4	74	2

Fall of Wickets
1-9, 2-101, 3-108, 4-111, 5-215, 6-273, 7-294, 8-369, 9-417
1-71, 2-258

WEST INDIES

	First Innings		Second Innings (following on)	
CH Gayle	c Gilchrist b McGrath	10	c Warne b Watson	33
DS Smith	b McGrath	88	c Warne b Lee	3
RR Sarwan	c Gilchrist b McGrath	21	c Gilchrist b Lee	31
BC Lara	lbw b Lee	30	c Hayden b Bracken	14
S Chanderpaul (capt)	c Bracken b Warne	2	lbw b Bracken	7
MN Samuels	c Gilchrist b McGrath	5	not out	17
*D Ramdin	not out	37	c Gilchrist b Lee	6
DB Powell	c Gilchrist b Warne	4	lbw b Bracken	0
FH Edwards	b Warne	2	b Bracken	0
CD Collymore	c Clarke b Warne	0	lbw b Lee	4
JJC Lawson	lbw b Warne	0	b Lee	1
Extras	lb 7, w 1, nb 3	11	lb 3, nb 10	13
	(all out 77 overs)	210	(all out 49 overs)	129

	First Innings				Second Innings			
	O	M	R	W	O	M	R	W
McGrath	22	3	72	4	11	3	22	0
Lee	15	4	59	1	14	4	30	5
Bracken	10	4	23	0	16	3	48	4
Warne	28	9	48	5	2	1	1	0
Clarke	2	1	1	0	-	-	-	-
Watson	-	-	-	-	6	0	25	1

Fall of Wickets
1-20, 2-74, 3-134, 4-149, 5-161, 6-174, 7-187, 8-204, 9-210
1-11, 2-53, 3-85, 4-99, 5-99, 6-105, 7-106, 8-106, 9-114

Umpires: IL Howell (New Zealand) & RE Koertzen (South Africa)
Toss: West Indies
Test Debut: MEK Hussey
Man of the Match: RT Ponting

Australia won by 379 runs

SECOND TEST – AUSTRALIA v. WEST INDIES
17–21 November 2005 at Hobart

WEST INDIES

	First Innings		Second Innings	
CH Gayle	lbw b McGrath	56	b McGrath	4
DS Smith	b Lee	4	c Ponting b McGrath	8
RR Sarwan	c Gilchrist b McGrath	2	c Gilchrist b Lee	32
BC Lara	lbw b Lee	13	c Gilchrist b Warne	45
S Chanderpaul (capt)	c Hodge b MacGill	39	c Gilchrist b Lee	10
MN Samuels	c Gilchrist b McGrath	5	c Hodge b Warne	29
DJJ Bravo	c Hodge b MacGill	3	b Warne	113
*D Ramdin	c Warne b MacGill	2	c Warne b MacGill	71
DB Powell	c Gilchrist b Lee	15	lbw b MacGill	0
FH Edwards	c Symonds b McGrath	0	not out	2
CD Collymore	not out	3	c Gilchrist b Warne	0
Extras	lb 3, w 1, nb 3	7	b 4, lb 12, w 1, nb 3	20
	(all out 68.3 overs)	149	(all out 122 overs)	334

	First Innings				Second Innings			
	O	M	R	W	O	M	R	W
McGrath	23	9	31	4	25	13	29	2
Lee	13.3	6	32	3	27	4	99	2
Symonds	10	4	17	0	5	1	9	0
Warne	11	2	48	3	39	4	112	4
MacGill	11	3	18	3	26	4	69	2

Fall of Wickets
1-15, 2-26, 3-60, 4-119, 5-119, 6-124, 7-126, 8-130, 9-141
1-4, 2-27, 3-62, 4-76, 5-133, 6-140, 7-322, 8-326, 9-332

AUSTRALIA

	First Innings		Second Innings	
ML Hayden	c Bravo b Collymore	110	(2) c Smith b Gayle	46
MEK Hussey	c Sarwan b Bravo	137	(1) not out	31
RT Ponting (capt)	b Edwards	17	not out	0
MJ Clarke	c sub b Edwards	5		
BJ Hodge	lbw b Collymore	60		
A Symonds	run out	1		
*AC Gilchrist	c sub b Bravo	2		
SK Warne	c Sarwan b Powell	1		
B Lee	c Ramdin b Edwards	18		
SCG MacGill	not out	20		
GD McGrath	run out	14		
Extras	lb 6, w 3, nb 12	21	nb 1	1
	(all out 109.4 overs)	406	(1 wkt 26.1 overs)	78

	First Innings				Second Innings			
	O	M	R	W	O	M	R	W
Edwards	27.4	2	116	3	5	1	16	0
Powell	24	2	117	1	7	1	21	0
Collymore	28	11	54	2	-	-	-	-
Bravo	23	2	96	2	7	1	21	0
Gayle	7	0	17	0	6	2	16	1
Sarwan	-	-	-	-	1.1	0	4	0

Fall of Wickets
1-231, 2-257, 3-271, 4-306, 5-315, 6-317, 7-324, 8-362, 9-377
1-77

Umpires: Aleem Dar (Pakistan) & RE Koertzen (South Africa)
Toss: West Indies
Test Debut: BJ Hodge
Man of the Match: MEK Hussey

Australia won by 9 wickets

THIRD TEST – AUSTRALIA v. WEST INDIES
25–29 November 2005 at Adelaide

WEST INDIES

	First Innings		Second Innings	
WW Hinds	c Hayden b Lee	10	st Gilchrist b Warne	15
DS Smith	c Hayden b Lee	7	c Ponting b Lee	0
RR Sarwan	c Symonds b Lee	16	lbw b Lee	62
BC Lara	b McGrath	226	(5) c Hayden b Warne	17
S Chanderpaul (capt)	c Gilchrist b Symonds	25	(6) c Hodge b Warne	4
DJJ Bravo	c Ponting b MacGill	34	(7) b Lee	64
DR Smith	c Symonds b MacGill	14	(8) lbw b Warne	0
*D Ramdin	lbw b McGrath	27	(9) c Gilchrist b Warne	28
DB Powell	lbw b McGrath	14	(4) b Warne	2
FH Edwards	c Hayden b Warne	10	c Warne b Lee	9
CD Collymore	not out	5	not out	1
Extras	b 2, lb 5, w 1, nb 9	17	lb 2	2
	(all out 111.2 overs)	405	(all out 81 overs)	204

	First Innings				Second Innings			
	O	M	R	W	O	M	R	W
McGrath	30	3	106	3	18	8	25	0
Lee	28	3	111	3	17	5	46	4
Symonds	16	5	44	1	2	0	9	0
Warne	19.2	2	77	1	33	9	80	6
MacGill	18	3	60	2	11	2	42	0

Fall of Wickets
1-16, 2-19, 3-53, 4-121, 5-237, 6-263, 7-333, 8-381, 9-388
1-2, 2-60, 3-72, 4-96, 5-96, 6-106, 7-106, 8-160, 9-203

AUSTRALIA

	First Innings		Second Innings	
JL Langer	c Ramdin b Edwards	99	c Smith DR b Collymore	20
ML Hayden	c Chanderpaul b Bravo	47	not out	87
RT Ponting (capt)	lbw b Bravo	56	c Sarwan b Collymore	3
BJ Hodge	lbw b Edwards	18	c Smith DR b Powell	23
MEK Hussey	not out	133	not out	30
A Symonds	b Bravo	9		
*AC Gilchrist	c Chanderpaul b Bravo	6		
SK Warne	c & b Bravo	0		
B Lee	c Ramdin b Bravo	9		
SCG MacGill	b Edwards	22		
GD McGrath	b Smith DR	5		
Extras	lb 7, w 2, nb 15	24	lb 3, w 1, nb 15	19
	(all out 123.3 overs)	428	(3 wkts 58 overs)	182

	First Innings				Second Innings			
	O	M	R	W	O	M	R	W
Edwards	23	4	114	3	11	1	52	0
Powell	24	6	80	0	14	2	40	1
Collymore	23	1	59	0	20	6	51	2
Bravo	27	7	84	6	-	-	-	-
Smith DR	17.3	3	59	1	1	0	1	0
Hinds	9	1	25	0	-	-	-	-
Sarwan	-	-	-	-	12	2	35	0

Fall of Wickets
1-97, 2-211, 3-228, 4-238, 5-271, 6-277, 7-277, 8-295, 9-388
1-51, 2-55, 3-110

Umpires: BF Bowden (New Zealand) & Aleem Dar (Pakistan)
Toss: West Indies
Man of the Match: BC Lara
Man of the Series: ML Hayden

Australia won by 7 wickets

SERIES AVERAGES
Australia v. West Indies

AUSTRALIA

Batting	M	Inns	NO	Runs	HS	Av	100	50	c/st
MEK Hussey	3	6	3	361	137	120.33	2	-	-/-
ML Hayden	3	6	1	445	118	89.00	2	1	5/-
RT Ponting	3	6	2	329	149	82.25	2	1	3/-
JL Langer	1	2	0	119	99	59.50	-	1	-/-
SCG MacGill	2	2	1	42	22	42.00	-	-	-/-
NW Bracken	1	1	0	37	37	37.00	-	-	1/-
BJ Hodge	2	3	0	101	60	33.66	-	1	4/-
B Lee	3	3	0	74	47	24.66	-	-	-/-
AC Gilchrist	3	3	0	52	44	17.33	-	-	15/1
SK Warne	3	3	0	48	47	16.00	-	-	5/-
SR Watson	1	1	0	16	16	16.00	-	-	-/-
GD McGrath	3	3	1	25	14	12.50	-	-	-/-
MJ Clarke	2	3	1	24	14*	12.00	-	-	1/-
A Symonds	2	2	0	10	9	5.00	-	-	3/-
SM Katich	1	1	0	0	0	0.00	-	-	-/-

Bowling	Overs	Mds	Runs	Wkts	Av	Best	5/inn	10m
NW Bracken	26	7	71	4	17.75	4-48	-	-
B Lee	114.3	26	377	18	20.94	5-30	1	-
GD McGrath	129	39	285	13	21.92	4-31	-	-
SK Warne	132.2	27	366	16	22.87	6-80	2	-
SR Watson	6	0	25	1	25.00	1-25	-	-
SCG MacGill	66	12	189	7	27.00	3-18	-	-
A Symonds	33	10	79	1	79.00	1-44	-	-
Also bowled: MJ Clarke 2-1-1-0.								

WEST INDIES

Batting	M	Inns	NO	Runs	HS	Av	100	50	c/st
BC Lara	3	6	0	345	226	57.50	1	-	-/-
DJ Bravo	2	4	0	214	113	53.50	1	1	2/-
D Ramdin	3	6	1	171	71	34.20	-	1	6/-
RR Sarwan	3	6	0	164	62	27.33	-	1	6/-
CH Gayle	2	4	0	103	56	25.75	-	1	1/-
MN Samuels	2	4	1	56	29	18.66	-	-	-/-
DS Smith	3	6	0	110	88	18.33	-	1	1/-
S Chanderpaul	3	6	0	87	39	14.50	-	-	2/-
WW Hinds	1	2	0	25	15	12.50	-	-	-/-
DR Smith	1	2	0	14	14	7.00	-	-	2/-
DB Powell	3	6	0	35	15	5.83	-	-	-/-
FH Edwards	3	6	1	23	10	4.60	-	-	-/-
CD Collymore	3	6	3	13	5*	4.33	-	-	2/-
JJC Lawson	1	2	0	1	1	0.50	-	-	-/-

Bowling	Overs	Mds	Runs	Wkts	Av	Best	5/inn	10m
DJ Bravo	57	10	201	8	25.12	6-84	1	-
CD Collymore	108	22	292	8	36.50	4-72	-	-
CH Gayle	60	9	156	3	52.00	2-74	-	-
FH Edwards	93.1	9	419	8	52.37	3-114	-	-
DR Smith	18.3	3	60	1	60.00	1-59	-	-
DB Powell	94	13	382	5	76.40	3-100	-	-
JJC Lawson	20	0	120	1	120.00	1-73	-	-
Also bowled: WW Hinds 9-1-25-0, RR Sarwan 13.1-2-39-0, MN Samuels 16-1-75-0.								

FIRST TEST – AUSTRALIA v. SOUTH AFRICA
16–20 December 2005 at Perth

AUSTRALIA

	First Innings			Second Innings	
JL Langer	c Smith b Ntini	37		b Pollock	47
ML Hayden	c Rudolph b Ntini	0		c Boucher b Langeveldt	20
RT Ponting (capt)	lbw b Pollock	71		(4) c Boucher b Ntini	53
BJ Hodge	c Boucher b Ntini	41		(5) not out	203
MEK Hussey	c Langeveldt b Ntini	23		(6) c Boucher b Pollock	58
A Symonds	b Nel	13		(7) c Gibbs b Langeveldt	25
*AC Gilchrist	c Gibbs b Ntini	6		(8) c Rudolph b Nel	44
SK Warne	lbw b Langeveldt	24		(9) lbw b Kemp	5
B Lee	not out	19		(3) lbw b Langeveldt	32
NW Bracken	c Boucher b Nel	10		not out	14
GD McGrath	c Boucher b Nel	0			
Extras	b 4, lb 2, w 2, nb 6	14		b 5, lb 4, w 1, nb 17	27
	(all out 75.2 overs)	258		(8 wkts dec 146.4 overs)	528

	First Innings				Second Innings			
	O	M	R	W	O	M	R	W
Pollock	19	6	46	1	36	6	98	2
Ntini	19	3	64	5	34	8	113	1
Langeveldt	17	1	100	1	31	3	117	3
Nel	17.2	3	29	3	28	2	104	1
Kemp	3	0	13	0	11	0	58	1
Rudolph	-	-	-	-	6.4	1	29	0

Fall of Wickets
1-0, 2-111, 3-117, 4-180, 5-185, 6-199, 7-210, 8-243, 9-258
1-37, 2-86, 3-129, 4-184, 5-316, 6-377, 7-444, 8-451

SOUTH AFRICA

	First Innings			Second Innings	
AB de Villiers	b Warne	68		(2) c Hodge b Warne	12
GC Smith (capt)	c Ponting b Bracken	34		(1) lbw b Bracken	30
HH Gibbs	b Lee	21		c Warne b Lee	33
JA Rudolph	c Langer b Lee	8		not out	102
AG Prince	lbw b Warne	28		lbw b Warne	8
JM Kemp	c Hodge b McGrath	7		c Ponting b Warne	55
*MV Boucher	c Hayden b Warne	62		not out	13
SM Pollock	b Lee	34			
A Nel	not out	4			
CK Langeveldt	lbw b Lee	0			
M Ntini	c Hodge b Lee	12			
Extras	b 4, lb 2, nb 12	18		b 18, lb 13, nb 3	34
	(all out 81.2 overs)	296		(5 wkts 126 overs)	287

	First Innings				Second Innings			
	O	M	R	W	O	M	R	W
McGrath	18	3	59	1	24	11	39	0
Lee	22.2	9	93	5	31	9	83	1
Bracken	12	3	46	1	19	5	37	1
Warne	29	4	92	3	47	21	83	3
Symonds	-	-	-	-	3	0	6	0
Hodge	-	-	-	-	2	0	8	0

Fall of Wickets
1-83, 2-127, 3-135, 4-145, 5-167, 6-187, 7-264, 8-282, 9-283
1-35, 2-55, 3-109, 4-138, 5-250

Umpires: SA Bucknor (West Indies) & B Doctrove (West Indies)
Toss: Australia
Man of the Match: BJ Hodge

Match drawn

SECOND TEST – AUSTRALIA v. SOUTH AFRICA
26–30 December 2005 at Melbourne

AUSTRALIA

	First Innings			Second Innings	
PA Jaques	c Rudolph b Pollock	2		(2) lbw b Nel	28
ML Hayden	c Smith b Pollock	65		(1) c Boucher b Kallis	137
RT Ponting (capt)	c Gibbs b Nel	117		lbw b Pollock	11
BJ Hodge	c Smith b Pollock	7		c Boucher b Nel	24
MEK Hussey	b Ntini	122		c Kallis b Smith	31
A Symonds	c Boucher b Nel	0		c Nel b Kallis	72
*AC Gilchrist	c Gibbs b Nel	2		c Prince b Kallis	0
SK Warne	c Boje b Nel	9		not out	0
B Lee	lbw b Ntini	4			
SCG MacGill	b Ntini	4			
GD McGrath	not out	11			
Extras	b 2, lb 4, w 2, nb 4	12		b 6, lb 3, nb 9	18
	(all out 119.3 overs)	355		(7 wkts dec 83 overs)	321

	First Innings				Second Innings			
	O	M	R	W	O	M	R	W
Pollock	26	5	67	3	23	5	60	1
Ntini	22.3	3	70	3	8	2	17	0
Kallis	21.5	4	69	0	11	0	58	3
Nel	31	6	84	4	20	3	71	2
Boje	18.1	3	59	0	14	0	65	0
Smith	-	-	-	-	7	0	41	1

Fall of Wickets
1-2, 2-154, 3-176, 4-207, 5-207, 6-213, 7-227, 8-239, 9-248
1-53, 2-81, 3-131, 4-193, 5-317, 6-321, 7-321

SOUTH AFRICA

	First Innings			Second Innings	
AB de Villiers	lbw b McGrath	61		(2) st Gilchrist b Warne	8
GC Smith (capt)	lbw b Lee	22		(1) c Gilchrist b McGrath	25
HH Gibbs	b Symonds	94		b Warne	9
JH Kallis	b Lee	23		c Gilchrist b Symonds	9
AG Prince	c Ponting b Warne	6		c Hayden b Warne	26
JA Rudolph	b Lee	13		b Symonds	4
*MV Boucher	lbw b Symonds	23		c Ponting b Warne	5
SM Pollock	lbw b Symonds	9		not out	67
N Boje	b Warne	12		b McGrath	13
A Nel	c Hussey b MacGill	14		c Gilchrist b McGrath	2
M Ntini	not out	10		b MacGill	2
Extras	b 2, lb 7, nb 15	24		lb 6, w 1, nb 4	11
	(all out 111 overs)	311		(all out 74 overs)	181

	First Innings				Second Innings			
	O	M	R	W	O	M	R	W
McGrath	27	13	57	1	15	3	44	3
Lee	28	5	92	3	11	4	23	0
Symonds	20	6	50	3	4	2	6	2
Warne	21	7	62	2	28	7	74	4
MacGill	15	3	41	1	16	7	28	1

Fall of Wickets
1-36, 2-122, 3-184, 4-192, 5-214, 6-260, 7-265, 8-281, 9-291
1-39, 2-45, 3-58, 4-64, 5-72, 6-82, 7-130, 8-166, 9-178

Umpires: SA Bucknor (West Indies) & Asad Rauf (Pakistan)
Toss: Australia
Test Debut: PA Jaques
Man of the Match: MEK Hussey

Australia won by 184 runs

THIRD TEST – AUSTRALIA v. SOUTH AFRICA
2–6 January 2006 at Sydney

SOUTH AFRICA

	First Innings		Second Innings	
AB de Villiers	c Gilchrist b Lee	2	(2) lbw b Lee	1
GC Smith (capt)	lbw b Lee	39	(1) lbw b McGrath	5
HH Gibbs	b McGrath	27	run out	67
JH Kallis	c McGrath b Symonds	111	not out	50
AG Prince	lbw b Warne	119	c Ponting b MacGill	18
JA Rudolph	c Gilchrist b McGrath	38	c McGrath b MacGill	4
*MV Boucher	c Gilchrist b MacGill	5	st Gilchrist b MacGill	11
SM Pollock	c Hodge b Lee	46	not out	26
J Botha	not out	20		
A Nel	c Hodge b Warne	12		
CK Langeveldt	not out	1		
Extras	b 9, lb 6, nb 16	31	b 3, lb 4, w 3, nb 2	12
	(9 wkts dec 154.4 overs)	451	(6 wkts dec 42 overs)	194

	First Innings				Second Innings			
	O	M	R	W	O	M	R	W
McGrath	34	17	65	2	15	2	61	1
Lee	30.4	7	82	3	10	3	48	1
Symonds	23	4	69	1	–	–	–	–
Warne	36	5	106	2	11	1	45	0
Hussey	2	0	12	0	–	–	–	–
MacGill	29	5	102	1	6	1	33	3

Fall of Wickets
1-16, 2-69, 3-86, 4-305, 5-344, 6-355, 7-394, 8-433, 9-449
1-4, 2-6, 3-92, 4-123, 5-129, 6-152

AUSTRALIA

	First Innings		Second Innings	
JL Langer	b Langeveldt	25	b Langeveldt	20
ML Hayden	b Langeveldt	4	c Smith b Botha	90
RT Ponting (capt)	b Kallis	120	not out	143
BJ Hodge	c Rudolph b Nel	6	not out	27
MEK Hussey	c Boucher b Botha	45		
A Symonds	lbw b Nel	12		
*AC Gilchrist	c Boucher b Nel	86		
SK Warne	c Boucher b Nel	0		
B Lee	c Smith b Kallis	17		
SCG MacGill	c Nel b Pollock	29		
GD McGrath	not out	1		
Extras	lb 10, w 2, nb 2	14	lb 1, w 2, nb 5	8
	(all out 95.1 overs)	359	(2 wkts 60.3 overs)	288

	First Innings				Second Innings			
	O	M	R	W	O	M	R	W
Pollock	25	3	109	1	14	2	55	0
Langeveldt	24	4	108	2	14	1	52	1
Nel	24.1	3	81	4	7	0	46	0
Kallis	15	4	25	2	2	0	8	0
Botha	7	2	26	1	12.3	0	77	1
Rudolph	–	–	–	–	11	0	49	0

Fall of Wickets
1-22, 2-35, 3-54, 4-184, 5-222, 6-226, 7-226, 8-263, 9-322
1-30, 2-212

Umpires: Aleem Dar (Pakistan) & BF Bowden (New Zealand)
Toss: South Africa
Man of the Match: RT Ponting
Man of the Series: RT Ponting

Australia won by 8 wickets

SERIES AVERAGES
Australia v. South Africa

AUSTRALIA

Batting	M	Inns	NO	Runs	HS	Av	100	50	c/st
RT Ponting	3	6	1	515	143*	103.00	3	2	5/-
BJ Hodge	3	6	2	308	203*	77.00	1	-	5/-
MEK Hussey	3	5	0	279	122	55.80	1	1	1/-
ML Hayden	3	6	0	316	137	52.66	1	2	2/-
JL Langer	3	4	0	129	47	32.25	-	-	1/-
AC Gilchrist	3	5	0	138	86	27.60	-	1	6/2
A Symonds	3	5	0	122	72	24.40	-	1	-/-
B Lee	3	4	1	72	32	24.00	-	-	-/-
NW Bracken	1	2	1	24	14*	24.00	-	-	-/-
SCG MacGill	2	2	0	33	29	16.50	-	-	-/-
PA Jaques	1	2	0	30	28	15.00	-	-	-/-
GD McGrath	3	3	2	12	11*	12.00	-	-	2/-
SK Warne	3	5	1	38	24	9.50	-	-	1/-

Bowling	Overs	Mds	Runs	Wkts	Av	Best	5/inn	10m
A Symonds	50	12	131	6	21.83	3-50	-	-
B Lee	133	29	415	13	32.38	5-93	1	-
SK Warne	172	45	462	14	33.00	4-74	-	-
SCG MacGill	66	16	204	6	34.00	3-33	-	-
GD McGrath	133	49	325	8	40.62	3-44	-	-
NW Bracken	31	8	83	2	41.50	1-37	-	-

Also bowled: BJ Hodge 2-0-8-0, MEK Hussey 2-0-12-0.

SOUTH AFRICA

Batting	M	Inns	NO	Runs	HS	Av	100	50	c/st
JH Kallis	2	4	1	193	111	64.33	1	1	1/-
SM Pollock	3	5	2	182	67*	60.66	-	1	-/-
HH Gibbs	3	6	0	251	94	41.83	-	2	4/-
AG Prince	3	6	0	205	119	34.16	1	-	1/-
JA Rudolph	3	6	1	169	102*	33.80	1	-	4/-
JM Kemp	1	2	0	62	55	31.00	-	1	-/-
GC Smith	3	6	0	155	39	25.83	-	-	5/-
AB de Villiers	3	6	0	152	68	25.33	-	2	-/-
MV Boucher	3	6	1	119	62	23.80	-	1	12/-
N Boje	1	2	0	25	13	12.50	-	-	1/-
M Ntini	2	3	1	24	12	12.00	-	-	-/-
A Nel	3	4	1	32	14	10.66	-	-	2/-
CK Langeveldt	2	2	1	1	1*	1.00	-	-	1/-
J Botha	1	1	1	20	20*	-	-	-	-/-

Bowling	Overs	Mds	Runs	Wkts	Av	Best	5/inn	10m
M Ntini	83.3	16	264	9	29.33	5-64	1	-
A Nel	127.3	17	415	14	29.64	4-81	-	-
JH Kallis	49.5	8	160	5	32.00	3-58	-	-
GC Smith	7	0	41	1	41.00	1-41	-	-
J Botha	19.3	2	103	2	51.50	1-26	-	-
CK Langeveldt	86	9	377	7	53.85	3-117	-	-
SM Pollock	143	27	435	8	54.37	3-67	-	-
JM Kemp	14	0	71	1	71.00	1-58	-	-

Also bowled: JA Rudolph 17.4-1-78-0, N Boje 32.1-3-124-0.

VB Series
(Australia, South Africa and Sri Lanka)

Match One
13 January 2006 at Melbourne (DS)
Australia 318 for 5 (50 overs) (DR Martyn 70,
A Symonds 66, SM Katich 60)
Sri Lanka 202 for 7 (50 overs)
(DPMD Jayawardene 50)
Australia won by 116 runs

Match Two
15 January 2006 at Brisbane
Australia 228 all out (49.5 overs)
(MEK Hussey 73, B Lee 57, SM Pollock 3 for 30)
South Africa 231 for 5 (48.5 overs)
(HH Dippenaar 74, MV Boucher 63*)
South Africa won by 5 wickets

Match Three
17 January 2006 at Brisbane
Sri Lanka 282 for 6 (50 overs) (KC Sangakkara 88,
J Mubarak 61)
South Africa 188 all out (44.2 overs) (MV Boucher 62,
JA Rudolph 53, CM Bandara 3 for 31)
Sri Lanka won by 94 runs

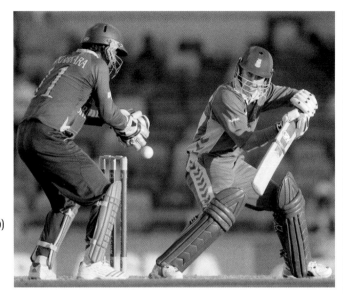

South Africa's Boeta Dippenaar pictured during his unbeaten
125 against Sri Lanka in Adelaide.

Match Four
20 January 2006
at Melbourne (DS)
Australia 245 all out
(49.2 overs) (PA Jaques 94,
AJ Hall 4 for 35)
South Africa 186 all out
(47 overs) (B Lee 5 for 22,
GB Hogg 3 for 32)
Australia won by 59 runs

Match Five
22 January 2006
at Sydney
Sri Lanka 309 for 7 (50
overs) (ST Jayasuriya 114,
KC Sangakkara 78,
DPMD Jayawardene 56)
Australia 258 all out
(50 overs) (MJ Clarke 67,
CM Bandara 4 for 58)
Sri Lanka won by 51 runs

**Kumar Sangakkara walks off
after scoring 88 in Brisbane.**

Match Six
24 January 2006 at Adelaide
South Africa 263 for 5 (50 overs) (HH Dippenaar 125*,
HH Gibbs 68)
Sri Lanka 254 for 8 (50 overs) (TM Dilshan 82*,
DPMD Jayawardene 52)
South Africa won by 9 runs

Match Seven
26 January 2006 at Adelaide
Sri Lanka 218 for 8 (50 overs)
(A Symonds 3 for 48)
Australia 219 for 5 (48.3 overs) (SM Katich 52)
Australia won by 5 wickets

Match Eight
29 January 2006 at Perth
Sri Lanka 233 for 8 (50 overs) (DPMD Jayawardene 69,
RP Arnold 56)
Australia 237 for 4 (41 overs) (AC Gilchrist 116,
SM Katich 82)
Australia won by 6 wickets

Match Nine
31 January 2006 at Perth
Sri Lanka 221 all out (47.4 overs) (ST Jayasuriya 86,
GC Smith 3 for 30)
South Africa 224 for 5 (45.1 overs) (HH Dippenaar 87,
M Muralitharan 3 for 44)
South Africa won by 5 wickets

Match Ten
3 February 2006 at Melbourne (DS)
Australia 281 for 7 (50 overs)
(A Symonds 65, MEK Hussey 62,
RT Ponting 53)
South Africa 201 for 9 (50 overs)
(B Lee 4 for 30)
Australia won by 80 runs

Match Eleven
5 February 2006 at Sydney
Australia 344 for 6 (50 overs)
(AC Gilchrist 88, DR Martyn 79,
RT Ponting 72)
South Africa 287 for 6 (50 overs)
(MV Boucher 76)
Australia won by 57 runs

Match Twelve
7 February 2006 at Hobart
Sri Lanka 257 for 9 (50 overs)
(MS Atapattu 80, KC Sangakkara
62, AJ Hall 3 for 50)
South Africa 181 all out (43.4 overs) (GC Smith 67,
CM Bandara 4 for 31)
Sri Lanka won by 76 runs

FINAL TABLE

	P	W	L	T	NR	RR	Pts
Australia	8	6	2	0	0	0.78	27
Sri Lanka	8	3	5	0	0	0.04	14
South Africa	8	3	5	0	0	-0.81	12

Best of Three to decide series winners

Match Thirteen – FIRST FINAL
10 February 2006 at Adelaide
Sri Lanka 274 for 8 (50 overs) (KC Sangakkara 83,
MS Atapattu 53, NW Bracken 3 for 61)
Australia 252 all out (49.1 overs) (MJ Clarke 80,
SM Katich 56, M Muralitharan 3 for 40)
Sri Lanka won by 22 runs

Match Fourteen – SECOND FINAL
12 February 2006 at Sydney
Australia 368 for 5 (50 overs) (A Symonds 151,
RT Ponting 124, MJ Clarke 54*, WPUJC Vaas 4 for 56)
Sri Lanka 201 all out (36 overs) (RP Arnold 64*,
DPMD Jayawardene 50, NW Bracken 4 for 30)
Australia won by 167 runs

Australia pose with the VB Trophy after completing a
2-1 win over Sri Lanka.

Sri Lanka's players celebrate a wicket, but it is Australian
captain Ricky Ponting who has the last laugh with a match-
winning 124 in the second final.

Match Fifteen – THIRD FINAL
14 February 2006 at Brisbane
Sri Lanka 266 for 9 (50 overs) (DPMD Jayawardene 86,
RP Arnold 76, KC Sangakkara 59, NW Bracken 3 for 44)
Australia 267 for 1 (45.3 overs) (AC Gilchrist 122,
SM Katich 107*)
Australia won by 9 wickets

Australia won the VB Series

BANGLADESH

BANGLADESH REPORT
By Qamar Ahmed

Amidst criticism about their ability to perform at international level, and appeals and pressure from various quarters including from the captain of Australia Ricky Ponting that they join Zimbabwe as a temporarily non-Test-playing nation, Bangladesh silenced their detractors with a near match-winning performance in a home Test at Fatullah against Australia.

If it had been achieved it would certainly have been the greatest upset of not only their own brief cricket history but that of Australia's too. Sadly for Bangladesh, though, the Australians were let out of jail by their captain Ponting's resilience with a fighting, unbeaten century that denied the minnows their crowning glory. 'The team does not really know how close they came to creating a major, major upset,' said their coach Dav Whatmore later. Australia's dramatic rally took them to a three-wicket victory in the end, and later they completed a 2-0 series win.

Up to that day in mid-April 2006, Bangladesh had lost 35 of their 40 Tests – and 24 of them by an innings. That is 60 per cent of the Tests they had played since becoming a full member of the International Cricket Council (ICC) in 2000. Their only win in a Test remains the one against Zimbabwe at home last year. A victory against Australia in a one-day international at Cardiff in the summer of 2005, however, was a day to remember as the nation celebrated.

At Fatullah, Bangladesh's 355 runs in a day and their huge 427 total in the first innings, based upon a brilliant 138 by Shahriar Nafees, had earned them a 158-run first innings lead. But Australia managed to save the follow-on as Adam Gilchrist hit 144 to rescue them from the depths of 93 for 6. Left-arm spinner Mohammad Rafique did most of the damage with 5 for 62.

Bangladesh failed in their second innings, being bowled out for only 148, but they did still manage to set Australia 307 to win. Australia were initially struggling at 225 for 5, but Ponting received solid support from tail-enders Brett Lee and Jason Gillespie – after Shane Warne and Adam Gilchrist had both fallen – to save his side from the ignominy

Left-handed opener Shahriar Nafees shocked both Australia's attack and the watching world with a magnificent 138 in the First Test.

OF BANGLADESH

By Qamar Ahmed

Before gaining independence in 1971, Bangladesh was in fact East Pakistan, a truncated wing of the country where football was the favourite pastime and cricket only a close second. Several factors, however, contributed to the growth in popularity of cricket in the region. First came Pakistan's victory at Lucknow in their inaugural series against India in 1952, and then the historic win against England at The Oval in 1954. When Pakistan, still a young cricket nation, then staged seven official Tests between 1955 to 1969 in what is now Bangladesh the game really caught on with the Bengali people. Regional representative cricket began in the region and I myself had the privilege of playing a number of first-class games against them for Sind Province.

After independence in 1971 the new country of Bangladesh continued to take an active interest in the game by hosting teams from neighbouring countries and MCC. They also organised themselves by establishing the Bangladesh Cricket Control Board in 1972 and later becoming an associate member of the ICC in 1977. This, in turn, allowed them to play in the ICC Trophy from 1979 onwards – and it was a competition they won in 1997, in Malaysia, to earn their right to play in fully fledged one-day internationals from 1998.

Not much notice was taken of them, however, until they faced Pakistan in the 1999 World Cup at Northampton where they staged a big upset, winning by 62 runs. This victory opened the door to their acceptance as a full member of the ICC in June 2000. Their historic inaugural Test was held in November of that year, against India.

That remained the highlight of their young Test-playing life until their home victory against India in a one-day international in the second of the three-match series by 15 runs. The whole nation went into rapturous euphoria celebrating a win against another top cricket-playing nation.

A Test win, however, eluded them, although they came very near to a surprising victory against Pakistan in Multan two years ago, before Inzamam-ul-Haq's century in the end deprived them of that glorious moment. But they did not have to wait long to experience the thrill of a first win in a Test. In January 2005 they finally achieved that elusive first Test victory against

Zimbabwe at Chittagong in their 35th Test – after a run of 31 defeats and three drawns.

I feel, however, that Bangladesh's gradual progress at international level reached a new high when they gored the mighty Australia – World Cup winners in 1987, 1999 and 2003 – at Cardiff in 2005 in a NatWest Series one-day match by five wickets. Australia, batting first, had set Bangladesh a target of 250 which the minnows reached with four balls to spare with the help of Mohammad Ashraful's run-a-ball hundred.

This surely was the defining moment of their quest to become a truly world-class cricket nation, and the biggest highlight to date of the past 25 years. It was a further mark of their growing maturity, of course, when they came close to beating Australia in a Test match too in April 2006. For Bangladesh, the best is very much still to come.

Australian captain Ricky Ponting congratulates Mohammad Ashraful on his century during Bangladesh's historic victory in the NatWest Series at Cardiff.

of an embarrassing defeat. Ponting's 31st Test hundred contained 13 fours in six hours of pure concentration and defiance.

Bangladesh, however, failed to maintain that kind of form in the Second Test at Chittagong as Jason Gillespie hit a maiden century – and then went on serenely to 201 not out – as Bangladesh lost by an innings and 80 runs.

Earlier in the season Bangladesh lost both their home and away series against Sri Lanka by a margin of 2-0. In addition, in the two one-day series, they were beaten 3-0 in Sri Lanka and 2-1 at home. On their tour of Sri Lanka they lost the First Test at the Premadasa Stadium in Colombo by an innings and 96 runs, their 23rd innings defeat in 39 Tests and eighth in the last ten Tests. Muttiah Muralitharan with eight wickets in the match was their main destroyer. They also lost the Second Test by an innings and 69 runs as they were bowled out in both the innings without reaching 200. The highlight of the Second Test were centuries for Sri Lanka for Thilan Samaraweera (138) and Tillekeratne Dilshan (168). Bangladesh captain Habibul Bashar described this series as 'the worst ever'.

Later, at home, results remained depressing as Bangladesh lost the First Test at Chittagong by eight wickets despite Mohammad Ashraful's 136. Muralitharan took 9 for 141 in the match. At Bogra a ten-wicket loss also cost them the series. Sri Lanka, set to make 120 to win, in the end knocked off the 43 runs still required on the fourth day in eight overs just in time before rain came.

Bangladesh, however, then enjoyed some consolation with a 4-0 clean sweep in a one-day series against the visiting Kenyans. Habibul Bashar, Mohammad Ashraful, Aftab Ahmed, Shahriar Nafees, Mashrafe bin Mortaza and Mohammad Rafique kept the Bangladesh flag flying during the season.

On the domestic front Rajshahi Division won both the first-class and one-day competition. Ehsanul Haque of Chittagong, with 955 runs in 17 innings at an average of 59.68, was the highest scorer of the season in first-class matches. Hasibul Hasan bagged 57 wickets. In one-day tournaments Faisal Hossain of Chittagong, with 423 runs in ten matches at 60.42, and Mohammad Sharif, with 26 wickets, were the most successful players of the season.

The steady left-arm spin of Mohammad Rafique has played an important part in Bangladesh's early history as a Test nation.

ONE-DAY INTERNATIONALS v. Sri Lanka

Match One

20 February 2006 at Bogra
Bangladesh 118 all out (35.5 overs)
(PDRL Perera 3 for 23, MF Maharoof 3 for 30)
Sri Lanka 119 for 5 (24.1 overs) (KC Sangakkara 50)
Sri Lanka won by 5 wickets

Match Two

22 February 2006 at Bogra
Sri Lanka 212 all out (49 overs) (ST Jayasuriya 96)
Bangladesh 213 for 6 (47 overs) (Mohammad Ashraful 51)
Bangladesh won by 4 wickets

Match Three

25 February 2006 at Chittagong
Sri Lanka 309 for 7 (50 overs) (KC Sangakkara 109,
KS Lokuarachchi 69, DPMD Jayawardene 51,
Mohammad Rafique 3 for 61)
Bangladesh 231 for 9 (50 overs) (Mohammad Ashraful 64)
Sri Lanka won by 78 runs

Sri Lanka won the series 2–1

ONE-DAY INTERNATIONALS v. Kenya

Match One

17 March 2006 at Bogra
Bangladesh 301 for 7 (50 overs) (Shahriar Nafees 91,
Aftab Ahmed 62)
Kenya 170 all out (48.1 overs) (Syed Rasel 3 for 31)
Bangladesh won by 131 runs

Match Two

20 March 2006 at Khulna
Kenya 161 all out (49.5 overs) (Syed Rasel 3 for 28)
Bangladesh 162 for 1 (23.5 overs) (Javed Omar 64*,
Aftab Ahmed 59*)
Bangladesh won by 9 wickets

Match Three

23 March 2006 at Fatullah
Bangladesh 231 all out (45.5 overs) (Shahriar Nafees 57,
Alok Kapali 55, SO Tikolo 3 for 32,
PJ Ongondo 3 for 40)
Kenya 211 all out (49.2 overs) (Mohammad Rafique 5 for
47, Mashrafe bin Mortaza 3 for 38)
Bangladesh won by 20 runs

Match Four

25 March 2006 at Fatullah
Kenya 232 for 9 (50 overs) (SO Tikolo 81*)

FIRST TEST – BANGLADESH v. SRI LANKA
28 February–3 March 2006 at Chittagong

BANGLADESH

	First Innings				Second Innings			
Javed Omar	c Samaraweera b Malinga			4	lbw b Fernando			31
Nafees Iqbal	b Bandara			34	c Sangakkara b Fernando			6
Habibul Bashar (capt)	lbw b Bandara			29	lbw b Bandara			12
Shahriar Nafees	b Maharoof			27	c Fernando b Muralitharan			38
Mohammad Ashraful	c Tharanga b Muralitharan			136	c Tharanga b Muralitharan			1
*Khaled Mashud	lbw b Muralitharan			6	c Dilshan b Muralitharan			15
Alok Kapali	c Tharanga b Muralitharan			16	lbw b Muralitharan			9
Mohammad Rafique	b Malinga			17	st Sangakkara b Muralitharan			40
Shahadat Hossain	c Tharanga b Malinga			13	c Malinga b Bandara			0
Syed Rasel	b Malinga			1	(11) not out			2
Enamul Haque jnr	not out			3	(10) lbw b Muralitharan			1
Extras	b 11, lb 4, w 3, nb 15			33	b 13, lb 3, w 3, nb 7			26
	(all out 91.5 overs)			**319**	(all out 58.5 overs)			**181**

	First Innings				Second Innings			
	O	M	R	W	O	M	R	W
Malinga	16.5	3	57	4	13	2	41	0
Maharoof	11	3	37	1	2	0	5	0
Fernando	17	4	50	0	4	1	10	2
Muralitharan	32	8	87	3	19.5	6	54	6
Bandara	13	0	61	2	20	2	55	2
Dilshan	2	0	12	0	-	-	-	-

Fall of Wickets
1-4, 2-76, 3-81, 4-146, 5-210, 6-248, 7-293, 8-308, 9-314
1-47, 2-56, 3-68, 4-69, 5-122, 6-131, 7-135, 8-150, 9-168

SRI LANKA

	First Innings				Second Innings			
MG Vandort	c Khaled Mashud b Rasel			0	not out			64
WU Tharanga	c M Ashraful b M Rafique			42	c Nafees b Rasel			19
*KC Sangakkara	c M Ashraful b E Haque jnr			69	c & b Enamul Haque jnr			46
DPMD J'wardene (capt)	c S Hossain b M Rafique			30	not out			23
TT Samaraweera	c Javed Omar b S Hossain			58				
TM Dilshan	lbw b Enamul Haque jnr			22				
MF Maharoof	b Shahadat Hossain			72				
CM Bandara	not out			19				
CRD Fernando	c Nafees b Shahadat Hossain			6				
M Muralitharan	c Nafees b Shahadat Hossain			5				
SL Malinga	run out			0				
Extras	lb 2, w 2, nb 11			15	b 5, lb 4, nb 2			11
	(all out 97.1 overs)			**338**	(2 wkts 37 overs)			**163**

	First Innings				Second Innings			
	O	M	R	W	O	M	R	W
Rasel	18	1	75	1	8	4	18	1
Shahadat Hossain	22	4	83	4	8	1	39	0
Mohammad Rafique	29	6	76	2	8	0	28	0
Enamul Haque jnr	24.1	5	76	2	9	1	50	1
Alok Kapali	1	0	6	0	2	0	6	0
Mohammad Ashraful	3	0	20	0	2	0	13	0

Fall of Wickets
1-0, 2-86, 3-149, 4-149, 5-178, 6-295, 7-316, 8-330, 9-338
1-25, 2-115

Umpires: Asad Rauf (Pakistan) & SA Bucknor (West Indies)
Toss: Bangladesh
Man of the Match: Mohammad Ashraful

Sri Lanka won by 8 wickets

Bangladesh 237 for 3 (41.3 overs) (Rajin Saleh 108*,
Habibul Bashar 64*)
Bangladesh won by 7 wickets

Bangladesh won the series 4–0

SECOND TEST – BANGLADESH v. SRI LANKA
8–11 March 2006 at Bogra

BANGLADESH

	First Innings		Second Innings	
Javed Omar	lbw b Muralitharan	35	c Sangakkara b Fernando	13
Nafees Iqbal	lbw b Muralitharan	26	c Sangakkara b Malinga	2
Habibul Bashar (capt)	c Tharanga b Muralitharan	69	lbw b Malinga	73
Shahriar Nafees	c Sangakkara b Malinga	9	c Maharoof b Muralitharan	6
Mohammad Ashraful	b Bandara	24	c Jayawardene b Bandara	13
Mushfiqur Rahim	lbw b Muralitharan	2	c Sangakkara b Bandara	0
*Khaled Mashud	c Sangakkara b Malinga	12	c Malinga b Muralitharan	6
Mohammad Rafique	c Muralitharan b Fernando	32	c Muralitharan b Malinga	64
Shahadat Hossain	c Muralitharan b Fernando	6	b Fernando	8
Enamul Haque jnr	not out	3	c Sangakkara b Fernando	3
Syed Rasel	c Bandara b Muralitharan	0	not out	1
Extras	b 3, lb 5, nb 8	16	b 1, lb 4, w 2, nb 5	12
	(all out 76.5 overs)	234	(all out 56.1 overs)	201

	First Innings				Second Innings			
	O	M	R	W	O	M	R	W
Malinga	20	1	73	2	14.1	1	51	3
Maharoof	4	0	22	0	-	-	-	-
Fernando	9	4	24	2	19	4	51	3
Muralitharan	30.5	8	79	5	13	1	62	2
Bandara	13	1	28	1	10	4	32	2

Fall of Wickets
1-52, 2-85, 3-106, 4-157, 5-172, 6-186, 7-208, 8-231, 9-233
1-15, 2-29, 3-46, 4-95, 5-95, 6-110, 7-162, 8-187, 9-198

SRI LANKA

	First Innings		Second Innings	
MG Vandort	lbw b Rasel	0	not out	40
WU Tharanga	c K Mashud b Shahadat Hossain	165	not out	71
CM Bandara	c Nafees Iqbal b S Hossain	2		
TT Samaraweera	c Khaled Mashud b S Hossain	20		
*KC Sangakkara	lbw b Shahadat Hossain	0		
DPMD J'wardene (capt)	c M Rahim b M Ashraful	49		
TM Dilshan	b Mohammad Rafique	33		
MF Maharoof	c K Mashud b E Haque jnr	7		
CRD Fernando	lbw b Enamul Haque jnr	5		
SL Malinga	c Nafees b Shahadat Hossain	12		
M Muralitharan	not out	8		
Extras	b 5, lb 4, w 2, nb 4	15	lb 5, w 3, nb 1	9
	(all out 103.3 overs)	316	(0 wkts 28 overs)	120

	First Innings				Second Innings			
	O	M	R	W	O	M	R	W
Rasel	20	8	50	1	5	0	21	0
Shahadat Hossain	21.3	2	86	5	8	2	43	0
Mohammad Rafique	32	9	84	1	9	2	32	0
Enamul Haque jnr	26	3	71	2	6	0	19	0
Mohammad Ashraful	4	1	16	1	-	-	-	-

Fall of Wickets
1-4, 2-13, 3-43, 4-43, 5-167, 6-232, 7-251, 8-263, 9-305

Umpires: Asad Rauf (Pakistan) & K Hariharan (India)
Toss: Bangladesh
Man of the Match: WU Tharanga
Man of the Series: M Muralitharan

Sri Lanka won by 10 wickets

SERIES AVERAGES
Bangladesh v. Sri Lanka

BANGLADESH

Batting	M	Inns	NO	Runs	HS	Av	100	50	c/st
Habibul Bashar	2	4	0	183	73	45.75	-	2	-/-
Mohammad Ashraful	2	4	0	174	136	43.50	1	-	2/-
Mohammad Rafique	2	4	0	153	64	38.25	-	1	-/-
Javed Omar	2	4	0	83	35	20.75	-	-	1/-
Shahriar Nafees	2	4	0	80	38	20.00	-	-	4/-
Nafees Iqbal	2	4	0	68	34	17.00	-	-	1/-
Alok Kapali	1	2	0	25	16	12.50	-	-	-/-
Khaled Mashud	2	4	0	39	15	9.75	-	-	4/-
Shahadat Hossain	2	4	0	27	13	6.75	-	-	1/-
Enamul Haque jnr	2	4	2	10	3*	5.00	-	-	1/-
Syed Rasel	2	4	2	4	2*	2.00	-	-	1/-
Mushfiqur Rahim	1	2	0	2	2	1.00	-	-	1/-

Bowling	Overs	Mds	Runs	Wkts	Av	Best	5/inn	10m
Shahadat Hossain	59.3	9	251	9	27.88	5-86	1	-
Enamul Haque jnr	65.1	9	216	5	43.20	2-71	-	-
Mohammad Ashraful	9	1	49	1	49.00	1-16	-	-
Syed Rasel	51	13	164	3	54.66	1-18	-	-
Mohammad Rafique	78	17	220	3	73.33	2-76	-	-
Also bowled: Alok Kapali 3-0-12-0.

SRI LANKA

Batting	M	Inns	NO	Runs	HS	Av	100	50	c/st
WU Tharanga	2	4	1	297	165	99.00	1	1	5/-
MG Vandort	2	4	2	104	64*	52.00	-	1	-/-
DPMD Jayawardene	2	3	1	102	49	51.00	-	-	1/-
MF Maharoof	2	2	0	79	72	39.50	-	1	1/-
TT Samaraweera	2	2	0	78	58	39.00	-	1	1/-
KC Sangakkara	2	3	0	115	69	38.33	-	1	7/1
TM Dilshan	2	2	0	55	33	27.50	-	-	1/-
CM Bandara	2	2	1	21	19*	21.00	-	-	1/-
M Muralitharan	2	2	1	13	8*	13.00	-	-	3/-
SL Malinga	2	2	0	12	12	6.00	-	-	2/-
CRD Fernando	2	2	0	11	6	5.50	-	-	1/-

Bowling	Overs	Mds	Runs	Wkts	Av	Best	5/inn	10m
M Muralitharan	95.4	23	282	16	17.62	6-54	2	-
CRD Fernando	49	13	135	7	19.28	3-51	-	-
SL Malinga	64	7	222	9	24.66	4-57	-	-
CM Bandara	56	7	176	7	25.14	2-32	-	-
MF Maharoof	17	3	64	1	64.00	1-37	-	-
Also bowled: TM Dilshan 2-0-12-0.

FIRST TEST – BANGLADESH v. AUSTRALIA
9–13 April 2006 at Fatullah

BANGLADESH

	First Innings		Second Innings	
Javed Omar	lbw b Gillespie	27	c Gilchrist b Gillespie	18
Shahriar Nafees	b MacGill	138	b Lee	33
Habibul Bashar (capt)	c Lee b MacGill	76	run out	7
Rajin Saleh	c sub b MacGill	67	c Hayden b Gillespie	33
Mohammad Ashraful	lbw b Gillespie	29	lbw b Clark	4
Aftab Ahmed	c Hayden b MacGill	29	lbw b MacGill	17
*Khaled Mashud	st Gilchrist b MacGill	17	b Gillespie	0
Mohammad Rafique	b MacGill	6	lbw b Warne	14
Mashrafe bin Mortaza	lbw b MacGill	6	b Warne	0
Shahadat Hossain	not out	3	not out	1
Enamul Haque jnr	c Hayden b MacGill	0	lbw b Warne	0
Extras	lb 16, w 2, nb 11	29	b 10, lb 7, nb 4	21
	(all out 123.3 overs)	427	(all out 50 overs)	148

	First Innings				Second Innings			
	O	M	R	W	O	M	R	W
Lee	19	5	68	0	8	1	47	1
Clark	25	4	69	0	4	2	8	1
Gillespie	23	7	47	2	11	4	18	3
Warne	20	1	112	0	13	4	28	3
MacGill	33.3	2	108	8	13	4	30	1
Clarke	3	0	7	0	1	1	0	0

Fall of Wickets
1-51, 2-238, 3-265, 4-295, 5-351, 6-398, 7-416, 8-417, 9-424
1-48, 2-58, 3-66, 4-77, 5-124, 6-128, 7-147, 8-147, 9-147

AUSTRALIA

	First Innings		Second Innings	
ML Hayden	lbw b Mashrafe bin Mortaza	6	run out	72
MEK Hussey	b Mohammad Rafique	23	b Enamul Haque jnr	37
RT Ponting (capt)	lbw b Shahadat Hossain	21	not out	118
DR Martyn	b Mohammad Rafique	4	b Mohammad Rafique	7
MJ Clarke	b Enamul Haque jnr	19	c K Mashud b M Rafique	9
*AC Gilchrist	c S Hossain b M Rafique	144	b Mohammad Rafique	12
SK Warne	c K Mashud b E Haque jnr	6	lbw b Mohammad Rafique	5
B Lee	lbw b Mashrafe bin Mortaza	15	c K Mashud b M bin Mortaza	29
JN Gillespie	b Mohammad Rafique	26	not out	7
SR Clark	lbw b Mohammad Rafique	0		
SCG MacGill	not out	0		
Extras	lb 4, nb 1	5	b 4, lb 7, w 1, nb 2	14
	(all out 95.2 overs)	269	(7 wkts 107 overs)	310

	First Innings				Second Innings			
	O	M	R	W	O	M	R	W
Mashrafe bin Mortaza	22	3	56	2	22	7	54	1
Shahadat Hossain	14	2	48	1	20	5	67	0
Mohammad Rafique	32.2	9	62	5	38	6	98	4
Enamul Haque jnr	25	4	83	2	27	5	80	1
Mohammad Ashraful	1	0	11	0	-	-	-	-
Rajin Saleh	1	0	5	0	-	-	-	-

Fall of Wickets
1-6, 2-43, 3-50, 4-61, 5-79, 6-93, 7-156, 8-229, 9-268
1-64, 2-173, 3-183, 4-205, 5-225, 6-231, 7-277

Umpires: Aleem Dar (Pakistan) & Nadeem Ghauri (Pakistan)
Toss: Bangladesh
Man of the Match: AC Gilchrist

Australia won by 3 wickets

SECOND TEST – BANGLADESH v. AUSTRALIA
16–20 April 2006 at Chittagong

BANGLADESH

	First Innings		Second Innings	
Javed Omar	lbw b Gillespie	2	lbw b Lee	19
Shahriar Nafees	c Lee b MacGill	15	(10) c Ponting b MacGill	0
Habibul Bashar (capt)	c Jaques b Gillespie	9	c Hayden b Warne	49
Rajin Saleh	b MacGill	71	c Ponting b Warne	5
Mohammad Ashraful	c Hayden b Warne	6	b Warne	29
Aftab Ahmed	c Gilchrist b Warne	18	c Gilchrist b MacGill	18
*Khaled Mashud	not out	34	lbw b MacGill	11
Mohammad Rafique	c Hayden b MacGill	19	c Warne b MacGill	65
Mashrafe bin Mortaza	c Gilchrist b Cullen	4	c Gillespie b Warne	1
Abdur Razzak	c Lee b MacGill	0	(2) c Gilchrist b Warne	79
Shahadat Hossain	c Gillespie b Warne	0	not out	3
Extras	lb 10, w 3, nb 6	19	b 7, lb 11, w 2, nb 5	25
	(all out 61.2 overs)	197	(all out 80.2 overs)	304

	First Innings				Second Innings			
	O	M	R	W	O	M	R	W
Lee	9	2	36	0	11	3	35	1
Gillespie	5	2	11	3	4	0	14	0
Warne	18.2	3	47	3	36	4	113	5
MacGill	22	4	68	3	22.2	3	95	4
Cullen	7	0	25	1	7	0	29	0

Fall of Wickets
1-0, 2-11, 3-17, 4-41, 5-102, 6-130, 7-152, 8-153, 9-193
1-25, 2-127, 3-137, 4-187, 5-201, 6-229, 7-230, 8-232, 9-235

AUSTRALIA

	First Innings	
ML Hayden	c sub b Mohammad Rafique	29
PA Jaques	c Razzak b M Rafique	66
JN Gillespie	not out	201
RT Ponting (capt)	run out	52
MEK Hussey	c S Hossain b Aftab Ahmed	182
MJ Clarke	not out	23
*AC Gilchrist		
SK Warne		
B Lee		
DJ Cullen		
SCG MacGill		
Extras	b 10, lb 10, w 5, nb 3	28
	(4 wkts dec 152.3 overs)	581

	First Innings			
	O	M	R	W
Mashrafe bin Mortaza	26	3	114	0
Shahadat Hossain	33	3	143	0
Mohammad Rafique	48.3	11	145	2
Abdur Razzak	30	5	99	0
Rajin Saleh	8	0	32	0
Aftab Ahmed	7	1	28	1

Fall of Wickets
1-67, 2-120, 3-210, 4-530

Umpires: Aleem Dar (Pakistan) & IL Howell (South Africa)
Toss: Bangladesh
Man of the Match: JN Gillespie
Man of the Series: JN Gillespie

Australia won by an innings and 80 runs

SERIES AVERAGES
Bangladesh v. Australia

BANGLADESH

Batting	M	Inns	NO	Runs	HS	Av	100	50	c/st
Shahriar Nafees	2	4	0	186	138	46.50	1	-	-/-
Rajin Saleh	2	4	0	176	71	44.00	-	2	-/-
Abdur Razzak	1	2	0	79	79	39.50	-	1	1/-
Habibul Bashar	2	4	0	141	76	35.25	-	1	-/-
Mohammad Rafique	2	4	0	104	65	26.00	-	1	-/-
Khaled Mashud	2	4	1	62	34*	20.66	-	-	3/-
Aftab Ahmed	2	4	0	82	29	20.50	-	-	-/-
Mohammad Ashraful	2	4	0	68	29	17.00	-	-	-/-
Javed Omar	2	4	0	66	27	16.50	-	-	-/-
Shahadat Hossain	2	4	3	7	3*	7.00	-	-	2/-
Mashrafe bin Mortaza	2	4	0	11	6	2.75	-	-	-/-
Enamul Haque jnr	1	2	0	0	0	0.00	-	-	-/-

Bowling	Overs	Mds	Runs	Wkts	Av	Best	5/inn	10m
Mohammad Rafique	118.5	26	305	11	27.72	5-62	1	-
Aftab Ahmed	7	1	28	1	28.00	1-28	-	-
Enamul Haque jnr	52	9	163	3	54.33	2-83	-	-
Mashrafe bin Mortaza	70	13	224	3	74.66	2-56	-	-
Shahadat Hossain	67	10	258	1	258.00	1-48	-	-

Also bowled: Mohammad Ashraful 1-0-11-0, Rajin Saleh 9-0-37-0, Abdur Razzak 30-5-99-0.

AUSTRALIA

Batting	M	Inns	NO	Runs	HS	Av	100	50	c/st
JN Gillespie	2	3	2	234	201*	234.00	1	-	2/-
RT Ponting	2	3	1	191	118*	95.50	1	1	2/-
MEK Hussey	2	3	0	242	182	80.66	1	-	-/-
AC Gilchrist	2	2	0	156	144	78.00	1	-	5/1
PA Jaques	1	1	0	66	66	66.00	-	1	1/-
ML Hayden	2	3	0	107	72	35.66	-	1	6/-
MJ Clarke	2	3	1	51	23*	25.50	-	-	-/-
B Lee	2	2	0	44	29	22.00	-	-	3/-
SK Warne	2	2	0	11	6	5.50	-	-	1/-
DR Martyn	1	2	0	11	7	5.50	-	-	-/-
SR Clark	1	1	0	0	0	0.00	-	-	-/-
SCG MacGill	2	1	1	0	0*	-	-	-	-/-
DJ Cullen	1	0	0	0	0	-	-	-	-/-

Bowling	Overs	Mds	Runs	Wkts	Av	Best	5/inn	10m
JN Gillespie	43	13	90	8	11.25	3-11	-	-
SCG MacGill	90.5	13	301	16	18.81	8-108	1	-
SK Warne	87.2	12	300	11	27.27	5-113	1	-
DJ Cullen	14	0	54	1	54.00	1-25	-	-
SR Clark	29	6	77	1	77.00	1-8	-	-
B Lee	47	11	186	2	93.00	1-35	-	-

Also bowled: MJ Clarke 4-1-7-0.

ONE-DAY INTERNATIONALS v. Australia

Match One
23 April 2006 at Chittagong
Bangladesh 195 all out (47 overs) (Habibul Bashar 52, GB Hogg 3 for 37)
Australia 196 for 6 (44 overs) (AC Gilchrist 76, Abdur Razzak 3 for 36)
Australia won by 4 wickets

Match Two
26 April 2006 at Fatullah
Australia 250 for 5 (50 overs) (A Symonds 103*, MJ Clarke 54, Mashrafe bin Mortaza 3 for 54)
Bangladesh 183 all out (48 overs) (Habibul Bashar 70, GB Hogg 3 for 34)
Australia won by 67 runs

Match Three
28 April 2006 at Fatullah
Bangladesh 124 all out (42.3 overs) (GB Hogg 3 for 17)
Australia 127 for 1 (22.4 overs) (MJ Cosgrove 74)
Australia won by 9 wickets

Australia won the series 3–0

NEW ZEALAND

NEW ZEALAND REPORT
By Bryan Waddle

The unique combination of politicians and the Cricket World Cup robbed New Zealand cricket of the chance at a balanced, successful season and left them reflecting on yet another mediocre year.

The New Zealand government refused to grant visas to Zimbabwe's players, forcing the cancellation of their return tour, while the desire to win the World Cup became the dominant focus for the Black Caps in a disjointed programme. Without the Zimbabwe tour, the West Indies stepped in to fill the gap, providing a more competitive series but still well below a challenging standard. Sri Lanka also returned to complete the one-day series that had been interrupted the previous year by the Boxing Day tsunami, but they too found it hard to capture the standard that makes them so formidable at home.

New Zealand played eight Test matches for a 50 per cent success rating, the wins coming over hapless Zimbabwe and the West Indies while the tour of South Africa saw New Zealand lapse into the ordinary form that has been typical of their recent record in the Republic.

Statistically the one-day programme was only marginally better: a 59 per cent success rate with 13 wins from 22 matches, and the highlight coming at Jade Stadium, Christchurch, in December. Chasing down 332 to win the final game of the Chappell-Hadlee series, New Zealand held, for a short time only, the record total in a one-day chase.

They had, in fact, come within three runs of setting a record three days earlier at Wellington's Westpac Stadium in search of 323 to win the second match. It started what proved to be New Zealand's most successful period, with ten wins from 12 games against the Australians, Sri Lankans and West Indians, despite the selection controversies that unsettled the team. A new selection panel had determined that rotation of players was a good tool to keep them fresh and

competitive with each other, but the constant changing of the side tended to undermine the players' confidence and created a climate of distrust and insecurity. The All Blacks had used the rotation concept successfully, but there is greater depth in the rugby ranks – a situation less apparent in cricket circles.

Despite the political pressure back home, the tour to Zimbabwe was a promising start although Zimbabwe could not offer the strength of opposition a developing Test side required. Massive innings victories, in two days in Harare and three days in Bulawayo, provided New Zealand with a false sense of wellbeing. That they did not play another Test for seven months did not help the development process either.

Nathan Astle, Lou Vincent, Daniel Vettori and Shane Bond thrived in the Zimbabwe environment. Astle, Vincent and Vettori showed sublime batting skills, while pace bowler Bond, seemingly injury-free, spearheaded an attack that without him was steady but seriously underpowered.

The final of the tri-nation series, against India, was an outstanding heavyweight bout between the two

Brendon McCullum and Daniel Vettori celebrate New Zealand's then record-breaking chase to beat Australia in the third one-day international at Christchurch.

visiting countries. Chasing 277, New Zealand reached the target in the 49th over due to a blistering opening stand of 121 in 18 overs by Astle and Stephen Fleming. New Zealand's success, though, was a precursor to the inconsistent form that plagued their year. This peak was followed by a trough in South Africa, in which they lost the one-day series 4-0 (with no result in the fifth match).

That result gave little cause for optimism when Australia arrived for the Chappell-Hadlee series and duly won the opening encounter by 147 runs, Brett Lee at his irresistible best taking 3 for 5 from six overs. But even great players have their reversals and, when New Zealand came close to victory in Wellington, Lee ended with 1 for 85 from his ten overs.

Ricky Ponting, Michael Clarke, Brad Hodge and Mike Hussey slayed the New Zealand attack in the final game, taking the Aussies to a massive 331 total. But Trans-Tasman rivalry was an important boost to the New Zealand performance and the short-lived record ODI score, 332, was achieved with an over to spare. Mick Lewis, who was later to be mauled by South Africa, had a taste of what was to follow, 77 runs coming from his nine overs for just one wicket.

Chris Cairns pulled stumps on his long career with an emotional farewell Twenty20 game at Eden Park against the West Indies. In keeping with the novelty game, it ended in a tie and had to be decided by a bizarre 'bowl-off', penalty style, which New Zealand won. Cairns wanted to end at the World Cup but his lack of form with the ball and lack of potency with the bat signalled the end of a career that began in 1989. He saw the writing on the wall after the four-match Sri Lankan series, won by New Zealand comfortably. Cairns quickly realised he was no longer the force that had made him one of the most exciting and destructive all-rounders of his era.

Without Brian Lara, the West Indies could not summon up enough spirit to test the Black Caps in the ODI series, losing 4-1. When the great left-hander did arrive for the Test series that followed, however, the West Indies were only spared the ignominy of a Kiwi clean sweep by five days of inclement weather in the final Test in Napier.

New Zealand, looking to the future, invested in some fresh batting talent during the series with Sri Lanka and West Indies. Pugnacious opener Jamie How and the tall, elegant right-hander Peter Fulton were preferred to more experienced players Lou Vincent and Mathew Sinclair.

It was those selections, though, which highlighted again the inconsistency and experimental nature of the New Zealand top order. Fulton gained a pass

New Zealand's finest all-rounder, Chris Cairns, confirmed his international retirement in 2006.

mark with a one-day hundred against Sri Lanka, batting at No. 4, but he was one of six players tried as Test match openers in the eight Tests played. Without continuity in selection at the top of the order, the best opening partnership in 12 innings was 50 in the Second Test against South Africa. Ironically that also led to New Zealand's best batting effort of the year, 593 for 8 declared, with Stephen Fleming scoring 262, his third Test double-century, and James Franklin making 122 not out batting at No. 9.

Franklin, indeed, could fairly claim to be New Zealand's leading all-rounder during the Test year, with 29 wickets at 27.34 and 262 runs at 37.43. Those figures are better than those of Astle, Scott Styris and Jacob Oram, although the latter was again plagued by injury that limited his contribution.

25 years OF NEW ZEALAND

By Brian Waddle

As a passionate sports fan well-versed in Trans-Tasman rivalry from an early age, I was well aware that cricket Down Under didn't need an underarm delivery to fuel the competitive spirit that exists between Australia and New Zealand. Between them though, Greg and Trevor Chappell contrived to create what proved to be a volatile relationship between opposing fans for quite a while during this past quarter-century, and ensured the passion remains high whenever the two countries meet.

The first day of February 1981 was seen as the 'lowest of low blows' despite it being within the laws, something New Zealanders were conveniently prepared to overlook in their outrage. It also signalled the one period in their recent history that New Zealand could claim any dominance over 'big brother'. Much of that was due to the contribution of the two greatest players New Zealand has produced in the past 100 years, let alone 25.

Richard Hadlee loved playing against Australia, and he saved many of his best performances for their back yard –

The peerless Sir Richard Hadlee: speed, stamina, skill and control all wrapped up in one bowling package.

such as a match haul of 15 for 123, including a career-best 9 for 52 in the first innings, at the Brisbane Test of 1985. Martin Crowe revealed his class in that Test too, with a dominant innings of 188 as New Zealand inflicted its heaviest defeat on Australia.

Hadlee and Crowe, in fact, contributed any number of memorable moments in New Zealand's recent cricket history, such as Hadlee's 374th Test wicket in Bangalore to wrest the world record at that point off Ian Botham, or him then becoming the first to break the 400-wicket barrier by removing Sanjay Manjrekar at Lancaster Park in 1990.

Crowe scored nine of his 17 Test hundreds outside New Zealand, with none better than the 188 at Bourda in Guyana in 1985 against the lethal West Indies attack of the mid-1980s. There was also a memorable 142 at Lord's in 1990, although his 299 against Sri Lanka at the Basin Reserve saw Crowe at his most majestic.

Equally memorable from that 1991 match was the partnership of 467 between Crowe and Andrew Jones, a record that stood for 15 years as the highest third-wicket stand in Tests. Yet, on the other hand, I can't recall a more exhilarating innings than Nathan Astle's fastest-ever Test double-century – 222 off a mere 168 balls on an unforgettable afternoon or power hitting against England at Christchurch in 2002.

Astle's audacious onslaught unfortunately did not help to win the Test, though neither did Mark Greatbatch's 146 not out at the WACA in 1989. But his innings of monumental patience, spread over 10 hours 55 minutes, did mean that New Zealand saved a Test that seemed destined for an innings defeat.

There are many more stunning highlights – Stephen Fleming's 274 not out in oppressive Colombo heat, New Zealand's first Test win at Lord's in 1999 and the series victory that went with it, plus Ian Smith's 173 not out against India at Eden Park in Auckland.

I could only marvel, meanwhile, at the muscular power of the two Cairns who played a prominent part through three decades: Chris, the all-rounder who didn't totally realise his full potential, and father Lance. Both were unique talents, with Chris more technically correct while also capable of some prodigious hitting. Lance's awesome power at the MCG in 1983, when he struck six sixes off Lillee, Hogg and MacLeay, sadly came in another of the lost causes which have too often been New Zealand's lot in Trans-Tasman battles.

ONE-DAY INTERNATIONALS v. Australia

Match One
3 December 2005 at Auckland
Australia 252 for 8 (50 overs) (RT Ponting 63,
SM Katich 54)
New Zealand 105 all out (27.4 overs) (B Lee 3 for 5,
SR Clark 3 for 19)
Australia won by 147 runs

Match Two
7 December 2005 at Wellington
Australia 322 for 5 (50 overs) (A Symonds 156,
MJ Clarke 82*)
New Zealand 320 all out (49.5 overs) (L Vincent 71,
CL Cairns 60, ML Lewis 3 for 56)
Australia won by 2 runs

Match Three
10 December 2005 at Christchurch
Australia 331 for 7 (50 overs) (MEK Hussey 88*,
RT Ponting 75, MJ Clarke 71, BJ Hodge 59,
CS Martin 3 for 65)
New Zealand 332 for 8 (49 overs) (SB Styris 101,
BB McCullum 50*, SR Clark 4 for 55)
New Zealand won by 2 wickets

Australia won the series 2–1

ONE-DAY INTERNATIONALS v. Sri Lanka

Match One
31 December 2005 at Queenstown
Sri Lanka 164 all out (47.2 overs) (SE Bond 3 for 29,
JDP Oram 3 for 31, KD Mills 3 for 31)
New Zealand 166 for 3 (37.2 overs) (PG Fulton 70*,
JM How 58)
New Zealand won by 7 wickets

Match Two
3 January 2006 at Christchurch
Sri Lanka 255 for 7 (50 overs) (WU Tharanga 103,
MS Atapattu 52)
New Zealand 256 for 5 (48 overs) (NJ Astle 90*)
New Zealand won by 5 wickets

Match Three
6 January 2006 at Wellington
New Zealand 224 for 9 (50 overs) (PG Fulton 50,
HJH Marshall 50, WPUJC Vaas 5 for 39)
Sri Lanka 203 all out (46.4 overs) (J Mubarak 53,
KC Sangakkara 52, SE Bond 3 for 39)
New Zealand won by 21 runs

Match Four
8 January 2006 at Napier
Sri Lanka 273 for 6 (50 overs) (MS Atapattu 69,
KC Sangakkara 58, CS Martin 3 for 62)
New Zealand 253 all out (48.2 overs) (PG Fulton 112,
WPUJC Vaas 4 for 48, PDRL Perera 3 for 56)
Sri Lanka won by 20 runs

New Zealand won the series 3–1

ONE-DAY INTERNATIONALS v. West Indies

Match One
18 February 2006 at Wellington
New Zealand 288 for 9 (50 overs) (NJ Astle 90,
JM How 66, SP Fleming 55)
West Indies 207 all out (47.3 overs) (RR Sarwan 56,
D Ganga 54)
New Zealand won by 81 runs

Match Two
22 February 2006 at Queenstown
West Indies 200 for 9 (50 overs) (WW Hinds 76)
New Zealand 204 for 7 (42 overs) (DL Vettori 53*)
New Zealand won by 3 wickets

Match Three
25 February 2006 at Christchurch
New Zealand 276 for 6 (50 overs)
(NJ Astle 118*, IDR Bradshaw 3 for 41)
West Indies 255 all out (49 overs)
(RR Sarwan 65, RS Morton 58, JS Patel 3 for 42,
SE Bond 3 for 47)
New Zealand won by 21 runs

Match Four
1 March 2006 at Napier
New Zealand 324 for 6 (50 overs) (L Vincent 102,
NJ Astle 81, SP Fleming 67, CH Gayle 3 for 50)
West Indies 233 for 8 (50 overs) (RS Morton 110*,
KD Mills 3 for 45)
New Zealand won by 91 runs

Match Five
4 March 2006 at Auckland
New Zealand 233 all out (49.3 overs) (SB Styris 90,
DR Smith 5 for 45)
West Indies 234 for 7 (49.4 overs)
(SE Bond 3 for 32)
West Indies won by 3 wickets

New Zealand won the series 4–1

FIRST TEST – NEW ZEALAND v. WEST INDIES
9–13 March 2006 at Auckland

NEW ZEALAND

	First Innings		Second Innings	
HJH Marshall	c Edwards b Taylor	11	c Ganga b Bradshaw	1
JM How	run out	11	c Ramdin b Bradshaw	37
PG Fulton	c Ganga b Bradshaw	17	b Edwards	28
SP Fleming (capt)	c Ramdin b Bradshaw	14	lbw b Bradshaw	33
NJ Astle	c Ramdin b Smith	51	(7) run out	13
SB Styris	not out	103	(5) c Bradshaw b Edwards	5
*BB McCullum	b Smith	19	(8) c Bravo b Gayle	74
DL Vettori	c Gayle b Smith	6	(9) c sub b Gayle	33
JEC Franklin	c sub b Gayle	14	(6) b Gayle	20
SE Bond	b Gayle	3	not out	18
CS Martin	c Ramdin b Bradshaw	0	b Gayle	0
Extras	b 4, lb 2, w 9, nb 11	26	lb 3, w 2, nb 5	10
	(all out 69.1 overs)	275	(all out 103.1 overs)	272

	First Innings				Second Innings			
	O	M	R	W	O	M	R	W
Edwards	15	1	76	0	21	3	65	2
Bradshaw	23.1	3	73	3	34	10	83	3
Taylor	8	2	39	1	1	0	6	0
Smith	18	2	71	3	17	6	44	0
Gayle	5	0	10	2	30.1	5	71	4

Fall of Wickets
1-23, 2-31, 3-54, 4-69, 5-140, 6-170, 7-199, 8-240, 9-261
1-11, 2-64, 3-73, 4-88, 5-118, 6-143, 7-146, 8-210, 9-272

WEST INDIES

	First Innings		Second Innings	
CH Gayle	c McCullum b Styris	25	c Fleming b Astle	82
D Ganga	c How b Martin	20	c How b Astle	95
IDR Bradshaw	c How b Styris	0	(9) c Fleming b Vettori	10
RR Sarwan	c Franklin b Bond	62	(3) c Styris b Bond	4
BC Lara	c sub b Bond	5	(4) b Bond	0
S Chanderpaul (capt)	c McCullum b Franklin	13	(5) c Fulton b Vettori	15
DJJ Bravo	c Bond b Martin	59	(6) lbw b Bond	17
DR Smith	c McCullum b Martin	38	(7) c Fleming b Bond	0
*D Ramdin	c & b Vettori	9	(8) c Franklin b Vettori	15
FH Edwards	c McCullum b Vettori	1	(11) not out	2
JE Taylor	not out	4	(10) b Bond	13
Extras	lb 7, w 1, nb 13	21	b 1, lb 3, w 1, nb 5	10
	(all out 71.2 overs)	257	(all out 102.3 overs)	263

	First Innings				Second Innings			
	O	M	R	W	O	M	R	W
Bond	19	4	57	2	27.3	7	69	5
Franklin	21	4	83	1	14	1	46	0
Martin	17	1	80	3	16	5	39	0
Styris	7	1	23	2	-	-	-	-
Vettori	7.2	3	7	2	35	11	92	3
Astle	-	-	-	-	10	4	13	2

Fall of Wickets
1-47, 2-48, 3-49, 4-60, 5-90, 6-179, 7-237, 8-248, 9-252
1-148, 2-157, 3-182, 4-211, 5-216, 6-218, 7-221, 8-246, 9-247

Umpires: DJ Harper (Australia) & R Koertzen (South Africa)
Toss: West Indies
Test Debuts: JM How, PG Fulton, IDR Bradshaw
Man of the Match: SE Bond

New Zealand won by 27 runs

SECOND TEST – NEW ZEALAND v. WEST INDIES
17–20 March 2006 at Wellington

WEST INDIES

	First Innings		Second Innings	
CH Gayle	c McCullum b Franklin	30	lbw b Vettori	68
D Ganga	c McCullum b Mills	15	c McCullum b Martin	23
RS Morton	lbw b Franklin	63	c Fleming b Franklin	7
BC Lara	c Fleming b Franklin	1	c Marshall b Astle	1
S Chanderpaul (capt)	c Fleming b Martin	8	c Fleming b Mills	36
DJJ Bravo	lbw b Franklin	9	c Astle b Martin	7
*D Ramdin	b Franklin	2	b Vettori	7
RN Lewis	c Fleming b Martin	22	c Astle b Mills	40
IDR Bradshaw	not out	20	c Styris b Franklin	2
DB Powell	c How b Mills	16	c How b Mills	7
FH Edwards	c Fleming b Mills	0	not out	0
Extras	b 2, lb 1, nb 3	6	w 6, nb 11	17
	(all out 61.4 overs)	192	(all out 90.5 overs)	215

	First Innings				Second Innings			
	O	M	R	W	O	M	R	W
Martin	14	1	66	2	27	8	65	2
Franklin	20	7	53	5	21	8	64	2
Mills	19.4	7	53	3	9.5	2	29	3
Vettori	5	2	13	0	20	4	40	2
Astle	3	2	4	0	13	4	17	1

Fall of Wickets
1-43, 2-45, 3-49, 4-80, 5-102, 6-108, 7-142, 8-165, 9-186
1-54, 2-75, 3-84, 4-115, 5-129, 6-156, 7-163, 8-189, 9-210

NEW ZEALAND

	First Innings		Second Innings	
HJH Marshall	c Chanderpaul b Bradshaw	3	not out	23
JM How	b Edwards	0	not out	9
PG Fulton	c Ramdin b Powell	75		
SP Fleming (capt)	c Bravo b Edwards	97		
NJ Astle	c Ramdin b Powell	65		
SB Styris	c Morton b Powell	8		
*BB McCullum	c Ramdin b Edwards	23		
DL Vettori	c Chanderpaul b Edwards	42		
JEC Franklin	not out	28		
KD Mills	c Ramdin b Edwards	10		
CS Martin	b Edwards	0		
Extras	lb 4, w 2, nb 15	21	nb 4	4
	(all out 106.3 overs)	372	(0 wkts 8.2 overs)	36

	First Innings				Second Innings			
	O	M	R	W	O	M	R	W
Edwards	15.3	2	65	5	-	-	-	-
Bradshaw	19	2	97	1	4	0	16	0
Powell	24	7	83	4	4.2	1	20	0
Gayle	18	4	46	0	-	-	-	-
Lewis	29	8	70	0	-	-	-	-
Morton	1	0	7	0	-	-	-	-

Fall of Wickets
1-3, 2-3, 3-168, 4-207, 5-219, 6-246, 7-332, 8-335, 9-372

Umpires: MR Benson (England) & DJ Harper (Australia)
Toss: West Indies
Man of the Match: SP Fleming

New Zealand won by 10 wickets

THIRD TEST – NEW ZEALAND v. WEST INDIES
25–29 March 2006 at Napier

WEST INDIES

	First Innings		
CH Gayle	c Fulton b Martin		30
D Ganga	b Bond		38
BC Lara	b Astle		83
RS Morton	not out		70
S Chanderpaul (capt)	run out		2
DJJ Bravo	not out		22
DR Smith			
*D Ramdin			
IDR Bradshaw			
FH Edwards			
DB Powell			
Extras	lb 3, nb 8		11
	(4 wkts 78.1 overs)		**256**

	First Innings			
	O	M	R	W
Bond	18	2	87	1
Franklin	15	1	66	0
Martin	10	2	39	1
Astle	14	5	23	1
Styris	13.1	5	27	0
Vettori	8	4	11	0

Fall of Wickets
1-37, 2-111, 3-171, 4-189

NEW ZEALAND

HJH Marshall
JM How
SP Fleming (capt)
PG Fulton
NJ Astle
SB Styris
*BB McCullum
DL Vettori
JEC Franklin
CS Martin
SE Bond

Umpires: MR Benson (England) & IL Howell (South Africa)
Toss: New Zealand
Man of the Match: No Award

Match drawn

SERIES AVERAGES
New Zealand v. West Indies

NEW ZEALAND

Batting	M	Inns	NO	Runs	HS	Av	100	50	c/st
SB Styris	3	3	1	116	103*	58.00	1	-	2/-
SP Fleming	3	3	0	144	97	48.00	-	1	9/-
NJ Astle	3	3	0	129	65	43.00	-	2	2/-
PG Fulton	3	3	0	120	75	40.00	-	1	2/-
BB McCullum	3	3	0	116	74	38.66	-	1	7/-
JEC Franklin	3	3	1	62	28*	31.00	-	-	2/-
DL Vettori	3	3	0	81	42	27.00	-	-	1/-
SE Bond	2	2	1	21	18*	21.00	-	-	1/-
JM How	3	4	1	57	37	19.00	-	-	5/-
HJH Marshall	3	4	1	38	23*	12.66	-	-	1/-
KD Mills	1	1	0	10	10	10.00	-	-	-/-
CS Martin	3	3	0	0	0	0.00	-	-	-/-

Bowling	Overs	Mds	Runs	Wkts	Av	Best	5/inn	10m
KD Mills	29.3	9	82	6	13.66	3-29	-	-
NJ Astle	40	15	57	4	14.25	2-13	-	-
DL Vettori	75.2	24	163	7	23.28	3-92	-	-
SB Styris	20.1	6	50	2	25.00	2-23	-	-
SE Bond	64.3	13	213	8	26.62	5-69	1	-
CS Martin	84	17	289	8	36.12	3-80	-	-
JEC Franklin	91	21	312	8	39.00	5-53	1	-

WEST INDIES

Batting	M	Inns	NO	Runs	HS	Av	100	50	c/st
RS Morton	2	3	1	140	70*	70.00	-	2	1/-
CH Gayle	3	5	0	235	82	47.00	-	2	1/-
D Ganga	3	5	0	191	95	38.20	-	1	2/-
RR Sarwan	1	2	0	66	62	33.00	-	1	-/-
RN Lewis	1	2	0	62	40	31.00	-	-	-/-
DJ Bravo	3	5	1	114	59	28.50	-	1	2/-
DR Smith	2	2	0	38	38	19.00	-	-	-/-
BC Lara	3	5	0	90	83	18.00	-	1	-/-
JE Taylor	1	2	1	17	13	17.00	-	-	-/-
S Chanderpaul	3	5	0	74	36	14.80	-	-	2/-
DB Powell	2	2	0	23	16	11.50	-	-	-/-
IDR Bradshaw	3	4	1	32	20*	10.66	-	-	1/-
D Ramdin	3	4	0	33	15	8.25	-	-	8/-
FH Edwards	3	4	2	3	2*	1.50	-	-	1/-

Bowling	Overs	Mds	Runs	Wkts	Av	Best	5/inn	10m
CH Gayle	53.1	9	127	6	21.16	4-71	-	-
DB Powell	28.2	8	103	4	25.75	4-83	-	-
FH Edwards	51.3	6	206	7	29.42	5-65	1	-
DR Smith	35	8	115	3	38.33	3-71	-	-
IDR Bradshaw	80.1	15	269	7	38.42	3-73	-	-
JE Taylor	9	2	45	1	45.00	1-39	-	-

Also bowled: RS Morton 1-0-7-0, RN Lewis 29-8-70-0.

SOUTH AFRICA

SOUTH AFRICA REPORT
By Telford Vice

South Africa's attempts to cope with Australia in 2005–06 resembled a penguin trying to do up a pair of shoelaces. The pluck of their first go at it, in Perth in December, was admirable. But that stout effort gave way to bathos, and from there it was a short waddle to pathos. By the time the teams met for the last of their six Test matches, in Johannesburg at the end of March, the joke was so over it almost didn't hurt to laugh.

Graeme Smith and Mickey Arthur spent a lot of the summer mouthing away about how the difference in strength and quality between the South African and Australian teams was as trifling as the fact that we

Graeme Smith is forced on to the defensive against New Zealand at Johannesburg.

say 'Howzit' and they say 'G'day'. The truth was that the gap was closer to the chasm that yawns betwixt hello and goodbye. Worse, for South Africans, was the lack of any real evidence that it would close any decade soon. That is a calamity in South Africa, where beating Australia is all that matters.

The countries' relationship is at least as complex as the thoughts Stephen Hawking might have if he took a bump to the head and decided the sky was about to fall. South Africans tell each other that Australians are arrogant prima donnas who are obsessed with measuring everything against an Australian scale, as in, 'Would you look at how flat Table Mountain is! The Adelaide Oval curator himself would be proud of it!' The only South Africans who won't agree with those sentiments are the thousands upon thousands who have become Australians. And there are many more aspirant Antipodeans where those came from, most of them only too ready to boo the living daylights out of people like Clyde Rathbone, Australia's Durban-born rugby star.

Then the Australians arrive for another tour and, if they overcome what seems to be a genetic predisposition to behave loutishly in Cape Town, we rediscover what a bloody fine bunch of blokes they are. The feeling, as far as we can tell, is entirely mutual.

But, last summer, things were depressingly different. Allegations of racism levelled at the South Africans by spectators in Australia became an ugly refrain. It didn't help that some Australians could not understand what the fuss was about. Perhaps their insensitivity could be explained by the fact that they have not recently negotiated their way from oppression to democracy, as South Africans have done. Australianised former South Africans were blamed, which clicked with the screwy psychology above. 'See,' dinkum South Africans said, 'only racists would move to a place as racist as Australia.' Then Mark Boucher steered the nastiness in a new direction when he said he had lost respect for some of the Australian players. That was too much for Justin Langer, who lashed back with a fit of naïve pique laden with hurt and confusion: how could anyone have anything less than total respect for anything Australian?

So there was little that was warmly blokish about the teams' onfield clashes last summer. Perth became

Makhaya Ntini, South Africa's outstanding bowler of the year, removes Simon Katich's leg stump at Centurion in the opening one-day international.

internet chatrooms as the losses mounted) could see that an absence of the fear of ruthlessness remains one of the factors that separated the Australians from the South Africans. The Australians left fewer ramparts standing for the South Africans to shelter behind in the Second Test in Melbourne and victory was theirs. When a knee injury ruled Ntini out in Sydney, where Ponting became the first player to score centuries in each innings of his 100th Test, the eventual 2-0 series scoreline was all but certain.

Worse was to come for South Africa in the VB Series when they won just three of their eight games and returned home early to leave Australia and Sri Lanka to contest the finals. The disappointment was palpable, but for a few hours at the Wanderers on the now famous date of 12 March it mattered not a jot. Were J. K. Rowling and Alfred Hitchcock able to collaborate they might have, on a good day, produced the electrifying drama of what in South Africa is known simply as 438. That was how many runs South Africa scored to beat Australia – by one wicket, with a ball to spare – in the fifth one-day international. One impossible shot after another exploded off the bat as the limits of what was achievable in 100 overs of cricket were rubbished faster than they were being reset. The celebration uncorked by the manner in which this triumph was achieved harked back to the heady days of the Springboks' World Cup win in 1995.

Less than a week later the braai smoke in the newly galvanised nation's backyard was again heavily laced with incredulity. But this time that was due to Australia needing less than three days to rip through Smith's team in the First Test in Cape Town. Debutant Stuart Clark, who gained his place on tour because Glenn McGrath decided to stay in Australia with his ill wife, took nine wickets on a responsive pitch. Ponting doubled up his hundreds again in Durban to join Sunil Gavaskar as the only men who have done so in three Test matches, and Shane Warne took six wickets in the second innings as Australia clinched the series in the gloom of the fifth evening.

It was all over early in the neon sunlight of the fifth morning in Johannesburg, where Langer – who was severely concussed by a bouncer from Ntini in the

an attritional trudge that the South Africans gained the better of, because the shape of the game was a good fit for the national character. It was also the first Test that South Africa had been granted at the WACA, a fact that had cricket's conspiracy theorists in a froth. Makhaya Ntini took the first of the five five-wicket hauls he would claim in the eight Tests he played in the season, and Jacques Rudolph scored a necessarily grim century to keep the danger of defeat at bay. Brad Hodge played his third Test just days before his 31st birthday, and he celebrated with an unbeaten double-century in the second innings. Hodge was noticeably less successful in the rest of the series – not good enough against the quick stuff, was the verdict – and he was left out of the tour party that would resume hostilities in South Africa in February.

Would that Arthur and Smith (who were codified as Mickey and Goofy in certain South African

25 years OF SOUTH AFRICA

By Telford Vice

Some might say the only South African cricket highlight worth celebrating from 25 years ago was the fact that the first of the rebel rabble had yet to sully our shores. That sorry stage was reached the next year, 1982, when Graham Gooch led a team to a country that P. W. Botha ruled with a forefinger of iron and a brain of bone. Nelson Mandela's freedom was still nine years away. Whites and blacks lived separate and brutally unequal lives, and cricket was duly fractured along racial lines.

Unification was achieved in 1991 with the formation of the United Cricket Board of South Africa. The phoenix rose from the ashes of the blaze ignited by the last of the shameful rebel tours, which was led by Mike Gatting in 1990. Progressive South Africans' hostile response to the tour – and the authorities' predictably vicious reaction to their outrage – shattered the white establishment's delusion that cricket was theirs to do with as they wished.

Against that background the mere fact that South Africa, who were rightly drummed out of Test cricket in 1970, played their first ever one-day international against India at Eden Gardens in Calcutta on 10 November 1991, looms among the most important milestones. The first shock of South Africa's World Cup debut in 1992 was the ease with which they beat Australia in the opening match in Sydney, and the last was the soggy semi-final defeat against England. In between we saw Peter Kirsten make light of his 36 years to reel off one important innings after another, and we were led to believe that Jonty Rhodes was a guided missile in disguise.

South Africa's most memorable Test match in the past 25 years was against Australia in Sydney in 1994. Australia needed just 117 to win, and they resumed on 63 for 4 on the final morning. But the day would belong to Fanie de Villiers who took 6 for 43 as Australia folded for 111, and a generation of South Africans had a moment to treasure. Perhaps the most important highlight, however, came in 1998, when Makhaya Ntini burst on to the scene. With his emergence, hopes that a team which represented the entire nation would also look like the nation, took a leap forward.

Jonty Rhodes takes another sharp catch on his way to becoming the world's finest fielder.

first innings – sat padded up as Australia snuck to victory by two wickets. Ponting was at a loss to explain what he would have done had Langer insisted on batting, 'If it comes to that again, I am just going to have to knock him out'. As if the theatre of all that wasn't enough to keep South Africans riveted, a stream of debatable umpiring decisions that seemed to assist the Australians only added to the tension. 'How does Steve Bucknor wink,' a listener asked in a text message to radio commentators that was read out on air. 'He opens one eye.'

One-sided though most of South Africa's encounters with Australia in 2005–06 were, they easily overshadowed the events of their other engagements. They cruised to victory in a home one-day series against New Zealand, and kept their edge keen in sharing a one-day rubber in India before the Australian assault began. Beating the New Zealanders in a Test series that stretched too far into winter for anyone's comfort – even the Kiwis wrapped up against the chill of May mornings in Johannesburg – provided balm for the bruises. It was welcome, but South Africa needed more than that to ease their pain.

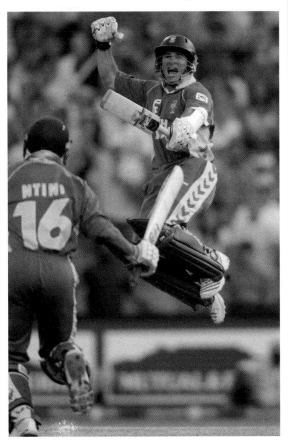

ONE-DAY INTERNATIONALS
v. New Zealand

Match One
23 October 2005 at Bloemfontein
New Zealand 249 for 8 (50 overs) (CD McMillan 66, A Nel 3 for 42)
South Africa 250 for 8 (49.3 overs) (JM Kemp 73)
South Africa won by 2 wickets

Match Two
28 October 2005 at Cape Town
South Africa 201 for 9 (50 overs) (JH Kallis 51, KD Mills 4 for 44)
New Zealand 182 all out (47.5 overs) (L Vincent 90, M Ntini 3 for 29, CK Langeveldt 3 for 35)
South Africa won by 19 runs

Match Three
30 October 2005 at Port Elizabeth
New Zealand 243 for 9 (50 overs) (SB Styris 78, SP Fleming 54, M Ntini 3 for 37)
South Africa 245 for 6 (49.2 overs) (HH Gibbs 81)
South Africa won by 4 wickets

Match Four
4 November 2005 at Durban
South Africa 79 for 2 (20 overs)
New Zealand
Match abandoned – no result

Match Five
6 November 2005 at Centurion
New Zealand 215 all out (49.3 overs) (L Vincent 66, AJ Hall 4 for 23)
South Africa 140 for 5 (28.1 overs) (GC Smith 66)
South Africa won by 5 wickets – DL Method: target 140 from 30 overs

South Africa won the series 4–0

The end of the greatest one-day match of all? Mark Boucher is airborne with delight as South Africa, amazingly, chase down Australia's 434 for 4 to win by one wicket at the Wanderers, with one ball to go.

ONE-DAY INTERNATIONALS
v. Australia

Match One
26 February 2006 at Centurion
Australia 229 for 8 (47 overs) (MEK Hussey 56,
MJ Clarke 53, SM Pollock 3 for 23)
South Africa 207 for 4 (37.3 overs) (GC Smith 119*)
*South Africa won by 6 wickets – DL Method: target 204
from 41 overs*

Match Two
3 March 2006 at Cape Town
South Africa 289 for 7 (50 overs) (HH Gibbs 66,
JM Kemp 51*)
Australia 93 all out (34.3 overs) (M Ntini 6 for 22,
A Nel 3 for 30)
South Africa won by 196 runs

Match Three
5 March 2006 at Port Elizabeth
Australia 254 for 6 (50 overs) (RT Ponting 62,
DR Martyn 51)
South Africa 230 all out (47.2 overs) (SM Pollock 69,
AB de Villiers 68, B Lee 4 for 48)
Australia won by 24 runs

Match Four
10 March 2006 at Durban
South Africa 246 for 9 (50 overs) (HH Dippenaar 101,
SM Pollock 53*)
Australia 247 for 9 (49.1 overs) (A Symonds 76,
R Telemachus 3 for 34)
Australia won by 1 wicket

Match Five
12 March 2006 at Johannesburg
Australia 434 for 4 (50 overs) (RT Ponting 164,
MEK Hussey 81, SM Katich 79, AC Gilchrist 55)
South Africa 438 for 9 (49.5 overs) (HH Gibbs 175,
GC Smith 90, MV Boucher 50*, NW Bracken 5 for 67)
South Africa won by 1 wicket

South Africa won the series 3–2

FIRST TEST – SOUTH AFRICA v. AUSTRALIA
16–18 March 2006 at Cape Town

SOUTH AFRICA

	First Innings		Second Innings	
GC Smith (capt)	c Gilchrist b Clark	19	(2) lbw b Warne	16
AB de Villiers	b Kasprowicz	8	(1) c Gilchrist b Lee	7
HH Gibbs	b Clark	18	b Lee	0
JH Kallis	c Hayden b Clark	6	c Gilchrist b Clark	36
AG Prince	c Hayden b Lee	17	c Gilchrist b Clark	27
JA Rudolph	c Gilchrist b Kasprowicz	10	b Warne	41
*MV Boucher	c Gilchrist b Clark	16	c Langer b Kasprowicz	2
AJ Hall	c Hayden b Lee	24	not out	34
N Boje	lbw b Clark	31	c & b Clark	14
A Nel	lbw b Lee	18	b Clark	4
M Ntini	not out	17	c Kasprowicz b Warne	6
Extras	lb 6, nb 15	21	w 3, nb 7	10
	(all out 63.5 overs)	**205**	(all out 63.5 overs)	**197**

	First Innings				Second Innings			
	O	M	R	W	O	M	R	W
Lee	14.5	2	37	3	17	5	47	2
Kasprowicz	13	0	44	2	12	0	39	1
Symonds	10	2	22	0	-	-	-	-
Clark	17	3	55	5	16	7	34	4
Warne	9	0	41	0	18.5	1	77	3

Fall of Wickets
1-24, 2-42, 3-48, 4-61, 5-76, 6-104, 7-124, 8-148, 9-173
1-20, 2-20, 3-37, 4-75, 5-92, 6-108, 7-158, 8-179, 9-183

AUSTRALIA

	First Innings		Second Innings	
JL Langer	lbw b Nel	16	b Ntini	34
ML Hayden	c Rudolph b Ntini	94	c Gibbs b Ntini	32
RT Ponting (capt)	c Hall b Kallis	74	lbw b Ntini	1
DR Martyn	c Boucher b Kallis	22	not out	9
MEK Hussey	c Boucher b Hall	6	not out	14
A Symonds	c Nel b Boje	55		
*AC Gilchrist	c Smith b Kallis	12		
SK Warne	c de Villiers b Boje	7		
B Lee	c Gibbs b Ntini	0		
MS Kasprowicz	not out	8		
SR Clark	c Gibbs b Nel	8		
Extras	lb 7, w 1	8	lb 5	5
	(all out 87.2 overs)	**308**	(3 wkts 27.1 overs)	**95**

	First Innings				Second Innings			
	O	M	R	W	O	M	R	W
Ntini	21	2	76	2	10	3	28	3
Nel	22.2	6	45	2	7	1	25	0
Hall	16	2	66	1	5	1	16	0
Boje	16	4	63	2	5.1	1	21	0
Kallis	12	0	51	3	-	-	-	-

Fall of Wickets
1-21, 2-175, 3-192, 4-214, 5-236, 6-272, 7-294, 8-294, 9-296
1-71, 2-71, 3-76

Umpires: Aleem Dar (Pakistan) & BR Doctrove (West Indies)
Toss: South Africa
Test debut: SR Clark
Man of the Match: SR Clark

Australia won by 7 wickets

SECOND TEST – SOUTH AFRICA v. AUSTRALIA
24–28 March 2006 at Durban

AUSTRALIA

	First Innings		Second Innings	
JL Langer	c Boucher b Kallis	35	c Pollock b Boje	37
ML Hayden	c de Villiers b Ntini	0	c Boucher b Ntini	102
RT Ponting (capt)	c Gibbs b Boje	103	c Boje b Pollock	116
DR Martyn	c Kallis b Ntini	57	not out	15
MEK Hussey	lbw b Kallis	75		
B Lee	c Boucher b Ntini	0		
A Symonds	lbw b Nel	13		
*AC Gilchrist	c Boucher b Nel	2	(5) c Nel b Boje	24
SK Warne	c de Villiers b Pollock	36		
MS Kasprowicz	c de Villiers b Nel	7		
SR Clark	not out	13		
Extras	b 8, lb 11, w 2, nb 7	28	lb 5, w 1, nb 7	13
	(all out 127.1 overs)	369	(4 wkts dec 82.4 overs)	307

	First Innings				Second Innings			
	O	M	R	W	O	M	R	W
Pollock	32	11	73	1	19	4	55	1
Ntini	24	4	81	3	15	2	62	1
Nel	31	8	83	3	14	3	58	0
Kallis	21.1	8	52	2	8	0	40	0
Boje	19	1	61	1	26.4	4	87	2

Fall of Wickets
1-0, 2-97, 3-198, 4-218, 5-219, 6-253, 7-259, 8-315, 9-327
1-49, 2-250, 3-278, 4-307

SOUTH AFRICA

	First Innings		Second Innings	
GC Smith (capt)	c Langer b Lee	0	(2) c Langer b Warne	40
AB de Villiers	c Hayden b Clark	50	(1) st Gilchrist b Warne	46
HH Gibbs	b Kasprowicz	9	c Warne b Clark	17
JH Kallis	c & b Clark	114	lbw b Warne	7
AG Prince	c Symonds b Warne	33	c Hussey b Clark	7
JA Rudolph	c Hussey b Warne	13	c Langer b Warne	36
*MV Boucher	b Lee	19	not out	51
SM Pollock	c Gilchrist b Lee	1	b Lee	4
N Boje	not out	6	c sub b Kasprowicz	48
A Nel	c Hayden b Lee	5	c Hayden b Warne	14
M Ntini	c Ponting b Lee	0	lbw b Warne	0
Extras	lb 3, nb 14	17	b 5, lb 8, nb 14	27
	(all out 88.4 overs)	267	(all out 99.5 overs)	297

	First Innings				Second Innings			
	O	M	R	W	O	M	R	W
Lee	19.4	5	69	5	22	6	65	1
Kasprowicz	14	0	60	1	12	2	51	1
Warne	25	2	80	2	35.5	9	86	6
Symonds	11	3	16	0	8	0	32	0
Hussey	1	0	2	0	1	0	4	0
Clark	18	4	37	2	21	6	46	2

Fall of Wickets
1-0, 2-10, 3-144, 4-200, 5-226, 6-255, 7-256, 8-257, 9-267
1-91, 2-98, 3-122, 4-122, 5-146, 6-170, 7-181, 8-253, 9-292

Umpires: SA Bucknor (West Indies) & BR Doctrove (West Indies)
Toss: Australia
Man of the Match: SK Warne

Australia won by 112 runs

THIRD TEST – SOUTH AFRICA v. AUSTRALIA
31 March–4 April 2006 at Johannesburg

SOUTH AFRICA

	First Innings		Second Innings	
AB de Villiers	c Martyn b Clark	12	b Clark	4
HH Gibbs	b Kasprowicz	16	c Martyn b Warne	53
HH Dippenaar	c Gilchrist b Clark	32	c Hayden b Clark	20
JH Kallis (capt)	b Lee	37	lbw b Clark	27
AG Prince	c Langer b Lee	93	c Symonds b Warne	9
JA Rudolph	c Hayden b Warne	25	(7) c Gilchrist b Clark	0
*MV Boucher	lbw b Warne	24	(8) c Gilchrist b Lee	63
SM Pollock	c Ponting b Clark	8	(6) c Gilchrist b Lee	44
N Boje	c Langer b Kasprowicz	43	c Symonds b Warne	4
A Nel	c Martyn b Lee	0	not out	18
M Ntini	not out	0	b Lee	0
Extras	lb 4, nb 9	13	b 6, lb 4, w 1, nb 5	16
	(all out 97.2 overs)	303	(all out 71.3 overs)	258

	First Innings				Second Innings			
	O	M	R	W	O	M	R	W
Lee	24	8	57	3	18.3	3	57	3
Clark	28	8	81	3	18	4	64	4
Kasprowicz	24.2	4	86	2	2	0	12	0
Warne	13	2	49	1	26	5	90	3
Symonds	8	2	26	1	5	0	18	0
Ponting	-	-	-	-	2	1	7	0

Fall of Wickets
1-26, 2-38, 3-97, 4-106, 5-161, 6-233, 7-251, 8-285, 9-303
1-9, 2-55, 3-100, 4-120, 5-130, 6-140, 7-186, 8-194, 9-258

AUSTRALIA

	First Innings		Second Innings	
JL Langer	retired hurt	0	absent hurt	
ML Hayden	c Gibbs b Ntini	3	(1) c de Villiers b Ntini	0
RT Ponting (capt)	c de Villiers b Ntini	34	c Boucher b Kallis	20
DR Martyn	c Nel b Ntini	21	lbw b Pollock	101
MEK Hussey	lbw b Boje	73	(2) lbw b Boje	89
A Symonds	lbw b Ntini	4	(5) c Boucher b Kallis	29
*AC Gilchrist	c Rudolph b Nel	12	(6) c Boucher b Ntini	0
SK Warne	c Pollock b Ntini	36	(7) c Boucher b Ntini	3
B Lee	c Boje b Ntini	64	(8) not out	24
MS Kasprowicz	c Gibbs b Pollock	2	not out	7
SR Clark	not out	0	(9) c Boucher b Ntini	10
Extras	b 5, lb 14, w 2	21	b 1, lb 9, nb 1	11
	(all out 62.5 overs)	270	(8 wkts 91.4 overs)	294

	First Innings				Second Innings			
	O	M	R	W	O	M	R	W
Ntini	18.5	2	100	6	26	4	78	4
Nel	15	2	42	1	2	1	4	0
Pollock	15	2	56	1	25.4	3	81	1
Kallis	10	2	43	0	18	6	44	2
Boje	4	1	10	1	19	5	65	1
de Villiers	-	-	-	-	1	0	12	0

Fall of Wickets
1-12, 2-68, 3-73, 4-89, 5-106, 6-174, 7-242, 8-260, 9-270
1-0, 2-33, 3-198, 4-228, 5-229, 6-237, 7-258, 8-275

Umpires: SA Bucknor (West Indies) & AL Hill (New Zealand)
Toss: South Africa
Man of the Match: B Lee
Man of the Series: SR Clark

Australia won by 2 wickets

SERIES AVERAGES
South Africa v. Australia

SOUTH AFRICA

Batting	M	Inns	NO	Runs	HS	Av	100	50	c/st
AJ Hall	1	2	1	58	34*	58.00	-	-	1/-
JH Kallis	3	6	0	227	114	37.83	1	-	1/-
MV Boucher	3	6	1	175	63	35.00	-	2	11/-
AG Prince	3	6	0	186	93	31.00	-	1	-/-
N Boje	3	6	1	146	48	29.20	-	-	2/-
HH Dippenaar	1	2	0	52	32	26.00	-	-	-/-
AB de Villiers	3	6	0	127	50	21.16	-	1	6/-
JA Rudolph	3	6	0	125	41	20.83	-	-	2/-
HH Gibbs	3	6	0	113	53	18.83	-	1	6/-
GC Smith	2	4	0	75	40	18.75	-	-	1/-
SM Pollock	2	4	0	57	44	14.25	-	-	2/-
A Nel	3	6	1	59	18*	11.80	-	-	3/-
M Ntini	3	6	2	23	17*	5.75	-	-	-/-

Bowling	Overs	Mds	Runs	Wkts	Av	Best	5/inn	10m
M Ntini	114.5	17	425	19	22.36	6-100	1	1
JH Kallis	69.1	16	230	7	32.85	3-51	-	-
A Nel	91.2	21	257	6	42.83	3-83	-	-
N Boje	89.5	16	307	7	43.85	2-63	-	-
SM Pollock	91.4	20	265	4	66.25	1-55	-	-
AJ Hall	21	3	82	1	82.00	1-66	-	-

Also bowled: AB de Villiers 1-0-12-0.

AUSTRALIA

Batting	M	Inns	NO	Runs	HS	Av	100	50	c/st
MEK Hussey	3	5	1	257	89	64.25	-	3	2/-
RT Ponting	3	6	0	348	116	58.00	2	1	2/-
DR Martyn	3	6	2	225	101	56.25	1	1	3/-
ML Hayden	3	6	0	231	102	38.50	1	1	8/-
JL Langer	3	5	1	122	37	30.50	-	-	6/-
B Lee	3	4	1	88	64	29.33	-	1	-/-
A Symonds	3	4	0	101	55	25.25	-	1	3/-
SK Warne	3	4	0	82	36	20.50	-	-	1/-
SR Clark	3	4	2	31	13*	15.50	-	-	2/-
MS Kasprowicz	3	4	2	22	7*	11.00	-	-	1/-
AC Gilchrist	3	5	0	50	24	10.00	-	-	11/1

Bowling	Overs	Mds	Runs	Wkts	Av	Best	5/inn	10m
SR Clark	118	32	317	20	15.85	5-55	1	-
B Lee	116	29	332	17	19.52	5-69	1	-
SK Warne	127.4	19	423	15	28.20	6-86	1	-
MS Kasprowicz	77.2	6	292	7	41.71	2-44	-	-
A Symonds	42	7	114	1	114.00	1-26	-	-

Also bowled: MEK Hussey 2-0-6-0, RT Ponting 2-1-7-0.

FIRST TEST – SOUTH AFRICA v. NEW ZEALAND
15–19 April 2006 at Centurion

SOUTH AFRICA

	First Innings				Second Innings			
GC Smith (capt)	lbw b Franklin			45	lbw b Martin			7
HH Gibbs	b Mills			6	c Styris b Franklin			2
HH Dippenaar	c Fulton b Mills			52	c Fleming b Oram			16
JH Kallis	b Franklin			38	c Vettori b Styris			62
AG Prince	c Styris b Mills			9	c McCullum b Franklin			11
AB de Villiers	b Franklin			27	c Franklin b Oram			97
*MV Boucher	c Fleming b Martin			18	b Mills			21
SM Pollock	c Styris b Mills			24	lbw b Vettori			10
N Boje	lbw b Franklin			23	c McCullum b Astle			31
DW Steyn	c Mills b Martin			13	not out			7
M Ntini	not out			1	lbw b Vettori			16
Extras	b 6, lb 4, w 3, nb 7			20	b 12, lb 2, nb 5			19
	(all out 95.4 overs)			276	(all out 98.1 overs)			299

	First Innings				Second Innings			
	O	M	R	W	O	M	R	W
Mills	18	7	43	4	21	5	57	1
Franklin	18	3	75	4	14	2	60	2
Martin	22.4	4	66	2	24	5	64	1
Oram	14	7	27	0	17	4	44	2
Vettori	18	2	44	0	15.1	0	42	2
Astle	5	2	11	0	5	1	15	1
Styris	-	-	-	-	2	0	3	1

Fall of Wickets
1-16, 2-95, 3-118, 4-130, 5-177, 6-197, 7-229, 8-233, 9-274
1-8, 2-19, 3-42, 4-73, 5-140, 6-194, 7-205, 8-270, 9-276

NEW ZEALAND

	First Innings				Second Innings			
HJH Marshall	b Ntini			6	c Boucher b Ntini			25
PG Fulton	c Boucher b Pollock			14	c Boucher b Ntini			4
SP Fleming (capt)	c & b Ntini			0	(4) c Kallis b Steyn			6
SB Styris	c Gibbs b Ntini			17	(5) c Boucher b Steyn			2
NJ Astle	c Boucher b Steyn			4	(6) c de Villiers b Ntini			2
JDP Oram	c Pollock b Steyn			133	(7) b Ntini			2
*BB McCullum	c Boje b Kallis			31	(8) c Dippenaar b Steyn			33
DL Vettori	c Prince b Ntini			81	(9) c Boucher b Steyn			38
JEC Franklin	c Boucher b Ntini			8	(10) not out			0
KD Mills	c Boje b Pollock			12	(3) c Dippenaar b Ntini			0
CS Martin	not out			1	b Steyn			0
Extras	lb 12, nb 8			20	lb 2, nb 6			8
	(all out 71.4 overs)			327	(all out 36 overs)			120

	First Innings				Second Innings			
	O	M	R	W	O	M	R	W
Ntini	19	2	94	5	14	3	51	5
Steyn	18.4	1	95	2	17	4	47	5
Pollock	15	4	45	2	5	1	20	0
Kallis	9	1	41	1	-	-	-	-
Boje	7	0	29	0	-	-	-	-
Smith	3	1	11	0	-	-	-	-

Fall of Wickets
1-8, 2-12, 3-32, 4-38, 5-45, 6-89, 7-272, 8-280, 9-322
1-5, 2-5, 3-17, 4-23, 5-26, 6-28, 7-73, 8-119, 9-119

Umpires: MR Benson (England) & DJ Harper (Australia)
Toss: South Africa
Man of the Match: M Ntini

South Africa won by 128 runs

SECOND TEST – SOUTH AFRICA v. NEW ZEALAND
27 April–1 May 2006 at Cape Town

NEW ZEALAND

	First Innings		Second Innings	
MHW Papps	b Nel	22	c Prince b Steyn	20
PG Fulton	c Boucher b Steyn	36	c Kallis b Ntini	11
SP Fleming (capt)	b Prince	262		
SB Styris	c Dippenaar b Ntini	11	(3) not out	54
NJ Astle	lbw b Ntini	50	(4) c Smith b Kallis	14
JDP Oram	run out	13	(5) not out	8
*BB McCullum	lbw b Ntini	5		
DL Vettori	c Nel b Ntini	11		
JEC Franklin	not out	122		
JS Patel	not out	27		
CS Martin				
Extras	b 4, lb 14, w 1, nb 15	34	lb 10, nb 4	14
	(8 wkts dec 165 overs)	593	(3 wkts 37 overs)	121

	First Innings				Second Innings			
	O	M	R	W	O	M	R	W
Ntini	43	5	162	4	8	2	25	1
Steyn	31	4	114	1	9	3	26	1
Nel	27	3	98	1	10	2	41	0
Kallis	15	4	45	0	5	3	5	1
Boje	29	4	89	0	5	1	14	0
Smith	17	2	61	0	-	-	-	-
Amla	1	0	4	0	-	-	-	-
Prince	2	0	2	1	-	-	-	-

Fall of Wickets
1-50, 2-62, 3-82, 4-188, 5-237, 6-259, 7-279, 8-535
1-34, 2-41, 3-81

SOUTH AFRICA

	First Innings	
GC Smith (capt)	c & b Patel	25
HH Dippenaar	b Patel	47
HM Amla	lbw b Vettori	149
JH Kallis	c Martin b Oram	71
AG Prince	not out	108
AB de Villiers	c Papps b Patel	13
*MV Boucher	c Fleming b Franklin	33
N Boje	lbw b Franklin	0
A Nel	lbw b Franklin	12
DW Steyn	st McCullum b Vettori	13
M Ntini	run out	11
Extras	b 15, lb 10, nb 5	30
	(all out 188 overs)	512

	First Innings			
	O	M	R	W
Martin	20	7	62	0
Franklin	33	5	95	3
Vettori	63	10	147	2
Patel	42	8	117	3
Styris	10	2	33	0
Oram	18	10	24	1
Astle	2	0	9	0

Fall of Wickets
1-36, 2-108, 3-252, 4-344, 5-361, 6-435, 7-435, 8-462, 9-495

Umpires: MR Benson (England) & EAR de Silva (Sri Lanka)
Toss: South Africa
Man of the Match: SP Fleming

Match drawn

THIRD TEST – SOUTH AFRICA v. NEW ZEALAND
5–7 May 2006 at Johannesburg

NEW ZEALAND

	First Innings		Second Innings	
MHW Papps	b Ntini	0	c Hall b Kallis	15
JM How	c de Villiers b Steyn	0	lbw b Steyn	4
SP Fleming (capt)	c Boucher b Ntini	46	c de Villiers b Kallis	37
SB Styris	c de Villiers b Ntini	0	c & b Steyn	42
NJ Astle	c Kallis b Steyn	20	c Boucher b Steyn	45
JDP Oram	lbw b Pollock	18	c Dippenaar b Steyn	27
*BB McCullum	c & b Steyn	0	c Boucher b Pollock	5
DL Vettori	lbw b Steyn	2	c de Villiers b Hall	60
JEC Franklin	c Boucher b Hall	19	b Pollock	19
KD Mills	not out	0	not out	0
CS Martin	c Smith b Ntini	1	c Amla b Hall	0
Extras	lb 9, w 1, nb 3	13	b 5, lb 17, w 3, nb 4	29
	(all out 44 overs)	119	(all out 78.5 overs)	283

	First Innings				Second Innings			
	O	M	R	W	O	M	R	W
Ntini	16	7	35	5	17	4	44	0
Steyn	12	3	43	3	22	3	91	4
Hall	9	2	21	1	12.5	1	50	2
Pollock	7	2	11	1	13	3	36	2
Kallis	-	-	-	-	14	1	40	2

Fall of Wickets
1-0, 2-0, 3-2, 4-57, 5-78, 6-78, 7-82, 8-118, 9-118
1-9, 2-40, 3-82, 4-158, 5-177, 6-190, 7-239, 8-283, 9-283

SOUTH AFRICA

	First Innings		Second Innings	
GC Smith (capt)	c McCullum b Franklin	63	c McCullum b Franklin	68
HH Dippenaar	b Martin	0	c McCullum b Martin	37
HM Amla	c Papps b Styris	56	b Mills	28
JH Kallis	b Martin	9	c How b Mills	13
AG Prince	c McCullum b Martin	4	not out	43
AB de Villiers	c Styris b Franklin	2	b Franklin	5
*MV Boucher	lbw b Franklin	0	b Franklin	6
SM Pollock	not out	32	not out	6
AJ Hall	lbw b Martin	5		
DW Steyn	b Martin	2		
M Ntini	c McCullum b Mills	8		
Extras	nb 5	5	b 4, lb 5, w 2, nb 3	14
	(all out 44 overs)	186	(6 wkts 47.3 overs)	220

	First Innings				Second Innings			
	O	M	R	W	O	M	R	W
Martin	15	2	37	5	17	1	64	1
Franklin	13	2	87	3	13.3	0	67	3
Oram	4	0	20	0	2	0	8	0
Mills	8	0	30	1	11	3	49	2
Astle	2	0	11	0	-	-	-	-
Styris	2	1	1	1	3	0	12	0
Vettori	-	-	-	-	1	0	11	0

Fall of Wickets
1-1, 2-99, 3-131, 4-131, 5-139, 6-139, 7-139, 8-145, 9-161
1-69, 2-130, 3-156, 4-167, 5-180, 6-202

Umpires: EAR de Silva (Sri Lanka) & DB Hair (Australia)
Toss: South Africa
Man of the Match: GC Smith
Man of the Series: M Ntini

South Africa won by 4 wickets

SERIES AVERAGES
South Africa v. New Zealand

SOUTH AFRICA

Batting	M	Inns	NO	Runs	HS	Av	100	50	c/st
HM Amla	2	3	0	233	149	77.66	1	1	1/-
AG Prince	3	5	2	175	108*	58.33	1	-	2/-
GC Smith	3	5	0	208	68	41.60	-	2	2/-
JH Kallis	3	5	0	193	71	38.60	-	2	3/-
SM Pollock	2	4	2	72	32*	36.00	-	-	1/-
HH Dippenaar	3	5	0	152	52	30.40	-	1	4/-
AB de Villiers	3	5	0	144	97	28.80	-	1	5/-
N Boje	2	3	0	54	31	18.00	-	-	1/-
MV Boucher	3	5	0	78	33	15.60	-	-	12/-
M Ntini	3	4	1	36	16	12.00	-	-	2/-
A Nel	1	1	0	12	12	12.00	-	-	1/-
DW Steyn	3	4	1	35	13	11.66	-	-	1/-
AJ Hall	1	1	0	5	5	5.00	-	-	1/-
HH Gibbs	1	2	0	8	6	4.00	-	-	1/-

Bowling	Overs	Mds	Runs	Wkts	Av	Best	5/inn	10m
AG Prince	2	0	2	1	2.00	1-2	-	-
M Ntini	117	23	411	20	20.55	5-35	3	1
SM Pollock	40	10	112	5	22.40	2-36	-	-
AJ Hall	21.5	3	71	3	23.66	2-50	-	-
DW Steyn	109.4	18	416	16	26.00	5-47	1	-
JH Kallis	43	9	131	4	32.75	2-40	-	-
A Nel	37	5	139	1	139.00	1-98	-	-

Also bowled: HM Amla 1-0-4-0, GC Smith 20-3-72-0, N Boje 41-5-132-0.

NEW ZEALAND

Batting	M	Inns	NO	Runs	HS	Av	100	50	c/st
SP Fleming	3	5	0	351	262	70.20	1	-	3/-
JEC Franklin	3	5	2	168	122*	56.00	1	-	1/-
JDP Oram	3	6	1	201	133	40.20	1	-	-/-
DL Vettori	3	5	0	192	81	38.40	-	2	1/-
SB Styris	3	6	1	126	54*	25.20	-	1	4/-
NJ Astle	3	6	0	135	50	22.50	-	1	-/-
PG Fulton	2	4	0	65	36	16.25	-	-	1/-
HJH Marshall	1	2	0	31	25	15.50	-	-	-/-
BB McCullum	3	5	0	74	33	14.80	-	-	7/1
MHW Papps	2	4	0	57	22	14.25	-	-	2/-
KD Mills	2	4	2	12	12	6.00	-	-	1/-
JM How	1	2	0	4	4	2.00	-	-	1/-
CS Martin	3	4	1	2	1*	0.66	-	-	1/-
JS Patel	1	1	1	27	27*	-	-	-	1/-

Bowling	Overs	Mds	Runs	Wkts	Av	Best	5/inn	10m
KD Mills	58	15	179	8	22.37	4-43	-	-
SB Styris	17	3	49	2	24.50	1-1	-	-
JEC Franklin	91.3	12	384	15	25.60	4-75	-	-
CS Martin	98.4	19	293	9	32.55	5-37	1	-
JS Patel	42	8	117	3	39.00	3-117	-	-
JDP Oram	55	21	123	3	41.00	2-44	-	-
NJ Astle	14	3	46	1	46.00	1-15	-	-
DL Vettori	97.1	12	244	4	61.00	2-42	-	-

ONE-DAY INTERNATIONALS
v. Zimbabwe

Match One
15 September 2006 at Bloemfontein
Zimbabwe 201 for 7 (50 overs) (V Sibanda 51)
South Africa 202 for 5 (43.5 overs) (HH Dippenaar 85*, JP Duminy 60)
South Africa won by 5 wickets

Match Two
18 September 2006 at East London
Zimbabwe 152 all out (49.4 overs)
South Africa 156 for 4 (27.4 overs)
South Africa won by 6 wickets

Match Three
20 September 2006 at Potchefstroom
South Africa 418 for 5 (50 overs) (MV Boucher 147*, LL Bosman 88, AN Peterson 80, JH Kallis 50)
Zimbabwe 247 for 4 (50 overs) (T Duffin 88, H Masakadza 55)
South Africa won by 171 runs

South Africa won the series 3–0

SRI LANKA

SRI LANKA REPORT
By Charlie Austin

Sri Lanka continued a period of transformation during the year under new coach Tom Moody. Fortunes were mixed with Test defeats to India and Pakistan and one-day series defeats to India and New Zealand, as well as Australia in the VB Series. But their cricket grew stronger under a new leader, Mahela Jayawardene, who galvanised the team, introducing a refreshing brand of intelligent, positive and aggressive cricket. By September, the team was in healthy shape, filled with self-belief, internally harmonious and injury-free.

Moody's successful start continued with a predictably straightforward home tour against Bangladesh, although concerns lingered about Sri

Lanka's inconsistent top order. But events took a turn for the worse with a freak watersports accident to Sanath Jayasuriya on a team-bonding trip. Jayasuriya's left-shoulder was dislocated and uncertainty over his fitness contributed to instability in the top order during their India tour. Sri Lanka started in disastrous fashion, surrendering early momentum before being steamrollered 1-6 in the ODI Series. Their bowlers were plundered mercilessly during the Power plays and the batsmen crumbled under the pressure.

The defeat precipitated an uncomfortable and internally rancorous period as the selectors responded ruthlessly, axing Jayasuriya for the Test matches, a move that prompted a government inquiry. The decision was publicly justified on the grounds of fitness but conflicting medical assessments encouraged conspiracy theories. Also, out of the blue, the selectors sacked Jayawardene and appointed Chaminda Vaas as vice-captain. Again, the motives of the move were questioned with senior players upset by the obvious interference of political forces. Team morale plummeted and a 2-0 defeat surprised few.

Confidence nosedived even further with a 1-3 ODI defeat against New Zealand, although the cricket was more keenly contested than the eventual scoreline. By the time the team arrived in Australia for the VB Series, Sri Lankan cricket was in crisis. Fans feared a string of embarrassing defeats and those concerns appeared justified when they were hammered by 116 runs by Australia in their opening game. But the first green shoots of recovery emerged as Jayasuriya, having recovered full fitness, was rushed to Sydney for Sri Lanka's second game against Australia.

Once again he proved Sri Lanka's talisman, smoking a blistering 114 from 96 balls just hours after landing. Sri Lanka's self-belief started to grow again and the team, although handicapped by Marvan Atapattu's increasingly acute back problems, sneaked through to the finals by virtue of two more wins against an out-of-sorts South Africa team. Then they stunned the home team with a hard-fought 22-run victory in the opening game of the finals. Australia responded emphatically, winning 2-1, but Sri Lanka returned home in more optimistic mood.

Sanath Jayasuriya is pictured during his innings of 114 against Australia in the VB Series match at Sydney.

A short tour to Bangladesh provided an opportunity to rest Atapattu, Muttiah Muralitharan and Vaas. It also gave the selectors the chance to quietly ease Vaas, who had struggled with on-field leadership, out of the vice-captaincy. The selectors choose Jayawardene as the new captain with Sangakkara as his deputy. The tour started well with a landslide win at Bogra, but then the Tigers hit back with a shock win, their first-ever against Sri Lanka. The series was secured but Sri Lanka were pushed hard by a Bangladeshi team clearly growing in stature.

Jayawardene's inauspicious start continued in a home series against Pakistan as their one-day form, normally so reliably at home, dipped. The rain-affected ODI series was lost 0-2 and then the Test series was squandered. Sri Lanka dominated the First Test but then Shoaib Malik launched a 121-over rearguard in the final two days, scoring 148. Mohammad Asif made Sri Lanka pay for the let-off, cutting through their top order in successive innings in Kandy, claiming 11 for 71. Prior to the match, Jayasuriya announced his retirement from Test cricket but the farewell game was marred by another injury: this time a painful dislocated thumb that robbed him of a final innings – or so we thought at the time.

When Sri Lanka arrived in England for their early-season tour the team management played down

expectations, Moody calling it a 'learning experience'. With Atapattu and Jayasuriya missing, the inexperienced batting looked vulnerable in English conditions. The warm-up games did little to dispel this notion and controversy – Sri Lanka's perennial bedfellow – soon erupted as the new chairman of selectors, the former fast bowler Ashantha de Mel, claimed that Jayasuriya had been forced into premature Test retirement by the previous panel and announced, just a couple of days before the First Test, that he was now sending him to England. The decision, a vote of no confidence in the young openers Upul Tharanga and Michael Vandort, irked the team management. But the issue was handled skilfully with Moody and Jayawardene standing firm, determined that the pre-tour plan to blood young players would continue.

But, three days into the opening Test at Lord's, de Mel's concerns looked justified. After a toothless bowling performance and a calamitous early collapse, Sri Lanka were left hanging on the ropes, forced to follow on 359 runs in arrears with seven sessions still remaining. But rather than seal their humiliation, the next two days proved to be the turning point of the summer, Sri Lanka's own Dunkirk, a remarkable 199-over escape that ranked as one of the greatest rearguards in Test history. Jayawardene led from the front with 61 in the first innings and an emotional 119 in the second, the start of a prolific period that finished with him scoring 1,264 runs at 57.45 during the year.

The mood within the Sri Lanka camp lifted immeasurably. Even though the Second Test was lost, Sri Lanka battled England close with Muralitharan claiming the first of four consecutive ten-wicket hauls. When Sri Lanka saw the dry pitch for the Third Test at Trent Bridge, they sensed an upset. The tail-enders once again frustrated England's bowlers, squeezing out just enough runs to let Muralitharan run riot in the second innings with 8 for 70, his finest performance during a 12-month period that included 108 wickets at 19.37 in 15 Tests.

With the Tests drawn 1-1, Sri Lanka swiftly claimed the upper hand in the ODIs with a bold strategy designed to exploit the Power plays and dismantle the confidence of England's injury-ravaged bowling attack. With Jayawardene, Tharanga and Jayasuriya all in superb form, the Sri Lankans romped to a 5-0 whitewash, completing their best-ever tour of England. It was all polished off with a record-breaking performance against Holland as

Another memorable moment in the astounding career of Muttiah Muralitharan. Here he leads Sri Lanka off after taking 8 for 70 against England at Trent Bridge in 2006.

Mahela Jayawardene during his epic 374 against South Africa in Colombo.

Jayasuriya smashed 157 from 104 balls, powering Sri Lanka to 443 for 9, the highest-ever score in ODIs.

On Sri Lanka's return the record-breaking spree continued during a two-match series against injury-hit South Africa, as Jayawardene scored 374 in the first Test, the highest score by a Sri Lankan – surpassing Jayasuriya's 340 against India in 1998 – and the fourth-highest in the game's history. He also shared a world-record stand with Sangakkara, the pair compiling an astonishing 624-run third-wicket partnership, not only an all-wicket record in Tests but also in first-class cricket. The second game was a cliffhanger as Sri Lanka were set a stiff 352-run target. Jayawardene led the way with a masterful 123, shepherding the lower order to the highest-ever successful chase in Sri Lanka and a 2-0 series victory.

The tour then came to a sudden end when a bomb attack forced the abandonment of the tri-nation ODI Series with the tourists and India as South Africa pulled out due to concerns that the players' safety could not be guaranteed. With the return of open conflict in the north and east between the government and Tamil Tigers, it raised the spectre of an uncertain financial future for Sri Lanka Cricket, which lost an estimated US$12 million in television and sponsorship revenues as a result of the unrest.

The financial loss was a major blow for the government-appointed Cricket Board during what hitherto had been an unusually controversy-free year. Appointed in 2005 after allegations of mismanagement were levied at the previous Board, they started to build stronger relations with the players and implement significant changes to the domestic game, including a slimming-down of the first-class structure to 14 teams, a substantial increase in match fees for first-class cricketers and a renewed focus on the introduction of new development structures.

With the government wary of holding fresh Board elections before changes are made to the constitution, the new atmosphere within Sri Lanka's cricket could not have finished the year more upbeat. The team left for the ICC Champions Trophy with the highest of ambitions.

ONE–DAY INTERNATIONALS v. Pakistan

Match One
17 March 2006 at Colombo (RPS)
Pakistan 201 for 8 (50 overs) (MF Maharoof 3 for 24, KS Lokuarachchi 3 for 47)
Sri Lanka
Match abandoned – no result

Match Two
19 March 2006 at Colombo (RPS)
Sri Lanka 130 all out (44.2 overs) (Naved-ul-Hasan 3 for 23)
Pakistan 134 for 6 (44.4 overs)
Pakistan won by 4 wickets

Match Three
22 March 2006 at Colombo (SSC)
Sri Lanka 224 all out (49.4 overs) (CK Kapugedera 50, Shahid Afridi 3 for 37)
Pakistan 229 for 6 (45.2 overs)
(Mohammad Yousuf 53, M Muralitharan 3 for 58)
Pakistan won by 4 wickets

Pakistan won the series 2–0

ONE–DAY INTERNATIONALS v. India

The series was abandoned due to the adverse weather conditions after only 3.4 overs had been bowled.

OF SRI LANKA

By Charlie Austin

Exactly 100 years after Ceylon played their first match against England, Sri Lanka entered the Test arena on 17 February 1982. Their Test career started with great pomp, plenty of dignitaries and a mountain of memorabilia, from a special stamp collection to plaques, mugs and a special gold coin for the toss between captains Keith Fletcher and Bandula Warnapura.

Ranjan Madugalle became the first Sri Lankan to pass 50 with 64 in the first innings while a teenage Arjuna Ranatunga batted four hours for his 54. When England collapsed to 223 all out and Sri Lanka followed with 152 for 3, a remarkable first win beckoned. But John Emburey triggered a dramatic collapse – the last seven wickets falling for eight runs – and England comfortably achieved their 171-run target.

Like so many touring teams, Lord's holds special memories for the Sri Lankans – dating right back to their first Test there in 1984 when a richly talented batting line-up, a virtual *Who's Who* of Sri Lanka's finest batsmen, paraded their talents. Sidath Wettimuny, an erudite man with a classical technique, led the way with a beautiful 190. Duleep Mendis, a belligerent strokeplayer, also starred with 111 in the first innings and 94 in the second. The match was drawn.

Sri Lanka had to wait until 1985 for their first Test win, achieved at home against neighbours India. The match finished with frenzied scenes as Colombo's offices emptied early on the final day and people descended on the P. Saravanamuttu Stadium to watch a thrilling climax. The match was dominated by Amal Silva, Sri Lanka's wicketkeeper, who opened the innings with 111 and then claimed nine dismissals in the match. Rumesh Ratnayake (9 for 125) and Ashantha de Mel (5 for 127), both lively fast bowlers, were responsible for bowling out the Indians twice.

After a bright start to their Test career, Sri Lanka struggled in the late 1980s and early 1990s as a number of great players, such as Sidath Wettimuny, Roy Dias, Duleep Mendis, Rumesh Ratnayake and Ashantha de Mel, retired. The new side was built around Arjuna Ranatunga and Aravinda de Silva but team preparation remained unfocused and amateurish. Finally, in April 1995, Sri Lanka were able to finance full-time professional coaching. Early appointments were successful as Dav Whatmore, the director of coaching at the Victoria Cricket Association, teamed up with physiotherapist Alex Kontouri to revolutionise the national team. The World Cup win of early 1996 was the greatest triumph for Ranatunga and Whatmore.

Sri Lankan victories overseas remain elusive but the team is now travelling with greater self-belief. The sweetest triumph abroad remains their remarkable win at The Oval in 1998, a match dominated by the wizardry of Muttiah Muralitharan who claimed 16 for 220, including 9 for 65 in the second innings. The match started bizarrely with Sri Lanka choosing to bowl first on the flattest of batting pitches. England piled up 445. Sri Lanka's strategy only became evident when their batsmen cracked 591 at four runs per over with Sanath Jayasuriya slamming 213. Muralitharan then wreaked havoc on a drying surface.

Sri Lanka, indeed, became Asia's most powerful Test nation during a golden run in 2001–02 that included nine straight victories – a consecutive sequence that included wins against India, Bangladesh, Zimbabwe, West Indies and Pakistan – lifting the team to third position in the world Test rankings. Captained by Jayasuriya, the team was fuelled by the prolific wicket-taking of Muralitharan – during 12 matches in 2001 he claimed 80 wickets.

Soon after Mahela Jayawardene and Kumar Sangakkara accepted senior responsibility for the national team, they celebrated by piling up a 624-run third-wicket partnership against South Africa, the highest in Test and first-class cricket. Jayawardene went on to score 374, Sri Lanka's highest individual score and the fourth-highest among all nations.

His finest hour? Muttiah Muralitharan pictured during his match-winning second innings 9 for 65 against England at The Oval in 1998.

FIRST TEST – SRI LANKA v. PAKISTAN
26–30 March 2006 at Colombo (SSC)

SRI LANKA

	First Innings		Second Innings	
WU Tharanga	lbw b Mohammad Asif	0	c Imran Farhat b Danish Kaneria	72
ST Jayasuriya	b Umar Gul	6	c K Akmal b Mohammad Asif	13
*KC Sangakkara	b Mohammad Asif	8	c Inzamam-ul-Haq b S Malik	185
DPMD J'wardene (capt)	c K Akmal b Umar Gul	1	c Abdul Razzaq b M Asif	82
TT Samaraweera	b Mohammad Asif	4	c Imran Farhat b Shahid Afridi	64
TM Dilshan	c Younis Khan b Danish Kaneria	69	not out	8
MF Maharoof	c Younis Khan b M Asif	46	not out	5
CM Bandara	b Danish Kaneria	16		
CRD Fernando	c Inzamam-ul-Haq b D Kaneria	16		
SL Malinga	c Inzamam-ul-Haq b S Afridi	8		
M Muralitharan	not out	0		
Extras	b 4, lb 6, w 1	11	b 10, lb 6, nb 3	19
	(all out 57.5 overs)	185	(5 wkts dec 128 overs)	448

	First Innings				Second Innings			
	O	M	R	W	O	M	R	W
Mohammad Asif	16	5	41	4	23	4	71	2
Umar Gul	12	2	41	2	20	1	73	0
Abdul Razzaq	10	1	43	0	12	1	43	0
Danish Kaneria	17.5	3	44	3	36	5	138	1
Shahid Afridi	2	0	6	1	21	0	57	1
Shoaib Malik	-	-	-	-	15	2	48	1
Imran Farhat	-	-	-	-	1	0	2	0

Fall of Wickets
1-0, 2-10, 3-18, 4-26, 5-32, 6-143, 7-149, 8-162, 9-177
1-53, 2-127, 3-285, 4-429, 5-438

PAKISTAN

	First Innings		Second Innings	
Shoaib Malik	c Tharanga b Maharoof	13	not out	148
Imran Farhat	c Bandara b Malinga	69	c Jayawardene b Muralitharan	34
Younis Khan	c Sangakkara b Maharoof	0	b Muralitharan	8
Faisal Iqbal	c Maharoof b Malinga	2	lbw b Maharoof	60
Inzamam-ul-Haq (capt)	c Sangakkara b Maharoof	31	c Dilshan b Muralitharan	48
Abdul Razzaq	b Maharoof	8	not out	20
Shahid Afridi	b Muralitharan	14		
*Kamran Akmal	c Tharanga b Muralitharan	27		
Umar Gul	lbw b Muralitharan	2		
Mohammad Asif	b Malinga	0		
Danish Kaneria	not out	0		
Extras	b 1, w 1, nb 8	10	b 6, lb 7, w 1, nb 5	19
	(all out 54.4 overs)	176	(4 wkts 121 overs)	337

	First Innings				Second Innings			
	O	M	R	W	O	M	R	W
Malinga	12	3	30	3	13	3	44	0
Maharoof	15	2	52	4	23	8	70	1
Fernando	3	0	20	0	15	3	40	0
Bandara	7	1	32	0	14	4	35	0
Muralitharan	17.4	4	41	3	42	13	94	3
Jayasuriya	-	-	-	-	13	3	37	0
Dilshan	-	-	-	-	1	0	4	0

Fall of Wickets
1-25, 2-25, 3-28, 4-122, 5-127, 6-138, 7-154, 8-160, 9-172
1-59, 2-71, 3-186, 4-267

Umpires: SJ Davis (Australia) & RE Koertzen (South Africa)
Toss: Pakistan
Man of the Match: KC Sangakkara

Match drawn

SECOND TEST – SRI LANKA v. PAKISTAN
3–5 April 2006 at Kandy

SRI LANKA

	First Innings		Second Innings	
WU Tharanga	c Younis Khan b M Asif	10	b Mohammad Asif	12
ST Jayasuriya	b Mohammad Asif	14	absent hurt	
*KC Sangakkara	c Faisal Iqbal b Danish Kaneria	79	(2) b Mohammad Asif	16
DPMD J'wardene (capt)	c Imran Farhat b M Asif	4	(3) b Abdul Razzaq	15
TT Samaraweera	b Mohammad Asif	65	(4) b Mohammad Asif	4
TM Dilshan	c Kamran Akmal b D Kaneria	22	(5) c Kamran Akmal b M Asif	11
MF Maharoof	c Younis Khan b Danish Kaneria	7	(6) lbw b Mohammad Asif	1
CM Bandara	c Kamran Akmal b M Asif	43	(7) c K Akmal b Abdul Razzaq	4
KMDN Kulasekara	c Kamran Akmal b M Asif	13	(8) c Umar Gul b Abdul Razzaq	6
SL Malinga	c Abdul Razzaq b Danish Kaneria	9	(9) not out	0
M Muralitharan	not out	1	(10) c Umar Gul b Abdul Razzaq	0
Extras	lb 4, w 1, nb 2, p 5	12	lb 3, w 1	4
	(all out 91.2 overs)	279	(all out 24.5 overs)	73

	First Innings				Second Innings			
	O	M	R	W	O	M	R	W
Mohammad Asif	23	7	44	6	12	6	27	5
Umar Gul	23	3	83	0	3	0	15	0
Iftikhar Anjum	11	1	54	0	3	1	8	0
Danish Kaneria	23.2	6	53	4	-	-	-	-
Abdul Razzaq	11	1	36	0	6.5	1	20	4

Fall of Wickets
1-18, 2-27, 3-61, 4-142, 5-178, 6-193, 7-238, 8-256, 9-271
1-22, 2-40, 3-46, 4-56, 5-57, 6-65, 7-72, 8-73, 9-73

PAKISTAN

	First Innings		Second Innings	
Imran Farhat	c Jayasuriya b Kulasekara	23	c Jayawardene b Kulasekara	65
*Kamran Akmal	c Jayawardene b Muralitharan	33	c Sangakkara b Malinga	24
Younis Khan	c Samaraweera b Maharoof	35	not out	73
Mohammad Yousuf	b Muralitharan	17	not out	14
Inzamam-ul-Haq (capt)	run out	15		
Faisal Iqbal	lbw b Muralitharan	5		
Abdul Razzaq	b Muralitharan	4		
Iftikhar Anjum	not out	9		
Umar Gul	c Sangakkara b Kulasekara	4		
Mohammad Asif	run out	0		
Danish Kaneria	c Sangakkara b Muralitharan	4		
Extras	b 4, lb 9, w 1, nb 7	21	lb 3, nb 4	7
	(all out 52.4 overs)	170	(2 wkts 43.2 overs)	183

	First Innings				Second Innings			
	O	M	R	W	O	M	R	W
Malinga	6	2	19	0	6.2	0	33	1
Maharoof	14	2	54	1	10	0	52	0
Kulasekara	16	3	45	2	12	3	34	1
Muralitharan	16.4	4	39	5	13	3	46	0
Bandara	-	-	-	-	2	0	15	0

Fall of Wickets
1-57, 2-71, 3-121, 4-125, 5-140, 6-149, 7-162, 8-166, 9-166
1-38, 2-152

Umpires: SJ Davis (Australia) & DJ Harper (Australia)
Toss: Pakistan
Man of the Match: Mohammad Asif
Man of the Series: Mohammad Asif

Pakistan won by 8 wickets

SERIES AVERAGES
Sri Lanka v. Pakistan

SRI LANKA

Batting	M	Inns	NO	Runs	HS	Av	100	50	c/st
KC Sangakkara	2	4	0	288	185	72.00	1	1	5/-
TM Dilshan	2	4	1	110	69	36.66	-	1	1/-
TT Samaraweera	2	4	0	137	65	34.25	-	2	1/-
DPMD Jayawardene	2	4	0	102	82	25.50	-	1	3/-
WU Tharanga	2	4	0	94	72	23.50	-	1	2/-
CM Bandara	2	3	0	63	43	21.00	-	-	1/-
MF Maharoof	2	4	1	59	46	19.66	-	-	1/-
CRD Fernando	1	1	0	16	16	16.00	-	-	-/-
ST Jayasuriya	2	3	0	33	14	11.00	-	-	1/-
KMDN Kulasekara	1	2	0	19	13	9.50	-	-	-/-
SL Malinga	2	3	1	17	9	8.50	-	-	-/-
M Muralitharan	2	3	2	1	1*	1.00	-	-	-/-

Bowling	Overs	Mds	Runs	Wkts	Av	Best	5/inn	10m
M Muralitharan	89.2	24	220	11	20.00	5-39	1	-
KMDN Kulasekara	28	6	79	3	26.33	2-45	-	-
SL Malinga	37.2	8	126	4	31.50	3-30	-	-
MF Maharoof	62	12	228	6	38.00	4-52	-	-

Also bowled: TM Dilshan 1-0-4-0, ST Jayasuriya 13-3-37-0, CRD Fernando 18-3-60-0, CM Bandara 23- 5-82-0.

PAKISTAN

Batting	M	Inns	NO	Runs	HS	Av	100	50	c/st
Shoaib Malik	1	2	1	161	148*	161.00	1	-	-/-
Imran Farhat	2	4	0	191	69	47.75	-	2	3/-
Younis Khan	2	4	1	116	73*	38.66	-	1	4/-
Inzamam-ul-Haq	2	3	0	94	48	31.33	-	-	3/-
Mohammad Yousuf	1	2	1	31	17	31.00	-	-	-/-
Kamran Akmal	2	3	0	84	33	28.00	-	-	6/-
Faisal Iqbal	2	3	0	67	60	22.33	-	1	1/-
Abdul Razzaq	2	3	1	32	20*	16.00	-	-	2/-
Shahid Afridi	1	1	0	14	14	14.00	-	-	-/-
Danish Kaneria	2	2	1	4	4	4.00	-	-	-/-
Umar Gul	2	2	0	6	4	3.00	-	-	2/-
Mohammad Asif	2	2	0	0	0	0.00	-	-	-/-
Iftikhar Anjum	1	1	1	9	9*	-	-	-	-/-

Bowling	Overs	Mds	Runs	Wkts	Av	Best	5/inn	10m
Mohammad Asif	74	22	183	17	10.76	6-44	2	1
Danish Kaneria	77.1	14	235	8	29.37	4-53	-	-
Shahid Afridi	23	0	63	2	31.50	1-6	-	-
Abdul Razzaq	39.5	4	142	4	35.50	4-20	-	-
Shoaib Malik	15	2	48	1	48.00	1-48	-	-
Umar Gul	58	6	212	2	106.00	2-41	-	-

Also bowled: Imran Farhat 1-0-2-0, Iftikhar Anjum 14-2-62-0.

FIRST TEST – SRI LANKA v. SOUTH AFRICA
27–31 July 2006 at Colombo (SSC)

SOUTH AFRICA

	First Innings			Second Innings	
HH Gibbs	b Fernando	19		(7) c & b Muralitharan	18
AJ Hall	b Fernando	17		lbw b Muralitharan	64
JA Rudolph	c J'wardene HAPW b Maharoof	29		(1) c Kapugedera b Fernando	90
HM Amla	st J'wardene HAPW b Murali	19		(3) lbw b Fernando	2
AG Prince (capt)	c J'wardene HAPW b Maharoof	1		(4) c J'wardene DPMD b Murali	61
AB de Villiers	c Kapugedera b Muralitharan	65		(5) lbw b Muralitharan	24
*MV Boucher	c Jayasuriya b Muralitharan	5		(6) c & b Jayasuriya	85
N Boje	lbw b Muralitharan	5		not out	33
A Nel	lbw b Fernando	0		b Muralitharan	0
DW Steyn	b Fernando	0		b Muralitharan	4
M Ntini	not out	0		b Malinga	16
Extras	b 4, lb 6	10		b 11, lb 4, w 2, nb 20	37
	(all out 50.2 overs)	169		(all out 157.2 overs)	434

	First Innings				Second Innings			
	O	M	R	W	O	M	R	W
Malinga	10	2	38	0	16.2	0	85	1
Maharoof	9	1	32	2	15	3	48	0
Fernando	13	2	48	4	24	6	69	2
Muralitharan	18.2	6	41	4	64	11	131	6
Dilshan	-	-	-	-	4	1	10	0
Jayasuriya	-	-	-	-	34	8	76	1

Fall of Wickets
1-32, 2-45, 3-78, 4-80, 5-112, 6-128, 7-148, 8-151, 9-151
1-165, 2-171, 3-185, 4-234, 5-312, 6-350, 7-401, 8-404, 9-412

SRI LANKA

	First Innings	
WU Tharanga	c Boucher b Steyn	7
ST Jayasuriya	lbw b Steyn	4
KC Sangakkara	c Boucher b Hall	287
DPMD J'wardene (capt)	b Nel	374
TM Dilshan	lbw b Steyn	45
CK Kapugedera	not out	1
*HAPW Jayawardene		
MF Maharoof		
SL Malinga		
CRD Fernando		
M Muralitharan		
Extras	b 16, lb 6, w 8, nb 8	38
	(5 wkts dec 185.1 overs)	756

	First Innings				Second Innings			
	O	M	R	W	O	M	R	W
Ntini	31	3	97	0	-	-	-	-
Steyn	26	1	129	3	-	-	-	-
Nel	25.1	2	114	1	-	-	-	-
Hall	25	2	99	1	-	-	-	-
Boje	65	5	221	0	-	-	-	-
Rudolph	7	0	45	0	-	-	-	-
Prince	2	0	7	0	-	-	-	-
de Villiers	4	0	22	0	-	-	-	-

Fall of Wickets
1-6, 2-14, 3-638, 4-751, 5-756

Umpires: MR Benson (England) & BF Bowden (New Zealand)
Toss: South Africa
Man of the Match: DPMD Jayawardene

Sri Lanka won by an innings and 153 runs

SECOND TEST – SRI LANKA v. SOUTH AFRICA
4–8 August 2006 at Colombo (PSS)

SOUTH AFRICA

	First Innings		Second Innings	
HH Gibbs	lbw b Vaas	0	c Jayasuriya b Muralitharan	92
AJ Hall	c Dilshan b Malinga	0	c J'wardene HAPW b Maharoof	32
HM Amla	lbw b Muralitharan	40	(4) run out	8
JA Rudolph	b Malinga	13	(3) run out	15
AG Prince (capt)	c J'wardene HAPW b Murali	86	c & b Muralitharan	17
AB de Villiers	c J'wardene HAPW b Maharoof	95	c Dilshan b Muralitharan	33
*MV Boucher	b Muralitharan	32	c Dilshan b Muralitharan	65
SM Pollock	not out	57	c Tharanga b Muralitharan	14
N Boje	c Sangakkara b Malinga	11	c J'wardene HAPW b Murali	15
DW Steyn	c Jayasuriya b Muralitharan	6	lbw b Muralitharan	0
M Ntini	c Malinga b Muralitharan	13	not out	5
Extras	w 1, nb 7	8	b 9, lb 4, w 1, nb 1	15
	(all out 89.5 overs)	361	(all out 107.5 overs)	311

	First Innings				Second Innings			
	O	M	R	W	O	M	R	W
Vaas	18	4	71	1	19	4	53	0
Malinga	18	4	81	3	12	1	55	0
Muralitharan	33.5	2	128	5	46.5	12	97	7
Maharoof	15	2	52	1	21	3	53	1
Jayasuriya	5	0	29	0	9	0	40	0

Fall of Wickets
1-0, 2-4, 3-31, 4-70, 5-231, 6-256, 7-273, 8-307, 9-327
1-76, 2-119, 3-131, 4-161, 5-206, 6-207, 7-235, 8-280, 9-282

SRI LANKA

	First Innings		Second Innings	
WU Tharanga	c Boje b Ntini	2	c Gibbs b Ntini	0
ST Jayasuriya	c Gibbs b Ntini	47	c Amla b Boje	73
KC Sangakkara	c Amla b Ntini	14	c Amla b Pollock	39
DPMD J'wardene (capt)	c Boucher b Steyn	13	c Gibbs b Boje	123
TM Dilshan	b Ntini	4	c Gibbs b Boje	18
CK Kapugedera	b Boje	63	c de Villiers b Boje	13
*HAPW Jayawardene	b Steyn	42	lbw b Hall	30
MF Maharoof	b Steyn	56	not out	29
WPUJC Vaas	c Boucher b Steyn	64	c de Villiers b Hall	4
SL Malinga	not out	8	(11) not out	1
M Muralitharan	c Hall b Steyn	0	(10) b Hall	2
Extras	lb 1, w 2, nb 5	8	b 4, lb 8, w 4, nb 4	20
	(all out 85.1 overs)	321	(9 wkts 113.3 overs)	352

	First Innings				Second Innings			
	O	M	R	W	O	M	R	W
Ntini	21	3	84	4	7.2	2	13	1
Steyn	13.1	1	82	5	22.4	2	81	0
Pollock	16	4	52	0	19	2	60	1
Hall	15	7	31	0	25	3	75	3
Boje	20	6	71	1	39.3	11	111	4

Fall of Wickets
1-16, 2-43, 3-74, 4-85, 5-86, 6-191, 7-191, 8-308, 9-317
1-12, 2-94, 3-121, 4-164, 5-201, 6-279, 7-341, 8-348, 9-350

Umpires: BF Bowden (New Zealand) & Aleem Dar (Pakistan)
Toss: South Africa
Man of the Match: DPMD Jayawardene
Man of the Series: M Muralitharan

Sri Lanka won by 1 wicket

SERIES AVERAGES
Sri Lanka v. South Africa

SRI LANKA

Batting	M	Inns	NO	Runs	HS	Av	100	50	c/st
DPMD Jayawardene	2	3	0	510	374	170.00	2	–	1/–
KC Sangakkara	2	3	0	340	287	113.33	1	–	1/–
MF Maharoof	2	2	1	85	56	85.00	–	1	–/–
ST Jayasuriya	2	3	0	124	73	41.33	–	1	4/–
CK Kapugedera	2	3	1	77	63	38.50	–	1	2/–
HAPW Jayawardene	2	2	0	72	42	36.00	–	–	6/1
WPUJC Vaas	1	2	0	68	64	34.00	–	1	–/–
TM Dilshan	2	3	0	67	45	22.33	–	–	3/–
WU Tharanga	2	3	0	9	7	3.00	–	–	1/–
M Muralitharan	2	2	0	2	2	1.00	–	–	2/–
SL Malinga	2	2	2	9	8*	–	–	–	1/–
CRD Fernando	1	0	0	0	0	–	–	–	–/–

Bowling	Overs	Mds	Runs	Wkts	Av	Best	5/inn	10m
M Muralitharan	163	31	397	22	18.04	7-97	3	2
CRD Fernando	37	8	117	6	19.50	4-48	–	–
MF Maharoof	60	9	185	4	46.25	2-32	–	–
SL Malinga	56.2	7	259	4	64.75	3-81	–	–
WPUJC Vaas	37	8	124	1	124.00	1-71	–	–
ST Jayasuriya	48	8	145	1	145.00	1-76	–	–

Also bowled: TM Dilshan 4-1-10-0.

SOUTH AFRICA

Batting	M	Inns	NO	Runs	HS	Av	100	50	c/st
SM Pollock	1	2	1	71	57*	71.00	–	1	–/–
AB de Villiers	2	4	0	217	95	54.25	–	2	2/–
MV Boucher	2	4	0	186	85	46.50	–	2	4/–
AG Prince	2	4	0	165	86	41.25	–	2	–/–
JA Rudolph	2	4	0	147	90	36.75	–	1	–/–
HH Gibbs	2	4	0	129	92	32.25	–	1	4/–
AJ Hall	2	4	0	113	64	28.25	–	1	1/–
N Boje	2	4	1	64	33*	21.33	–	–	1/–
HM Amla	2	4	0	69	40	17.25	–	–	3/–
M Ntini	2	4	2	34	16	17.00	–	–	–/–
DW Steyn	2	4	0	10	6	2.50	–	–	–/–
A Nel	1	2	0	0	0	0.00	–	–	–/–

Bowling	Overs	Mds	Runs	Wkts	Av	Best	5/inn	10m
DW Steyn	61.5	4	292	8	36.50	5-82	1	–
M Ntini	59.2	4	194	5	38.80	4-84	–	–
AJ Hall	65	12	205	4	51.25	3-75	–	–
N Boje	124.3	22	403	5	80.60	4-111	–	–
SM Pollock	35	6	112	1	112.00	1-60	–	–
A Nel	25.1	2	114	1	114.00	1-114	–	–

Also bowled: AG Prince 2-0-7-0, AB de Villiers 4-0-22-0, JA Rudolph 7-0-45-0.

WEST INDIES

WEST INDIES REPORT
By Tony Cozier

At the height of another of its perennial predicaments, West Indies cricket was thrown into a state of excitement, expectation and eventual confrontation by its first experience of the newest, shortest form of the game that had already proved its popularity elsewhere. The contrast between the inauguration and success of the privately run Stanford 20/20 Tournament, conceived and financed by Antigua-based American tycoon Allen Stanford, and the travails of the West Indies Cricket Board (WICB) was stark, and the coincidence ironic. In the week in July that its auditors reported to the WICB that its accumulated debt has reached US$34.9 million, Stanford's event, the richest tournament the game has ever known, anywhere, was in full swing a few miles away from the WICB headquarters in Antigua.

Three months earlier, both captain Shivnarine Chanderpaul and WICB chief executive Roger Braithwaite had resigned. While, for the third time during his turbulent career, Brian Lara was appointed skipper, Braithwaite's post stayed vacant. In addition, the WICB and the West Indies Players

Association (WIPA) remained at loggerheads over terms for retainer contracts for the leading players. Chanderpaul, thrust into a position in which he was clearly uncomfortable a year earlier, quit after heavy defeats in successive series in Australia and New Zealand. Hope that Lara would, at last, inspire a revival in his final chance as leader were prompted by immediate victories over depleted Zimbabwe, 5-0, and India, 4-1, in the two back-to-back series of one-day internationals at home but such optimism was soon tempered in the Tests against the Indians who secured their second triumph in nine series in the Caribbean, and the first since 1976, with the only outright result in four in the final match at Sabina Park.

West Indian disappointment was compounded by Lara's persistent, petulant criticism of selectors and pitches, comments for such he was obliged by the WICB to publicly apologise. The dreadful record of the West Indies A team in late summer in England only heightened anxiety for the future.

It was against this background that Stanford, a big, brash Texan who has based part of his global banking and investment operations, along with two regional airlines, in Antigua for more than two decades, launched his event. It carried team and individual prize money, along with grants to participating boards, that totalled US$28 million, a sum that would have instantly erased the WICB's deficit. Stanford bumped it up by several millions through promotion and marketing and with the stunning announcement of a one-off, US$5 million, winner-take-all match between his so-called Superstars and South Africa.

However, the latter proposal eventually ended in cancellation and led to a heated exchange between him and WICB president Ken Gordon and a fall-out between Clive Lloyd and Michael Holding, two icons of a glorious era, after Lloyd quit Stanford's group and Holding resigned from the WICB's cricket committee. But the 20/20 tournament, contested on the purpose-built ground that is part of Stanford's financial complex adjacent to Antigua's international airport, involved 19 territories, more than had ever

Eye on the ball: Brian Lara (left) and Shivnarine Chanderpaul add more runs to the West Indies cause.

competed in a domestic event. Among them were the Bahamas, Bermuda, the US and British Virgin Islands and the Cayman Islands, all previously outside the mainstream. Stanford arranged for live television coverage throughout the Caribbean and sold rights for the final to Sky Sports in Britain. Other international networks carried packaged highlights. It was the first tournament in the Caribbean played under lights and boisterous crowds, with numerous women and children among the many new fans, filled the ground to its 5,000 capacity most nights. West Indies cricket had never known anything like it.

Guyana, led by Rajneesh Saran, beat Trinidad and Tobago in a pulsating final when the left-hander Narsingh Deonarine hoisted the penultimate ball for six over midwicket. It earned their players the top prize of US$1 million, with an additional US$200,000 for the Guyana Board. The Trinidad and Tobago team pocketed US$500,000 and their Board US$100,000 as runners-up. The previous October, all Guyana received for beating Barbados in the WICB's annual 50-overs-an-innings final was the KFC Cup. Since it was sponsored for the first time, by Kentucky Fried Chicken, a few buckets of spiced wings and drumsticks might have been added for good measure.

Comparisons between Stanford and Kerry Packer, the similarly brazen Australian media mogul who rocked the game with his World Series Cricket three decades earlier, were inevitable. While Packer's purpose to gain television rights was clear, Stanford's was less so. He simply stated that his aim was for the tournament to be 'a catalyst for a resurgence of the love for the game, and that it will signal a return to the glory days'. He employed 14 of the finest West Indies players of various generations, from the 81-year-old Sir Everton Weekes to the 37-year-old Ian Bishop, as his board of directors, a shrewd PR move, and assigned each to a competing team.

But from the start, there were misgivings over the Texan's involvement. In a statement, the six territorial boards worried that it might 'create duplication and division'. Stanford sought to assuage them with a pledge that his plans would 'not overshadow or conflict with any of the WICB's existing programmes'. His tournament was placed at the start of the hurricane season to avoid a clash with the official season and players of the official 'A' team tour of England were declared ineligible.

But the relationship between the two was always tenuous and the fall-out came over the clash of dates of Stanford's $5 million South Africa match, set for 10 November in Antigua, and the First Test on the official West Indies tour of Pakistan, set to start on

Jerome Taylor (right) leaps high in dramatic celebration as he and fellow fast bowler Corey Collymore greet the dismissal of India's Munaf Patel in the Jamaica Test.

11 November. Although Stanford produced a letter from ICC's cricket manager, Clive Hitchcock, to then WICB chief executive Braithwaite, dated 22 January, approving dates for the planned encounter as 10, 11 and 12 November, the WICB said it could not get the Pakistan Board to agree to altering its dates.

The ramifications were immediate. Lloyd, the former revered captain who had been elected to the WICB's Board and the head of its cricket committee a few weeks earlier, quit Stanford's Board because of his 'concerns for West Indies cricket'. Holding, who was not on Stanford's team, resigned from the WICB's cricket committee following disagreements with Gordon and Lloyd over the Pakistan tour issue. The conflict placed Stanford's future involvement in West Indies cricket in understandable doubt. Whatever his motives, he matched his talk with his money and it would be a significant financial loss to a sport so desperately short of cash that the WICB was obliged to close its academy in 2005 and severely cut costs, including trimming its first-class competition, the Carib Beer Cup, by half.

25 years OF *WEST INDIES*

By Tony Cozier

The statistics are staggering but they accurately reflect one of international sport's most dramatic declines. They also explain the emotional upheaval that all who have followed West Indies cricket over the past quarter-century have had to endure. In the 15 years from 1980 to 1995, when Australia handed them their first defeat in 27 series, the West Indies won 59 and lost only 15 of their 106 Tests. In the decade that has followed, the figures are almost identically reversed – 59 defeats against 29 victories in 114 matches.

In the previous period, there were two 5-0 clean sweeps over England, the so-called 'blackwashes'. The indignity has been returned since, not only by England, but also by Australia, South Africa, Pakistan and Sri Lanka as well. In the first period, there was only one total under 100. In the second, there have been seven. And so on.

If the record in the shorter game was somewhat less imposing, for the teams triumphantly led by Clive Lloyd and Viv Richards, there was no doubt who then ruled the cricket roost. They were heady days that provided memories to last a lifetime, if not sufficient to erase the disappointments that followed. Yet, in good times and bad, several of the finest players the game has known have been West Indian, as have the most enduring records. There was no more self-assured or intimidating batsman in his time than Richards, no more durable or reliable opening pair than Gordon Greenidge and Desmond Haynes who went in first in 89 Tests, no more revered captain or explosive strokemaker than Lloyd.

No team in history has matched the firepower Lloyd had at his disposal to destroy opposition batting. Andy Roberts, Michael Holding, Joel Garner, Colin Croft and Malcolm Marshall formed a lethal combination, all fast and clinical in execution, yet each largely different in physique and method. Marshall ended with 376 wickets, Holding, Garner and Roberts with more than 200 each. Croft's 125 came in a career shortened by injury to 27 Tests.

Lloyd played the last of his 110 Tests in 1985. Holding and Garner retired two years later. Richards, Greenidge, Marshall and the exceptional wicketkeeper/batsman Jeffrey Dujon all exited together in 1991. Such a transition inevitably led to the subsequent nosedive, gradual at first but gathering pace as each succeeding defeat eroded confidence.

It is astounding that, in such troubled times, three individuals rose above the rubble to place their names alongside the all-time greats. Brian Lara's incredible record of high-scoring and the wicket-taking consistency of the fast-bowling association of Curtly Ambrose and Courtney

Walsh counterbalanced the gloom and doom that enveloped the West Indies in recent hard times.

If Lara, the sublime left-hander, was unable to inspire a revival in his three stints as captain, his record scores of 375 in 1994 and 400 not out ten years later and a plethora of other rapturous innings have made him Test cricket's leading scorer. He alone has kept the batting torch burning that was initially lit by George Headley and handed down through the generations to the Three Ws, Garry Sobers and Richards.

And the indefatigable Walsh, the first bowler to 500 Test wickets, and Ambrose, his uncompromising accomplice with 405 wickets at under 21 runs apiece, maintained the West Indies' legacy of fast bowling first established more than 50 years earlier by Learie Constantine, George Francis, George John and Manny Martindale.

Walsh and Ambrose have now taken their leave. Lara is 37 and strongly hinting at a farewell next year. Their successors are not readily identifiable. The immediate future, sadly, is no brighter than the present.

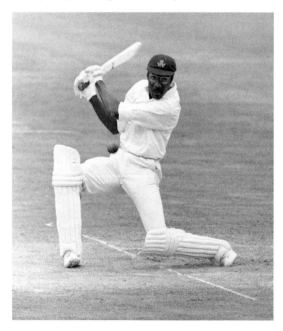

Clive Lloyd played 110 Tests for West Indies, and captained them in 74. Of those Tests under his command, 36 were won and a mere 12 lost.

As Carib is the beer of Trinidad, it was appropriate that the 2006 tournament should be dominated by Trinidad and Tobago which won both the Cup, determined by the round-robin matches between the six teams, and the Challenge, contested on a knockout basis between the top four teams. It ended a 21-year wait for the Trinidadians whose previous success was in 1985 in what was then the Shell Shield. Since then, even Lara had been unable to inspire them to a repeat. This season, however, they were skilfully led by Daren Ganga who credited a strong team spirit for the double triumph. They went into their last match in the round-robin, away to traditional powerhouse Barbados, needing outright victory to take the Cup – and achieved it by the indisputable margin of 264 runs. They then reversed their only first-round loss, by beating the Windward Islands in the Challenge semi-final by 391 runs, and, after Barbados pipped Guyana in the other semi, outplayed them again in the final by 125 runs.

The previous season, Barbados had plunged from top in both competitions to bottom. It was an unenviable trick now duplicated by Jamaica who went down in three of their five matches (by 282 runs to Trinidad and Tobago). Their batting was the downfall. There was not a single century-maker in their five matches, an embarrassment shared by the Windward Islands and Leeward Islands. It was a general problem. Undermined by dubious pitches at inadequate grounds, batsmen struggled so that there were only 15 hundreds in the 17 matches. Barbados's captain, the left-hander Ryan Hinds, who was the season's leading scorer with 720 runs at 65.45, compiled two centuries in the same match, 168 and 156 against the Leewards. Bowlers consequently prospered, especially spinners. Left-arm chinaman specialist Dave Mohammed's 45 wickets at 14.57 runs each for Trinidad and Tobago and Windward Islands' captain Rawl Lewis's 30 at 18.33 with his leg spin earned them both Test recalls.

It was much the same in the 50-over competition, the KFC Cup. The 17 matches yielded only four hundreds, all for Guyana. Sarwan counted three, with the other by the left-handed opener Sewnarine Chattergoon coming in their victory over Barbados in the final in Georgetown.

ENGLAND A IN WEST INDIES
By Pat Gibson

They say that winning is all that matters in sport these days but the England A tour of the West Indies proved otherwise. They were beaten in both the four-day and one-day series, yet by the end of the summer 12 of the 14 players in the original squad, plus one of the four replacements, had gone on to play Test or one-day international cricket.

As early as lunchtime on the first day of the first four-day game in Antigua, Alastair Cook and James Anderson had turned their backs on the waving palms of the Caribbean and were heading for the heat and dust of India to reinforce the Test team. Owais Shah followed them two days later and, within hours of the limited-overs series being completed in Barbados, Vikram Solanki, Kabir Ali, Gareth Batty and Sajid Mahmood were dashing off to the airport to join the one-day squad. Chris Read, who had to return home after the second four-day match because his house had been broken into for the second time in 18 months, regained his rightful place as England's wicketkeeper-batsman in the series against Pakistan, and Ed Joyce, Jamie Dalrymple, Michael Yardy, Rikki Clarke and Stuart Broad were all called up for the one-day side.

Since the main purpose of the A team is to supply players to the senior sides as and when they are required, the tour could therefore be considered a conspicuous success even though the results against their West Indies counterparts suggested that they still had a lot to learn.

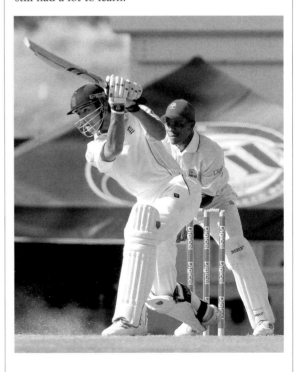

England A captain Vikram Solanki led his team well despite constant disruption caused by Test and one-day international call-ups.

England A celebrate a wicket taken by Rikki Clarke (behind Ravi Bopara on the left).

There was no doubt that the early disruption took its toll in the first four-day game after Vikram Solanki, the captain, Read and Batty had played well to put England A in a commanding position. They eventually set West Indies A 365 to win and Marlon Samuels and Sylvester Joseph put on 194 for the fourth wicket before Carlton Baugh and Jermaine Lawson kept their nerve to clinch a one-wicket win.

Solanki did his best with his depleted resources to level the series in the second game in St Lucia but again he was to be thwarted by Joseph, his opposite number. A disciplined Solanki and a bristling Read both scored hundreds, and Broad took a wicket with his first ball at this level, but Joseph and Sewnarine Chattergoon put on 162 for the fourth wicket to ensure the match was drawn.

The one-day series began with the first floodlit game ever to be staged in the Caribbean but only Joyce provided any illumination for England A, volunteering to keep wicket after Read had gone home and scoring the first of three successive fifties as an opening batsman. Clarke provided a tantalising glimpse of his potential by coming up with a match-winning all-round performance in the second game and, after West Indies A had gone ahead again in Barbados, Dalrymple showed his character by helping Solanki to square the series once more. So it

was all to play for in the last match and England A were found wanting as Baugh struck 71 off 73 balls to take West Indies A to a four-wicket victory.

It was a disappointing finale for Peter Moores, the ECB academy director and A team coach, and David Parsons, England's first spin-bowling coach, who was his assistant, but Solanki put the tour in perspective. 'We came here to try to win both the four-day and the one-day series and unfortunately we did neither, but hopefully all the players have learnt a lot from the trip,' he said. 'To compete as we did with all the chopping and changing that went on is testimony to the players' character.'

Pat Gibson covered the England A tour of the West Indies for The Times.

ONE-DAY INTERNATIONALS
v. Zimbabwe

Match One
29 April 2006 at St John's
Zimbabwe 151 for 9 (50 overs) (CJ Chibhabha 55)
West Indies 154 for 5 (38.2 overs)
West Indies won by 5 wickets

Match Two
30 April 2006 at St John's
West Indies 242 for 9 (50 overs) (RR Sarwan 55)
Zimbabwe 144 all out (46.2 overs) (CJ Chibhabha 67, JE Taylor 4 for 24)
West Indies won by 98 runs

Match Three
6 May 2006 at Guyana
West Indies v. **Zimbabwe**
Match abandoned – no result

Match Four
7 May 2006 at Guyana
West Indies 333 for 6 (50 overs) (S Chanderpaul 93, RS Morton 79, BC Lara 56)
Zimbabwe 251 for 7 (50 overs) (E Chigumbura 60, V Sibanda 52)
West Indies won by 82 runs

Match Five
10 May 2006 at Gros Islet
Zimbabwe 152 all out (49.2 overs)
West Indies 156 for 0 (27.4 overs) (CH Gayle 95*, S Chattergoon 54*)
West Indies won by 10 wickets

Match Six

13 May 2006 at Port of Spain
West Indies 263 for 6 (50 overs) (RS Morton 109, RR Sarwan 54, S Chanderpaul 51*)
Zimbabwe 72 for 2 (12.1 overs)
Match abandoned - no result

Match Seven

14 May 2006 at Port of Spain
West Indies 266 for 8 (50 overs) (RR Sarwan 91)
Zimbabwe 162 all out (49 overs) (DR Smith 4 for 29)
West Indies won by 104 runs

West Indies won the series 5–0

ONE-DAY INTERNATIONALS
v. India

Match One

18 May 2006 at Kingston
West Indies 251 for 6 (45 overs) (CH Gayle 123)
India 254 for 5 (44.5 overs) (R Dravid 105, M Kaif 66*)
India won by 5 wickets

Match Two

20 May 2006 at Kingston
West Indies 198 for 9 (50 overs) (RR Sarwan 98*)
India 197 all out (49.4 overs) (Yuvraj Singh 93)
West Indies won by 1 run

Match Three

23 May 2006 at St Kitts
India 245 for 9 (50 overs) (V Sehwag 97, M Kaif 61)
West Indies 248 for 6 (49.5 overs) (RR Sarwan 115*, S Chanderpaul 58)
West Indies won by 4 wickets

Match Four

26 May 2006 at Port of Spain
India 217 for 7 (50 overs)
(M Kaif 62, Yuvraj Singh 52)
West Indies 218 for 4 (44 overs) (BC Lara 69, DJJ Bravo 61*)
West Indies won by 6 wickets

Match Five

28 May 2006 at Port of Spain
West Indies 255 for 6 (50 overs) (DJJ Bravo 62*, RR Sarwan 52, CH Gayle 51)
India 236 all out (48 overs) (V Sehwag 95)
West Indies won by 19 runs

West Indies won the series 4–1

FIRST TEST – WEST INDIES v. INDIA
2–6 June 2006 at St John's

INDIA

	First Innings		Second Innings	
W Jaffer	c Ramdin b Edwards	1	b Bradshaw	212
V Sehwag	c Lara b Collymore	36	c Gayle b Collymore	41
VVS Laxman	c Ramdin b Bravo	29	c Bradshaw b Mohammed	31
R Dravid (capt)	c Lara b Collymore	49	c Bradshaw b Mohammed	62
Yuvraj Singh	b Mohammed	23	c Chanderpaul b Gayle	39
M Kaif	c Ramdin b Bravo	13	not out	47
*MS Dhoni	c Lara b Collymore	19	c Ganga b Mohammed	69
A Kumble	b Bravo	21		
S Sreesanth	not out	29		
VR Singh	c Sarwan b Bravo	2		
MM Patel	b Edwards	0		
Extras	lb 8, w 2, nb 9	19	lb 5, w 6, nb 9	20
	(all out 92.5 overs)	241	(6 wkts dec 150.5 overs)	521

	First Innings				Second Innings			
	O	M	R	W	O	M	R	W
Edwards	18.5	3	53	2	5.4	2	16	0
Bradshaw	24	3	83	0	40	9	108	1
Collymore	17	7	27	3	23	8	50	1
Gayle	4	0	6	0	22	6	67	1
Bravo	22	9	40	4	26.2	4	98	0
Mohammed	7	1	24	1	29.5	5	162	3
Sarwan	-	-	-	-	4	0	15	0

Fall of Wickets
1-10, 2-51, 3-72, 4-126, 5-155, 6-179, 7-180, 8-227, 9-231
1-72, 2-147, 3-350, 4-375, 5-419, 6-521

WEST INDIES

	First Innings		Second Innings	
CH Gayle	c Dravid b Kumble	72	lbw b Kumble	69
D Ganga	lbw b Patel	9	c Yuvraj Singh b Kumble	36
RR Sarwan	lbw b Kumble	58	c Kumble b Sreesanth	1
BC Lara (capt)	c Yuvraj Singh b Patel	18	lbw b Sreesanth	0
S Chanderpaul	c Dhoni b Sehwag	24	c Dravid b Kumble	62
DJJ Bravo	st Dhoni b Sehwag	68	c Dhoni b Sehwag	28
*D Ramdin	c Dhoni b Patel	26	c Dravid b Sehwag	8
IDR Bradshaw	c Yuvraj Singh b Singh	33	c Dhoni b Patel	10
D Mohammed	not out	19	b Mohammed	52
FH Edwards	c Dhoni b Singh	4	not out	1
CD Collymore	lbw b Kumble	0	not out	1
Extras	b 2, lb 14, w 2, nb 22	40	b 5, lb 8, nb 17	30
	(all out 98.3 overs)	371	(9 wkts 95 overs)	298

	First Innings				Second Innings			
	O	M	R	W	O	M	R	W
Sreesanth	16	1	96	0	19	10	49	2
Patel	28	7	80	3	20	4	55	1
Singh	15	1	61	2	11	3	35	0
Kumble	27.3	6	86	3	34	8	107	4
Sehwag	12	2	32	2	11	2	39	2

Fall of Wickets
1-18, 2-137, 3-159, 4-182, 5-255, 6-282, 7-331, 8-359, 9-370
1-67, 2-68, 3-72, 4-171, 5-202, 6-220, 7-226, 8-277, 9-297

Umpires: Asad Rauf (Pakistan) & SJA Taufel (Australia)
Toss: India
Debut: VR Singh
Man of the Match: W Jaffer

Match drawn

SECOND TEST – WEST INDIES v. INDIA
10–14 June 2006 at Gros Islet

INDIA

	First Innings		
W Jaffer	c Bravo b Collins	43	
V Sehwag	c & b Collins	180	
VVS Laxman	c Ramdin b Collins	0	
R Dravid (capt)	c Lara b Sarwan	146	
Yuvraj Singh	b Collins	2	
M Kaif	not out	148	
*MS Dhoni	c Ganga b Bradshaw	9	
IK Pathan	c Ganga b Gayle	19	
A Kumble	b Taylor	14	
MM Patel			
VR Singh			
Extras	b 4, lb 7, w 4, nb 12	27	
	(8 wkts dec 148.2 overs)	**588**	

	First Innings			
	O	M	R	W
Collins	28	5	116	4
Taylor	24.2	4	88	1
Bravo	10	0	66	0
Collymore	21	1	92	0
Bradshaw	26	6	80	1
Sarwan	18	1	83	1
Gayle	21	6	52	1

Fall of Wickets
1-159, 2-161, 3-300, 4-306, 5-485, 6-517, 7-555, 8-588

WEST INDIES

	First Innings		Second Innings	
CH Gayle	c Dhoni b Kumble	46	c Dhoni b Pathan	2
D Ganga	lbw b Patel	16	b Kumble	26
RR Sarwan	lbw b Patel	0	(4) c Dhoni b Patel	1
BC Lara (capt)	c Dhoni b Kumble	7	(3) lbw b Sehwag	120
S Chanderpaul	lbw b Pathan	30	c Pathan b Kumble	54
DJJ Bravo	c Dravid b Kumble	25	c Yuvraj Singh b Kumble	47
*D Ramdin	c Dhoni b Patel	30	not out	17
IDR Bradshaw	c & b Sehwag	20	lbw b Patel	3
JE Taylor	c Kaif b Sehwag	23	not out	0
PT Collins	c Dravid b Sehwag	0		
CD Collymore	not out	2		
Extras	b 5, lb 2, nb 9	16	lb 5, nb 14, p 5	24
	(all out 85.1 overs)	215	(7 wkts 119 overs)	294

	First Innings				Second Innings			
	O	M	R	W	O	M	R	W
Pathan	11	2	43	1	15	1	50	1
Patel	17	4	51	3	21	7	49	2
Kumble	30	12	57	3	42	11	98	3
Singh	10	3	23	0	11	0	39	0
Sehwag	16.1	5	33	3	30	9	48	1
Yuvraj Singh	1	0	1	0	-	-	-	-

Fall of Wickets
1-36, 2-36, 3-55, 4-106, 5-106, 6-167, 7-178, 8-209, 9-210
1-2, 2-51, 3-52, 4-181, 5-252, 6-277, 7-291

Umpires: Asad Rauf (Pakistan) & SJA Taufel (Australia)
Toss: India
Man of the Match: V Sehwag

Match drawn

THIRD TEST – WEST INDIES v. INDIA
22–26 June 2006 at St Kitts

WEST INDIES

	First Innings		Second Innings	
CH Gayle	b Patel	83	c Dhoni b Sreesanth	3
D Ganga	b Patel	135	not out	66
RR Sarwan	lbw b Sreesanth	116	c Dravid b Sreesanth	23
BC Lara (capt)	lbw b Patel	10	st Dhoni b Kumble	19
S Chanderpaul	not out	97	c & b Kumble	11
DJJ Bravo	c Dhoni b Harbhajan Singh	21	c Sreesanth b Kumble	9
MN Samuels	c Harbhajan Singh b Sehwag	87	st Dhoni b Harbhajan Singh	20
*D Ramdin	c Jaffer b Harbhajan Singh	3	not out	8
JE Taylor	c Yuvraj Singh b Harbhajan Singh	2		
PT Collins	c Dravid b Harbhajan Singh	1		
CD Collymore	b Harbhajan Singh	0		
Extras	lb 14, w 1, nb 11	26	b 4, lb 7, w 1, nb 1	13
	(all out 170 overs)	581	(6 wkts dec 32 overs)	172

	First Innings				Second Innings			
	O	M	R	W	O	M	R	W
Patel	32	5	134	3	7	0	43	0
Sreesanth	31	8	99	1	6	1	19	2
Kumble	47	8	140	0	12	0	60	3
Harbhajan Singh	44	6	147	5	7	0	39	1
Sehwag	16	3	47	1	-	-	-	-

Fall of Wickets
1-143, 2-346, 3-356, 4-371, 5-406, 6-562, 7-570, 8-576, 9-581
1-3, 2-46, 3-81, 4-102, 5-120, 6-152

INDIA

	First Innings		Second Innings	
W Jaffer	c Lara b Bravo	60	c Gayle b Collins	54
V Sehwag	c Lara b Collymore	31	lbw b Collymore	65
VVS Laxman	c Ramdin b Collins	100	c Lara b Collins	63
R Dravid (capt)	lbw b Taylor	22	not out	68
Yuvraj Singh	c Ramdin b Taylor	0	(6) not out	8
M Kaif	b Taylor	0		
*MS Dhoni	lbw b Collymore	29	(5) c Gayle b Taylor	20
A Kumble	c Collins b Collymore	43		
Harbhajan Singh	not out	38		
S Sreesanth	c Lara b Collins	0		
MM Patel	c Ganga b Bravo	13		
Extras	b 8, lb 5, nb 13	26	b 9, lb 8, w 1, nb 2	20
	(all out 107 overs)	362	(4 wkts 85 overs)	298

	First Innings				Second Innings			
	O	M	R	W	O	M	R	W
Taylor	26	3	118	3	11	1	40	1
Collins	29.3	4	117	2	18	1	66	2
Collymore	25	4	63	3	15	3	40	1
Bravo	17.3	6	38	2	7	1	36	0
Gayle	2	0	3	0	14	2	31	0
Samuels	7	1	10	0	20	3	68	0

Fall of Wickets
1-61, 2-124, 3-157, 4-159, 5-159, 6-220, 7-297, 8-311, 9-315
1-109, 2-143, 3-243, 4-273

Umpires: BG Jerling (South Africa) & RE Koertzen (South Africa)
Toss: West Indies
Man of the Match: D Ganga

Match drawn

FOURTH TEST – WEST INDIES v. INDIA
30 June – 2 July 2006 at Kingston

INDIA

	First Innings		Second Innings	
W Jaffer	b Taylor	1	c sub b Taylor	1
V Sehwag	c Sarwan b Collins	0	lbw b Taylor	4
VVS Laxman	c sub b Bravo	18	c Lara b Collymore	16
R Dravid (capt)	c Ramdin b Collymore	81	b Collymore	68
Yuvraj Singh	lbw b Taylor	19	c Lara b Collymore	13
M Kaif	c Lara b Taylor	13	b Collins	6
*MS Dhoni	c Bravo b Collymore	3	b Taylor	19
A Kumble	b Bravo	45	c Bravo b Collymore	10
Harbhajan Singh	not out	9	c Lara b Collymore	9
S Sreesanth	b Taylor	0	c Lara b Taylor	16
MM Patel	c Ramdin b Taylor	0	not out	0
Extras	b 2, lb 2, w 5, nb 2	11	b 4, lb 3, w 1, nb 1	9
	(all out 87.4 overs)	200	(all out 65.1 overs)	171

	First Innings				Second Innings			
	O	M	R	W	O	M	R	W
Collins	19	7	34	1	22	8	61	1
Taylor	18.4	4	50	5	15	4	45	4
Bravo	24	3	68	2	4	1	10	0
Collymore	19	11	17	2	24.1	9	48	5
Chanderpaul	5	0	17	0	–	–	–	–
Gayle	2	0	10	0	–	–	–	–

Fall of Wickets
1-1, 2-3, 3-34, 4-58, 5-78, 6-91, 7-184, 8-197, 9-200
1-1, 2-6, 3-49, 4-63, 5-76, 6-122, 7-141, 8-154, 9-171

WEST INDIES

	First Innings		Second Innings	
CH Gayle	b Sreesanth	0	c Laxman b Sreesanth	0
D Ganga	lbw b Harbhajan Singh	40	b Sreesanth	16
BC Lara (capt)	c Jaffer b Sreesanth	26	lbw b Patel	11
MN Samuels	st Dhoni b Kumble	2	(7)lbw b Kumble	5
S Chanderpaul	c Dhoni b Patel	10	lbw b Kumble	13
DJJ Bravo	c Yuvraj Singh b Harbhajan Singh	0	b Kumble	33
RR Sarwan	c Kaif b Harbhajan Singh	7	(4)c Dravid b Sreesanth	51
*D Ramdin	c Yuvraj Singh b Harbhajan Singh	10	not out	62
JE Taylor	run out	6	lbw b Kumble	20
PT Collins	c Sehwag b Harbhajan Singh	0	lbw b Kumble	3
CD Collymore	not out	0	c Dhoni b Kumble	0
Extras	w 1, nb 1	2	lb 2, nb 3	5
	(all out 33.3 overs)	103	(all out 69.4 overs)	219

	First Innings				Second Innings			
	O	M	R	W	O	M	R	W
Sreesanth	9	3	34	2	15	2	38	3
Patel	12	5	24	1	12	2	26	1
Kumble	8	3	32	1	22.4	3	78	6
Harbhajan Singh	4.3	0	13	5	16	3	65	0
Sehwag	–	–	–	–	4	0	10	0

Fall of Wickets
1-0, 2-42, 3-53, 4-72, 5-80, 6-81, 7-88, 8-99, 9-103
1-0, 2-27, 3-29, 4-56, 5-126, 6-128, 7-144, 8-180, 9-219

Umpires: BG Jerling (South Africa) & RE Koertzen (South Africa)
Toss: India
Man of the Match: R Dravid
Man of the Series: R Dravid

India won by 49 runs

SERIES AVERAGES
West Indies v. India

WEST INDIES

Batting	M	Inns	NO	Runs	HS	Av	100	50	c/st
D Mohammed	1	2	1	71	52	71.00	–	1	-/-
D Ganga	4	8	1	344	135	49.14	1	1	4/-
S Chanderpaul	4	8	1	301	97*	43.00	–	3	1/-
CH Gayle	4	8	0	275	83	34.37	–	3	3/-
D Ramdin	4	8	3	164	62*	32.80	–	1	8/-
RR Sarwan	4	8	0	257	116	32.12	1	2	2/-
DJJ Bravo	4	8	0	231	68	28.87	–	1	3/-
MN Samuels	2	4	0	114	87	28.50	–	1	-/-
BC Lara	4	8	0	211	120	26.37	1	–	13/-
IDR Bradshaw	2	4	0	66	33	16.50	–	–	2/-
JE Taylor	3	5	1	51	23	12.75	–	–	-/-
FH Edwards	1	2	1	5	4	5.00	–	–	-/-
PT Collins	3	4	0	4	3	1.00	–	–	2/-
CD Collymore	4	6	3	3	2*	1.00	–	–	-/-

Bowling	Overs	Mds	Runs	Wkts	Av	Best	5/inn	10m
CD Collymore	144.1	43	337	15	22.46	5-48	1	–
JE Taylor	95	16	341	14	24.35	5-50	1	–
FH Edwards	24.3	5	69	2	34.50	2-53	–	–
PT Collins	116.3	25	394	10	39.40	4-116	–	–
DJJ Bravo	110.5	24	356	8	44.50	4-40	–	–
D Mohammed	36.5	6	186	4	46.50	3-162	–	–
CH Gayle	65	14	169	2	84.50	1-52	–	–
RR Sarwan	22	1	98	1	98.00	1-83	–	–
IDR Bradshaw	90	18	271	2	135.50	1-80	–	–

Also bowled: S Chanderpaul 5-0-17-0, MN Samuels 27-4-78-0.

INDIA

Batting	M	Inns	NO	Runs	HS	Av	100	50	c/st
R Dravid	4	7	1	496	146	82.66	1	4	8/-
M Kaif	4	6	2	227	148*	56.75	1	–	2/-
Harbhajan Singh	2	3	2	56	38*	56.00	–	–	1/-
W Jaffer	4	7	0	372	212	53.14	1	2	2/-
V Sehwag	4	7	0	357	180	51.00	1	1	2/-
VVS Laxman	4	7	0	257	100	36.71	1	1	1/-
A Kumble	4	5	0	133	45	26.60	–	–	2/-
MS Dhoni	4	7	0	168	69	24.00	–	1	13/4
IK Pathan	1	1	0	19	19	19.00	–	–	1/-
Yuvraj Singh	4	7	1	104	39	17.33	–	–	7/-
S Sreesanth	3	4	1	45	29*	15.00	–	–	1/-
MM Patel	4	4	1	13	13	4.33	–	–	-/-
VR Singh	2	1	0	2	2	2.00	–	–	-/-

Bowling	Overs	Mds	Runs	Wkts	Av	Best	5/inn	10m
V Sehwag	89.1	21	209	9	23.22	3-33	–	–
Harbhajan Singh	71.3	9	264	11	24.00	5-13	2	–
A Kumble	223.1	51	658	23	28.60	6-78	1	–
MM Patel	149	34	462	14	33.00	3-51	–	–
S Sreesanth	96	25	335	10	33.50	3-38	–	–
IK Pathan	26	3	93	2	46.50	1-43	–	–
VR Singh	47	7	158	2	79.00	2-61	–	–

Also bowled: Yuvraj Singh 1-0-1-0.

ZIMBABWE

ZIMBABWE REPORT
By Telford Vice

No one would have been surprised had the price of beer doubled while the nation awaited the last ball of the third one-day international between Zimbabwe and Bangladesh on 2 August 2006. Brendan Taylor's feet were, as usual, planted as permanently as the trees that towered just inside the walls of Harare Sports Club and almost as wide apart. Many yards away, Mashrafe bin Mortaza leaned into his run. Zimbabwe, who were eight wickets down, needed five to win. Taylor, bat cocked in his idiosyncratic horizontal backlift, lowered his chin as the bowler approached. Mortaza pictured in his mind a swift, stealthy yorker that would reveal itself only when it smashed Taylor's wicket. Instead, he bowled a full toss, which Taylor coolly smote high over the midwicket boundary.

The noise from the joyous chaos as the Zimbabwe dressing room uncorked itself on to the field jerked the attention of the bristling soldiers beyond the trees and the walls away from their primary task of keeping Robert Mugabe safe from the citizenry. In the stands gaggles of uniformed schoolchildren discovered they had another reason to celebrate besides being granted a day away from their desks. Even in the Red Lion, the boundary-side pub where the last of the Rhodesians gather to mutter their unreconstructed views, cheers that were once smirks escaped from ruddy faces. In the Keg and Maiden next door, however, the barmen might have been too occupied with adjusting the price of beer on their cash registers to pay much heed to what was happening outside.

Up on the Bangladeshis' balcony, Dav Whatmore's moustache seemed to take on a denser shade of dark, and everyone around him was rendered catatonic with disappointment. For neutrals, these scenes were struck through with poignancy. Not because Zimbabwe had secured an improbable win, and certainly not because they had done so against a side that had anointed themselves favourites and gracelessly predicted that they would win the series 5-0. The shadow of sadness came from the fact that, in claiming this victory as their own, Zimbabweans seemed to spend all the happy moments that cricket had given them for several years. That one win, albeit a last-ball thriller, should spark such pandemonium spoke of many more

Zimbabwe's Brendan Taylor (left) celebrates with batting partner Blessing Mahwire after seeing his side to a thrilling two-wicket victory against Bangladesh in Harare.

Tatenda Taibu looks on as India's Rahul Dravid sweeps. Taibu later quit the international game, adding to Zimbabwe's woes.

bleak days past, and to come. Among the most empty of them was 24 November 2005, when Tatenda Taibu resigned the Zimbabwe captaincy. Taibu cited dissatisfaction with the performance of administrators and with new contracts that significantly lowered the players' guaranteed income. The last straw might have been the threats of violence made against him and his family.

Two weeks later police arrested Peter Chingoka and Ozias Bvute, respectively chairman and managing director of Zimbabwe Cricket (ZC), in connection with foreign currency irregularities. They were held for two days and released without charge, but ZC was subsequently fined the equivalent of £700 for illegally using an offshore banking account to pay for a consignment of cricket balls from Pakistan. Police are reportedly investigating several other similar charges against Chingoka and Bvute. They survived a procedural attempt to remove them from power that was mounted by then ZC vice-chairman Ahmed Ebrahim, and another few

weeks down this troubled road a player strike broke out. The strike ended when the players – most of them young and inexperienced, and unpaid for months – capitulated and accepted ZC's terms. On 6 January 2006 the Zimbabwean government took control of cricket. To some this represented a forward step: at last, they thought, an entity more powerful than that controlled by Chingoka and Bvute had stepped in. Could positive change be far behind? It could. Among the first decisions made by Zimbabwean cricket's new masters was to retain Chingoka and Bvute in their posts. Another was to withdraw the team from the Test arena, which meant the thrashing they would surely endure in the West Indies in May could be absorbed one day at a time. A 5-0 scoreline duly followed. But there was some respite when Zimbabwe beat Canada and Bermuda in a tournament in Trinidad.

Which brings us back to the events of 2 August 2006. The 'Boy's Own' ending to that match gave Zimbabwe their second success in a series they would go on to win 3-2. In doing so, they looked, sounded and performed like that rare beast in Zimbabwe: a collection of young men focused entirely on playing to the best of their abilities. But how long will it last? The edgy uncertainty was plain in coach Kevin Curran's tone as he pondered the question. 'In this country things aren't dealt with like they are in a first-world country,' he said to all round agreement.

The most difficult job in world cricket? Kevin Curran is the man charged with working miracles as coach of Zimbabwe.

OF ZIMBABWE

By Telford Vice

There is wicked irony in the fact that Zimbabwe, the ICC's most pressing problem, was decreed a Test-playing country to solve one of the ICC's previous most pressing problems. When Zimbabwe was admitted to the game's most exclusive club in 1992, the highest level of cricket played there might well have been recognised as first-class in most full-member countries, but there were probably fewer cricketers of first-class quality in the whole of Zimbabwe than could be counted on the parks of Port of Spain or Delhi or Adelaide on any given afternoon. But the ICC needed a serious presence in Africa, and apartheid South Africa was not the answer.

Fourteen years down the line, prospects for cricket in Zimbabwe look bleaker than ever, what with administrators who are most kindly described as authoritarian, the haemorrhage of players to other countries or out of the game, and the perennial unhappiness of those who choose or have no choice but to remain. Most of Zimbabwean cricket's best moments, then, are not recent. One of the finest came on 9 June 1983 at Trent Bridge, when Zimbabwe beat Australia in their inaugural one-day international, which was also their first World Cup match. Zimbabwe scored 239 for 6 from 60 overs, and they held the Australians to a reply of 226 for 7. Duncan Fletcher, their captain, scored 69 not out and took 4 for 42.

The Zimbabweans would lose their next 18 ODIs – all of them World Cup games – before they beat England in the 1992 World Cup in Albury, where Eddo Brandes took 4 for 21. Seven months later Dave Houghton led Zimbabwe in their inaugural Test, against India in Harare. John Traicos, who had played three Tests for South Africa, was the only Zimbabwean not on debut. Houghton scored 121 not out, and Traicos' 5 for 86 earned Zimbabwe a first-innings lead of 149 in a match that was eventually drawn. Five more draws and four losses later Zimbabwe earned their first Test victory when they beat Pakistan by an innings and 64 runs in Harare in February 1995. Grant Flower scored 201 not out and there were centuries for his brother Andy, and Guy Whittall. A 20-year-old Heath Streak took nine wickets in the match.

Sadly, Zimbabwe would win just seven more of their 83 Tests to date, while their reputation as a plucky one-day side has taken a beating since a player strike in 2004 ended the careers of a generation of experienced international cricketers.

England's John Crawley is the second victim of Eddo Brandes' hat-trick during the third one-day international at Harare in 1996–97.

ONE-DAY INTERNATIONALS
v. Kenya

Match One
25 February 2006 at Bulawayo
Kenya 227 for 9 (50 overs) (KO Otieno 74,
TM Odoyo 54)
Zimbabwe 231 for 2 (43.3 overs) (BRM Taylor 60*,
H Masakadza 58*, T Duffin 53)
Zimbabwe won by 8 wickets

Match Two
26 February 2006 at Bulawayo
Kenya 284 for 7 (50 overs) (SO Tikolo 98,
AJ Ireland 3 for 46)
Zimbabwe 205 all out (46.2 overs) (K Meth 53, HP
Rinke 52, PJ Ongondo 3 for 26)
Kenya won by 79 runs

Match Three
1 March 2006 at Harare
Kenya 134 all out (42.5 overs) (EC Rainsford 3 for 16)
Zimbabwe 69 (22.5 overs) (PJ Ongondo 4 for 14,
TM Odoyo 3 for 13)
Kenya won by 65 runs

Match Four
3 March 2006 at Harare
Zimbabwe 231 for 9 (44 overs) (HP Rinke 72,
PJ Ongondo 3 for 32, TM Odoyo 3 for 50)
Kenya 122 all out (36.5 overs) (KO Otieno 69,
R Higgins 4 for 21)
Zimbabwe won by 109 runs

Match Five
4 March 2006 at Harare
Zimbabwe v. **Kenya**
Match abandoned – no result

Series drawn 2–2

ONE-DAY INTERNATIONALS
v. Bangladesh

Match One
29 July 2006 at Harare
Bangladesh 246 for 7 (50 overs) (Shahadat Hossain 78,
E Chigumbura 4 for 61)
Zimbabwe 248 for 8 (49.1 overs) (S Matsikenyeri 89,
E Chigumbura 70*, Mashrafe bin Mortaza 4 for 41)
Zimbabwe won by 2 wickets

Match Two
30 July 2006 at Harare
Bangladesh 238 for 8 (50 overs) (Farhad Reza 50)
Zimbabwe 176 all out (44.4 overs)
Bangladesh won by 62 runs

Match Three
2 August 2006 at Harare
Bangladesh 236 all out (49 overs) (Rajin Saleh 54,
Aftab Ahmed 53)
Zimbabwe 238 for 8 (50 overs) (BRM Taylor 79*)
Zimbabwe won by 2 wickets

Match Four
4 August 2006 at Harare
Bangladesh 206 for 9 (50 overs)
Zimbabwe 212 for 3 (41.4 overs) (GM Strydom 58)
Zimbabwe won by 7 wickets

Match Five
6 August 2006 at Harare
Zimbabwe 197 all out (49.3 overs) (H Masakadza 75,
Rajin Saleh 4 for 16)
Bangladesh 201 for 2 (44.4 overs) (Shahriar Nafees 118*)
Bangladesh won by 8 wickets

Zimbabwe won the series 3–2

OTHER INTERNATIONAL MATCHES

AUSTRALIA v. ICC WORLD XI
14–17 October 2005 at Adelaide

AUSTRALIA

	First Innings		Second Innings	
JL Langer	b Harmison	0	c Smith b Kallis	22
ML Hayden	c Kallis b Muralitharan	111	b Harmison	77
RT Ponting (capt)	c Kallis b Flintoff	46	c Boucher b Flintoff	54
MJ Clarke	c Sehwag b Vettori	39	b Harmison	5
SM Katich	run out	0	c & b Muralitharan	2
*AC Gilchrist	lbw b Flintoff	94	c Kallis b Muralitharan	1
SR Watson	lbw b Muralitharan	24	c Boucher b Flintoff	10
SK Warne	c Kallis b Flintoff	5	c Dravid b Flintoff	7
B Lee	c Smith b Flintoff	1	c Muralitharan b Harmison	3
GD McGrath	not out	0	c Smith b Muralitharan	2
SCG MacGill	not out	0	not out	0
Extras	b 5, lb 11, w 3, nb 6	25	b 7, lb 7, nb 2	16
	(all out 90 overs)	345	(all out 65.3 overs)	199

	First Innings				Second Innings			
	O	M	R	W	O	M	R	W
Harmison	18	3	60	1	12.3	2	41	3
Flintoff	18	3	59	4	16	2	48	3
Kallis	7	1	35	0	3	1	3	1
Muralitharan	30	3	102	2	24	5	55	3
Vettori	17	3	73	1	10	0	38	0

Fall of Wickets
1-0, 2-73, 3-154, 4-163, 5-260, 6-323, 7-331, 8-339, 9-344
1-30, 2-152, 3-160, 4-167, 5-167, 6-170, 7-177, 8-192, 9-195

ICC WORLD XI

	First Innings		Second Innings	
GC Smith (capt)	c Gilchrist b Lee	12	b McGrath	0
V Sehwag	c Katich b Warne	76	c Gilchrist b MacGill	7
R Dravid	c Gilchrist b McGrath	0	c Hayden b Warne	23
BC Lara	lbw b McGrath	5	c Gilchrist b Watson	36
JH Kallis	c Hayden b Warne	44	not out	39
Inzamam-ul-Haq	st Gilchrist b MacGill	1	lbw b Lee	0
A Flintoff	c Lee b MacGill	35	c sub b MacGill	15
*MV Boucher	c Gilchrist b Warne	0	c Hayden b Warne	17
DL Vettori	not out	8	c Ponting b MacGill	0
SJ Harmison	c Clarke b MacGill	1	lbw b MacGill	0
M Muralitharan	c Langer b MacGill	2	st Gilchrist b MacGill	0
Extras	b 1, lb 1, w 1, nb 3	6	b 1, lb 2, nb 4	7
	(all out 47.1 overs)	190	(all out 50 overs)	144

	First Innings				Second Innings			
	O	M	R	W	O	M	R	W
McGrath	12	4	34	2	6	3	8	1
Lee	8	1	54	1	10	2	42	1
Watson	6	0	38	0	–	–	–	–
Warne	12	3	23	3	19	4	48	3
MacGill	9.1	0	39	4	15	4	43	5

Fall of Wickets
1-27, 2-31, 3-43, 4-134, 5-135, 6-147, 7-151, 8-183, 9-184
1-0, 2-18, 3-56, 4-69, 5-70, 6-122, 7-143, 8-144, 9-144

Umpires: RE Koertzen (South Africa) & SJA Taufel (Australia)
Toss: Australia
Man of the Match: ML Hayden

Australia won by 210 runs

SUPER SERIES
Australia v. ICC World XI

Match One
5 October 2005 at Melbourne (DS)
Australia 255 for 8 (50 overs) (SM Katich 58,
DL Vettori 4 for 33)
ICC World XI 162 all out (41.3 overs)
(KC Sangakkara 64, SR Watson 3 for 43)
Australia won by 93 runs

Match Two
7 October 2005 at Melbourne (DS)
Australia 328 for 4 (50 overs) (AC Gilchrist 103,
RT Ponting 66, DR Martyn 54)
ICC World XI 273 all out (45.3 overs)
(KC Sangakkara 61, CH Gayle 54, NW Bracken 3 for 43)
Australia won by 55 runs

Match Three
9 October 2005 at Melbourne (DS)
Australia 293 for 5 (50 overs) (MEK Hussey 75*,
RT Ponting 68, SR Watson 66*)
ICC World XI 137 all out (27.5 overs) (B Lee 4 for 30,
SR Watson 4 for 39)
Australia won by 156 runs

Australia won the series 3–0

TRIANGULAR TOURNAMENT
(Bermuda, Canada and Zimbabwe)

Match One
16 May 2006 at Port of Spain
Zimbabwe 218 for 8 (50 overs)
(HP Rinke 72)
Canada 75 all out (28.5 overs)
Zimbabwe won by 143 runs

Match Two
17 May 2006 at Port of Spain
Canada 157 for 9 (49 overs)
Bermuda 153 for 7 (42.3 overs)
*Bermuda won by 3 wickets – DL Method: target 150
from 44 overs*

Match Three
18 May 2006 at Port of Spain
Zimbabwe 338 for 7 (50 overs) (BRM Taylor 98,
V Sibanda 78, T Duffin 60)
Bermuda 144 for 7 (50 overs) (IH Romaine 62)
Zimbabwe won by 194 runs

FINAL TABLE

	P	W	L	NR	RR	Pts
Zimbabwe	2	2	–	–	+3.370	10
Bermuda	2	1	1	–	–1.970	4
Canada	2	–	2	–	–1.628	0

FINAL – 20 May 2006 at Port of Spain
Zimbabwe 259 for 7 (50 overs) (V Sibanda 116,
BRM Taylor 55)
Bermuda 176 all out (47.2 overs)
Zimbabwe won by 83 runs

ONE-DAY INTERNATIONAL
Ireland v. England

13 June 2006 at Belfast
England 301 for 7 (50 overs) (ME Trescothick 113,
IR Bell 80)
Ireland 263 for 9 (50 overs) (AC Botha 52)
England won by 38 runs

ONE-DAY INTERNATIONAL
Scotland v. Pakistan

27 June 2006 at Edinburgh
Scotland 203 for 8 (50 overs) (RR Watson 80,
NFI McCallum 68)
Pakistan 205 for 5 (43.5 overs)
(Mohammad Yousuf 83*)
Pakistan won by 5 wickets

ONE-DAY INTERNATIONALS
Holland v. Sri Lanka

Match One
4 July 2006 at Amstelveen
Sri Lanka 443 for 9 (50 overs) (ST Jayasuriya 157,
TM Dilshan 117*)
Holland 248 all out (48.3 overs)
(TBM de Leede 51)
Sri Lanka won by 195 runs

Match Two
6 July 2006 at Amstelveen
Sri Lanka 313 for 8 (50 overs) (WU Tharanga 72,
TM Dilshan 66)

Holland 258 all out (49 overs) (KS Lokuarachchi 4 for 44)
Sri Lanka won by 55 runs

Sri Lanka won the series 2–0

EUROPEAN CUP

The following were the only matches classed as official
One-Day Internationals in the European Cup.

5 August 2006 at Ayr
Ireland 240 for 8 (50 overs) (EJG Morgan 99)
Scotland 155 all out (41.3 overs)
Ireland won by 85 runs

6 August 2006 at Ayr
Holland 137 for 8 (20 overs)
Scotland 138 for 6 (19.5 overs)
Scotland won by 4 wickets

8 August 2006 at Ayr
Ireland 274 all out (50 overs) (AC Botha 56,
NJ O'Brien 53, WK McCallan 50*)
Holland 125 for 5 (19 overs)
(RN ten Doeschate 56*)
Match abandoned – no result

ONE-DAY INTERNATIONALS
Canada v. Kenya

Match One
5 August 2006 at Toronto
Kenya 237 for 9 (50 overs) (JK Kamande 68,
SO Tikolo 50, S Thuraisingam 4 for 35)
Canada 129 all out (38.2 overs)
Kenya won by 108 runs

Match Two
6 August 2006 at Toronto
Canada 94 all out (33.2 overs) (HA Varaiya 4 for 25)
Kenya 97 for 5 (32.2 overs)
Kenya won by 5 wickets

Kenya won the series 2–0

ONE-DAY INTERNATIONALS
Canada v. Bermuda

Match One
19 August 2006 at Toronto
Canada 145 all out (39.5 overs)
Bermuda 150 for 4 (40 overs)
Bermuda won by 6 wickets

Match Two
21 August 2006 at Toronto
Bermuda 272 for 7 (50 overs) (IH Romaine 101)
Canada 261 all out (49.1 overs) (IS Billcliff 59,
JM Davison 55, H Durham 4 for 45)
Bermuda won by 11 runs

Bermuda won the series 2–0

ONE-DAY INTERNATIONALS
Kenya v. Bangladesh

Match One
12 August 2006 at Nairobi
Kenya 168 all out (49.1 overs)
Bangladesh 170 for 4 (30.1 overs)
(Mohammad Ashraful 67*)
Bangladesh won by 6 wickets

Match Two
13 August 2006 at Nairobi
Kenya 184 all out (46.3 overs) (TM Odoyo 84,
Syed Rasel 4 for 22)
Bangladesh 185 for 8 (46 overs) (TM Odoyo 4 for 36)
Bangladesh won by 2 wickets

Match Three
15 August 2006 at Nairobi
Kenya 118 all out (41.2 overs)
(Mashrafe bin Mortaza 6 for 26)
Bangladesh 120 for 4 (27 overs)
Bangladesh won by 6 wickets

Bangladesh won the series 3–0

UNITECH CUP

14 & 15 August 2006 at Colombo (RPS)
Sri Lanka v. **South Africa**
Match abandoned

16 August 2006 at Colombo (RPS)
Sri Lanka v. **India**
Match abandoned

The rest of the tournament was cancelled

DLF CUP (Australia, India and West Indies)

Match One
12 September 2006 at Kuala Lumpur
Australia 279 for 9 (50 overs) (MJ Clarke 81,
RT Ponting 54)

West Indies 201 all out (34.3 overs) (S Chanderpaul 92,
CH Gayle 58, SR Watson 4 for 43)
Australia won by 78 runs

Match Two
14 September 2006 at Kuala Lumpur
India 309 for 5 (50 overs) (SR Tendulkar 141*,
IK Pathan 64)
West Indies 141 for 2 (20 overs)
*West Indies won by 29 runs – DL method: target 113
from 20 overs*

Match Three
16 September 2006 at Kuala Lumpur
Australia 244 all out (49.2 overs) (SR Watson 79,
MJ Clarke 64)
India 35 for 5 (8 overs) (MG Johnson 4 for 11)
Match abandoned – no result

Match Four
18 September 2006 at Kuala Lumpur
Australia 272 for 6 (50 overs) (MEK Hussey 109*,
BJ Haddin 70)
West Indies 273 for 7 (47.2 overs) (BC Lara 87,
CH Gayle 79)
West Indies won by 3 wickets

Match Five
20 September 2006 at Kuala Lumpur
India 162 all out (39.3 overs) (SR Tendulkar 65,
DR Smith 4 for 31)
West Indies 146 all out (41 overs)
India won by 16 runs

Match Six
22 September 2006 at Kuala Lumpur
Australia 213 all out (48.1 overs) (ML Hayden 54)
India 195 all out (43.5 overs) (D Mongia 63*,
B Lee 5 for 38)
Australia won by 18 runs

FINAL TABLE

	P	W	L	T	NR	RR	Pts
Australia	4	2	1	0	1	+0.55	11
West Indies	4	2	2	0	0	-0.31	9
India	4	1	2	0	1	-0.26	6

FINAL
24 September 2006 at Kuala Lumpur
Australia 240 for 6 (50 overs) (DR Martyn 52,
A Symonds 52)
West Indies 113 all out (34.2 overs) (B Lee 4 for 24)
Australia won by 127 runs

ENGLAND: FIRST-CLASS COUNTIES FORM CHARTS

DERBYSHIRE

DURHAM

ESSEX

GLAMORGAN

GLOUCESTERSHIRE

HAMPSHIRE

KENT

LANCASHIRE

LEICESTERSHIRE

MIDDLESEX

NORTHAMPTONSHIRE

NOTTINGHAMSHIRE

SOMERSET

SURREY

SUSSEX

WARWICKSHIRE

WORCESTERSHIRE

YORKSHIRE

DERBYSHIRE CCC

FIRST-CLASS MATCHES
BATTING

Match	SD Stubbings	Hassan Adnan	PS Jones	CR Taylor	G Welch	MJ Di Venuto	TR Birt	DJ Pipe	ID Hunter	AG Botha	MA Sheikh	GG Wagg	AKD Gray	GM Smith	KJ Dean	LJ Goddard	MJ North	PM Borrington	J Needham	T Lungley	WA White	Extras	Total	Wickets	Result	Points
v. Oxford UCCE	12	73*		102		88	5			24*												17	321	4		
(The Parks) 15-17 April	44			0*		0				62*												16	122	2	D	
v. Surrey	7	88	0	45	0	60	99	16	6	100	51*											20	492	10		
(The Oval) 19-22 April																									D	12
v. Sri Lanka	43	12		34	2		4	15		3	6	29		0						27*		44	219	10		
(Derby) 29 April-1 May	6	32*		53	15*		83			7												12	208	4	L	
v. Glamorgan	97	9	16	121	10	26	0	0	11	0	36*											9	335	10		
(Cardiff) 3-6 May	52	33	5	10	15	33	1	20	4*	2	8											9	192	10	W	20
v. Worcestershire	8	42	0	11	94	56	39	57	5*	0	0											26	338	10		
(Worcester) 10-12 May	9	0	8	9	4*	58	7	12	8	3	13											18	149	10	W	20
v. Leicestershire	119	2		23	4*	93	119	15*			1											25	401	6	D	10
(Derby) 17-19 May																										
v. Northamptonshire	10*			4		23	16*															5	58	2	D	7
(Northampton) 24-27 May																										
v. Glamorgan	98	52	3	18	15	18	16	28	0		38		6*									35	327	10		
(Derby) 6-9 June	8	4	9	14	63	95	12	3	4*		15		25									30	282	10	L	6
v. Gloucestershire	7	73	12*	9	19	37	181	11		19*		10										24	402	8		
(Bristol) 14-17 June	17	29	23*	51	9	0	89	16		0		23*										29	286	8	D	11
v. Essex	23	21	4*		2	48	130	0		2	37	5	12									28	312	10		
(Derby) 20-22 June	48	3	5*		2	1	3	0		2	46	1	29									22	162	10	L	6
v. Somerset	19	20	34*	60	20	4		24	48		17						132					18	396	10		
(Taunton) 14-17 July	124	42		74	13	6		32*			20*						75					29	415	7	W	21
v. Leicestershire	24	117	27	0	5	6		89	9*		0		4				80					25	386	10		
(Leicester) 19-22 July	50			4		161*							24				0*					24	263	3	D	11
v. Worcestershire	11	33	17*	40	11	16		46	1		87		45				17					27	351	10		
(Chesterfield) 26-29 July	0	7	8	15	14	99		12	0*		50		14				161					29	409	10	D	10
v. Somerset	97	3	1		9	48	50	35*	0		5		17	23								28	316	10		
(Derby) 8-11 August	7	18			11	118	51	84*			41		46	17								20	413	10	W	20
v. Gloucestershire	8	15		16*		104	34			59				86		35*						43	400	6	D	12
(Derby) 17-20 August																										
v. Northamptonshire	0	12	9	41			63	6*		0		16		0	0	3						17	167	10		
(Derby) 30 August-2 September	64	8		103			32*					31*										48	286	3	D	7
v. Essex	42	60	4	22						11	0		2	0*		0			0			19	184	10		
(Chelmsford) 9-11 September	0	32	12	19						10	36		29	1*		37			29			12	218	10	L	1
v. Surrey	2	23	28	20						2		94		39	18	91		18			18*	32	385	10		
(Derby) 20-23 September	0	30	2	6						0		6		0		43*		38			19*	18	162	8	L	6

	SD Stubbings	Hassan Adnan	PS Jones	CR Taylor	G Welch	MJ Di Venuto	TR Birt	DJ Pipe	ID Hunter	AG Botha	MA Sheikh	GG Wagg	AKD Gray	GM Smith	KJ Dean	LJ Goddard	MJ North	PM Borrington	J Needham	T Lungley	WA White					
Matches	18	18	17	15	15	14	14	14	14	12	9	9	8	5	5	4	3	1	1	1	1					
Innings	32	29	21	26	23	23	24	20	13	21	13	14	11	9	5	6	6	2	2	1	2					
Not Out	1	2	6	0	5	1	2	4	6	2	3	1	2	1	2	2	1	0	0	1	2					
High Score	124	117	34*	121	94	161*	181	89	48	100	51*	94	29	86	18	91	161	38	29	27*	19*					
Runs	1056	893	227	908	353	1198	1059	515	102	470	270	317	162	227	19	209	465	56	29	27	37					
Average	34.06	33.07	15.13	34.92	19.61	54.45	48.13	32.18	14.57	24.73	27.00	24.38	18.00	28.37	6.33	52.25	93.00	28.00	14.50	-	-					
100s	2	1	0	3	0	3	3	0	0	1	0	0	0	0	0	0	2	0	0	0	0					
50s	6	5	0	4	2	7	6	3	0	4	1	1	0	1	0	1	2	0	0	0	0					
Catches/Stumpings	12/0	4/0	4/0	10/0	8/0	19/0	7/0	43/7	6/0	14/0	1/0	3/0	0/0	4/0	0/0	8/0	6/0	0/0	0/0	1/0	0/0					

Home Ground: Derby
Address: County Ground, Nottingham Road, Derby, DE21 6DA
Tel: 01332 383211
Fax: 01332 290251
Email: sue.evans@debyshireccc.com
Directions: *By road:* From the South & East, exit M1 junction 25, follow the A52 into Derby, take the fourth exit off the Pentagon Island. From the North, exit M1 junction 28, join the A38 into Derby, follow directional signs, the cricket ground is seen on the left approaching the city. From the West, on A50 follow signs for A52 Nottingham and on leaving the city centre inner ring road take the second exit off the Pentagon Island into the ground.

Capacity: 9,500
Other grounds used: Chesterfield
Year Formed: 1870

Chief Executive: Tom Sears
General Manager: Keith Stevenson
Director of Cricket: Dave Houghton
Academy Director & 2nd XI Coach: Karl Krikken
Captain: Graeme Welch
County Colours: Blue, brown and gold

Honours
County Championship
1936
Sunday League/NCL/Pro40
1990
Benson & Hedges Cup
1993
Gillette Cup/NatWest/C&G Trophy
1981

Website:
www.derbyshireccc.com

DERBYSHIRE CCC

FIRST-CLASS MATCHES
BOWLING

Match	PS Jones	G Welch	ID Hunter	AG Botha	GG Wagg	MA Sheikh	AKD Gray	WA White	KJ Dean	T Lungley	TR Birt	GM Smith	Hassan Adnan	MJ North	SD Stubbings	J Needham	Overs	Total	Byes/Leg-byes	Wickets	Run outs
v. Oxford UCCE (The Parks) 15-17 April	11.4-5-21-2	9-1-30-2	12-5-22-4						8-2-23-1								40.4	104	8	10	1
	17.5-4-46-1	18-6-40-3	21-3-64-0	22-5-77-3					12-1-55-1								90.5	300	18	8	
v. Surrey (The Oval) 19-22 April	17-5-48-2	19-5-72-3	18-5-63-0	12-4-58-0		22.5-8-65-5											88.5	308	2	10	
	25-5-78-1	26-8-58-2	22-3-89-1	54-11-159-3		22-9-48-0						6-1-24-1					155	476	20	8	
v. Sri Lanka (Derby) 29 April-1 May		6-3-14-1		2-1-1-0		6-2-18-0	10-1-33-1		11.5-2-32-2	12-4-59-2	0.1-0-1-0						47.5	166	9	7	1
		11-2-43-0		14-1-65-2		11-2-41-1	13-1-50-1		5-1-23-0	4-0-29-0							58.1	262	10	4	
v. Glamorgan (Cardiff) 3-6 May	19-4-86-2	14-1-62-1	15.1-5-47-4	27-8-83-3		10-4-34-0											85.1	315	3	10	
	20-14-25-6	8-3-26-0	22.4-10-52-3	17-4-48-0		8-3-17-1											75.4	184	16	10	
v. Worcestershire (Worcester) 10-12 May	17-3-58-3	17-5-50-1	20-5-92-4	9.4-1-24-1		18-9-44-1											81.4	278	10	10	
	15-1-62-4	11-2-33-4	4.2-0-33-1			10-3-32-1											40.2	174	14	10	
v. Leicestershire (Derby) 17-19 May	11-4-30-1		12-5-11-1	16-7-26-2		14-1-49-0	2-0-2-0										55	137	19	4	
																	-	-	-	-	
v. Northamptonshire (Northampton) 24-27 May	30.4-6-109-4	22-9-57-2	30-5-93-4			22-6-67-0	26-8-53-0										130.4	386	7	10	
																	-	-	-	-	
v. Glamorgan (Derby) 6-9 June	29-3-106-1	21-4-81-2	23-2-97-2			15-4-64-2	28.2-6-106-3					2-0-5-0					116.2	470	16	10	
	10-2-33-1		7-2-24-0			2-1-5-0	16.2-3-62-2										37.2	140	11	4	1
v. Gloucestershire (Bristol) 14-17 June	31.4-8-105-4	31-4-83-0	14-4-58-0			25-4-71-2	38-7-121-3						1-0-4-0				140.4	456	14	10	
	6-0-36-0	10-0-54-1				8-0-45-1	21-2-83-1					11-0-49-1	5-0-24-0				61	300	9	4	
v. Essex (Derby) 20-22 June	22-2-120-3	26-8-58-2		10-2-32-0	26-4-74-3	25-6-50-1	12-4-37-1										121	386	15	10	
	6-0-24-0			4-0-24-1	3-1-17-0		6-0-27-1										19	92	0	2	
v. Somerset (Taunton) 14-17 July	19-2-88-4	20-3-72-3		19.5-4-92-2	16-1-56-0		7-2-16-0							2-0-6-0			83.5	340	10	9	
	12-2-48-0	6.4-1-24-3		6-2-12-0	12-3-38-6												36.4	127	5	10	1
v. Leicestershire (Leicester) 19-22 July	30-7-112-2	26.2-6-88-2		24-3-93-1	18-1-105-3		12-3-45-1								24-7-43-1		134.2	515	29	10	
																	-	-	-	-	
v. Worcestershire (Chesterfield) 26-29 July	24-4-108-1	27-9-81-1	11-2-60-1	41.2-13-117-6	18-4-75-1										16-1-42-0		137.2	497	14	10	
			4-0-37-0	3-0-11-0	7-1-33-1												14	82	1	1	
v. Somerset (Derby) 8-11 August	18.1-2-45-4	13-3-28-1	13-4-28-3		8-1-39-2												52.1	151	11	10	
	28.1-3-119-4	27.3-3-109-1		26-2-111-1	9-2-43-0	13.3-2-88-2						2-0-11-0					106.1	498	17	10	2
v. Gloucestershire (Derby) 17-20 August	25-8-76-4	10-5-24-0	17-4-52-2	4.3-1-9-1	22-5-74-3												78.3	240	5	10	
	4-1-6-2	7-0-25-0	17-5-53-1	4-0-30-0							7-1-35-0	12-3-49-0	1-0-4-1			1-0-2-0	57	208	4	4	
v. Northamptonshire (Derby) 30 August-2 September	20-1-88-1		16-2-58-1	26-4-96-4	13-2-57-1				15-0-81-1			8.5-0-27-1					98.5	424	17	10	1
																	-	-	-	-	
v. Essex (Chelmsford) 9-11 September	25-5-80-2			21-3-106-0	24-7-96-1					27-9-115-0	1-0-10-0	16-2-60-0				15-1-88-0	129	580	25	3	
v. Surrey (Derby) 20-23 September	25-6-76-0			21-9-32-3	19-2-70-0			14-4-35-4	10-2-31-1			5-0-17-0					94	275	14	8	
	5-1-38-0			14-0-86-1	10-0-52-1			7-0-48-2	1-0-4-0			3-1-18-1					40	273	27	5	

	PS Jones	G Welch	ID Hunter	AG Botha	GG Wagg	MA Sheikh	AKD Gray	WA White	KJ Dean	T Lungley	TR Birt	GM Smith	Hassan Adnan	MJ North	SD Stubbings	J Needham
Overs	524.1	391.3	369	332.3	213.3	218.5	191.4	21	89.5	16	25.1	46.5	9	42	1	15
Maidens	108	98	79	74	34	62	37	4	17	4	2	6	0	8	0	1
Runs	1871	1198	1328	1124	904	650	635	83	364	88	119	182	37	91	2	88
Wickets	59	36	36	29	24	15	14	6	6	2	2	2	1	1	0	0
Average	31.71	33.27	36.88	38.75	37.66	43.33	45.35	13.83	60.66	44.00	59.50	91.00	37.00	91.00	-	-

FIELDING

50	DJ Pipe (43 ct, 7 st)
19	MJ Di Venuto
14	AG Botha
12	SD Stubbings
10	CR Taylor
8	G Welch
8	LJ Goddard
7	TR Birt
6	ID Hunter
6	MJ North
4	PS Jones
4	Hassan Adnan
4	GM Smith
3	GG Wagg
1	MA Sheikh
1	T Lungley
0	KJ Dean
0	AKD Gray
0	PM Borrington
0	J Needham
0	WA White

Final Division Two Table

	P	W	L	D	Bat	Bowl	Pts
Surrey	16	10	2	4	62	44	262.00
Worcestershire	16	8	4	4	58	43	229.00
Essex	16	7	4	5	62	40	220.00
Leicestershire	16	5	4	7	47	41	185.50
Derbyshire	16	4	4	8	51	41	178.50
Northamptonshire	16	3	5	8	52	37	163.00
Gloucestershire	16	3	6	7	51	36	155.50
Glamorgan	16	2	7	7	51	41	146.50
Somerset	16	3	9	4	43	40	140.00

(Derbyshire deducted 1.00 point v. Somerset, 8 August; and
0.50 points v. Somerset, 14 July for a slow over rate)

DURHAM CCC

FIRST-CLASS MATCHES
BATTING

Match	DM Benkenstein	GR Breese	JP Maher	P Mustard	G Onions	GJ Muchall	OD Gibson	CD Thorp	ML Lewis	BW Harmison	GM Scott	JJB Lewis	N Killeen	GJ Pratt	JA Lowe	GT Park	MM Iqbal	SJ Harmison	PJ Wiseman	M Davies	KJ Coetzer	LE Plunkett	GD Bridge	ML Turner	Extras	Total	Wickets	Result	Points
v. Kent (Canterbury) 19-22 April	22	11	25	130	17*	219	33	12				20	5	52											29	575	10	W	22
v. Lancashire (Riverside) 26-29 April	37	26	22	10	0	102	6	10				33	5*	25											13	289	10		
	88	33	63	4	10	1	11	19				2	0*	20											21	272	10	L	5
v. Middlesex (Riverside) 10-13 May	19	8	106	78	22*	17	38	4	6			21		8											21	348	10		
	48	2	8	9	4	5	17	9	5*			99		20											35	261	10	W	20
v. Nottinghamshire (Trent Bridge) 17-20 May	73	16	33	19	4*	88	49*					61		26			18								17	404	8	D	12
v. Sussex (Riverside) 23-24 May	18	0	23	15	4	0	8		0*			5	9			8									20	110	10		
	7	4	22	0	9	0	2		2			28	0			3*									3	80	10	L	3
v. Oxford UCCE (The Parks) 31 May-2 June		0							110	90					29	5*	4*				35				15	288	5		
		45						41	12	133					12	2*	0*				63				20	328	6	W	
v. Warwickshire (Edgbaston) 7-10 June	144*	1	10	45	40	4	81	0	0			12	12												10	359	10		
	23*	33	12	13	2	1	6	2	0			24	21												4	141	10	L	7
v. Kent (Stockton-on-Tees) 13-15 June	12	15	27	41*	8	61	4		14			21	4			0									20	227	10		
	70	31	99	3	4	1	0		1*			2	8			20									29	268	10	L	4
v. Hampshire (Rose Bowl) 20-22 June	22	44	7	19	15*	4	2	75				7	10							10					19	234	10		
	61	5	57	43	4	17	37*	28				40	22							0					39	353	10	W	18
v. Yorkshire (Riverside) 14-16 July	93	21	16	17	0	36	53	0	0*			4	6												12	258	10		
	96	63	19	0	6*	1	13	0	5			25	0												20	248	10	L	5
v. West Indies A (Riverside) 21-23 July	47			19	18					105	14			4*	30	19	0					28	5		21	310	10		
	26			4	5					1	2			0	22	34	5*						43		6	148	10	L	
v. Middlesex (Lord's) 26-29 July	125	110	46	1	4	68	12	5	16*	1					5										14	407	10		
	47	7	35	16		41	24*	9*	2						25										14	220	7	D	12
v. Nottinghamshire (Riverside) 1-4 August	0	4	2	81	3	5		68*	1	0			7	6											18	195	10		
	39	0	10	8	26	5		11	5*	8			34	0											11	157	10	L	3
v. Sussex (Hove) 16-18 August	2	2	35	58	4	17		0	6*	4						0			19						3	150	10		
	24	2	33	103	13	13		0	9*	29						1			5						15	247	10	L	1
v. Warwickshire (Riverside) 22-24 August	79	29	6	31	7*	17		4	0	65	34	1													11	284	10		
	31		101*		0					61*															3	196	3	W	19
v. Hampshire (Riverside) 7-9 September	31	15	0	15		19	24	2	19*	9	40	2													19	195	10		
	6	47	29	46		13	21*	27	38	75	2	8													22	334	10	L	3
v. Lancashire (Old Trafford) 13-16 September	33	43	95	11*	0		0			48	53		6				45			4					34	372	10		
		28*									0						34*								7	69	1	D	10
v. Yorkshire (Headingley) 20-23 September	151	6	2	0	3		155			0	77			0			77			6*					41	518	10		
	26		7							33*	7						100*								8	181	3	D	10

	DM Benkenstein	GR Breese	JP Maher	P Mustard	G Onions	GJ Muchall	OD Gibson	CD Thorp	ML Lewis	BW Harmison	GM Scott	JJB Lewis	N Killeen	GJ Pratt	JA Lowe	GT Park	MM Iqbal	SJ Harmison	PJ Wiseman	M Davies	KJ Coetzer	LE Plunkett	GD Bridge	ML Turner
Matches	17	17	16	16	16	15	13	12	11	9	9	9	9	6	5	4	4	2	2	2	1	1	1	1
Innings	31	29	30	27	26	28	22	21	18	17	18	16	12	10	10	8	8	3	2	2	2	1	2	0
Not Out	2	0	2	2	6	0	4	2	9	2	0	0	3	0	0	4	3	1	1	0	0	0	0	0
High Score	151	110	106	130	40	219	155	75	38	110	133	99	34	52	30	100*	20	18	6*	10	63	28	43	0
Runs	1500	623	978	816	232	778	596	326	127	563	551	355	72	193	130	316	53	29	10	10	98	28	48	0
Average	51.72	21.48	34.92	32.64	11.60	27.78	33.11	17.15	14.11	37.53	30.61	22.18	8.00	19.30	13.00	79.00	10.60	14.50	10.00	5.00	49.00	28.00	24.00	-
100s	3	1	2	2	0	2	1	0	0	2	1	0	0	0	0	1	0	0	0	0	0	0	0	0
50s	7	1	4	3	0	3	2	2	0	3	3	2	0	1	0	1	0	0	0	0	1	0	0	0
Catches/Stumpings	8/0	14/0	12/1	53/1	3/0	11/0	5/0	4/0	4/0	5/0	7/0	5/0	2/0	7/0	4/0	4/0	2/0	0/0	0/0	2/0	0/0	0/0	0/0	0/0

Home Ground: Chester-le-Street
Address: County Ground, The Riverside, Chester-le-Street, County Durham, DH3 3QR
Tel: 0191 3871717
Fax: 0191 3871616
Email: reception@durhamccc.co.uk
Directions: *By rail:* Chester-le-Street (approx 5 minutes by taxi or a 10-minute walk). *By road:* Easily accessible from junction 63 of the A1(M).

Capacity: 10,000
Other grounds used: Darlington CC, Hartlepool CC, Stockton CC
Year formed: 1882

Chief Executive: David Harker
Director of Cricket: Geoff Cook
First XI Coach: Martyn Moxon
Captain: Dale Benkenstein
County colours: Yellow, blue and burgundy

Honours
None yet

Website:
www.durhamccc.co.uk

DURHAM CCC

FIRST-CLASS MATCHES
BOWLING

	G Onions	OD Gibson	CD Thorp	ML Lewis	GR Breese	N Killeen	DM Benkenstein	MM Iqbal	SJ Harmison	GM Scott	LE Plunkett	ML Turner	M Davies	GD Bridge	PJ Wiseman	GJ Muchall	KJ Coetzer	Overs	Total	Byes/Leg-byes	Wickets	Run outs
v. Kent (Canterbury) 19-22 April	20-3-91-3	26-7-81-2	23-9-50-1		8-3-14-1	30-11-63-1	11-3-29-2											118	340	12	10	
	11-0-47-2	13.4-2-58-3		6-2-11-2		13-2-28-2	8-2-19-1		3-1-7-0									54.4	179	9	10	
v. Lancashire (Riverside) 26-29 April	24-2-117-2	28.5-1-106-4	23-8-58-2			9-1-43-1	19-5-47-1		10-2-40-0									113.5	421	10	10	
	16-4-46-2	17-4-34-1	12-1-48-1			18-3-87-0	13-0-39-1		1-0-6-0									77	268	8	6	1
v. Middlesex (Riverside) 10-13 May	16-2-82-4	13-1-66-0	15-9-19-3	13.1-4-48-2	6-2-14-1													63.1	242	12	10	
	11.3-1-56-4	14-5-49-2	8-1-28-1	15-2-63-2	2-0-5-0		9-4-22-1											59.3	232	9	10	
v. Nottinghamshire (Trent Bridge) 17-20 May	19-2-65-3	9.1-2-38-1			15-1-60-2	32-9-89-4				15-4-52-0								90.1	313	9	10	
v. Sussex (Riverside) 23-24 May	17.2-1-67-2	15-4-51-1		13-4-43-3		1-0-11-0			17-5-43-4									63.2	229	14	10	
v. Oxford UCCE (The Parks) 31 May-2 June			17-4-38-1			7-0-42-0	18-4-54-1		16-0-71-0	6-0-40-0				16-0-51-2	12-5-39-0		3-0-19-0	95	362	8	4	
			12-2-47-0			6-0-38-1	14-2-37-0		10-1-36-4					7-0-35-0	12-2-51-1			61	253	9	7	1
v. Warwickshire (Edgbaston) 7-10 June	17-7-45-3	18-4-45-4	13-5-25-1	18-4-49-1	3-1-3-0				8-1-31-0									77	208	10	10	1
	18-3-72-2	22.2-7-39-3	12-2-33-0	23-8-56-1	27-4-75-4				4-1-10-0									106.2	310	25	10	
v. Kent (Stockton-on-Tees) 13-15 June	10.2-3-43-3	16-7-25-3		6-2-24-1	7-1-18-0		20-10-52-3	2-0-11-0										61.2	179	6	10	
	18-3-86-1				16-1-73-1		4-0-39-0	10-2-57-2						2-0-22-0				70.4	411	24	10	
v. Hampshire (Rose Bowl) 20-22 June	16-6-37-1	20-5-79-2	18.3-7-55-6		3-0-27-0		11-3-37-0						8-5-9-1					76.3	256	12	10	
	6.4-1-16-2	11-5-27-0	12-3-42-5				5-2-16-3											34.4	104	3	10	
v. Yorkshire (Riverside) 14-16 July	14-3-46-0	17-1-85-3	15-5-35-2	23-7-84-2	13-1-40-1		4-0-24-1											86	339	25	10	1
	14-4-48-0	18-4-62-4	18-3-53-3	22-4-81-3	21-4-56-0													93	312	12	10	
v. West Indies A (Riverside) 21-23 July	18.3-4-85-3					13.1-1-55-2	18-2-63-2			5-0-33-0	6.5-1-24-2				16-5-73-1			82.3	364	15	10	
	8-3-31-1					6-0-18-0	4.1-0-27-1			2-0-13-0						1-0-4-0		21.1	95	2	2	
v. Middlesex (Lord's) 26-29 July	15-6-45-5	9-2-27-2	11-2-37-1	15-7-42-0			5.1-3-24-2											55.1	176	1	10	
	24-3-91-1	27-5-90-2	25-10-79-3	25.5-3-89-3	21-1-100-1		11-3-40-0											133.5	503	14	10	
v. Nottinghamshire (Riverside) 1-4 August	9-1-37-4		4-0-31-0	7.3-0-31-2					12-3-38-3									32.3	139	2	10	1
	16-3-56-1		11-2-42-0	14-4-43-2	9.3-2-21-0				13-1-45-0									63.3	214	7	4	1
v. Sussex (Hove) 16-18 August	26-7-76-0		22-7-49-1	22-5-78-2	36-5-133-2		15-4-47-1	21-1-132-0										142	530	15	6	
v. Warwickshire (Riverside) 22-24 August	17-4-58-1		18-5-57-4	18-4-68-1	1-0-2-0		14-7-24-1		9-0-54-1				7-2-39-2					84	314	12	10	
	8-3-50-1		11-2-32-1	10-2-52-3			14-4-29-5											40.4	164	1	10	
v. Hampshire (Riverside) 7-9 September		14-0-101-2	16-2-87-1	18-2-69-4	10-1-36-0		23.1-7-45-2		10-1-54-0				6-2-24-0					97.1	425	9	10	1
		11-1-60-1	5-3-12-0	14-4-50-1	22-4-85-3		11-3-38-0		1-0-4-0				5-1-23-0					69	278	6	5	
v. Lancashire (Old Trafford) 13-16 September	19-1-80-1	27-6-75-2							44-8-162-4	8-3-17-0			8.1-1-30-0	26-5-103-0				132.1	482	15	8	
v. Yorkshire (Headingley) 20-23 September	31-5-151-2	27-2-150-1			36-8-95-1	20-2-103-1				5-0-35-0				30-6-127-1				149	677	16	7	1

	G Onions	OD Gibson	CD Thorp	ML Lewis	GR Breese	N Killeen	DM Benkenstein	MM Iqbal	SJ Harmison	GM Scott	LE Plunkett	ML Turner	M Davies	GD Bridge	PJ Wiseman	GJ Muchall	KJ Coetzer
Overs	440.2	394.4	327.3	292.3	371.3	234	146.1	81.1	32	44.1	6.5	23	32	16	56	3	3
Maidens	85	77	94	67	61	55	38	6	9	6	1	0	12	5	11	0	0
Runs	1704	1458	968	1031	1297	671	552	417	95	237	24	86	99	73	230	26	19
Wickets	54	49	39	35	27	19	14	9	4	3	2	2	2	1	1	0	0
Average	31.55	29.75	24.82	29.45	48.03	35.31	39.42	46.33	23.75	79.00	12.00	43.00	49.50	73.00	230.00	-	-

FIELDING

54	P Mustard (53 ct, 1 st)
14	GR Breese
13	JP Maher (12 ct, 1 st)
11	GJ Muchall
8	DM Benkenstein
7	GJ Pratt
7	GM Scott
5	JJB Lewis
5	OD Gibson
5	BW Harmison
4	GT Park
4	JA Lowe
4	ML Lewis
4	CD Thorp
3	G Onions
2	N Killeen
2	M Davies
2	MM Iqbal
0	SJ Harmison
0	GD Bridge
0	LE Plunkett
0	KJ Coetzer
0	ML Turner
0	PJ Wiseman

Final Division One Table

	P	W	L	D	Bat	Bowl	Pts
Sussex	16	9	2	5	49	47	242.00
Lancashire	16	6	1	9	58	46	224.00
Hampshire	16	6	3	7	48	48	207.00
Warwickshire	16	6	5	5	42	43	189.00
Kent	16	4	4	8	43	44	175.00
Yorkshire	16	3	6	7	43	41	154.00
Durham	16	4	8	4	39	43	153.50
Nottinghamshire	16	4	7	5	40	37	153.00
Middlesex	16	1	7	8	47	42	133.50

(Derbyshire deducted 0.50 points v. Sussex, 23 May for a slow over rate)

ESSEX CCC

FIRST-CLASS MATCHES
BATTING

	A Flower	JS Foster	ML Pettini	RC Irani	RS Bopara	JD Middlebrook	TJ Phillips	AJ Tudor	RN ten Doeschate	V Chopra	AJ Bichel	AR Adams	D Gough	GW Flower	AP Palladino	AN Cook	GR Napier	MS Westfield	WI Jefferson	JS Ahmed	Extras	Total	Wickets	Result	Points
v. Loughborough UCCE	112*	101*	72							23				53							61	422	3		
(Chelmsford) 15-17 April			21*			6	1		105*	23				4							16	176	4	D	
v. Northamptonshire	51	0	12	2	9	59		4			16		52*			88	52				36	381	10		
(Chelmsford) 19-22 April	7		7	20*	7											103*					14	158	3	D	11
v. Glamorgan	169	4	22	73	159	19	6		102*		15*					35					35	639	8		
(Cardiff) 26-29 April																								W	22
v. Leicestershire	5	30	19	2		21	49		33			18		1	0*		62				2	242	10		
(Chelmsford) 3-5 May	26	25	30	24		0	0		25			7		59	7		17*				2	222	10	L	4
v. Somerset	161	26*	22	141*	29	27			50					8							13	400	4		
(Taunton) 10-13 May	1	82*	124	15	27	20	4*		50					8							16	347	7	W	21
v. Gloucestershire	0	0	33	87	1		37	21	30	106	44*				0						29	388	10		
(Chelmsford) 23-26 May	19*		8		19					50*											6	102	2	D	11
v. Surrey	13	34	44	122*	14	2	0	0		42		75			0						19	365	10		
(Whitgift School) 31 May-3 June	111	4	4	20	5	8	16	0	4	20	38				0*						14	244	10	L	7
v. Worcestershire	0	0	48	0	67*		0	5	5	53	16	50									39	283	10		
(Chelmsford) 14-17 June	5	61	25	97	127		31	93	0	4	1	12*									30	486	10	L	4
v. Derbyshire	84	19	30	8	50	31	11		26	65	35		1*								26	386	10		
(Derby) 20-22 June	6*		40	6*						39											1	92	2	W	21
v. Gloucestershire	190	0	59	12	5	73*			7	27			37	58							61	548	10		
(Bristol) 13-16 July	24*	39	6*	14					6												9	98	3	W	22
v. Glamorgan	3	64	29	145	37	15	7			25		9*		101					5		22	462	10	D	9
(Chelmsford) 19-22 July																									
v. Northamptonshire	271*	60	8	41	38	45	46	0			74			3	0						34	620	10	D	10
(Northampton) 26-29 July																									
v. Somerset	19	3	37	80	4	1	44	0					12	27			0*				25	252	10		
(Southend) 2-5 August	60	39*	23	61	33	24	29	26*						42				32			30	399	8	W	19
v. Surrey	24	74	97	38	94	113	38*	0		14	14						0				24	530	10	W	22
(Chelmsford) 16-18 August																									
v. Worcestershire	5	80	6	66	12	13	20	12		70	9							9*			28	330	10		
(Worcester) 30 August-2 September	29		26	8*	28*					5	6										14	116	4	D	9
v. Derbyshire	136*		208*		10			144		42											40	580	3	W	22
(Chelmsford) 9-11 September																									
v. Leicestershire	5	103	11	7	11	44	4	22	45		75*					132					27	486	10		
(Leicester) 20-23 September			114*													66*					6	186	0	L	6

	A Flower	JS Foster	ML Pettini	RC Irani	RS Bopara	JD Middlebrook	TJ Phillips	AJ Tudor	RN ten Doeschate	V Chopra	AJ Bichel	AR Adams	D Gough	GW Flower	AP Palladino	AN Cook	GR Napier	MS Westfield	WI Jefferson	JS Ahmed
Matches	17	17	17	16	15	15	14	11	9	9	8	8	7	7	6	3	3	3	1	1
Innings	27	21	29	23	24	17	17	13	12	16	8	9	7	11	6	5	3	4	1	0
Not Out	6	4	3	5	3	1	2	1	2	1	1	2	4	0	2	2	1	2	0	0
High Score	271*	103	208*	145	159	113	49	144	105*	106	75*	75	52*	101	7	132	62	32	5	-
Runs	1536	822	1218	1075	806	494	336	362	403	569	265	230	173	364	7	424	131	41	5	0
Average	73.14	48.35	46.84	59.72	38.38	30.87	22.40	30.16	40.30	37.93	37.85	32.85	57.66	33.09	1.75	141.33	65.50	20.50	5.00	-
100s	7	2	3	3	2	1	0	1	2	2	0	0	0	1	0	2	0	0	0	0
50s	3	6	3	6	3	2	0	1	1	4	2	1	2	3	0	2	2	0	0	0
Catches/Stumpings	18/0	65/3	15/0	1/0	12/0	6/0	16/0	2/0	4/0	7/0	4/0	1/0	7/0	5/0	5/0	1/0	1/0	0/0	1/0	

Home Ground: Chelmsford
Address: County Ground, New Writtle Street, Chelmsford, Essex, CM2 0PG
Tel: 01245 252420
Fax: 01245 254030
Email: administration.essex@ecb.co.uk
Directions: *By rail:* Chelmsford Station (8 minutes' walk away). *By road:* M25 then A12 to Chelmsford. Exit Chelmsford and follow AA signs to Essex Cricket Club.

Capacity: 6,000
Other grounds used: Colchester, Southend-on-Sea
Year formed: 1876

Chief Executive: David East
Cricket Operations Manager: Alan Lilley
Club Coach: Graham Gooch
Captain: Ronnie Irani
County colours: Blue, gold and red

Honours
County Championship
1979, 1983, 1984, 1986, 1991, 1992
Sunday League/NCL/Pro40
1981, 1984, 1985, 2005, 2006
Refuge Assurance Cup
1989
Benson & Hedges Cup
1979, 1998
Gillette Cup/NatWest/C&G Trophy
1985, 1997

Website:
www.essexcricket.org.uk

ESSEX CCC

FIRST-CLASS MATCHES
BOWLING

	JD Middlebrook	TJ Phillips	AJ Bichel	RN ten Doeschate	AJ Tudor	D Gough	AR Adams	RS Bopara	AP Palladino	GW Flower	MS Westfield	JS Ahmed	A Flower	GR Napier	AN Cook	Overs	Total	Byes/Leg-byes	Wickets	Run outs
v. Loughborough UCCE	22.3-7-51-4	11-5-29-1		12-3-43-2					9-2-28-0	7-3-24-1		14-2-50-2		12-2-33-0		87.3	264	6	10	
(Chelmsford) 15-17 April	31-12-70-5	13-2-53-2		8-1-32-1					6-1-30-0			7-2-26-0		7-1-18-0		72	237	8	8	
v. Northamptonshire	20-2-59-0			13-2-53-2			25.5-7-82-5	24-4-66-3	15-1-54-0					13-2-67-0		110.5	397	16	10	
(Chelmsford) 19-22 April	16-0-83-1			19-2-99-4			14-4-43-1	15-5-42-0	10-2-46-1					12-4-39-0		86	364	12	7	
v. Glamorgan	12-5-30-2	22.5-2-69-3		21-3-79-2			22-5-58-2	25-7-59-1	7-1-32-0							109.5	337	10	10	
(Cardiff) 26-29 April	16-8-16-1	25-3-103-3		17-3-51-2			12-4-31-2	17-6-31-1	7-2-20-1							94	272	20	10	
v. Leicestershire	21-2-66-0	15-3-57-2		14-0-81-1				29-5-79-1		24.4-6-68-6	2-1-15-0			11-0-40-0		116.4	417	11	10	
(Chelmsford) 3-5 May		0.4-0-6-0						4-0-19-0		5-1-16-1				1-0-6-1		10.4	48	1	2	
v. Somerset	20-2-69-2	29-6-86-2		20-0-86-1			24-4-93-1	22.3-3-79-1	22-7-53-3							137.3	471	5	10	
(Taunton) 10-13 May	17-0-68-0	21-1-100-2		4-0-20-0			7-3-11-1	5.2-1-19-1	13-2-54-1							67.2	275	3	5	
v. Gloucestershire		8-2-27-2		19-6-75-3	19-2-74-1		26.1-5-77-3	13-3-56-1	27-4-80-0							112.1	396	13	10	
(Chelmsford) 23-26 May		12-6-28-1		16-2-57-2	9.5-1-61-3		19-2-72-4	6-0-35-0	16-4-66-0							78.5	323	4	10	
v. Surrey	23-5-72-1	22-3-91-1		31-2-143-5			25-8-59-2	20-3-19-0	9-2-40-1							113	433	9	10	
(Whitgift School) 31 May-3 June	6-0-29-2	11-3-41-0		11-1-67-2			9.2-2-25-0		6-3-9-0							43.2	178	7	4	
v. Worcestershire		38-5-168-3		17-1-114-0	26-5-115-1	25.5-4-73-2	29.5-1-113-1	10-0-62-0					1-1-0-0			145.5	650	5	7	
(Chelmsford) 14-17 June		4-0-33-0			4-0-28-1	4-0-22-0	5.4-1-34-0									18.4	121	4	1	
v. Derbyshire	28-9-55-1	8-0-22-0	17.1-5-54-2		22-6-76-4	14-2-57-0		9.5-3-36-2								99	312	12	10	1
(Derby) 20-22 June	12-5-23-1	5.3-1-23-1	17-5-38-6		6-0-27-0	15-6-33-2										55.3	162	18	10	
v. Gloucestershire	38-9-94-2		23.3-0-101-1		20-5-64-3	26-4-87-3		2-0-12-0		11-1-36-1						120.3	394	0	10	
(Bristol) 13-16 July	22-7-63-1		18-5-50-3		11-2-41-0	12-1-50-0		7-2-16-3		15.1-6-28-3						85.1	251	3	10	
v. Glamorgan	39-10-88-2		33-8-95-2		22-2-117-2	29-3-104-4		11-3-27-0		5-0-27-0				7-2-20-1		139	474	16	10	
(Chelmsford) 19-22 July	31-9-95-1		6-3-13-0		7-2-13-0	4-0-11-0		7-1-30-0		14-3-58-3						76	251	11	5	
v. Northamptonshire	44-4-174-3	34-2-147-0	24-5-102-1		23-5-92-0			11-1-49-0	23-2-88-1							159	660	8	5	
(Northampton) 26-29 July		7-1-24-0			5-1-13-0			3-0-18-1	5-2-15-0	4-2-2-0						24	77	5	1	
v. Somerset	3-2-2-0	1-1-0-0			19-4-67-5	19.3-4-41-4		4-1-22-1				18-1-72-4				46.3	133	1	10	
(Southend) 2-5 August	22-2-97-2	17.3-4-53-3			12-1-47-1	9-2-32-0										78.3	307	6	10	
v. Surrey	11-1-24-1	12-4-34-0	22-5-80-3		15-4-66-1			21.5-4-75-5				10-2-47-0				91.5	330	4	10	
(Chelmsford) 16-18 August	24-5-51-3	18-3-47-1	14.4-1-53-3		10-4-16-1							6-1-15-1				72.4	198	16	10	1
v. Worcestershire	16-2-77-1	28-2-110-1	21.3-0-111-3		15-1-72-1			12-2-63-0				6-1-28-0				98.3	473	12	6	
(Worcester) 30 August- 2 September	24-8-71-1	13-0-49-1	19-4-77-1		9-0-47-1			7-0-44-0				3-0-18-1				75	331	25	5	
v. Derbyshire	6-0-25-0	11-1-41-5	18-3-45-3		12-2-35-0		12-4-30-2	1-0-2-0								60	184	6	10	
(Chelmsford) 9-11 September	15-4-63-3	10.1-2-49-2	13-1-37-1		10-2-37-3		7-2-26-1									55.1	218	6	10	
v. Leicestershire	8-1-36-0	18-3-54-0	21-4-86-2		11.5-3-69-0			21-8-61-2							2-1-4-0	93.5	372	23	4	
(Leicester) 20-23 September	16-1-55-1	14-2-71-1	13-4-49-1		13.1-1-72-1	5-1-18-0		7-0-25-0							70.1	301	7	5	1

Overs	563.3	429.4	280.5	249.1	293.4	232.1	278.1	223.3	165.4	58.1	43	21	8	56	2					
Maidens	122	67	53	31	53	46	63	38	36	16	5	4	3	9	1					
Runs	1706	1615	991	1115	1195	724	830	902	547	190	180	76	20	203	4					
Wickets	41	37	32	28	28	25	21	19	13	8	6	2	1	1	0					
Average	41.60	43.64	30.96	39.82	42.67	28.96	39.52	47.47	42.07	23.75	30.00	38.00	20.00	203.00	–					

FIELDING

68	JS Foster (65 ct, 3 st)
18	A Flower
16	TJ Phillips
15	ML Pettini
12	RS Bopara
7	GW Flower
7	V Chopra
6	JD Middlebrook
5	AP Palladino
5	AN Cook
4	AR Adams
4	RN ten Doeschate
2	AJ Tudor
1	D Gough
1	RC Irani
1	GR Napier
1	MS Westfield
1	JS Ahmed
0	AJ Bichel
0	WI Jefferson

Final Division Two Table

	P	W	L	D	Bat	Bowl	Pts
Surrey	16	10	2	4	62	44	262.00
Worcestershire	16	8	4	4	58	43	229.00
Essex	16	7	4	5	62	40	220.00
Leicestershire	16	5	4	7	47	41	185.50
Derbyshire	16	4	4	8	51	41	178.50
Northamptonshire	16	3	5	8	52	37	163.00
Gloucestershire	16	3	6	7	51	36	155.50
Glamorgan	16	2	7	7	51	41	146.50
Somerset	16	3	9	4	43	40	140.00

GLAMORGAN CCC

FIRST-CLASS MATCHES
BATTING

Match	MJ Powell	DL Hemp	RDB Croft	MA Wallace	RE Watkins	DS Harrison	DA Cosker	MJ Cosgrove	AG Wharf	DD Cherry	JEC Franklin	N Peng	RN Grant	HT Waters	AP Davies	BB McCullum	GP Rees	BJ Wright	KD Tudge	SP Jones	AJ Harrison	Extras	Total	Wickets	Result	Points
v. Essex	38	31	7	47*	87			31	12		39	25			1					0		19	337	10		
(Cardiff) 26-29 April	36	36	71	48	5			4	7		2	28			7					4*		24	272	10	L	4
v. Derbyshire	100	0	2	52	7		0	114	5		6	0	2*									27	315	10		
(Cardiff) 3-6 May	10	0	41*	6	5	1	18	5			56	2	16									24	184	10	L	6
v. Leicestershire	73	38	27	2	18		8	5	19	66			7		11*							23	297	10		
(Leicester) 9-12 May	4*	86	0		1			54*		91			12									19	267	5	D	8
v. Worcestershire	4	29	10	37	8	4		61	2	33	8				14*							29	239	10		
(Worcester) 23-26 May	20	10		31*	41			71*		40		49										19	281	5	D	8
v. Somerset	31	12	17	5	7	9*	3	19	49	20	37											14	223	10		
(Swansea) 31 May-1 June	4	21	10	9	0	4*	11	5	4	6	4											25	103	10	L	4
v. Derbyshire	90	19	8	0		8*	0	233	9	3	36	33										31	470	10		
(Derby) 6-9 June	38*	8		34*				21		20		6										13	140	4	W	22
v. Northamptonshire	40	99	18	64		3	20*	1	60	27	3	8										11	354	10		
(Northampton) 14-17 June	6	5	10	7		2	0*	5	4	2	6	6										3	56	10	L	7
v. Surrey	27	21	72	0	19	36	28*	63	60			59	2									23	410	10		
(Swansea) 20-23 June	4*	21*			48			80														15	168	2	D	12
v. Leicestershire	127	29	17	1	20	12	1*	14			43	3				160						22	449	10		
(Cardiff) 14-17 July	4	7	0*	20	6			33*			23	34				16						11	154	7	D	11
v. Essex	202	14	14	64	6	64	11*				7		44			13					3	32	474	10		
(Chelmsford) 19-22 July	0	21	22	72	7*						53*					63						13	251	5	D	10
v. Gloucestershire	299	102		5	59			14*		94						20	1					53	647	7		
(Cheltenham) 26-29 July																34*	4*					6	44	10	W	22
v. Worcestershire	12	26	25	48	39	27	0		86		31		28						3*			15	340	10		
(Colwyn Bay) 2-5 August	5	16	44*	27	38	3	8		8		9		12						4			17	191	10	L	6
v. Somerset	34	43		15*	37*		8			77							20					6	240	5		
(Taunton) 15-18 August																									D	8
v. Surrey	18	0	71*	22	21	40	39	5			26		9	0								18	269	10		
(The Oval) 30 August-1 September	43	155	7	0	9	5	9*	16			1		3	0								7	255	10	L	5
v. Northamptonshire	27	0	21	9	30	13	8		71	2			5*		2							16	204	10		
(Northampton) 7-9 September	19	22	47	9	0	31	28		3	16			0*				57					16	248	10	L	4
v. Gloucestershire	12	132	40*	64	36	20	1			121		21			0			72				78	597	10		
(Cardiff) 20-23 September																									D	11
Matches	16	16	16	16	14	13	13	10	10	9	9	8	7	5	4	3	3	1	1	1	1					
Innings	29	29	24	27	25	16	16	19	15	17	15	15	11	7	6	6	5	1	2	2	1					
Not Out	3	1	5	4	2	3	6	2	2	0	1	0	0	2	3	1	1	0	1	1	0					
High Score	299	155	72	72	87	64	39	233	86	121	94	59	44	5*	16	160	57	72	4	4*	3					
Runs	1327	1003	601	698	554	281	168	856	397	532	346	357	196	7	51	306	84	72	7	4	3					
Average	51.03	35.82	31.63	30.34	24.08	21.61	16.80	50.35	30.53	31.29	24.71	23.80	17.81	1.40	17.00	61.20	21.00	72.00	7.00	4.00	3.00					
100s	4	3	0	0	0	0	0	2	0	1	0	0	0	0	0	1	0	0	0	0	0					
50s	2	2	3	5	2	1	0	6	3	3	2	2	0	0	0	1	1	1	0	0	0					
Catches/Stumpings	7/0	18/0	9/0	41/3	12/0	4/0	9/0	5/0	9/0	4/0	4/0	10/0	3/0	1/0	1/0	3/0	1/0	2/0	0/0	0/0	0/0					

Home Ground: Cardiff
Address: Sophia Gardens, Cardiff, CF11 9XR
Tel: 0871 2823401
Fax: 0871 2823405
Email: info@glamorgancricket.co.uk
Directions: *By rail:* Cardiff Central train station.
By road: From North, A470 and follow signs to Cardiff until junction with Cardiff bypass then A48 Port Talbot and City Centre. Cathedral Road is situated off A48 for Sophia Gardens.

Capacity: 4,000
Other grounds used: Swansea, Colwyn Bay, Abergavenny
Year formed: 1888

Chief Executive: Mike Fatkin
Chairman: Paul Russell
First XI Coach: John Derrick
Captain: Robert Croft
County colours: Navy blue and yellow/gold

Honours
County Championship
1948, 1969, 1997
Sunday League/NCL/Pro40
1993, 2002, 2004

Website:
www.glamorgancricket.com

GLAMORGAN CCC

FIRST-CLASS MATCHES
BOWLING

	RDB Croft	DS Harrison	DA Cosker	JEC Franklin	RE Watkins	AG Wharf	HT Waters	AP Davies	MJ Cosgrove	RN Grant	AJ Harrison	SP Jones	DD Cherry	KD Tudge	Overs	Total	Byes/Leg-byes	Wickets	Run outs
v. Essex (Cardiff) 26-29 April	33.3-1-139-1				19-2-77-1	26-5-82-2		39-3-147-2		13-0-82-1		28-4-96-1			158.3	639	16	8	
v. Derbyshire (Cardiff) 3-6 May	37-8-86-3		34.5-7-69-3		8-3-36-0		22-7-49-2	21-7-55-1	9-2-35-0						131.5	335	5	10	1
	34-10-51-4		30.4-7-78-4		3-2-10-1		4-0-18-0	9-2-33-1							80.4	192	2	10	
v. Leicestershire (Leicester) 9-12 May	39-6-106-2		28.2-1-93-1		25-5-78-2	31-8-100-1		29-9-70-2	15-2-53-1						167.2	525	25	10	1
v. Worcestershire (Worcester) 23-26 May		20.4-3-76-5			13-1-40-4	13-0-62-1		16-1-69-0							62.4	252	5	10	
	3-1-5-2	10.2-3-33-2			4-1-19-2	11-4-27-1		10-2-28-2							38	117	5	9	
v. Somerset (Swansea) 31 May-1 June	7.2-0-30-1	13-3-32-1	14-4-38-3	14-3-53-4	6-1-19-1	10-2-33-0									64.2	210	5	10	
	1-0-4-0	8-2-24-1	3.4-0-31-0	5-1-27-3	2-0-16-0	2-0-15-0									21.4	118	1	4	
v. Derbyshire (Derby) 6-9 June	34.5-14-56-5	23-6-49-1	29-9-61-2	20-2-80-1		9-0-56-0			4-1-8-1						119.5	327	17	10	
	39-10-73-4	3-1-2-0	41-7-119-4	8-1-27-0		12-3-39-1									103	282	22	10	1
v. Northamptonshire (Northampton) 14-17 June	2-0-2-1	23-7-61-1		13-3-49-4		15-0-56-3				3-1-8-1					56	178	2	10	
	47.5-11-99-4	19-0-77-1	39-7-86-3	14.5-27-0		17-2-82-1				6-0-15-1					142.5	400	14	10	
v. Surrey (Swansea) 20-23 June	13-4-33-2	22-2-97-4	9-2-20-0		10-0-53-1	26.3-1-126-3				3-0-13-0					83.3	348	6	10	
	39-5-140-3	23-5-73-0	35-2-96-1		11-2-37-0	25.2-4-67-4				8-1-25-0					141.2	448	12	8	
v. Leicestershire (Cardiff) 14-17 July	55-6-186-3	30-7-83-1	44-2-138-3		19-2-67-3	20-1-74-0									168	560	10	10	
	22-5-105-1	6-2-21-0	18-2-74-0		8-2-22-0										54	228	6	3	2
v. Essex (Chelmsford) 19-22 July	45-9-104-4	22-9-43-0	37.2-11-105-2		25-7-59-2	19-3-44-0				4-1-9-1	21-3-81-1				173.2	462	17	10	
v. Gloucestershire (Cheltenham) 26-29 July	37.2-4-120-6	21-3-63-0	22-2-73-1		17-3-89-2	6-0-44-0	14-4-34-1								117.2	443	20	10	
	29.5-5-67-7	13.2-2-51-2	22.4-5-51-1		9-1-31-0		11-2-32-0								85.5	244	12	10	
v. Worcestershire (Colwyn Bay) 2-5 August	28.4-5-86-3	26-8-56-2			24-3-102-2	20-1-98-1			8-0-31-0					7-1-21-0	123.4	460	8	10	1
	20-2-90-1	19-1-95-0			12-0-47-1	9-1-48-0				11-0-36-1		3.5-0-15-1		6-0-37-0	80.5	382	14	5	1
v. Somerset (Taunton) 15-18 August	19.3-5-63-3	2.1-1-2-0	9-2-35-0		25.5-5-115-2			29-7-86-5		3-0-10-0	3-1-14-0				91.3	330	5	10	
v. Surrey (The Oval) 30 August-1 September	21-3-90-2	23-4-86-2	17-3-46-0	24.1-5-68-5	9-1-47-0		17-2-74-1					2-0-8-0			113.1	433	14	10	
	11-2-75-0	16-1-74-3	15-0-61-1	15-1-72-0			4-1-23-0								61	309	4	5	1
v. Northamptonshire (Northampton) 7-9 September	22-1-86-1	17-3-73-0	20-4-73-2	13-1-82-3	4-1-13-0		14.3-4-33-4						0.4-0-4-0		90.3	369	9	10	1
	5.4-2-30-0	8-0-33-1	0.2-0-2-0	2-0-14-0											16.4	84	1	1	
v. Gloucestershire (Cardiff) 20-23 September	26-2-98-0	29-8-95-4	21-2-100-1	23.3-6-67-3	17-3-55-1		17-2-87-0								133.3	525	23	10	1
	29-4-88-3	23-8-88-4	12-3-37-1	13-3-56-1	3-0-24-0		4-1-10-0								84	308	5	9	

	RDB Croft	DS Harrison	DA Cosker	JEC Franklin	RE Watkins	AG Wharf	HT Waters	AP Davies	MJ Cosgrove	RN Grant	AJ Harrison	SP Jones	DD Cherry	KD Tudge
Overs	702.3	420.1	502.5	251.4	230.5	262.5	111.3	124	70	25.5	21	28	0.4	13
Maidens	125	88	82	45	36	37	24	24	7	2	3	4	0	1
Runs	2112	1387	1486	950	922	983	380	402	234	128	81	96	4	58
Wickets	66	35	33	31	19	19	12	8	5	3	1	1	0	0
Average	32.00	39.62	45.03	30.64	48.52	51.73	31.66	50.25	46.80	42.66	81.00	96.00	-	-

FIELDING

44	MA Wallace (41 ct, 3 st)
18	DL Hemp
12	RE Watkins
10	N Peng
9	RDB Croft
9	AG Wharf
9	DA Cosker
7	MJ Powell
5	MJ Cosgrove
4	DD Cherry
4	DS Harrison
4	JEC Franklin
3	BB McCullum
3	RN Grant
2	BJ Wright
1	AP Davies
1	GP Rees
1	HT Waters
0	SP Jones
0	AJ Harrison
0	KD Tudge

Final Division Two Table

	P	W	L	D	Bat	Bowl	Pts
Surrey	16	10	2	4	62	44	262.00
Worcestershire	16	8	4	4	58	43	229.00
Essex	16	7	4	5	62	40	220.00
Leicestershire	16	5	4	7	47	41	185.50
Derbyshire	16	4	4	8	51	41	178.50
Northamptonshire	16	3	5	8	52	37	163.00
Gloucestershire	16	3	6	7	51	36	155.50
Glamorgan	16	2	7	7	51	41	146.50
Somerset	16	3	9	4	43	40	140.00

(Glamorgan deducted 0.50 points v. Essex, 26 April; and
1.00 point v. Worcs, 23 May for a slow over rate)

GLOUCESTERSHIRE CCC

FIRST-CLASS MATCHES

BATTING

Match	APR Gidman	CM Spearman	SJ Adshead	SP Kirby	CG Taylor	WPC Weston	HJH Marshall	Kadeer Ali	MA Hardinges	J Lewis	MCJ Ball	IJ Harvey	ID Fisher	MGN Windows	CG Greenidge	JMM Averis	WD Rudge	V Banerjee	DA Burton	DO Brown	Extras	Total	Wickets	Result	Points
v. Somerset (Bristol) 18-21 April	103	109	7	3	10	54		16	21*	15	45		20								34	437	10		
																								W	22
v. Surrey (The Oval) 3-5 May	5	3	23	6*	8	102					16	0		0	0	21					23	207	10		
	39*	13	22	0	0	28					0	ah		1	0	8					24	135	10	L	2
v. Northamptonshire (Bristol) 10-12 May	8	11	4	5	7	54		8	102*	5			6	5							17	232	10		
	12	5			5	21			12*				38*	†							9	102	4	W	18
v. Essex (Chelmsford) 23-26 May	4	19	36	3	66	62		16		33*		114	12	8							23	396	10		
	10	30	58	0	27	23			107*	29	27		0	4							8	323	10	D	11
v. Worcestershire (Bristol) 2-5 June	6	192	13	1	24	13	102	35		12	50*				2						21	471	10		
	5*	14	6*		58	61	9														10	163	4	D	11
v. Derbyshire (Bristol) 14-17 June	59	30	13	19*	39	3*rh	84	68	0	57	58										26	456	10		
	31*	47	32*		121	ah	2	55													12	300	4	D	11
v. Leicestershire (Leicester) 20-23 June	32	35	49	2*	29		0*	42	24	31	1	17									20	282	10		
	115*	36			1		83					72*									16	323	3	W	19
v. Essex (Bristol) 13-16 July	87	70	68	3*	9		28	27	38	0	45	2									17	394	10		
	4	51	16*		30		43	3	0	40	4	48									11	251	10	L	6
v. Worcestershire (Worcester) 20-23 July	25	15	20	0*		44	112	6		15	0	14			20						5	276	10		
	27	24	22*	4		29	20	8		0	14	5			3						13	169	10	L	5
v. Glamorgan (Cheltenham) 26-29 July	3	106	41	1*	30	18	127	60		6	17	2				†					32	443	10		
	66	7	26	1	23	9	53	0		23	1	21*									14	244	10	L	6
v. Leicestershire (Cheltenham) 2-5 August	58	28	55	4*		36	21	10		14	31	3					1				21	282	10		
	120	39	8		4		168	8		0	32*	35*									25	439	7	L	4
v. Northamptonshire (Northampton) 8-11 August	63	140	24	8	0	7	1	32		6						39					22	350	6		
	17*	137	14		37	87	133	145		1*							8*				25	596	6	D	10
v. Derbyshire (Derby) 17-20 August	35	0	0	13*	17	46	1	33	†	17		19	33								26	240	10		
	0*	0	56		0	70	76*														6	208	4	D	7
v. Somerset (Taunton) 22-24 August	11	18	1		5	69	31	4	6*	4					0	0					12	161	10		
	17	16	10		3	11	0	24	50	23					7	0*					11	172	10	L	3
v. Surrey (Bristol) 6-9 September	52	100	0	3*	14	130	56	32	13							53	0				6	459	10		
	20	45	79*	10*	4	0	76	36	38							6					15	329	8	D	12
v. Glamorgan (Cardiff) 20-23 September	92	26	29	2	54		79	18	101									7	52*	34	31	525	10		
	118	4	11	17*	28		73	23	0									5*	1	22	6	308	9	D	10
Matches	16	16	16	15	14	13	11	11	11	11	10	9	5	5	5	4	4	3	1	1					
Innings	31	31	28	22	27	24	21	22	15	14	15	15	8	9	8	7	2	5	2	2					
Not Out	6	0	5	11	0	1	1	1	2	2	1	5	2	1	0	0	1	2	1	0					
High Score	120	192	79*	19*	121	130	168	145	107*	57	58	114	45	48	20	53	8*	7	52*	34					
Runs	1244	1370	687	106	705	911	1218	834	444	242	215	561	168	127	42	128	9	12	53	56					
Average	49.76	44.19	29.86	9.63	26.11	39.60	60.90	39.71	34.15	20.16	15.35	56.10	28.00	15.87	5.25	18.28	9.00	4.00	53.00	28.00					
100s	4	6	0	0	1	2	5	1	2	0	0	2	0	0	0	0	0	0	0	0					
50s	7	2	4	0	4	6	7	5	1	1	1	2	0	0	0	1	0	0	1	0					
Catches/Stumpings	2/0	18/0	47/2	3/0	12/0	7/0	6/0	6/0	0/0	4/0	16/0	4/0	1/0	2/0	3/0	0/0	0/0	1/0	0/0	0/0					

Key: ah absent hurt; rh retired hurt; † replaced by J Lewis

Home Ground: Bristol
Address: County Ground, Nevil Road, Bristol, BS7 9EJ
Tel: 01179 108000
Fax: 01179 241193
Email: reception@glosccc.co.uk
Directions: By road: M5, M4, M32 into Bristol, exit at second exit (Fishponds/Horfield), then third exit – Muller Road. Almost at end of Muller Road (bus station on right), turn left at Ralph Road. Go to the top, turn left and then right almost immediately into Kennington Avenue. Follow the signs for County Cricket.

Capacity: 8,000
Other grounds used: Gloucester, Cheltenham College
Year formed: 1870

Chief Executive: Tom Richardson
Chairman: Ray Parsons
Director of Cricket: Andy Stovold
Head Coach: Mark Alleyne
Captain: Jon Lewis
County colours: Blue, brown, gold, green and red

Honours
Sunday League/NCL/Pro40
2000
Benson & Hedges Cup
1977, 1999, 2000
Gillette Cup/NatWest/C&G Trophy
1973, 1999, 2000, 2003, 2004

Website:
www.glosccc.co.uk

GLOUCESTERSHIRE CCC

FIRST-CLASS MATCHES
BOWLING

	SP Kirby	J Lewis	MCJ Ball	MA Hardinges	APR Gidman	IJ Harvey	JMM Averis	ID Fisher	V Banerjee	CG Greenidge	CG Taylor	WD Rudge	HJH Marshall	Kadeer Ali	DO Brown	DA Burton	Overs	Total	Byes/Leg-byes	Wickets	Run outs
v. Somerset	14-2-49-0	14.3-4-38-7		5-0-32-1		7-2-21-2					3-2-11-0						40.3	143	3	10	
(Bristol) 18-21 April	16-4-51-0	15-5-37-3	13-1-54-0	17-4-69-2	5-1-21-1	16-2-39-3											85	287	5	10	1
v. Surrey	30-2-132-1		42.1-7-134-6		16-0-85-1		24-4-111-0				28-0-146-0	4-0-18-0					144.1	639	13	8	
(The Oval) 3-5 May																					
v. Northamptonshire	20.3-7-67-2		4-2-3-0	18-7-52-2		15-2-40-3					15-4-50-3						72.3	219	7	10	
(Bristol) 10-12 May	10-3-27-1	16.5-2-36-5		6-2-23-1		8-1-25-3											40.5	114	3	10	
v. Essex	23.2-5-91-3		11-0-50-1	21.4-7-72-2	19.8-8-38-3	12-3-31-0					23-4-91-1						109.2	388	10	10	
(Chelmsford) 23-26 May	8-1-39-0			4-2-5-1	4-0-30-0						5-0-24-1	3-1-4-0					24	102	0	2	
v. Worcestershire	23-4-105-0		29.5-5-107-2	27-3-127-4	18.4-2-72-1	18.2-5-61-1				13-2-91-0	3-0-18-0						132.5	587	6	8	
(Bristol) 2-5 June	16-4-54-3		21-1-86-2	11-1-40-1						15-2-56-3							63	247	11	9	
v. Derbyshire	19.1-4-87-4	25-5-92-1	25.2-8-67-1	15.4-4-70-1	17-6-45-1						1-0-5-0			7-1-22-0			110.1	402	14	8	
(Bristol) 14-17 June	20.4-2-97-2	24.5-4-73-3	17.2-3-72-2	10-2-37-0													72.5	286	7	8	1
v. Leicestershire	18-4-78-2	27.4-6-93-4	13-3-36-0	23-5-82-1	16-3-40-2	12-6-25-1											109.4	371	17	10	
(Leicester) 20-23 June	20-3-73-1	23-12-36-4	10.3-3-36-3	10-2-44-1	6-0-23-1	7-2-16-0											76.3	233	5	10	
v. Essex	34-11-94-4	32-3-93-3		21-4-64-0	15-6-27-1	16-5-51-0		48-5-178-2			2-0-20-0			1-0-4-0			169	548	17	10	
(Bristol) 13-16 July	7.5-1-36-1	7-0-27-2						8-0-32-0									22.5	98	3	3	
v. Worcestershire	19-2-64-2	19-5-77-6	1-0-1-0		5-1-29-1	11-3-37-0				9-1-58-1							64	271	5	10	
(Worcester) 20-23 July	18-3-72-3	20.3-1-93-4	14-2-24-3		4-0-19-0	4-3-5-0				1.3-0-17-0							62	232	2	10	
v. Glamorgan	28-3-117-1	7-0-28-0	60-19-113-2		24-4-103-1		44.3-3-166-2					19-0-99-1		2-0-9-0			184.3	647	12	7	
(Cheltenham) 26-29 July	1.4-0-29-0	2-0-15-0															3.4	44	0	0	
v. Leicestershire	32-7-117-4		34.4-7-84-3		4-0-11-0	16-4-27-0	26-2-110-3					20-2-95-0	7-2-27-0				139.4	482	11	10	
(Cheltenham) 2-5 August	7-2-27-1		11-0-63-2				10.5-0-74-0	14-3-70-2									42.5	241	7	6	1
v. Northamptonshire	32.3-5-99-5	29-7-109-1		19-4-63-0			31-5-108-1				15-0-75-2	20-0-117-1		4-1-22-0			150.3	628	35	10	
(Northampton) 8-11 August											10.4-4-19-0		11-3-16-0				21	35	0	0	
v. Derbyshire	18.4-2-74-2	16-2-69-1			8.2-1-41-1	17-3-75-0	33-4-87-2				21-3-43-0						114	400	11	6	
(Derby) 17-20 August																	-	-	-	-	
v. Somerset		29-6-104-2		26-6-106-1	16-3-38-2		24.4-5-79-4	24-5-76-0			1-0-4-0						120.4	409	2	10	1
(Taunton) 22-24 August																	-	-	-	-	
v. Surrey	20-4-45-2			19-5-67-1	14-3-40-1		18-2-75-4	15-3-45-2		8-2-25-0			2-1-4-0				86	288	16	10	
(Bristol) 6-9 September	28-6-95-2			16-2-61-2	3-2-1-0		24.1-1-133-2	31-6-129-3									112	470	22	9	
v. Glamorgan	32.2-4-125-3			21-4-55-2	18-5-36-0			42-10-150-4			5-0-25-0		6-1-16-1		9-2-30-0	20-1-129-0	153.2	597	31	10	
(Cardiff) 20-23 September																	-	-	-	-	

	SP Kirby	J Lewis	MCJ Ball	MA Hardinges	APR Gidman	IJ Harvey	JMM Averis	ID Fisher	V Banerjee	CG Greenidge	CG Taylor	WD Rudge	HJH Marshall	Kadeer Ali	DO Brown	DA Burton
Overs	517.4	322.2	307.5	270.4	232	142.2	107.4	201.2	112	109.3	76	59	26	14	9	20
Maidens	95	65	61	57	49	38	15	19	24	13	12	2	7	2	2	1
Runs	1944	1090	930	1011	762	378	473	755	400	533	267	311	63	57	30	129
Wickets	49	48	27	23	17	13	10	10	9	9	2	2	1	0	0	0
Average	39.67	22.70	34.44	43.95	44.82	29.07	47.30	75.50	44.44	59.22	133.50	155.50	63.00	-	-	-

FIELDING

49	SJ Adshead (47 ct, 2 st)
18	CM Spearman
16	MCJ Ball
12	CG Taylor
7	WPC Weston
6	Kadeer Ali
6	HJH Marshall
4	J Lewis
4	IJ Harvey
3	CG Greenidge
3	SP Kirby
2	MGN Windows
2	APR Gidman
1	ID Fisher
1	V Banerjee
0	JMM Averis
0	MA Hardinges
0	WD Rudge
0	DO Brown
0	DA Burton

Final Division Two Table

	P	W	L	D	Bat	Bowl	Pts
Surrey	16	10	2	4	62	44	262.00
Worcestershire	16	8	4	4	58	43	229.00
Essex	16	7	4	5	62	40	220.00
Leicestershire	16	5	4	7	47	41	185.50
Derbyshire	16	4	4	8	51	41	178.50
Northamptonshire	16	3	5	8	52	37	163.00
Gloucestershire	16	3	6	7	51	36	155.50
Glamorgan	16	2	7	7	51	41	146.50
Somerset	16	3	9	4	43	40	140.00

(Gloucestershire deducted 1.00 point v. Northants, 10 May; and 0.50 points v. Worcs, 20 July for a slow over rate)

HAMPSHIRE CCC

FIRST-CLASS MATCHES
BATTING

	JHK Adams	JP Crawley	AD Mascarenhas	N Pothas	MA Carberry	DJ Thornely	SM Ervine	SK Warne	JTA Bruce	SD Udal	CC Benham	CT Tremlett	BV Taylor	MJ Brown	GA Lamb	RJ Logan	TG Burrows	JA Tomlinson	JJ McLean	KJ Latouf	DA Griffiths	Extras	Total	Wickets	Result	Points
v. Lancashire	2	20	0	6	30	31	44*		5	8				23	4							21	194	10		
(Old Trafford) 18-21 April	26*													21*								7	54	0	D	7
v. Sussex	13	18	11	9	43	18	38		5*	3	4			0								6	168	10		
(Rose Bowl) 26-28 April	17	14	7	1	39	42	2		1*	13	23			37								15	211	10	L	3
v. Middlesex	11	55	38	100	29	65	34	22	16*	28		0										28	426	10		
(Rose Bowl) 3-5 May	14*				0*																	4	18	0	W	22
v. Warwickshire	40	96	5	67*	102	42	7	17	0	4	5											20	405	10		
(Edgbaston) 9-12 May	85	0	41	9	11	30*	23															19	218	6	W	21
v. Loughborough UCCE	11										34		2*	133	29	4	20	3	60	29	16*	37	378	9		
(Rose Bowl) 17-19 May																									D	
v. Kent	0	43	34	96	17	13	12	9	17			0*	0									30	271	10		
(Rose Bowl) 24-27 May	4	83*	20		7	34	16*	3					2									7	176	6	D	9
v. Yorkshire	30	54	3	10	52	76	0	0					0*	0	0							23	248	10		
(Headingley) 31 May-3 June	168*	19	2	23	62	71									32*							27	404	5	W	18
v. Nottinghamshire	21	106	25	117	15	19	13	19	4	17*		0										45	401	10		
(Rose Bowl) 7-9 June	80	116			23	10*																22	251	3	W	22
v. Durham	29	93	1	17	20	21	0	25	0*		13	12										25	256	10		
(Rose Bowl) 20-22 June	32	31	0	7	12	4	0	12	0*		0	0										6	104	10	L	5
v. Nottinghamshire	262*	148			49	50*					35											28	572	10		
(Trent Bridge) 14-17 July	4	23	11	43*	8	0	46	11			15											12	173	8	D	11
v. Yorkshire	29	173	39	7	99	27	2	30			56	4*	3									24	493	10		
(Rose Bowl) 26-28 July	5*			10*																		0	15	0	W	22
v. Kent	38	189	131	52	0	52	15	44*														33	554	7		
(Canterbury) 2-5 August																									D	12
v. Middlesex	7	70	34	102*	104	9	42	16*			1											17	402	7		
(Lord's) 8-11 August	29	13	0	74*	1	45	6	61*			39											15	283	7	D	12
v. Warwickshire	58	29	15		29	19	23		0*	14	5	18					11					14	235	10		
(Rose Bowl) 16-19 August	23	18	2		6	65	10		0*	28	95	9					18					12	286	10	L	4
v. Sussex	4	39	10	122*	7	5	25	53		3	62	1										16	347	10		
(Hove) 31 August-3 September	11	45	48*	62	1		50*				0											18	235	5	D	10
v. Durham	4	150	28	54	3	10	49		0*		91	0										31	425	10		
(Riverside) 7-9 September	84	29	0	5*	98		14*				30											18	278	5	W	22
v. Lancashire	32	63	17	4			7	30*	4		28			13	0			0				17	215	10		
(Rose Bowl) 20-23 September																									D	8

	JHK Adams	JP Crawley	AD Mascarenhas	N Pothas	MA Carberry	DJ Thornely	SM Ervine	SK Warne	JTA Bruce	SD Udal	CC Benham	CT Tremlett	BV Taylor	MJ Brown	GA Lamb	RJ Logan	TG Burrows	JA Tomlinson	JJ McLean	KJ Latouf	DA Griffiths
Matches	17	16	16	15	15	15	15	13	13	10	9	9	6	5	3	3	2	2	1	1	1
Innings	31	27	24	22	28	25	22	17	14	9	15	10	6	8	4	3	3	2	1	1	1
Not Out	5	1	0	7	2	3	3	5	8	1	0	1	3	1	1	0	0	0	0	0	1
High Score	262*	189	131	122*	104	76	50*	61*	17	28	95	23	3	133	32*	4	20	3	60	29	16*
Runs	1173	1737	474	973	938	759	464	371	52	118	504	76	5	229	61	8	49	3	60	29	16
Average	45.11	66.80	19.75	64.86	36.07	34.50	24.42	30.91	8.66	14.75	33.60	8.44	1.66	32.71	20.33	2.66	16.33	1.50	60.00	29.00	–
100s	2	6	1	4	2	0	0	0	0	0	0	0	0	1	0	0	0	0	0	0	0
50s	4	7	0	5	5	6	1	2	0	0	4	0	0	0	0	0	0	0	1	0	0
Catches/Stumpings	18/0	8/0	4/0	56/2	8/0	12/0	14/0	16/0	2/0	3/0	9/0	0/0	1/0	3/0	2/0	1/0	5/0	0/0	0/0	0/0	0/0

Home Ground: Southampton
Address: The Rose Bowl, Botley Road, West End, Southampton, SO30 3XH
Tel: 02380 472002
Fax: 02380 472122
Email: enquiries@rosebowlplc.com
Directions: From the North: M3 Southbound to junction 14, follow signs for M27 Eastbound (Fareham and Portsmouth). At junction 7 of M27, filter left onto Charles Watts Way (A334) and from there follow the brown road signs to the Rose Bowl. From the South: M27 to junction 7 and follow the brown road signs to the Rose Bowl.

Capacity: 9,950
Year formed: 1863

Chief Executive: Roger Bransgrove
Director of Cricket: Tim Tremlett
Captain: Shane Warne
County colours: Navy blue, old gold

Honours
County Championship
1961, 1973
Sunday League/NCL/Pro40
1975, 1978, 1986
Benson & Hedges Cup
1988, 1992
Gillette Cup/NatWest/C&G Trophy
1991, 2005

Website:
www.hampshirecricket.com

HAMPSHIRE CCC

FIRST-CLASS MATCHES
BOWLING

	SK Warne	AD Mascarenhas	JTA Bruce	CT Tremlett	SM Ervine	DJ Thornely	SD Udal	BV Taylor	JA Tomlinson	RJ Logan	MA Carberry	GA Lamb	N Pothas	JHK Adams	JP Crawley	CC Benham	DA Griffiths	Overs	Total	Byes/Leg-byes	Wickets	Run outs
v. Lancashire (Old Trafford) 18-21 April		21-8-40-1	22.3-4-52-4		11-2-38-2	5-2-11-1	4-1-7-0			16-3-71-2								79.3	224	5	10	
																		-	-	-	-	
v. Sussex (Rose Bowl) 26-28 April		13-4-34-0	19-9-35-2	16-7-30-0	16-4-57-3	13-5-38-3	7.3-2-12-2											84.3	211	5	10	
		11-0-28-0	17-6-59-3	12.3-4-24-1	13.3-3-60-2	11-2-52-2	9-2-27-2											74	262	12	10	
v. Middlesex (Rose Bowl) 3-5 May		8-2-12-0	7.3-1-33-2		5-0-20-2			12-2-32-6										32.3	98	1	10	
	37.1-5-99-7	10-1-26-0		14-2-47-0	11.3-2-61-1	5-0-16-0	20-3-65-1	12-0-61-1										109.1	344	4	10	
v. Warwickshire (Edgbaston) 9-12 May	27.2-9-52-5	16-5-38-2	11-1-42-2	10-2-34-0	15-5-28-0		12-6-15-1											91.2	217	8	10	
	33-12-58-2	7-2-8-0	15-5-37-2	16.5-2-50-3	11-5-25-1		17-8-23-2											99.5	213	12	10	
v. Loughborough UCCE (Rose Bowl) 17-19 May								8.3-4-14-0	7-2-28-0	7-1-27-0							6-2-29-0	28.3	101	3	0	
v. Kent (Rose Bowl) 24-27 May	15.4-2-38-4	16-4-35-2	16-1-49-1		15-3-43-2	8-4-10-0		11-2-41-1										81.4	223	7	10	
	11-4-16-1	4-0-9-1	5-1-9-0		8-1-35-2			6-0-23-0										34	94	2	4	
v. Yorkshire (Headingley) 31 May-3 June	28.1-8-68-4	17-4-51-0	20-3-55-1			7-1-14-1		22-4-64-2		15-1-58-1	1-0-4-0	3-0-13-0		2-0-8-0				115.1	350	15	10	1
	25-1-83-3	14-1-47-2	12-1-60-1			12-1-34-2		14-2-42-0		5-0-22-0								82	301	13	8	
v. Nottinghamshire (Rose Bowl) 7-9 June	1-0-2-0	12-4-25-4	10-2-52-2			9-0-31-0	2.4-0-7-2	8-1-25-2										42.4	147	5	10	
	18.1-3-53-3	9-3-15-0	16-3-43-5			9-2-41-0	8-1-21-1	6-3-16-0										74.1	206	6	10	
v. Durham (Rose Bowl) 20-22 June	11-1-56-0	15-7-25-3	8-1-33-1	13.2-1-51-3	16-3-45-2	5-3-17-1								4-0-13-0				68.2	234	7	10	
	17-1-46-1	32-5-93-4		28.1-5-101-3	8-2-23-0	24-10-61-2												113.1	353	16	10	
v. Nottinghamshire (Trent Bridge) 14-17 July	36-6-128-3	8-2-19-1		25-9-43-4	12-0-66-0	3-0-7-0	17-2-97-1											101	362	2	10	1
	24-4-92-1	19-6-35-2		21-3-50-1	15-5-44-0	8-2-37-0	16-2-60-0											103	318	4	5	
v. Yorkshire (Rose Bowl) 26-28 July	4-0-22-0	19-5-65-6		9.3-3-25-3	14-3-45-1	7-2-19-0				7-3-11-0								60.3	195	8	10	
	21.3-1-100-3	12-3-48-1		15-0-69-4	14-1-57-2					10-1-35-0								72.3	311	2	10	
v. Kent (Canterbury) 2-5 August	11.4-1-26-3	19-10-29-1	11-4-31-0	16-3-56-2	6-2-18-1	17-2-62-2	13-2-54-1											93.4	285	9	10	
	32-13-54-0	8-2-24-0	17-3-59-0		9-2-42-0	8-2-20-0	15-4-39-0				4-0-16-0			6-2-12-0	2-1-5-0	2-0-8-0		103	281	2	0	
v. Middlesex (Lord's) 8-11 August	29.4-2-88-4	26-9-53-4	22-5-79-0		23-9-72-0	19-5-60-2	11-0-37-0							1-0-7-0				131.4	422	21	10	
	16-0-43-0	12-2-47-1	5-1-23-0		9-1-37-1	11-3-26-1	7-0-20-0				2-0-9-0			5-0-16-1	1.1-0-26-0	3-0-21-0		75.1	309	11	4	
v. Warwickshire (Rose Bowl) 16-19 August		25-6-60-0	16-2-86-0	26-4-89-6	9-1-40-0	16-2-42-2	22.5-5-73-2											114.3	401	3	10	
		8-0-39-5	5-1-26-1	6-0-29-0	1-0-11-0		5-0-14-1											25	121	2	8	1
v. Sussex (Hove) 31 August-3 September	42.3-7-136-6	11-3-19-0		24-1-100-1	21-1-52-2	6-1-22-0		25-3-82-1								2-0-17-0		122.3	448	20	10	
																		-	-	-	-	
v. Durham (Riverside) 7-9 September	8.2-1-21-2	12-4-22-1	10-0-60-2	16-5-51-3	8.4-3-24-1	3.2-0-12-0												58.2	195	5	10	1
	23.3-1-135-5	6-1-19-0	11-2-33-3	9-2-33-0							15-0-85-2		5-0-22-0					69.3	334	7	10	
v. Lancashire (Rose Bowl) 20-23 September	35-6-105-0	24-5-64-2	24-5-85-4						17-4-64-2			22-0-95-2		4-1-19-0				126	438	6	10	
	15-3-50-1	13-5-45-0	13-4-21-2		16-0-76-0				15-4-54-2			10-1-27-0	3-1-8-0	9-2-46-1	1-0-7-0			97	339	5	6	

	SK Warne	AD Mascarenhas	JTA Bruce	CT Tremlett	SM Ervine	DJ Thornely	SD Udal	BV Taylor	JA Tomlinson	RJ Logan	MA Carberry	GA Lamb	N Pothas	JHK Adams	JP Crawley	CC Benham	DA Griffiths					
Overs	523.4	429	327	264.2	296.1	199	209	116.3	39	43	22	35	19	25.1	5	5	6					
Maidens	91	111	67	51	60	49	41	22	10	5	0	1	3	4	0	0	2					
Runs	1571	1074	1109	835	1060	578	646	364	146	178	114	135	58	141	29	37	29					
Wickets	58	43	38	34	26	22	15	12	4	3	2	2	1	1	0	0	0					
Average	27.08	24.97	29.18	24.55	40.76	26.27	43.06	30.33	36.50	59.33	57.00	67.50	58.00	141.00	-	-	-					

FIELDING

58	N Pothas (56 ct, 2 st)
18	JHK Adams
16	SK Warne
14	SM Ervine
12	DJ Thornely
9	CC Benham
8	JP Crawley
8	MA Carberry
5	TG Burrows
4	AD Mascarenhas
3	SD Udal
3	MJ Brown
2	JTA Bruce
2	GA Lamb
1	RJ Logan
1	BV Taylor
0	CT Tremlett
0	JA Tomlinson
0	KJ Latouf
0	DA Griffiths
0	JJ McLean

Final Division One Table

	P	W	L	D	Bat	Bowl	Pts
Sussex	16	9	2	5	49	47	242.00
Lancashire	16	6	1	9	58	46	224.00
Hampshire	16	6	3	7	48	48	207.00
Warwickshire	16	6	5	5	42	43	189.00
Kent	16	4	4	8	43	44	175.00
Yorkshire	16	3	6	7	43	41	154.00
Durham	16	4	8	4	39	43	153.50
Nottinghamshire	16	4	7	5	40	37	153.00
Middlesex	16	1	7	8	47	42	133.50

(Hampshire deducted 1.00 point v. Warwicks, 16 August for a slow over rate)

KENT CCC

FIRST-CLASS MATCHES
BATTING

Match	DI Stevens	MJ Walker	M van Jaarsveld	DP Fulton	RWT Key	MM Patel	SJ Cook	NJ O'Brien	A Khan	RH Joseph	NJ Dexter	GO Jones	JC Tredwell	JM Kemp	T Henderson	DJJ Bravo	AJ Hall	JL Denly	RS Ferley	MJ Saggers	DJ Chambers	DA Stiff	MJ Dennington	SMJ Cusden	PG Dixey	JA Iles	Extras	Total	Wickets	Result	Points
v. Durham (Canterbury) 19-22 April	62	27	83	62	23	19	27	3	0*	4	6																24	340	10		
	7	14	37	13	1	61	2	13	15*	0	5																11	179	10	L	5
v. Middlesex (Lord's) 26-29 April	15	123	63	30	4	2	6	10	11	0*			13														31	308	10		
	35*	84*	104	77	19																						37	356	3	W	20
v. Lancashire (Old Trafford) 3-5 May	10	41	87	40		8	6			4	34	29	2	54*													12	327	10		
	0	2	15	7		0*	10			0	5	60	7	7													11	124	10	L	6
v. Yorkshire (Canterbury) 10-13 May	3	60	82	75	81		0	6		29	39			124*	14												20	533	10		
																														D	11
v. Cambridge UCCE (Fenner's) 17-19 May	52						37				116							115	0	2*	12						26	360	7		
											62*							107*									15	184		D	
v. Hampshire (Rose Bowl) 24-27 May	10	26	15	0	28	4	4	38	2					16			61*										19	223	10		
	17*	1	24	18	17									9*													8	94	4	D	8
v. Warwickshire (Tunbridge Wells) 31 May-3 June	24	57	9	10	12		0	26*	0		10	28					27										31	234	10		
			57*	31	98*																						11	197	1	W	18
v. Durham (Stockton-on-Tees) 13-15 June	1	2	59	27	0	11	0	0*					16	0			36										27	179	10		
	70	6	2	29	4	0	62	0*					47	118			45										28	411	10	W	17
v. Nottinghamshire (Canterbury) 20-23 June	7	141	108	65	31		8				131*						68*										41	600	6		
																														D	10
v. Sussex (Hove) 13-16 July	118	87	10	0	16	9	16	10*						6	4	23											37	336	10		
	43	70*	23	2	36	13								0	31*	31											31	280	7	D	10
v. Lancashire (Canterbury) 18-21 July	25	197	6	29	16	0	10	38						13		76							2*				28	440	10		
	16	1	59	64	2	16*	7	19*						11		6											14	215	8	W	22
v. Hampshire (Canterbury) 2-5 August	8	52	34	14	27	1		5*					0	35	59	6											19	285	10		
				134*	136*																						11	281	0	D	7
v. Yorkshire (Headingley) 16-19 August	31	6	61*	6	40		71					0		8*													7	230	6		
																														D	8
v. Nottinghamshire (Trent Bridge) 22-24 August	15	65	2	57	20	6	30	12*	4					17		8											15	251	10		
	2	17	10	14	31	17	0	0*	4					8		33											24	160	10	L	5
v. Sussex (Canterbury) 5-8 September	24	48	116	4	15	2	1	0	1		2*		2														26	241	10		
	54	66	9	6	0	2	7	30*	4		15		1														14	208	10	L	4
v. Warwickshire (Edgbaston) 13-16 September	61	19	79	25	25	28	4*	0				50		21				86									23	421	10		
	61*	103*	61	49														13									24	311	3	D	12
v. Middlesex (Canterbury) 20-23 September	126*	104	2	155					35*					59				66	22								34	603	6		
																														D	12
Matches	17	16	16	15	14	13	11	10	9	9	8	7	7	6	6	5	4	3	3	2	1	1	1	1	1	1					
Innings	27	26	27	26	25	16	14	13	10	12	12	10	10	9	9	8	5	5	3	2	1	0	1	0	1	0					
Not Out	4	3	2	1	2	2	0	1	7	4	4	1	1	3	1	0	2	1	0	1	0	0	1	0	0	0					
High Score	126*	197	116	155	136*	61	71	62	38	29	131*	60	47	124*	59	76	68*	115	22	2*	12	0	2*	0	0	0					
Runs	897	1419	1217	969	731	179	196	241	98	63	463	254	126	369	146	208	237	387	36	2	12	0	2	0	0	0					
Average	39.00	61.69	48.68	38.76	31.78	12.78	14.00	20.08	32.66	7.87	57.87	28.22	14.00	61.50	18.25	26.00	79.00	96.75	12.00	2.00	12.00	–	–	–	–	–					
100s	2	5	3	2	1	0	0	0	0	0	2	0	0	2	0	0	0	2	0	0	0	0	0	0	0	0					
50s	6	8	10	6	2	1	1	1	0	0	1	3	0	1	1	2	2	0	0	0	0	0	0	0	0	0					
Catches/Stumpings	18/0	9/0	36/0	7/0	8/0	4/0	1/0	19/8	1/0	1/0	3/0	12/1	7/0	10/0	2/0	0/0	3/0	1/0	0/0	0/0	1/0	0/0	0/0	0/0	3/0	0/0					

Home Ground: Canterbury
Address: St Lawrence Ground, Old Dover Road, Canterbury, CT1 3NZ
Tel: 01227 456886
Fax: 01227 762168
Email: jon.fordham.kent@ecb.co.uk
Directions: From the North, From M20 junction 7 turn left onto A249. At M2 junction 5 (Sittingbourne) bear right onto M2. At junction 7 (Boughton Street) turn right on to A2. Follow this to junction with A2050, turn left. Follow yellow signs to cricket ground. From the South, From M20 junction 13 bear right onto A20. Follow this road to junction with A260. Bear left and continue to junction with A2 (north). Continue to junction with A2050 and then proceed as north.
Capacity: 10,000
Other grounds used: Beckenham, Maidstone, Tunbridge Wells
Year formed: 1870

Chief Executive: Paul Millman
Director of Cricket: Graham Ford
Coaching Co-Ordinator: Simon Willis
Captain: Robert Key
County Colours: Red, yellow and black

Honours
County Championship
1906, 1909, 1910, 1913, 1970, 1978
Joint Champions 1977
Sunday League/NCL/Pro40
1972, 1973, 1976, 1995, 2001
Benson & Hedges Cup
1973, 1978
Gillette Cup/NatWest/C&G Trophy
1967, 1974

Website:
www.kentccc.com

KENT CCC

FIRST-CLASS MATCHES
BOWLING

Match	A Khan	MM Patel	SJ Cook	JC Tredwell	RH Joseph	DI Stevens	AJ Hall	JM Kemp	RS Ferley	T Henderson	DJJ Bravo	NJ Dexter	MJ Saggers	JL Denly	MJ Dennington	SMJ Cusden	NJO'Brien	JA Iles	DA Stiff	M van Jaarsveld	MJ Walker	DP Fulton	RWT Key	Overs	Total	Byes/Leg-byes	Wickets	Run outs
v. Durham (Canterbury) 19-22 April	32-2-115-0	28-5-100-4	19-2-85-1		29-7-124-3	10-0-55-0							20-5-76-2											138	575	20	10	
																								–	–	–	–	
v. Middlesex (Lord's) 26-29 April	23-4-82-1	12-1-42-0	18-4-48-1		22.1-2-62-4	6-0-14-1	20-3-72-3														5-1-18-1			101.1	333	13	10	
	17.1-3-58-4	12-1-52-0	15-1-48-0		23-3-67-4	9-1-19-0	12-1-51-1																	93.1	327	14	10	
v. Lancashire (Old Trafford) 3-5 May			23-6-60-2	27.3-3-102-2	25-5-84-2		24-3-63-2					21-4-40-2										1-1-0-0		121.3	363	14	10	
			6-0-31-0	7-1-34-3	7-2-18-0	2.2-1-5-1																		22.2	89	1	4	
v. Yorkshire (Canterbury) 10-13 May			27-8-67-4		26-5-86-0	17.3-3-36-4	20-3-56-1		14-3-42-0			17-2-55-1					6-1-17-0							127.3	382	23	10	
			9-1-21-0		7-0-23-0	14-3-33-1	2-0-7-1		42-10-94-0											19-2-60-0	3-0-13-0			96	263	12	2	
v. Cambridge UCCE (Fenner's) 17-19 May				4-0-17-0			10-1-36-0					5-0-25-0		14-4-40-2	15-4-29-1	15-1-62-2	8-6-10-0	9.3-0-53-1						80.3	276	4	6	
												3-0-9-0		6-2-20-1	11-4-21-2	3-0-21-0	0.3-0-4-1	5-0-27-1	6-2-22-0					34.3	176	5	5	
v. Hampshire (Rose Bowl) 24-27 May		2-0-10-1	22-6-62-2		19.5-4-68-3	17-5-35-2	30-10-62-2	5-1-13-0																95.5	271	21	10	
		9-0-54-2	6-0-40-0		2-0-18-0	8-2-31-1	9-3-27-3																	34	176	6	6	
v. Warwickshire (Tunbridge Wells) 31 May-3 June	20-5-43-2	20-6-48-3		29-8-51-1		4-0-17-0	18.2-7-43-3	9-1-25-1																100.2	237	10	10	
	7-2-29-0	28.3-5-68-3		28-6-61-4			10-1-19-2	4-1-8-0																77.3	192	7	10	1
v. Durham (Stockton-on-Tees) 13-15 June	23-3-70-3	1-0-4-0				27.4-4-71-4	18-5-39-1	12-3-33-2																81.4	227	10	10	
	17-3-52-3	26-2-83-4		19.2-7-58-2		3-0-8-0	7-2-38-0	3-0-5-0																75.2	268	19	10	1
v. Nottinghamshire (Canterbury) 20-23 June	36-11-100-5	45-6-103-1	22-7-66-1			8-4-16-0	31.1-5-100-3					3-0-16-0								1-0-9-0	4-1-6-0			150.1	439	23	10	
	6-2-12-0	20-6-44-1	8-1-18-1			4-0-7-0	5-1-6-0					13-5-26-1								3-0-7-0	9-1-36-0	1-0-3-0	1-0-3-0	70	167	5	3	
v. Sussex (Hove) 13-16 July	28-3-75-3	37.4-7-101-4		17-1-56-1		3-0-14-0				20-4-57-1	16-1-74-1													121.4	399	22	10	
	16-2-60-1	36-4-122-4		17-1-90-0		2-1-6-1				8-2-30-0	6-0-51-0									4-0-26-0				89	393	8	6	
v. Lancashire (Canterbury) 18-21 July	17-2-73-3	3-1-7-0				2-0-8-0				14-5-29-4	9-0-50-0		12.5-4-38-3											57.5	218	13	10	
	26-4-129-4	24-0-68-0				15-4-72-2				27-5-87-2	6-2-16-0		15-3-52-2							1-0-1-0				114.4	436	11	10	
v. Hampshire (Canterbury) 2-5 August	27-4-86-3	31.3-5-108-1				23.4-5-73-1				24-7-84-1	19-3-92-0		15.2-1-59-0							5-1-37-1				145.3	554	15	7	
v. Yorkshire (Headingley) 16-19 August	17-1-50-2	18.5-3-38-2	20-5-36-5			8-0-25-0						21-1-118-0	8-0-40-1											92.5	310	3	10	
																								–	–	–	–	
v. Nottinghamshire (Trent Bridge) 22-24 August		17-1-64-0	28-4-101-2			17-0-80-0	13-4-25-1				30-7-100-1	24.1-4-112-6									1-1-0-0			130.1	496	14	10	
																								–	–	–	–	
v. Sussex (Canterbury) 5-8 September			18-4-60-1	16-0-84-4	17.2-4-57-5	15-1-48-0						6-0-25-0												72.2	289	15	10	
			14.2-5-26-2	20-3-81-6	6-0-26-0	8-2-16-0																		48.2	161	3	8	
v. Warwickshire (Edgbaston) 13-16 September			18-2-55-2	19.4-2-74-6	30-6-82-1	16-1-67-1	3-1-18-0					6-0-19-0												92.4	318	3	10	
			2-0-9-0			13-0-10-0																		3.3	19	0	0	
v. Middlesex (Canterbury) 20-23 September			13-2-56-0	33-5-143-1	13-3-49-2	4-1-12-0			31.2-3-136-6					3-1-8-1										97.2	413	9	10	
			4-2-8-0	26-2-85-1	13-1-58-0	4-1-7-0			25-2-70-3			1-0-9-0		7-1-17-0										80	264	10	5	1

	A Khan	MM Patel	SJ Cook	JC Tredwell	RH Joseph	DI Stevens	AJ Hall	JM Kemp	RS Ferley	T Henderson	DJJ Bravo	NJ Dexter	MJ Saggers	JL Denly	MJ Dennington	SMJ Cusden	NJO'Brien	JA Iles	DA Stiff	M van Jaarsveld	MJ Walker	DP Fulton	RWT Key
Overs	312.1	389.3	294	269.5	244.5	235.5	128.3	111	122.2	144	88.1	89	43.1	36	26	18	0.3	13	15.3	29	33	1	1
Maidens	51	55	60	43	37	39	34	16	19	31	10	16	8	8	8	1	0	6	2	3	6	0	0
Runs	1034	1171	925	927	897	688	334	333	378	505	435	281	149	104	50	83	4	37	75	114	116	3	3
Wickets	34	32	28	26	24	19	14	11	9	9	8	6	5	4	3	2	1	1	1	1	1	0	0
Average	30.41	36.59	33.03	35.65	37.37	36.21	23.85	30.27	42.00	56.11	54.37	46.83	29.80	26.00	16.66	41.50	4.00	37.00	75.00	114.0	116.0	–	–

FIELDING

36	M van Jaarsveld
27	NJO'Brien (19 ct, 8 st)
18	DI Stevens
13	GO Jones (12 ct, 1 st)
10	JM Kemp
9	MJ Walker
8	RWT Key
7	DP Fulton
7	JC Tredwell
4	MM Patel
3	AJ Hall
3	NJ Dexter
3	PG Dixey
2	T Henderson
1	SJ Cook
1	A Khan
1	JL Denly
1	RH Joseph
1	DJ Chambers
0	MJ Saggers
0	RS Ferley
0	DA Stiff
0	DJJ Bravo
0	MJ Dennington
0	SMJ Cusden
0	JA Iles

Final Division One Table

	P	W	L	D	Bat	Bowl	Pts
Sussex	16	9	2	5	49	47	242.00
Lancashire	16	6	1	9	58	46	224.00
Hampshire	16	6	3	7	48	48	207.00
Warwickshire	16	6	5	5	42	43	189.00
Kent	16	4	4	8	43	44	175.00
Yorkshire	16	3	6	7	43	41	154.00
Durham	16	4	8	4	39	43	153.50
Nottinghamshire	16	4	7	5	40	37	153.00
Middlesex	16	1	7	8	47	42	133.50

LANCASHIRE CCC

FIRST-CLASS MATCHES
BATTING

	IJ Sutcliffe	MB Loye	SG Law	MJ Chilton	TC Smith	G Keedy	G Chapple	DG Cork	LD Sutton	KW Hogg	NJ Astle	OJ Newby	BJ Hodge	PJ Horton	GD Cross	SJ Mahmood	M Kartik	SJ Marshall	SJ Mullaney	A Flintoff	SJ Croft	KR Brown	JM Anderson	Extras	Total	Wickets	Result	Points
v. Hampshire (Old Trafford) 18-21 April	39	0	30	11	26	1*	70	7	1		4			8										27	224	10		
																											D	8
v. Durham (Riverside) 26-29 April	6	114	45	44	2	5*	82	16	58					21	7									21	421	10		
	17	3	111*	57	1*		27	23						19										10	268	6	W	22
v. Kent (Old Trafford) 3-5 May	5	44	39	131	0	4	0		11	19*				79	4									27	363	10		
	27	14	4	33					1*					5*										5	89	4	W	21
v. Durham UCCE (Durham) 10-12 May	3					3*			5			1*	133*rh	53	7			34	44		17	2		26	328	8		
	70*													42*								32		1	145	1	D	
v. Yorkshire (Headingley) 16-19 May	12	138	101	4	1*	4*	35	11	46	12				27										26	417	9		
																											D	12
v. Nottinghamshire (Old Trafford) 24-27 May	50	53	0	11	6	2	31	1	13		12*			115										14	308	10		
																											D	10
v. Sussex (Liverpool) 6-9 June	10	80	21	4	1	11*	47	53	23					47		0								20	317	10		
	45*	10*		10																				4	69	1	W	20
v. Warwickshire (Edgbaston) 14-16 June	69	5	121	3	35*	1		1	2	44	19			2										15	317	10		
	8	15	31*	8							20*													2	84	3	W	20
v. Middlesex (Lord's) 21-24 June	40	4	17	93	2	8*		1	72	70	15			161										22	505	10		
	34*			39*																				13	86	0	W	22
v. Kent (Canterbury) 18-21 July	10	6	53	31		2*	0	10					7		72	3				4				20	218	10		
	6	98	85	1		2*	50	23					84		2	22				37				26	436	10	L	4
v. Nottinghamshire (Trent Bridge) 26-29 July	10	35	0	44	0	0*	39	22			29	0		10										11	200	10		
	139*	108	0	50			2*	4*			2													9	314	5	W	18
v. Sussex (Hove) 2-5 August	23	4	130	0	28	2	27	1*			41						68		3					15	342	10		
	2	148*	5	29	0	0*	32	10			20						3		3					38	290	9	D	9
v. Yorkshire (Old Trafford) 8-11 August	23	100	32	2	3	0	27		151*	60	24	0												19	441	10		
																											D	12
v. Middlesex (Old Trafford) 17-20 August	1	107	64*	35	26	0	0	21	27	24	44													13	362	10		
																											D	11
v. Warwickshire (Blackpool) 30 August-2 September	159	10	61	18	2*		22	10	45	20	64							2*						43	456	9		
																											D	12
v. Durham (Old Trafford) 13-16 September	1	78	50	69	40*		29	154	36		2													23	482	8		
																											D	11
v. Hampshire (Rose Bowl) 20-23 September	27	67	79	38	49		42	9	46	26							40						7*	8	438	10		
	11	55	24	1	12		18*	111*	86															21	339	6	D	12
Matches	17	16	16	16	15	15	14	14	13	8	8	7	6	4	4	4	3	2	1	1	1	1	1					
Innings	27	24	23	25	18	16	19	17	16	8	12	7	7	7	6	5	2	3	1	2	1	2	1					
Not Out	4	2	3	1	5	10	1	2	3	1	0	2	2	2	0	0	1	0	0	0	0	0	1					
High Score	159	148*	130	131	49	11*	82	154	151*	70	86	19	161	79	72	22	40	34	44	37	17	32	7*					
Runs	847	1296	1103	766	234	45	580	354	666	254	429	51	505	227	162	36	42	40	44	41	17	34	7					
Average	36.82	58.90	55.15	31.91	18.00	7.50	32.22	23.60	51.23	36.28	35.75	10.20	101.00	45.40	27.00	7.20	42.00	13.33	44.00	20.50	17.00	17.00	-					
100s	2	6	4	1	0	0	0	1	2	0	0	0	0	3	0	0	0	0	0	0	0	0	0					
50s	3	6	6	4	0	0	3	1	2	2	3	0	0	2	0	0	0	0	0	0	0	0	0					
Catches/Stumpings	11/0	6/0	16/0	13/0	14/0	4/0	6/0	11/0	38/3	1/0	3/0	1/0	4/0	3/0	13/4	1/0	1/0	0/0	1/0	2/0	1/0	0/0	1/0					

Key: rh retired hurt

Home Ground: Old Trafford
Address: Old Trafford, Manchester, M16 0PX
Tel: 0870 0625000
Fax: 0870 0624614
Email: enquiries@lccc.co.uk
Directions: *By rail:* Manchester Piccadilly or Victoria then Metro link to Old Trafford. *By road:* M63, Stretford slip-road (junction 7) on to A56; follow signs.
Capacity: 21,500
Other grounds used: Blackpool, Liverpool
Year formed: 1864

Chairman: Jack Simmons
Chief Executive: Jim Cumbes
Cricket Manager: Mike Watkinson
Captain: Mark Chilton
County colours: Red and white

Website:
www.lccc.co.uk

Honours
County Championship
1881, 1897, 1904, 1926, 1927, 1928,
1930, 1934. Joint champions 1879,
1882, 1889, 1950
Sunday League/NCL/Pro40
1970, 1989, 1998, 1999
Benson & Hedges Cup
1984, 1990, 1995, 1996
Gillette Cup/NatWest/C&GTrophy
1970, 1971, 1972, 1975, 1990, 1996, 1998

LANCASHIRE CCC

FIRST-CLASS MATCHES
BOWLING

	G Keedy	DG Cork	G Chapple	TC Smith	SJ Mahmood	OJ Newby	KW Hogg	M Kartik	BJ Hodge	SJ Marshall	NJ Astle	MJ Chilton	A Flintoff	SG Law	IJ Sutcliffe	JM Anderson	SJ Mullaney	Overs	Total	Byes/Leg-byes	Wickets	Run outs
v. Hampshire (Old Trafford) 18–21 April	8-1-21-0	19-4-47-1	19-5-46-3	13-4-29-3		9-1-40-2												68	194	11	10	1
	2-0-6-0	7-1-14-0	6-2-13-0	5-3-4-0		2-0-14-0												22	54	3	0	
v. Durham (Riverside) 26–29 April	22.3-3-67-1		27.4-5-74-4	21-4-72-4	22-5-62-0							2.3-1-1-1						95.4	289	13	10	
	28-5-82-2	13-3-36-0	22-6-54-4	9-3-29-0	18.4-7-46-4							3-0-7-0						93.4	272	18	10	
v. Kent (Old Trafford) 3–5 May	28-5-71-4		23-6-59-0	20-5-59-0	24.3-4-71-3		19-5-56-2											114.3	327	11	10	1
	13.2-3-44-4		10-5-13-2	7-1-20-0	11-2-24-4		5-0-12-0											46.2	124	11	10	
v. Durham UCCE (Durham) 10–12 May	15.2-2-40-6						14-1-39-1	20-6-33-2			15-7-21-1						5-0-15-0	69.2	159	11	10	
	12.4-2-25-1						8-2-21-2	4-1-11-0			14-6-27-2						5-0-21-0	43.4	108	3	5	
v. Yorkshire (Headingley) 16–19 May	18-3-40-3	19-2-58-1	24-9-58-1	25-12-57-4			14-5-44-1					2-0-12-0			1-0-1-0			100	265	8	10	
	14-0-42-0	9-2-18-0	9-3-23-0	9-1-24-0			9-1-30-1	6-0-20-0										59	177	7	1	
v. Nottinghamshire (Old Trafford) 24–27 May	6-1-28-1	25.3-7-49-2	18-3-64-2	21-7-46-1		12-2-58-4												82.3	253	8	10	
	4-0-19-0	7-1-25-0	7-3-10-0	8-4-11-2		9-3-33-2		2-0-2-0										37	102	3	4	
v. Sussex (Liverpool) 6–9 June	13-3-38-2	13.5-4-44-2	17-5-35-4	12-5-39-1		13-1-59-1												68.5	218	3	10	
	10-0-32-2	4-0-26-0	12-3-47-3	6-3-8-0		10.3-0-52-5												42.3	166	1	10	
v. Warwickshire (Edgbaston) 14–16 June	6.4-0-18-2	25-7-53-6			15-9-31-1		10-2-31-1	19-9-27-0										75.4	173	13	10	
	30.5-5-81-6	14-3-43-0			7-0-20-1		5-1-11-0	11-1-31-0	16-5-21-3									83.5	225	18	10	
v. Middlesex (Lord's) 21–24 June	8-2-20-1	15-2-61-4		13-4-27-1			5.3-1-16-2	10-2-35-2					2-0-15-0					51.3	161	2	10	
	23-2-72-3	26.4-3-85-4		20-3-59-1			16-2-68-0	10-1-58-0	11-1-54-2									108.4	426	15	10	
v. Kent (Canterbury) 18–21 July	39.3-4-128-1	23-6-76-1	21-5-75-1		20-2-79-3							8-1-17-1	19-4-46-2					130.3	440	20	10	
	26.5-9-61-4	19-6-45-1	15-1-56-2		12-3-34-1								4-0-11-0					76.5	215	8	8	
v. Nottinghamshire (Trent Bridge) 26–29 July	22-0-80-2	16.3-1-74-3	20-7-76-1		20-2-69-3	15-0-72-1						4-0-14-0	1-0-5-0					98.3	397	7	10	
		14-5-38-3	22-10-35-6		7-0-26-0	1-0-5-0												44	114	10	10	1
v. Sussex (Hove) 2–5 August	45-9-116-3	22.5-5-54-4	26-5-71-1		30-7-98-2					13.3-4-47-0	6.3-0-22-0			3-0-11-0				146.5	439	20	10	
	20-0-80-4	9-0-35-0	13-3-45-0		8-1-32-0					16-0-68-1	2-0-6-0			5-0-24-1				73	294	4	6	
v. Yorkshire (Old Trafford) 8–11 August	18-0-68-1		22.4-5-60-4	23-3-83-3			13-1-47-0	19-4-50-2				5-1-22-0						100.4	345	15	10	
	59-11-156-3		23-7-56-0	18-3-37-0			19-4-69-4	19-8-51-1				10-1-31-0	8-2-12-1	4-0-15-0				160	450	23	9	
v. Middlesex (Old Trafford) 17–20 August	36.4-6-126-4	24-5-42-0	13-3-30-1	20-6-58-1			21-5-52-2					13-4-35-1						127.4	350	7	9	
																		-	-	-	-	
v. Warwickshire (Blackpool) 30 August–2 September		16.5-6-35-2	18-6-32-1	13-7-40-2			14-6-38-2	25-5-60-2				6-3-19-1						92.5	231	7	10	
		1-1-0-0	1-1-0-0															2	0	0	0	
v. Durham (Old Trafford) 13–16 September	28-8-72-1	23-7-52-3	25-6-64-1	22-5-71-2						35.3-7-89-3		1-0-3-0						134.3	372	21	10	
	8.4-2-27-0	5-1-14-1	2-0-5-0	4-2-4-0						8-3-12-0								27	69	7	1	
v. Hampshire (Rose Bowl) 20–23 September		17-4-47-4	9-3-23-0	7-3-20-3						23.3-7-73-1		3-2-9-1				10-2-38-0		69.3	215	5	10	1
																		-	-	-	-	
Overs	566.2	389.1	425.2	383	131.4	138.3	194	92	35	58.3	58.3	18.3	23	12	1	10	10					
Maidens	88	86	117	107	24	20	54	22	6	17	12	3	4	0	0	2	0					
Runs	1660	1071	1124	1073	427	523	528	234	97	163	178	52	56	50	1	38	36					
Wickets	61	42	41	35	21	19	15	6	5	4	4	2	2	1	0	0	0					
Average	27.21	25.50	27.41	30.65	20.33	27.52	35.20	39.00	19.40	40.75	44.50	26.00	28.00	50.00	-	-	-					

FIELDING

41	LD Sutton (38 ct, 3 st)
17	GD Cross (13 ct, 4 st)
16	SG Law
14	TC Smith
13	MJ Chilton
11	DG Cork
11	IJ Sutcliffe
6	MB Loye
6	G Chapple
4	G Keedy
4	BJ Hodge
3	NJ Astle
3	PJ Horton
2	A Flintoff
1	JM Anderson
1	KW Hogg
1	SI Mahmood
1	SJ Croft
1	OJ Newby
1	M Kartik
1	SJ Mullaney
0	SJ Marshall
0	KR Brown

Final Division One Table

	P	W	L	D	Bat	Bowl	Pts
Sussex	16	9	2	5	49	47	242.00
Lancashire	16	6	1	9	58	46	224.00
Hampshire	16	6	3	7	48	48	207.00
Warwickshire	16	6	5	5	42	43	189.00
Kent	16	4	4	8	43	44	175.00
Yorkshire	16	3	6	7	43	41	154.00
Durham	16	4	8	4	39	43	153.50
Nottinghamshire	16	4	7	5	40	37	153.00
Middlesex	16	1	7	8	47	42	133.50

LEICESTERSHIRE CCC

FIRST-CLASS MATCHES
BATTING

	CW Henderson	PA Nixon	JK Maunders	HD Ackerman	JL Sadler	DD Masters	DDJ Robinson	SCJ Broad	D Mongia	DL Maddy	JN Snape	Mohammad Asif	RAG Cummins	TJ New	CJ Liddle	AR Griffith	NGE Walker	SG Clark	JHK Naik	J Allenby	MC Rosenberg	Mansoor Amjad	MAG Boyce	A Habib	PW Harrison	DT Rowe	Extras	Total	Wickets	Result	Points
v. Surrey	14	20	87	15		6*	9	24	4	43	4	1															17	244	10		
(Leicester) 26-29 April	0	31*	7	55	1	13	11	15	97	29	21																34	314	10	L	4
v. Essex	0	18	0	111	15		53		165	2	29	3	0*														21	417	10		
(Chelmsford) 3-5 May			4*	14*			13		16																		1	48	2	W	22
v. Glamorgan	26	70*	71		77	19		14	161	26	19	8												4			30	525	10	D	12
(Leicester) 9-12 May																															
v. Derbyshire			0	13	52*				10	1	30*																31	137	4	D	6
(Derby) 17-19 May																															
v. Somerset	29	72	27	25	18	0	2			41	3		4*				12										21	254	10		
(Taunton) 24-27 May		71*	7	64	29					49	5							23*									6	254	5	D	9
v. Northamptonshire	2	40*	78	92	0	12		6		26		15	6				0										17	294	10		
(Oakham School) 31 May-3 June			80	55*				54*		47																	8	244	2	D	9
v. Surrey	46*	1	27	58	13	0	31	20	20	6			8														21	251	10		
(The Oval) 7-10 June	34	12	7	23	12	12	106	12	22			0*	9														10	259	10	L	3
v. Gloucestershire	40	21	6	58	82	19	4	12	7					52		41*											29	371	10		
(Leicester) 20-23 June	14	0	6	59	24*	7	7	0	62					25		6											23	233	10	L	7
v. Pakistan	0		0	92		34			129*	5	4	5	0*	11									4				31	315	9		
(Leicester) 1-3 July	1		4	51		13		14	5	0*	67	0											6				30	191	10	L	
v. Glamorgan	42	60	32	309*	36	18	29	15	0	0						1											18	560	10		
(Cardiff) 14-17 July			34	62	15*		90	20*																			7	228	3	D	11
v. Derbyshire		7	64	79	36	52	21	65*	1		90					34	0										66	515	10	D	12
(Leicester) 19-22 July																															
v. West Indies A	34							12					10	59	4*		0	13		46	15				0	0	12	205	10		
(Leicester) 26-28 July	11*						92							85			10			22	33*				5		13	271	5	D	
v. Gloucestershire	41*	103	180	62	20	7	4	4	1							1						27					32	482	10		
(Cheltenham) 2-5 August	42*	68*	5	46	20		17						7									25					11	241	6	W	22
v. Worcestershire			25	3	30*		40*																				3	101	2		
(Leicester) 16-19 August	36	50	18	17	81		34	9*	83				1*														28	357	7	W	16
v. Northamptonshire	13	144*	11	216	69		15	12	0				0*						1								34	515	8		
(Northampton) 22-25 August	23*	22*	20	50	13		19	5	12																		11	175	6	D	10
v. Somerset	4	15	0	53	2	43	2		4					1*				21									19	170	10		
(Leicester) 1-4 September	62*	21	3	82	58		22		86*																		26	360	5	W	17
v. Worcestershire	25	7	30	111*	9	8	28		11				13	1			0										16	259	10		
(Worcester) 6-9 September	6	4	74	72	19	0	47		6				5*	0													19	258	10	L	5
v. Essex			7		128*		80	0	0											103*							54	372	4		
(Leicester) 20-23 September		38*	49	38	7		39		51											68*							11	301	5	W	21
Matches	17	16	16	15	15	14	13	12	11	11	8	7	7	6	6	5	5	3	3	2	1	1	1	1	1	1					
Innings	24	23	29	28	26	16	25	15	18	19	11	8	8	12	6	6	6	5	2	4	2	2	2	1	2	1					
Not Out	6	8	1	4	5	1	1	2	3	1	1	2	4	0	3	2	0	1	0	2	1	0	0	0	0	0					
High Score	62*	144*	180	309*	128*	52	106	65*	165	97	90	21	13	85	4*	41*	21	23*	13	103*	33*	27	6	4	5	0					
Runs	545	895	959	1808	1024	219	738	211	800	538	219	58	38	414	6	84	38	45	14	239	48	52	10	4	5	0					
Average	30.27	59.66	34.25	75.33	48.76	14.60	30.75	16.23	53.33	29.88	21.90	9.66	9.50	34.50	2.00	21.00	6.33	11.25	7.00	119.50	48.00	26.00	5.00	4.00	2.50	0.00					
100s	0	2	1	4	1	0	1	0	3	0	0	0	0	0	0	0	0	0	0	1	0	0	0	0	0	0					
50s	1	6	6	14	8	0	3	1	2	4	1	0	0	5	0	0	0	0	0	1	0	0	0	0	0	0					
Catches/Stumpings	7/0	43/3	9/0	14/0	15/0	6/0	10/0	6/0	2/0	16/0	3/0	4/0	2/0	2/0	0/0	2/0	1/0	2/0	2/0	1/0	1/0	0/0	1/0	2/0	1/0						

Home Ground: Grace Road, Leicester
Address: County Ground, Grace Road, Leicester, LE2 8AD
Tel: 0871 2821879
Fax: 0871 2821873
Email: enquiries@leicestershireccc.co.uk
Directions: *By road:* Follow signs from city centre, or from southern ring road from M1 or A6.
Capacity: 5,500
Other grounds used: Oakham School
Year formed: 1879

Chief Executive: Paul Maylard-Mason
Head Coach/Academy Director: Paul Whitticase
Senior Coach: Tim Boon
Club Captain: Jeremy Snape
County Colours: Dark green and scarlet

Honours
County Championship
1975, 1996, 1998
Sunday League/NCL/Pro40
1974, 1977
Benson & Hedges Cup
1972, 1975, 1985
Twenty20 Cup
2004, 2006

Website:
www.leicestershireccc.com

LEICESTERSHIRE CCC

FIRST-CLASS MATCHES
BOWLING

Match	CW Henderson	SCJ Broad	DD Masters	Mohammad Asif	NGE Walker	RAG Cummins	CJ Liddle	DL Maddy	AR Griffith	D Mongia	JK Maunders	JN Snape	SG Clark	DT Rowe	JHK Naik	PA Nixon	DDJ Robinson	J Allenby	Mansoor Amjad	Overs	Total	Byes/Leg-byes	Wickets	Run outs
v. Surrey (Leicester) 26-29 April	10-1-43-0	22.5-2-94-5	22-11-33-1	28-4-76-2				15-1-53-1		3-0-23-0	12-2-29-0									112.5	370	19	10	1
	21-1-64-0	7-0-48-1	14-4-47-3	17-4-40-2				12-0-37-1				12.5-1-38-0								83.5	287	13	7	
v. Essex (Chelmsford) 3-5 May	16-4-56-1		14-4-44-2	15.1-0-56-5		6-0-44-1		5-1-14-0		6-1-26-1										62.1	242	2	10	
	24-6-69-5		20-3-23-1	22-5-74-1		20-4-54-3				1-1-0-0										87	222	2	10	
v. Glamorgan (Leicester) 9-12 May	38.2-9-77-4	21-8-49-2	20-5-45-2	26-8-61-2				13-5-39-0		6-3-5-0										124.2	297	21	10	
	37-12-75-1	3-0-19-0	15-6-25-0	12-4-29-1				18-2-71-2		8-4-8-1		15-4-24-0								108	267	11	5	
v. Derbyshire (Derby) 17-19 May	17-4-40-0	16.2-1-89-0	40-10-89-4	32-4-109-1				15-3-51-0												120.2	401	23	6	1
	-																			-	-	-	-	
v. Somerset (Taunton) 24-27 May	19-4-58-1	20-4-62-4	21-5-48-1	25-5-94-2				4-0-9-1					6-1-29-1							95	314	14	10	
	-																			-	-	-	-	
v. Northamptonshire (Oakham School) 31 May-3 June	22.4-3-75-2	16-4-48-2	23-4-91-2	22-6-67-3									6-0-40-1							89.4	331	9	10	
	32-8-75-4	11-1-48-0	14-4-33-0	31-3-132-5							11-3-27-0									99	334	19	9	
v. Surrey (The Oval) 7-10 June	54.2-5-235-3	36-11-112-1	33-3-117-0	10-2-50-1							33-7-105-2	8-1-28-0								174.2	668	21	7	
	-																			-	-	-	-	
v. Gloucestershire (Leicester) 20-23 June	3-0-10-0	19.4-2-83-5	19-3-78-1						21-3-49-1	9-1-23-1	7-0-27-1									78.4	282	12	9	
	20.5-3-66-0	15-1-78-0	17-3-57-3						19-2-81-0	8-1-23-0	2-0-10-0									81.5	323	8	3	
v. Pakistan (Leicester) 1-3 July	26-7-101-1			24-5-47-3	16-1-94-0	14-4-34-0							5-1-18-0							85	304	10	4	
	5-0-42-0			7-0-45-0	9-0-37-0	10-3-27-2				5-0-24-0			4.2-0-29-0							40.2	207	3	2	
v. Glamorgan (Cardiff) 14-17 July	32-3-115-3	27-1-113-1	21-2-57-2							26-5-82-1	26.1-6-62-2	1-0-5-0								133.1	449	15	10	1
	13.4-4-45-0	9-1-21-2	3-0-14-0							11-3-34-3	8-5-14-1	3-0-19-1								47.4	154	7	7	
v. Derbyshire (Leicester) 19-22 July		24-8-89-5	24-6-53-1		17-3-74-2					25.4-3-95-2	16-4-33-0	1-0-6-0	5-0-23-0							112.4	386	13	10	
		19.4-7-71-1	10-2-17-0		12-2-48-0					17-7-39-0	20-10-44-0		7-1-27-2							85	263	17	3	
v. West Indies A (Leicester) 26-28 July	39-4-138-4				21-5-46-4	13-2-51-0		6-1-16-0						9-4-22-1	16-3-55-1					104	349	21	10	
	-																			-	-	-	-	
v. Gloucestershire (Cheltenham) 2-5 August	25-6-76-5	20.4-8-47-4	21-7-60-0							14-2-52-1									8-0-37-0	88.4	282	10	10	
	27-3-90-1	24-6-88-5	19-2-73-0							25-2-91-1			3-0-20-0						16-1-65-0	114	439	12	7	
v. Worcestershire (Leicester) 16-19 August	19-4-57-2	20-4-96-2					16-0-61-0		10.3-1-51-1	24-5-98-2			6-0-29-0		11-3-51-0					106.3	456	13	8	1
	-																			-	-	-	-	
v. Northamptonshire (Northampton) 22-25 August	29-6-110-3	15.5-4-62-0					11-1-51-0	18-3-60-1	13-5-38-0		3-0-9-0				3-0-9-0					92.5	353	14	4	
	21.3-2-90-2	13-0-63-4					5-2-12-0	5-1-25-0							9-0-66-0					53.3	259	3	6	
v. Somerset (Leicester) 1-4 September	3-2-4-0		18-6-32-1	24-8-59-5	10-3-32-1	11.4-3-42-3		4-1-18-0												70.4	192	5	10	
	9.3-2-25-3		13-7-23-2	8-2-22-0	11-3-36-3	8-0-40-1														49.3	148	2	10	
v. Worcestershire (Worcester) 6-9 September	8-0-35-0		22-7-73-2	15-2-77-1	7-1-45-0	12-1-45-2	15-5-45-1				9.2-4-15-4									88.2	331	2	10	
	18-0-89-2		10.5-2-42-0	18.1-3-49-1	11-0-67-1	11-1-49-1	25-8-70-3				10-2-21-0									104	378	11	8	
v. Essex (Leicester) 20-23 September	29.5-5-114-2		32-13-58-3		27-5-83-2		24-6-105-1	19-6-52-1			7-0-25-1							8-2-23-0		146.5	486	26	10	
																5-0-69-0	4.4-0-117-0			9.4	186	0	0	

	CW Henderson	SCJ Broad	DD Masters	Mohammad Asif	NGE Walker	RAG Cummins	CJ Liddle	DL Maddy	AR Griffith	D Mongia	JK Maunders	JN Snape	SG Clark	DT Rowe	JHK Naik	PA Nixon	DDJ Robinson	J Allenby	Mansoor Amjad
Overs	620.4	360.2	465.5	240.1	152.1	143	126.4	174.3	182.4	160.1	68.2	53.1	12	9	39	5	4.4	8	24
Maidens	108	67	129	45	30	20	24	39	32	46	9	7	1	4	6	0	0	2	1
Runs	2054	1381	1232	788	498	579	478	564	621	417	219	183	69	22	181	69	117	23	102
Wickets	49	44	32	25	14	13	11	11	11	8	6	3	2	1	1	0	0	0	0
Average	41.91	31.38	38.50	31.52	35.57	44.53	43.45	51.27	56.45	52.12	36.50	61.00	34.50	22.00	181.00	-	-	-	-

FIELDING

46	PA Nixon (43 ct, 3 st)
16	DL Maddy
15	JL Sadler
14	HD Ackerman
10	DDJ Robinson
9	JK Maunders
7	CW Henderson
6	DD Masters
6	SCJ Broad
4	Mohammad Asif
3	JN Snape
2	TJ New
2	NGE Walker
2	D Mongia
2	JHK Naik
2	J Allenby
2	RAG Cummins
2	PW Harrison
2	CJ Liddle
1	A Habib
1	SG Clark
1	MC Rosenberg
1	DT Rowe
1	Mansoor Amjad
0	MAG Boyce
0	AR Griffith

Final Division Two Table

	P	W	L	D	Bat	Bowl	Pts
Surrey	16	10	2	4	62	44	262.00
Worcestershire	16	8	4	4	58	43	229.00
Essex	16	7	4	5	62	40	220.00
Leicestershire	16	5	4	7	47	41	185.50
Derbyshire	16	4	4	8	51	41	178.50
Northamptonshire	16	3	5	8	52	37	163.00
Gloucestershire	16	3	6	7	51	36	155.50
Glamorgan	16	2	7	7	51	41	146.50
Somerset	16	3	9	4	43	40	140.00

(Leicestershire deducted 0.50 points v. Derbyshire, 17 May for a slow over rate)

MIDDLESEX CCC

FIRST-CLASS MATCHES
BATTING

	NRD Compton	ET Smith	J Louw	CEW Silverwood	OA Shah	EC Joyce	JWM Dalrymple	BL Hutton	SB Styris	CT Peploe	BJM Scott	DC Nash	PN Weekes	CB Keegan	EJG Morgan	CJC Wright	Mohammad Ali	MM Betts	AJ Strauss	A Richardson	Extras	Total	Wickets	Result	Points
v. Oxford UCCE	5	134			85	96	24				20*	9									22	395	6		
(The Parks) 20-22 April	101		11				100				33*	7			11						8	271	5	D	
v. Kent	13	36	1	2	12	130	17	47			12					10	19*				34	333	10		
(Lord's) 26-29 April	124	2	2	1*	16	9	64	8			14					42	19				26	327	10	L	6
v. Hampshire	0	32	12	0			0	24			0	0				12*	7		0		11	98	10		
(Rose Bowl) 3-5 May	31	22	35	4			27	20			23	8				13*	4		141		16	344	10	L	3
v. Durham	48	5	0	10*	68	14	36	9			4	0								9	39	242	10		
(Riverside) 10-13 May	33	3	25	8	11	8	71	4			49	7								0*	13	232	10	L	4
v. Warwickshire	40	166	28		73	9	69	24	13		39			34*							25	520	9		
(Lord's) 24-27 May																								D	12
v. Sussex	4	0	5	24*	126	42	28	18			0		4		1						14	266	10		
(Horsham) 31 May-3 June	1	0	10	50	4	92	37	16			1		8		23*						14	256	10	L	5
v. Yorkshire	34	0	34*	2	30	155	4	59	33	43	0										21	415	10		
(Southgate) 7-9 June		44			0	7*		19*													4	74	2	W	22
v. Nottinghamshire	69*	31	5	13	66			22	20	9	6			7	0						28	276	10		
(Trent Bridge) 13-15 June	11	4	0	8	1		ah	7	0	6				5	7*						0	49	10	L	5
v. Lancashire	8	0	20	11	19				19			52*	22	4	0						6	161	10		
(Lord's) 21-24 June	9	114	2	17*	36				133	46	39	10	2		0						18	426	10	L	1
v. Warwickshire	52	30	0	2*	10	211	43	0	2			68	7								21	446	10		
(Edgbaston) 14-17 July	102*	19			20	6	33	78*													22	280	4	D	12
v. Sussex	1	75	10*	0	85	68	60	70	7		12				27						51	466	10		
(Southgate) 19-22 July	86	31	0*	0*	26	4	14	16	0		16				5						10	208	9	D	12
v. Durham	56	1	22*	3	0	16	6	28	†		1		1		38						4	176	10		
(Lord's) 26-29 July	190	10	10	0	57	19	8	84			47*		21		38						19	503	10	D	7
v. Hampshire	11	24	0	7	91	54	40	63		41	49*	6									36	422	10		
(Lord's) 8-11 August	15	147*			6	92		5			24*										20	309	4	D	11
v. Lancashire	21	10	2*		103	32		39	16			68*	36	5	8						10	350	9		
(Old Trafford) 17-20 August																								D	11
v. Yorkshire	1	56	16	20	0			11	64	5	19		128*	25							31	376	10		
(Scarborough) 30 August-2 September	17	15	7	7	22			105	5	20*	14		5	0							7	224	10	D	11
v. Nottinghamshire	105*	28	3	23	26			0	34	0	0			0	4						7	230	10		
(Lord's) 6-9 September	2	147	42	16	35			27	16	38	11			10	25*						18	387	10	L	3
v. Kent	25	7	12	43	43	99	20		6			64	35		34*						25	413	10		
(Canterbury) 20-23 September	100	16			52	10	26					22*	4*								34	264	5	D	10
Matches	17	17	17	16	15	12	11	11	10	10	9	8	8	7	6	5	5	2	1	1					
Innings	31	31	27	24	28	21	18	20	17	14	15	14	15	10	11	8	8	4	2	2					
Not Out	3	1	5	6	0	1	0	1	1	1	2	4	4	1	0	3	4	0	0	1					
High Score	190	166	42	50	126	211	96	105	133	46	49	68*	128*	34*	38	42	23*	7	141	9					
Runs	1315	1209	314	271	1038	1162	653	583	677	204	248	460	348	111	144	133	87	18	141	9					
Average	46.96	40.30	14.27	15.05	37.07	58.10	36.27	30.68	42.31	15.69	19.07	46.00	31.63	12.33	13.09	26.60	21.75	4.50	70.50	9.00					
100s	6	5	0	0	2	3	0	2	1	0	0	0	1	0	0	0	0	0	1	0					
50s	4	2	0	1	7	6	5	1	5	0	0	4	0	0	0	0	0	0	0	0					
Catches/Stumpings	7/0	12/0	1/0	4/0	11/0	10/0	5/0	16/0	14/0	2/0	28/2	14/2	0/0	3/0	1/1	0/0	3/0	1/0	2/0	0/0					

Key: ah absent hurt
† replaced by JMM Dalrymple

Home Ground: Lord's
Address: Lord's Cricket Ground, London, NW8 8QN
Tel: 0207 289 1300
Fax: 0207 289 5831
Email: enquiries@middlesexccc.com
Directions: By underground: St John's Wood on Jubilee Line. By bus: 13, 82, 113 stop along east side of ground; 139 at south-west corner; 274 at top of Regent's Park.
Capacity: 28,000

Other grounds used: Southgate, Uxbridge, Richmond
Year formed: 1864

Chief Executive: Vinny Codrington
Head Coach: John Emburey
Captain: Ben Hutton
County Colours: Navy

Website:
www.middlesexccc.co.uk

Honours
County Championship
1903, 1920, 1921, 1947, 1976, 1980, 1982, 1985, 1990, 1993. Joint champions 1949, 1977
Sunday League/NCL/Pro40 1992
Benson & Hedges Cup 1983, 1986
Gillette Cup/NatWest/C&G Trophy 1977, 1980, 1984, 1988, 1989

MIDDLESEX CCC

FIRST-CLASS MATCHES
BOWLING

	CEW Silverwood	J Louw	JWM Dalrymple	CB Keegan	SB Styris	CT Peploe	Mohammad Ali	CJC Wright	PN Weekes	MM Betts	A Richardson	BL Hutton	DC Nash	ET Smith	NRD Compton	EC Joyce	OA Shah	Overs	Total	Byes/Leg-byes	Wickets	Run outs
v. Oxford UCCE (The Parks) 20-22 April	12-1-38-1	15-4-42-4	9-0-27-1				6.5-2-14-1	8-1-33-2				7-0-25-1						57.5	185	6	10	
	7-1-14-1	6-3-23-0					6-2-15-2	5-2-4-0	6-0-19-1							6-3-18-0		36	99	6	4	
v. Kent (Lord's) 26-29 April	17-3-55-3	20-5-69-1	17-6-33-3				13.5-2-71-2	15-3-64-1				3-2-6-0						85.5	308	10	10	
	16-2-42-1	19-1-83-2	26-4-77-0				15-1-49-0	10-0-48-0				2-1-14-0					4.4-0-26-0	92.4	356	17	3	
v. Hampshire (Rose Bowl) 3-5 May	20-2-86-2	29-5-117-5	16-1-52-0				18.4-1-70-1			17-3-59-2		9-0-35-0						109.4	426	7	10	
			1-0-1-0									1.4-0-17-0						2.4	18	0	0	
v. Durham (Riverside) 10-13 May	27-4-88-4	30-6-99-2	22-4-57-2						9-1-29-2		18-4-71-0	8-1-21-0						106	348	4	10	
	19.2-3-47-5	21-7-46-0	23-2-70-1								22-6-50-4							93.2	261	27	10	
v. Warwickshire (Lord's) 24-27 May	27-5-92-3	25-3-102-2	24-5-52-1	25-5-76-3	13-3-65-0													114	401	14	9	
v. Sussex (Horsham) 31 May-3 June	20.5-5-61-3	21-4-65-1	20-2-81-3	17-4-80-0			18-4-61-1					8-2-20-2						104.5	376	8	10	
	19-4-74-0	21-2-87-3	18-2-69-3	17-4-50-2			9-0-56-2					3-0-19-0					1-0-2-0	88	370	13	10	
v. Yorkshire (Southgate) 7-9 June	22.2-6-51-6	22-10-30-2	22-4-55-1			19-3-70-0	24-6-89-1					1-0-13-0			1-0-9-0		5-1-29-1	116.2	355	9	10	
	7-1-13-2	8-3-21-1	16-1-56-3				14.5-4-31-4											45.5	130	9	10	
v. Nottinghamshire (Trent Bridge) 13-15 June	22.4-5-79-5		24-7-74-3			14-5-51-0	19-6-44-0		17-2-100-2									96.4	358	10	10	
v. Lancashire (Lord's) 21-24 June	30-5-105-1	33-8-121-1				27.3-6-71-6	12-2-45-0	28-5-117-1	12-1-29-1									142.3	505	17	10	
	5-1-13-0	5-0-27-0					6-2-18-0	5.3-0-20-0										21.3	86	8	0	
v. Warwickshire (Edgbaston) 14-17 July	23-3-97-2	23.5-3-82-3	21-3-64-0	24-4-78-3	14-2-40-2		18-6-30-0											123.5	391	20	10	
	5-0-28-0	8-1-24-0	19-4-57-2	7-1-20-1														52	154	7	4	
v. Sussex (Southgate) 19-22 July	25-4-84-4	33-6-141-3	23-2-102-1			20-2-66-0	23.3-5-89-1						4.5-0-53-1	5-0-60-1	6-0-94-1	4-0-60-0	3-0-14-0	127.3	507	11	10	1
	6-2-7-0	5-0-27-0	8-1-26-0			5-0-14-0	13-2-34-0											56.5	379	4	3	
v. Durham (Lord's) 26-29 July	23-3-83-3	20-2-85-1	3-0-12-0	23.1-6-90-5	18-3-65-1	17-3-64-0												105.1	407	7	10	
	19-4-67-0	6-0-29-0		14.4-4-29-3	13-3-33-0	15-4-55-4											1-0-1-0	67.4	220	7	7	
v. Hampshire (Lord's) 8-11 August	26-8-70-3	20-2-82-0	17-2-56-1	28.1-4-111-2	20-6-57-1							8-0-17-0						119.1	402	9	7	
	18-6-41-3	12.5-0-65-0		15-3-69-1	10-1-45-2							12-2-53-1						67.5	283	10	7	
v. Lancashire (Old Trafford) 17-20 August		16-0-89-3		15.2-0-76-2	9-0-33-1	26-3-109-3						5-0-21-1				4-0-21-0		75.2	362	13	10	
v. Yorkshire (Scarborough) 30 August-2 September	21.1-2-63-5	25-5-76-3	16-5-53-0	14-2-38-1			11-2-41-0	15-3-39-1				2-0-8-0						104.1	326	8	10	
	7-4-12-0	9-6-6-0					5-1-7-0					2-0-11-0						23	39	3	0	
v. Nottinghamshire (Lord's) 6-9 September	25-4-91-3	34-4-132-3				30-3-120-0			25-2-144-2	21-1-73-0		8-0-49-0					1-0-26-0	144	642	7	9	1
v. Kent (Canterbury) 20-23 September	34-7-90-3	24-3-66-0				50-4-205-2				23-1-113-0	24-2-67-0	4-0-25-0				5-0-21-1		164	603	16	6	

	CEW Silverwood	J Louw	JWM Dalrymple	CB Keegan	SB Styris	CT Peploe	Mohammad Ali	CJC Wright	PN Weekes	MM Betts	A Richardson	BL Hutton	DC Nash	ET Smith	NRD Compton	EC Joyce	OA Shah
Overs	504.2	535.4	319.4	200.4	198.3	282.2	115.2	103	108.3	26	40	58.4	4.5	5	7	19	15.4
Maidens	95	100	47	39	37	55	17	11	9	4	10	6	0	0	0	3	1
Runs	1591	1890	976	736	670	944	453	506	338	88	121	263	53	60	103	120	98
Wickets	63	43	25	19	18	12	10	7	5	4	4	3	1	1	1	1	0
Average	25.25	43.95	39.04	38.73	37.22	78.66	45.30	72.28	67.60	22.00	30.25	87.66	53.00	60.00	103.00	120.00	–

FIELDING

30	BJM Scott (28 ct, 2 st)
16	DC Nash (14 ct, 2 st)
16	BL Hutton
14	SB Styris
12	ET Smith
11	OA Shah
10	EC Joyce
7	NRD Compton
5	JWM Dalrymple
4	CEW Silverwood
3	CB Keegan
3	Mohammad Ali
2	AJ Strauss
2	CT Peploe
2	EJG Morgan (1 ct, 1 st)
1	MM Betts
1	J Louw
0	PN Weekes
0	A Richardson
0	CJC Wright

Final Division One Table

	P	W	L	D	Bat	Bowl	Pts
Sussex	16	9	2	5	49	47	242.00
Lancashire	16	6	1	9	58	46	224.00
Hampshire	16	6	3	7	48	48	207.00
Warwickshire	16	6	5	5	42	43	189.00
Kent	16	4	4	8	43	44	175.00
Yorkshire	16	3	6	7	43	41	154.00
Durham	16	4	8	4	39	43	153.50
Nottinghamshire	16	4	7	5	40	37	153.00
Middlesex	16	1	7	8	47	42	133.50

(Middlesex deducted 1.50 points v. Hampshire, 8 August for a slow over rate)

NORTHAMPTONSHIRE CCC

FIRST-CLASS MATCHES

BATTING

Match	U Afzaal	DJG Sales	BM Shafayat	BJ Phillips	L Klusener	SD Peters	MJ Nicholson	JF Brown	CJL Rogers	MH Wessels	RA White	MS Panesar	SP Crook	DH Wigley	SC Ganguly	C Pietersen	GG White	Extras	Total	Wickets	Result	Points
v. Essex (Chelmsford) 19-22 April	5	75	118	9	126*	8	5		9	9		2	0					31	397	10		
	28	157*	43	1	62	7	29*		9	11								17	364	7	D	11
v. Cambridge UCCE (Fenner's) 27-29 April	26		7		53			1	5	62	4	31*	4	6		20		26	245	10		
	100*		6		34				3	12	141		20*					13	329	5	W	
v. Somerset (Northampton) 3-5 May	26	88	101	11	147*		26	3	36	1	0	1						9	449	10		
																					W	22
v. Gloucestershire (Bristol) 10-12 May	40	22	15	47*	5	33	3	0	16	8			12					18	219	10		
	2	4	0	6	0	10	18	0	4	49			6*					15	114	10	L	4
v. Derbyshire (Northampton) 24-27 May	68	0	18	7	49	33	106*	9	30	6							37	23	386	10		
																					D	8
v. Leicestershire (Oakham School) 31 May-3 June	1	46	32	72	122	0	18	0*	9	22						0		9	331	10		
	53	31	66	3	51*	63	40	0*	7	0						0		20	334	9	D	10
v. Glamorgan (Northampton) 14-17 June	20	20	15	14	15	3	6	0	54	28*	10							8	178	10		
	151	42	59	25	0	6	35	0*	36	9	0							37	400	10	W	17
v. Worcestershire (Worcester) 21-24 June	8	8	0	1	21	9	0			12	0	0*				2		6	67	10		
	27	38	49	10	28	4	19			59*	0	12				0		8	254	10	L	1
v. Surrey (Northampton) 14-17 July	136*	23	0	8	32		0	6		34	15				6	12		28	300	10		
	0	4	6	52	58		0	10		22	7				2	39*		23	223	10	L	6
v. Pakistan (Northampton) 20-22 July	71*		30			142				15								11	269	3		
	8	15	2	39		0		4	9	11				14	5*	20*		13	140	9	L	
v. Essex (Northampton) 26-29 July	35	225	23		124*	178					48*				9			18	660	5		
	20*		19			26*												12	77	1	D	11
v. Surrey (The Oval) 2-5 August	13	1	91	65	31	15	19*	0	59		30		1					22	347	10		
	142	21	16	13	0	1	53*	4	75		9		28					24	386	10	L	3
v. Gloucestershire (Northampton) 8-11 August	51	10	0		44	76	11	20*	319		8		41	2				46	628	10		
	15*					20*												0	35	0	D	12
v. Leicestershire (Northampton) 22-25 August	44	67	58*		4*	104			53									23	353	4		
	82	25	67	0	16*	44			17				4*					4	259	6	D	12
v. Derbyshire (Derby) 30 August-2 September	27	27	6	1	128	12	25		112			2	44	4*				36	424	10		
																					D	12
v. Glamorgan (Northampton) 7-9 September	16	42	14	29	131	13	18	0	77				0*	11				18	369	10		
			19*			31			33*									1	84	1	W	21
v. Somerset (Taunton) 12-15 September	49*	35	1	0	0	63	23	8	128		0		0					19	326	10		
	0	93	14		33*	69			222*									22	453	4	D	9
v. Worcestershire (Northampton) 20-23 September	0	96	18	75	16	38	20*		28		34		0	0				17	342	10		
	51	4	2	14*	8	27	0		19		1		14	0				3	143	10	L	6
Matches	18	17	17	17	16	16	15	15	14	10	9	9	8	8	4	3	2					
Innings	32	27	30	25	26	30	20	19	24	17	14	11	10	10	6	4	3					
Not Out	6	1	2	2	7	2	4	5	2	2	1	3	2	2	1	2	0					
High Score	151	225	118	75	147*	178	106*	20*	319	62	141	34	44	28	9	39*	37					
Runs	1315	1219	887	515	1251	1122	454	85	1360	353	288	93	138	73	24	91	37					
Average	50.57	46.88	31.67	22.39	65.84	40.07	28.37	6.07	61.81	23.53	22.15	11.62	17.25	9.12	4.80	45.50	12.33					
100s	4	2	2	0	6	3	1	0	4	0	1	0	0	0	0	0	0					
50s	6	5	5	4	3	5	1	0	5	2	0	0	0	0	0	0	0					
Catches/Stumpings	6/0	13/0	20/3	6/0	9/0	11/0	6/0	3/0	12/0	27/1	4/0	1/0	5/0	5/0	0/0	0/0	0/0					

Home Ground: Northampton
Address: Wantage Road, Northampton, NN1 4TJ
Tel: 01604 514455
Fax: 01604 514488
Email: commercial@nccc.co.uk
Directions: Junction 15 from M1 onto A508 (A45) towards Northampton. Follow the dual carriageway for approx 3 miles. Keeping in left-hand lane, take next exit from dual carriageway marked A428 Bedford and Town Centre. Move into middle lane approaching the roundabout at bottom of slip road. Take second exit following signs for Abington/Kingsthorpe on to Rushmere Road. Follow Rushmere Road (A5095) across the junction with Billing Road and continue straight on through Abington Park to traffic lights at main junction with Wellingborough Road.
Capacity: 4,250
Other grounds used: Campbell Park, Milton Keynes, Stowe School
Year formed: 1878

Chief Executive: Mark Tagg
Chairman: Lynn Wilson
First XI Manager: Kepler Wessels/David Capel
Captain: David Sales
County Colours: Claret and gold

Honours
Benson & Hedges Cup
1980
Gillette Cup/NatWest/C&G Trophy
1976, 1992

Website:
www.nccc.co.uk

NORTHAMPTONSHIRE CCC

FIRST-CLASS MATCHES
BOWLING

Match	MJ Nicholson	MS Panesar	JF Brown	BJ Phillips	L Klusener	DH Wigley	SP Crook	U Afzaal	SC Ganguly	RA White	BM Shafayat	C Pietersen	CJL Rogers	DJG Sales	GG White	Overs	Total	Byes/Leg-byes	Wickets	Run outs
v. Essex (Chelmsford) 19–22 April	26-7-92-1	26-5-76-1	23-7-69-3	21.5-4-70-4			14-1-57-1									110.5	381	17	10	
	6-1-18-0	19-6-47-0	5-1-12-1	7-3-17-1			11-0-59-1							1-0-1-0		49	158	4	3	
v. Cambridge UCCE (Fenner's) 27–29 April		20-6-45-1	24-10-36-2	11-3-29-1		15-2-51-3	12-4-39-1					7-0-36-0				89	249	13	10	2
		10-5-28-0	6-1-22-0	14-7-29-6		7.5-2-27-2	8-2-17-1									45.5	132	5	10	1
v. Somerset (Northampton) 3–5 May	11-2-47-0	20-6-52-1		25.3-4-82-5	13-3-28-2	8-1-44-2										77.3	258	5	10	
	12-2-50-2	26.3-12-32-5		19-6-47-2	4-1-11-1											61.3	145	5	10	
v. Gloucestershire (Bristol) 10–12 May	22-12-43-3		26-8-39-4	9-2-41-0	18.4-1-67-3		9-2-37-0									84.4	232	5	10	
	8-1-22-1		8-2-22-1	7-2-20-1	9-2-20-0		2.5-0-18-1									34.5	102	0	4	
v. Derbyshire (Northampton) 24–27 May	4-1-23-0			9-5-9-0	7-4-5-2	7-5-8-0									5-1-8-0	32	58	5	2	
v. Leicestershire (Oakham School) 31 May–3 June	24-7-59-2		25-5-88-1		19-7-30-0	25-5-69-6					1-0-8-0				8-0-29-0	102	294	11	10	
	12-2-31-1		27-5-72-0		8-1-28-0	12-3-46-1		1-0-8-0				2-0-14-0			13-0-42-0	75	244	3	2	
v. Glamorgan (Northampton) 14–17 June	20-6-67-3	36-7-90-3	31.4-12-63-2	20-6-51-1		18-1-74-1										125.4	354	9	10	
	9.2-1-23-6	8-1-11-3		4-0-7-1												26.2	56	0	10	
v. Worcestershire (Worcester) 21–24 June	38.3-8-127-3	58-10-211-3		32-4-121-1	2-0-11-0				9-3-23-0			7-0-33-0				146.3	543	17	9	2
v. Surrey (Northampton) 14–17 July	24-5-84-4		8-1-47-0	20-1-59-3	9-0-33-0				11-2-36-1			16-1-62-1				88	328	7	10	1
	14-1-31-1		38-3-177-3	16.5-3-55-1	4-0-23-0				10-2-29-1		3-0-26-0	23-3-75-0				108.5	424	8	6	
v. Pakistan (Northampton) 20–22 July			16-6-41-0	14-2-55-1			22.5-9-77-5			6-1-19-1		0.2-0-6-0	5.4-0-39-1			64.5	250	13	9	1
			6-2-34-0	7-1-13-0			12-2-36-0	8.2-0-52-1				7-0-25-2				40.2	160	0	3	
v. Essex (Northampton) 26–29 July	26-6-70-0		53-9-146-3	19-4-64-2	19-4-68-0		26-2-115-2	13-0-61-0	6-1-24-0	10-0-57-2						172	620	15	10	1
v. Surrey (The Oval) 2–5 August	37-6-143-0		52-4-187-2	20-2-63-0	8-2-27-1		21-0-117-0		17.3-0-71-1	15-2-51-0						170.3	669	10	5	1
			7-0-34-2						7-1-25-1							14	65	6	3	
v. Gloucestershire (Northampton) 8–11 August	23-4-62-7		22-1-77-0			19.3-1-104-2	16-0-89-1			5-0-15-0			14-4-44-0			85.3	350	3	10	
	23-2-84-2		49-12-143-0			19-4-103-1	19-1-95-0		15-2-75-3	7-1-44-0						146	596	8	6	
v. Leicestershire (Northampton) 22–25 August	30-6-84-1		28-5-80-1		13-2-48-0		21-1-105-2			5-1-34-0			4-0-16-1			137	515	31	8	1
	10-3-38-0		3-0-17-0				11-1-46-3									41	175	9	6	
v. Derbyshire (Derby) 30 August–2 September	12-9-12-4	14-3-41-2		8.3-3-10-3	5-2-12-0	10-1-45-1	9-2-32-0									58.3	167	15	10	
	17-2-59-0	27-12-39-0		11-4-28-1	4-2-15-0	15-4-49-1	8-0-48-0	9-3-19-1						1-0-1-0		92	286	28	3	
v. Glamorgan (Northampton) 7–9 September	19-10-41-2	25-11-67-5	11-3-19-0		13-7-21-2	3-0-17-0	6.1-0-24-0			5-2-13-0						77.1	204	14	10	
	21-5-68-2	43-15-73-4	28.5-10-46-3		7-1-25-0		4-0-13-1									108.5	248	10	10	
v. Somerset (Taunton) 12–15 September	26-4-83-1		41-8-160-1	24-6-78-1	7-3-15-0		25-0-113-2	32-6-93-0	8-0-34-1			3-1-11-0				166	625	28	8	1
v. Worcestershire (Northampton) 20–23 September		37.3-6-101-5	37-12-92-3	3-1-8-0	5-1-14-0	5-1-17-0	9-1-26-2			4-1-15-0						100.3	281	8	10	
		21.4-3-76-5	20-0-75-0	3-0-16-0	1-0-1-0		2-0-18-0	3-0-5-0								50.4	205	14	5	
Overs	474.5	444.4	594	374.2	206.3	185	175.1	119.5	42	48	17.2	51.4	21	2	26					
Maidens	113	117	129	89	41	30	13	16	9	3	0	4	5	0	1					
Runs	1471	1171	1765	1081	699	796	782	471	131	227	86	212	71	2	79					
Wickets	46	43	35	34	19	18	17	7	3	3	2	2	1	0	0					
Average	31.97	27.23	50.42	31.79	36.78	44.22	46.00	67.28	43.66	75.66	43.00	106.00	71.00	–	–					

FIELDING

28	MH Wessels (27 ct, 1 st)
23	BM Shafayat (20 ct, 3 st)
13	DJG Sales
12	CJL Rogers
11	SD Peters
9	L Klusener
6	U Afzaal
6	BJ Phillips
6	MJ Nicholson
5	DH Wigley
5	SP Crook
4	RA White
3	JF Brown
1	MS Panesar
0	SC Ganguly
0	C Pietersen
0	GG White

Final Division Two Table

	P	W	L	D	Bat	Bowl	Pts
Surrey	16	10	2	4	62	44	262.00
Worcestershire	16	8	4	4	58	43	229.00
Essex	16	7	4	5	62	40	220.00
Leicestershire	16	5	4	7	47	41	185.50
Derbyshire	16	4	4	8	51	41	178.50
Northamptonshire	16	3	5	8	52	37	163.00
Gloucestershire	16	3	6	7	51	36	155.50
Glamorgan	16	2	7	7	51	41	146.50
Somerset	16	3	9	4	43	40	140.00

NOTTINGHAMSHIRE CCC

FIRST-CLASS MATCHES
BATTING

	DJ Bicknell	DJ Hussey	MA Ealham	GP Swann	RJ Sidebottom	JER Gallian	WR Smith	PJ Franks	SP Fleming	AJ Harris	D Alleyne	CE Shreck	CMW Read	SR Patel	GJ Smith	RJ Warren	MHA Footitt	JA Mierkalns	A Singh	GD Clough	PJ McMahon	Extras	Total	Wickets	Result	Points
v. MCC (Lord's) 14-17 April	36	21	25	8	1	20	29	30*					12		0	0						9	191	10		
	0	19	112*			171	39						110*			4						16	471	5	W	
v. Yorkshire (Trent Bridge) 19-22 April	95	31	2		0*	5	60	1					102*		0	93						28	417	8	D	9
v. Durham UCCE (Durham) 27-28 April	48			28	21*		68	54		4	0			173	2	27			0			22	447	10	W	
v. Warwickshire (Trent Bridge) 3-6 May	0	2	4	15*	1	25	2	38		0	57				0							13	157	10		
	17	21	56	30	26	8	16	1		3	109*				0							29	316	10	L	3
v. Sussex (Hove) 9-11 May	28	15	52	37	21*	19	16	7		2		0			9							23	229	10		
	28	3	3	14	6*	15	13	3		15					7							10	120	10	L	4
v. Durham (Trent Bridge) 17-20 May	40	15	7	2	18*	114	41	12	7	19			23									15	313	10	D	9
v. Lancashire (Old Trafford) 24-27 May	30	19	33	26		4	10	1	42	6*			53		17							12	253	10		
	28	38*				7	2		0				22*									5	102	4	D	9
v. Hampshire (Rose Bowl) 7-9 June	15	26	2	15		16	14	13	10	11		0*	14									11	147	10		
	22	13	0	0		67	40	15*	29	2		1	1									16	206	10	L	3
v. Middlesex (Trent Bridge) 13-15 June	40	107	41	62		0	4	8	75			0	0				0*					21	358	10	W	21
v. Kent (Canterbury) 20-23 June	85	32	4	85	31	7			51	41	0*			67	0							36	439	10		
	25	20*				42			63*	10												7	167	3	D	9
v. Hampshire (Trent Bridge) 14-17 July	77	4	101*	54	3	23			81	0	0			1	2							16	362	10		
	9	150*	15*			18			0		99			6								21	318	5	D	8
v. Lancashire (Trent Bridge) 26-29 July	6	150	83	27	4	4			53	28*	20	1	9									12	397	10		
	7	18	10	5	0	8			15	14	10	1*	16									10	114	10	L	7
v. Durham (Riverside) 1-4 August	18	12	9	11	33	1			11	5	1	0*		32								6	139	10		
	21				18	1			89*	18				56*								11	214	4	W	17
v. Warwickshire (Edgbaston) 8-11 August	9	0	6	23	20	0	8	55			61	2*		16								8	208	10		
	55	0	18	42	1	54	64	60			16	5*		5								24	344	10	L	4
v. West Indies A (Trent Bridge) 16-18 August	44				50	2	10*			2				66*				18				13	205	5	D	
v. Kent (Trent Bridge) 22-24 August	19	164	92	15	7		3		101	14	8	1*		27								45	496	10	W	22
v. Middlesex (Lord's) 6-9 September	1	19	15	2*			141	64	192	0	15			156								37	642	9	W	22
v. Yorkshire (Headingley) 13-16 September		117	2	24	1		41	20	25	0	7	0*		8								18	263	10		
		86*	0	23	0		0	1	29	0	54	0		16								4	213	10	L	5
v. Sussex (Trent Bridge) 20-22 September	20	31	1		5		28	10	0	2	11	0*		35								22	165	10		
	28	10	39		3		6	16	4	10	0	0*		22								12	150	10	L	1
Matches	18	17	17	15	15	14	14	14	13	13	12	12	10	8	6	5	2	1	1	1	1					
Innings	29	28	26	21	22	24	21	20	22	17	20	16	16	12	6	8	1	1	1	0	0					
Not Out	0	4	3	1	6	0	0	3	2	2	1	10	3	2	0	0	1	0	0	0	0					
High Score	95	164	112*	85	33	171	141	64	192	28*	109*	5*	110*	173	17	93	0*	18	0	0	0					
Runs	851	1143	732	546	222	679	575	376	992	119	543	11	451	612	21	140	0	18	0	0	0					
Average	29.34	47.62	31.82	27.30	13.87	28.29	27.38	22.11	49.60	7.93	28.57	1.83	34.69	61.20	3.50	17.50	-	18.00	-	-	-					
100s	0	5	2	0	0	2	1	0	2	0	1	0	2	2	0	0	0	0	0	0	0					
50s	4	1	4	3	0	3	2	3	8	0	4	0	2	2	0	1	0	0	0	0	0					
Catches/Stumpings	2/0	14/0	13/0	9/0	7/0	17/0	8/0	1/0	17/0	2/0	29/5	4/0	32/0	3/0	1/0	3/0	0/0	0/0	0/0	1/0	0/0					

Home Ground: Trent Bridge
Address: Trent Bridge, Nottingham, NG2 6AG
Tel: 01159 823000
Fax: 01159 455730
Email: administration.notts@ecb.co.uk
Directions: By road: Follow signs from ring road towards city centre.
Capacity: 14,500 (16,000 during international matches)
Other grounds used: Cleethorpes
Year formed: 1841

Chief Executive: Derek Brewer
Director of Cricket: Mick Newell
Captain: Stephen Fleming
County colours: Green and gold

Website:
www.trentbridge.co.uk

Honours
County Championship
1883, 1884, 1885, 1886, 1907, 1929, 1981, 1987, 2005
Sunday League/NCL/Pro40
1991
Benson & Hedges Cup
1976, 1989
Gillette Cup/NatWest/C&G Trophy
1987

NOTTINGHAMSHIRE CCC

FIRST-CLASS MATCHES
BOWLING

	CE Shreck	RJ Sidebottom	MA Ealham	AJ Harris	GP Swann	PJ Franks	GJ Smith	DJ Hussey	MHA Footitt	GD Clough	SR Patel	PJ McMahon	Overs	Total	Byes/Leg-byes	Wickets	Run outs
v. MCC		16-6-42-4	14-7-26-3		1-0-4-0	11.2-2-34-2	13-3-57-1						55.2	168	5	10	
(Lord's) 14–17 April		18-2-77-3	10-4-34-1		21-7-88-1	15-0-87-2	17-2-54-2	1-0-5-1					82	352	7	10	
v. Yorkshire													–	–	–	–	
(Trent Bridge) 19–22 April													–	–	–	–	
v. Durham UCCE	5.2-3-6-5	7-4-7-2						9-2-28-3					21.2	46	5	10	
(Durham) 27–28 April	4-3-1-2				16-3-48-3	10-3-29-1		18.2-7-75-4			5-0-29-0		53	194	12	10	
v. Warwickshire		22.5-5-73-2	18-6-45-2	27-9-53-5	23-9-37-0	14-6-28-1							104.5	248	12	10	
(Trent Bridge) 3–6 May		21-2-77-1	16-6-43-3	13-0-51-3	17-3-47-2	12-1-60-1							79	285	7	10	
v. Sussex		16-6-38-2	13.3-7-17-2	12-3-33-1	15-4-25-2	9-5-24-2		1-0-5-1					66.3	143	3	10	
(Hove) 9–11 May		13-7-17-0	12.4-0-29-4	10-4-16-1	43-8-114-4	12-1-50-0		4-0-10-1					94.4	247	11	10	
v. Durham		22-5-65-0	24-10-53-3	33.2-7-133-2	28-6-66-0	20-0-83-2							127.2	404	4	8	
(Trent Bridge) 17–20 May													–	–	–	–	
v. Lancashire			29-6-75-5	34.5-7-76-4	12-1-39-0	24-3-85-0	16.2-8-28-1						116.1	308	5	10	
(Old Trafford) 24–27 May													–	–	–	–	
v. Hampshire	32.3-2-94-5		20-6-70-1	30-3-114-4	15-2-46-0	20-4-72-0							117.3	401	5	10	
(Rose Bowl) 7–9 June	13-2-60-1		14-3-45-0	4.1-0-20-0	18.1-1-51-2	9.5-0-56-0		5-1-17-0					64.1	251	2	3	
v. Middlesex	27-5-98-4		17.5-7-48-4			20-4-61-2			11-0-62-0				75.5	276	7	10	
(Trent Bridge) 13–15 June	14-5-31-8		8-4-8-0		1.4-0-7-1	4-1-3-0							27.4	49	0	9	
v. Kent	37-10-124-2	32-10-76-2	29-3-97-1		46-7-152-1		28-7-89-0	4-0-35-0					176	600	27	6	
(Canterbury) 20–23 June													–	–	–	–	
v. Hampshire	34-10-110-1	32-6-88-1	28-7-74-1		30-2-136-0		27-3-103-0	5-0-37-0					156	572	24	3	
(Trent Bridge) 14–17 July	10-0-35-4	8-0-43-2	5-2-10-1		10-0-42-0		7-0-33-1						40	173	10	8	
v. Lancashire	13-1-57-2	18-3-57-3	13.2-3-32-2	12-3-46-3									56.2	200	8	10	
(Trent Bridge) 26–29 July	14-4-69-0	22-4-73-0	11-3-35-0	11-3-36-2		38-15-81-4		5.4-2-20-1					106.4	314	4	5	
v. Durham	21-6-67-6	18-9-43-2	9-2-21-2	8-2-48-0	1-0-2-0								57	195	14	10	
(Riverside) 1–4 August	13.5-2-64-4	11-4-21-2	11-3-36-2	8-0-35-2									43.5	157	1	10	
v. Warwickshire	25-4-95-1	29-6-74-3	21.1-7-59-5		38-9-96-1	10-1-37-0					1-0-8-0		124.1	381	12	10	
(Edgbaston) 8–11 August	12-1-45-0	14-6-32-2	8-2-23-1		25-9-54-4	4-0-23-1		1-0-9-0			5.1-0-22-1		69.1	230	22	9	
v. West Indies A			15-4-52-2			14-0-45-1			12-1-45-5	13-4-56-2		1-0-6-0	55	211	7	10	
(Trent Bridge) 16–18 August													–	–	–	–	
v. Kent	24-6-70-2	25-9-53-4	17.1-4-54-3	16-4-50-1	2-0-6-0					4-1-11-0			88.1	251	7	10	
(Trent Bridge) 22–24 August	13-1-70-2	16-7-22-5	10-2-22-0	12.3-3-40-3									51.3	160	6	10	
v. Middlesex	22-5-79-5	16-5-54-1		15-1-53-2		13-3-40-2					12-7-16-0		66	230	4	10	
(Lord's) 6–9 September	30-5-84-1	27-9-62-3		23-7-73-3		14-4-69-1		12.2-0-66-2					120.2	387	17	10	
v. Yorkshire	23.2-8-63-4	31-6-70-3		21-2-75-1	17-5-28-2	17-2-58-0					2-0-5-0		111.2	306	7	10	
(Headingley) 13–16 September	14-3-59-0	21-5-55-3		8-1-38-0	22-4-78-1	4-1-6-0							69	238	2	5	1
v. Sussex	24-3-141-2	30-8-90-0		27-8-103-1		20-1-121-0		6-0-32-0			20-3-67-1		127	560	6	5	1
(Trent Bridge) 20–22 September													–	–	–	–	

Overs	426	485.5	359.4	345.5	439.5	279.1	135.2	45	23	13	49.1	1					
Maidens	89	134	104	70	95	42	27	3	1	4	11	0					
Runs	1512	1307	956	1151	1247	1071	467	236	107	56	158	6					
Wickets	61	50	46	38	28	18	12	6	5	2	2	0					
Average	24.78	26.14	20.78	30.28	44.53	59.50	38.91	39.33	21.40	28.00	79.00	–					

FIELDING

34	D Alleyne (29 ct, 5 st)
32	CMW Read
17	JER Gallian
17	SP Fleming
14	DJ Hussey
13	MA Ealham
9	GP Swann
8	WR Smith
7	RJ Sidebottom
4	CE Shreck
3	RJ Warren
3	SR Patel
2	DJ Bicknell
2	AJ Harris
1	GJ Smith
1	PJ Franks
1	GD Clough
0	A Singh
0	MHA Footitt
0	PJ McMahon
0	JA Mierkalns

Final Division One Table

	P	W	L	D	Bat	Bowl	Pts
Sussex	16	9	2	5	49	47	242.00
Lancashire	16	6	1	9	58	46	224.00
Hampshire	16	6	3	7	48	48	207.00
Warwickshire	16	6	5	5	42	43	189.00
Kent	16	4	4	8	43	44	175.00
Yorkshire	16	3	6	7	43	41	154.00
Durham	16	4	8	4	39	43	153.50
Nottinghamshire	16	4	7	5	40	37	153.00
Middlesex	16	1	7	8	47	42	133.50

SOMERSET CCC

FIRST-CLASS MATCHES
BATTING

Match	MJ Wood	AR Caddick	CM Willoughby	JC Hildreth	WJ Durston	CM Gazzard	CL White	PD Trego	AV Suppiah	KA Parsons	RL Johnson	NJ Edwards	JD Francis	DJ Cullen	SHP Spurway	ME Trescothick	SRG Francis	RJ Lett	MK Munday	JL Langer	ID Blackwell	Extras	Total	Wickets	Result	Points
v. Gloucestershire	9	2	21	9	2	21	36	4			9*		2			12						16	143	10		
(Bristol) 18-21 April	27	7*	0	8	21	9	172	15			11		4			4						9	287	10	L	3
v. Worcestershire	36	39*	0	28	74	22	65	51			51		27			0						13	406	10		
(Worcester) 26-28 April	44	0*	4	10	35	4	0	0			13		1			5						4	120	10	W	22
v. Northamptonshire	0	13	4	10	2	9	26	1				10		24*		154						5	258	10		
(Northampton) 3-5 May	24	1	2	0	41	5	19	18				12		4*		12						7	145	10	L	5
v. Essex	49	0		57	0	21	41	102	27	153	1		11*									9	471	10		
(Taunton) 10-13 May	1			69	69*	5*	58		10	59												4	275	5	L	6
v. Leicestershire	11	25	6*	4		35	0	31	99	0	40										49	14	314	10	D	10
(Taunton) 24-27 May																										
v. Glamorgan	6	0	5*	24	4	12	86	15	26	1			7									24	210	10		
(Swansea) 31 May-1 June	9			0	52*				5	46*												6	118	4	W	18
v. Worcestershire	8	7	2	34	89	1	131*	8	16	5			19									26	346	10		
(Taunton) 7-10 June	27	43	47	17	40	0	1	67	37				16*									14	313	10	L	4
v. Surrey	14	16	1*	42	7	32	4	110	9	54	22											31	342	10		
(Bath) 14-16 June	69	10*	0*	0	23	20	108	4	26	10	0											6	276	10	L	6
v. Derbyshire	2	0	17*		19	1	135	50	9*rh			30					36			18		23	340	9		
(Taunton) 14-17 July	14	13*	4		4	16	19	4	ah			4					4			30		15	127	10	L	6
v. Surrey	54	7			34*	14	0	71				77	41							342		48	688	8	D	10
(Guildford) 19-22 July																										
v. Essex	0	21	1*	11	10	0	26	0	5		44							4				11	133	10		
(Southend) 2-5 August	50	1	0*	43	31	16	111	1	20		20							0				14	307	10	L	3
v. Derbyshire	5	0	1	4	4	8	15	4	16			75					4*					15	151	10		
(Derby) 8-11 August	5	10	0	40	73	0	260*	11	30			2					38					29	498	10	L	3
v. Glamorgan	20	68	12*	41	46	28			1	45		8					3	50				8	330	10	D	8
(Taunton) 15-18 August																										
v. Gloucestershire	60	5	0	71	60*				46	47	6	32		8	46							28	409	10	W	22
(Taunton) 22-24 August																										
v. Leicestershire	73	2	0*	33	8				5	39	4				22			1	0			5	192	10		
(Leicester) 1-4 September	0	23	0	16	1				30	16	35				13			6	5*			3	148	10	L	3
v. Northamptonshire	5	28*		227*	73			98	10	3		12			83						43	43	625	8	D	12
(Taunton) 12-15 September																										

	MJ Wood	AR Caddick	CM Willoughby	JC Hildreth	WJ Durston	CM Gazzard	CL White	PD Trego	AV Suppiah	KA Parsons	RL Johnson	NJ Edwards	JD Francis	DJ Cullen	SHP Spurway	ME Trescothick	SRG Francis	RJ Lett	MK Munday	JL Langer	ID Blackwell
Matches	16	16	15	14	13	13	12	12	12	10	8	7	5	4	3	3	3	3	3	2	2
Innings	27	25	22	24	23	22	22	20	19	15	12	10	9	6	4	6	5	4	4	3	2
Not Out	0	5	9	1	3	2	2	0	0	2	1	0	0	4	0	0	1	0	1	0	0
High Score	73	68	47	227*	89	35	260*	135	99	153	51	77	41	24*	83	154	38	50	5*	342	49
Runs	622	341	127	798	765	305	1190	596	563	511	211	309	131	81	164	187	85	65	9	390	92
Average	23.03	17.05	9.76	34.69	38.25	15.25	59.50	29.80	29.63	39.30	19.18	30.90	14.55	40.50	41.00	31.16	21.25	16.25	3.00	130.00	46.00
100s	0	0	0	1	0	0	5	3	0	1	0	0	0	0	0	1	0	0	0	1	0
50s	5	1	0	3	7	0	3	2	4	2	1	2	0	0	1	0	0	1	0	0	0
Catches/Stumpings	8/0	5/0	2/0	11/0	15/0	32/0	6/0	5/0	6/0	9/0	2/0	4/0	5/0	1/0	7/0	5/0	1/0	0/0	0/0	1/0	0/0

Key: ah absent hurt; rh retired hurt

Home Ground: Taunton
Address: County Ground, St James Street, Taunton, Somerset, TA1 1JT
Tel: 01823 272946
Fax: 01823 332395
Email: info@somersetcountycc.co.uk
Directions: By road: M5 junction 25, follow A358 to town centre. Signposted from there.

Capacity: 6,500
Other grounds used: Bath
Year formed: 1875

Chief Executive: Peter Anderson
Head Coach: Mark Garaway
Captain: Ian Blackwell
County colours: Black, white and maroon

Honours
Sunday League/NCL/Pro40
1979
Benson & Hedges Cup
1981, 1982
Gillette Cup/NatWest/C&G Trophy
1979, 1983, 2001
Twenty20 Cup
2005

Website:
www.somersetcountycc.com

SOMERSET CCC

FIRST-CLASS MATCHES
BOWLING

	CM Willoughby	AR Caddick	RL Johnson	PD Trego	CL White	KA Parsons	WJ Durston	DJ Cullen	SRG Francis	ID Blackwell	MK Munday	AV Suppiah	JD Francis	NJ Edwards	JC Hildreth	Overs	Total	Byes/Leg-byes	Wickets	Run outs
v. Gloucestershire	33.4-7-125-5	34-7-104-1	28-2-105-1	19-4-65-1	6-1-17-1											120.4	437	21	10	1
(Bristol) 18-21 April																-	-	-	-	
v. Worcestershire	19-6-40-1	18.2-5-40-5	15-4-41-2	10-1-26-2	1-0-9-0											63.2	161	5	10	
(Worcester) 26-28 April	14-3-43-3	12.1-4-25-4	14-2-53-2	7-2-17-1												47.1	138	0	10	
v. Northamptonshire	16-4-44-1	26-4-113-1		16-2-70-0	17-0-71-2		8-2-10-1	43-10-137-5								126	449	4	10	
(Northampton) 3-5 May																-	-	-	-	
v. Essex		20-3-79-3	15-1-57-0	14-2-31-0	12-2-44-0	25-0-15-0	11-0-45-1	26-4-84-0				6-0-41-0				106.5	400	4	4	
(Taunton) 10-13 May		24-7-64-2	19.4-2-69-1	12-4-48-1	9-0-49-1	6-0-21-0	1-0-6-0	14-0-54-1				5-0-26-0				90.4	347	10	7	1
v. Leicestershire	27-10-86-4	20.5-4-58-3	8-0-25-2	16-3-38-1	4-1-6-0	3-0-10-0			6-1-17-0					3-0-12-0		84.5	254	14	10	
(Taunton) 24-27 May	23-4-70-2	28-5-85-2	10.3-2-38-1	7-0-29-0	2-0-8-0							4-0-11-0				77.3	254	1	5	
v. Glamorgan	17-6-39-3	22.3-5-79-3		3-0-19-1		13-5-43-3		10-2-33-0								65.3	223	10	10	
(Swansea) 31 May-1 June	10.5-2-24-3	16-3-55-5				6-4-9-1										32.5	103	15	10	1
v. Worcestershire	32-5-104-6	26-1-145-0		18-1-106-0	20-0-74-0	10.5-0-33-3	4-0-21-0	26-1-73-1				13-2-50-0				149.5	618	12	10	
(Taunton) 7-10 June	2-0-20-0			2.3-0-22-0												4.3	42	0	0	
v. Surrey	16-4-52-4	23-3-93-3	11-1-62-1	5.5-0-24-2		3-0-23-0						1-0-1-0				59.5	266	11	10	
(Bath) 14-16 June	17-6-40-3	22-2-102-0	10.2-1-49-1	4-0-23-0	7-0-40-0		3.3-0-31-2					5.4-1-36-0		2-0-15-0		71.3	356	20	6	
v. Derbyshire	29-8-106-3	30-7-99-3		8-2-40-0	21.5-2-63-1	3-0-15-0			21-8-61-3			1-0-1-0				113.5	396	11	10	
(Taunton) 14-17 July	27-7-80-1	21-3-78-1		17-5-44-2	19-0-92-1				11-1-32-0			20-3-62-1	1-0-9-0			116	415	18	7	1
v. Surrey	33-5-107-2	35-5-166-0		23.5-1-87-3	34-2-148-5							27-0-126-0	14-0-64-0	2-0-12-0		168.5	717	7	10	
(Guildford) 19-22 July																-	-	-	-	
v. Essex	22-10-46-3	25-6-82-5		21-4-74-1	6-2-16-1						7-1-24-0					81	252	10	10	
(Southend) 2-5 August	20-4-68-1	26-5-110-3		13-1-48-0	4-1-8-0		14-1-57-1				21-1-83-3	3-0-13-0				101	399	12	8	
v. Derbyshire	22-10-48-3	24-4-87-1		8.4-0-53-2	21-2-57-3				14-2-57-1							89.4	316	14	10	
(Derby) 8-11 August	15-1-85-2	20-2-89-2		17-2-101-2	3-0-21-0		19-5-56-1		3-0-44-0			2.2-1-13-1				79.2	413	4	8	
v. Glamorgan	17-3-84-3	21-5-87-1			5-0-24-1				6-2-43-0							49	240	2	5	
(Taunton) 15-18 August																-	-	-	-	
v. Gloucestershire	15-5-44-7	16-4-60-0	7-0-30-2		7-1-27-1							1-1-0-0				46	161	0	10	
(Taunton) 22-24 August	9-1-40-2	12-0-49-2	13-4-37-5		7-1-34-1							3-0-9-0				44	172	3	10	
v. Leicestershire	13-2-47-2	18-5-46-5	14-5-38-2		8-1-32-1											53	170	7	10	
(Leicester) 1-4 September	21-4-108-0	28-8-91-3	16-4-48-1		10-1-31-0	9-1-41-1						4-0-29-0				88	360	12	5	
v. Northamptonshire	19-3-92-2	22-4-76-4	8.1-0-28-1		7-3-17-0		10-1-33-1		21-2-63-2							87.1	326	17	10	
(Taunton) 12-15 September	9-1-45-0	19-0-97-1	6-0-37-0		6-0-26-0		33-4-116-2		19-4-59-1			12-1-58-0		1-1-0-0		105	453	15	4	

Overs	498.3	609.5	195.4	242.5	186.5	97.4	112.3	119	55	46	59	91	1	3	5					
Maidens	121	111	28	34	13	16	14	17	13	7	2	9	0	1	0					
Runs	1687	2259	717	965	723	360	416	381	237	139	262	385	9	12	27					
Wickets	66	63	22	19	15	11	10	7	4	3	3	2	0	0	0					
Average	25.56	35.85	32.59	50.78	48.20	32.72	41.60	54.42	59.25	46.33	87.33	192.50	-	-	-					

FIELDING

32	CM Gazzard
15	WJ Durston
11	JC Hildreth
9	KA Parsons
8	MJ Wood
7	SHP Spurway
6	AV Suppiah
6	CL White
5	AR Caddick
5	ME Trescothick
5	PD Trego
5	JD Francis
4	NJ Edwards
2	RL Johnson
2	CM Willoughby
1	JL Langer
1	SRG Francis
1	DJ Cullen
0	ID Blackwell
0	MK Munday
0	RJ Lett

Final Division Two Table

	P	W	L	D	Bat	Bowl	Pts
Surrey	16	10	2	4	62	44	262.00
Worcestershire	16	8	4	4	58	43	229.00
Essex	16	7	4	5	62	40	220.00
Leicestershire	16	5	4	7	47	41	185.50
Derbyshire	16	4	4	8	51	41	178.50
Northamptonshire	16	3	5	8	52	37	163.00
Gloucestershire	16	3	6	7	51	36	155.50
Glamorgan	16	2	7	7	51	41	146.50
Somerset	16	3	9	4	43	40	140.00

(Somerset deducted 0.50 points v. Glos, 18 April; and
0.50 points v. Leics, 1 September for a slow over rate)

SURREY CCC

FIRST-CLASS MATCHES
BATTING

	MA Butcher	SA Newman	JN Batty	AD Brown	IDK Salisbury	MR Ramprakash	ND Doshi	Mohammad Akram	Azhar Mahmood	R Clarke	JGE Benning	NC Saker	MP Bicknell	J Ormond	TJ Murtagh	SJ Walters	A Kumble	CP Schofield	JW Dernbach	RS Clinton	Extras	Total	Wickets	Result	Points
v. Durham UCCE	47	89	23	87	47*	67					122*										51	533	5		
(The Oval) 15-17 April		144*	67				12*														15	238	1	D	
v. Derbyshire	2	66	22	26	14	71	0*	1	37	59			0								10	308	10		
(The Oval) 19-22 April	19	90	96	15	2	12	1*	46	130					41*							24	476	8	D	9
v. Leicestershire	77	9	54	25	1	113	6*		1	45				6	4						29	370	10		
(Leicester) 26-29 April	85*	75	41	0	8	22			0	4					37*						15	287	7	W	21
v. Gloucestershire	47	81	4	4	4	292			39	112			15*								41	639	8		
(The Oval) 3-5 May																								W	22
v. Worcestershire	74	74	69	17	3*	118			16*	38	52										40	501	7		
(The Oval) 17-20 May	20			11					40*	57*	0										8	136	3	L	8
v. Essex	71	97	87	27	14		1*	2	42	13	35	24									20	433	10		
(Whitgift School) 31 May-3 June	4	1	32		48				12*	63*											18	178	4	W	22
v. Leicestershire	105	8	39	215	73				0	165		27*									36	668	7		
(The Oval) 7-10 June																								W	22
v. Somerset	5	25	13	63	0	87*	0		39	0	0	15									19	266	10		
(Bath) 14-16 June	19	14	27	126*		51			77	4		5*									33	356	6	W	19
v. Glamorgan	136	22	0	4	42	20	9	21*	14	11			59								10	348	10		
(Swansea) 20-23 June	1	27	73	73	26*	156	16*		0	29			26								21	448	8	D	10
v. Northamptonshire	30	23	8	113	1	51	5*	1	47	13											15	328	10		
(Northampton) 14-17 July	4	8	133	44*		155			52	10											18	424	6	W	20
v. Somerset	84	32	17	13	50	167	3		98	214	0						6*				33	717	10		
(Guildford) 19-22 July																								D	10
v. Northamptonshire	147	143	18	27		301*			15*	6											12	669	5		
(The Oval) 2-5 August	8*	0	19	2*	30																6	65	3	W	22
v. Worcestershire	0	64	104	112	6	196	6	0	40*	12							8				28	576	10		
(Worcester) 8-10 August																								W	22
v. Essex	6	41	4	36	74		32	6	5			58*				41				11	16	330	10		
(Chelmsford) 16-18 August	6	25	12	63	14		2	8*	26			9				4				12	17	198	10	L	5
v. Glamorgan	151	35	5	2	7	77	14	0*	101	22								3			16	433	10		
(The Oval) 30 August-1 September	108	13	0	107*		31			32*	13											5	309	5	W	22
v. Gloucestershire	64	44	5	14		75	22*		7	0						7		16	9		25	288	10		
(Bristol) 6-9 September	35	4	50	43		51	2*		22	47						67		95	4*		50	470	9	D	9
v. Derbyshire	51*rh	67	0	14	16				0	22	30			41*	6			0*			28	275	8		
(Derby) 20-23 September	59*	83	3	8	21*						26			41							32	273	5	W	19
Matches	17	17	17	16	16	15	14	14	13	11	8	7	4	4	3	3	3	2	2	1					
Innings	29	29	29	27	19	24	13	11	20	18	13	10	6	4	3	6	2	3	3	2					
Not Out	4	1	0	4	4	2	8	4	4	3	2	1	2	2	2	0	1	0	2	0					
High Score	151	144*	133	215	74	301*	32	21*	101	214	122*	58*	59	41*	41*	67	8	95	9	12					
Runs	1465	1404	1025	1264	363	2278	106	64	600	970	488	192	156	62	82	166	14	114	13	23					
Average	58.60	50.14	35.34	54.95	24.20	103.54	21.20	9.14	37.50	64.66	44.36	21.33	39.00	31.00	82.00	27.66	14.00	38.00	13.00	11.50					
100s	5	2	2	5	0	8	0	0	1	3	2	0	0	0	0	0	0	0	0	0					
50s	8	10	7	4	2	9	0	0	2	3	2	1	1	0	0	1	0	1	0	0					
Catches/Stumpings	17/0	13/0	44/9	9/0	11/0	13/0	3/0	3/0	18/0	12/0	4/0	4/0	2/0	0/0	2/0	3/0	4/0	2/0	0/0	0/0					

Key: rh retired hurt

Home Ground: The Brit Oval
Address: The Brit Oval, Kennington, London, SE11 5SS
Tel: 0207 582 6660
Fax: 0207 735 7769
Email: enquiries@surreycricket.com
Directions: *By road:* The Brit Oval is located south of the Thames in Kennington on the A202, near the junction with the A3 and A24, just south of Vauxhall Bridge and 10 minutes from Victoria and Waterloo (Eurostar). *By rail:* Take South West Trains to Vauxhall which is a short walk from the ground. The station is well served by trains from throughout Surrey and Hampshire as well as from the Greater London area. Connections include Clapham Junction and Waterloo.

Capacity: 16,500
Other grounds used: Guildford, Whitgift School
Year formed: 1845

Chief Executive: Paul Sheldon
Cricket Manager: Steve Rixon
Captain: Mark Butcher
County colours: Blue, white and yellow

Website:
www.surreycricket.com

Honours
County Championship
1890, 1891, 1892, 1894, 1895, 1899, 1914, 1952, 1953, 1954, 1955, 1956, 1957, 1958, 1971, 1999, 2000, 2002
Joint Champions 1950
Sunday League/NCL/Pro40
1996, 2003
Benson & Hedges Cup
1974, 1997, 2001
Gillette Cup/NatWest/C&G Trophy
1982, 1992
Twenty20 Cup
2003

SURREY CCC

FIRST-CLASS MATCHES
BOWLING

	IDK Salisbury	ND Doshi	Mohammad Akram	Azhar Mahmood	A Kumble	R Clarke	NC Saker	CP Schofield	TJ Murtagh	MP Bicknell	J Ormond	JW Dernbach	AD Brown	JGE Benning	SJ Walters	MA Butcher	Overs	Total	Byes/Leg-byes	Wickets	Run outs
v. Durham UCCE (The Oval) 15-17 April	33.1-7-70-3	19-8-19-1	20-8-40-6						11-4-40-0		19-5-27-0			4-0-24-0			106.1	227	7	10	
																	-	-	-	-	
v. Derbyshire (The Oval) 19-22 April	23.1-2-69-2	38-4-135-1	3.2-0-17-0	28.4-10-69-5		17-0-94-0					32-8-93-2						142.1	492	15	10	
v. Leicestershire (Leicester) 26-29 April	22-7-40-1	10.1-4-21-3		14-5-36-1		10-2-32-1				16-6-48-3	16-3-52-1						88.1	244	15	10	
	22.5-1-82-2	4-0-18-0		24-5-66-2		20-7-44-3				9-1-37-0	18-6-39-3						97.5	314	28	10	
v. Gloucestershire (The Oval) 3-5 May	14-5-29-3	4.2-0-8-1		18-7-43-2		17-4-44-2					8-2-18-0			11-0-58-2			72.2	207	7	10	
	5-0-17-0	9-3-18-2		12.5-5-34-6		9-3-20-0								7-1-32-1			42.5	135	14	9	
v. Worcestershire (The Oval) 17-20 May	36.1-5-104-3	36-7-91-6	15-1-73-0	17-3-56-0		2-1-4-0							2-0-9-0				108.1	353	16	9	
	7-0-60-2	7.5-0-68-4	6-0-53-0	10-0-79-1		1-0-22-0											31.5	287	5	8	1
v. Essex (Whitgift School) 31 May-3 June	17.3-1-46-5	13-2-50-1	22-2-83-0	17-3-52-1		22-8-68-3				14-3-56-0					5-3-5-0		105.3	365	10	10	
	25-5-52-2	21.3-1-74-3	12-3-32-2	12-0-43-2		7-1-26-0				7-3-10-0							89.3	244	2	10	1
v. Leicestershire (The Oval) 7-10 June	18-6-35-3	8-3-22-1		14-0-64-1	11-1-37-0	16-4-45-4				13-4-30-1				1-0-9-0			80	251	18	10	
	33-12-64-4	17.1-2-60-2		20-6-61-3	2-0-9-0	8-2-28-0				7-2-20-1							88.1	259	8	10	
v. Somerset (Bath) 14-16 June	5-0-34-0		25.1-5-81-4			11-1-43-1	8-1-37-0				27-7-93-5				5-0-43-0		81.1	342	11	10	
	14.4-3-36-4		19-5-76-2			9-1-41-0	16-1-79-4				13-3-31-0				3-0-10-0		74.4	276	3	10	
v. Glamorgan (Swansea) 20-23 June	31-4-81-1	29-3-106-3		21.3-4-64-3		14-0-93-3					16-3-49-0			2-0-44-0			111.3	410	17	10	
	9-1-22-0	10-0-49-2		5-0-25-0		3-0-5-0					4-1-14-0						33	168	9	2	
v. Northamptonshire (Northampton) 14-17 July	22-5-67-3	14-4-40-0	15.1-3-53-3	19-2-61-2		8-2-22-1	11-1-38-1										89.1	300	19	10	
	16.4-4-62-3	7-0-33-1	14-4-49-3			8-2-31-0											52.4	223	13	10	
v. Somerset (Guildford) 19-22 July	40-1-181-2		21-3-79-0		17-0-101-0	36-3-127-1	24-3-88-1			16-2-73-0			8.5-1-25-3				162.5	688	14	8	1
																	-	-	-	-	
v. Northamptonshire (The Oval) 2-5 August	26.5-2-83-3	16-4-42-2		14-3-55-2	11-1-59-0	28-10-83-3	2-0-15-0										97.5	347	10	10	
	26-4-84-0	20-4-62-1		20-4-64-0	16-4-47-1	34.2-6-100-8	2-0-9-0										118.2	386	20	10	
v. Worcestershire (Worcester) 8-10 August	31-7-89-4			8-1-32-0	12-3-56-1	33-8-80-5	4-0-29-0						2-0-9-0				90	304	9	10	
	14-3-37-3			10-0-42-1	15-3-53-4	8.3-0-28-2											47.3	165	5	5	
v. Essex (Chelmsford) 16-18 August	13-2-56-0	38.5-4-135-4	28-2-98-1	28-6-72-3			22-1-101-1							12-1-31-0		7-3-21-1	148.5	530	16	10	
																	-	-	-	-	
v. Glamorgan (The Oval) 30 August-1 September	12-3-42-1	11-3-30-1	15-6-46-2	11-0-49-2			8-2-31-2	21-6-63-1									78	269	8	10	1
	12-2-49-2	18-5-42-2	6-0-30-1	9-4-37-1			3-0-14-1	16-1-82-3									64	255	1	10	.
v. Gloucestershire (Bristol) 6-9 September		36-11-117-4		30-10-79-1			20-4-107-2	24.2-3-78-3			9-2-55-0			4-0-21-0	5-0-8-1		123.2	459	2	8	
		30-3-92-3					12-1-63-0	12-0-73-1			18-2-67-3			7-2-18-0			84	329	8	8	
v. Derbyshire (Derby) 20-23 September	28.3-7-88-2	30-13-58-1					22.4-2-73-3		25-6-82-2				17.2-5-43-1	3-0-12-0	8-2-9-1		134.3	385	15	10	
	19-7-53-4	21-2-44-2					8-1-41-0		6-1-16-2								54	162	8	8	

	IDK Salisbury	ND Doshi	Mohammad Akram	Azhar Mahmood	A Kumble	R Clarke	NC Saker	CP Schofield	TJ Murtagh	MP Bicknell	J Ormond	JW Dernbach	AD Brown	JGE Benning	SJ Walters	MA Butcher
Overs	577.3	468.5	365	336.4	139.5	188	146.4	73.2	67	101	93	44.2	23.5	42	26	5
Maidens	106	90	72	69	27	34	16	10	18	26	24	9	2	4	7	0
Runs	1732	1434	1294	1161	418	738	657	296	223	303	229	165	74	237	69	8
Wickets	62	51	42	31	19	18	14	8	7	7	6	4	3	3	2	1
Average	27.93	28.11	30.80	37.45	22.00	41.00	46.92	37.00	31.85	43.28	38.16	41.25	24.66	79.00	34.50	8.00

FIELDING

53	JN Batty (44 ct, 9 st)
18	Azhar Mahmood
17	MA Butcher
13	MR Ramprakash
13	SA Newman
12	R Clarke
11	IDK Salisbury
9	AD Brown
4	A Kumble
4	JGE Benning
4	NC Saker
3	Mohammad Akram
3	ND Doshi
3	SJ Walters
2	MP Bicknell
2	CP Schofield
2	TJ Murtagh
0	J Ormond
0	RS Clinton
0	JW Dernbach

Final Division Two Table

	P	W	L	D	Bat	Bowl	Pts
Surrey	16	10	2	4	62	44	262.00
Worcestershire	16	8	4	4	58	43	229.00
Essex	16	7	4	5	62	40	220.00
Leicestershire	16	5	4	7	47	41	185.50
Derbyshire	16	4	4	8	51	41	178.50
Northamptonshire	16	3	5	8	52	37	163.00
Gloucestershire	16	3	6	7	51	36	155.50
Glamorgan	16	2	7	7	51	41	146.50
Somerset	16	3	9	4	43	40	140.00

SUSSEX CCC

FIRST–CLASS MATCHES
BATTING

	RR Montgomerie	CD Hopkinson	MW Goodwin	CJ Adams	JD Lewry	Mushtaq Ahmed	MJ Prior	RSC Martin-Jenkins	MH Yardy	LJ Wright	Yasir Arafat	RJ Kirtley	Naved-ul-Hasan	OP Rayner	CD Nash	AJ Hodd	DJ Spencer	NRK Turk	TE Linley	SA Heather	Extras	Total	Wickets	Result	Points
v. Warwickshire (Hove) 19-22 April	2	39	37	23	13	42*		4	48	54						18	16				6	302	10		
	9	7	214*						159*												28	417	2	D	9
v. Hampshire (Rose Bowl) 26-28 April	9	45	0	64	12*	1		3	12	6			38			8					13	211	10		
	35	5	5	31	5*	2		91	38	20			8			3					16	262	10	W	18
v. Yorkshire (Headingley) 3-6 May	14	65	0	12	2*	13	124	29	23	2		1									16	301	10		
	1	41	23	44			55*	17*	11												3	195	5	W	20
v. Nottinghamshire (Hove) 9-11 May	8	2	29	6	0*	1	33	17	25	13		2									7	143	10		
	29	74	5	37	0	0*	42	22	7	3			11								17	247	10	W	17
v. Sri Lanka (Hove) 18-21 May	27	32						0			28*			101	11	0	17	24	0	0	22	262	10	D	
v. Durham (Riverside) 23-24 May	28	20	42	19	0*	8	2	49	17	1		7									36	229	10	W	18
v. Middlesex (Horsham) 31 May-3 June	26	62	55	31	0	27*	3	37		59			64	0							12	376	10		
	98	4	57	59	5*	6	77	27		13			3	4							17	370	10	W	21
v. Lancashire (Liverpool) 6-9 June	56	2	1	30	1*	22	37	3		28		2			29						7	218	10		
	27	4	2	68	1*	14	9	6		4		12			7						12	166	10	L	4
v. Yorkshire (Arundel Castle) 21-23 June	9	25	235	107	0*	11	4	32	12		86	14									15	550	10	W	22
v. Kent (Hove) 13-16 July	0	20	82	3	17*		15		134	0	31	36		23							38	399	10		
	69	57	122				108		4	3	5*			5*							20	393	6	D	11
v. Middlesex (Southgate) 19-22 July	0	8	69	115	27*	12	43		97	43	67			0							26	507	10		
	61	68	156	16*					66*												12	379	3	D	12
v. Warwickshire (Edgbaston) 27-30 July	45	36	0	63	0	2	52	0	4		22	1*									21	246	10		
	65	2	8	16	3	8	9	20	67		23	6*									29	256	10	L	4
v. Lancashire (Hove) 2-5 August	4	0	40	31	0	13	112	73	63	51*	27										25	439	10		
	100	14	103	28			6		6	13*	15*										9	294	6	D	11
v. Durham (Hove) 16-18 August	69	64	88	155			41	45*	2		40*										26	530	6	W	22
v. Hampshire (Hove) 31 August- 3 September	27	15	107	75	1	2	36	28		34	16*				67						40	448	10	D	12
v. Kent (Canterbury) 5-8 September	1	3	51	75	2	25*	30	0		18	0				42						42	289	10		
	4	9	16	38		13*	19	5		22	3*				28						4	161	8	W	19
v. Nottinghamshire (Trent Bridge) 20-22 September	82	0	99	72			77*	84*	119												27	560	5	W	22
Matches	17	17	16	16	16	15	14	14	12	11	8	8	8	5	4	3	2	1	1	1					
Innings	28	28	27	25	19	19	22	21	20	17	12	10	8	6	6	4	2	1	1	1					
Not Out	0	0	1	1	11	5	2	3	2	2	3	5	0	1	0	0	0	0	0	0					
High Score	100	74	235	155	27*	42*	124	91	159*	59	86	36	64	101	67	18	17	24	0	0					
Runs	905	723	1649	1218	89	222	934	592	914	313	390	118	134	133	184	29	33	24	0	0					
Average	32.32	25.82	63.42	50.75	11.12	15.85	46.70	32.88	50.77	20.86	43.33	23.60	16.75	26.60	30.66	7.25	16.50	24.00	-	-					
100s	1	0	6	3	0	0	3	0	3	0	0	0	0	1	0	0	0	0	0	0					
50s	7	6	7	7	0	0	4	3	4	3	2	0	1	0	1	0	0	0	0	0					
Catches/Stumpings	17/0	10/0	4/0	28/0	10/0	2/0	34/11	1/0	9/0	7/0	1/0	2/0	1/0	6/0	0/0	8/0	1/0	0/0	0/0	1/0					

Home Ground: Hove
Address: County Ground, Eaton Road, Hove, BN3 3AN
Tel: 0871 2822000
Fax: 01273 771549
Email: simon.dyke@sussexcricket.co.uk
Directions: By rail: Hove station is a 10-minute walk.
By road: Follow AA signs. Street parking at no cost.
Capacity: 5,500

Other grounds used: Horsham, Arundel Castle
Year formed: 1839

Chief Executive: Hugh Griffiths/Gus Mackay
Director of Cricket: Peter Moores
Captain: Chris Adams
County colours: Red, black and white

Honours
County Championship
2003, 2006
Sunday League/NCL/Pro40
1982
Gillette Cup/NatWest/C&G Trophy
1963, 1964, 1978, 1986, 2006

Website:
www.sussexcricket.co.uk

SUSSEX CCC

FIRST-CLASS MATCHES
BOWLING

	Mushtaq Ahmed	JD Lewry	Yasir Arafat	Naved-ul-Hasan	RJ Kirtley	LJ Wright	RSC Martin-Jenkins	OP Rayner	DJ Spencer	MH Yardy	TE Linley	CD Nash	CJ Adams	CD Hopkinson	NRK Turk	Overs	Total	Byes/Leg-byes	Wickets	Run outs
v. Warwickshire (Hove) 19-22 April	43-5-128-2	28.2-14-58-1				25-4-88-2	33-10-78-4		13-1-70-1	2-0-5-0						144.2	449	22	10	
																-	-	-	-	
v. Hampshire (Rose Bowl) 26-28 April	5-2-6-1	14-1-56-2		23.2-9-63-5		8-2-19-0	14-10-19-2									64.2	168	5	10	
	15.2-1-64-7	13-1-31-1		19-3-52-1		5-0-32-1	7-2-23-0									59.2	211	9	10	
v. Yorkshire (Headingley) 3-6 May	28.3-7-68-3	13-3-34-2		18-5-86-4		8-2-23-1	15-3-32-0									82.3	272	19	10	
	11-1-79-0	22-10-49-3		22-5-62-7		5-1-14-0	7-1-12-0									67	221	5	10	
v. Nottinghamshire (Hove) 9-11 May	28.5-6-72-6	17-5-38-1		24-4-89-3		7-3-10-0	4-2-5-0									80.5	229	15	10	
	18.3-4-58-3	10-2-23-3		13-4-29-4			4-2-2-0									45.3	120	8	10	
v. Sri Lanka (Hove) 18-21 May				31-5-103-1	25-7-68-1		30-5-115-0	24-3-82-1		27-7-56-1	17-1-63-1		4.4-1-17-0	3-0-9-0		161.4	521	8	5	
				1-0-2-1				1-0-3-0								2	5	0	1	
v. Durham (Riverside) 23-24 May	13-4-25-5	11-4-27-0		12.5-5-28-4		7-3-6-1	9-5-6-0									52.5	110	18	10	
	7-4-12-5	3-0-9-0		9.1-0-42-5		3-1-5-0	7-1-9-0									29.1	80	3	10	
v. Middlesex (Horsham) 31 May-3 June	29-6-92-4	12.4-2-36-1		10-2-69-1		13-2-39-3	5-1-17-0	2-0-10-0								71.4	266	3	10	1
	24-3-110-6	20-6-49-2				15-1-60-2	5-2-15-0	4-0-14-0								68	256	8	10	
v. Lancashire (Liverpool) 6-9 June	32.4-4-112-5	23-5-75-5		20-4-74-0		4-0-38-0						1-1-0-0		2-0-19-0		79.4	317	13	10	
		4-1-13-0		8-1-25-1		4-1-11-0										19	69	1	1	
v. Yorkshire (Arundel Castle) 21-23 June	18.1-3-58-3	19-6-54-4	9-2-40-1	20-7-53-2		11-5-19-0		1-0-4-0								78.1	238	10	10	
	27.4-5-109-3	21-1-67-3	11-3-36-2	13-3-41-1		6-1-23-1										78.4	287	11	10	
v. Kent (Hove) 13-16 July		27-8-54-2	29-3-84-5	18-4-3-72-2		12-6-33-0		10-1-47-0		5-0-16-0			1-0-2-0			102.4	336	28	10	1
		13-4-29-0	17-3-58-2	15-3-37-1		6-0-21-1		31-15-89-3		8-2-29-0						90	280	17	7	
v. Middlesex (Southgate) 19-22 July	42-1-168-0	18-5-55-1	21.4-3-94-5			16-1-58-2		9-1-33-1		14-0-43-1						120.4	466	15	10	
	27-12-74-3	13-1-39-1	18-6-71-2			7-1-13-0		8-4-8-2								73	208	3	9	1
v. Warwickshire (Edgbaston) 27-30 July	25-4-92-1	21-10-45-0	22-4-77-4	26-6-82-3			21-5-41-2									115	375	38	10	
	18.3-6-39-5	13-0-32-0	12-2-38-3	9-2-25-1			3-1-6-1									55.3	140	0	10	
v. Lancashire (Hove) 2-5 August	18.5-4-76-0	25.1-5-68-6	21-2-97-3			4-0-25-0	7.1-2-27-0			11-2-37-1						87.1	342	12	10	
	37-11-84-3	24-6-61-2	19-2-85-3			8-2-30-1	9-6-16-0			1-0-5-0						98	290	9	9	
v. Durham (Hove) 16-18 August	17-4-64-5	16.2-4-55-4	8-4-21-1				8-4-7-0									49.2	150	3	10	
	12-1-57-3	17-2-73-3	16.2-3-64-4				4-2-6-0	4-0-32-0		1-0-8-0						54.2	247	7	10	
v. Hampshire (Hove) 31 August-3 September	33-4-98-3	13.5-2-48-3	20-2-96-3			13-2-45-1	10-2-48-0						1-0-2-0			90.5	347	10	10	
	12-2-46-0	14-5-24-2	19-6-33-1			23-9-54-0	12-1-42-2						5-2-13-0	3-1-12-0		88	235	11	5	
v. Kent (Canterbury) 5-8 September	22-6-58-6	15-1-38-2	15.1-1-85-2			11-1-43-0	6-2-12-0									69.1	241	5	10	
	27-2-74-7	19-1-39-1	13-2-40-0			12-3-24-2	1-0-9-0						1-0-9-0			73	208	13	10	
v. Nottinghamshire (Trent Bridge) 20-22 September	19.2-4-60-4	14-2-42-2		11-0-36-1		6-2-12-1	4-1-4-2									54.2	165	11	10	
	11.3-2-48-9			3-0-29-0		10-2-56-1				3-0-12-0						27.3	150	5	10	

	Mushtaq Ahmed	JD Lewry	Yasir Arafat	Naved-ul-Hasan	RJ Kirtley	LJ Wright	RSC Martin-Jenkins	OP Rayner	DJ Spencer	MH Yardy	TE Linley	CD Nash	CJ Adams	CD Hopkinson	NRK Turk
Overs	623.5	494.2	271.1	165.2	236.4	178	216.1	98	38	46	27	25	1	9.4	3
Maidens	118	117	48	37	53	36	72	26	4	4	7	4	0	2	0
Runs	2031	1321	1019	585	748	582	489	348	155	159	56	87	2	48	9
Wickets	102	57	41	35	18	15	14	6	2	2	1	1	0	0	0
Average	19.91	23.17	24.85	16.71	41.55	38.80	34.92	58.00	77.50	79.50	56.00	87.00	-	-	-

FIELDING

45	MJ Prior (34 ct, 11 st)
28	CJ Adams
17	RR Montgomerie
10	JD Lewry
10	CD Hopkinson
9	MH Yardy
8	AJ Hodd
7	LJ Wright
6	OP Rayner
4	MW Goodwin
2	Mushtaq Ahmed
2	RJ Kirtley
1	DJ Spencer
1	RSC Martin-Jenkins
1	Naved-ul-Hasan
1	Yasir Arafat
1	SA Heather
0	CD Nash
0	NRK Turk
0	TE Linley

Final Division One Table

	P	W	L	D	Bat	Bowl	Pts
Sussex	16	9	2	5	49	47	242.00
Lancashire	16	6	1	9	58	46	224.00
Hampshire	16	6	3	7	48	48	207.00
Warwickshire	16	6	5	5	42	43	189.00
Kent	16	4	4	8	43	44	175.00
Yorkshire	16	3	6	7	43	41	154.00
Durham	16	4	8	4	39	43	153.50
Nottinghamshire	16	4	7	5	40	37	153.00
Middlesex	16	1	7	8	47	42	133.50

WARWICKSHIRE CCC

FIRST-CLASS MATCHES
BATTING

	UL Trott	NV Knight	HH Streak	AGR Loudon	IJ Westwood	MA Wagh	NM Carter	DR Brown	JE Anyon	JO Troughton	TR Ambrose	T Frost	PL Harris	MJ Powell	TD Groenewald	MM Ali	LM Daggett	IR Bell	LC Parker	N Tahir	FA Klokker	NS Poonia	DL Vettori	CR Woakes	AJ Shantry	Extras	Total	Wickets	Result	Points
v. Cambridge UCCE (Fenner's) 15-17 April	55	79	28*	124			33			5	4	56	16*													32	432	7		
				29*						21*		5														3	58	1	D	
v. Sussex (Hove) 19-22 April	109	73	20	51	4	4	7	6*		58	42										40					35	449	10		
																													D	12
v. Yorkshire (Edgbaston) 26-29 April	43	30	9	73	25		10	0*		73	13	3		10												27	316	10		
	177*	126		29	7		36				12*															10	399	5	W	20
v. Nottinghamshire (Trent Bridge) 3-6 May	30	0	0		14		53	2*	11	3		36				68		8								23	248	10		
	84	20	27*		5		5	1	10	12		29				3		79								10	285	10	W	18
v. Hampshire (Edgbaston) 9-12 May	0	20	4	15	21	2	15	0*		103	19	10														8	217	10		
	6	34	12*	11	23	23	26	4		25	29	6														14	213	10	L	3
v. Middlesex (Lord's) 24-27 May	139	14	6	68		16	5*	69		9	13*					14							27			21	401	9		
																													D	11
v. Kent (Tunbridge Wells) 31 May-3 June	0	0		11		48	27	10	2	29	66*				7	20										17	237	10		
	40	24	0		8	6	38	1	22	34*					3											8	192	10	L	4
v. Durham (Edgbaston) 7-10 June	7	37	12	13		12	30	2	0		20*				0	53										22	208	10		
	14	41	37	14	5	20	8	6			96				2*	32										35	310	10	W	18
v. Lancashire (Edgbaston) 14-16 June	7	0	29		26	4	0	18*	2	63						5	0									19	173	10		
	33	80	1		27	13	0	0	7	22*						6	12									24	225	10	L	3
v. Middlesex (Edgbaston) 14-17 July	16	10	44*	19		111	15	6	3	4	133	0														30	391	10		
	46*	36				44	8	10*	3																	7	154	4	D	9
v. Yorkshire (Scarborough) 19-21 July	7	3	68*	31		18	0	22		4				32	0			9								7	201	10		
	43	58	16*		80	5	2	4	1					0	14	0										16	239	10	L	3
v. Sussex (Edgbaston) 27-30 July	9	123	16	19	24	5	18*	4		67	0			42												48	375	10		
	19	19	5	4	53	7	0			11*	0			15												6	140	10	W	21
v. West Indies A (Edgbaston) 2-4 August				10	178	48					50					16	5	30	8*			35		4	4*	26	414	9	W	
v. Nottinghamshire (Edgbaston) 8-11 August	46	9	31	6	81	20	16	2*		63	17							73								17	381	10		
	15	5	44	3	29	70	0*			34								0								24	230	9	W	21
v. Hampshire (Rose Bowl) 16-19 August	4	78	16	10	0	128	36			36	16				16*			28								33	401	10		
	17	19	11	0	2*	47	18*			0	2							0								5	121	10	W	22
v. Durham (Riverside) 22-24 August	18	33	19	13		18	18			0	27				76	68	0*									24	314	10		
	69	0	2	55	0	2	4			19					7	4	1*									1	164	10	L	6
v. Lancashire (Blackpool) 30 August-2 September	0	32		31	67	15	11			0	20					11	12*			21						11	231	10		
				0*	0*																					0	0	0	D	8
v. Kent (Edgbaston) 13-16 September	75	52	56	3	0	3	13			77	9*		7						7							16	318	10		
		15*		3*																						1	19	0	D	10
Matches	17	17	15	14	13	13	13	11	11	10	9	8	8	6	6	6	5	4	4	3	1	1	1	1	1					
Innings	29	30	24	22	23	24	20	19	17	18	14	13	11	11	9	9	9	7	7	3	1	1	1	1	1					
Not Out	2	1	6	0	3	2	4	1	6	1	1	5	1	1	2	0	4	0	0	1	0	0	0	0	1					
High Score	177*	126	68*	73	178	128	36	69	18*	103	133	96	32	56	76	68	12*	79	73	21	40	35	27	4	4*					
Runs	1128	1070	513	458	850	648	250	368	60	390	443	431	140	256	157	177	37	214	140	36	40	35	27	4	4					
Average	41.77	36.89	28.50	20.81	42.50	29.45	15.62	20.44	5.45	22.94	34.07	53.87	14.00	25.60	22.42	19.66	7.40	30.57	20.00	18.00	40.00	35.00	27.00	4.00	-					
100s	3	2	0	0	2	2	0	0	0	1	1	0	0	0	0	0	0	0	0	0	0	0	0	0	0					
50s	4	6	2	4	4	1	0	2	0	2	3	4	0	1	1	2	0	2	1	0	0	0	0	0	0					
Catches/Stumpings	20/0	22/0	5/0	9/0	5/0	2/0	1/0	4/0	3/0	4/0	30/4	20/0	3/0	4/0	1/0	2/0	1/0	2/0	4/0	1/0	3/0	0/0	0/0	3/0	0/0					

Home Ground: Edgbaston
Address: County Ground, Edgbaston, Birmingham, B5 7QU
Tel: 0870 0621902
Fax: 0121 4464544
Email: info@edgbaston.com
Directions: *By rail:* New Street station, Birmingham.
By road: M6 to A38(M) to city centre, then follow signs to county ground.
Capacity: 20,000

Other grounds used: Stratford upon Avon
Year formed: 1882

Chief Executive: Dennis Amiss MBE
Director of Coaching: John Inverarity
Captain: Heath Streak
County colours: Blue and white

Honours
County Championship
1911, 1951, 1972, 1994, 1995, 2004
Sunday League/NCL/Pro40
1980, 1994, 1997
Benson & Hedges Cup
1994, 2002
Gillette Cup/NatWest/C&G Trophy
1989, 1993, 1995

Website:
www.thebears.co.uk

WARWICKSHIRE CCC

FIRST-CLASS MATCHES

BOWLING

Match	HH Streak	NM Carter	DR Brown	PL Harris	JE Anyon	AGR Loudon	LM Daggett	N Tahir	JO Troughton	AJ Shantry	TD Groenewald	IR Bell	CR Woakes	MM Ali	IJ Westwood	IJL Trott	NV Knight	MA Wagh	MJ Powell	DL Vettori	Overs	Total	Byes/Leg-byes	Wickets	Run outs
v. Cambridge UCCE (Fenner's) 15-17 April	16-5-39-1	23-8-39-0	17-5-26-2		22-8-58-4				3.4-0-15-2	10-4-20-1											91.4	224	27	10	
	-																				-	-	-	-	-
v. Sussex (Hove) 19-22 April	22-4-72-5	15-4-39-0	19-3-68-3		16.5-1-66-1	14-5-39-0			4-1-15-1												90.5	302	3	10	
	22-8-52-0	20-8-71-1	15-6-21-0		25-7-74-0	31-3-95-0			12-3-41-0										11-0-45-0		136	417	18	2	1
v. Yorkshire (Edgbaston) 26-29 April	16-1-47-3	20-6-48-2			17-3-60-1	6-3-15-1					14-4-36-2										73	216	10	10	1
	28.3-5-77-2	27-4-120-2			22-6-66-2	27-7-65-2					16-5-34-0								1-0-4-0		135.3	433	9	10	
v. Nottinghamshire (Trent Bridge) 3-6 May	16-6-40-2		17-4-49-4	12.3-3-33-3								6-2-18-1	2-1-11-0								53.3	157	6	10	
	26-4-78-3		20-7-49-0	27-8-48-4		17-6-60-1						5-2-10-1	16-3-52-0								111	316	19	10	1
v. Hampshire (Edgbaston) 9-12 May	21-3-66-0	28-8-58-1	35-6-97-4		16-1-42-0	36-1-109-5			2-0-3-0										6-0-16-0		144	405	14	10	
	9.2-3-22-2	6-0-29-0	9-1-61-3			5-0-33-0			3-0-24-0							2-0-22-1			1-0-15-0		35.2	218	12	6	
v. Middlesex (Lord's) 24-27 May	33-11-113-3	25.3-4-104-2	26-6-85-2			12-1-51-0						12-1-59-2								31-4-92-0	139.3	520	16	9	
	-																				-	-	-	-	-
v. Kent (Tunbridge Wells) 31 May-3 June		15-3-46-2	27.5-11-45-4		15-4-35-0	10-4-13-0	24-6-81-4														91.5	234	14	10	
		10-2-30-0	9-2-21-0		9.5-2-26-0	22-3-63-1	3-0-14-0	12-2-38-0													65.5	197	5	1	
v. Durham (Edgbaston) 7-10 June	18-2-80-2		21-3-64-2		21.5-4-59-2	10-4-54-0	16-5-52-2		4-0-16-1			7-0-24-1									101.5	359	10	10	
	11-2-44-1		7-1-16-1		15-1-36-2	2-0-11-0	2-0-9-0														49.4	141	4	10	
v. Lancashire (Edgbaston) 14-16 June	26.5-7-37-3		24-3-82-2		21-2-74-1		10-2-37-0		12-2-26-2					15-4-50-2							108.5	317	11	10	
	8-1-30-2						4-2-9-0		5-0-22-1					1.4-0-23-0							18.4	84	0	3	
v. Middlesex (Edgbaston) 14-17 July	24-3-69-1	24-2-91-2	21-5-47-1	36-5-109-3	20-5-65-0		18.3-1-53-3														143.3	446	12	10	
	10-1-30-0	18.1-3-54-1	5.4-0-37-0	23-2-77-1	0.2-0-0-0		12.5-1-34-2		8.3-0-33-0												78.3	280	15	4	
v. Yorkshire (Scarborough) 19-21 July	19-2-93-0	31-7-101-4	20-2-80-1	44-12-134-5								16-1-78-0			4-0-12-0						134	536	38	10	
	-																				-	-	-	-	-
v. Sussex (Edgbaston) 27-30 July	11-1-52-0	17.4-4-63-6		8-4-23-1	17-1-78-3		5-0-25-0														58.4	246	5	10	
	11-4-38-1	13.1-2-46-2		38-13-73-5	25-3-63-2		6-1-18-0														93.1	256	18	10	
v. West Indies A (Edgbaston) 2-4 August							17.1-4-57-2			14-6-49-5	14-2-59-1		13-2-64-2								58.1	235	6	10	
						10-5-16-4	15-4-62-1			10-5-16-2	16-4-31-1			10-0-38-1	0.5-0-0-1						61.5	173	10	10	
v. Nottinghamshire (Edgbaston) 8-11 August	5-0-29-0	9-1-43-3			13-4-36-1	20-4-49-5															61	208	6	10	1
	18-5-49-1	15.5-3-58-1			34-14-60-1	25-8-83-5		26-5-79-2							1-1-0-0						119.5	344	15	10	
v. Hampshire (Rose Bowl) 16-19 August	16-8-32-0	10-1-40-1			40.1-14-80-6			18-1-53-2			7-1-26-0										91.1	235	4	10	1
	20-4-73-6							14-4-50-1			14-1-66-1										73.3	286	10	10	1
v. Durham (Riverside) 22-24 August	5-3-13-0		20-5-56-3		34.4-11-94-6	4-0-14-0	10-0-36-1				4-0-17-0			12-1-44-0							89.4	284	10	10	
			11-3-36-1		8-0-28-0	3-0-11-0	9-1-54-2				6-0-29-0			4.5-0-35-0							41.5	196	3	3	
v. Lancashire (Blackpool) 30 August- 2 September		27-2-146-0		21-6-52-1					10-0-36-0	25-4-92-1	22-8-107-7		2-1-4-0								117	456	19	9	
		-																			-	-	-	-	-
v. Kent (Edgbaston) 13-16 September	30-6-84-2	32-5-130-4		22-4-52-0	13-0-37-1				20.5-1-98-3					2-1-8-0							119.5	421	12	10	
	4-1-15-1	5-0-36-0							13-2-51-0					18-2-91-0	18-2-46-2	1-0-6-0	9-0-41-0	3-0-14-0			71	311	11	3	

	HH Streak	NM Carter	DR Brown	PL Harris	JE Anyon	AGR Loudon	LM Daggett	N Tahir	JO Troughton	AJ Shantry	TD Groenewald	IR Bell	CR Woakes	MM Ali	IJ Westwood	IJL Trott	NV Knight	MA Wagh	MJ Powell	DL Vettori
Overs	446.4	392.2	324.3	347.2	342.2	339.2	115.4	98	97.1	24	117	30	23	74.2	23	3	9	3	19	31
Maidens	100	77	73	91	71	49	25	19	17	11	22	5	2	13	3	0	0	0	0	4
Runs	1374	1392	940	905	1011	1023	405	375	351	65	396	111	102	318	58	28	41	14	80	92
Wickets	41	34	33	31	31	29	16	13	9	7	6	5	3	3	2	1	0	0	0	0
Average	33.51	40.94	28.48	29.19	32.61	35.27	25.31	28.84	39.00	9.28	66.00	22.20	34.00	106.00	29.00	28.00	-	-	-	-

FIELDING

34	TR Ambrose (30 ct, 4 st)
22	NV Knight
20	T Frost
20	IJL Trott
9	AGR Loudon
5	HH Streak
5	IJ Westwood
4	DR Brown
4	MJ Powell
4	JO Troughton
4	LC Parker
3	FA Klokker
3	JE Anyon
3	PL Harris
3	CR Woakes
2	MA Wagh
2	IR Bell
2	MM Ali
1	N Tahir
1	NM Carter
1	LM Daggett
1	TD Groenewald
0	DL Vettori
0	AJ Shantry
0	NS Poonia

Final Division One Table

	P	W	L	D	Bat	Bowl	Pts
Sussex	16	9	2	5	49	47	242.00
Lancashire	16	6	1	9	58	46	224.00
Hampshire	16	6	3	7	48	48	207.00
Warwickshire	16	6	5	5	42	43	189.00
Kent	16	4	4	8	43	44	175.00
Yorkshire	16	3	6	7	43	41	154.00
Durham	16	4	8	4	39	43	153.50
Nottinghamshire	16	4	7	5	40	37	153.00
Middlesex	16	1	7	8	47	42	133.50

WORCESTERSHIRE CCC

FIRST–CLASS MATCHES
BATTING

	VS Solanki	SM Davies	BF Smith	SC Moore	Z Khan	GJ Batty	GA Hick	RJ Sillence	Kabir Ali	MS Mason	PA Jaques	RW Price	L Vincent	MN Malik	DKH Mitchell	SA Wedge	Extras	Total	Wickets	Result	Points
v. Somerset (Worcester) 26-28 April	34	0	9	24	0	9	8		0	14			0*				11	161	10		
	5	37	0	24	30*	10	6		0	10			4				7	138	10	L	3
v. Derbyshire (Worcester) 10-12 May	110	49	5	0	12		6	20	15			34*	0		2		25	278	10		
	0	5	18	24	10		4	9	13			56	6*		11		18	174	10	L	5
v. Surrey (The Oval) 17-20 May	16	61*	34	75	18	4	26		14	0*	61	0					44	353	9		
	11	1	46*	57	6*	0	20				107	5					26	287	8	W	20
v. Glamorgan (Worcester) 23-26 May	31	11	21	16	4	10	23	27	25*		73			2			9	252	10		
	4	12	5	53*	5	1	7	0	19		6			0*			5	117	9	D	9
v. Gloucestershire (Bristol) 2-5 June	222	192	5	14		12*	20	32	0		58						32	587	8		
	29	22	59	15	12*	14*	64	12	0		7	0					13	247	9	D	12
v. Somerset (Taunton) 7-10 June	5	11	203	53	1*	15	182	20	1		88	1					38	618	10		
				27*							15*						0	42	0	W	22
v. Essex (Chelmsford) 14-17 June	32	18	50	62		112*	37	36	38*		244						21	650	7		
	40*			16							60*						5	121	1	W	22
v. Northamptonshire (Worcester) 21-24 June	23	14	21	29	3	68	139	18		0*	202						26	543	9	W	22
v. Gloucestershire (Worcester) 20-23 July	60	14	19	20	2	36	40	40		7*		6	0				27	271	10		
	6	12	106	0	8	0	8	51		29*		0	0				12	232	10	W	19
v. Derbyshire (Chesterfield) 26-29 July	140	107	45	63	7	79	8	0		4		3*	14				27	497	10		
	22*			26									33*				1	82	1	D	12
v. Glamorgan (Colwyn Bay) 2-5 August	49	27	35	2	13	37		63		21	33			35	134*		11	460	10		
	36	77	72*	82							92				7		16	382	5	W	22
v. Surrey (Worcester) 8-10 August	17	23	0	44	4	10		27		0	95			17	54*		13	304	10		
	56	0	28	0	9	37*		0		0	7			4	17		7	165	10	L	5
v. Leicestershire (Leicester) 16-19 August	0	140	21	97	7*	98	33		31				5				24	456	8	L	5
v. Essex (Worcester) 30 August-2 September	122	46	19	16		16*	104	1*					114				35	473	6		
	30	33	42	3		46*	105*						32				40	331	5	D	12
v. Leicestershire (Worcester) 6-9 September	72	51	36	3	4	35	11	31	2	0*			78				8	331	10		
	16	28	0	26	5*	33*	72	36	1				141				20	378	8	W	20
v. Northamptonshire (Northampton) 20-23 September	14	11	7	30	1	37	70	64	1			1*	36				9	281	10		
	50	2	9	59		25*	30*						16				14	205	5	W	19
Matches	16	16	16	16	16	15	14	13	11	10	8	8	6	6	4	2					
Innings	29	27	27	30	21	24	23	19	16	11	15	10	11	9	8	0					
Not Out	2	1	2	2	6	8	2	1	2	5	2	3	1	3	2	0					
High Score	222	192	203	97	30*	112*	182	64	38*	29*	244	56	141	35	134*	0					
Runs	1252	1004	915	960	161	744	1023	487	168	85	1148	106	469	68	282	0					
Average	46.37	38.61	36.60	34.28	10.73	46.50	48.71	27.05	12.00	14.16	88.30	15.14	46.90	11.33	47.00	-					
100s	4	3	2	0	0	1	4	0	0	0	3	0	2	0	1	0					
50s	4	3	3	9	0	3	3	3	0	0	7	1	1	0	2	0					
Catches/Stumpings	12/0	58/5	23/0	6/0	4/0	14/0	36/0	5/0	1/0	2/0	8/0	3/0	5/0	0/0	3/0	0/0					

Home Ground: New Road, Worcester
Address: County Ground, New Road, Worcester, WR2 4QQ
Tel: 01905 748474
Fax: 01905 748005
Email: info@wccc.co.uk
Directions: From the M5 Junction 7, follow the brown 'broken stumps' logos to WCCC.
Capacity: 4,500

Other grounds used: None
Year formed: 1865

Chief Executive: Mark Newton
Director of Cricket: Steve Rhodes
Academy Director: Damian D'Oliveira
Captain: Vikram Solanki
County colours: Green, black and white

Honours
County Championship
1964, 1965, 1974, 1988, 1989
Sunday League/NCL/Pro40
1971, 1987, 1988
Benson & Hedges Cup
1991
Gillette Cup/NatWest/C&G Trophy
1994

Website:
www.wccc.co.uk

WORCESTERSHIRE CCC

FIRST-CLASS MATCHES
BOWLING

Match	Z Khan	GJ Batty	MS Mason	Kabir Ali	RJ Sillence	MN Malik	RW Price	VS Solanki	SA Wedge	BF Smith	L Vincent	SC Moore	PA Jaques	Overs	Total	Byes/Leg-byes	Wickets	Run outs
v. Somerset (Worcester) 26-28 April	25.1-8-100-4	8-0-26-0	24-4-65-1	26-5-99-2		18-5-104-3								101.1	406	12	10	
	16.3-4-40-6	5-0-13-0		7-3-16-1	6-1-19-1	12-3-29-2								46.3	120	3	10	
v. Derbyshire (Worcester) 10-12 May	22.1-6-60-6			21-6-69-2		13-1-49-0	17-3-76-1	25-6-58-1				2-0-14-0		100.1	338	12	10	
	16.2-7-58-3			17.4-3-43-7			6.4-2-25-0	13-5-16-0						53.4	149	7	10	
v. Surrey (The Oval) 17-20 May	27-7-110-1	27-3-120-3	13-5-34-0	29-7-101-2			25.3-4-104-1					3-1-11-0		124.3	501	21	7	
	1-0-8-1			1-0-13-0						3-0-39-1		3-0-61-1	0.2-0-15-0	8.2	136	0	3	
v. Glamorgan (Worcester) 23-26 May	26-10-65-4	3-2-4-0		24-6-74-3	10.5-3-36-1	9-0-46-2								72.5	239	14	10	
	20-6-88-3	10.2-1-39-0		17-4-56-2	7-1-28-0	9-2-46-0						2-0-22-0		65.2	281	2	5	
v. Gloucestershire (Bristol) 2-5 June	26-3-122-1	31-3-101-2		23.3-3-78-5	15-0-65-2		17-2-74-0	1-0-7-0		2-0-9-0				115.3	471	15	10	
	15-3-35-0			9-2-34-1	2-1-3-0		16-2-51-1							58	163	7	4	
v. Somerset (Taunton) 7-10 June	21-1-93-1	12-4-22-0		26-5-87-2	22.1-3-96-7		12-1-33-0							93.1	346	15	10	
	11-2-48-1	36-8-119-6		13-4-50-2	5-1-21-0		24-8-67-1							89	313	8	10	
v. Essex (Chelmsford) 14-17 June	27-7-138-9		14-5-38-0	11.1-2-34-1	13-2-48-0		4-1-9-0	1-0-3-0						70.1	283	13	10	
	27-1-122-2		46-14-98-2	21-7-84-3	25.2-4-98-2			8-2-18-0	12-0-53-1					139.2	486	13	10	
v. Northamptonshire (Worcester) 21-24 June	8-1-27-5	1-1-0-0	9.2-4-19-2		2-0-6-0					5-2-11-3				25.2	67	4	10	
	21-9-59-1	16-4-52-3	20.2-5-59-5		8-2-33-0			1-1-0-0		10-1-44-0				76.2	254	7	10	1
v. Gloucestershire (Worcester) 20-23 July	23.1-6-74-5	23-3-38-2	25-6-72-2		10-2-24-0		15-2-44-1				6-1-19-0			102.1	276	5	10	
	23-7-60-2	7-2-25-0	22.2-6-45-8		4-0-11-0		4-1-8-0				4-0-10-0			64.2	169	10	10	
v. Derbyshire (Chesterfield) 26-29 July	17-2-57-1	23-4-67-1	20.2-5-49-5		6-0-40-0		25-1-93-2	4-0-18-0				2-0-12-0		97.2	351	15	10	1
	30-5-95-3	44-13-91-2	17-3-57-1		8.4-2-28-1		34-3-94-0	4-1-16-2						139.4	409	28	10	1
v. Glamorgan (Colwyn Bay) 2-5 August	24-2-95-3	22-7-71-3		16-2-71-1	9-0-38-0		13.2-2-49-3	1-0-7-0						85.2	340	9	10	
	16-2-68-1			13-1-56-4	3.4-0-9-3		11-2-43-2							43.4	191	15	10	
v. Surrey (Worcester) 8-10 August	36-6-142-3	28-3-119-2	20-3-100-1		26-6-95-3		19-4-67-1	10-2-34-0						139	576	19	10	
	–													–	–	–	–	
v. Leicestershire (Leicester) 16-19 August	12-2-63-2	3.5-1-12-0		7-4-13-0	3-1-10-0						1-1-0-0			26.5	101	3	2	
	18-4-80-1	16-2-51-0		11-1-54-1	11-1-66-0			27.4-3-89-4			3-0-12-1			86.4	357	5	7	
v. Essex (Worcester) 30 August-2 September	26-4-95-3	17-3-58-2		24-7-49-2	16-1-45-0	19-6-41-2		7-0-15-1				2-0-5-0		111	330	22	10	
	13.5-3-35-1	10-6-10-1		12-1-36-1		3-1-10-1		6-1-13-0						44.5	116	12	4	
v. Leicestershire (Worcester) 6-9 September	20.3-5-54-3	11-3-30-2	19-3-47-2	16-3-69-2	7-1-22-1			4-1-17-0				3-0-10-0		80.3	259	10	10	
	19-5-62-0	24-9-50-2	19.4-7-35-3		21-2-94-5									88.4	357	7	10	
v. Northamptonshire (Northampton) 20-23 September	21-3-81-2	28-3-109-4		17-4-41-0	11-4-28-3		26-11-44-0	3-0-17-1			1-0-8-0			107	342	14	10	
	9-1-34-0	14-4-43-4		7-1-25-1			15.3-5-38-4	0.3-0-0-1						46	143	3	10	

	Z Khan	GJ Batty	MS Mason	Kabir Ali	RJ Sillence	MN Malik	RW Price	VS Solanki	SA Wedge	BF Smith	L Vincent	SC Moore	PA Jaques
Overs	618.4	496.1	296.1	337.1	220.4	137	279.4	52.3	27	5	22	10	0.2
Maidens	132	112	71	68	35	30	54	8	3	0	2	1	0
Runs	2268	1439	910	1161	792	536	813	165	108	48	76	108	15
Wickets	78	43	41	40	23	17	15	5	4	1	1	1	0
Average	29.07	33.46	22.19	29.02	34.43	31.52	54.20	33.00	27.00	48.00	76.00	108.00	–

FIELDING

63	SM Davies (58 ct, 5 st)
36	GA Hick
23	BF Smith
14	GJ Batty
12	VS Solanki
8	PA Jaques
6	SC Moore
5	RJ Sillence
5	L Vincent
4	Z Khan
3	RW Price
3	DKH Mitchell
2	MS Mason
1	Kabir Ali
0	MN Malik
0	SA Wedge

Final Division Two Table

	P	W	L	D	Bat	Bowl	Pts
Surrey	16	10	2	4	62	44	262.00
Worcestershire	16	8	4	4	58	43	229.00
Essex	16	7	4	5	62	40	220.00
Leicestershire	16	5	4	7	47	41	185.50
Derbyshire	16	4	4	8	51	41	178.50
Northamptonshire	16	3	5	8	52	37	163.00
Gloucestershire	16	3	6	7	51	36	155.50
Glamorgan	16	2	7	7	51	41	146.50
Somerset	16	3	9	4	43	40	140.00

YORKSHIRE CCC

FIRST-CLASS MATCHES

BATTING

	MJ Lumb	DS Lehmann	A McGrath	C White	JN Gillespie	JJ Sayers	GJ Kruis	TT Bresnan	GL Brophy	RKJ Dawson	MAK Lawson	SM Guy	MJ Wood	AW Gale	A Rashid	SA Patterson	MP Vaughan	JAR Blain	MJ Hoggard	ME Claydon	JE Lee	A Shahzad	Extras	Total	Wickets	Result	Points
v. Nottinghamshire (Trent Bridge) 19-22 April																										D	6
v. Warwickshire (Edgbaston) 26-29 April	11	6	48	23	6*	11		17	40	10			15				12						17	216	10		
	71	150	84	24	17*	10		9	19	1			18				10						20	433	10	L	4
v. Sussex (Headingley) 3-6 May	1	64	80	37	6	8		11	0		25	5					0*						35	272	10		
	69	87	20	7	1	8		6	4*		9	0					0						10	221	10	L	5
v. Kent (Canterbury) 10-13 May	3	193	5	79	7*	1	1	33		12		6	11										31	382	10		
	24*		123*		5								92										19	263	2	D	10
v. Lancashire (Headingley) 16-19 May	20	33	64	1	45	23	28*	13	1				13				2						22	265	10		
			81*		75*								14										7	177	1	D	9
v. Hampshire (Headingley) 31 May-3 June	67	37	0	57	44		0*	91	6	7			9				1						31	350	10		
	5	18	127	35	2*			14*	13	5			0				56						26	301	8	L	7
v. Middlesex (Southgate) 7-9 June	144	35	0		1		1	31	8	8	0*		0				99						28	355	10		
	12	26	2		34*		7	10	3	12	3		2				4						15	130	10	L	7
v. Sussex (Arundel Castle) 21-23 June	2	12	0	104	12		0*		4	56			10				14	4					20	238	10		
	15	130*	58	49	10		0		0	0			4				4	1					16	287	10	L	3
v. Durham (Riverside) 14-16 July	14	58	140*	5	18	4	0	3	1	8										38			50	339	10		
	18	49	61	66	7*	56	0	5	27	4										0			19	312	10	W	20
v. Warwickshire (Scarborough) 19-21 July	57		15	28	25	72	10*	3	97					149	10	8							62	536	10	W	22
v. Hampshire (Rose Bowl) 26-28 July	31	41	1	4	29	31	2		31		4			0			6*						15	195	10		
	105	4	65	0	8	43	0*		1		44			27			6						8	311	10	L	1
v. Lancashire (Old Trafford) 8-11 August	2	130	65	9	43	48	21*		0		7					2					1		17	345	10		
	68	27	102	116	36	5	4*		0		1					46					21*		24	450	9	D	10
v. Kent (Headingley) 16-19 August	15	172	41	3	4	9	9*			21	4			10	0								22	310	10	D	9
v. Middlesex (Scarborough) 30 August-2 September	17	43	49	10		122*	2			10	33				1				7			2	30	326	10		
			17*			15*																	7	39	1	D	10
v. Nottinghamshire (Headingley) 13-16 September	10	4	147	15	2	0*				15	2			11	63	17							20	306	10		
	84*	48		16		37				15	19*			16	7								11	238	5	W	20
v. Durham (Headingley) 20-23 September	98	339	62	22	5	3		19*	52*					24									53	677	7	D	11
Matches	16	15	15	15	14	13	13	10	10	8	7	6	6	5	5	5	3	3	3	2	1	1					
Innings	25	23	24	23	21	21	17	14	16	13	10	8	10	9	6	7	6	3	5	2	2	1					
Not Out	2	1	3	1	6	3	9	1	0	1	2	2	0	0	0	1	0	0	1	0	1	0					
High Score	144	339	140*	147	45	122*	28*	91	97	56	44	52*	92	149	63	46	99	12	7	38	21*	2					
Runs	963	1706	1293	859	370	590	85	249	251	127	124	150	177	219	115	85	178	24	12	38	22	2					
Average	41.86	77.54	61.57	39.04	24.66	32.77	10.62	19.15	15.68	10.58	15.50	25.00	17.70	24.33	19.16	14.16	29.66	8.00	3.00	19.00	22.00	2.00					
100s	2	6	4	3	0	1	0	0	0	0	0	0	0	1	0	0	1	0	0	0	0	0					
50s	7	3	9	3	0	3	0	1	1	1	0	1	1	0	1	0	2	0	0	0	0	0					
Catches/Stumpings	10/0	1/0	18/0	5/0	1/0	7/0	2/0	4/0	26/3	2/0	5/0	15/5	6/0	2/0	2/0	1/0	0/0	2/0	1/0	0/0	0/0	0/0					

Home Ground: Headingley
Address: Headingley Cricket Ground, Leeds, LS6 3BU
Tel: 0870 4296774
Fax: 0113 2784099
Email: cricket@yorkshireccc.com
Directions: From M1 South leave at junction 43 to M621 as far as junction 2. From M62 West leave at junction 27 to take M621 as far as junction 2. From M62 East leave at junction 29 to join M1 northbound to junction 2 of M621. At junction 2 of the M621 follow the signs for Headingley stadium along A643. Follow Leeds Inner Ring Road (A58(M)) to A660 which is signposted to Headingley stadium. Signs along this route will indicate when you have reached the Headingley area and on Test match days additional temporary signing will direct you to the free Park & Ride car park to the north of Headingley at Beckett Park.
Other grounds used: Scarborough
Year formed: 1863

Chief Executive: Stewart Regan
Director of Cricket: David Byas
Captain: Craig White
County colours: Blue and gold

Website:
www.yorkshireccc.com

Honours
County Championship
1867, 1869, 1870, 1893, 1896, 1898, 1901,
1902, 1905, 1908, 1912, 1919, 1922, 1923,
1924, 1925, 1931, 1932, 1933, 1935, 1937,
1938, 1939, 1946, 1949, 1959, 1960, 1962,
1963, 1966, 1967, 1968, 2001
Sunday League/NCL/Pro40
1983
Benson & Hedges Cup
1987
Gillette Cup/NatWest/C&G Trophy
1965, 1969, 2002

YORKSHIRE CCC

FIRST-CLASS MATCHES
BOWLING

Match	GJ Kruis	JN Gillespie	TT Bresnan	MAK Lawson	A Rashid	A McGrath	DS Lehmann	MJ Hoggard	RKJ Dawson	JAR Blain	C White	ME Claydon	SA Patterson	MJ Lumb	JJ Sayers	A Shahzad	JE Lee	Overs	Total	Byes/Leg-byes	Wickets	Run outs
v. Nottinghamshire (Trent Bridge) 19-22 April			25.1-7-85-3			20-2-64-3	7-1-23-0		13-0-53-0	19-0-95-1		21-1-92-1						105.1	417	5	8	
																		-	-	-	-	
v. Warwickshire (Edgbaston) 26-29 April		22.1-4-50-1	21-5-81-0			22-7-62-4		8-1-20-0	20-3-72-2	6-3-11-2								99.1	316	20	10	1
		19-4-72-2	15-2-73-1			19-1-65-2	13-1-48-0	17-2-78-0		8-0-41-0								95	399	10	5	
v. Sussex (Headingley) 3-6 May		28-8-54-2	21-4-53-2			5-1-11-1	8-1-20-1	30-11-63-3	18-1-69-0		4.3-0-8-1							114.3	301	13	10	
		14-4-27-1	11-1-60-1			3-0-17-0	6-0-12-1	15-0-58-2			7-0-18-0							56	195	3	5	
v. Kent (Canterbury) 10-13 May	27-5-91-1	31-9-86-0	26-5-67-1			17-4-38-1	21-2-60-1		43-3-151-4		10.5-0-26-1			2-0-7-0				177.5	533	7	10	1
																		-	-	-	-	
v. Lancashire (Headingley) 16-19 May	29-4-135-2	33-7-97-2	22-2-65-3			10-0-28-0	5-0-9-0			12-0-79-2								111	417	4	9	
																		-	-	-	-	
v. Hampshire (Headingley) 31 May-3 June	20-3-71-3	19-6-39-2	19-3-36-4			10-0-47-1	6-0-13-0		18-3-41-0									92	248	1	10	
	21-3-75-1	24-6-66-0	18.2-2-74-0			18-0-73-2	16-0-70-2		14-3-37-0									111.2	404	9	5	
v. Middlesex (Southgate) 7-9 June	19-2-59-2	22-7-58-1	11-2-33-0	19.2-1-98-2		4-1-9-1	14-1-40-2		33-2-102-1		11-1-40-2							122.2	415	16	10	1
	3-0-15-0	4-0-15-0				4.3-1-14-0					5-0-30-2							16.3	74	0	2	
v. Sussex (Arundel Castle) 21-23 June	35-6-108-3	35-9-89-4				21-1-107-1	17-0-76-0	22-5-75-0	20-5-82-1				1-0-6-0					151	550	7	10	1
																		-	-	-	-	
v. Durham (Riverside) 14-16 July	14-2-59-2	17-1-74-2	16-2-58-5			4-1-17-0						11-2-42-1						62	258	8	10	
	18-1-95-3	14.2-2-37-6	11-3-23-1			3-0-6-0		7-0-38-0				11-3-37-0						64.2	248	12	10	
v. Warwickshire (Scarborough) 19-21 July	19-4-57-0	17-5-52-4	14-3-37-3		1.2-0-8-1	5-1-17-0							9-1-25-1					65.2	201	5	10	1
	17-3-56-0	14-3-29-1	16-4-40-3		28-6-67-6								5-0-26-0					81	239	12	10	
v. Hampshire (Rose Bowl) 26-28 July	25-4-96-0	29-9-85-2		34.4-1-150-6		25-6-67-1	7-0-25-1						21-7-56-0					141.4	493	14	10	
				2-0-8-0									1.4-0-7-0					3.4	15	0	0	
v. Lancashire (Old Trafford) 8-11 August	28-7-97-5	26-4-82-1		27.4-0-121-2		5-0-22-0	13-0-33-1						17-3-39-1			9-0-36-0		125.4	441	11	10	
																		-	-	-	-	
v. Kent (Headingley) 16-19 August	17-5-39-3	18-6-48-0		6-0-26-0	11-1-46-2	13-2-45-1							3-0-21-0					68	230	5	6	
																		-	-	-	-	
v. Middlesex (Scarborough) 30 August-2 September	27-4-67-5			12-0-61-1	20-3-59-1	11-1-30-0		26-2-92-3								12-1-45-0		108	376	22	10	
	8-1-19-0			22-0-88-6	26.4-3-96-4			4-0-16-0										60.4	224	5	10	
v. Nottinghamshire (Headingley) 13-16 September	15-4-60-1	14-2-47-2		11.5-0-42-4		20-1-76-3							6-2-29-0					66.5	263	9	10	
	10-1-31-2	8-1-22-1		22.4-0-85-4		25-3-74-3	1-0-1-0											66.4	213	0	10	
v. Durham (Headingley) 20-23 September	24-5-92-3	21-4-63-2	12-2-43-0	38-0-148-1	34.2-2-144-4	3-1-8-0												132.2	518	20	10	
	5-1-20-2	5-2-8-0		10.5-1-70-0	14-2-59-1	5-0-20-0												39.5	181	4	3	

	GJ Kruis	JN Gillespie	TT Bresnan	MAK Lawson	A Rashid	A McGrath	DS Lehmann	MJ Hoggard	RKJ Dawson	JAR Blain	C White	ME Claydon	SA Patterson	MJ Lumb	JJ Sayers	A Shahzad	JE Lee
Overs	381	434.3	258.3	207	180.2	216	146.3	97	196	59	32.2	43	62.4	1	2	12	9
Maidens	65	103	47	3	21	28	8	18	20	3	4	6	13	0	0	1	0
Runs	1342	1210	828	897	629	734	472	304	701	287	75	171	203	6	7	45	36
Wickets	38	36	27	26	25	18	9	8	8	5	4	2	2	0	0	0	0
Average	35.31	33.61	30.66	34.50	25.16	40.77	52.44	38.00	87.62	57.40	18.75	85.50	101.50	-	-	-	-

FIELDING

29	GL Brophy (26 ct, 3 st)
20	SM Guy (15 ct, 5 st)
18	A McGrath
10	MJ Lumb
7	JJ Sayers
6	MJ Wood
5	C White
5	MAK Lawson
4	TT Bresnan
2	JAR Blain
2	RKJ Dawson
2	GJ Kruis
2	AW Gale
2	A Rashid
1	DS Lehmann
1	MJ Hoggard
1	JN Gillespie
1	SA Patterson
0	MP Vaughan
0	A Shahzad
0	ME Claydon
0	JE Lee

Final Division One Table

	P	W	L	D	Bat	Bowl	Pts
Sussex	16	9	2	5	49	47	242.00
Lancashire	16	6	1	9	58	46	224.00
Hampshire	16	6	3	7	48	48	207.00
Warwickshire	16	6	5	5	42	43	189.00
Kent	16	4	4	8	43	44	175.00
Yorkshire	16	3	6	7	43	41	154.00
Durham	16	4	8	4	39	43	153.50
Nottinghamshire	16	4	7	5	40	37	153.00
Middlesex	16	1	7	8	47	42	133.50